MANAGING & ORGANIZATIONS

AN INTRODUCTION TO THEORY & PRACTICE

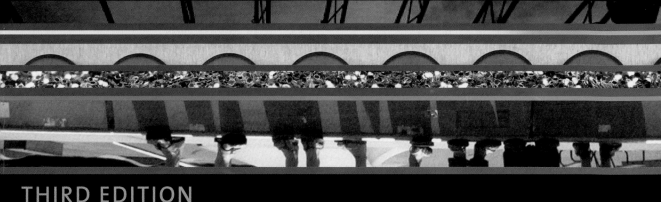

THIRD EDITION

STEWART CLEGG MARTIN KORNBERGER TYRONE PITSIS

Los Angeles | London | New Delhi
Singapore | Washington DC

First edition published 2004
Second edition published 2008
Reprinted 2009

This third edition published 2011
Reprinted 2012

SAGE Publications Ltd
1 Oliver's Yard
55 City Road
London EC1Y 1SP

SAGE Publications Inc.
2455 Teller Road
Thousand Oaks, California 91320

SAGE Publications India Pvt Ltd
B 1/I 1 Mohan Cooperative Industrial Area
Mathura Road
New Delhi 110 044

SAGE Publications Asia-Pacific Pte Ltd
3 Church Street
#10-04 Samsung Hub
Singapore 049483

Library of Congress Control Number: 2011940970

British Library Cataloguing in Publication data

A catalogue record for this book is available from the British Library

ISBN 978-0-85702-040-6
ISBN 978-0-85702-041-3 (pbk)

Typeset by C&M Digitals (P) Ltd, Chennai, India
Printed and bound in Great Britain by Ashford Colour Press Ltd

MANAGING & ORGANIZATIONS

SAGE has been part of the global academic community since 1965, supporting high quality research and learning that transforms society and our understanding of individuals, groups, and cultures. SAGE is the independent, innovative, natural home for authors, editors and societies who share our commitment and passion for the social sciences.

Find out more at: **www.sagepublications.com**

'*This is an exciting book.* It covers the most important concepts in good currency. The coverage is based on the best and most relevant research. It connects with practical problems. It is written in language that is clear and accessible. It contains innovative exercises to help the readers expand their knowledge beyond simply reading this book.'
Chris Argyris, James B. Conant Professor Emeritus, Harvard University and Monitor Group

'*This is truly the most exhaustive textbook on organization and management that ever existed.* It conveys complex messages avoiding complicated style; it moves gracefully between the summaries of theories and examples from practice, between models to imitate and errors to be avoided, between micro and macro lenses applied to organizational phenomena. While obviously meant as a travel guide – a thorough and detailed manual for the beginners, it offers many unexpected insights and pearls of wisdom even for the most seasoned travelers interested in knowledge of and about management.'
Barbara Czarniawska, M.A., E.D., Professor of Management Studies, Göteborg University

'*Managing and Organizations* succeeds at being practical and honest in its treatment of working in and with organizations. It challenges students to build their competencies and insights step by step while deepening their awareness of opportunities for genuine achievement while working through workplace conflicts and politics.'
Denise M. Rousseau, H. J. Heinz II Professor of Organizational Behavior and Public Policy, Director, Project on Evidence-based Organizational Practices, Carnegie Mellon University

'A textbook on managing thinking and practice that takes the reader into "real life", within and outside organizations. It is conceived as a travel guide that allows to connect and make connections between what is already known and what may be discovered and enjoyed during the voyage. It is friendly and challenging, simple and complex at the same time. And, most important, it is faithful: it delivers what is promised in the first lines of its introduction.'
Silvia Gherardi, University of Trento, Italy

'Here it is, the second edition of one of the best and most intriguing introductions to the complex processes of managing in organizations to be written in the past decade ... It offers a perfect mix of practical information and well-thought-out and challenging theoretical insights, which will help the reader to reflect critically on the complex processes of managing and organizing.'
Hans Doorewaard, University of Nijmegen, The Netherlands

'The book is up-to-date yet historically grounded. It is easy to read yet richly textured. It maps the territory of organizational studies in clear and

useful ways. Its lively format, excellent examples, and topical coverage make it a unique and highly relevant text for becoming a thoughtful practitioner of organizations.'
Jane Dutton, Robert L. Kahn, Distinguished University Professor of Business Administration and Psychology, University of Michigan

'The book is a true pleasure to read! It is an excellent "travel guide to the world of management", not only because of its wealth of detailed information and insight, but also because it makes you want to travel! Don't leave home without it! And if you don't go, read it at home!'
Kristian Kreiner, Professor – Copenhagen Business School – Department of Organization, Director – Center for Management Studies of the Building Process – Realdania Research

'Managing and Organizations is a real adventure … *it is a novel, innovative and unconventional textbook, which will not only inform but will also entertain* … a real must in understanding the process of management and organizational behavior.'
Professor Cary L. Cooper, CBE, Professor of Organizational Psychology and Health at Lancaster University Management School, and Editor in Chief of the *Blackwell Encyclopedia of Management*

'Critical and practical, scholarly and aesthetically enjoyable … Students on Master courses and reflective practitioners will find insight, inspiration and encouragement to think differently about what has been seen as a pretty dry area. *What more could be expected of a learning and teaching resource?*'
Richard Weiskopf, Department of Organization and Learning, School of Management, Innsbruck University

'Most textbooks discuss *in vitro* organizations: bloodless, lifeless, distorted and inanimate, hence ready for study and dissection. This volume is different. Written as a "realist's guide to management", it pictures organizations as they are in the "real world": alive, paradoxical, emotional, insecure, self-confident, responsible, irresponsible. This book, in other words, contains life, the life of organizations. *To read this book is to live that life.*'
Miguel Pina e Cunha, Universidade Nova de Lisboa

'In an age where there is saturation of textbooks on Managing and Organizing, particularly due to their limited impact on management practice, this book provides a truly refreshing perspective.'
Elena Antonacopoulou, Professor of Organizational Behaviour, University of Liverpool Management School

'This book is both scholarly and fun. It may even give textbooks a good name! I thoroughly recommend it to all students and lecturers who want something more enjoyable, insightful and enduringly satisfying than McManagement takeaways or force-fed ivory tower correctness.'
Richard J. Badham, Professor of Management, Macquarie Graduate School of Management

SUMMARY OF CONTENTS

CONTENTS

11 MANAGING SUSTAINABLY: ETHICS AND CORPORATE SOCIAL RESPONSIBILITY   403

Morals, Conduct, Responsibility   403

PART THREE
MANAGING ORGANIZATIONAL STRUCTURES AND PROCESSES

12 MANAGING ONE BEST WAY?   445

Thinkers, Principles, Models   445

13 MANAGING BEYOND BUREAUCRACY   485

Dysfunctions, Institutions, Isomorphism   485

14 MANAGING ORGANIZATIONAL DESIGN   519

Design, Environment, Fit   519

Gentlemen, he said,
I don't need your organization, I've shined your shoes,
I've moved your mountains and marked your cards
But Eden is burning, either brace yourself for elimination
Or else your hearts must have the courage for the changing of the guards.

Bob Dylan (1978), 'Changing of the guards'

ABOUT THE AUTHORS

Stewart Clegg   Stewart is Professor of Management and Research Director of the Centre for Organization and Management Studies at the University of Technology, Sydney Business School. For over forty years he has been extremely active in teaching and researching organizations and management from a sociological perspective.

His major research interests have always centred on power relations in organizations and in theory. He is the author of many books, including *Strategy: Theory and Practice* (2011), a further collaboration with Martin Kornberger, amongst others, as well as being the editor of a great many volumes, including the award-winning *Handbook of Organization Studies* (2006). In addition he is editor of the series *Advances in Organization Studies*. He has published many articles in leading journals.

He lives in Sydney and travels extensively in Europe, Asia and the Americas, usually finding time to catch up with good friends and good music, especially if one of his favourites happens to be in town. He believes in the potential of the sociological imagination to illuminate social reality. To this end he has tried, with his co-authors, to make understanding management and organizations relevant, accessible and stripped of pretension.

Martin Kornberger   Martin received his PhD in Philosophy from the University of Vienna in 2002. After a decade in Sydney he currently lives in Vienna and works at Copenhagen Business School. With an eclectic bookshelf behind him, his eyes are firmly focused on organizations: How do we manage them? How do we strategize their futures? How do organizational cultures shape insiders? How do brands engage with outsiders? What makes some organizations more innovative than others? And what ways are there to make organizations behave more ethically?

Martin has written several other books including *Brand Society* (2010) which explores how brands transform practices of production and consumption; and *Strategy: Theory and Practice* (2011) with Stewart Clegg, Chris Carter and Jochen Schweitzer.

His research has been published in leading journals including *Accounting, Organizations and Society; Public Administration; Strategic Organization; British Journal of Management; Organization Studies; Organization; Human Relations; Management Learning; Sociological Review; AAAJ; Journal of Business Ethics; Scandinavian Journal of Management; Industrial Relations Journal; European Management Review; Gender Work and Organization; Journal of Management Inquiry* and others.

Tyrone S. Pitsis   Tyrone is Co-Director of Strategy and Society at the Newcastle University Business School, UK where he teaches Strategy and Change Management. He is also a visiting academic at EDHEC, France and University of Sydney, Australia

His major area of research is in the phenomenology of inter-organizational collaboration, strategic foresight and organizational and managerial innovation. He is the author of *The Handbook of Organizational and Managerial Innovation* (2012), as well as several research book chapters, encyclopedic entries and publications in journals such as *Organizational Science* and *Organization Studies*. He has been a recipient of research awards, including from the British Academy of Management, and the Emerald Science Citation of Excellence Award with Stewart Clegg and Kjersti Bjorkeng. In 2011 he was elected Chair: Practice Theme Committee of the Academy of Management

He lives in Newcastle upon-Tyne and travels extensively in Europe, Australia and North America. Tyrone originally started his working life as a chef, starting off as a kitchen hand and worked his way up to an Executive Chef in award-winning restaurants and hotels. He now cooks as little as possible. Aside from his family, Tyrone could not live without his iPod and cannot imagine life without music.

ACKNOWLEDGEMENTS

All book authors need good friends, patient colleagues, and great loves. Starting with the last first, Stewart had Lynne, Jonathan, and William, Martin had Jessica, and Tyrone had Sharon and gained Theodore and Joseph.

In addition to those who are close to us, we want to thank all the people who featured in the first edition, with the following revised acknowledgements. We should start with Cleusa Lester. Everyone who knows Cleusa (or Cleo) realizes, even if they cannot imagine all of the incredibly important roles she plays, that she is absolutely fabulous. Being Brazilian is not the least! We were sorry to see her return to her home country. Since Cleo left Nancy Chan and Lisa Adiprodjo have been of great assistance. Among the patient friends, good colleagues, and others who have helped us, provided feedback, or just been supportive, we would like to mention, alphabetically, Anjana Anandakumar, Emma Bowyer, Geoff Breach, Chris Carter, Andrew Chan, Jonathan Clegg, Lynne Clegg, William Clegg, Chris Coupland, David Courpasson, Miriam Dornstein, Dan Evans, Jessica Fergusson, Kevin Foley, John Garrick, Ranjan George, Ray Gordon, John Gray, Julie Gustavs, Winton Higgins, Simon Hoerauf, Brian Hunt, Joan S. Ingalls, Emanuel Josserand, Ken Kamoche, Kevin Keough, Karl Kruselniscki, Linda Leung, Adam Morgan, Michael Muetzelfeldt, Katherine Peil, Bruce Petty, Paul O. Radde, Tim Ray, Carl Rhodes, Anne Ross-Smith, John Sillince, David Silverman, John Stokes, Emanuela Todeva, Marc Tyrell, Robert van Krieken, Johannes Weissenbaeck, Adam Yazxhi, Joanne Young, and also the members of the Friends of Positive Psychology listserve.

It seems almost unfair to single out anyone in particular from this list, but we should acknowledge some specific contributions to the first edition: Anjana Anandakumar for her initial proofreading, alerting us to continuity problems, as well as giving us insight into what should go into our glossary, and her help in preparing the PowerPoint slides; Emma Bowyer's knowledge was a great help in keeping us focused on our readers; Chris Carter, for providing the very careful and thorough reading, as well as the many small word-sketches of ideas and input to the material on culture and globalization, especially; David Courpasson and Dan Evans, as well as the students who took the subject, for providing an opportunity to test out some of the ideas from the first edition of the book in the classroom with the 2003 MBA Summer School at EM-Lyon in Managing with Power and Politics; Miriam Dornstein for her panoptic capability for telling us where we were getting lost in our text; Kevin Foley for his ability to detect structural weaknesses and omissions – not all of which might have been rectified to his 'standards'; Ranjan George, for inviting Stewart to Sri Lanka to develop curriculum material for the Open University of Sri Lanka, which formed an initial challenge within which some of the convictions that shaped this book were gestated; Ray Gordon, for the police case on the website; John Gray for his alertness to our occasional lapses into a particular type of metaphysical bathos; Julie Gustavs for her sharp eye for detail; Emanuel Josserand for his assistance in researching the current state of play in the French bread industry; Carl Rhodes for his support and enthusiasm; John Sillince for his identification of a number of theoretical absences in our arrangement of the material; and Joanne Young for her detailed commentary on early drafts and suggestions for the title. We would also like to thank all the IML students who presented ideas for the original website, especially Antoine Tremoulet and Ian Tanedo, whose ideas we enjoyed most and who built the first website for us. We carried some ideas over. Without the great images that Jonathan Clegg and Jessica Fergusson made available, the book would not have been as interesting. Penultimately, a very special thanks to Johannes and Simon from PLAY, with whom Martin thought a lot about why so many books are so boring and, as a result, started thinking about some new ideas that are reflected in the underlying structure for this book; and finally, from Stewart to Jonathan, because, through working with his visual creativity, he learned to be more fluent with words.

We also appreciate the great support and guidance that we have had at Sage from many people, including Rachel Eley, Alan Maloney, Ruth Stitt, Natalie Aguilera, Ian Eastment, Seth Edwards, Ben Sherwood, Alison Mudditt, Sanford Robinson (not forgetting the great copy-editing job done by all the copy editors we have worked with on various editions), and especially Kiren Shoman. She is a persistent editor who was able to persuade Stewart to do something that he had agreed, in principle and in contract, to do a long time ago with some other potential collaborators (for both Sue Jones and Rosemary Nixon, who should also be acknowledged as earlier editors) but which, for various reasons, he never got around to doing. As it transpired, Stewart is delighted to have written the book with Martin and Tyrone. He doesn't think he could have had a more enjoyable partnership for the project. Finally, there may have been some other people we should have thanked and acknowledged but have overlooked. Sorry if that is the case, but do let us know.

We would like to single out a few people for special mention. First, we would like to thank all the people who provided us with great case studies: James B. Avey, Kjersti Bjørkeng, Arne Carlsen, Gerard Fairtlough, Reidar Gjersvik, Annelies Hodge, Brett C. Luthans, Tord F. Mortensen, Emil A. Røyrvik, Ace Simpson, Marie-France Turcotte, Grete Wennes, and Tara S. Wernsing. Second, we have some more generic thanks for the support of the various heads of the Management Discipline Group in Sydney, and Chris Carter for lots of help and good times in Edinburgh and St Andrews. More especially, we want to thank Ursulla Glunk, Ad van Iterson, and Robert Roe at Maastricht University, and Chris Carter, now from the University of

Newcastle, for their very helpful comments on an earlier draft of the first chapter. Also, more specifically, in Sydney, we want to thank Ed Wray-Bliss, Mel Edwards and Jonathan Pratt for critical feedback on an earlier edition and Sebastian Graham and Emma Lovelly for their feedback and help in making the second edition even better. Also, in Sydney (but now in Oxford) William Clegg helped us greatly by reading the manuscript and suggesting revisions from a student perspective as well as working on the permissions. In Lyons, we say thanks to Grégoire Croidieu for the trip to the *Boulangerie de l'Ille Barbe*! In Birmingham, Bhomali Grover was a great help. Finally, thanks to everyone in Sydney, Lyons, Maastricht, and Copenhagen who helped out with the photos – you know who you are – even if you didn't always make the final cut due only ever to photographer error – you know who he was! Rachel Eley has done a great job of steering the book through Sage's production process along with the various copy editors: a big thanks!

Institutionally, we would like to thank various organizations and people that have hosted us and our endeavours over the editions: University of Technology, Sydney; Aston Business School, Birmingham; The University of Maastricht; Copenhagen Business School; University of Paris-Dauphine; University of Innsbruck; University of St Andrews; EM-Lyon Business School; the University of Versailles Saint Quentin-en-Yvelines; Universidade Nova, Lisbon; Vriej Universieit, Amsterdam; The American Psychological Association; Professor Edward L. Deci, Professor Kennon M. Sheldon, and Dr Tim Sharp.

Finally, Stewart would like to thank the University of Umea, where he spent a month in 2010 as the Erasmus Mundos Fellow; the Institute of Advanced Study, Durham University, UK, where he was a Distinguished Fellow in 2010; and the University of Cambridge Judge Business School, where he was the Montzelomo Visiting Professor in 2011.

Stewart, Martin, and Tyrone
University of Technology, Sydney, Australia
and Universidade Nova, Lisbon
Copenhagen Business School, Denmark
University of Newcastle, UK

INTRODUCTION

Welcome to the new world of management and organization theory! We will take you on a trip through some main roads, back streets, secret places, and exciting viewpoints, to explore management thinking and practice. But let us begin at the beginning …

THE IDEA

The three of us all worked in the School of Management at the University of Technology, Sydney, where this book was conceived. Martin and Stewart are also Visiting Professors at Copenhagen Business School, and Stewart is also a Visiting Professor at Universidade Nova, Lisbon, in Portugal; at the Universidade do Estado de Santa Catarina, in Florianopolis, Brazil, and at EM-Lyon in France. In each of these places the ideas that form this book have been rehearsed and practiced. We would like to thank all the students and colleagues at UTS and elsewhere for their insights and inspiration. Drawing on this global experience we believe we have written a book that can travel as readily as we do. We have written a textbook that introduces management as we conceive of it. It is a realist's guide to management, and this is what makes it so different from many other books. It is not a work of desiccated science fiction, creating an 'as if' world where technical dreams come true and the reality of life lived in organizations rarely intrudes. We tell it like it is, but we also suggest how to do it better; thus we offer a book that proposes a new approach to management and treats it in an open and refreshing way.

The book provides not only an account of theories, but also an introduction to their practice – one

that we hope you will find enjoyable. To make it more so, we have used examples from everyday life and culture, such as football and skating, as well as discussions of management and organization theories. The book provides a resource for making connections, a book that will connect with you and will connect you to lots of other interesting ideas and people. It is meant to be serious but also fun. It is undoubtedly scholarly, but it is also accessible. It is a book to use. In short, we think that you will find this book challenging but also engaging.

THE GUIDE

The idea that structures the book is quite simple. Think of a travel guide. It provides you with all the necessary information you need to know to enjoy your trip. Of course, sometimes it is tricky to read, with lots of details and comparisons, maps, and tables. But it also gives you a flavour of the country you will visit, its lifestyle, culture, and attractions. To package this into a formula, what a guidebook does is provide you with necessary information, but it also fascinates, inspires, and motivates you to explore more and to see things from different perspectives. So we decided that we wanted to write a travel guide to the world of management, containing reliable maps of the terrain, highlighting some critical viewpoints, and outlining ways forward, as well as exploring some of the nooks and crannies and byways while observing the main thoroughfares. We wanted to provide you with a resource book that helps you to navigate through this world and encourages you to explore not only new, exciting, and brilliant aspects, but also some dark sides as well. And it is a guide with great interconnectivity: check out the material at the end of the chapters and visit the Companion Website and you will see what we mean.

HOW TO USE THE BOOK

We have divided the book into three parts, which we have envisaged rather as a photographer focusing a camera. First, we begin with the close-up focus, with issues related to managing the individual in the organization, matters that are close at hand to the individual, such as teams, groups, leading, coaching, mentoring, human resource management, and cultures at work. Then, in the second part of the book we open up the perspective a little wider, to take in more of the scene that surrounds individuals at work, by looking at the organizational practices that they are necessarily involved in when being organized. Here, the themes are broader, involving managing power and politics, communications, knowledge and learning, and highly contemporary and salient issues of corporate social responsibility, sustainability and ethics, as well as the constant issue of innovation and change. The third part of the book opens up the full landscape view. We look at how the historical landscape underlying present practices was formed, beginning with the long-standing search for the elixir of the one best way to manage, a search that never will and never can arrive at its destination. We pause for a while to focus on some of the most pervasive features in this landscape – the persistence of bureaucracy, despite its many critiques, and the widespread rationalization of this landscape by the simple systems of McDonaldization. Organizational design does not stop with bureaucracy and McDonaldization, of course, so we also consider some of the new organizational forms that have emerged subsequent to the development of these designs, right up to contemporary concerns with virtual organization. Increasingly, tomorrow's managers will have to manage in a global context, considering the impact of globalization and the issues that it raises, and will raise, for any successful contemporary manager. Increasingly, in the contemporary world, organizations cannot be treated as if they stand apart from the momentous forces shaping our everyday life as employees, consumers, and citizens, which have major implications for employment relations, the world of work, and its management.

Welcome to the guided tour of *Managing and Organizations: An Introduction to Theory and Practice*. This tour will take you through the main sections and special features of the text.

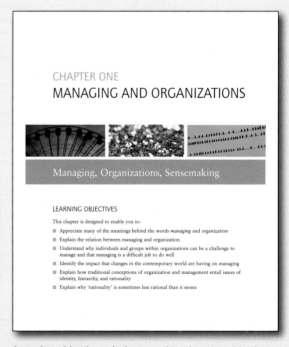

Learning objectives: A clear set of key learning objectives are provided for each chapter.

[Page preview 1]

A little Danish wisdom:

Life must be understood backwards; but ... it must be lived forward.
(Søren Kierkegaard, Danish existential philosopher, 1813–1855)

INTRODUCTION

The book that you have started to read will be, for many readers, a first introduction to the theory and practice of managing and organizations. While you may be familiar with organization practices of many kinds, you may not be familiar with the theories that may be behind those practices or that enable us to make sense of them. Thus, in this introductory chapter we will do two main things:

1 Define the relation between our two key terms of 'managing' and 'organization'.
2 Stress the importance of 'sensemaking' and 'rationality' both for management practice and as central organization devices.

We will argue that while it is important to have management tools and techniques in place to run organizations effectively, we should never lose sight of the fact that it is people who are doing the managing. However much managers may believe that the management systems and tools that they have designed and adopted are well thought out, people still have to use them. In using them people will make different sense of these devices and the contexts in which they are deployed – this is what we call sensemaking. What connects the activity of managing to the structures, practices, and processes of organizations is sensemaking. That is why we have chosen it as the central theme of this introductory chapter and why it will recur so frequently as a theme in the book.

Let us begin with the subtitle first – with the theory word before we move to consider *practice*.

WHY THEORY?

Margin: A theory is an account of how things work, which is, at its best, coherent in its terms and applicable to phenomena that it seeks to interpret, understand, and explain.

You may find theory difficult and wonder why we have to have it. The point is, however, that we are all tied up in theories of one kind or another. The way your university or college is organized is underpinned by a theory, just as much as is the McDonald's that you might have worked in while at school, the production line that your grandfather may have laboured on, or the organizations in which your parents are employed. How we make sense of these things depends on the theory we use. We live within the designs and assumptions of past theory about effort and its organization every day at work. However, if we are aware of the theories that hold us

Introduction: The introduction provides you with the overall framework of each chapter. It provides a map of the journey you are about to undertake within each topic area, the key ideas, their histories, present and future.

[Page preview 2]

and surgery can modify that quite markedly. We may have a definite personality, but, once again, ill health, drugs, diet, and life experiences can reshape the ways that we present ourselves to the world, often quite dramatically.

Some celebrities in popular culture are famous for their shifting iconography, the way they style themselves and hint at their changing personality. Within our unique bodies most of us like to think we have a uniquely free will. Only we are master or mistress of ourselves, a sentiment particularly strong in toddlers, but certainly not absent from more mature manifestations of will. To think otherwise is to accept that the fates, the stars, the gods, society, or some other transcendent entity guides our lives as preordained. Often, our glimpses of celebrity seem to offer another, more exciting world than that which we live in. But even celebrity does not escape routine: rehearsals, performances, organizing glamour weddings in between checking in and out of rehab, the divorce courts, and the gym. As individuals we have power to shape organizational practice; we can vote in elections or choose to support various products. Each time we make a purchase we make a decision whether or not to support a particular organization's products. However, individual choice is constrained. These constraints may be as obvious as a police officer forcing you to comply with the rules imposed by the structure of the state, or as discrete as the behaviour encouraged by the language one uses in conversation with one's peers.

When we become organization members each of us has to surrender some of our autonomy to the control of others and other things such as schedules, machines, routines, and deadlines. In return we receive wages, salaries, or fees, identifying us as workers, staff, or independent professionals. Actually, we receive far more than mere income. We are able to bask, as unique individuals, in the ambience of a unique organization. Its brand helps define who we are: we are US Customs Officers, or Australian Tax Officers, or London Police Officers; we are Oxford academics or college professors; we are Vogue models or Chelsea football players. Sometimes we bask in a reflected light: we may be Chelsea football fans rather than supporters of Arsenal, wear Armani rather than Dolce & Gabbana, or wear Nike rather than Adidas. We can attach our identities as individuals to organizations quite easily.

MANAGING

Framing managing

A key term in theory is the idea of there being a frame through which we understand things. We will use this introduction to develop some key terms with which to understand this book.

All managing involves framing: separating that which deserves focus from that which does not. One thing that managers have to do all the time is to differentiate between the relevant and the irrelevant, just as do the authors of textbooks, trying to manage their expectations of their readers. To do this we, much as managers, frame some things as more relevant than others.

We can differentiate between managing as a practice, as something that we do, and organizations as a goal-oriented collectivity, in which we

Margin: A frame is a term that comes from the cinema: a director frames a shot by including some detail and omitting other detail. A frame defines what is relevant.

Frames enable us to framing. They focus us in on specific relevancies: by framing we decide on what is relevant from the infinite number of stimuli, behavioural cues, sense data, and information that surround us.

Managing is an active, relational practice which involves doing things. The things that managers do are supposed to contribute to the achievement of the organization's formal goals.

Organizations are systematically arranged frameworks relating people, things, knowledge, and technologies, in a design intended to achieve specific goals.

Marginal definitions: Key terms clearly and concisely defined in page margins of every chapter in order to aid understanding.

[Page preview 3]

Organizations can be thought of as huge repositories of rules. These rules often have different origins and rationalities supporting them, and, as a result, they may often come into conflict. From the above examples it is also clear that these organizational rules originate from both individuals comprising organizations as well as from the social relations and institutions embedded within organizations. These produce

some unlikely similarities: consider the following questions.

1 What essential features does a kindergarten share with a university?
2 In what ways could a university be compared with a fast food restaurant?
3 In what ways might a McDonald's be similar to a car factory?

Check out the Companion Website www.sagepub.co.uk/managingandorganizations3 for free access to an article by Parker and David Jary (1995) if you want to learn why some universities and McDonald's have some things in common.

Organizations go on while members change

Organizations have an embedded, structural reality that endures irrespective of their members. People may come and people may go but the organization retains an identity separate from the individuals who comprise it. Think of the educational institution in which you are reading this book: every year a new cohort of students enters, staff retire or resign, and new staff are employed, but the university or college carries on regardless. The same routines – enrolment, lectures, tutorials, seminars, and assessments – are carried out year to year irrespective of who is doing them.

Organizations are huge repositories of rules

Let us take a closer look at what we mean by 'rules'. Here are some common distinctions:

1 *Formal rules:* You will arrive at a certain time and leave at a certain time. This is often a really stupid rule as it slows everyone down as the roads clog with people all trying to get to the organization at the same normal time – often making many people late. Should people be able to come and go as they please at work?
2 *Professional rules:* These are the rules that you have internalized, perhaps as a result of a professional accreditation, achieved in, or in conjunction with, your higher education. But sometimes the organization that employs you will require things of you that simply cannot be done as and when is required using the internalized rules. Which rules should you follow – the professional rules or those of the employing organization, if there is a clash between them?
3 *Legal rules:* These may be directives that are explicit, compulsory, and have a clear source and target within the organization. For instance, you shall not use organizational resources for personal purposes. But even a simple rule such as this can be difficult to follow. Should you not call friends and relations on the office phone?

Marginal references to journal articles: Stimulating papers from key journals on the topics covered are provided free to you and your students on the book's Companion Website.

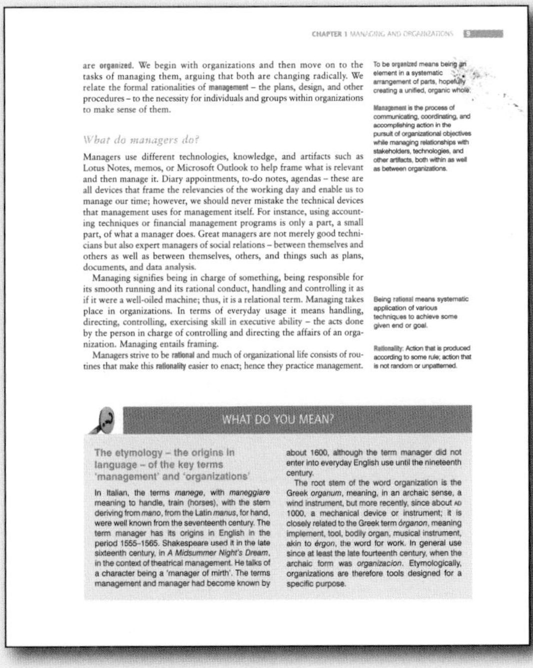

[Page preview 4]

are organized. We begin with organizations and then move on to the tasks of managing them, arguing that both are changing radically. We relate the different rationalities of management – the plans, design, and other procedures – to the necessity for individuals and groups within organizations to make sense of them.

What do managers do?

Managers use different technologies, knowledge, and artifacts such as Lotus Notes, memos, or Microsoft Outlook to help frame what is relevant and then manage it. Diary appointments, to-do notes, agendas – these are all devices that frame the relevancies of the working day and enable us to manage our time; however, we should never mistake the technical devices that management uses for management itself. For instance, using accounting techniques or financial management programs is only a part, a small part, of what a manager does. Great managers are not merely good technicians but also expert managers of social relations – between themselves and others as well as between themselves, others, and things such as plans, documents, and data analysis.

Managing signifies being in charge of something, being responsible for its smooth running and its rational conduct, handling and controlling it as if it were a well-oiled machine; thus, it is a relational, functional term. Managing takes place in organizations. In terms of everyday usage it means handling, directing, controlling, exercising skill in executive ability – the acts done by the person in charge of controlling and directing the affairs of an organization. Managing entails framing.

Managers strive to be rational and much of organizational life consists of routines that make this rationality easier to enact; hence they practice management.

Margin: To be organized means being an element in a systematic arrangement of parts, hopefully creating a unified, organic whole.

Management is the process of communicating, coordinating, and accomplishing action in the pursuit of organizational objectives while managing relationships with stakeholders, technologies, and other artifacts, both within as well as between organizations.

Being rational means systematic application of various techniques to achieve some given end or goal.

Rationality: Action that is produced according to some rule; action that is not random or unpatterned.

WHAT DO YOU MEAN?

The etymology – the origins in language – of the key terms 'management' and 'organizations'

In Italian, the terms *manege*, with *maneggiare* meaning to handle, train (horses), with the stem deriving from *mano*, from the Latin *manus*, for hand, were well known from the seventeenth century. The term *manager* has its origins in English in the period 1555–1565. Shakespeare used it in the late sixteenth century, in *A Midsummer Night's Dream*, in the context of theatrical management. He talks of a character being a 'manager of mirth'. The terms management and manager had become known by

about 1600, although the term manager did not enter into everyday English use until the nineteenth century.

The root stem of the word organization is the Greek *organum*, meaning, in an archaic sense, a wind instrument, but more recently, since about AD 1000, a mechanical device or instrument; it is closely related to the Greek term *órganon*, meaning implement, tool, bodily organ, musical instrument, akin to *érgon*, the word for work. In general use since at least the late fourteenth century, when the archaic form was organization. Etymologically, organizations are therefore tools designed for a specific purpose.

What do you mean? Boxed text designed to expand upon key concepts within each chapter in order to facilitate learning and understanding.

What's the point? Within each chapter boxed text can be found illustrating the relevance and significance of key concepts covered in the text.

Mini case: Boxed mini cases for active learning and practical reinforcement of difficult or challenging concepts.

Question time: A boxed selection of fun and challenging exercises, tests, and surveys on specific key concepts.

Summary and review: This section simply does what it says. We review the main concepts and issues we covered in the chapter in order to be sure that you are clear on what was covered, and why.

End of chapter exercises: Group and individual based exercises designed to provide practical and reflective learning on key issues, concepts and phenomena covered in each chapter.

Additional resources: A selection of handpicked resources such as novels, texts, movies, music, and other forms of media that explain and expand upon chapter contents.

Web section: An excellent array of web-based resources such as website links and YouTube clips that illustrate and emphasize key issues covered in the book.

Looking for a higher mark? An annotated list of engaging and challenging journal articles that can be accessed for free on the Companion Website are provided at the end of every chapter.

Case study: Each chapter ends with an innovative case study with questions designed for reflective learning and the reinforcement of key concepts.

Glossary: At the end of the book you will find a detailed glossary of all the key concepts covered in the book.

COMPANION WEBSITE

Be sure to visit the Companion Website at www.sagepub.co.uk/managingandorganizations3 to find a range of teaching and learning material for both lecturers and students including the following:

For Lecturers:

1 **Instructor's notes:** A password-protected instructor's manual is provided on the website with teaching notes, including:

   a **A tutor's guide** indicating how the subject might best be taught with insights into debriefing the exercise and case studies found within the textbook.
   b **Assessment resources:** A wide range of multiple choice, short- and long-answer assessment questions with test generation capabilities. This section also includes model answers for long- and short-answer questions.
   c **Teaching resources:** An array of extra case studies, and in-class exercises with methods and debriefing sheets, to aid in the quality of the learning experience for students.

2 **PowerPoint slides:** PowerPoint slides for each chapter for use in class are also provided in the instructor's manual on the website. The slides can be edited by instructors to suit teaching styles and needs.

3 **Teacher interaction portal:** A portal direct to the authors for textbook-related feedback, continuous improvement, recommendations, case contributions, and general Q&A.

For Students:

1 **Online readings:** Full access is provided to selected journal articles related to each chapter, summaries of which are given on the website and at the end of each chapter.

2 **Links to relevant websites:** Direct links to related websites for each chapter are provided as appropriate.

3 **Flashcard glossary:** The full glossary for Managing and Organizations is online in flashcard format. You can use these flashcards to test your knowledge and revise the key concepts in the text.

4 **Interactive multiple choice questions:** A sample of selective multiple choice questions are available for students to test and challenge themselves.

5 **Interaction portal:** Direct access to the authors to offer your own pictures that you believe represent key concepts, to communicate your glowing praise, or suggestions for improvements, and general Q&A.

PART ONE

MANAGING PEOPLE IN ORGANIZATIONS

CHAPTER ONE
MANAGING AND ORGANIZATIONS

Managing, Organizations, Sensemaking

LEARNING OBJECTIVES

This chapter is designed to enable you to:

- Appreciate many of the meanings behind the words *managing* and *organization*
- Explain the relation between managing and organization
- Understand why individuals and groups within organizations can be a challenge to manage and that managing is a difficult job to do well
- Identify the impact that changes in the contemporary world are having on managing
- Explain how traditional conceptions of organization and management entail issues of identity, hierarchy, and rationality
- Explain why 'rationality' is sometimes less rational than it seems

BEFORE YOU GET STARTED . . .

A little Danish wisdom:

Life must be understood backwards; but … it must be lived forward.
(Søren Kierkegaard, Danish existential philosopher, 1813–1855)

INTRODUCTION

The book that you have started to read will be, for many readers, a first introduction to the theory and practice of managing and organizations. While you may be familiar with organization practices of many kinds, you may not be familiar with the theories that may lie behind those practices or that enable us to make sense of them. Thus, in this introductory chapter we will do two main things:

1   Define the relation between our two key terms of 'managing' and 'organization'.
2   Stress the importance of 'sensemaking' and 'rationality' both for management practice and as central organization devices.

We will argue that while it is important to have management tools and techniques in place to run organizations effectively, we should never lose sight of the fact that it is people who are doing the managing. However much managers may believe that the management systems and tools that they have designed and adopted are well thought out, people still have to use them. In using them people will make different sense of these devices and the contexts in which they are deployed – this is what we call sensemaking. What connects the activity of managing to the structures, practices, and processes of organizations is sensemaking. That is why we have chosen it as the central theme of this introductory chapter and why it will recur so frequently as a theme in the book.

Let us begin with the subtitle first – with the theory word before we move to consider *practice*.

WHY THEORY?

A **theory** is an account of how things work, which is, at its best, coherent in its terms and applicable to phenomena that it seeks to interpret, understand, and explain.

You may find **theory** difficult and wonder why we have to have it. The point is, however, that we are all tied up in theories of one kind of another. The way your university or college is organized is underpinned by a theory, just as much as is the McDonald's that you might have worked in while at school, the production line that your grandfather may have laboured on, or the organizations in which your parents are employed. How we make sense of these things depends on the theory we use. We live within the designs and assumptions of past theory about effort and its organization every day at work. However, if we are aware of the theories that hold us

IMAGE 1.1   Theory and shopping

captive we at least have the chance to understand the ties that bind us, and, maybe, we might even be able to change them.

You need to be clear about the theory that you are using just as much as you need to be clear about the theories that frame the organizations in which you are working. Remember, theory makes sense of the world – and theory need not be scary!

WHAT IS PRACTICE?

Practice is what connects disparate actors, material things, and ideas (see Antonacopoulou (2008) for a much fuller analysis of the idea of practice). In practice, managers situate themselves and are situated within knowledge that enables them to be coordinating, controlling, and communicating with various others. These others may be thought of as stakeholders – people who have an interest in the organization, such as employees, share-holders, customers, suppliers, and governments. In addition, they are interacting with various things: with immaterial artifacts such as software, systems, models, and accounting principles as well as with material arti-facts such as buildings, computers, and machines.

These relations often form routines in organizations that are reflected in historically evolved collective patterns of interconnected actions, activities, and modes of knowing. These collective patterns are governed by a purpose, certain rules, formal and informal routines – in short, organization – which are embedded in technological and societal contexts. Although not necessarily the most important part of this complex scheme of things, these arrangements all depend on individuals designing, maintaining, and reproducing them. So let us look at individuals next, before we get to the main title – *Managing and Organizations*.

INDIVIDUALS IN A SOCIETY OF ORGANIZATIONS

Individuals wrapped up in chains

The French philosopher Jean Jacques Rousseau (1712–1778) wrote that 'Man is born free, but everywhere he is in chains.' When he wrote these words in pre-revolutionary France in *The Social Contract* (2006 [1762]), the 'bonds' he had in mind were those of feudal, monarchical, and religious privilege. The modern world, in contrast, has been shaped by the principles of *liberté*, *égalité*, and *fraternité* (liberty, equality, and fraternity). If Rousseau could be transported forward into the present, would he find then that the chains binding individuality have been dissolved by more than two centuries of progress?

In the contemporary world the bonds of organizations shape our lives: from being born in a hospital, entered into the Registry of Births, Marriages, and Deaths – which tracks the whole population and changes in it – enrolled in formal schooling in kindergarten from an early age, proceeding through primary, secondary, and then higher education, to be employed by an organization to earn a salary or wage, perhaps going to festivals, concerts, cinemas, or joining clubs for recreation, being a member of various spiritual, social, and sporting organizations, checking train and bus timetables, flying on airlines for holidays, having children of our own, enrolling them in school, seeing them into work, growing old, looking forward to the pension or superannuation, planning the retirement experience, perhaps moving into a 'sunset home' in our old age, and then dying, and being re-entered for the last time into that Registry of Births, Marriages, and Deaths.

Almost every aspect of our everyday life – and, indeed, our deaths – will be shaped by organizations of one kind or another. Billions of individuals – all of who can lay claim to uniqueness – are every day being organized as members of organizations – as employees but also as students, customers, and clients. While each of us is both alike and unique – our essential biology is remarkably similar, irrespective of ethnicity, marked only by gender differences – is this also the case of the many organizations through which we pass?

Consider those organization types that you have already experienced. One, mentioned already, deals with your birth, marital status, and death while the other concerns your education. The Registry of Births, Marriages, and Deaths and the university both chart individual progress through life through entries in databases. The university deals with a slice of life while the Registry deals with the whole of life. Both employ many experts in different fields to enter and interpret the data. Each has quite sophisticated routines in place for registering the information that they then attend to, from records of births signed by medical practitioners to classroom records of attendance, assessments performed, and grades recorded. The uniqueness

IMAGE 1.2   Rousseau: 'Man is born free but everywhere he is in chains'

of each individual is the subject of a vast amount of organizational effort in the modern world, rendering that uniqueness into statistics, into data, creating a record that is, from some perspectives, the sum of you.

What are individuals?

Being an individual means that each body – and all that it contains – is as unique as the fingerprints we leave or the DNA that constructed us. You can only really ever be you and not another person – although as an actor you may assume the identity of another person. Identity is a concept that cannot be defined easily, other than to say that identity refers to the way a person constructs, interprets, and understands who they are in relation to others in their life world. Identity may be more or less stable, more or less fragmented, more or less problematic, and more or less secure. The personal identities that we emphasize in one space may be very different from those that we emphasize in another. Thus, the identity that we develop and project at work may be very different from that which we project when clubbing or playing a sport. We have multiple identities.

Not all acting occurs only on stage or on screen. In everyday life we often are said to be actors, acting out parts, learning to be siblings, lovers, parents, and members of many and various organizations. So our identity is not fixed but fluid, within the genetic inheritance that defines our uniqueness. We may have a relatively fixed genetic appearance but exercise, diet, styling, aging, and surgery can modify that quite markedly. We may have a definite personality, but, once again, ill health, drugs, diet, and life experiences can reshape the ways that we present ourselves to the world, often quite dramatically.

Some celebrities in popular culture are famous for their shifting iconography, the way they style themselves and hint at their changing personality. Within our unique bodies most of us like to think we have a uniquely free will. Only we are master or mistress of ourselves, a sentiment particularly strong in toddlers, but certainly not absent from more mature manifestations of will. To think otherwise is to accept that the fates, the stars, the gods, society, or some other transcendent entity guides our lives as preordained. Often, our glimpses of celebrity seem to offer another, more exciting world than that which we live in. But even celebrity does not escape routine: rehearsals, performances, organizing glamour weddings in between checking in and out of rehab, the divorce courts, and the gym. As individuals we have power to shape organizational practice; we can vote in elections or choose to support various products. Each time we make a purchase we make a decision whether or not to support a particular organization's products. However, individual choice is constrained. These constraints may be as obvious as a police officer forcing you to comply with the rules imposed by the structure of the state, or as discrete as the behaviour encouraged by the language one uses in conversation with one's peers.

When we become organization members each of us has to surrender some of our autonomy to the control of others and other things such as schedules, machines, routines, and deadlines. In return we receive wages, salaries, or fees, identifying us as workers, staff, or independent professionals. Actually, we receive far more than mere income. We are able to bask, as unique individuals, in the ambience of a unique organization. Its brand helps define who we are: we are US Customs Officers, or Australian Tax Officers, or London Police Officers; we are Oxford academics or college professors; we are Vogue models or Chelsea football players. Sometimes we bask in a reflected light: we may be Chelsea football fans rather than supporters of Arsenal, wear Armani rather than Dolce & Gabbana, or wear Nike rather than Adidas. We can attach our identities as individuals to organizations quite easily.

MANAGING

Framing managing

A key term in theory is the idea of there being a **frame** through which we understand things. We will use this introduction to develop some key terms with which to understand this book.

All managing involves **framing**: separating that which deserves focus from that which does not. One thing that managers have to do all the time is to differentiate between the relevant and the irrelevant, just as do the authors of textbooks, trying to manage their expectations of their readers. To do this we, much as managers, frame some things as more relevant than others.

We can differentiate between **managing** as a practice, as something that we do, and **organizations** as a goal-oriented collectivity, in which we

---

A **frame** is a term that comes from the cinema: a director frames a shot by including some detail and omitting other detail. A frame defines what is relevant.

Frames enable us to do **framing**. They focus us in on specific relevancies: by framing we decide on what is relevant from the infinite number of stimuli, behavioural cues, sense data, and information that surround us.

Managing is an active, relational practice which involves doing things. The things that managers do are supposed to contribute to the achievement of the organization's formal goals.

Organizations are systematically arranged frameworks relating people, things, knowledge, and technologies, in a design intended to achieve specific goals.

are **organized**. We begin with organizations and then move on to the tasks of managing them, arguing that both are changing radically. We relate the formal rationalities of **management** – the plans, design, and other procedures – to the necessity for individuals and groups within organizations to make sense of them.

> To be **organized** means being an element in a systematic arrangement of parts, hopefully creating a unified, organic whole.

What do managers do?

Managers use different technologies, knowledge, and artifacts such as Lotus Notes, memos, or Microsoft Outlook to help frame what is relevant and then manage it. Diary appointments, to-do notes, agendas – these are all devices that frame the relevancies of the working day and enable us to manage our time; however, we should never mistake the technical devices that management uses for management itself. For instance, using accounting techniques or financial management programs is only a part, a small part, of what a manager does. Great managers are not merely good technicians but also expert managers of social relations – between themselves and others as well as between themselves, others, and things such as plans, documents, and data analysis.

> **Management** is the process of communicating, coordinating, and accomplishing action in the pursuit of organizational objectives while managing relationships with stakeholders, technologies, and other artifacts, both within as well as between organizations.

Managing signifies being in charge of something, being responsible for its smooth running and its rational conduct, handling and controlling it as if it were a well-oiled machine; thus, it is a relational term. Managing takes place in organizations. In terms of everyday usage it means handling, directing, controlling, exercising skill in executive ability – the acts done by the person in charge of controlling and directing the affairs of an organization. Managing entails framing.

> Being **rational** means systematic application of various techniques to achieve some given end or goal.

Managers strive to be **rational** and much of organizational life consists of routines that make this **rationality** easier to enact; hence they practice management.

> **Rationality:** Action that is produced according to some rule; action that is not random or unpatterned.

WHAT DO YOU MEAN?

The etymology – the origins in language – of the key terms 'management' and 'organizations'

In Italian, the terms *manege*, with *maneggiare* meaning to handle, train (horses), with the stem deriving from *mano*, from the Latin *manus*, for hand, were well known from the seventeenth century. The term manager has its origins in English in the period 1555–1565. Shakespeare used it in the late sixteenth century, in *A Midsummer Night's Dream*, in the context of theatrical management. He talks of a character being a 'manager of mirth'. The terms management and manager had become known by about 1600, although the term manager did not enter into everyday English use until the nineteenth century.

The root stem of the word organization is the Greek *organum*, meaning, in an archaic sense, a wind instrument, but more recently, since about AD 1000, a mechanical device or instrument; it is closely related to the Greek term *órganon*, meaning implement, tool, bodily organ, musical instrument, akin to *érgon*, the word for work. In general use since at least the late fourteenth century, when the archaic form was *organizacion*. Etymologically, organizations are therefore tools designed for a specific purpose.

Managers always manage as interpretive individuals, as people who are trying to make sense of things – and sometimes these things may be confusing, ambiguous, and puzzling. Things become even more puzzling and ambiguous at times of rapid change. We will discuss the major trends shaping, and being shaped by, organizations and their impact on managing later in this chapter. We consider technological changes; the shifting international division of labour; globalization; the compression of conceptions of time and space; and the emergence of new generational values.

Although the origins of the term manager are manual – the stress on handling things – it would be quite wrong to think that management is a job that is principally premised on manual labour. Instead, it is largely a job that involves interpreting, understanding, directing, cajoling, communicating, leading, empowering, training, politicking, negotiating, enthusing, encouraging, focusing, explaining, excusing, obfuscating, communicating – a job full of action words that are all to do with the manager as a speaking subject, a person who manages to shape and express directions, in writing and in speech. The mastery of different forms of meaningful expression, in writing, talk, and images, is usually referred to as a mastery of discourse. Central to discourse is rhetoric; indeed, a skilled master of business will be a master of rhetoric. Rhetoric means the tools of persuasion and argumentation, the ways of producing agreement and of making a point. **Managers** have to be skilled at talking because their expressive capabilities will be the most used and useful assets that they have. In a world of individuals, all capable of going their own way, the manager's task is to steer, guide, and persuade people to pull together in a common enterprise – an organization – when this may not be the instinctive desire of those being addressed. To be an effective manager requires a combination of *power* and *knowledge*: power to be able to bend others to executive will and knowledge enough to be able to interpret both the nature of that will, resistance to it, and the effects of changing circumstances, contexts, and contingencies on its implications. Managers must constantly be interpreting the people, technologies, and environments that they enact and with whom they interact. Hence, managers must blend technical skills with sophisticated social skills to be effective.

Managers are middletons: they intercede between executive authority, howsoever lodged, and those whose task it is to execute it. Historically, they were the supervisors, comprising the staff – those who had superordinate vision over subordinates, who were the hired 'hands'.

ORGANIZATIONS

Organization characteristics

Organizations all differ in what they do. Think of some of the organizations that you will have encountered thus far in life. Schools, designed to educate; police, intended to regulate, or media, functioning to communicate. Irrespective of the rationale of any specific organization, they will all be purposive, with specific objectives and goals, giving rise to the following characteristics:

1 The organization and its actions are consciously shaped by the organization's design, expressed through its routine practices and specific structure.

2 The organization is not time- and motion-less: changes will occur as organizations revise their practices intermittently in the light of experience.

3 The organization will be future oriented, as the members of the organization seek to achieve a desired and planned future. Often this future will be expressed in terms of key performance indicators or targets.

4 The organization will employ hierarchy and a division of labour to create distinct and related roles that are laterally separated and stratified vertically. A hierarchy is a systematic arrangement of powers of command and control with reciprocal obligations of obedience and consent lodged in those being managed.

5 Responsibilities are defined for roles, and actions, roles, and responsibilities are revised in the light of experience as future actions unfold.

6 As future action unfolds the preferential weighting of actions, roles, and responsibilities is systematically revised by programmes of change management or organization reform.

Behind all organizations' roles, relations and responsibilities are rules: organizations are built on rules. Rules provide for rationality. A rule tells how things have been done in the past and how they should be done in the future. If organizations follow rules it is thought that they will minimize opportunities for error. Rules protect organization members; they ensure rationality.

Brunsson (2006: 13), a leading European management thinker, suggests that organizational actions are not just guided by formal instructions and directives but also by informal rules. Additionally, as Brunsson (2006: 14) suggests, experience-based learning and imitation will also play a role. The first often tells us how to short cut rules that we find inconvenient. We follow the rule but, on reflection, think that there is a better way of doing it. Learning to drive is like this – when you pass the driving test you have to 'do driving according to rule' in a way that you will probably never do as you become a more experienced driver, and your driving becomes more fluid. So you drive without risk or danger on a country road a little above the speed limit because you are an experienced and safe driver and there is little traffic on the road. When the speeding ticket arrives in the mail a few weeks later you wish that you had followed the speed rules, or more likely had seen that speed camera so that you could slow down until out of range. Rules, especially as they have legitimate authoritative sanctions attached to them, which are then applied to you, can be a powerful experience – especially when rules are paired with punishment (you speed, you get a fine).

QUESTION TIME

Organizations can be thought of as huge repositories of rules. These rules often have different origins and rationalities supporting them, and, as a result, they may often come into conflict. From the above examples it is also clear that these organizational rules originate from both individuals comprising organizations as well as from the social relations and institutions embedded within organizations. These produce some unlikely similarities: consider the following questions.

1 What essential features does a kindergarten share with a university?
2 In what ways could a university be compared with a fast food restaurant?
3 In what ways might a McDonald's be similar to a car factory?

Check out the Companion
Website www.sagepub.co.uk/
managingandorganizations3
for free access to an article by
Parker and David Jary (1995) if
you want to learn why some
universities and McDonald's have
some things in common.

Organizations go on while members change

Organizations have an embedded, structural reality that endures irrespective of their members. People may come and people may go but the organization retains an identity separate from the individuals who comprise it. Think of the educational institution in which you are reading this book: every year a new cohort of students enters, staff retire or resign, and new staff are employed, but the university or college carries on regardless. The same routines – enrolment, lectures, tutorials, seminars, and assessments – are carried out year to year irrespective of who is doing them.

Organizations are huge repositories of rules

Let us take a closer look at what we mean by 'rules'. Here are some common distinctions:

1 *Formal rules*: You will arrive at a certain time and leave at a certain time. This is often a really stupid rule as it slows everyone down as the roads clog with people all trying to get to the organization at the same normal time – often making many people late. Should people be able to come and go as they please at work?
2 *Professional rules*: These are the rules that you have internalized, perhaps as a result of a professional accreditation, achieved in, or in conjunction with, your higher education. But sometimes the organization that employs you will require things of you that simply cannot be done as and when is required using the internalized rules. Which rules should you follow – the professional rules or those of the employing organization, if there is a clash between them?
3 *Legal rules*: These may be directives that are explicit, compulsory, and have a clear source and target within the organization. For instance, you shall not use organizational resources for personal purposes. But even a simple rule such as this can be difficult to follow. Should you not call friends and relations on the office phone?

4 *Standards*: Many organizations do many things according to standards authorized by explicit rules that are designed by independent standard-setting organizations, such as British Standards, Standards Australia or the International Standards Organization. These may cover many things from the correct lighting and plumbing standards, through health and safety standards, to quality standards or environmental standards. Standards can be very powerful devices in shaping similar behaviours in many organizations. What standards can you think of that shape organizational behaviour?

5 *Informal social rules*: For instance, about clothing. Men will wear jackets, shirts, and trousers and women may wear shirts, trousers, and skirts, but men usually do not because that would be 'cross-dressing'. In most organizations it is OK for women to wear trousers but this was not always the case. What happens if the men are Scotsmen, or Pacific Islanders? Is it then OK to wear 'skirts', if they are called kilts, *sulu*, *pareau*, *lavalava*, or *sarong*? If they are men in hot climates, are shorts acceptable? How long should they be? Should they be worn with socks? Should the socks be long or short? Should the shoes be white, black, or can they be sandals? These informal rules can be quite complicated.

QUESTION TIME

Choose three of the following organizations: what do they have in common?

- Hospitals
- Correctional organizations
- Schools
- Railways
- The police service
- Orchestras and bands
- Military organizations
- Banks
- Disneyland
- Airlines
- Rock festivals

Organizations' arrangements are usually thought of as attempts at systematically rational approaches to goal achievement. Most organizations strive to be rational – that is, to be consciously designed to achieve specific ends in an ordered and systematic way, such as fitness, punishment, and training – sometimes even in one organization, such as the military.

Hierarchy is often seen as a necessary feature of any complex organization, involving delegation and authority, with communication, coordination, and control centralized on the top management team. Additionally, in most organizations, different roles are clearly distinguished and prescribed. Members and non-members are usually clearly differentiated, whether the latter are defined as clients, customers, patients, or civilians.

Organizational identity

The notion of an **organizational identity** usually means that organizations are assumed to have clear boundaries, a large degree of autonomy, and distinctive characteristics that differentiate them from other organizations.

Organizations have distinct identities. Corporate organizations often strive to shape their **organizational identities** in ways that reflect their conception of the corporate image.

In addition, they often seek to present a coherent corporate identity to the world. That an organization should prove to be a source of identity is not so surprising. Since the late nineteenth century it has been established that corporate bodies – organizations – have a distinct 'legal personality'. Attributes such as logos create familiar signs and symbols, which help to reinforce the brand. Most people have a fairly clear idea quite quickly of what organization they work for or are visiting. Some of what these organizations do as everyday activity helps define them: the accounts they keep, the orders they ship, the web pages they maintain. Other, more intangible elements, which are often referred to as 'organization culture', which we discuss in Chapter 6, are also important.

Brunsson (2006) suggests that identity, whether attached to the qualifier of either organizational or individual, is typically used to alert us to the unique properties and characteristics that individuals and organizations use to differentiate their unique features. All notions of identity are relational: distinguishing something means denoting a difference from something else just as much as it may be an affirmation of likeness and similarity with others. Organizational identities are becoming increasingly complicated: firms that enter into alliances to deliver products, projects, and services blur the boundaries of their unique identity. Alliances are one of the most common of the new organizational forms (see Chapter 14), involving the forging of innovative collaborations, partnerships, and networks. For instance, many companies such as Oracle have hundreds of licensing arrangements with other companies as channels to market. Fashion leaders such as Benetton (Clegg, 1990) comprise a core firm that remains independent but linked to many suppliers and outlets by IT. The suppliers receive detailed small-batch orders for specific models and sizes of garment, using information derived from the sophisticated IT that each franchised outlet uses to send sales data to Benetton HQ.

MINI CASE

Zara

Zara operates a vertically integrated demand and supply chain – a *network* of organizations that collaborate to deliver a product or service to an end-user or market. Zara studies its customers' demand in the stores and tries instantly to modify just-in-time production schedules to meet the shifting patterns of demand. Zara's designers can 'interpret' the latest catwalk fashions from Paris, London, New York, or Milan and have them on the racks in five weeks. Zara uses IT to communicate directly with suppliers and designers in Spain. Shop managers use personal micro-computing devices to check on the latest clothes designs and place their orders in accordance with the demand they observe in their stores. Zara's speed is the secret of their success.

What management and organization aspects of Zara's business model help to make it so successful? Use the web to research the case.

IMAGE 1.3   Zara –
Europe's most successful
fashion chain

Many other firms, especially in high-technology organizations and in major project-based organizations, working on projects such as major pieces of infrastructure, use alliances between different organizations to produce a consortium of skills that in alliance can do what none of them can do independently (see Pitsis et al., 2003). None of these types of organizations are characterized by a clear-cut identity that maps easily to any one legal identity. Their identity is tied up with the networks that they form and is indistinguishable from them.

Organizations as professional institutions

Especially in knowledge-intensive organizations that employ many professionals, such as universities, hospitals, high-technology firms, and R&D (research and development) labs, it is often the professional boundaries and identities that are most meaningful for the individual employee. Their identity might stem more from the profession they belong to than the organization they work in. Further, organizations are subject to many institutional demands from their environment and, as many organizations share the same environment of legislation and standards, they tend to end up looking very similar – they all have the same ISO standards in place, they all have to comply with EEO (Equal Employment Opportunity) legislation and OHSS (Occupational Health and Security) laws, and so on. Large consulting companies, for example, offer similar solutions to the various problems that they face and so they end up with similar recipes: quality management, business process re-engineering, or knowledge management. As we will explore in Chapter 13, these institutional tendencies make organizations less distinctive and more alike.

Institutions are recognizable in as much as specific practices are widely followed, accepted largely without debate, and exhibit properties of endurance.

According to Scott (2001), one of the main scholars in the field, **institutions** are social structures that persist and endure and, in doing so, strongly shape the way that people, especially professionals, in organizations do the things they do. Institutions have been conceptualized as being made up of various elements. If the emphasis is on *cognitive* elements then we tend to talk of common mental maps or archetypes among professionals; if the emphasis is on more normative elements, then we focus on the informal rules and expectations that surround an institution, while regulative elements usually refer to either state regulation, often coercive in kind, or more subtle regulation by institutionalized standards, such as ISO 9000. These, together with associated activities and resources, provide stability and meaning in our sense of the organization of work, business, and everyday life.

Institutions are formed from habituated action that is routinely repeated and sometimes changed. The agents of change are often referred to as institutional entrepreneurs, and may be either particular individuals or organizations, such as Richard Branson and Virgin, changing business models in related fields such as trains and airlines by cross-pollinating ideas from one field to the other.

Hierarchy implies status differentia based on relations of super- and subordination and associated privileges and distinctions.

The reality of complex organization means that **hierarchy** does not always work well. Sectional interests often prevail. At the operational level what it makes sense to do is what appears to be in a department's best interests rather than that of the organization as a whole. Interestingly, this has been a recurrent phenomenon in very hierarchical organizations, such as military, intelligence, and government bureaucracies, where departments and services have competed for political attention and resources, such as seeking funding for new battleships rather than new tanks, or for domestic surveillance rather than foreign operations. Where the parts are completely coordinated and controlled from the centre then important cues can be missed, ensuring a lack of flexibility and adaptability, as the behavioural theorists of the firm realized (Cyert and March, 1963). It is at the boundaries and interface of the organization with other organizations – suppliers and customers, information analysts and service providers, other companies and civil society groups – that crucial behavioural cues can be enacted and shape action – but not if everyone is following central management dictate. In some management textbooks the job of being a manager looks pretty simple: it is the task of managers to have an overview of everything that is going on and steer the organization accordingly. Of course, this is absolutely unrealistic in anything but a small business – and even there it is sometimes difficult to work out where one's stock is being pilfered, or why customers are not returning.

Total control rarely occurs in any organization – if it did, there would be no need for the extensive literature on the gap between decision-making and implementation that we discuss in Chapter 7. As Brunsson (2006: 32) suggests, the implementation gap can in fact be a good thing – it creates space for subordinate and marginal views to get a hearing. Also, it allows managers to talk the talk that people expect without the risks of walking the walk – the risk that their decisions will lead to action is minimized. As Brunsson says, this can be especially useful 'when organizational action is expensive or awkward, or when organizations encounter inconsistent demands from their environment' (Brunsson, 2006: 32).

Often, an organization's managers will say one thing and do something different. There can be several reasons for this. First, they are creating cover for what they really want to do; second, they may be quite wrong in what they want to do and their subordinates or those on the margins are trying to tell them so, because they are closer to the action and have a better insight into what can be done. Smart managers will listen and do something different, accepting good advice in good spirit. Not so smart ones will probably carry on regardless.

Smart managers know that their actions and those of the people around them shape – or should shape – their preferences. Those who cultivate the illusion of acting emphatically, carrying a metaphorical big stick, usually come unstuck. They seek to act out their projects but in a way that can only be a kind of fantasy that does not connect with the reality in which they find themselves. Typically, managers report to a **top management team**, which in turn reports to an ultimate governing body: a board of directors, a university council, or (in government) a cabinet, for example. Again, as Brunsson (2006: 33) suggests, if the top management team's managers want to be able to implement decisions they are better making them in alignment with the preferences of their subordinates rather than against them.

> The **top management team** comprises the senior executives in any organization, the people who set strategy, direction, and purpose.

What do top management teams do? In profit-oriented organizations the crucial factor is to maintain a sustainable flow of earnings and profits; for other organizations, it is more complex. In not-for-profit organizations there is a great deal more to manage than the bottom line.

Some organization theorists suggest that it is not just financial **capital** that needs to be managed but also other kinds. In the case of a university, for example, there are different types of capital, each of which needs to be managed. There is the financial capital, required to ensure that the university is a 'going concern', and there is also, very importantly, social capital (above all, that intangible thing called 'reputation'). Social capital refers to whom you know rather than what you own or what you know; social capital is the set of relations and knowledge embedded in those relations that you are able to mobilize. For instance, in business schools students not only learn from the formal curriculum but also make social contacts that they can relate to later in their business career.

> **Capital** is an abstract concept that might take many material forms. Traditionally, it was thought of purely in economic terms, as wealth invested in an asset with the intention of delivering a return to the owner of that asset. As such, capital implies complex sets of relations of ownership and control of the asset and employment in its service.

Recently, it has become common to talk of intellectual capital, meaning knowledge that is worth something, that can earn its owner a return on the investments made in acquiring it. The most obvious example would be where one has intellectual property rights to benefit from a specific innovation or invention.

SENSEMAKING

What is sensemaking?

Top management teams are supposed to set a common frame within which organization members, customers, suppliers, investors, etc., can make

Sensemaking: Managers have to be highly skilled and competent in managing to make sense of what they do. In management, the key competency has become known as *sensemaking*, which has been defined by Weick (2008) as the ongoing retrospective development of plausible images that rationalize what people are doing.

Check out the Companion Website www.sagepub.co.uk/ managingandorganizations3 for free access to an article by Karl Weick if you want to learn more about sensemaking.

common sense of the organization – what it is and what it does. If the members of an organization cannot negotiate some commonsense and shared understanding, goal achievement is difficult.

We all make sense of everything around us all of the time. Organization and management theorists refer to this as **sensemaking**. One way to think of sensemaking is to compare it with driving: as you drive you interpret and try to make sense of other road users' and pedestrians' intentions and behaviours, as well as of all the traffic signs around you. You are constantly making sense of a mass of detail, data, and interpretation.

Much of what happens in organizations entails a constant process of sensemaking. Organizations are a little like a busy intersection through which a great deal of traffic is moving. Managers may be thought of as 'drivers' – they seek to steer things, make things happen as they are intended to. Some managers are driving for performance, for instance production managers; others are driving marketing or sales; some others are driving human resource management.

Sensemaking characteristics

What are the characteristic activities that bind such different kinds of managing together? Consider the definition of sensemaking given in the margin above and explore each of its terms in a little more detail:

1 *Ongoing*: We are always making sense – we never stop doing so, even when asleep – our dreams are ways of making sense of deep issues that we must deal with in our wakeful moments. Our sense of what we are experiencing is always of the moment – fleeting, experiential, changing, and contextual.

2 *Retrospective*: We make sense of something as it is elapsing and we are constantly reviewing the sense we make in terms of additional sense data.

3 *Plausible*: We never make perfect but provisional sense, sense that is good enough for the matter and people at hand. It allows us to go on with what we are trying to do. While accuracy may be desirable, reasonable constructions that are continuously updated work better as directional guides, especially when things are changing fast.

4 *Images*: We often work with representations of things – models, plans, and mental maps – as we navigate our way around unfamiliar territory. We hear what the other is saying and try to accommodate it to things we already know and carry round with us as our stock of knowledge.

5 *Rationalize*: We rationalize the meaning of things that are confusing to make them clearer and justifiable.

6 *People*: Although organizations contain many things that act which are not people – such as computers and keypads – it is people who do the sensemaking.

7 *Doing*: We do things through thinking and action, which define one another. Weick uses a rhetorical question, 'How can I know what I think until I see what I say?' The point he is making is that when people act they discover their goals, which may be different even when we think we are dealing with the same cues.

We all make sense of things all the time and sometimes the sense that we make may be quite different from another person's – even though we might think we are dealing with the same cues. In organizations, managers should aim to have their employees make the same sense.

We make individual sense of what's happening around us. We use our sense data – sight, sound, touch, taste, and smell – to assemble impressions of unfolding events and then we use our cognitive capacities to make a pattern from the data. The sense we make is always *our* sense – *you* make the sense – but you never do so in isolation. You use many cues to make sense: past experience; what others say they think is happening; likely stories that you are familiar with that seem to fit the pattern that appears to be forming; and so on. People will not use these cues in a uniform way, because they are individuals and, as a result, people can make wildly different senses from the same set of cues.

Why are organizations interested in sensemaking?

Organizations have a considerable interest in their members making common sense. Any organization appears to be only as good as its people, products, and services, and if these people are consistently 'on message', making a sense that is common across customers, suppliers, shareholders, and employees, then this is a vital factor in assisting the organization to produce consistent products and services. Common sensemaking is important for organizations.

It is because common sensemaking is important for organizations that a vital part of the management task is to try and produce many cues for common sensemaking. An important part of the manager's job is to create, adapt, and use common frames of meaning that characterize the organization and its members. However, making sensemaking common is no easy matter in a world of individuals. We are all, in principle, free to interpret things as we please. But of course, practically, we usually try to obey the law when doing so; we follow habits and routines; we interpret using familiar categories and concepts that are customary in our language. Managers also employ many different tools to help develop common sense. Have you ever received or experienced any communications from your university, old school, sporting club, or favourite shops that could have shaped your sensemaking practices?

As we have said, management is not dissimilar to driving. Driving is not only a complex activity in itself, involving acute hand, feet, eye, and brain coordination, but it takes place in a complex environment of signs. Some of these signs are advisory; others are prescriptive. These signs are cues for you to use to manage your flow in the traffic on the road. When you drive, you immediately enter into a complex system – the car – of whose workings your knowledge is likely to be less scientific and more a matter of 'know-how'. Once you are driving the car you are interacting with a great many other road users as well as interacting with the environment that they share with you. As you share this environment you also constitute it because the sense that you make of the road becomes a factor for the sensemaking of all those other drivers in proximity to you.

You constitute a part of the environment for these others as they constitute a part of it for you. You cannot control what these other drivers do but you can signal your intentions in many subtle ways such as the way that you drive and the traffic signals that you give. Meanwhile, your driving is framed by all the prescriptions that surround you: Slow Down! 50 km zone! Stop!

Road signs are visible cues and artifacts that provide prescriptions for driving. They seek to shape the environment in which we do driving. When we drive we make sense of the signs and cues that surround us. Managing is similar. Organizations want their members to drive in unison and harmony, with a common understanding, and no nasty accidents. They provide many cues and artifacts that try and frame this common sense. The most obvious ones would be uniforms, which visually position the individuals they employ as members. Hence, many organizations, such as large-scale bureaucracies, including the churches, police, military, hospitals, railways, and airlines, dress their members in uniforms. Thus, we may say that organizations often reinforce the way that they shape the identity of their members by dressing them up in uniforms. Probably the first uniforms were military ones – it helped to distinguish who was friend and who was foe on the field of battle – but we find uniforms today in many walks of life, from small settings such as car rental counters or restaurants, to large complex organizations such as hospitals or armies. In some of these organizations the subtle distinctions between gradations of rank are encoded in uniform: take a look at Images 1.4 and 1.5 – can you see any signs of different status in common identity?

The uniforms are sometimes more symbolic and culturally valued than they are functional; the soldiers in the picture guard the Royal Palaces in Copenhagen and, rather like the guards at England's Buckingham Palace, have to wear a uniform and headgear that is neither comfortable nor practical – but it has enormous symbolic value, denoting them as Royal Guardsmen. More often than not the function of uniforms is as much symbolic as functional; the other photo shows bar and restaurant staff in a corporate uniform. When we see people wearing clothing that identifies them corporately as members of an organization we know that management is positioning them not just as employees but as employees who 'belong' to the organization.

Management seeks to establish rules and rational routines that will make individual sensemaking predictable. Uniforms help to do this because they code in a shorthand way what rank people have, what they might know and do.

Tools and sensemaking

Most managers try to be people who are not just managing but doing the best that they can with the best tools and advice available. Just like drivers, they are trying to follow the signs, interpret the complex situation, make sense of it all, and get somewhere – that is their goal – as they do so. Drivers do so using a tool – the car – and their capacity for sensemaking.

IMAGE 1.4 and 1.5   Being clothed in and by organizations

Managers also use tools to get things done: accounting systems, resource planning models, and so on. These tools are designed to be rational instruments to aid managing. But, just as the car is a tool, and will not go anywhere if it is not driven, so it is with management tools. They only work insofar as they are made sense of and driven. Managers are the drivers and those people with whom they interact in and around the organization are the sensemakers.

Tools do nothing on their own; they have to be used; they have to be made sense of in terms of the specific context of their application, the time available to do something, the information that is at hand, the skills and capabilities that are available. Thus, managing is actively constructed – made sense of – by ordinary people going about their everyday organizational life, using such resources as come to hand – including rational tools, instruments, and designs. But the important thing is the *use to which they are* put – not that they *merely exist* – and that there is a distinct individual who is the user and who is making sense of the context and situations of use. A number of factors thus enter into sensemaking.

WHAT DO YOU MEAN?

Aspects of sensemaking

Sensemaking is a complex phenomenon. It involves:

- *Social context*: Sensemaking is influenced by the actual, implied, or imagined presence of others. If other people think that a particular interpretation makes sense then you are more likely to do so as well.
- *Personal identity*: A person or group's sense of who they are is important in sensemaking. Certain situations may subvert or reinforce this sense of identity. Think of yourself reading this book. By now you should be thinking that managing – which might have seemed such a new idea – is now more familiar because you are able to relate it to your identity as a driver.
- *Retrospection*: What people notice in elapsed events, how far back they look, and how well they remember the past, all influence sensemaking. Organizationally, this is extremely important because, sometimes, the most important decisions are often the least apparent: decisions made by minutes secretaries – what to keep and what to discard – can provide the basis for any later sense that can possibly be made by organization members. While these are not strategic or conspicuous decisions they construct the organizational past.
- *Salient cues*: When we read detective novels and try to work out 'who done it' we are doing sensemaking. Managers will use

sketches of what is going on and who is who in making sense, which they have derived from their past experiences; thus they project their pasts onto their futures.
- *Ongoing projects*: Stuff is always happening. We provide structure to divide the unfolding of events into different patterns. Often situations are structured in such a way as to assist you in doing this: for instance, football is a game of two halves; symphonies have different movements. In a football game, for example, one goal can change the whole meaning and tempo of a game.
- *Plausibility*: To make sense is to answer the question, 'What's the story here?' Sensemaking is about creating meaning that is sufficient to carry on with current projects.
- *Enactment*: Actions can modify that which is being observed. Something seems to be overheating and you take steps to cool it. Your action enacts your understanding of the situation – it's overheating – and what you do changes the situation – now it's cooling down.
- *Drafting*: Sensemaking involves redrafting an emerging story so that it becomes more comprehensive as events unfold and are interpreted.
- *Doing*: Sensemaking involves framing details as relevant, to isolate particular themes in an emerging story and provide an answer to the question, 'What's going on?'

(Adapted from Weick, 1995; 2008)

Sensemaking is endemic in organizational life. Organizations are full of plausible stories – rumour, gossip, official statements, business plans, and websites – each sensible in its own way but none necessarily coherent with the others. People talk all the time at work. Much of what they say is formal: the transmission of instructions and information; the making and taking of orders; the analysis of data and artifacts; debating issues in meetings, or making speeches and presentations. Yet, *even more is not formal*, which is to say that it is neither constitutive of, nor mandated by, the occupational and organizational roles that organization members fill.

Everyday talk in organizations engages an infinite variety of topics as matter for discourse. Some of these relate to the currency of intimacy: talk of one's appearance, family, friends, and significant others; while others deal with more generalized others to be found in sports, media stories, politics, or a new movie. Sometimes this talk makes a difference to the formal organizational world: the resignation due to stress, illness, or the holiday necessary to recuperate from a gruelling project. Mostly it is just about being at work.

Multiple sources of sensemaking in organizations

Organizations often have multiple sources of formal meaning regarded as official. For instance, many organizations contain members who are represented by **unions**, which will formulate views on official policy of the organization that is equally formal and official but may well conflict with that of management. In a pluralist organizational setting, it is recognized that management and the unions will often hold competing but legitimate views on an issue. Unions are formal organizations that need to be managed; just as other organizations they use IT, maintain websites, and offer benefits and services to members.

Some people consider unions that seek to bargain collectively for the betterment of the rights and conditions of their members as illegitimate representations of irrational interests queering the pitch for the rational employer and loyal employee to collaborate harmoniously. Unions are secondary organizations because they can only ever organize in a space already organized by employers. To the extent that these employment spaces become increasingly global, the creation of solidarity by the union becomes far more difficult to manage.

Unions are sensemaking devices that many employers and conservative political parties antagonistically oppose because they regard the sense they make as a restraint on the free market. From this perspective labour is a commodity to be bought, sold, and used (or not used) just as any other commodity, and its sale should be at a market rate determined only for individual cases rather than at some collectively bargained price.

Management, employers, and the political parties that seek to represent their interests often regard unions with hostility, despite the many positive things that unions can achieve, such as legitimate grievance resolution, which can often minimize turnover with all its attendant costs, or obliging employers to be more innovative in the use of capital because the price of labour cannot be pushed lower. They want to exclude union sensemaking

Unions can be defined as an association of wage-earning employees mobilized and organized in order to represent their constituents' interests. These interests can often be counter to the interests of employers, but not always necessarily so.

Managerialism is the view that organizations should be normatively integrated by shared values expressed within a single source of authority, legitimacy, and decision-making embedded in the managerial hierarchy and serving the interests of the owners of that organization.

An **ideology** is a coherent set of beliefs, attitudes, and opinions. The meaning is often pejorative, with a contrast drawn between ideology and science.

from the picture. Often employers, managers, and the parties that seek to represent them have a unitarist frame of reference that espouses what is termed **managerialism**. The belief in management as a means capable of solving any problem elevates the necessity of management into an **ideology** of the modern world.

Where the owners are shareholders then the assumption is that the decisions that management makes can always be rationalized by reference to the maximization of shareholder value. In such a conception of the organization, resistance to management decisions is regarded as illegitimate and irrational.

In recent years managerialism – or new public management as it is known in the public sector – has come to pervade most aspects of organizational life. Managerialism involves the attempt to remake organizations in an idealized image revolving around a strong corporate culture, entrepreneurialism, quality, and leadership, and focused on achieving targets. The targets are often measured through audits – of culture, quality, job satisfaction, customer satisfaction, etc. These can be used to rank organizations according to a range of criteria. Power (1999) has argued that this is a sign that we live in an 'audit society' in which rankings of organizations are increasingly common, and where league tables determine the sense that is made of organizational performance.

How organization relations actually pan out will always depend on the specific sensemaking that we find in local situations, discourses, and practices. For instance, Scandinavian managers would expect to be union members; British and other English-language managers would not. Their attitudes to unions will differ in consequence.

When managerialism is expressed politically at the national level it can take the shape of a systematic mobilization of bias against collective representation, contracts, and rights, stressing instead the individual nature of employment contracts and effort bargains. When it is expressed politically at the organization level it is usually through the discourses of human resource management (HRM) in which mechanisms that create employee commitment to the organization are stressed, such as performance-related pay, regular performance appraisals, team working, empowerment, and skill development programs (see Chapter 5).

Among the major sensemaking tools in use in organizations are rational management plans, designs, structures, and theories – it is these that provide the categories and labels with which managing is done. Sometimes these work smoothly and paper over the little cracks that may occur in our understanding of the situation. We should expect to find a great deal of managerialism and rational planning in the organizational world. For one thing, trying to fix everyone's sensemaking on management's terms is a powerful device but, equally, we might also expect that some people might have a fair degree of cynicism and contestation about managerial interpretations when doing so.

Different types of sensemaking occur especially where things are uncertain or where things are not as we would have expected them to be, when sense just breaks down, or cannot be made, and normal expectations do not work. The computer messages that the system transmits are just plain puzzling and seem wrong, your colleagues are acting strange (what do they know that you don't?), and so on. When we make sense of breaches in everyday understanding, suggests Weick (2008), we look first for reasons that will enable us to keep on doing whatever it was that we were doing – we are averse to change. We make sense using devices such as what everybody knows, or apply rational analysis, or we ask others what they think is going on.

Sensemaking can be a matter of life and death

Organizations are often difficult places to make sense in, especially as we cross their rational boundaries. Consider the example of hospitals. Despite being focused on patient care they can in fact be dangerous for the patients. One reason for this is that the patient's body becomes the point of intersection of many different professional practices, such as radiography, anaesthetics, operative care, post-operative care, and so on. At each handover point there will be inscriptions – readings, charts, data printouts, briefings – that are passed from one team to another. Unfortunately, these present lots of opportunities for people to make different sense of the situation. Sometimes inscriptions will be misunderstood, sometimes improperly read or communicated, sometimes they will be faulty, and sometimes they just get it wrong. Organizations are full of handoff situations: when inspection comes into play; when training takes over; when memos are sent and instructions issued from one subunit to another. All of these offer ample opportunity for recipients to make plausible sense of incomplete details – and hopefully, not have to be accountable subsequently for the sense that they did, or did not, make at the time (Weick and Sutcliffe, 2003).

Sensemaking produces what we take to be rational

So, sensemaking is what all people in organizations will do routinely while they go about their busy organizational lives. Essentially, it is a process of pattern-making. We fit clues and cues together and make meaning out of them. We trace a frame, enabling us to connect things together and make a coherent and connected picture, often using metaphors to do so. Once we have the frame then we can make sense. Metaphors frame understanding to produce rationality.

One metaphor has long been dominant where management is concerned: the metaphor of engineering. The idea of there being a specific managerial rationality first emerged in the 1880s in the USA (Shenhav, 1999) from which early management writers created a new language of rationality, one that American engineer Frederick Taylor (1967 [1911]) popularized in the famous *Principles of Scientific Management*.

The father of modern management, Taylor insisted that under rational management 'all of the planning which under the old system was done by the workman, as a result of his personal experience, must out of necessity under the new system be done by management' (Taylor, 1967 [1911]: 38). Here decision-making is taken to be the domain of the superior intellect of the manager such that the manager (usually) can deploy a scientific rationality in order to find the 'one best way' proposed by Taylor's approach.

The divorce between decision and execution has been a central tenet of management science. Usually, the model of decision-making is described as a perfectly well-organized, rational, and logical process. Problems are defined, the relevant information is analysed, possible solutions are generated, and the optimal solution is decided upon and implemented. Deming's 'plan–do–check–act' (PDCA) cycle is an excellent example of how this is done in many contemporary organizations (see Deming, 2000). Organization members become disciplined and reflexive extensions of the corporate mind, able to exercise discretion, but in corporately prescribed ways. Much of modern management thinking follows this vector. It is framed by a simple assumption that what management does is nearly always necessarily and inherently rational.

METAPHORS FRAMING RATIONALITY

Metaphors use terms other than those of the subject under discussion to describe it. 'Dream-machine' is a recognizable metaphor.

Check out the Companion Website www.sagepub.co.uk/ managingandorganizations3 for free access to an article by Joep P. Cornelissen, Mario Kafouros, and Andrew R. Lock (2005) if you want to learn more about metaphors.

The **division of labour** produces a more specialized labour force. Instead of everybody trying to be a jack-of-all-trades and a master of none, capable of doing everything in an organization, labour becomes more specialized by breaking down large jobs into many tiny components.

While the essential tool of the driver is the car, the essential tool of the manager is often said to be rationality. However, while cars are very tangible and real, rationality is always a **metaphor**. A metaphor cannot be pointed to as if it were the new BMW in the street outside, although when asked about the car, the owner might use a metaphor to describe it, such as saying it is a 'dream-machine'.

Creating a metaphor always involves the literal meaning of a phrase or word being applied to a new context in a figurative sense, says Grant (2008: 896). Metaphors influence the way we describe, analyse, and think about things. As Morgan (1986) has argued, it is the metaphor of the machine that is most preponderant in its application to managing and organizations. So when rationality is attributed to managers and organizations it is often done so in terms of machine-like properties, such as 'the organization runs on clockwork'. We will look at three influential metaphors used in thinking about managing organizations as rational enterprises.

Metaphors of division

A very specific idea of rationality, one tied up with the **division of labour**, became embedded as the common sensemaking of modern management. Discussion of the division of labour goes back at least to Adam Smith (1723–1790), with his praise for the rationally divided pin-factory and its labours in *The Wealth of Nations* (1961 [1776]). Economic growth, according to Smith, is rooted in the increasing division of labour. Where there is a division of labour, each employee becomes an expert in one task, saving time in task-switching and thus increasing efficiency.

A smart organization divides all its tasks in terms of different roles and responsibilities and assigns these to different occupational titles, suggested Smith. In turn, these titles describe in shorthand the jobs that people are supposed to do.

Smith's ideas connected with many currents in the US, the home of modern management. In the military, especially strong after the US Civil War, West Point engineers were very influential in promulgating efficient engineering solutions to many problems. One man, in particular, F. W. Taylor, fused the engineering stream with one that emerged from the Deep South. Many of the practices used to manage slaves were based upon the idea that the people being managed were basically stupid and that therefore the means of control and direction needed to be very simple. Taylor adopted the idea that the best worker was a simple creature and he sought to design efficiently engineered solutions for designing and managing work based on the assumption that these simple employees were not to be trusted. What intelligence they had, he thought, often became manifest in cheating on their employers.

Metaphors of the organ

Another key metaphor for modern management and organizations is the assumption that organizations are analogous to an **organ**.

Putting the organ into organization, some people like to think about organizations as having brains and other organic characteristics. The brains are usually seen to be in the 'head quarters' (headquarters), the hands on the factory floor, and so on, all working in a harmony and unison designed by the brain. Such metaphors are essentially organic – they assume that the organization is akin to an organism – and have been around for a long time. They are especially popular with top management teams who think that they are the brains of the organization.

The problems with conceiving of organizations as an organ are evident. Only the top management team is allowed to have ideas; everybody else has to follow these. Thus, there is little scope for innovation to arise from anywhere other than the top. If good ideas emerge from elsewhere the odds are they will not be captured. Often they are not sought. A desperate Henry Ford asked why he always got stuck with the whole person rather than with a pair of hands. Hands were what he hired, but troublesome bodies with querulous minds were what he so often got, despite many systematic attempts by the Ford organization and the agencies it hired to screen out troublemakers and those morally unfit and insufficiently temperate in their habits for the regime on Ford's production line. The metaphorical body corporate easily reduces the literal body of the worker to be considered only as exemplary if the worker behaves as a puppet to the commands issued through the managerial pulling of strings (ten Bos and Rhodes, 2003).

Organizations conceived as an **organ** are seen as a collective body in which all the component parts should function much as do healthy organs in a human or animal body.

Metaphors of choice and rationality

Rational choice is a concept that adopts the view that all social interaction is a basically economic transaction undertaken by self-interested, goal-oriented individuals who exercise choice among alternative known outcomes that are based on their knowledge of, and the incentives that exist in, their immediate environment.

Sometimes it is assumed that everyone who works in whatever job they do does so because of a **Rational choice**, otherwise they would exit. Of course, this is to deny the many ways in which opportunities are structured historically, economically, socially, culturally, religiously, and so on.

Rational choice theories, beloved of economists, assume that individuals have an established preference or utility order. The rational person, it is assumed, will always maximize individual benefits and reduce costs in the choices that they make. There are many things wrong with the assumption that individuals exercise rational choice. The criticisms point to the neglect of individuals:

Ideas and preferences: These are always socially and organizationally formed and cannot be treated as independent and voluntary casual variables. You are Jewish or Muslim and abhor pork, for example, while I am Hindi and cannot bring myself to eat beef.

Motivations: Individuals sometimes have interests not only in their self and particular others, such as family members, but sometimes act on behalf of members of particular categories of person, such as women (feminist organizations; battered women's shelters), or religious orders (youth or social clubs). Individuals often act from rational motives that are not economically self-interested. Individuals' rational preferences are frequently shaped by irrational factors, such as emotions: think of the sports teams you love and hate.

Knowledge: Individuals never have perfect knowledge of alternatives and thus cannot weigh up preferences rationally.

Calculations: Individuals do not have an economic calculus for every action; some actions have value that is expressed morally, ethically, and socially rather than economically.

Habit: Many actions are considered very poorly, or very quickly, as matters of instinct or habit.

To talk of bounded rationality means accepting that there are limitations and constraints on human behaviour. People are cognitively limited, producing satisfactory rather than optimally rational decisions (March and Simon, 1958; Simon, 1957), which is referred to as 'satisficing', meaning accepting decisions that are both sufficient and satisfying. Conditions of uncertainty are often characteristic of decision-making situations. In situations of uncertainty individuals act inconsistently (and thus irrationally).

Individuals' choices made in the spirit of self-interest do not necessarily maximize the collective benefit; poor managerial choices can destroy things of great value, such as employment, careers, shareholder value, the environment, and social harmony. Indeed, if one takes a longer term perspective, choices made in the spirit of self-interest may not be of benefit over a longer period: for example, burning fossil fuels can further climate change; using common land to feed one's animals, because it is a free resource, leads to the depletion of the resource.

Social scientists are skeptical about the capacity of human decision-making to be utterly rational. Instead they prefer to see people as only ever rational within the bounds of their knowledge and ignorance. They see people as characterized by **bounded rationality**.

From a bounded perspective, rationalized practices are seen as essentially cultural, expressed through managerial talk and writing (Dobbin, 1994).

Fligstein (2002) showed how different managerial groups sought to promote their own expertise as the basis for organizational rationality in the emerging multi-divisional form of organizations that superseded bureaucracy, as we discuss in Chapter 14. The crucial thing is to appear to be rational by having all of the symbols of rationality in place.

We could not express ourselves fully if we did not use metaphors. Yet, as we can see in these three cases, metaphors can be dangerous. Each of the metaphors that we have looked at assumes that rationality inheres in each of them. However, these assumptions of rationality dissolve when the metaphors are interrogated. In fact, we find that rational divisions of labour can produce irrational employees; that the organization conceived as a rational organ can stultify innovation; and that rational choices can sometimes be irrational.

WHY ARE ASSUMPTIONS OF RATIONALITY SO INFLUENTIAL?

Rationalist views are attractive to many managers. Such views place them in control. They tell them they know what they are doing. They make them feel authoritative. They place them clearly in the centre of their own frame. They legitimate these frames. They make them feel important – big men and tough women in business – even as their pretensions may be mocked by their subordinates, contradicted by their failures to make the world of work correspond to the ideal model, and compromised by the endless ways in which they have to ad hoc and cobble together compelling accounts of what they have been doing, which they know do not correspond with the reality that they have lived.

Sometimes, as some feminist critics suggest, managerial rationality seems a peculiarly masculine view of the world (Freeman, 1984), which we discuss in terms of gendered communication in Chapter 8. The rational attributes of decision-making are equated with male characteristics by contrast to the way that women have been represented as being emotional, capricious, unsystematic, and irrational (also see Calás and Smircich, 2006).

To maintain a rational model of organization would mean being able to closely control events and people, according to a tight script, even at a distance. As we will see in Chapters 11, 12 and 13, this is the very essence of bureaucracy. But any organization that ran like this would be not only a disaster in any environment subject to change but also impossible. It would be a disaster because there would be no deviance, no opportunity for learning or innovation (see Chapters 9 and 10), just a kind of *Stepford Wives* rationality (Oz, 2004). It would be impossible because we cannot help making sense, and we cannot help but make sense using a plurality of devices, as social beings. It takes a lot of training to have total tunnel vision; many failed organizations seemed to have thought it worthwhile to attempt it in pursuit of rationality.

How do organizations' managers know that they are being rational? Brunsson (2006: 34) suggests that they can do so by following rules, or imitating the ways in which other organizations operate, or through experimenting. Following rules is a sure-fire way of keeping out of trouble, even if the results are unfortunate, as we will see in Chapter 12. In reality, rule following is usually less about getting things done and more to do with keeping out of trouble. Similarly, if managers imitate what other managers who are perceived as being successful do, they can claim legitimacy for their actions – even if they fail – while experimentation may mean that they hit on something that they could never have arrived at intentionally (see Chapter 13).

Rational models are best thought of as descriptions of action that will usually be compelling for most organizational audiences – thus they are a handy tool with which to provide accounts of action – but they are not necessarily the best basis for determining what managing *actually* consists of. The metaphors of rationality have great legitimacy – in part because they have been around for a long time and in part because they have been associated with strong programmes for reforming organizations.

Irrationality literally means the non-interpretability of a rule or rules underlying action; in practice, it more often means action whose rationality runs counter to that which is dominant and authorized.

The opposite of rationality is **irrationality**. Given that the most powerful people in any situation usually get to define what rationality is, then it is not surprising that they also define what rationality is not, and thus what is irrational. Irrationality usually looks a lot like what the powerful oppose or that which opposes them. For instance, when managers implementing reforms encounter widespread resistance to change they tend to see the resistance as irrational. Resistance to change serves as additional evidence for managers of the rightness of the reforms being resisted and so a vicious cycle of more control generating more resistance often ensues (see Chapter 7).

A belief in rationality can become a self-fulfilling prophecy: if what managers define as rational is resisted then the resistance simply shows the irrationality that has to be reformed (Fleming, 2008). There are two types of resistance to change:

- *Resistance by omission*: Passive attempts at undermining what is being presented as rationality by withholding consent or support, demonstrating a lack of legitimacy of the rationality in question.

- *Resistance by commission*: More active attempts at blocking, thwarting, or otherwise sabotaging what the organization is trying to position as its rationality (Fleming, 2008).

Resistance can sometimes be thought of as an attempt to assert an alternative rationality. Claims to management knowledge that position it as rational often assume all other claims are merely the promotion of sectional, self-interested, and irrational strategies. Such views presuppose a unitary framework: that there is one correct way of seeing things. The unitary view of organizations is a major strategy in promoting managerial rationalities. Often, the argument is that where there is resistance then more work must be done in building commitment on the part of HRM (see Chapter 5);

otherwise, people would not resist! According to this view, if reason prevailed there would be total commitment and no resistance.

Many social scientists suggest that rather than restrict the category of rationality to plans that rarely work out in practice we should instead study the practical, situated rationality that people display in their everyday life – what is sometimes referred to as mundane reality. Hence, there are rationalities, rather than rationality per se. People make sense through their understanding of the world, their interpretations of other people and those things that populate their world. They have many categories and devices for making sense of this world; some of these will be shared with other members of the organization and some will not. Some will be regarded as legitimate by the organization while others will not. Organization members build their practices on their understandings.

We should not just study the formal rationality that characterizes modern organizations – the plans, documents, and devices of the top management team – but we should look at what people actually do with and to these. In other terms, rationalities will be plural, they will consist of both the words and the deeds that are done – and sometimes not done – in and around organizations.

Many of the strategic errors that managers make can be attributed to the fact that they manage as if the world depicted and represented in their tools and plans was actually as controlled and controllable as these make it appear to be. Rarely, given the ingenuity that we all bring to sensemaking, can this illusion be sustained, because we rarely use a shared common sense to make sense. We work from different interests, different disciplines, and different knowledge, with different power relations, striving to make sense using those terms that make sense to us. Of course, if we are all doing this, then we should expect managing to be a highly politicized and contested activity – which is precisely what management is.

THE CHANGING CONTEXTS OF MANAGING AND ORGANIZATIONS

We all learn to make sense of the situations we are in. However, just like a fast-flowing river, these situations are often changing in imperceptible ways. Before too long we find that the ways we have been using to make sense leave us out of our depth! Managers find that what they took for granted no longer helps them survive as well as it did in the past. Well-established direct techniques of the past, such as management by rules and instructions, by oversight and surveillance, by command and control, on the part of hierarchical managers, are changing. Today, what they seem to be changing to is use of more indirect techniques, such as managing in and through vision, mission, culture, and values, leading to a lot less imperative instruction and command and a great deal more dialogue and discussion. When everyone can be connected to anyone everywhere, when the value basis of employees is shifting radically, and when the organization laces

Check out the Companion Website www.sagepub.co.uk/ managingandorganizations3 for free access to an article by James G. March (2007) if you want to learn more about how the study of organizations and organizing has changed since the Second World War.

Paradigm: A coherent set of assumptions, concepts, values, and practices that constitute a way of viewing reality for the community that shares them, especially in an intellectual discipline, in which the views are widely shared as a result of training and induction into the methods of the discipline. In more mature disciplines, there is usually a single dominant or normal paradigm, whereas less developed disciplines are characterized by a plurality of paradigms because there is a lack of shared agreement on what the discipline entails.

Outsourcing occurs when an organization decides to contract a service provider who specializes in a particular area of service provision to do more economically and efficiently something that it previously did itself, such as catering, cleaning, maintenance, or IT.

itself over the globe and employs many of the diverse peoples that the globe has to offer, the old certainties are harder to hold on to.

Having considered sensemaking, we now move on to consider the contexts in which people work. We will first look at the generic changes that we think are important; then we will look at their impact on managing and organizations, relating them to specific chapters later in the book. The reasons why **paradigms** for management are changing are several. We need, however, to distinguish between academic paradigms and business paradigms. The former are ways of theorizing about an activity; in the case of the latter they would be the activity itself. For something to be a paradigm it must be accepted as an ideal model and exemplar, something that shows people how to practice something.

Organizations and technological changes

The shift to a digital world means that digital capabilities enable organization to be moved offshore – hence the spectacular rise of Bangalore in India as an IT and call centre 'district' – a region of the global economy in which a particular part of organizational activity is often done for many firms, using the English-language skills of Indian graduates, as well as those of the many fine computer and engineering graduates produced in this vast sub-continent. Of course, the main reason is that wage costs in India are far less than, say, Indiana or Aberdeen. Since it is much cheaper to live there, employers pay far less.

Outsourcing involves contracting the provision of certain services to a third-party specialist service provider rather than seeking to deliver the service from within one's own organization. Usually, outsourcing is entered into to save costs and to deliver efficiencies and productivity benefits. By not concentrating on services and tasks that are peripheral to the main business, an organization can better focus on those things it needs to do well while leaving the peripheral tasks to organizations that specialize in the delivery of those services. Often, areas such as HRM, catering, IT, and equipment and facilities maintenance are outsourced.

Outsourcing is not a new phenomenon: in major production industries such as automotives, the outsourcing of initially non-core and latterly core functions and services has been progressively used since the 1930s (Macaulay, 1966). The development of outsourcing, burrowing away at the innards of organizations, hollowing them out, and networking them into other organizations' capabilities and competencies, is often regarded as being a part of a shift that has been underway in organizations since the late twentieth century. The outsourcing of sectors such as IT and telecommunications, and business processing, occurred with the dawning of advanced digital telecommunications services. The imperative to outsource – as distinct from the opportunity to do so – was a result of other dynamics of the digital age, which we will shortly consider: primarily globalization and increased competition, leading to a continual need to improve efficiency from productivity and to increase service levels. Thus, vertically integrated services were no longer seen as the best organizational arrangements for gaining competitive advantage. Extending the organization's capabilities, whether core or non-core, to a third party became synonymous with efficient and effective management.

Many new industries have developed on the back of the digital revolution, often referred to as knowledge-intensive industries, those which we find at the forefront of contemporary global competition, such as Google, IBM, Microsoft, and Dell. In these organizations we find new organizational forms that challenge the older, more bureaucratic structures of the past, new organization structures that we will explore in Chapter 14.

Digital capabilities have transformed the world – some journalists such as Friedman (2005), of the *New York Times*, suggest that digital capabilities have made the world 'flat' – by which he means that advances in technology and communications now link people all over the globe. This may explain the rapid development of India and China, and the growth of global businesses that exploit the opportunities of the Internet to create and design goods and services on a 24/7 cycle – globally – taking advantage of different time zones to work on accounts, data, and designs seamlessly. The world has speeded up to a state of immediacy: any reader of this book would know how to find the authors in a matter of seconds and send them feedback immediately. (We would like you to let us know what you think about the book – we like to hear from our customers!)

Managing technological changes   Shorter life cycles, virtual connectivity, and dissagregation spell many changes in ways of managing. The dominant trend is that there has been an increasing separation of routine processes from more essential work, which is often reflected in a spatial division of labour. Thus, for instance, as we will see in Chapter 14, in call centres the work is as routine and scripted as in any work process designed in an early twentieth-century bureaucracy by one of F. W. Taylor's scientific managers (see Chapters 12 and 13). The means for storing the rules may have shifted from paper to software and the nature of the work may be less physical, but there are still essential similarities.

There are consequences for other jobs when much of the routine is extracted and repositioned elsewhere. The remaining core staff – rather than those that are peripheral – will need to be more skilled than before. They will be working in technological environments subject to rapid and radical change. New competencies and skills will be required. Managing will mean more developmental work oriented to renewing staff's specific skills and general competencies rather than seeing that they follow the rules, issuing imperative commands, and generally exercising authority. Managing will mean negotiating the use and understanding of new technologies, contexts, and capabilities, and facilitating the understanding of those who will be operating with the new tools and environments. As Sandberg and Targama (2007: 4) note, citing Orlikowski's (1993) influential work on Japanese, European and US firms, many technology implementation projects fail because of what the employees do – or do not – understand. Changing technological paradigms mean that managers must be able to make sense of the new technology for all those who will use it.

Traditionally, organizations were neither very responsive nor flexible because of their bureaucratic nature, as we will see in Chapter 12. They had tall hierarchical structures, relatively impermeable departmental silos, and many rules. Such organizations offer little incentive for innovation and, typically, innovation was frowned on because precedents went against the rules. Such organizations could hardly be responsive – they were not designed to be.

More responsive organizations should have employees who are capable of problem solving rather than having to refer any problem, deviation, or precedent to a higher authority. Such people need to be trained and engaged in styles of managing and being managed that reinforce empowerment, using far more positive than negative approaches to power, as we will see in Chapter 7.

New technologies attach a premium to a flexible, timely approach to customer requirements. In order that such flexibility can exist in an organization it has to be premised on ways of managing employees that allow them to be responsive to customer requirements in developing products and services. As we will see in Chapter 13, the critique of bureaucracy has been particularly acute in the areas of public sector management. Especially in the Anglo-Saxon countries, from the 1980s onwards, the extensive adoption of strategies of deregulation, privatization, and contracting out, often on the back of significant changes in technology, have led to profound changes in the nature of public sector work. Something known as new public management (Osborne and Gaebler, 1992) has had a profound impact on the public sector, in the public (or civil) service, education, universities, and health care, especially. The clarion call has been for more entrepreneurial managers and less rule following. Whether this is a good or bad thing has been the subject of lively debate, which we discuss in Chapter 13.

Changing relations of service and production

Look at your computer; check the clothes you are wearing; what about your shoes? Where do your things come from? Bet they were made in several countries and none of them may be where you live. Bet also that China was one of the countries. Today, 'Made in China' is a ubiquitous label – we find it on virtually any manufactured product that we are likely to wear or use in the office or home.

Supermarkets such as Wal-Mart represent the end of a supply chain that invariably starts somewhere in China. The concentration of much global manufacturing in China is a relatively recent phenomenon, which really gathered pace in the 1990s. Just as much of service work has been disaggregated into lower value-adding elements such as call centres that can be located anywhere, much of what was once produced by a domestic blue-collar labour force in the then heartlands of Europe or the USA, is now produced globally, often in China.

One consequence of the shifting international division of labour is that the developed world is increasingly based on the production of services rather than goods. Material things – such as computers, clothes, and household goods – are increasingly being produced in the developing world. One consequence is that the nature of work and organizations is changing rapidly in both worlds. In the developing world peasants are rapidly becoming factory workers; in the developed world there has been an explosive growth in what is referred to as knowledge work, done by knowledge workers in knowledge-intensive firms. Chief among these are IT firms (Alvesson, 1995; Starbuck, 1992), global consultancy, law, and accounting firms, as well as the universities, technical colleges, and schools that produce the new knowledge workers.

Shifting locations, shifting managing   An increase in knowledge-intensive work means that organizations have to employ – and manage – different kinds of employees. Brains not brawn, mental rather than manual labour, are the order of the day. Employees need to be capable of working with sophisticated databases, software, and knowledge management systems. These have to be related to customer requirements often on a unique and tailored basis that deploys a common platform while customizing it for specific requirements. Thus, technical and relational skills will be at a premium.

   Knowledge-intensive work, according to Alvesson's (2004) research, depends on much subtle tacit knowledge as well as explicit mastery. In such a situation, working according to instruction and command will not be an effective way of managing or being managed, especially where the employee is involved in design and other forms of creative work on a team basis, often organized in projects. In such situations, increasingly common in contemporary work, 'because of the high degree of independence and discretion to use their own judgement, knowledge workers and other professionals often require a leadership based on informal peer interaction rather than hierarchical authority' (Sandberg and Targama, 2007: 4). As we will explore in Chapters 4 and 5, some of the old theories and approaches to leadership and project work need updating.

Going global

Digital technologies, together with a growing international division of labour between economies specialized on services and production, make the world economy increasingly globalized. Competition is based less on traditional comparative advantage as a result of what economists call 'factor endowments', such as being close to raw materials, and more on competitive advantages that arise from innovation and enterprise. IT means that enterprise and innovation can now be globally organized. No industry is more indicative of this than the financial services industry, where firms such as American Express, Citicorp, and HSBC span the globe. These multinational behemoths operate as integrated financial services providers almost everywhere. Global competition goes hand in hand with outsourcing in industries such as these, as such firms exploit technology to disaggregate 'back-office' routine functions and locate them in cheaper labour markets, as we discuss in Chapter 15.

Managing globally   Doing business internationally in real time, enabled digitally, produces ample opportunity for cultural *faux pas* and misunderstanding. Work groups may be working in serial or in parallel with each other on projects that are networked globally. Global organization means managing diversity: it means developing appropriate ways of managing people who may be very different from each other – from different national, ethnic, religious, age cohort, educational achievement levels, social status, and gender backgrounds (Ashkenasy et al., 2002). One consequence of globalization and diversity is that HRM must be both increasingly international and equipped to deal with diversity, as we will see in Chapter 5.

Diversity is increasingly seen as an asset for organizations: people with diverse experiences can contribute more varied insights, knowledge, and experience than a more homogeneous workforce. (In the terms that we use in Chapters 6, 7 and 10 we can say that it is a good thing to introduce more polyphony into organizations.) An evident reason is that if a business wishes to sell globally it must understand all the specificities of the local markets into which it seeks to trade. One good way of doing this is to ensure that the organization has employees that understand that market. Moreover, in certain markets, such as the Middle East, where etiquette and rituals are of considerable importance in everyday interactions, then it is enormously beneficial to have employees who do not have to learn through making costly mistakes because they have an intuitive understanding. Moreover, as we will see in Chapter 11, organizations whose members are not representative of the populations the organizations draw on and serve risk being seen as discriminatory in their recruitment policies. There are ethical issues concerned in managing diversity.

Changing conceptions of time and space

Technological developments such as the Internet and other telecommunications seem to make the whole world something that can be present here and now – as users of Google Earth no doubt know. E-mail can fly around the world in seconds, as quite a few people can testify who have pressed the send button inadvertently on something they might have preferred not to share globally.

While time and space are two fundamental coordinates of the way we relate to the world, the ways in which we make this representation are not fundamental but socially constructed. The earliest concerns of modern global management were with the centrality of clock time in the time and motion studies of F. W. Taylor. Indeed, in these studies the central motif was that of time–space relations, as we will see in Chapter 12. Stopwatches measured in terms of microseconds to prescribe ways of doing tasks. Space was rigidly defined in order to maximize the speed of work. These notions of space and time as phenomena under strict organizational control are hardly relevant in the age of the Internet. With a computer, camera, and broadband connection any organization member can simulate immediacy with anyone anywhere in the world similarly equipped.

In such a situation time and space are eclipsed. Organizations can be global, navigating anywhere.

Managing time and space   Immediacy through the eclipse of space presents problems. Work is much more accountable and transparent as others can be online anytime, anywhere, challenging the understandings that the other has developed. Often these understandings will be embedded in a sense made in a cultural, linguistic, religious, ethnic, and age and gendered context that is simply foreign to partners elsewhere. Great cultural sensitivity, as well as a capacity to handle circadian rhythms, is needed in the interest of global business. In such contexts there will be a great deal of doing by learning as managers seek to make sense of others whose cues are not only unfamiliar but often mediated by the limitations of Internet communication. Managing communication in these circumstances poses especial challenges, as we will see in Chapter 8.

Changing demographics; changing values

The era from the 1960s onwards has been dominated by the 'boomer' generation, who are now slowly moving out of the workforce, to be replaced with people drawn from Generation X and Y. Generation X, broadly defined, includes anyone born from 1961 to 1981. In the West, Generation X grew up with the Cold War as an ever-present backdrop. During their childhood they saw the dismantling of the post-war settlement and the advent of neo-liberal economics (such as Thatcherism) and the collapse of communism. They often grew up in single-parent households, without a single clear or guiding moral compass. They had to negotiate the hard years of global industrial restructuring when they were seeking their first jobs; they experienced the economic depression of the 1980s and early 1990s; and saw the decline of traditional permanent job contracts offering clear career structures. Instead of careers they were invited to accept insecure short-term contracts, unemployment, or junk jobs in McDonaldized organizations, or to get educated. Many of them ended up overeducated and underemployed, with a deep sense of insecurity. Not expecting that organizations will show them much commitment, they offer little themselves.

Generation Y includes anyone born in the late 1980s and 1990s, sometimes to professional boomer couples who left childrearing later than previous generations or, as a result of boomer males mating with much younger women, maybe entering into reproduction the second or third time around. Young people born in this bracket are the first digital generation for whom the computer, Internet, mobile, iPods, DVDs, and the Xbox were a part of what they took for granted growing up. While Generation X was shaped by de-industrialization in the West and the fall of communism globally, Generation Y developed into maturity during the War on Terror, grew up reading *Harry Potter*, and, until 2008, enjoyed relatively prosperous economic times, in part because of the success – for the West – of globalization. If you want to know more about the generations and the differences they are inscribed in, you could talk to your parents or grandparents – if they haven't already talked to you about these things!

Managing changing values   The employment of Generation X members offers real challenges for managers seeking to motivate and gain commitment from employees. As we will see in Chapter 3, the issues of commitment and motivation are increasingly central to managing. The X generation will be more cynical than its predecessors and less likely to accept rhetoric from management that is not backed up by actions. For Generations X and Y, according to Sennett (1998: 25), there is a predisposition towards high uncertainty and risk-taking as defining features of the challenges they want from work because they do not expect commitment. In part this is because they do not expect anything solid or permanent: they have seen casino capitalism at close quarters as brands they grew up with moved offshore or were taken over, or radically changed by new ownership, and so tend to distrust prospects of long-term or predictable futures.

Using traditional management control and command devices to manage people who desire to explore is not appropriate. Instead, the emphasis will have to be on creativity and innovation, as we explore in Chapter 10.

If there is one value that binds these disparate generations together it is the sense that the previous generations have really made a mess of the planet; green values are very strongly held, and saving the environment through sustainability is high on the list of value preferences. Consequently, as we discuss in Chapter 11, issues of corporate social responsibility, especially those addressed to sustainability, are high on the values agenda. Such changes pose major implications for how organizations attract, select, retain, and treat employees, as we see in Chapter 5 on HRM.

Check out the Companion Website www.sagepub.co.uk/ managingandorganizations3 for free access to an article by Ronald Paul Hill (2002) if you want to learn more about how generations should make a difference to the ways that managers learn and are taught.

USING *MANAGING AND ORGANIZATIONS*

The basic argument of this text is now established. In this book, as we have foreshadowed, we will introduce you to the main lines of management and organization theory, and we will situate these in the major changes marking the present-day world. These, we will argue, make the ideal of the wholly rationalistic organization evermore difficult to believe in principle and secure in practice. However, most of what you will learn as a management student makes assumptions about the rationality of organizations and management. We will outline these assumptions, and the associated arguments, in each case.

We will not assume that there are two types of entity involved in organizations: the organization's (objective) systems and the (subjective) people within it. This kind of thinking, often called dualistic in the social science literature, leads to the view that if you change the objective systems then the subjects framed within these systems will change in ways that the objective changes should predict. If you start from these premises then the appropriate strategy is to seek relationships between changes in the objective conditions and the effects of these on organizational behaviour – what the people in organizations actually do.

By contrast we argue that if we do not understand the sense that the subjects make of objective changes we will understand and manage very little. What people choose to do will depend on their understanding of the contexts and the resources that they find at hand. The choices are theirs and their choices are grounded in their understanding, in their stocks of personal knowledge, in the way that they socially construct reality, as well as in the way that they are constrained by other people's social constructions.

Managing will rarely if ever correspond with the management presumed in rational plans and principles. Management consists of a series of devices and resources for making sense while managing. Managers seek to be rational but they can never be sure that they will be. As the old phrase has it, even the best laid plans can go awry as the immutable individuality of different ways of making sense, of interpreting and making meaning of the world, intervenes. Managers use sensemaking to construct the situation that they are in. They draw on professional disciplines, organization rules and routines, as well as everyday stocks of knowledge, to make this sense. Even though organizations have hierarchies that seek to sustain top management's ways of making sense as the natural attitude of those who are subordinate, there are so many competing sources of sensemaking that the social construction of a shared reality is always an enterprise that is likely to crack up and break down.

People who share only organization membership, but neither gender, ethnicity, age cohort, religion, families, interests, friends, pastimes, nor anything else, are hardly likely to find it easy to make common sense other than in a superficial way, without rational designs, plans, and structures binding them together.

Organizations go to great lengths to try and ensure that stocks of knowledge are shared as widely as possible within the organization, as we will see in subsequent chapters, and do so in ways that are reflected in each of the subsequent chapters:

1   Creating induction programmes (Chapter 2), which socialize individuals into an organizational frame of reference; they train individuals in teamwork and groupwork (Chapter 3).
2   Hosting leadership development, coaching, and training for common understanding (Chapter 4).
3   Building highly rationalistic HRM plans and seeking to implement them (Chapter 5).
4   Emphasizing strong, common cultures (Chapter 6).
5   Designing lots of rules to frame everyday behaviour in the organization (Chapter 7).
6   Managing power, politics, and decision-making so that plans are implemented, not resisted, and so sectional and specific interests are well aligned with rational plans (Chapter 7).
7   Communicating these rational plans, their culture, and other messages to organization members (Chapter 8).
8   Capturing all of what their members know and embedding it in management systems as they try and practice organizational learning (Chapter 9).

9 Managing change, introducing and effectively using new technologies, and ensuring innovation (Chapter 10).

10 Incorporating new mandates arising from social issues and concerns articulated by new stakeholders and influential social voices, such as sustainability, ethics, and corporate social responsibility (Chapter 11).

11 Implementing global management principles in the organization (Chapter 12).

12 Adjusting the structure of their organization to fit the contingencies it has to deal with, be they size, technology, or environment (Chapters 12 and 13).

13 Designing the organization in order to empower (some) people and distribute (some) knowledge while not empowering or sharing with others (Chapter 14).

14 Managing to manage globally, to manage globalization, and to deal with the added complexities that managing in a global world entails (Chapter 15).

SUMMARY AND REVIEW

In this chapter we have introduced some key ideas as well as many of the topics that will frame the remaining chapters.

We have introduced the two key terms that comprise the title of the book: *managing* and *organizations*. We chose to begin with organizations, as this is the more conventional point of departure. Next, we considered managing, the other key word in the title of the book. Managing is an activity, something that we all do. We all manage our everyday lives, more or less competently. While managers are specialists in managing – it is the job that they are paid to do – this does not make everyone else they work with a non-manager. They do not give up managing their affairs because someone called a 'manager' has come on the scene.

The core competency of managing is *sensemaking*: making sense of others, of situations, of material things and immaterial ideas, plans, and documents. It is possible to make sense on one's own but it is not advisable. Sensemaking is what we do when we make sense of situations, people, and things. Most of what is important about situations, people, and things is the sense that others are making of them, and if we do not have a good grasp of the range of sensemaking that is going on we cannot begin to act as effective managers. Being an effective manager means getting things done, and to get things done

we have to act with and through others: we must form alliances and coalitions, use power, build relations, develop cultures, and so on.

We never manage in a metaphorical 'green field'. There is always too much history, too much past sense that people have made of the same situation or situations that they define as being similar. That's how people make sense – they make comparisons using what they know. People bring past experience to bear on the situations in which they find themselves. Different people often make different sense of what appears to be the same situation. Managing has to deal with these different definitions of the situation.

Organization is, in many ways, a prescribed state, and a great deal of management and organization theory seeks to prescribe its states. But managing is never static, always dynamic. *Managing means accomplishing organization in action.* If rules are not followed, if routines are not repeated, if standards are not reproduced, then the organization is not being achieved in the terms that those who seek to control think it should be. Contrary to much conventional thinking, lack of control may not be such an error. Creativity and innovation rarely come only from following rules or orders: it is often the exclusion of error, according to plans, that makes organizations more fallible and likely to fail, precisely because they have minimized opportunities for learning.

For the individual, becoming an employee in an organization means renouncing some degree of freedom of choice and freedom of sensemaking. As the old adage has it, you have to fit in – and organizations will go to great lengths to try and ensure that you do, from selection, through training, to performance-related pay. Much of HRM is oriented to achieving desired organizational behaviour. As an employee, you have to make sense on terms that are largely prescribed for you – and for those who are managing you and those whom you are managing. There will always be areas of agreement and areas of conflict and some things that just do not make much sense.

Managers use many artifacts with which to manage: organization charts, standards, routines, rules, technologies, and, above all, formally planned and prescribed ways of relating to and using all these devices. Because of sensemaking they may actually use these devices in creative and different ways. The devices used by managers do not prescribe what management does: managers choose how they will use what they use and what they seek to position it as meaning, just as do all those other people in and around their organizations – subordinates, colleagues, rivals, suppliers, customers, etc., who have an interest in the situation being defined and managed.

Sensemaking is always more problematic when situations are changing rapidly and their definition is contested or unclear. The world of organizations is changing rapidly at the present time such that ever since the development of new digital technologies, particularly the Internet in the mid-1990s, writers have been noting that paradigms of management were changing (Clarke and Clegg, 1998). In this book we focus not only on new technologies but also on changing international divisions and specialization in the production of goods and services, and the skill implications of these for managers; we also look at the effects of globalization and the increased diversity that this creates for organizations to manage; also, we consider the role of changing values, particularly those concerning corporate social responsibility and sustainability, values often held dearly by the younger generations, and consider what it means to manage in a world that is not only speeding up but becoming evermore integrated. All these trends are deeply corrosive of traditional modes of organization.

EXERCISES

1 Having read this chapter you should be able to say in your own words what each of the following key terms means. Test yourself or ask a colleague to test you.

- Managing
- Technologies
- Values
- Organizations
- Sensemaking

- Identity
- Rationality
- Hierarchy
- Metaphors

2 What do you think are the major changes that are shaping the contemporary world and what do you think their impact is on management?

3 What happens to one's sense of individuality in organizations?

4 How is your world flat?

ADDITIONAL RESOURCES

1 If you want to find out more about 'sensemaking', then the key resource is Weick's (1995) book, called *Sensemaking in Organizations*. It is not an introductory book, though, and may be hard going if you are new to this subject.

2 Three excellent books on problems with the rational model of organizations have been written by the Swedish theorist, Nils Brunsson. These are *The Irrational Organization* (1985), *The Organization of Hypocrisy* (1989), and *Mechanisms of Hope* (2006). Together they form a remarkable trio of organization analysis at its best. Again, however, they are not for the introductory student. There is also an interview with Nils Brunsson on www.sagepub.co.uk/managingandorganizations3.

3 Rational choice theory is dissected economically and clearly by Zey (2008a).

4 If you want to know more about the major changes shaping the contemporary world of business you could take a look at Clarke and Clegg's (1998) *Changing Paradigms*. It is dated now, but still has several interesting points to make about globalization, digitalization, and so on. This book is not too difficult for the introductory student.

5 A good overview of approaches to understanding and sensemaking in organizations is

provided by Sandberg and Targama (2007), in their excellent book *Managing Understanding in Organizations*.

WEB SECTION

1 Our Companion Website is the best first stop for you to find a great deal of extra resources, free PDF versions of leading articles published in Sage journals, exercises, video and pod casts, team case studies and general questions, and links to teamwork resources. Go to www.sagepub.co.uk/managingandorganizations3.

2 For state of the art briefings on how to manage organizations effectively, please visit the Henry Stewart Talks series of online audiovisual seminars on Managing Organizations, edited by Stewart Clegg: www.hstalks.com/r/managing-orgs, in particular, Talk #1: Introducing the field of managing organizations, by Stewart Clegg.

3 A great resource site is www.criticalmanagement.org/. It is packed with useful and searchable bibliographic references and links as well as pod casts.

4 We assume that most readers of this book will be either students in business or intending to be so. If this is the case then you might find the following website useful: http://www.business-administrationdegree.com.

5 A good site for the fashion retailers, Zara, is to be found at: http://www.zara.com/.

6 Yale University hosts a site with many interesting and relevant interviews, articles and debates – well worth exploring: http://yaleglobal.yale.edu/.

7 Good pages on sensemaking are to be found at http://communication.sbs.ohio-state.edu/sense-making/.

8 Pearltrees has an interesting site on sensemaking: http://www.pearltrees.com/#/N-u=1_16309&N-f=1_343513&N-s=1_343513&N-p=2062093&N-pw=1.

9 There is a special issue of the journal *Organization Studies*, one of the consistently best journals in the field, on 'Making sense of organizing: In honor of Karl Weick', which is available at http://oss.sagepub.com/content/vol27/issue11/, if your institution has viewing rights. Otherwise, the issue is Volume 27, Number 11, 2006.

10 An important research article on sensemaking and organization by Karl Weick, Kathleen M. Sutcliffe, and David Obstfeld is available from http://tinyurl.com/2dsopq.

LOOKING FOR A HIGHER MARK?

Reading and digesting these articles that are available free on the Companion Website www.sagepub.co.uk/managingandorganizations3 can help you gain deeper understanding and, on the basis of that, a better grade.

1 Universities are similar to McDonald's – or at least, some are! This is the conclusion that Parker and Jary come to in a 1995 paper on 'The McUniversity: organization, management and academic subjectivity', *Organization*, 2 (2): 319–338.

2 In an article highlighted in the chapter, by Karl Weick (2006), titled 'Faith, evidence, and action: better guesses in an unknowable world', *Organization Studies*, 27 (11): 1723–1736, there is a good and accessible account of his approach.

3 The paper by Joep P. Cornelissen, Mario Kafouros, and Andrew R. Lock (2005) 'Metaphorical images of organization: how organizational researchers develop and select organizational metaphors', *Human Relations*, 58 (12): 1545–1578, is a useful place to extend your knowledge.

4 How management ideas are used in management practice is a topic of perennial interest, given the role of business schools and subjects such as the one that you are probably doing now! Andrew Sturdy's (2004) 'The adoption of management ideas and practices: theoretical perspectives and possibilities', *Management Learning*, 35 (2): 155–179, is a good place to get an overview of some current views.

5 Of all the significant contemporary management thinkers, James March stands out for the elegance of his ideas and expression: see James G. March (2007) 'The study of organizations and organizing since 1945', *Organization Studies*, 28 (1): 9–19.

6 Generations do make a difference in management, according to Ronald Paul Hill (2002). See what he has to say in his article, 'Managing across generations in the 21st century: important lessons from the ivory trenches', *Journal of Management Inquiry*, 11 (1): 60–66.

CHAPTER TWO
MANAGING INDIVIDUALS

Seeing, Being, Feeling

LEARNING OBJECTIVES

This chapter is designed to enable you to:

■ Develop an understanding of how psychology contributes to organizational behaviour
■ Describe the process of perception and understand how it can affect performance at work
■ Outline how values drive individual behaviour
■ Outline a range of personality theories
■ Explain how positive psychology can improve people's workplaces

BEFORE YOU GET STARTED . . .

A few words from Anna Quindlen, Pulitzer Prize winning American journalist:

When you leave college, there are thousands of people out there with the same degree you have; when you get a job, there will be thousands of people doing what you want to do for a living. But you are the only person alive who has sole custody of your life. (Quindlen, 2000)

INTRODUCTION

In the last few years we have seen a succession of natural and human made disasters and changes ranging from destructive floods and earthquakes, global financial meltdowns, increasing civil unrest in the Middle East and Europe, and a shift in economic power trending towards China, Brazil, India, and Russia. At the same time advances in technology, particularly in communications technology, are transforming the ways in which we not only do business, but how we relate and communicate as societies. As organizations face unparalleled levels of complexity and uncertainty that come with such challenges, they must become more agile and responsive, not only to survive but also to lead and capitalize on the opportunities available to them during seemingly turbulent times. It is no secret that people – how they relate to one another, work together, and share ideas – are at the very core of the ability for organizations to be innovative, responsive, adaptive, and successful. What we hope will be evident in all the chapters of this textbook is that the relational aspects of managing and organizing, while often treated as 'the soft stuff', are probably going to be the most difficult part of your life as a manager. Indeed, most of the problems you will experience at work will be related to people, the things they do, or don't do, and the way you relate to and with them. In organizations today a 'one size fits all' management approach will not work. Contemporary managers can no longer rely on hierarchy and nominal roles to manage people; there is no longer a divine right to manage, and so managing has become an increasingly difficult, political, and challenging endeavour. It is so for one very good reason: people are complex. It is imperative, therefore, that managers are acquainted with some of the core ideas that have originated from psychology and are now applied to managing and organizations, often in taken for granted ways.

In this chapter we will explore the core ideas central to managing individuals, particularly from a psychological perspective. Psychological properties can be analysed at both an individual and a group level, both of which are critical to managing people at work. We will explain the basic psychological concepts and principles we believe are central for managing individuals in organizations – we will look at groups and teams in Chapter 3. In this chapter we will discuss perception and how perception can affect how we behave and think about things. We humans are not the perfectly designed creatures we believe ourselves to be; how we perceive things, what we attend to and ignore, how we interpret people and make decisions about them is prone to many types of errors. For this reason understanding the process of perception is critical in helping us become better managers.

Second, we take a close look at values because they are the fundamental building blocks for managing culture, diversity, and communication (all topics covered in detail throughout this textbook). You need to consider how our values are formed and how they can drive us throughout our working lives; how they bind us but also how they separate and isolate us from others, and how they can lead to conflict between people and societies. Third, personality is important because it is seen as the essence that makes each of us who we are, determines how we behave, and shapes how we feel. We ask, 'Can we categorize people as types, or are each and every one of us unique individuals?'

Finally, we close the chapter by looking at emotions from a 'positive psychology' (PP) perspective. We will concentrate on a topic, the pursuit of which is enshrined in at least one nation's constitution. Before we explore these fascinating topics, let us first build an understanding of psychology and its application at work.

PSYCHOLOGY AT WORK

Psychology first explicitly emerged in Greece more than 2,500 years ago when philosophers tried to explain the nature of the self, the soul, and personality. The word psychology has a classical etymology.

Psychology seeks to answer the question: 'Why are we the way we are?' It concerns itself with all aspects of the workings of the mind (such as perception, attention, thought, memory, and affect at the intrapersonal and interpersonal levels of analysis), and also with understanding the brain's development, its possibilities, degradation and limitations.

> The term **psychology** is derived from the Greek word *psyche*, meaning one's own thoughts and feelings, and the English suffix 'ology' derived from the Greek *logos*, meaning reason, which in English is rendered as 'ology', denoting a field of study.

The application of psychology at work has occurred through the fields of applied industrial and organizational psychology. However, more generally it is in the field of **organizational behaviour** that the theory, research and practice in psychology have been applied to organizational life.

OB involves understanding, researching and addressing organizational behaviour phenomena from a multidisciplinary perspective including psychology, sociology, anthropology, economics and political science to name but a few.

> **Organizational behaviour (OB)** refers to the study of human behaviour in organizational contexts. OB is an applied discipline that concerns itself with individual level, group level and organizational level processes and practices that inhibit or enable organizational performance.

In this textbook we epitomize the interdisciplinary nature of the OB field. The book is written by a sociologist who has worked in management for nearly 20 years and has a behavioural science background (Stewart); a philosopher and strategist who works in both the management and the design field (Martin); and a psychologist (Tyrone), who also works in management. In Chapters 2 to 5 we predominantly draw upon psychology's contributions to OB; later, some of the other influences will be more apparent – they are all part of the rich blend that comprises the study of managing and organizations today. Now, on with the show.

Who am I?

Stop and reflect for a moment about who you are. Before you read on, answer the question 'Who am I?', and write down and list the things that you believe make you who you are … go on, do it!

....

....

....

....

....

....

Now, look at your list. What sorts of things make you who you are? Did you describe yourself in terms of roles (daughter, son, student, volunteer, mother, father, etc.) and profession (accountant, lawyer, chef, etc.)? Did you describe yourself in terms of character and emotions (good, happy, depressed, honest, confident, shy, etc.)? By appearance (fat, skinny, tall, short, ugly, pretty, etc.)? By institutional affiliation (Christian, Muslim, Jewish, Buddhist, Conservative, Liberal, Democrat, Green, etc.), or by beliefs and perceptions (pro-versus anti-abortion, pro-versus anti-immigration, etc.)? Or even by demography (Generation X, Y, gender, marital status, or by where you live or come from, etc.)?

Keep your list handy and when you complete this chapter, revisit your list. What would you add, change or take away from your original list?

How would you answer the question 'Who am I'? knowing what you know now after reading this chapter – and maybe even the entire book?

So, why are we the way we are? We can all answer this question to a degree, but how we answer it depends upon our beliefs about human nature. Over the last 100 or so years, there has been a great deal of theory, research, and practice in psychology that addresses these questions. Our intention is to guide you to what you need to know in relation to psychology at work.

In almost all fields of psychology, two main themes drive theory and research. The first theme centres on the nature versus nurture debate. At issue is whether we are genetically encoded to be the way we are, and so how well you achieve in specific spheres of life depends on your genetic dispositions – your personality, ability to be a leader, to be caring or aggressive. The second theme focuses on the idea that we come into this world *tabula rasa* – that is, with a clean slate – and that we learn our personality, we learn to become leaders, and that we are influenced by social contexts such as the socioeconomic status of our families, their culture, social support, the environment in which we grow up, our schooling, and so on.

The opposing views of nature versus nurture frame much of what you will learn in the field of organizational behaviour because psychology informs much of organizational behaviour theory, research, and practice. Some theorists and researchers hold dearly to one or the other view. Others, like us, however, prefer more moderate, integrative theories about what makes us who we are. Our view is that we are born with aspects of what constitutes us but that much of who we are is learned over time and that context has a profound impact on development. How you approach the question of nature and nurture influences how you manage people and the underlying assumptions you make about how people might, or might not, behave at work.

An important theme that has emerged in organizational behaviour theory and research suggests that nurture is overridden because of the fundamental drives that underpin human nature. Such ideas are derived from Charles Darwin and his theory of evolution; in particular the importance of behaviours that perpetuate the survival of the species. Some evolutionary arguments stress the 'selfish gene' perspective: that we are programmed for competition in a fundamental struggle to perpetuate our genes over those of others. Others stress that fitness and survival depend far more on the fact that we are social animals seeking affiliation and human relations; hence, we are more committed to cooperation than competition to ensure our survival as a species. These two related but somewhat opposing views of evolution underpin many of the ideas in management research and theory today.

Many management scholars and theorists use Darwinian theory to validate and substantiate their claims about human nature as being based in a competitive instinct and struggle. Evolutionary psychology has made substantial inroads into management research and theory such that it is now steeped in the Darwinian tradition of 'survival of the fittest'. Some of those who believe in the survival of the fittest as a competitive concept are the first to claim a liver or a kidney transplant. In the ideal world of survival of the fittest, of course, such individuals would be left to die because they are simply not fit enough. Conversely, some of those who believe that the fittest survivors are those best able to cooperate are the first to complain when their taxes are raised to provide more public goods.

Before Darwin published *On the Origin of Species by Means of Natural Selection, or the Preservation of Favored Races in the Struggle for Life* in 1859, Adam Smith (1961 [1776]), a political economist and philosopher of the Scottish Enlightenment who is credited with being the father of capitalism, argued that progress and economic growth occur because human behaviour is based on self-interest, which is best served by the operation of free and unfettered markets in the supply of goods and services. For example, if we as consumers want more leisure time and express a preference for this through our purchasing decisions in markets – maybe by buying vacations and appliances rather than saving money – then business people who market vacations or innovations in labour-saving devices will be rewarded. We buy and sell in markets that achieve balance between the supply and demand of goods such that, in the long term, efficiencies will prevail, and the price mechanism will maintain equilibrium. By being self-interested, we create demand preferences that markets emerge to meet; these markets benefit all of society because they create a self-regulating economic system where benefits trickle down by way of jobs, economic growth, prosperity and innovations.

Fundamental self-interest does not necessarily provide welfare or products or services that cannot be privately owned to generate income and so, the argument goes, government must become involved in providing such public goods. When a 16-year-old single parent has produced a baby and needs some support to sustain herself and her child, no business will assist her because there is no profit in giving resources away unless someone is paying them to do so. Hence, government typically provides social security and basic support. Of course, in doing so, in the long term, this is a subsidy to business in general because it enables the reproduction of another recruit to the next generation of workers and consumers. It is not surprising that social responsibility and economic, social, and environmental sustainability have long been perceived as the duty of government to regulate or a task for charity and other 'do-gooders' (see Chapter 11).

The views of Adam Smith have certainly been influential. Look at any newspaper story on corporate behaviour to see parallels with notions of survival of the fittest, the centrality of self-interest, and the primal pursuit of economic wealth as the end of human activity. Today, this bundle of beliefs assumes that self-interested economic action is the only rational basis for human behaviour. Hence, it is a small step to arguing that our rationalities are formed this way as a constitutive feature of our human nature. Using Darwin and Smith as authorities, some scholars, such as Nicholson (2000), would argue that competition is genetically a human predisposition. Despite the global financial crisis (GFC), and its effect in raising questions about the viability of unfettered market behaviour, we still see behaviours being lauded that stress a return to business as usual, with exorbitant CEO salaries and payouts, together with a continuation of gender and racial inequalities in management ranks as well as resistance to sustainable, corporate social responsibility.

All ideas, such as the survival of the fittest through competition or cooperation, as well as debates about nature and nurture, underpin and are underpinned by our beliefs or working theories about how the world, and the things within it, operate. Our values and beliefs are integral to all these working theories and assumptions about work, organizations, and society. These values, beliefs, and assumptions are inherent in the workplace and become an important component of the management of people and organizations. Psychology provides part of the answer to understanding and dealing with the tensions and opportunities that present themselves in the workplace. We will now consider these in more detail.

We will begin with a central concern in psychology, that of perception. How we take information in, process it, store it, add to it, and use it are fundamental issues for research and theory into human perception. Feeding into the idea of perception is how we experience and make sense of ourselves and others in our world, particularly in terms of what drives our behaviours and attitudes to work, society and life in general. Our discussion of personality will lead us to the exploration of values. Values refer to those things we value more strongly than others. Sometimes our values are aligned to those people we relate with, while sometimes our values systems are opposed to those with whom we have to relate in our jobs. Values, as the drivers of behaviour, are integral not only to management but to organizational life in general. Here the concept of personality becomes a core concern, particularly given that there is an obsession with selecting and developing the 'right' people for the job; moreover, our dealing with different personalities from the unique positioning of our own personality complicates our ability to practice management. Ultimately, our aim as managers should be to create positive, productive working environments, in which *all* kinds of performativity can flourish healthily and so we will close with a discussion on the idea of positive emotions at work.

First, however, in order to fully understand how values drive behaviour, how we make sense of our own and other people's personality, and even how we can achieve happiness, we need to understand how the process of perception works. In the next section we will discuss the process of perception, its structures and common errors.

PERCEPTION AT WORK

In general terms, all management starts from **perception** because we manage what we think we perceive to be happening.

Figure 2.1 represents a basic model of information processing: the model shows in a simplified way the perceptual process of how we deal with stimuli in our environment. Let us use an example in order to help us make sense of this model. Let us assume you are at a party, and the music (*stimulus A*) played has been excellent all night – Lady GaGa, The Killers, and Snow Patrol, as well as some of the old stuff like Blur and Marilyn Manson, and even ancient stuff like Bob Dylan and the Beatles. You notice one of your fellow students (*stimulus B*), whom you find very attractive, is alone and you go over and strike up a conversation – you find you both have so much in common that you attend to every word (*attention*). So much so that you forget that the music is playing, even though your absolute favourite song is playing (*filtering*) – filtering can be intentional or sub-conscious and essentially is the same thing as *selective perception*, or the process of selectively gathering and processing information that is consistent with one's values, belief, and attitudes. The more you listen to the person the more you find you have in common, the more attractive they appear to you, and the more they reinforce what you believe about their attractiveness, and so this information that is selectively attended to is stored and processed in relation to existing schemas (*organization*). The cognitive process of organization happens through **schemas.**

The next step in the model is *interpretation*, all the information you have gathered and organized about this attractive person (attractiveness, smiling, common interests, body language), has been grouped into a set of schemas that comprise a possible relationship (be it sexual or loving), and so you *store* all this information as reality or as representative of what you are experiencing. The problem is that people interpret stimuli in different ways, sometimes not in the same way you do. What you did not notice is crucial: what you did not notice was that this person found you friendly, and recognized you from the lectures – it was not romantic interest but

Perception is the process of receiving, attending to, processing, storing, and using stimuli to understand and make sense of our world. The stimuli can be experiences through any and all of the senses such as sight, sound, smell, taste, and touch.

Schemas are sets of cognitive constructs developed through social interactions that organize our thoughts, feelings, and attention (Baldwin, 1992; Epstein and Baucom, 2002).

FIGURE 2.1
A basic information processing model of perception (adapted from Reed, 2007)

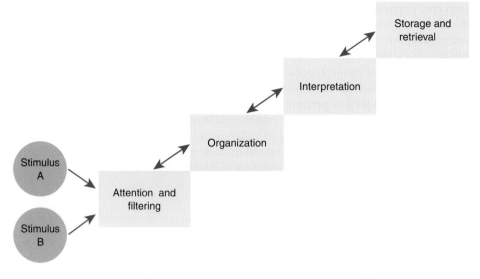

Person schemas are structures of meaning that affect thinking, planning and behaviour concerning others; there are idealized person schemas which serve as prototypes which we compare all other persons with (see Horowitz, 1991).

Self-schemas are specific self-conceptions we hold about ourselves and we believe are self-descriptive and highly important to possess (Fong and Markus, 1982; Markus, 1977).

Script schemas refer to schemas about how we operate upon our world and understand and remember information.

simple affability that person exhibited towards you. But to be sure, they utter those words you never expected to hear 'Oh, here is my partner, I'll introduce you, you'll really get along'. All that information you stored about a possible love interest is *retrieved* and reinterpreted. What you once thought 'real' is no longer real, and so you must reanalyse and update your information as you come crashing back from a momentary alternative reality. Of course, some people don't do this, and still hold on to the original belief – in this example, if you did this you probably would find yourself charged with stalking or being labelled 'a creep'.

A very important component of the perceptual information processing story told above are schemas because in many ways they underscore much of what we cover in this chapter – our values, personality, and emotions can all be linked to schemas (also referred to as schemata or scripts). Schemas are used to structure and organize information that we experience in our social world and are often hierarchical (my car is a Mini Cooper, a Mini Cooper is a small car, a car is an automobile, an automobile is a vehicle, a vehicle is a mode of transport). There are several types of schemas, including **person schemas** and **self-schemas**.

You may perceive yourself as an open, honest and attractive person and so it is not surprising to you that the person at the party also finds you attractive: self-schemas are critical in our personality, and include idealized self- or projected self- (an ideal self-) schemas.

Other kinds of schema include script, social and role schemas. We all have several scripts, deriving from **script schemas**, and these scripts allow us to function in our daily lives – we have scripts for going to a restaurant, scripts for going to university, scripts for how we ride our bikes, and so on (Schank and Abelson, 1977). In all these situations there are *conditions* (such as going to the restaurant because you are hungry, you have money for food, and the restaurant has food), *standard roles* for main actors (you are the star playing lead role of customer) and supporting actors (waitress, chef, and other customers), *props* (tables and chairs, etc.), and *results* (the main actor has less money, but is no longer hungry) (Reed, 2009). We develop these scripts from **social schemas** and **role schemas**.

Once our schemas become established they become increasingly difficult to change and falsify; that is, we tend to pay attention to information that reaffirms or fits our schemas, rather than questioning our schemas whenever we experience information that contradicts them (Reed, 2009) . As an example, read the sentence in the What Do You Mean? box below. This example works with people who possess good English language skills. The brain reads the first and last letter, matches it to the words on either side and quickly calls up language scripts that fit the general idea of the passage. 'The hamun brian' makes no sense (unless you actually know someone called Hamun Brian), so your brain searches for the closest match – 'the human brain'.

Social schemas, as the name suggests, refers to our social knowledge (such as knowledge about public affairs, laws, politics, media and the arts, and anything else socially important).

Role schemas refer to schemas about appropriate and inappropriate behaviour in specific contexts (for example, a woman's role as a mother, daughter, professional, wife, friend, etc.).

WHAT DO YOU MEAN?

The hamun brian is so azaming, as lnog as the frist and lsat lteter is the smae yuo wlil mkae snese of the snetecne!

This sentence is an example of how schemas are organized and influence perception through selective perception. Your brain will automatically complete information for you so that things will make sense – most people will see 'The human brain is so amazing...'. However, if you read the sentence exactly as the letters appear you will find most of the sentence is nonsense. What you think you see, and what is actually there, are two different things.

(© Tyrone S. Pitsis (2012))

For cognitive psychologists schemas are, as already mentioned, the underlying constructs that contain information about our values, how we perceive ourselves as people, how we perceive others, how we adjust and respond to change, how we operate in our world, and how we experience emotions. Schemas are so powerful that they are proving to be one of the most important components of cognitive-behavioural therapy. Schema therapy is used to uncover and deconstruct the underlying thought processes and structures of people, and transplant destructive schemas with more psychologically healthy schemas (Giesen-Bloo et al., 2006; Young et al., 2003); it can even be used to better understand how we might negotiate peace between conflicting parties (Leahy, 2011). We will revisit schemas in this context when we look at personality and also the pursuit of happiness later on; let us now look at how perception and schemas can be problematic, especially in workplace contexts.

There is probably no better example of how schemas structure our understandings, beliefs, and values more than the science vs religion, evolution vs creationism debate. The argument for and against intelligent design (ID) is one of those debates. There has been a growing and powerful movement within the United States, which seeks to include ID as a core part of the education curriculum. At best the proponents of ID want it taught along with Darwinian evolutionary theory, at worst they want it to totally replace teachings on evolution. The main argument is that God (an intelligent entity) designed the world and humans, and that much of this design can be scientifically tested and supported to a) prove God exists, and b) to prove evolutionary theory is wrong. Here is an example of the arguments used.

> The Christian world view begins with the Creation, with a deliberate act by a personal Being who existed from all eternity. This personal dimension is crucial for understanding Creation. Before bringing the world into existence, the Creator made a choice, a decision: He set out a plan, an intelligent design. (Colson and Pearcey, 1999)

More recently in March 2011, a Republican State Representative for Texas, Bill Zedler, introduced the Bill HB 2454, which was aimed at protecting the rights of people to teach ID.

Science, of course, rejects the ideas espoused in ID, and organizations and institutions such as the National Science Teachers' Association and the US National Academy of Science have responded by claiming that ID is not a science, and in fact some call it junk science. Ironically, the very things that proponents of ID argue for and against contradict their arguments for intelligent design – for example, the existence and wiping out of most dinosaurs, mental and physical illness, and the fact that every single human being on earth can be traced back to Adam and Eve (which means we are all the result of in-breeding), is hardly evidence of intelligent design. It seems people do not necessarily rely on facts or evidence but more on common held beliefs that are experienced and interpreted to be true. Common errors in how people perceive the world appear to be rife.

The concept of the **halo effect** was first developed by psychologist Edward Thorndike (1920) and refers to the process by which if we ascribe certain characteristics to a person in one situation based on one trait, we tend to apply those characteristics to that person in other situations and to other traits.

Stereotyping refers to the process of grouping objects into simplistic categories based on one's generalized perceptions of those objects.

PERCEPTION AND COMMON ERRORS

Armed with a basic understanding of perception and the perceptual process and structure let us now define and explore some common errors we make in judgements, interpretations, assumptions, and beliefs about our social world, the people within it, and our place in it. In this chapter we will discuss stereotyping, self-fulfilling prophecies, the **halo effect**, attribution error, and cognitive dissonance. All these errors have important implications not just for our roles as managers, but in life more generally.

The first perceptual error is **stereotyping**. In reality while many textbooks present stereotyping as an error, stereotyping serves as an important process for dealing with information in a timely manner, and is not always negative.

Stereotyping occurs most commonly in the absence of enough social cues in order to make an informed assessment (Jackson, 2011; Kawakami et al., 1998). Stereotypes are problematic when the objects we stereotype are complex, as people tend to be. Think of the terms 'Jock', 'Nerd', 'Greenie', and so on – these are all stereotypes. The most common issues concerning stereotyping centre on culture and race. Examples of language around stereotyping include overt statements that are benign, perceived as fact but still false and covertly racists: 'Irish love potatoes', 'The English don't bathe', 'Americans are loud and obnoxious', 'Asians study hard and drive expensive cars'. Alternatively, and most often, stereotyping can be racist and overtly offensive. 'Mexicans are lazy', 'Arabs are terrorists', and so on.

Stereotyping also concerns people's roles based on gender. For example, currently in Australia, the United Kingdom and the United States there is still a gender gap in terms of equal pay – even after 100 years of the women's rights movement. While the situation is definitely improving, women are paid on average approximately 80 per cent of what men are paid for the same role and position (Iyer and Ryan, 2006; Joo-Kee, 2006; Taylor, 2006). When we ask our management students in the classroom about their opinions concerning such gender pay inequity, those opinions vary; some students argue that because women can become pregnant they are not a good investment and so should be paid less. Others argue that the inequity occurs because of sexist, male-dominant culture, which has no place in modern society. Research suggests that mothers are *perceived* to be less competent and less committed to their work, even though there is no evidence to support such a stereotype: surprisingly, it is women who were more likely to perceive mothers in this way (Benard and Correll, 2010).

Often, to avoid stereotyping, people have been asked to stop or suppress their stereotyping behaviour. In studies on prejudiced people it was found that while suppression works in the short term, it tends to work only with highly motivated individuals who want to stop stereotyping people. In the long term, even when people are motivated they tend to revert back to stereotyping people (Wyer, 2007). Indeed, people with unprejudiced beliefs tend not to stereotype, irrespective of whether they are motivated to do so or not (Wyer, 2007), and even when they lack social cues they still tend to avoid stereotypes (Kawakami et al., 1998). Such individuals can contribute to positive work places and positive identity construction (see Dutton et al., 2010). Seeking out more information about others, learning about other cultures and subcultures, knowledge and experience of other people, discussion and open communication, and practising empathy and compassion are all ways we can avoid stereotyping people.

The next perceptual error arises from self-fulfilling prophecies. The **self-fulfilling prophecy** affects both how we perceive others and how we act when we interact with them, but it also affects how we perceive and act ourselves. One of the most famous studies of self-fulfilling prophecy was Robert Rosenthal's and Lenore Jacobson's (1992) seminal study on the *Pygmalion Effect* – an experiment that would in all likelihood not be allowed in today's world. In their experiment the researchers randomly

The concept of the **self-fulfilling prophecy** was originally conceptualized by the sociologist, Robert Merton (1957), to refer to the process by which a person who holds a belief or expectation, irrespective of the validity of that belief or expectation, causes that prediction to come true because people behave and act as if it is true.

selected 20 per cent of students from 18 different classrooms and told the teachers that these chosen students were gifted, and that these students would show improvements in academic ability over time. The students were returned to class and by the end of the year the students did show significant improvement.

What caused this improvement? Teachers treated the gifted students differently because they were perceived as gifted. These students sat closer to the teachers, and were given more attention by the teachers and were, generally, treated differently to the non-select group. The 'normal' students were perceived as less bright and these students were given less time to answer questions, and had certain qualities attributed to their behaviour because they were differentiated. The implications for us as managers is that we can easily allow our self-fulfilling prophecies to cloud our judgement about people, so we may label some people as performers and team players and others as non-performers, or not team players – we therefore start to treat people differently and the prophecy becomes fulfilled. In order to avoid such self-fulfilling prophecies, we need to be careful that how we judge people is based on sound information, is done accurately and uses critical reflection, equity, and fairness.

As with the self-fulfilling prophecy, the halo effect also involves bias in judgement that affects behaviour.

An example might be the expectation that a comedian who is funny on stage will be funny in all other contexts, is generally happier than most of us, and more positive, and would be fun to hang around with. Or because a person drives an expensive looking car and wears a suit they must be rich and successful. In terms of businesses and organizational behaviour, the halo seems to be rife. Hype surrounding businesses that are perceived to be successful creates a halo around them. For example, Cisco was one of the most popular companies and was often used as an exemplar of how businesses should operate – until of course Cisco developed financial problems (Rosenzweig, 2007). Similarly, ENRON had been awarded a number of accolades, even just before its historic collapse, and so we should be skeptical and careful about how we use examples as proof of success. Interestingly, a similar, and less covered concept is the **devil effect**.

The final two perceptual errors we are prone to make are attribution errors and cognitive dissonance. Let us begin with attribution error; in order to do this we should first discuss attribution theory.

Attribution theory addresses how we explain away our own behaviour and the behaviours of others in our lives based upon two general types of attributions. Later on we will look at internal and external locus of control, which is a social cognitive theory of personality. In essence locus of control is an attribution theory of personality. Attribution theory involves three general components, with **internal/external attributions** being one of those.

Another component of attribution is stability: if we perceive the attributed causes as *stable*, then we would expect the same result from that behaviour next time. Conversely, if the attributed cause is *unstable*, then we would expect outcomes to vary next time. The final component is controllability: if

The **devil effect** refers to generally ascribing negative interpretations of people based on one negative trait in one situation (think of the former prisoner who cannot get a job when he divulges this information, even though he has done his time).

Attribution theory in its simplest definition refers to how people 'attribute' cause to their own and other people's behaviour (Heider, 1958).

Internal attribution refers to attributing the cause of an individual's behaviour to internal or dispositional factors such as being mean or being generous.

External attribution refers to attributing the cause of an individual's behaviour to an external or situational factor such as being 'Catholic', 'Jewish', or 'Muslim'.

we believe the situation is *controllable* then we would assume that next time we could control the outcome; if the situation is *uncontrollable* then we believe it probably cannot be altered, irrespective of our efforts (see Weiner, 1980; 1992). Research shows how we attribute negative motivations to people we disagree with and more favourable perceptions towards those we agree with. Thus if we agree with a war, or with gay marriage, for example, we are more likely to attribute positive motivations towards people who also support our perceptions and attitudes, and we are also more likely to be attracted to them and they are more likely to be attracted to us (Greifeneder et al., 2011).

Within attribution we are prone to two key errors. The first is the **fundamental attribution error**.

When we see someone fail or behave in certain ways we believe it is due to their personality, attitude, or disposition. For example, over recent years research has shown that when discussing rape crimes people have apportioned blame to the victims of rape due to their choice of clothing, being under the influence of drugs and/or alcohol and therefore not in control of their own behaviour, and choice of profession, rather than to external causes such as the criminal act and anti-social behaviour of another person (Vanderveen, 2006). Related to attribution error is the notion of **self-serving bias**.

Let us say you go for a job interview and you get it, and you may believe that you got it because you did well in the interview, you have all the skills and abilities necessary and you can do the job. Conversely, let us say you missed out on the job, you may attribute your failure to the poor interview questions, or that someone on the interview panel did not like you, or the questions were stupid, or the position has already been filled internally. The fundamental attribution error and self-serving bias are important concepts that we need to reflect on when managing people, and especially when we are making judgements about their behaviours based upon their internal attributions. Practising empathy by putting yourself in other people's shoes or trying to understand their perspective, and trying to account for the external causes of behaviour are good ways to avoid attribution errors.

The final perceptual error is **cognitive dissonance**. Most commonly we do not experience dissonance until we experience conflicting or disconfirming information. For example, a devout person may question their faith after experiencing tragedy in their life; they question their belief in God, and their religion. They may ask, 'Why would God do this to me?' Similarly, Albert Einstein developed his theory of relativity but when his theories were used to develop weapons of mass destruction he felt anxiety and regret – his assumptions were that his theories would lead to new forms of power generation, not the possible destruction of humanity and the death of millions (Braun and Krieger, 2005).

Leon Festinger (1957) was one of the first people to develop and study cognitive dissonance theory. Festinger's study, even though quite old, is not only critical to understanding cognitive dissonance, it is fascinating. Along with a number of colleagues he studied the behaviour and cognitions of a cult that claimed to know the date that the world would end, and that it would end by

Check out the Companion Website www.sagepub.co.uk/ managingandorganizations3 for free access to an article by Glenn D. Reeder and his colleagues (2005) if you want to learn about some interesting research on George Bush and his decision to go to war in Iraq and on attitudes towards gay marriages and abortions.

The **fundamental attribution error** is the tendency to make internal attributions when explaining the causes of the behaviour of others.

When a **self-serving bias** comes into play, people attribute their own successes to internal causes and their failure to external causes.

Cognitive dissonance refers to the anxiety and discomfort we experience when we hold inconsistent and conflicting sets of cognitions (or schemas).

flooding. A number of people were convinced, and joined the cult, some of them were totally committed, others were less so. After the date of doom passed, and there was no flood or destruction what do you think happened? Those people who were on the periphery believed they had been conned, or left the cult. But a number of people became even more committed to the cult claiming that it was actually their faith and prayers that stopped the floods.

When experiencing cognitive dissonance, therefore, people will either seek to reconcile their feelings of anxiety and discomfort by changing their beliefs, or reinterpreting the information that contradicts their beliefs (Festinger, 1957; Festinger and Carlsmith, 1959). There are some interesting implications that emerge out of cognitive dissonance. Let us say you choose to study a subject, and you find the subject really difficult and you struggle and put lots of effort in, and pass but do not do well. Now let us also say you study another subject that you find very easy, you don't need to study hard, and you still do exceptionally well. What dissonance theory shows is that the first case creates dissonance because you choose a subject and find it difficult, you therefore reduce dissonance by saying 'even though it's a hard subject, I really am getting a lot out of it, so it's worth it'. Conversely, your emotions concerning the subject that you did well in are less intense. Cognitive dissonance is important when we give feedback to people, because their commitment to the task, their beliefs, opinions, and expectations will determine how they react to the feedback.

Interestingly, we rarely question what we know, how we came to know it, and what we think we know about things, because we take things such as our knowledge, experiences, values, and belief systems for granted; as a result we selectively perceive and reinterpret what we experience to fit what we already know (Pitsis and Clegg, 2007; Weick, 2004). The process of perception is important, and it shows that we can often make errors. Often these errors are because of our ideas being based on unreflexive beliefs about things and we make assumptions or inferences based on these

QUESTION TIME

Assumptions and inferences

1 Often people talk in dualisms (for example, black and white thinking, A or B, either/or ...) If the world is that simple, try this exercise: for each item try writing in the concept that would belong in the middle point.

a. Good _____ Evil
b. Safe _____ Unsafe
c. Honest _____ Dishonest
d. Us _____ Them
e. Happy _____ Sad

Because we find it hard to reflect on the way in which we categorize people and their behaviours, if they do not fit one extreme we tend to categorize them into the opposite extreme. Try and think of as many situations in which you may do this sort of categorizing of people.

(Continued)

(Continued)

2 Often we do not distinguish between our inferences and observations when we are perceiving objects. Look at the picture below, which of the following are observations that are true about the picture:

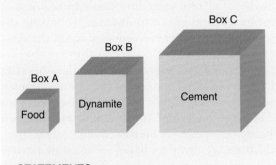

STATEMENTS

1 Box A has things to eat in it
2 There are three boxes

3 Box B should be handled with care
4 Box C is larger than box A and B
5 Box C is heavy

The fact is that only statements 2 and 4 are observations, the rest are inferences based on our assumptions and interpretations. We assume food is in box A because it says food on the box, we assume box C is heavy, and we assume box B is dangerous because of our knowledge about dynamite. Next time you make judgements; see if you can distinguish between observation and inference. How do inferences affect your observations? Can we ever really separate inferences from observations? (An age old question in the philosophy of science.)

These exercises are adapted from the Oklahoma State University's Speech Communication Interaction Program.

systems of beliefs rather than informed decision (challenge yourself with the two examples in the Question Time box).

A final word; all the things we have discussed under perception are in many ways what makes us human. Our inadequacies, creativeness, eccentricity, are what makes us all unique and the reality is that some of the most influential theorists, researchers, and leaders on earth have interpreted things and made sense of things in very different ways from most of us. Further, many of these issues of perception are essential to handling the nearly infinite stimuli our mind receives. Perception and cognition are definitely exciting fields for research and theory. You should now have solid foundations for the rest of this chapter because much of what we cover is underpinned by perception and schemas (ideas about ourselves, others, and about our social world). So, let us now look at the idea of values because these not only frame how we perceive the world, they also affect how we act upon it.

VALUES: MANAGING ME, MYSELF, AND I

For many scholars, values can be thought of as the building blocks of culture (Howard, 1988). However, values can also be understood within the context of people management; to form, sustain, and improve relationships with people, or to motivate people, we must understand what is and what is not important to them. Values not only drive behaviour but also affect, and are affected by, how we perceive and make sense of our world. To a great extent, management is about managing people in a coordinated way to ensure that organizational outcomes are realized while also ensuring that one's own and others' values are met. Understanding values is a fundamental attribute for managing today. Moreover, we should also have an understanding and appreciation of how our values filter information and create knowledge, colouring the world we perceive as tinted lenses do. Not everyone sees things the same way.

Although there are many theories and approaches to values, here we look in detail at Shalom Schwartz's (1992) account of the role that universal values play at the personal level. We choose to highlight Schwartz for two reasons: first, because his work underpins much of the values research evident in organizational behaviour today, yet his role is underemphasized, even though he developed his theory of values based on a sample of over 60,000 people around the world (Schwartz, 1994); and second, his work is influential and well respected in psychology. Indeed, we believe that over the next few years Schwartz's model of values will become a dominant tool for understanding people's values – be they employees or customers – and aligning the organization's own values to those values. Unlike the values models that we will consider in Chapter 6 on managing culture, Schwartz's values model clearly distinguishes between individual level and cultural level values – something that cannot be said about the models of Hofstede, Trompenaars or Hampden-Turner – which are much more oriented to the broader cultural level of analysis. In the next section, we provide you with the necessary background to values theory to help you start managing values.

Values

So what are **values**?

People are social animals living in a state of tension between values associated with their individuality and values associated with social conformance (Aronson, 1960). Values can create tension because some values that drive our behaviour as individuals are not consistent with others that regulate our behaviour socially.

For example, superstar football players earn more money in a week than most people earn in a lifetime. They have the means to have whatever they desire and to live a lavish lifestyle in competition with other fit, wealthy young men. Not surprisingly, these young men express both highly competitive and team-based values. Sometimes their competitive values as young men competing for success can clash with social norms. In addition, sometimes the team norms of sharing with your teammates may conflict with social norms respecting the individuality and privacy of others, particularly as one comes into contact with others from outside one's field

Values are a person's or social group's consistent beliefs about something in which they have an emotional investment. Schwartz defines values as desirable goals, varying in importance, which serve as guiding principles in people's lives (Schwartz, 1992; 1994).

who are, nonetheless, relatively overawed followers of it. A number of high-profile cases of sexual assault by professional sportsmen underscore this point. For instance, from a social values perspective, one might see young football players as overpaid, oversexed, and undereducated louts, whereas from an individual values perspective, they are supercompetitive and thus appropriately rewarded, but they have some problems adjusting to societal rather than team values.

Values have a personal component and a social component. Sometimes what we value as individuals might not be valued by society and vice versa – the interaction of personal (self-schema) and social values (social schema) can result in tension because values are something people feel strongly about. Typically, individuals become very upset when they feel their values are threatened or compromised.

In essence, this is where the role of a manager is most difficult – managing and sharing understanding about values, whether they are those of a co-worker, a customer, a superior, or other organizations. Understanding values is critical in aligning organizational behaviour and managing people. For example, if you were the English football team manager getting ready for the FIFA World Cup in Brazil in 2014, how would you manage the private lives of your players when they are lived in the public face of the paparazzi? Any desires the players have can be satisfied easily because they are so wealthy, so bored when not playing or training, and so ready for whatever action is going down.

Schwartz (1992) identifies some values as '**trans-situational**'.

For instance, if you value life and freedom above all else, and one day you see a march protesting about your country going to war, it is likely that you will join this march to protest. Another day, you may be at the football stadium watching your team win another amazing victory. At this time, your values for life and freedom may not be at the forefront of your thoughts, but does this mean that you no longer value life and freedom, or hold them any less important?

Trans-situational values are those that, irrespective of the situation in which you find yourself, your values do not change; you take them with you wherever you go.

Values appear to have a strong motivational aspect to them. Rokeach (1968; 1973) argued that values guide our behaviours throughout life. Accordingly, Schwartz (1992) identified a number of motivational value types organized according to sets of associated values. He identified ten universal values that he believed all people and peoples would hold in common. Some of these values are mutually exclusive, but most are what Schwartz calls 'continuous', meaning that they overlap. Because values overlap, people behave or respond differently to certain things in life. Study each of the representations of Schwartz's value types in Table 2.1 for a moment, and look at their associated values.

You may recall that we said the ten values types are universal and that we all hold these values, irrespective of culture. Often, values are discussed in the same breath as culture and we will explore values in relation to culture later (see Chapter 6), but what is important to note is that values have often been talked about as being cultural, that is, that culture determines values; however, a significant body of research suggests that culture does not determine values (Schwartz, 2011).

TABLE 2.1 Schwartz's values by type and their associated meanings

Value type	Description	Associated values
ACHIEVEMENT	Valuing of personal success by demonstrating one's competence according to social standards	**Success** (goal achievement) **Capability** (competence, effectiveness, efficiency) **Ambition** (hard work) **Influence** (the ability to influence people and events)
BENEVOLENCE	Preservation and enhancement of the welfare of people with whom one is in frequent personal contact	**Helpfulness** (working for the welfare of others) **Honesty** (genuineness, sincerity) **Forgivingness** (willingness to pardon others) **Loyalty** (faithful to friends, group) **Responsibility** (dependable, reliable)
CONFORMITY	Restraint of actions, inclinations, and impulses that are likely to upset or harm others and that might violate social expectations or norms	**Politeness** (courtesy, good manners) **Obedience** (dutiful, meet obligations) **Self-discipline** (self-restraint, resistance to temptation) **Honouring parents and elders** (showing respect)
HEDONISM	Pleasure and sensuous gratification for oneself	**Pleasure** (gratification of one's desires) **Enjoyment in life** (enjoyment of food, sex)
POWER	One's social status and prestige, control, or dominance over people and resources	**Social power** (control over others, dominance) **Authority** (the right to lead or command) **Wealth** (material possessions, money)
SECURITY	Safety, harmony, and stability of society, of relationships, and of self	**Family security** (safety for loved ones) **National security** (protection from enemies) **Social order** (stability of society) **Cleanliness** (neatness, tidiness) **Reciprocation of favours** (avoidance of indebtedness)
SELF-DIRECTION	Independent thought and action	**Creativity** (uniqueness, imagination) **Freedom** (freedom to think and act) **Independence** (self-dependence, self-reliance, self-sufficiency) **Curiosity** (exploring) **Choose own goals** (select own direction in life and be free to choose)
STIMULATION	Excitement, novelty, and challenge in life	**Daringness** (risk-taking) **A varied life** (challenge, novelty, change) **An exciting life** (stimulating experiences)

(Continued)

TABLE 2.1　*(Continued)*

Value type	Description	Associated values
TRADITION	Respect, commitment, and acceptance of the customs and ideas that traditional culture or religion provides	**Humility** (modesty, self-effacement) **Acceptance of one's portion in life** (submission to and acceptance of one's life's circumstances) **Devotion** (hold to religious faith and belief) **Respect for tradition** (preservation of time-honoured customs) **Moderate** (avoiding extremes of feeling or action)
UNIVERSALISM	Understanding, appreciation, tolerance, and protection for the welfare of all people and for nature	**Broad-minded** (tolerant of different ideas and beliefs) **Wisdom** (a mature understanding of life) **Social justice** (correcting injustice, care for the weak) **Equality** (equal opportunity for all) **A world at peace** (free of war and conflict) **A world of beauty** (beauty of nature and the arts) **Unity with nature** (fitting into nature) **Protecting the environment** (preserving nature)

Sources: Adapted from Schwartz (1992; 1996) and Rohan (2000)

Much research supports Schwartz's views of **values** and has shown that we all, more or less, have the same sets of values – irrespective of culture, gender, and religion (Schwartz, 1996). However, we differ in the priorities we assign to our values (Rohan, 2000). Research has shown that how values are prioritized can lead to conflict between people from the same political party when their values are prioritized differently (Keele and Wolak, 2006); and how we prioritize our values has a strong influence on whether we trust or distrust our institutions such as churches, governments, and so on (Devos et al., 2002).

For this reason, there has been a lot of interest over the last decade in understanding values, especially in organizational settings, and Schwartz's model of values is growing in stature and popularity (Knafo et al., 2011; Lindeman and Verkasalo, 2005; Lönnqvist et al., 2006; Sagiv and Schwartz, 2000; Tsui et al., 2007). We explore values in greater detail later (see also pp. 221–242), when we look at the chapters on managing human resources (pp. 174–180), managing cultures (pp. 240–242), and managing sustainably (pp. 409–413). Parashar et al. (2004) provide an accessible and readable account of values, and present a study conducted on students' values, their perceptions about what values are important in society and how they might affect their actions as future professionals.

Value priorities refer to the order of values in terms of their importance to us as individuals.

Check out the Companion Website www.sagepub.co.uk/ managingandorganizations3 for free access to an article by Sapna Parashar and colleagues (2004), which provides some insights into values, their definition, and underlying constructs, and how they are developed over time.

A question of values

Using Schwartz's values, let us look at an example of how people might think and act according to their value priorities. Imagine a person who works for a major IT company meets a client for the first time in a meeting – let us call them Anne (the national manager of a chain of book stores) and Samantha (the customer relations manager of the IT firm). The two of them will have a lot to do with each other over the next few years as their associated companies are now in a joint venture. Let us assume Anne's values rate highly on tradition, power, and conformance, but low on universalism, so she respects and upholds her cultural and religious traditions and believes they are dominant, and that people who violate or threaten such traditions should be converted to her views or should be punished. Like Anne, Samantha also highly rates values of tradition and conformance but, rather than having power

as a priority, she views universalism as a higher-order value. Take a look at the associated values for power and universalism in Table 2.1; do you think that over time Samantha and Anne will find it difficult to get along? What do you think might happen after they start discussing issues important to them? Sure, they might agree that it's a nice sunny day, that Brad Pitt is a hunk, and that Angelina's new African baby is too cute – but what about if they start discussing issues such as whether asylum seekers from different religious backgrounds should enter their country? Of course, as managers we would hope that they only ever discuss work matters, but in close working relationships such a wish would be very difficult to uphold. This is where values are very important because we tend to prefer people who have the same value priorities as we do, and often we find it difficult to tolerate people with different value priorities.

PERSONALITY

Personality refers to the stable patterns of behaviour and internal states of mind that help explain a person's behavioural tendencies (Monte, 1991).

Why do managers need to know about personality, and what is a **personality**, anyway? Management, above all, is about managing people. And people, unlike machines or numbers, have individual personalities.

Most of us are already everyday theorists of personality – we make observations about people's actions and behaviours, and we categorize people accordingly, on an almost daily basis. Consider the following example. A group of friends go to the university bar every Friday night. One friend, Jo, is always joking and making people laugh; another friend, Sal, is quiet and reserved. Jo is a 'fun' person, and people might say Jo is extroverted. Sal, however, is perceived as introverted. Their individual personalities influence how others react and behave in response to them, both in the bar and at work.

In the workplace, depending on the task, Sal and Jo's different personalities will have a profound effect on how those they work with perform their work and the quality of their working relationships. For this reason alone, the ability to manage diverse personalities is an important repertoire for a manager's set of skills. In addition to values, personality is important in understanding why and how humans behave, think, and feel as they do, and people's personalities can have a strong impact on what they choose to do and how they perform at work (George, 1992), how well they suc-ceed in life (Rode et al., 2006), and on their academic achievement (Jolijn Hendriks et al., 2011).

In this section, we consider a handful of theories that have emerged from quite distinct backgrounds. The fascinating story of how personality has been theorized has many twists and turns. We look at four broad accounts: the **trait**, the sociocognitive, the psychoanalytical, and the humanist. There are many others but these are the four dominant ways that personality is theorized; each approach views the subject matter of personality from a quite distinct perspective.

> Traits refer to a mixture of biological, psychological, and societal influences that characterize a person's thoughts and actions throughout their lives.

You are what you are: the trait approach

The trait approach develops from the perspective that personality is some-thing that can be clearly identified, operationalized, and measured.

The trait perspective became popular in the 1930s, when Allport and Odbert (1936) sought to identify all the traits that might describe people. To do this, they decided to look in a dictionary. They found about 18,000 words that could be used as descriptors, and subsequent psychologists have sought to reduce and condense this enormous list. The most popular approach is through **factor analysis**.

> Factor analysis is a statistical method used to describe variability amongst variables by identifying inter-correlation coefficients that indicate underlying factors.

Let us revisit Jo. Jo might be funny, friendly, easy to get along with, and might also enjoy experiencing new things and taking risks. Each of these traits reflects Jo's personality. Traits that cluster together are called a *factor*. In this example, the factor would be 'extraversion'.

By far the best-known trait theory using factorial analysis is McCrae and Costa's (1996) 'Big Five' personality factors. The Big Five person-ality factor approach has been found to be one of the most reliable trait-based approaches to personality measurement (Endler and Speer, 1998; Howard and Howard, 2006; Schmitt et al., 2007). Almost every textbook on personality, organizational behaviour, and management includes the Big Five, also sometimes referred to as the NEO-PI, and OCEAN. The five factors and their associated meanings are presented in Table 2.2.

You are what we think: the sociocognitive approach

The sociocognitive approach seeks to explain how learning, social behav-iour, and cognition compose and shape our personality. Its popularity started with the work of Alfred Bandura and his concept of **reciprocal deter-minism** (Bandura, 1986).

> By reciprocal determinism, Bandura meant that our personality is a product of our behaviour, our thoughts, and our feelings in interaction with our environment.

For example, Samantha might come from a very quiet and reserved home. She has grown to like peace and quiet, and this has helped make up much of her personality. The fact that the bar is loud and crowded makes Sam uncomfortable, so she becomes quieter and more reserved. It is not that she is unsociable: Sam may be sociable and friendly at home but not in the bar because it is the wrong milieu for her personality.

TABLE 2.2   The Big Five personality factors

Factor	Description
Emotional stability	Emotional stability includes whether a person is calm vs anxious, self-satisfied vs self-pitying, secure vs insecure, emotionally stable vs emotionally unstable
Extraversion	Extraversion refers to whether a person is sociable vs reserved or assertive vs timid
Openness	Openness refers to a person's approach to life – whether they are independent vs conforming, broad-minded vs narrow-minded, creative vs practical
Agreeableness	Agreeableness refers to how people get along with others – whether they are warm-hearted vs ruthless, trusting vs distrusting, helpful vs uncooperative
Conscientiousness	Conscientiousness refers to high vs low tolerance for risk, well organized vs disorganized, well disciplined vs impulsive

Sources: Adapted from McCrae and Costa (1996) and Costa and McCrae (1999)

One of the most appealing sociocognitive theories of personality is known as the *locus of control*, developed by Rotter (1966). You can complete Rotter's Locus of Control Survey in the Question Time box below.

QUESTION TIME

Rotter's Locus of Control Scale

Answer the questions honestly and choose only one option (A or B) per question.

1. a. Children get into trouble because their parents punish them too much.
    b. The trouble with most children nowadays is that their parents are too easy with them.
2. a. Many of the unhappy things in people's lives are partly due to bad luck.
    b. People's misfortunes result from the mistakes they make.
3. a. One of the major reasons why we have wars is because people don't take enough interest in politics.
    b. There will always be wars, no matter how hard people try to prevent them.
4. a. In the long run people get the respect they deserve in this world.
    b. Unfortunately, an individual's worth often passes unrecognized no matter how hard they try.

5. a. The idea that teachers are unfair to students is nonsense.
    b. Most students don't realize the extent to which their grades are influenced by accidental happenings.
6. a. Without the right breaks one cannot be an effective leader.
    b. Capable people who fail to become leaders have not taken advantage of their opportunities.
7. a. No matter how hard you try some people just don't like you.
    b. People who can't get others to like them don't understand how to get along with others.
8. a. Heredity plays the major role in determining one's personality.
    b. It is one's experiences in life which determine what they're like.
9. a. I have often found that what is going to happen will happen.
    b. Trusting to fate has never turned out as well for me as making a decision to take a definite course of action.

(Continued)

(Continued)

10 a. In the case of the well-prepared student there is rarely if ever such a thing as an unfair test.
    b. Many times exam questions tend to be so unrelated to course work that studying is really useless.

11 a. Becoming a success is a matter of hard work, luck has little or nothing to do with it.
    b. Getting a good job depends mainly on being in the right place at the right time.

12 a. The average citizen can have an influence in government decisions.
    b. This world is run by the few people in power, and there is not much the little guy can do about it.

13 a. When I make plans, I am almost certain that I can make them work.
    b. It is not always wise to plan too far ahead because many things turn out to be a matter of good or bad fortune anyhow.

14 a. There are certain people who are just no good.
    b. There is some good in everybody.

15 a. In my case getting what I want has little or nothing to do with luck.
    b. Many times we might just as well decide what to do by flipping a coin.

16 a. Who gets to be the boss often depends on who was lucky enough to be in the right place first.
    b. Getting people to do the right thing depends upon ability, luck has little or nothing to do with it.

17 a. As far as world affairs are concerned, most of us are the victims of forces we can neither understand, nor control.
    b. By taking an active part in political and social affairs the people can control world events.

18 a. Most people don't realize the extent to which their lives are controlled by accidental happenings.
    b. There really is no such thing as 'luck'.

19 a. One should always be willing to admit mistakes.
    b. It is usually best to cover up one's mistakes.

20 a. It is hard to know whether or not a person really likes you.
    b. How many friends you have depends upon how nice a person you are.

21 a. In the long run the bad things that happen to us are balanced by the good ones.

    b. Most misfortunes are the result of lack of ability, ignorance, laziness, or all three.

22 a. With enough effort we can wipe out political corruption.
    b. It is difficult for people to have much control over the things politicians do in office.

23 a. Sometimes I can't understand how teachers arrive at the grades they give.
    b. There is a direct connection between how hard I study and the grades I get.

24 a. A good leader expects people to decide for themselves what they should do.
    b. A good leader makes it clear to everybody what their jobs are.

25 a. Many times I feel that I have little influence over the things that happen to me.
    b. It is impossible for me to believe that chance or luck plays an important role in my life.

26 a. People are lonely because they don't try to be friendly.
    b. There's not much use in trying too hard to please people, if they like you, they like you.

27 a. There is too much emphasis on athletics in high school.
    b. Team sports are an excellent way to build character.

28 a. What happens to me is my own doing.
    b. Sometimes I feel that I don't have enough control over the direction my life is taking.

29 a. Most of the time I can't understand why politicians behave the way they do.
    b. In the long run the people are responsible for bad government on a national as well as on a local level.

Score one point for each of the following:

2 (a), 3 (b), 4 (b), 5 (b), 6 (a), 7 (a), 9 (a), 10 (b), 11 (b), 12 (b), 13 (b), 15 (b), 16 (a), 17 (a), 18 (a), 20 (a), 21 (a), 22 (b), 23 (a), 25 (a), 26 (b), 28 (b), 29 (a)

The higher the score, the higher the external locus of control (maximum score is 23).

The lower the score, the higher the internal locus of control.

You may remember our discussion on schemas, and attribution theory, internal, external attributions and attribution errors – these are all concepts in locus of control. To get a feeling for the locus of control approach, consider the following example. You are walking along the street and you trip. You look back at the spot where you tripped and notice there is a brick on the path. Do you say, 'Oh, I'm such an idiot because I didn't see that brick', or do you say, 'Argh, what idiot put that brick there?'

In one case, you internalize your behaviour (it is your fault for falling over), and in the other you externalize (the reason you fell over is someone else's stupidity). In the former, we describe an internal locus of control, which refers to the belief that you control your own fate. In the latter, we describe an external locus of control, which is the perception that outside forces, or even chance, predominantly determine your fate – your fate is outside your control.

Internals have a high level of achievement, they are much more independent, enjoy better psychological and physical health, and have much better coping strategies (Myers, 2001). Moreover, internals perform better on most subjective and objective measures of organizational behaviour (Beukman, 2005; Spector, 1982). Interestingly, high external people cope better and are happier when they eventually enter old age homes where life is structured and controlled (Cicirelli, 1987), and high externals tend to create a social environment and prefer to lead and be led in an autocratic way (Beukman, 2005).

Locus of control has been shown to be very important in terms of how people behave in organizations and how well they cope with uncertainty and change (Chen and Wang, 2007; Herscovitch and Meyer, 2002; Spector,

IMAGE 2.1 Peeling back to the internal locus of control

1982). Those with high internal locus of control are better able to deal with work conditions of high uncertainty and stress (Rahim, 1997). Ng and Feldman (2011) found that internal locus people are more likely to feel embedded within their organization, while external people are more likely to move because they are much more influenced by external forces.

Of course, as in all theories there are counter arguments. While much of the research supports the idea of locus of control towards an internal or external orientation, to simplify behaviour as either internally or externally oriented is somewhat dualist. It might not be that people are either internal or external, but rather are both simultaneously. Research is suggesting that locus of control can be altered through cognitive behavioural training methods, which suggests locus of control is a mindset socialized and learned over time (Wolinsky et al., 2010), and hence alterable.

You are what you don't know: the psychoanalytical approach

The psychoanalytical approach to personality is typified by unconscious desires and defence mechanisms aimed at fighting pent-up sexual anxiety and the pervasive fear of death. Unlike the other approaches to personality, the psychoanalytic approach focuses on the 'battle' between the subconscious and conscious awareness as critical to constructing our personality. Sigmund Freud is considered the father of the psychoanalytical approach to personality. Freud is a theorist who is one of the most loathed (by many psychologists and some feminists) and, at the same time, one of the most admired (by many artists, writers, and psychiatrists). Certainly, Freud, along with figures such as Charles Darwin and Adam Smith, did much to define the ways in which we understand the nature of the reality that we experience today.

Freud believed personality was made up of thoughts and actions emerging from what he called the *unconscious*. The unconscious surfaces in dreams and slips of the tongue, because it contains desires, thoughts, and feelings that are 'unconscionable' and often repressed. For Freud, absolutely nothing happens by accident; an explanation is usually to be found hidden in the unconscious. It is deep in the unconscious that we store our troubled feelings and thoughts, and the mind keeps them hidden by working in a number of remarkable ways.

According to Freud, there are three ways in which our mind is structured. First, the unconscious mind (the *id*) operates on the pleasure principle and is driven by desires such as hunger, sex, and aggression. The *id* must be controlled, or it will be impossible to delay gratification. Second, there is the *ego*, which allows us to cope with our world based on the *reality principle* (the principle that, as we grow, we become aware of the real environment and the need to adapt to it). It recognizes desires and satiates them, but in ways that ensure minimal pain and destruction. The *ego* is the 'control room' of our personality. Third, there is the *superego* – our social and personal monitor, constantly judging our behaviour, thoughts, and feelings, looking at how we should behave through the eyes of all those others around us who constitute our society. The superego and the id are

IMAGE 2.2   Fragmented self

usually in battle, so the ego must ensure that the two are reconciled – and, as we shall see, this is where all the trouble starts.

For Freud, absolutely nothing happens by accident.

Freud (1935) believed personality development coincided with certain psychosexual stages. For example, at the oral stage (up to about 1½ years of age), a child is fixated with oral pleasures, such as sucking, gumming, and chewing, whereas at the anal stage (around 1½ to 2½ years of age), the child becomes fixated on the anal stage of development, focusing on anything to do with what comes out of the anus. Fart jokes work well with the anally fixated – think of the Terrence and Phillip characters from the cartoon *South Park*. From about 3 to 6 years, the child is in the phallic stage (you can see why feminists might dislike Freud given the 'phallocentric' nature of his theory!) and gains arousal and pleasure from stimulation of the genital region. Then, from around the age of 6 until puberty, people go into a sort of hibernation – or what Freud calls *latency* – where everything lies dormant. Finally, individuals enter the genital phase as they hit puberty and start getting interested in sex.

Quite a lot of the language you hear today has its origins in Freudian theory based on the sexual stages of development – for example, the notion of a Freudian slip, an Oedipus complex, penis envy, fixation, repression, and many other concepts in everyday use. Table 2.3 provides a description of some of the concepts related to three of the psychosexual stages (oral, anal, and phallic).

TABLE 2.3   Freud's three stages of development

Stage	Description
Oral	If we are traumatized or disciplined during the oral phase, we become fixated at that stage. So an oral person becomes fixated with pleasures of the mouth, which can be quite sensual. They constantly place things in their mouths, tend to overeat, and possibly smoke. Orally fixated people tend to become artists. Or they can deny their overdependence on oral pleasures and tend to become aggressive to compensate – so maybe they end up as a bouncer at a bar or a black belt in judo
Anal	Being punished during the anal stage tends to make a person what Freud calls 'anally retentive'. Such people discover that they can control their parents by refusing to go to the toilet or by going to the toilet at inappropriate times and in inappropriate places. Such individuals are quite stringent, control oriented, and tend to choose a career in accounting or something similar. Or they might become anally expulsive – highly disorganized and messy
Phallic	The phallic phase is where we start seeing some real problems. For example, based on the ancient Greek fable of Oedipus, who killed his father and married his mother, Freud believes males develop an Oedipus complex. Because mothers tend to clean up after their children, children get sexual gratification and arousal from maternal attention. Slowly, the male child develops sexual feelings for his mother and hatred for his father, who is perceived as a competitor for maternal affections. These feelings create intense anxiety and guilt in children, and they come to fear castration by their fathers. The only way to cope with such overwhelming feelings is to repress and hide all these fears deep down in the unconscious

Source: Adapted from Hall and Lindzey (1957: 29–75)

Obviously, if Freud's ideas stopped at the psychosexual stages of personality, everyday life would be a challenge, and the anxiety, guilt, and fear we would constantly feel would be unbearable. However, in addition, Freud argued that there exists an intricate system of checks and balances that enable us to operate in our world – the defence mechanisms that allow us to reinterpret reality and to fool ourselves that everything is fine. There are a number of defence mechanisms; here, we look briefly at three: repression, reaction formation, and projection (adapted from Myers, 2001: 494).

First, through *repression* we block all our incestual thoughts and feelings and try to present a smooth facade to the world. However, repression is an imperfect mechanism because some thoughts still slip out. Freud believed such thoughts would manifest themselves through symbolism or in slips of the tongue. For example, the fact that many missiles are designed in a shape similar to a penis suggests to some psychoanalysts that men create these weapons of mass destruction because of their repressed sexual feelings and aggression.

Second, we use *reaction formation* to block our impulses and feelings by acting in ways opposite to them. One common social problem today is the violence that some young men perpetrate towards homosexuals (gay bashing). Freudians would argue that such young men are trying to cope with their homosexual thoughts and feelings by causing violence to the very people they fear they might be. Thus, being macho both enables them to repress any anxieties and to demonstrate, by overcompensating, their own sense of the sexuality that they wish to project to the world.

Third, *projection*: when we have feelings and thoughts that are threatening for us, we project them onto others. For example, a distrustful and incompetent office administrator may treat everyone who comes into their office with distrust and see them as incompetent. Such a person denies his or her own incompetence by projecting it onto others.

Although Freud produced one of the most interesting personality theories, there is inconsistent evidence supporting his notions. Even so, there is no doubt that he has been, historically, one of the most influential psychological theorists and practitioners. His concepts have had considerable intellectual appeal and remain the most salient aspect of Freud's work. Still, Freud's theory takes a very negative view of humanity and overemphasizes sexual desire as the main motivator behind behaviour and thought. Imagine reprimanding an employee by saying that he is fixated at the phallic stage of development and is acting the way he is because he wants to sleep with his mother and kill his father – that might not go down too well! Fortunately, there are other personality theories that approach the subject from a more positive view – the humanist approach.

You are what you grow: the humanist approach

The humanist places our sense of self at the centre of personality. The aim of the humanist is to ensure that humans fully realize personal growth and

IMAGE 2.3 Symbols of/on the self

potential. The humanist tradition experienced its greatest growth in the 1960s as psychologists became increasingly critical of the overreliance on objectivity in trait-based approaches to studying personality, where paper and pencil inventories and factor analysis de-humanized psychology. They were equally wary of Freud's overly negative orientation, with its view that our personalities are mainly based on suppression of deviant thoughts and incestual sexual desires. By far the best-known humanist psychologists are Carl Rogers (1967) and Abraham Maslow (1968) (see also pp. 149–151 and 323).

Most critical for Maslow and Rogers is the notion of how we express the self-concept. When we try to answer the question 'Who am I?' the self-concept refers to our thoughts and feelings about ourselves. We view ourselves as being in the world in a number of ways. First, we have an actual self and an idealized self, and we strive to reduce the gap between the two by becoming as close to our idealized self as possible. When we act in ways consistent with our ideal self, we have a positive self-image. If we feel there are gaps between our ideal self and actual self, we have a negative self-image.

Rogers approached personality from the perspective that we are all unique and fundamentally 'good' people, all striving for what Maslow termed *self-actualization*. For Rogers, the key to positive self-image is the environment within which we grow because it provides three basic conditions enabling that growth:

- People must be *genuine*, *honest*, and *open* about their own feelings.

- People must be *accepting*, in that they value themselves and others. Even one's own failings should be seen with a positive regard, or what Rogers referred to as 'Unconditional Positive Regard'.

- The final important aspect for Rogers is empathy; *empathy* concerns how we communicate our feelings to the world and how we, in turn, share and reflect on these meanings. Empathy is very important in concepts such as emotional intelligence (see also pp. 74) and is an integral part of our ability to function in the social world.

Personality and management

Personality is clearly complex; although we all have one, it is by no means clear what it is or how it should best be conceived, and many very successful people are adept at masking the true nature of their personality. Rather like the mask in Image 2.1, they present a smooth but inscrutable front to the world. But if so much about personality is hidden or unclear, how are we supposed to use it as a tool to manage people?

Perhaps the best thing to do is to take a few pointers from each theory. Try to identify the traits that those with whom you work exhibit, and try to adjust your expectations and behaviour appropriately. Be sensitive to people's conceptions of the locus of control. Appreciate that some people will be more anal retentive in their dispositions than others, and try to deal with them in a way that takes this into account. Understand that not all behaviour is obvious and measurable, and that people sometimes are driven due to subconscious and repressed reasons. Also, try to be a practical humanist and facilitate human growth and potential.

POSITIVE PSYCHOLOGY: EMOTIONS AND HAPPINESS

At the beginning of this journey through perception, values, and personality we pointed out that we will predominantly take a psychological perspective. Psychology is commonly associated with the study of the deviant and the abnormal but is becoming increasingly interested in more positive phenomena. Although the essence of positive psychology has been advocated since William James, the concept can be attributed to Martin E. P. Seligman and Mihaly Csikszentmihalyi, who describe that:

> The field of positive psychology at the subjective level is about valued subjective experiences: wellbeing, contentment, and satisfaction (in the past); hope and optimism (for the future); and flow and happiness (in the present). At the individual level, it is about positive individual traits: the capacity for love and vocation, courage, interpersonal skill, aesthetic sensibility, perseverance, forgiveness, originality, future mindedness, spirituality, high talent, and wisdom. At the group level, it is about the civic virtues and the institutions that move individuals towards better citizenship: responsibility, nurturance, altruism, civility, moderation, tolerance, and work ethic. (2000: 5)

In its simplest form, **positive psychology** is the study, research, and theorizing of the psychological bases for leading the best life possible through positive thinking, feelings, and behaviour. In a management sense, positive psychology seeks to understand and to foster civic virtues, social responsibility, altruism, tolerance, happiness, and psychological wellbeing.

Check out the Companion Website www.sagepub.co.uk/ managingandorganizations3 for free access to an article by Barbara Held (2004) if you want to learn that positive psychology may not be as positive as some of its adherents suggest.

Positive psychology (PP), in the form of positive organizational behaviour (POB), is growing and attracting attention in management theory, research, and practice. In essence, it is an overnight success that was one hundred years in the making (Pitsis, 2008c). Historically, psychology predominantly concerned pathology and treatment of a variety of mental illnesses. As such, its initial application to disciplines such as OB also bound management psychology to pathology. Psychology centred on abnormality below the norm, and its explicit aim was to find ways to help the individual become 'normal'. Positive psychology is more interested in helping people be abnormal but above the norm. One area in which PP is internationally recognized is in the pursuit of happiness, but of course this is only a small part of what PP scholars are interested in. Even so it is one of the most contentious areas, if only because happiness has become a massive industry.

Not everyone is enamoured with positive psychology; indeed, some people are critical of certain sectors of the positive psychology movement. Barbara Held (2004), for example, believes that positive psychology paradoxically presents itself in a negative light. She believes some within the positive psychology movement are negative or dismissive of ideas or views that run counter to the movement's dominant message: (a) negativity about negativity itself, which is explored by way of researching health psychology, happiness, and coping styles rather than depressions etc; and (b) negativity about the wrong kind of positivity, namely, allegedly unscientific positivity, especially that which Seligman purports to find within humanistic psychology.

Happiness is something that PP seeks to spread and so it will be the focus of this final section of the chapter. Before we delve into happiness, let us briefly look at the general topic of **emotions**. First, we'll look at what they are and then check the differences between 'reading emotions' and 'feeling emotion'.

Emotions are by definition feelings in response to or expectation of an object or event.

Emotions are complex, and at the same time both highly personal and social. It is often assumed that emotions arise as a result of an instrumentally irrational cognitive process and that they are thus superfluous to the rational job of managing. We now know that this is not the case and that emotions enter into a great deal of how managers manage.

Early works on emotions perceived them to be related to instinct and survival and so were presented as quite basic, simple displays of emotional responses to threat or courtship (such as anger, fear, sadness). However, by the late 1990s emotion researchers and theorists provided insights that go beyond the earlier accounts of emotions as solely tied to simple displays of emotions (see for example, Campos et al., 1999). Cognition, rational and irrational, is a critical component of emotions and it is quite feasible that a person can feel many different kinds of emotions at any one time (Sroufe, 1979), or more importantly can mask emotions for a range of reasons such as the closeness they feel to other people, or due to the power status of

MINI CASE

Try this interesting experiment. Take a few photos of your friends in natural settings – try and get them when they are naturally laughing or happy. Then instruct some other friend to assume a certain attitude or disposition (e.g. happiness). Record what they have chosen to enact. Load the pictures on your computer.

Now, show the pictures and hand out a list of emotions to another group of people. Ask each person to attach an emotion to a face. Also have them assess whether they believe the emotion being displayed in each picture is authentic or fake, and ask them to provide a short reason as to why they believe this to be the case.

How consistent and accurate are people in the attribution of emotions?

Note: We do not necessarily condone the consumption of alcohol at all, and accept no responsibility if you are influenced by the following story, but when Tyrone was a psychology student he and his friends used to play a very similar game, but would have to drink shots of vodka every time they gave the incorrect answer.

others (Diefendorff et al., 2011). Diefendorff and colleagues found that when in the presence of people with high levels of power status, people will mask strong negative emotions such as anger and emphasize positive ones such as happiness. Clearly, humans are much more complex in their behaviours and emotional displays and so a simple smile sometimes is not simply a smile.

The understanding of emotions has been problematic. Ekman, for example (Ekman and Friesen, 1986), objectively studied emotions by observing facial expressions and found facial expressions to be consistent across cultures. But so what? When you smile do you always feel happy?

Sometimes we smile even though we are unhappy, or we smile back at someone in order to be friendly. We will tend to mimic the emotions of our 'in-group' – the group we feel affiliation towards – irrespective of whether we actually feel that emotion (van der Schalk et al., 2011). We may display emotions when we find a person attractive (O'Doherty et al., 2003), or we want to sell them something (Sutton and Rafaeli, 1988), and any other reason you might think of.

Anthropologists have shown that smiling might be interpreted as friendly and happy, yet culturally it might actually mean that the person smiling is nervous or anxious – as is the case with some Indonesian and Australian indigenous cultures. Of course, other times a smile might actually mean a person is happy; but can you ever really know if the display of happiness means the person actually is happy? The ability to read and regulate emotions is a major concern for organizational and management researchers and theorists.

Being able to read people's emotions is recognized as an important social skill; moreover, the ability to manage one's own and other people's emotions has become a popular domain of interest. Most recently the concept of **emotional intelligence** has become increasingly popular. Many textbooks include a discussion of emotional intelligence, and almost always that discussion comes under personality.

The concept of **emotional intelligence** has been popularized by Daniel Goleman (1997), who conceives of it as the capacity to recognize our own emotions and the emotions of others, and the ability to manage our emotions in our relationships with others.

John D. Mayer, along with Peter Salovey, wrote profusely on EQ in the early 1990s. Mayer argued that the popular literature's assertion – 'that highly emotionally intelligent people possess an unqualified advantage in life – appears overly enthusiastic at present and unsubstantiated by reasonable scientific standards' (Mayer, 1999: 1). More importantly, Mayer believes emotional intelligence is just that, a factor of intelligence, not a personality factor at all. Moreover, tests designed to measure emotional intelligence are still not as reliable as they should be, and claims that emotional intelligence leads to significant outcomes in terms of performance, or other life outcomes, are overstated – it seems only to account for 2 per cent to 25 per cent of the variance in outcomes. In other words, 98 per cent to 75 per cent of important life outcomes cannot be explained by emotional intelligence – even those surveys developed by Mayer, Salovey, Caruso and Sitarenios (2001; 2003). Hence, all the really positive things you read about emotional intelligence should be treated with a little caution – it works, but not to the degree many authors of popular books might assume.

The difference between **moods** and emotions is duration – a mood is thought to last longer, and mood states can take time to develop. Emotions are seen as a response to an event, or emotional episode; the emotion subsides (sometimes within minutes), but a mood state remains for hours and even weeks.

It should be made clear that the reading of emotions and the experience of emotions are very different things. Think about being severely depressed – the constant feelings of sadness, fatigue, and lack of motivation can be severely debilitating, and even lethal. Just by anecdotal logic we can assume that by no longer feeling depressed, you go about your daily life in a very different way. Emotions definitely affect certain life outcomes (when scientists use bland 'unemotional' words like 'life outcomes' they mean things like success, failure, life, death, alcoholism, drug abuse, and so on. Emotions include love, anger, hatred, shame, happiness, sadness, fear, resentment, joy. You will often hear the word **moods**, and for many people it is hard to distinguish between the two (Parkinson et al., 1996).

IMAGE 2.4   A happy face and a sunny disposition

Shiny happy people

There are few emotions that are as hotly debated in the social sciences as happiness. Life, business, and leadership coaching firms, psychotherapists, organizations, self-help books and DVDs, and university research centres have been established around the emotion of happiness. But what does happiness actually mean? **Happiness** is a very slippery concept, and most people would describe it as feeling 'good' or feeling positive.

The term 'good' could mean anything in a subjective sense, such as a general feeling that life is good (however good is defined), but here we consider 'good' to mean positive emotions and feelings with regards to one's overall quality of life. Veenhoven (2004) sees quality of life as integral to happiness. He breaks down quality of life (happiness) into two parts, which are represented in Figure 2.2. First there is a distinction between chances of a good life (life chances), and the actual outcomes of life (life results); second, he distinguishes between environmental (outer) qualities and individual (inner) qualities.

Happiness, in Veenhoven's model, is a function of: (a) the type of environment we live in (top left quadrant), and whether that environment provides opportunities for growth and happiness; (b) the purpose of life

Happiness can generally be defined as positive thoughts and feeling about one's life and can range from elation (being present when your team wins a grand final at the weekend), to a general feeling of satisfaction and contentment with one's life; it includes feeling calm, contented, satisfied, fulfilled, inspired, positive, and free.

	OUTER QUALITIES	INNER QUALITIES
LIFE CHANCES	Livability of environment	Life-ability of the person
LIFE RESULTS	Utility of life	Appreciation of life

FIGURE 2.2   Four qualities of life (Veenhoven, 2004)

(bottom left), and whether we feel we have a higher purpose in life and are living according to our values; (c) life-ability of the person (top right), which includes health, capabilities, adaptive ability (optimism, coping, resilience, and so on); and (d) appreciation of life (bottom right), which refers to satisfaction with life, and is typically a subjective experience. Happiness, therefore, requires a positive environment, purpose and values, health and feelings of being capable and competent, and appreciation of and satisfaction with life (Veenhoven, 2010; Veenhoven, 2011).

But why be happy? A number of studies have shown that happy people tend to be healthier (Ward and Coates, 2006), and they have greater opportunities in life, especially when people are part of a happy community, as happy communities tend to be healthier, wealthier (Ross, 2005; Subramanian et al., 2005), and generally do better in life. There is, however, a slight problem with some of these studies on happiness and health. The issue is that unhealthy people seem to rate themselves as unhappy and happy people rate themselves as healthy, but is it the health that is causing the mood state or is it the mood state that is causing the health? More importantly, it has been argued that happiness increases productivity at work and leads to several other positive organizational outcomes.

Does happiness actually lead to organizational productivity? This seems like a simple question, but it has a very complex and hotly debated response. The fact is, despite what you might read, we do not really have a definitive answer to this question – indeed, if we think about it, happiness may not be conducive to certain types of performance. For example, wealth is known to have low correlation with happiness (Kahneman et al., 2006) and feelings of wellbeing, but wealth does have a high correlation with good health (Bloom and Canning, 2000), which makes the health–happiness link a little confusing. However, the field of research on happiness and work-related outcomes is new, and slowly research is beginning to address the issue of reliability, validity, and scholarship (i.e. serious academic, rigorous, and well-designed study, Cameron et al., 2003b).

Finally, can we teach happiness? Fortunately we can and people have been working on increasing happiness for a long time. While the interest in happiness is old, the design, use, and validation of happiness training are relatively new. One of the most fruitful approaches to happiness is schema therapy – which is similar to cognitive-behavioural therapy that addresses how we think, feel, and act by promoting consistency across those three areas. Aaron T. Beck uses cognitive-behavioural theory in order to help people overcome depression – aside from medication; CBT seems to be one of the most successful approaches to dealing with mental health problems (Westbrook and Kirk, 2005), and the application of parallel principles to happiness shows promising signs (Seligman et al., 2005).

While there is growing evidence that happiness can be taught, pursuing interventions that make you happy should be seen as critical (Norrish and Vella-Brodrick, 2006). Even if it adds no measurable value to an organization's performance, general feelings of wellbeing are something that the individual might wish to pursue (see the What Do You Mean? box below).

One cliché you may often hear is, 'Money can't buy you happiness', but is this really true? Someone once responded to this statement by saying, 'Money might not buy you happiness, but it sure buys you a better quality of misery'. Counter to several decades of research that suggests money does not actually buy happiness, the most recent research suggests money does actually buy you happiness (Blanchflower and Oswald, 2011). So, the next annoying person who says, 'Money does not buy you happiness', tell them to read this book: but get them to buy it, because that makes Stewart, Martin, and Tyrone happy too.

WHAT DO YOU MEAN?

Get happy!

In order to help people experience sustained happiness, clinical psychologist and happiness guru, Dr Timothy Sharp, proposes the CHOOSE model of happiness. To develop and enhance your experience of happiness implement some of these steps:

C = Clarity (of goals, direction, and life purpose): Happy people set clear goals and determine clear and specific plans to ensure these goals become reality. So clarify your life plan now (because no one else will do it for you!).

H = Healthy living (activity and exercise, diet and nutrition, and sleep): Health forms a crucial part of the foundation to happiness. It's hard to be happy if you're literally sick and tired all the time. So do whatever you can to be healthy and you'll also boost your chances of being happy.

O = Optimism (positive but realistic thinking): There's no doubt that happy people think about themselves, others, and the world differently. Among other things, they search for more positives. The good news is that this is something you can learn to do, so start practising now.

O = Others (the key relationships in your life): Research strongly indicates that happy people have both more and better quality relationships. So make sure you devote time to developing and fostering your key relationships.

S = Strengths (your core qualities and attributes): Rather than spending all their time trying to 'fix' their 'weaknesses', happy people spend more time identifying and utilizing their strengths. Find out what you're good at and do it as much as possible.

E = Enjoy the moment (live in, and appreciate the present): The past is history, tomorrow's a mystery, and today's a gift – that's why they call it 'the present'. Live in the moment and enjoy life more.

As we bring this chapter to a close, we will consider just one last and important concept on happiness from a sociocognitive point of view: Tim Wilson and Dan Gilbert discuss the concept of **affective forecasting**, and cognitive errors that occur in forecasting: impact bias and focalism.

Sometimes the prospect of a negative event in the future elicits negative emotion in the present, and so you refrain from action (for example, we may fear bad news from a full body health check up, and so we keep putting it off). Of course, sometimes we also overpredict the value of positive goals because we think that the future event will elicit lots of positive feelings for us (for example, we may look forward to a big party at the weekend). When we pursue things we often make a cognitive error called **impact bias.**

Affective forecasting refers to the process of making basic decisions in the present based on predictions about your emotions in some future act or event.

Impact bias may be considered to be the overestimation of the intensity and duration of the feelings actually experienced when we achieve that future event or goal.

Focalism refers to the tendency to underestimate the extent to which other events will influence our thoughts and feelings (Lench, Safer, and Levine, 2011).

Check out the Companion Website www.sagepub.co.uk/ managingandorganizations3 for free access to an article by Kent Lam and colleagues (2005) if you want to learn more about how affective forecasting varies culturally.

One cause of the impact bias is **focalism**. Another is our failure to antici-pate how quickly we will make sense of things that happen to us in a way that speeds emotional recovery. In an interesting study conducted on affec-tive forecasting Kent Lam and his colleagues (2005) found that there are cultural differences in the impact bias process of affective forecasting. It seems that some cultures that think more holistically are less likely to be affected by focalism (the tendency to overascribe affect to upcoming events). The study found 'Westerners' are more likely to focalize than 'East Asians'; however, it was also found that Westerners who were helped to 'de-focus' were as likely as Asians to make only moderate affective forecasts.

In other words, when we are pursuing happiness, we need to be cogni-zant or aware of the fact that we sometimes attach too much emotional weight to that event, and so we can actually end up being disappointed when the event or goal achieved does not meet our expectations. Furthermore, positive feelings are not experienced 24 hours a day, but rather it is more likely you will experience a range of emotions over the day.

Realistically, how likely would it be that any future event will provide you with everlasting happiness and joy? Thus, in the pursuit of happiness we must be aware that the feeling subsides, and sometimes our pursuits might not necessarily make us as happy as we once thought. Conversely, negative events are never as terrible (in terms of our ability to cope) as we think. What Wilson and Gilbert (2005) argue is that we often find ways to cope internally with situations as they arise. In the end, you create your future emotional state in the way that you approach and make sense of your place in that future.

QUESTION TIME

How happy are you?

This survey measures how happy you feel. Please read each of the following groups of statements and select the one statement in each group that best describes the way you have been feeling for the past week, including today.

1. a. I feel miserable almost all the time.
    b. I often feel miserable.
    c. I usually feel neutral.
    d. I usually feel pretty good.
    e. I feel great almost all the time.
2. a. I find life to be boring all the time.
    b. I'm pretty bored with most aspects of life.
    c. I find life boring at times but at other times, it interests me.

d. I'm interested in most aspects of life.
e. I find life and living to be absolutely fas-cinating.

3. a. I have no direction or life purpose.
    b. I'm unsure about my life direction and purpose.
    c. Sometimes I feel like I know my life purpose.
    d. I'm pretty clear about my life purpose and direction.
    e. My life purpose and direction are crystal clear.
4. a. I have no energy and feel tired almost all the time.
    b. I often feel tired and lethargic.
    c. I usually have enough energy to do what I need to do.

(Continued)

(Continued)

d. Most of the time I feel energetic and enthusiastic.

e. I'm bursting with energy and enthusiasm almost all the time.

5 a. I'm extremely pessimistic about the future.

b. There are times when I feel pessimistic about the future.

c. I'm not sure about the future, one way or the other.

d. I'm pretty optimistic about the future.

e. I'm extremely optimistic and excited about the future.

6 a. I don't have any close friends.

b. I have a few friends but none I really consider close.

c. I have a few good friends and family members with whom I'm close.

d. I have quite a few good friends.

e. I have lots of good friends and feel I easily connect with everyone.

7 a. I don't think I have any strengths at all.

b. I'm not sure whether or not I have any strengths.

c. I'm getting to know my strengths.

d. I know my strengths and try to use them when I can.

e. I know exactly what my strengths are and I use them all the time.

8 a. I never enjoy myself no matter what I'm doing.

b. I find it difficult to enjoy life in the moment.

c. I try to enjoy life as much as I can.

d. I enjoy myself most of the time.

e. I thoroughly enjoy every moment.

9 a. I have absolutely nothing for which to be grateful.

b. There's not much in my life for which I'm grateful.

c. I'm grateful for a few things in my life.

d. I have quite a few things in my life for which I'm grateful.

e. I'm extremely grateful for so many things in my life.

10 a. I've accomplished nothing.

b. I've not accomplished much in life.

c. I've accomplished about as much as the average person.

d. I've accomplished more in life than most people.

e. I've accomplished a great deal more in life than most people.

Score each question from 1 to 5 where (a) equals 1 and (e) equals 5 (your maximum score, therefore, should be 50 and your minimum 10).

If you scored 40 or above – you're doing extremely well. Keep up the great work.

If you scored 30–39 – you're doing pretty well but might like to review the questions on which you scored 3 or below and consider how you might improve in these areas.

If you scored below 29 – you could be much happier!

© 2007 The Happiness Institute (http://www.the happinessinstitute.com)

SUMMARY AND REVIEW

Organizational behaviour is a vast and complex field. It represents the cohabitation of psychology with management, and in this chapter we have barely scratched the surface. Our task has not been to provide you with a complete account of OB – there are other books that do that – but simply to suggest some ways in which psychology and its insights may be useful in understanding management and work. We have painted over a broad canvass, nonetheless. In this chapter we have addressed perception, values, and personality theory. We have looked at the new currents in organizational psychology, which stress positive organizational behaviour, and visited the fascinating importance that emotions such as happiness have in and for organizations.

EXERCISES

1 Having read this chapter you should be able to say in your own words what each of the following key terms means:

- Attribution error
- Attribution theory
- Big Five personality
- Competing values
- Halo effect
- Information processing model
- Organizational behaviour
- Perception
- Positive psychology
- Stereotyping
- Values

- Internal/external locus of control
- Nature/nurture
- Emotions
- Schemas
- Personality
- Happiness
- Id, ego, and superego
- Cognitive dissonance
- Affective forecasting
- Impact bias

2 The commitment to happiness exercise. Research shows that when we do things out of love and passion, and that fit our values, we tend to be happier and healthier. This exercise is used in Tyrone's Executive MBA subject on organizational behaviour and students respond to this very favourably. The exercise is designed to help you do more of what's important to you. Do each part of this exercise on your own:

a List everything that you can think of that is important to you. Be specific and honest. These things can be extrinsic material (money, car, guitar, etc.), intrinsic or intangible (love, family, friendship, happiness, etc.), spiritual (God etc.). Really whatever you think is important to you.

_____ _____ _____ _____
_____ _____ _____ _____
_____ _____ _____ _____
_____ _____ _____ _____
_____ _____ _____ _____
_____ _____ _____ _____

b Now, you must choose the top five things that are most important to you and rank them from 1–5. This is difficult, but it is to help you to sort out your priorities. Once you list the top five things you must also write three things that you currently do each week which prove that the things you have listed are the most important to you. For example, let us say you said financial wealth is one of those. Then you should be able to say: 1) I put money into my savings account, 2) I personally contribute money each week to my retirement fund, 3) I own property, and so on. If you cannot list three things that you do each week that contribute directly to your financial wealth then maybe it's not as big a priority as you say. Do this for each of your top five.

1 _____ 3 things I do _____
3 things I do _____
3 things I do _____
2 _____ 3 things I do _____
3 things I do _____
3 things I do _____
3 _____ 3 things I do _____
3 things I do _____
3 things I do _____
4 _____ 3 things I do _____
3 things I do _____
3 things I do _____
5 _____ 3 things I do _____
3 things I do _____
3 things I do _____

c Now, if you cannot list three things that you currently do for each of your top five, on a piece of paper write down three things you will start doing right away to show that your behaviour is consistent with what you list as most important in your life.

d Once you verbalize your commitments to what you say is important to you, start a journal and keep track of how you show your commitment to what is important to you. Remember that sometimes we cannot always commit to things as much as we like, so it would be unrealistic to commit everyday. In addition, some days are harder than others are, so look more for a general commitment over a period of time. However, by keeping the journal we start being more realistic and honest with ourselves.

ADDITIONAL RESOURCES

1 If you are interested in positive organizational scholarship, a very well-written, and excellent foundational text is Cameron, Dutton, and Quinn (2003a) 'Foundations of Positive Organizational Scholarship'. This text provides an excellent grounding and introduction to the work being done in positive psychology. We also highly recommend Cameron and Spreitzer (2011) *Oxford Handbook of Positive Organizational Scholarship.*

2 *Memento* (directed by Christopher Nolan, 2001) is an outstanding psychological thriller that deals with perception, memory, obsession, and toxic emotions in the form of obsession and revenge. The film is about an insurance fraud assessor who searches for his wife's killer; however, he suffers from a serious form of amnesia and must rely on a complex array of memory substitutes (such as Post-it notes, tattoos, and photographs, etc.). Be warned it is a demanding film because the story line actually runs backwards. Similarly we recommend *Inception* (directed by Christopher Nolan, 2010), which deals with temporality, reality, and even affective forecasting.

3 A great film that deals with attribution error, stereotyping, and personality is the movie *Crash* (directed by Paul Haggis, 2006). The film is about a number of people interconnected in certain ways and deals with covert and overt forms of racism, human behaviour, and character. The tag line to the film is, 'You think you know who you are, you have no idea!' and the story follows a number of people in Los Angeles, CA, including a police detective with a drugged mother and a thieving brother, two car 'jackers' who philosophize on society and race, a white district attorney and his over-pampered wife, a racist white cop and his sick father, and the cops idealistic younger partner, a successful Hollywood director and his wife who deal with the racist cop, a Persian-immigrant father, a

Hispanic locksmith and his young daughter who is afraid of bullets for good reason.

WEB SECTION

1 Our Companion Website www.sagepub.co.uk/managingandorganizations3 contains a great deal of excellent resources, links, exercises, cases, and self-testing. Be sure to visit it, and look under Chapter 1 for lots more great things on managing the individual in organizations.

2 For state of the art briefings on how to manage organizations effectively, please visit the Henry Stewart Talks series of online audiovisual seminars on Managing Organizations, edited by Stewart Clegg: www.hstalks.com/r/managing-orgs. Check out especially Talk #2 by Tyrone Pitsis on *An introduction to managing people in organizations.*

3 http://personality-project.org/personality.html is an excellent website titled the personality project. From here you can access personality surveys, definitions, and explanations.

4 Check out the website of the Academy of Management (AOM) at www.aomonline.org. It contains some excellent resources for students, and more than 25 per cent of the AOM's membership is management students.

5 Professor Martin Seligman is director of the Positive Psychology Center at the University of Pennsylvania. You can join the web portal Authentic Happiness and access a large number of resources on happiness, wellbeing, and so on, access groups and other positive psychological societies, research centres and resources. The resources on the Authentic Happiness site are free to use as long as you register. You can do so at http://www.authentichappiness.sas.upenn.edu/.

6 Visit www.youtube.com for some great videos illustrating many of the concepts we covered in this chapter: some clips are funny, some are quite stupid, some are well made, and many are not. We recommend the following:

a For an interesting study on how travel and emotions affect our perception of time watch http://www.youtube.com/watch?v=bG6nZY9Bxy0.

b This six-minute clip runs through several optical illusions. See if you can guess any before the answer is provided? http://www.youtube.com/watch?v=Y5J6_UO67c0.

c For an interesting training video on office values, watch the following ten-minute clip http://www.youtube.com/watch?v=pEOz7nxky6Y. Let us hope your managers can be this inspiring and values driven, especially concerning the guidelines to living life.

LOOKING FOR A HIGHER MARK?

Reading and digesting these articles will help you gain a deeper understanding of some of the concepts we have covered in this chapter. We chose these articles because they challenge your thinking and in so doing might help you gain a better grade.

1 In an interesting study conducted on affective forecasting Kent Lam and his colleagues found that there are cultural differences in the impact bias process of affective forecasting. The article is: Lam, K. C. H., Buehler, R., McFarland, C., Ross, M. and Cheung, I. (2005) 'Cultural differences in affective forecasting: the role of focalism. *Personality and Social Psychology Bulletin*, 31 (9): 1296–1309. The paper is available for download on the Companion Website www.sagepub.co.uk/managingandorganizations3.

2 Glenn D. Reeder and his colleagues conducted some interesting research including using George Bush and his decision to go to war in Iraq, and attitudes towards gay marriages and abortions. Their study shows how we attribute negative motivations on people we disagree with and more favourable perceptions towards those we agree with. Thus if we agree with the war, or with gay marriage, we are more likely to attribute positive motivations towards people who also support our perceptions and attitudes. The article by Reeder, G. D., Pryor, J. B., Wohl, M. J. A., and Griswell, M. L. (2005) 'On attributing negative motives to others who disagree with our opinions', *Personality and Social Psychology Bulletin*, 31 (11): 1498–1510 can be downloaded from the Companion Website for free: www.sagepub.co.uk/managingand organizations3.

3 What are values, and how do they develop? Once they are developed how do they influence us in our future. Sapna Parashar and friends provide some insights into values, its definition, and underlying constructs and how they are developed over time. They provide an accessible and readable account of values, and present a study conducted on students' values, their perceptions about what values are important in society and how they might affect their actions as future professionals. The paper by Parashar, S., Dhar, S., and Dhar, U. (2004) 'Perception of values: a study of future professionals', *Journal of Human Values*, 10 (2): 143–152, can be accessed from the Companion Website www.sagepub.co.uk/managingandorganizations3.

4 Not everyone is enamoured with positive psychology, some people are critical of some sectors of the positive psychology movement. Barbara Held (2004), for example, believes that positive psychology paradoxically presents itself in a negative light. She believes some within the positive psychology movement is negative or dismissive of ideas or views that run counter to the movement's dominant message: (a) negativity about negativity itself, which is explored by way of researching health psychology, happiness, and coping styles rather than depressions etc; and (b) negativity about the wrong kind of positivity, namely, allegedly unscientific positivity, especially that which Seligman purports to find within humanistic psychology. You can read more on the issue by downloading the article by Held, B. S. (2004) 'The negative side of positive psychology', *Journal of Humanistic Psychology*, 44 (1): 9–46, from the Companion Website www.sagepub.co.uk/managingandorganizations3.

CASE STUDY

MANAGING INDIVIDUALS

The Case of Oslo Philharmonic Orchestra[1]

There is something mysterious about concert halls. All concert halls, not only the Victorian ones: dark corridors, silent-signs, thick doors, and the bright and alluring stage. The mystique is even more noticeable when the orchestra appears. Musicians in black and white, concentrated and grave looking. After a minute or two the first violin player (concert master) stands up. A tone is given somewhere in the ensemble – and everyone follows in tuning. Then a new silence: everyone stands up – the conductor arrives on the stage …

The largest orchestra in Norway, Oslo Philharmonic Orchestra, contains 109 musicians, performing as a large group, struggling and searching for a homogeneous sound day after day, concert after concert. Starting every week with a new conductor, sometimes one the orchestra already knows – even maybe the chief conductor, other times a stranger. Sometimes the teamwork pays off – in magic moments of melding together into one. But the large group is most of all 109 individuals, or even 110 including the conductor, trained towards perfection, maybe with a solo career in mind. Most of them are still in training for individual perfection, often by silent competition with the neighbouring musician at their side.

Musicians in Oslo Philharmonic Orchestra differ widely in their career outlooks, motivations, and horizons as well as their paths into their organization. Some are just starting while others are near the end of their careers. Some have moved into their present position by working up the ranks, some are fresh from music school, while others have principal positions that will last a lifetime. Not all are equally ambitious or motivated, nor are they on the same level musically, technically or emotionally. They may despise and envy one another, disagree about music and the merits of conductors, and even be in open competition with their colleagues for prestigious or

better positions within their respective orchestral sections.[2]

The nature of work in a symphony orchestra may therefore be described as a dichotomous experience for musicians: at times it is extremely exciting, challenging, and satisfying; at other times, full of stress, disappointment, and boredom. Orchestral musicians are highly skilled specialists who have trained from an early age. Once in an orchestra, musicians must contend with the social dynamics of a huge group that is an amalgamation of diverse individuals, and in an organizational setting that is complex and competitive. The most mysterious part is how it is possible to make this highly specialized and individual work into an integrated and collaborating unity.

The history of this particular orchestra goes back to the eighteenth century, under other names and forms than the orchestra we know today, formally established in 1919 as *Filharmonisk Selskap.* Famous composers and conductors such as Edvard Grieg, Johan Halvorsen, and Carl Nielsen were all part of the orchestral music scene in Oslo in the eighteenth and nineteenth centuries, developing the orchestra. In more modern times, Mariss Jansons, the chef conductor for the 20-year period to 2000, is recognized by many as the most important individual in stretching the orchestra's quality and quantity of repertoire. He has also been important in stretching the management opportunity set.

The guest conductors (on a weekly basis) and the chief conductor (leading the orchestra for about ten weeks a year) have an unquestionably important role in the orchestra's performance and development. Although there are some universal rules to the art of conducting, the conductors differ greatly in personal qualities and in musical orientation. The dominant picture of a great conductor is still the one of the lonely and gifted genius, a picture often used to describe Mariss Jansons.

We can feel the energy increase in the orchestra sometimes a week before Mariss arrives. Because we know it is going to be that good and that challenging. He forms me as a musician – by his ambitions for the orchestra and for every one of us.[3]

There are wonderful stories of other, greater conductors, but with less pedagogical skills. The musicians in the Oslo Philharmonic Orchestra tell stories of 'tyrannical artistic leaders' with high expectations and ambitions. Some leaders are described as having dangerous tempers and unpredictable behaviours. Individual members of the orchestra have experienced intense critique in front of the entire orchestra but there is never any noticeable protest or protection of the individual in this context. The stories of these conductors are often told with a touch of pride and as a history of success, probably because they all are willing to pay the price for an unforgettable concert. Because the musicians face a different leader every week, they must be flexible. They have to adapt to different interpretations of the same symphony and tolerate these variations. In this way an orchestra may be one of few organized professional groups that is explicitly trained in following a leader, no matter what the circumstances.

Everyday rehearsals and concerts on Thursdays and Fridays are held at Oslo Concert Hall, while the administrative department, with about 19 administrative employees, is located in another building. Here you also find the administrative director, in charge of the entire organization. The story of 'following the leader' does not, however, apply to him. In any case of non-artistic decision, the orchestra seems to follow a different logic.

Outside the concert hall, every decision is based on democracy: everyone should and will be heard.

Despite the fact that is it me that has the total responsibility for this organization, I have to give the chief conductor room enough to be creative and to be an excellent performer. The rest of the year I also have to deal with a group of 109 strong individuals that feel that they have a right to be in charge – as a community. I have to live with the fact that my management room is reduced.[4]

During a one-year period the chief conductor, the board leader, and the administrative director all left their positions – in that order. The orchestra remained the same – 109 individuals.

Questions

1 Imagine you are recently employed as the administrative director. How will you start to establish the relation and teamwork with the main artistic leader (the chief conductor)?
2 What do you think is the main challenge you have to deal with as a director?
3 What do you think are the main tensions, natural and unnatural, in an orchestra like this?
4 How can you, as a top manager, deal with these tensions?

Case prepared by Dr Grete Wennes, Associate Professor, Trondheim Business School, Norway.

NOTES

1   The case is based on the dissertation 'Beauty and the Beast' and the case is therefore presented from a researcher's point of view. Wennes, Grete (2002) 'Skjønnheten og udyret: Kunsten å lede kunstorganisasjonen'. Norwegian School of Economics and Business Administration, Bergen.

2   See more in Falkner (1973) of the diversity in symphonic orchestras.

3   String player in Oslo Philharmonic Orchestra (in Wennes, 2002).

4   Administrative director in Oslo Philharmonic Orchestra (in Wennes, 2002).

CHAPTER THREE
MANAGING TEAMS AND GROUPS

Cohabitation, Collaboration, Consternation

LEARNING OBJECTIVES

This chapter is designed to enable you to:

- Define the meanings of teams and groups
- Describe the concept of group dynamics and the process of group development
- Categorize common problems in teamwork
- Understand how to identify and resolve team conflict
- Describe toxic emotions and how to deal with them in organizations and teams

Advice from Mahatma Gandhi:

A small group of determined spirits with an unquenchable thirst for their mission can alter the course of history.

INTRODUCTION

Our world continues to become increasingly complex and ambiguous. Resources are becoming scarcer, and globalization is opening up exciting possibilities, while at the same time increasing the level of risk and complexity in managing organizations. With complexity comes the need to address problems in collaborative ways, and where once upon a time the aim was to ensure team members were as similar as possible, current complex problems (often referred to as 'wicked problems' because they have no simple solution) require diversity of knowledge, skills, philosophies, and practices in order to achieve success. Not surprisingly the use of **teams** has grown because they allow greater flexibility in decision-making and adaption to change, and provide better decisions and even better performance outcomes than do individuals operating under such contexts. Sometimes teams can be the most rewarding ways of doing things, but at other times teamwork can be frustrating, riddled with conflict, and even counterproductive. The reality is that every single one of us will work as part of a team at some stage in our lives – be it playing sport, doing ballet, or while studying or working.

In Chapter 2 we considered the problems of perception and how perceptual errors can affect our judgements and evaluations of people. These processes are even more complex in teams because we are dealing with multiple people simultaneously, all of whom are expected to be aligned to the same objectives and goals. It is therefore important for us to have a general understanding of teams, their psychological properties, how they influence us, and how teams work.

We will explore our definition of teams in greater detail. Management academics like to distinguish between a team and a **group**; even though the differences between teams and groups are subtle, they are important differences in some contexts. However, in this chapter we sometimes use the terms interchangeably because in the development of psychology, all teams have traditionally been referred to as groups.

Let us look at an example. Jenny, Mary, Sarah, and Joanne all play for the Mount Pleasant Rangers – a local football team that has made it into the finals. Every day, the players get together and practice their shots at goal, their long and short passing, and their game plan. The coach also makes sure that the players imagine themselves winning, holding up the trophy after the game. She points out to her team how important it is that they understand each other's roles and positions, and stresses that even though some of them do not get along that well, they need to work together to

A **team** can be defined as two or more people psychologically contracted together to achieve a common organizational goal in which all individuals involved share at least some level of responsibility and accountability for the outcome.

A **group** can be defined as two or more people working towards a common goal, but there is no psychological contract between them; the outcomes are less dependent on all the members working together, and there is usually no shared responsibility and accountability for outcomes.

achieve that all-important win. On finals day, people from all around Mount Pleasant leave their houses for the game. The traffic is bad; some people are driving on sidewalks, others are waiting for an hour or so for a bus, and some are walking. Obviously, these groups of people are all there for a common purpose – to get to the stadium to see their team play – but they are not bound by any **psychological contract**. If the people on the bus never get to the stadium, it does not affect the people who get there by walking or driving. In this example, the Rangers are a team, and the fans are a group.

In reality, a team is a form of work group and so in this chapter we will use the terms group and teams interchangeably to mean groups at work in which people are dependent upon others in their team in achieving outcomes. Interdependence among people in teams poses many challenges and opportunities to managers because it means increased saliency has to be given to managing issues such as personalities and values; coordinating behaviours; establishing direction, roles, and responsibilities; and resolving conflict. Put simply, teams are not only difficult things to be part of, but also full of leadership challenges. To help you better understand the complexities of teams, we look at how group psychology came about, mainly in the form of group dynamics. We then consider how an individual can be affected by groups of people, and how and why teams are used.

A **psychological contract** can be defined as the assumptions, beliefs, and expectations held between one person and another or within a group, organization, or some other collective entity, about the nature and function of the relationship between them. Typically a psychological contract refers to a contract made in the context of work.

TEAM AND GROUP DYNAMICS

Elsewhere in this book we discuss some well-established approaches to management–employee relations (see Chapters 5 and 12). Two key perspectives are the scientific management (or Taylorism) and human relations traditions. We cannot examine teams at work without engaging with the assumptions of these two managerial ideologies (you can refer to Chapter 12 for in-depth discussion about these approaches).

Scientific management essentially takes a very instrumental view of management–employee relations. The manager is assumed to know the best method or 'one best way' of getting the job done: a team will have no role in deciding what gets done and how it is to be done outside perhaps how much gets produced. Moreover, the use of teams in which people work closely together in a social group to complete tasks is avoided, if not frowned upon. Scientific management emphasizes clearly demarcated lines of management and worker roles, and states that work should be hierarchically divided; that is, workers and managers must be clearly demarcated. The human relations approach partly grew out of resistance to the ideas inherent in scientific management and emphasizes the role of teams, and the importance of social relationships in affecting workplace performance. Groups are seen as a critical part of the human relations philosophy, which includes notions such as the following: people want to be liked, respected, and valued; management's role is to ensure that people feel part of the team; all staff and teams should be involved in decision-making and provide staff with self-direction; and management should clearly define objectives and expected outcomes, and seek input or buy-in from staff when making such decisions (Mayo, 1946).

Teams, for the human relations school, are critical, but many 'feel-good' statements are made about teams. Some influential theorists, researchers, and authors argue that many organizations have unreal expectations of teams; in fact, they say, it can take up to ten years for an organization to transform itself into one with effective teams (Greenberg and Baron, 2003). Others are even more critical, such as Graham Sewell (2001), who argued that the idea of teamwork is often accepted without question as a 'good thing' based on the legend that we have always worked in teams. Such ideas can have the effect of downplaying individuality and individualism. Hence if someone chooses not to be part of a team, or prefers to work alone, they can be labelled as problematic and 'not a team player'.

Teamwork, therefore, can be extremely difficult because it is so open to interpersonal psychological issues. Certain psychological properties of teams can attract and bind individuals, or they can orient people towards destructive behaviours, causing some managers to question the value of teams because they require substantial management time and resources. In other words, teams can demand a lot of management time and effort, mainly because when teams are used, they are not designed or managed to great effect.

There are many psychological underpinnings to groups and teams, so we will now discuss how these function mainly from a psychological perspective. The specific study of teams and especially their psychological properties is called group dynamics. **Group dynamics** is a concept popularized by Knowles and Knowles (1972) and refers to the underlying attitudes, perceptions, and behaviours of groups.

Group dynamics is concerned with how groups form, their structure, processes, and how they function as a unit. Group dynamics is relevant in both formal and informal groups of all types. In essence group dynamics is concerned with the study and analysis of any form of interaction that occurs within group contexts.

Included within group dynamics are questions about why and how teams are formed, how they develop, how they work (or do not work), how they are sustained, their challenges, and their eventual demise. So let us take a close look at group dynamics.

The things that bind: why we form groups

Why do we form groups? First, let us consider the notion of safety in numbers. In evolutionary terms, forming groups rather than existing alone is a very important way in which many animals ensure survival. Ants and bees have very large, highly structured, and organized societies, comprising many groups of worker ants or bees, queens, and armies. Small fish in the ocean and animals in the wild (such as the impala, buffalo, and zebra) all travel in large groups for safety.

In the tradition of Charles Darwin, imagine yourself as an animal aware that a predator might be waiting to make you their lunch. If there were a series of points on your journey where attack was more likely, your chances of surviving would be greater if you travelled in large numbers than if you were on your own – especially if you were fitter, smarter, and could run faster than the others. However, to say that we form groups simply to avoid getting killed is a bit too simplistic. Psychologically, being part of a group is critical to our survival in other very important ways.

Second, we form groups because of a sense of belongingness. If you pick up any psychological textbook and turn to the chapter on psychological disorders (abnormal psychology), you will notice one remarkable thing: all the disorders (regardless of their cause) are considered problems for individuals because they cannot function effectively as part of society. Being part of a group is necessary for healthy psychological development and identity. In their classic text *The Social Psychology of Organizations*, Daniel Katz and Robert L. Kahn state the following:

> By being part of something beyond the physical self, the individual can achieve a sense of belongingness and can participate in accomplishments beyond individual powers. Moreover, affiliating with others can extend the ego in time as well as space, for individuals can see their contribution to the group as enduring over time even though they themselves may not survive. (Katz and Kahn, 1978: 374)

Being part of a group, therefore, is important for our own psychological needs because it provides us with a sense of self beyond our physical life. We all belong to one form of group or another – a family, a group of friends, a work team, a student group, a union, a special interest group, a religious group, a nationality, and so on. We feel that we either belong or do not belong to those groups for myriad reasons.

With the thought-exercise below, you will notice that for almost all of us, whether we feel part of a team or not is based on whether we are made to feel we belong, whether our interests and values are similar, and whether we fit in. Organizationally, when thinking about teamwork, the manager might design a team that cultivates the feelings in the first column and reduces the feelings in the second column. By identifying, or not identifying, with certain

IMAGE 3.1   Teams at work

teams, we are effectively creating a distinction between 'us' and 'them'. Each of us is treated as either in or apart from the group. When part of a group, we, in turn, probably treat others in the same 'us' and 'them' terms.

QUESTION TIME

Team feelings

Take a few moments to think about the groups you feel you belong to or are a part of. You do not need to identify these groups to anyone unless you want to – just think about them.

In the first column below list the reasons why you feel included as part of these groups.

After you complete that list, think about the groups that you feel you do not belong to or that you feel excluded from and, using the second column of the table, list the reasons why you feel that you do not belong.

I feel I *do* belong because:

_____
_____
_____
_____
_____
_____
_____
_____

I feel I *do not* belong because:

_____
_____
_____
_____
_____
_____
_____
_____
_____
_____
_____

Now, with some friends, compare and contrast your answers. What do you notice about why people felt they did or did not belong to each group? Can you see any common themes emerging? Are there any major differences?

In-group bias refers to the process by which members of a group favour or treat members of their own group with preference over others.

Out-group refers to those people within one's own group, or in another group, who are treated inequitably or more negatively because they are not seen as belonging to one's own in-group.

Much research has shown that in group settings we tend to favour certain individuals when making decisions. This phenomenon is called the **in-group bias**. In-group bias occurs because one's own group members are perceived to possess qualities and attributes not possessed by **out-group** members. Such bias can be between groups (favouring members of your own group) and even within groups (favouring select members of your group over other members of your group) (Hogg, 1996; Turner, 1987). Creating and reinforcing an 'us' and 'them' distinction has often been used as a way of uniting teams towards performance, especially by getting a team to compete against 'other' teams, thus creating strong identification with one's own team, or in-group. Over time, strong identification with your group can lead to quite problematic relations, such as prejudice and distrust, and even hatred and anger, towards members of different out-groups (see Whitely, 1999).

TABLE 3.1   Types of teams in organizations

Advice and involvement teams	Management decision-making committees, quality control (QC) circles, staff involvement teams
Production and service teams	Assembly teams, maintenance, construction, mining, and commercial airline teams, consulting teams, sales and health-care teams
Project and development teams	Research teams, new product development teams, software development teams
Action and negotiation teams	Military combat units, surgical teams, trade union negotiating teams

Source: Adapted from West (2008)

Overall, team cohesion and identification is important, but bear in mind that it can pose problems that make managing teams a complex art.

Types of groups

Having developed an understanding as to why we form groups, let us now look at different kinds of groups that we may experience over time. Typically there are two categories of groups in organizations, **formal groups** and **informal groups**.

There are many kinds of formal groups, for example a surgical team in a hospital, a production team in a factory, a policy team within government, a construction project team, or even a team of students working on a group assignment. An informal group is one that forms outside the formal structuring of work roles and activities.

For example, informal groups are a group of workmates who meet for lunch every week, union members within an organization, a group of workmates who play in a football team at weekends, or even a number of people who form a coalition within the organization to resist, reduce, or alter the power or interests of others in the organization.

Most groups tend to be **closed groups**. For example, most teams in an organization will contain people skilled or capable in key areas. A surgical team will include surgeons, anaesthetists, and nurses – all skilled in specific aspects of the surgical task. Obviously, to be part of this team you must have completed a range of university degrees in medicine, nursing, and so on. Moreover, the surgeon may belong to a national association, such as the Royal College of Surgeons, which has strict requirements in all aspects of joining and maintaining membership (including entry requirements, ongoing exams, and fees and charges). Moreover, being a member of such a group provides one with accreditation, as well as a certain level of prestige and professional trust within the community.

Some groups are relatively open, called, not surprisingly, **open groups**. Some of the most common open groups can be found in online communities. YouTube is a perfect example in which people share favourite movies, ideas, and productions. YouTube members vary from professional movie-makers through to total amateurs from all over the world. Of course, in

Formal groups refer to those groups where people have been specifically selected and are recognized as a team in order to complete a task, innovate, solve a problem, or provide a service or a product.

Informal groups are groups that are not necessarily sanctioned or even accepted by the organization and its management, but which still play a significant role in organizational outcomes.

Closed groups have several limitations or barriers to joining, maintaining, and ceasing membership.

Open groups usually have free membership and no barriers to exit, and attract people due to shared interest.

reality even open teams are limited in membership in terms of available and accessible technologies, same interests, and, as we will see shortly, in terms of operating within accepted behavioural norms.

Table 3.1 above lists the most common types of teams used in organization.

QUESTION TIME

The power of self-comparison in groups

The aim of this exercise is to develop your understanding of how we often make social comparisons. Try the exercise out on a group of friends or work colleagues (they are not allowed to use the Internet etc.). Tell your friends you did a general knowledge test and you want to see how they would have performed (but do not say if you did well or poorly). Have them answer the following questions but tell them to keep the answers to themselves. Explain that the general knowledge test is in two parts, simple A and difficult B, and that you will compare scores at the end.

Part A

1 What or who is Scooby Doo?

a. A cartoon dog
b. A street sweeping vehicle
c. A rap band

2 Which of the following is *not* a *Star Wars* character?

a. Yoda
b. Darth Vader
c. Spock

3 Which number is the last number in the following sequence: 2, 4, 6, 8, __?

a. 10
b. 12
c. 14

Before you read out the answers ask people to rate themselves on a scale of 1–5 in terms of how they believe they performed in this task compared with the others in the group. The ratings are 1 = better, 3 = about the same, 5 = worse. Get them to call out this rating and you write it down.

Now read out the answers and tell them to give themselves one point for each correct answer, but not to let anyone know how they performed. The answers are 1A, 2C, 3A. Now move on to part B.

Part B

1 Agronulocytosis is

a. A part of a plant?
b. The process of fermenting fruit for alcohol?
c. A type of microorganism?
d. A side effect from drugs?

2 Which of the following is the largest in terms of size?

a. The United Kingdom
b. Malta
c. Italy
d. The Great Barrier Reef of Queensland

3 How many medals did Australia win in the 2006 Winter Olympics?

a. None, Australia does not compete in the Winter Olympics
b. Two – one Gold and one Bronze
c. None
d. One – a Gold Medal

Once again ask people to rate how they believe they did compared with the others in the group, where 1 = much better, 3 = about the same, and 5 = much worse. Read out the answers, and tell people to give themselves two points for each correct answer: 1D, 2D, 3B. Now look at the rating people provided. Did anyone believe they would do worse or better on the easy section (Part A), and did people believe they would do worse or better on the hard section (Part B)? If a task is easy, why would people assume they would do better than others would? Would others not tend to find the task easier? If it is hard, why would they assume they would perform worse than others would? Where is the logic in that? Would most people not find the task more difficult? We are always comparing ourselves with others and can make wild and incorrect judgements about ourselves compared with others in our groups.

GROUP PROPERTIES AND PROCESSES

So far we have considered some of the reasons why we join groups, and the kinds of groups that exist in organizations. Group dynamics research and theory have identified some key properties and processes of teams that are integral to how they perform on given tasks. In this section we will discuss issues of social impact and group size, social facilitation, conformance and obedience, the problems of groupthink and social loafing.

Social impact and group size

In groupwork **social impact** has been identified as an important factor in the richness and quality of communication between people interacting together (Latané, 1981; Latané and Wolf, 1981).

> **Social impact** refers to the strength of ties between individuals interacting in a group, the spatio-temporal closeness of the individuals, and the size of the group.

Social impact theory is concerned with how a social system influences people to behave and think in certain ways. In other words, how people in teams perform is a function of how well they know each other, trust each other and get along, how interrelated their jobs are in terms of space and time, and how large the group is – the larger the group, the lower the social impact.

Group size is a critical component in how groups perform. Online groups, often referred to as online communities (e.g. YouTube.com), would be perceived typically to have a low social impact and are therefore usually seen as unable to get complex tasks completed because they lack close ties, are spatio-temporally distant, and can be of an immense size – even millions of people – thus lacking the closeness one would find in a small group.

There are, however, exceptions to the argument that large groups lack the social impact and meaningfulness of small groups. TEDx is a wonderful example of how people all over the world, from the most famous through to everyday people, can connect online in very rich and meaningful ways through TEDx talks and conferences: be they large scale production or local TEDx talks that are held all over the globe (visit www.ted.com/tedx). Thinking about groups has often ignored the fact that computer-mediated communications now vary widely, and new IT can provide chatting and voice or video conferencing tools where people can interact synchronously as well as asynchronously through multimedia, such as Skype, i-chat, msn messenger among others. In addition, social networking sites allow members of large groups to form smaller informal groups that focus on special interests.

Usually virtual communities are not designed to achieve specific organizational goals and objectives, and can sometimes even run counter to stated organizational goals. Members of virtual communities, unlike virtual teams, are usually bound together by similar interests, and so they are usually centred on social exchange, knowledge and information sharing rather than task completion. Even though they are not usually task-oriented, virtual communities do offer a lot of possibilities for organizations because they can be a great way that organizations can share knowledge, creativity, learning, and ideas (Frey and Lüthje, 2011; Gudergan et al., 2005; Lampel and Bhalla, 2007; Suh and Shin, 2010).

A virtual team has fewer people than an online community and so is perceived to be a more effective group than is an online community. Moreover, the virtual team exists to achieve results for the organization or group of organizations. Even so, a virtual team continues to be perceived as less effective in most situations than a face-to-face team. Researchers believe poor performance is due to the poor training and coaching of people in using collaborative technologies, and especially in developing and coping with high levels of empowerment and self-direction. While virtual teams work best when members have had at least some face-to-face meetings, research has found that fewer, rather than more, face-to-face meetings work best when the teams are highly empowered (Kirkman et al., 2004). In other words, if you are going to have people work in low social impact teams they should be empowered, motivated, self-directed, and skilled and knowledgeable: otherwise it is highly likely that the team will not perform.

Indeed, this case is true irrespective of whether a team is virtual or face to face. Face-to-face group communications have their problems, which can be just as serious and problematic. Where virtual teams experience problems because of the lack of social presence of others, face-to-face teams experience problems because of the presence of others, lack of psychological contracts, and inappropriate group size. Let us take a brief but closer look at these.

It appears that in face-to-face teams the 'Goldilocks' principle applies to group size – teams must not be too big, or too small, but 'just right'. What does just right mean? The answer to this question is not as simple as some people make it out to be. Typically there are a number of questions that we need to consider when deciding on group size:

- *What is the nature of the task?* For example, is the task complex and ambiguous and does it demand a great amount of resources, skills, knowledge, and expertise? A larger group might mean a greater pool of resources, expertise, skills, and knowledge. There is a trade-off in terms of group size and the available pool of talent. A larger group will have a greater pool of talent to choose from; however, a larger group will require clearer leadership and coordination as more people can mean greater chances of conflict.

- *What is the nature of the physical space within which the team will operate?* If space is limited a large group will mean space is cramped and uncomfortable.

- *Is there likely to be high turnover of staff?* A small team cannot afford one or two people to leave, so is the team large or skilled enough to cope with dropouts?

- *Is the team to be self-led or will there be a formal leader established?* Large teams will find it harder to be self-led and so structures and systems will need to be implemented in order to direct large teams. Smaller teams tend to be better for self-led tasks as people tend to share leadership in smaller groups.

The majority of group research suggests that the optimal size of an effective and productive team is between three and seven people. There have been effective teams with as many as 20 people. More recently, research suggests that a team of three is sufficient for performance on moderately difficult decision-making tasks (Laughlin et al., 2006); however, the research is recent and requires greater investigation.

The size of a team is very important. In terms of social impact it means that in larger groups it will be more difficult to communicate and coordinate interpersonal behaviours and actions towards group goals and objectives. Conversely, the task is also a critical component because a team that is working on a complex and demanding task but is too small in size will be stretched beyond the limits of its abilities. Similarly, a team that is too large, and is especially working on routine tasks, will perform less well and less efficiently due to overcrowding – simply put, there are 'too many chefs cooking the soup'.

Check out the Companion Website www.sagepub.co.uk/ managingandorganizations3 for free access to an article by K. Granstrom and D. Stiwne (1998) that expands upon Janis's notion of groupthink, which considers how groupthink can lead to depressive team behaviours and thinking and identifies some symptoms and methods for overcoming depressive groupthink.

Social facilitation

As social influence and impact suggest, groups of people have a profound effect upon individual behaviour and the overall performance of the team. Social facilitation is a concept that is as old as the discipline of psychology itself. In the late 1800s, Norman Triplett observed that children fishing would wind in their reel much faster when other children were present (Myers, 2001). The phenomenon of an increase in performance in the presence of others, known as social facilitation, is similar to the effect found in the Hawthorne studies by human relations theorists (see also pp. 464). Almost always, however, social facilitation occurs on fairly simple tasks only, or on tasks a person is experienced in doing. If the tasks are complex or the person performing them is a novice, social facilitation produces performance that is actually worse in social settings than when the person works alone. Thus, how you introduce and train new team members needs careful consideration and thought. Also, people who can do something competently alone may not necessarily perform competently in the presence of others. Training and experience, therefore, can be a critical aspect to successful teamwork, as all sportspeople who play competitive team sports know.

IMAGE 3.2   Up early and on the water by 5 a.m. – making a team work

FIGURE 3.1
Solomon Asch's experiment
demonstrating conformity.
Which line is identical to the
standard line: A, B, or C?

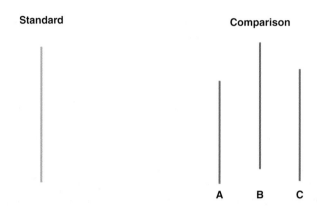

Conformance and obedience

In 1955, Solomon Asch published in the journal *Scientific American* what has become a classic study, in which he reported an interesting and simple experiment about how groups influence individuals. Asch had prearranged a group of five people who were seated in a room. Another individual, who had been recruited for the study, would arrive at the experiment to find this group already seated at the table. The individual was told that the group consisted of other people who were recruited for the experiment. What the individual did not know was that everyone in the group was a confederate of the experimenter. After the subject (who was the real focus of the experiment) sat down with the group, the experimenter began the study by telling the members of the group that he would show them a standard line and a set of comparison lines (similar to the lines in Figure 3.1). The group had to decide which comparison line was identical to the standard line, and each person spoke in turn, with the individual who was the subject of the experiment being asked to speak last. The process was repeated a couple of times. On each occasion, the answer was obvious, but each person in the group would answer in a way that was clearly incorrect – for example, they would all say C is identical to the standard line. Now if you were the individual who was the real focus of the study, how do you think you would answer? You think you would say B, would you not? Well, do not be so sure, because over the course of the experiment approximately one-third of the individuals agreed with the group – even though all the information available showed that the answer was incorrect.

Often, of course, conformity is absolutely necessary. Imagine a workplace in which no one conformed to the rules concerning health and safety, for instance, and no one followed policy on decision-making. Imagine the chaos; you would be in a workplace that looked a lot like the Wild West with its lawlessness, bandits, and outlaws. Even so, many people tend to follow or conform blindly to the group even when what the group is doing is clearly wrong. Conformity might help explain why so few people resist their organizations and why a group may tolerate or engage in unethical and socially irresponsible behaviours (see also Chapter 11 for an in-depth discussion on ethics and responsibility).

Groupthink

Similar to conformity, **groupthink** is a term coined by Irving Janis, who was intrigued by how teams arrive at devastating decisions – even when the teams appear to be prestigious, well educated, or carefully selected (Janis, 1982). Since Janis's study, many researchers have found that groupthink occurs across broad levels of an organization. Even when the team culture of a senior leadership team is made up of experts of equal power and status, it can become too strong. When this occurs, the team reinterprets information so that members can avoid any thinking that might disrupt the strong team culture, sometimes leading to a belief that, together, the team can overcome any obstacle faced (Clegg et al., 2002), but of course, sometimes such thinking can actually help teams overcome obstacles, such as a team that strongly believes in the vision and mission of what they are trying to achieve (Pitsis et al., 2003).

> **Groupthink** refers to the tendency of members of a group to seek and maintain harmony in a group, at the cost of ignoring or avoiding important decisions that may disrupt harmony.

To avoid groupthink the team might encourage people to voice their opinion by establishing that any critique of the team's decision is welcome and encouraged, or a team can allocate a role of devil's advocate in which one or two people actively question ideas in an informed and critical way. One especially effective way to avoid groupthink is to encourage reflective learning by sending team members on reflective retreats in which they discuss and interrogate the process of decision-making in their team.

MINI CASE

No space for groupthinking at NASA

By far one of the most famous cases of groupthink is Esser and Lindoerfer's (1989) analysis of the *Challenger* space disaster. On a freezing day in 1986, NASA engineers instructed key NASA administrators to abort the takeoff of the Space Shuttle *Challenger* because conditions were unsafe. NASA had a proud history of leading the space race, a very strong culture of invulnerability and success, cohesion, and close personal contact. There was extreme pressure for this flight to succeed due to future funding issues, time pressures, and world expectations. After the instruction to abort, the engineers and other members of the NASA team involved in the launch finally gave what appears to be a unanimous decision to continue with the flight. It ended in tragedy, with the crew all being killed in an explosion shortly after takeoff.

Once the federal inquiry began, a number of team members started to try and apportion blame across the organization.

Tragically, groupthink can be so pervasive that even accidents such as the *Challenger* disaster have little effect on enacting change. In 2003, we saw similar events at NASA when the Space Shuttle *Columbia* broke up during its re-entry into Earth's atmosphere, killing all aboard.

• What advice would you give NASA in order to avoid such examples of groupthink?

Social loafing

One of the reasons that people exert less effort in some group situations is that people feel less accountable for their behaviours when they know other people will pick up the slack (Harkins and Szymanski, 1989). For instance, when everyone around you is applauding a performance, you do not need to do so demonstratively because your applause will neither add much nor be missed if it cannot be heard. (Though if everyone at a performance thought this way, what would happen?)

There are many reasons why people might appear to be social loafers in an organizational setting, such as lack of confidence, being poorly matched to the job, or having personal problems such as family relationship or health problems. However, although **social loafing** is an important issue, especially for student teams doing an assignment, in a team at work it is quite unlikely that people will be able to loaf socially for a long period of time without other team members seeking to correct the situation. Theoretically, one would assume that social loafing would be much less likely to exist in work teams because team pressures can be a powerful source of conformance (Barker, 2002).

Even when social loafing does occur, it is easy to counter by, for example, ensuring that team members have clear roles, responsibilities, and accountability. Also, you can ensure that there are clear goals set for individuals and the team, and that team and individual performance are measured. When team rewards are based on individual contributions, allow team members to decide how members will be punished for failure to perform. In general, do not use teamwork for simple, routine, or meaningless tasks or in situations in which the whole team is dependent on the performance of only one or two members. For example, many department stores use sales teams; however, in sales there are often one or two individuals that have the ability to close or complete the sales transactions. In such situations, a team is only a team by name. It is probably more effective to use individuals in competition with each other rather than a team that relies on cohesion and the equal input of many individuals.

Of course, we are not suggesting more complex teamwork makes it less likely that social loafing will occur. Research has shown that when teams work on non-linear tasks, such as ad hoc decision-making, it is often the case that social loafers will coexist with active members of the team. Often the management response to the existence of social loafing is to tighten managerial control; however, rather than using a dictatorial team management style, cooperation in ad hoc decision-making groups can function robustly and efficiently (Kameda et al., 2011).

DEVELOPING TEAMS

Up to here we have discussed groups and teams, the types of teams that exist in organizations, and explained some of the reasons why we form teams. We then considered some of the key team dynamics inherent in

Social loafing – colloquially known as shirking, bludging, free riding, or laziness – is a phenomenon that we have all experienced. It refers to a situation in which members of a group exert less work effort than their peers.

teamwork and how this dynamics affects how individuals behave in teams, and how individual behaviour affects teams. In this section we investigate how teams form and develop, and differentiate between stage and process models of team development. We then place emphasis on the social psychology of team roles because knowing our roles and responsibilities in team settings is crucial to performance. We then move on to some practical discussion of managing tensions in teams.

Teams

First, let us take a look at the stages of team development. West (2008) identified four key dimensions upon which all teams can be differentiated. First, *degree of permanence* refers to the duration that teams are expected to operate as a team. The temporal life of teams can vary from quite short assignments to long-term tasks. For example, project teams may be formed for tasks that can vary from a few weeks to several years. Other teams may be required to work together in short shifts, such as a team of chefs in a restaurant or a team of airline cabin and cockpit crews who are together for only a few hours.

Second, teams vary on expectations of skill levels required over time. Consider a specialist medical team that provides care to expectant mothers with medical complications – not only are the required skill levels high, but they must also be constantly developed to keep up with technological changes and improvements in the knowledge of care and treatment of a variety of medical complications. Other teams may require few skills other than knowledge or experience around a given topic (as is the case with a jury).

Third, autonomy and influence refer to the level of real power and influence possessed by the team members. A team of five 17-year-old McDonald's staff may have little autonomy and influence in what gets done and how it is to be done, whereas McDonald's top management team is very powerful.

Finally, teams differ in terms of the nature of the task involved. Tasks can be routine, as would be the case on a car assembly line, whereas a senior leadership team may develop the strategy for a company for the next two decades.

We will add a fifth dimension that is not included in West's list, that of spatio-temporal context. By spatial context we mean that members of a team may interact in close physical proximity or they may interact from distant or remote physical locations. By temporal context we mean that people may operate in synchronous time (at the same time), or in asynchronous time (at different times). For example, an emergency disaster response crew will work in close proximity at the disaster site together at the same time, sharing not only space but also time. Conversely, a virtual team of engineers may be globally dispersed, working at different times of the day via computer-mediated communications (e-mail, virtual collaborative software) and in different time zones. Some of the engineers might never have met face to face. Teams that operate in this way are often referred to as **virtual teams**.

Virtual teams are teams that operate across space, time, and organizational boundaries in order to complete a project. Typically they use computer-mediated communication technologies and collaborative software in order to communicate and share information.

Virtual teams are predominantly knowledge based in that each member contributes their knowledge, expertise, and experience to the specific task at hand (see the What Do You Mean? box below).

So, to summarize, all teams can be differentiated based upon five key dimensions:

1   Degree of permanence.
2   Skills/competencies.
3   Autonomy and influence.
4   Level of task from routine to strategic
5   Spatio-temporal context.

WHAT DO YOU MEAN?

The Clegg, Kornberger, and Pitsis virtual team

While the three of us usually work at the same organization, in the same building (and even on the same floor), as with the first edition, for the creation of the third edition of this book you are reading we operated as a virtual team. Stewart worked in the United Kingdom, Australia, and Denmark, while Martin was in Denmark, and Tyrone was in Sydney. Sometimes, when one of us was writing, because of the different time zones, others were asleep, which made the production of the text faster than it might otherwise have been.

When Tyrone was writing the words that you are reading right now, Stewart was getting ready for bed. When Stewart woke up nine hours later the chapter was in his inbox, waiting for him to add his contribution and comments, before it was sent to the editorial team at Sage in London.

As a virtual team, enabled by our technologies and the Internet, Stewart, Martin, and Tyrone and the other team members were able to work on a twenty-four-hour cycle from different parts of the Earth, at different times.

Team stages

One of the most famous models of team development is Tuckman's (1965) stages of group development. As an educational psychologist, Tuckman was able to observe how people operate in teams, and develop a theory of team development that identified four key stages that all teams go through. These are the forming, storming, norming, and performing stages of group development. Later Tuckman collaborated with Mary Anne Jensen and together they added a final stage called 'adjourning'. Table 3.2 represents each of the stages and summarizes the key characteristics of each stage.

Many books that describe Tuckman and Jensen's (1977) stages of group development critique the model as outdated because it assumes team development occurs in a linear, functional manner. Another reason the model is critiqued has been because it is prescriptive, in that it is telling us what 'should' happen, rather than descriptive – what is happening. However, the power of the model is not to be found in terms of the 'stages' of group

TABLE 3.2   Stages of group development

Stage	Characteristics
Forming	As the name suggests, as people form groups they tend to try and avoid conflict and seek to gain acceptance by others. The group seems to lack a sense of urgency as people try to get to know one another, but in reality a lot is happening at this stage of group development. People are actually sizing each other up, working out status, power, and roles. However, because this is an early stage of group development, there is little action as people avoid issues and actions that might create conflict
Storming	Eventually the group will have to disband, fade away, or move towards action. Once these things start happening people begin to vie for position, they align with in-group members, and conflict may start to emerge as people attempt to deal with contentious issues relating to group outcomes and processes. Individuals in the group can only remain nice to each other for so long, as important issues start to be addressed. Sometimes members work towards cohesion in order to get things done, but a lot of problems concerning group dynamics emerge at this stage. Sometimes issues are repressed but continue to fester until they explode into overt conflict. It is here where the third stage, norming, begins to evolve
Norming	At this stage people start to get an understanding of their roles and responsibilities, what they can and cannot do, how they do it, and who does it. Once norms are established, new members must abide by these norms or face becoming outcast and being pushed out of the team. These norms become embedded and taken for granted and once established become very difficult to change. It is therefore important to ensure the norms reflect the intentions of what the group was established to achieve
Performing	Once the team has established its norms and a sense of cohesion is achieved the team is ready to perform. If you remember earlier we defined a team as one in which people are interdependently linked. That is, the task requires all people to perform in order for the team's outcomes to be realized. A team can only reach the performing stage when people are able to work well together, know and trust each other, and care enough about each other and what they are doing to adapt and change as needed in order to get things done. A performing team is identifiable when people are comfortable in airing their concerns, and the team members work through problems and issues without severe conflict
Adjourning	In the adjourning stage the team has completed its tasks and everyone should be basking in the glow of a job well done. People exchange ideas about the tasks, say their goodbyes, or find ways to stay in touch with team members, and must cope with a sense of 'break-up' and loss that they experience as the team dissipates. Of course, some teams such as project teams only adjourn in the sense that they have completed their given task, but remain a formal team that goes on to work on new projects

development but rather that it provides us with a relatively simple framework for understanding that certain things are happening at certain stages and that these influence the effectiveness of the team. For example, knowing that everyone is operating to the same norms around deadlines, quality of work, values, and so on might be integral to successful task completion. In this sense, by thinking about the stages and what goes on in each stage, managers can identify and reflect on what is happening, and what things need to be considered during each stage.

QUESTION TIME

Looking at each stage of group development, what do you believe are some important issues that team members should be thinking about, discussing, and developing?

Try and list two or three for each stage. For example, at the adjourning stage we might ask, 'How can learning from the process of teamwork be shared among team members so that we can improve our ability to work in teams and perform well on task completion in the future?'

_____
_____
_____
_____
_____
_____

Teamwork as a reflexive process

While the team stages help us to understand what might be happening at different stages of group development in order to make the team more effective, in reality the process of team working is much more complex. One interesting way to think of teamwork is to view it as an ongoing process of **reflexivity.**

Reflexivity is the process of thinking about the effect of one's role, assumptions, and behaviour on a given action or object and considering the effect that the action has upon how we continue to think and behave.

Reflexivity is similar to a journey in which we start off a certain way, act out certain things, and then stop to think about how we acted and how the action affects future action. For example, let us say you and a friend are in a team together, and let us say that your role is to provide information for making decisions on allocating funding to certain departments, and your friend's role is to ensure that the meetings stay on track and on time. You might find that you always go way over your allotted time, and you constantly find yourself being cut off by your friend. Moreover, you find that the rest of the team members agree with your friend, that you waste too much time, and that your presentations should be shorter and better organized. You may get very angry and storm out, but after a while you may calm down and accept that there are certain things you can do to be better prepared and present the most important information during those meetings. So, you do this and in the next meeting people commend you on a job well done, and that the changes in the structure of your presentation are much easier to follow and to understand. Through reflexivity, you performed a task, reflected on the task, changed what you did, and performed the task again.

While Tuckman and Jensen's (1977) model paints a picture of teamwork and team formation as a linear process where we can isolate and identify where a team is in terms of its stages of development, others argue that team working should be thought of as a complex and dynamic process (West, 2008; Wiedow and Konradt, 2011). For example, when we work in teams a great deal of cognitive processing and sensemaking is going on. How do we work together as individuals; are we getting along; do we know how to do the job; are our expectations realistic; do we have the required resources and people, and so on? Such questions do not happen in a static way, but evolve and continue throughout the life cycle of the team's development. As all this processing goes on, each team member is constantly adapting, changing, processing, and integrating what they know, do, and think in relation to the task at hand – in this sense teamwork involves a high level of team task reflexivity (West, 2008). By team task reflexivity we mean that a team will be effective not so much by adhering to certain rules around stages of team development, but that team members reflect upon their task objectives, strategies, processes, and environments, and adapt and improve these aspects of their functioning in order to achieve their outcomes.

West (2008) identifies a number of problems that teams face if they are not reflexive about how they are performing tasks, including that non-reflexive teams will:

- Tend to comply unquestioningly with organizational demands and expectancies.
- Accept organizational limitations and only operate within these limitations.
- Fail to discuss or challenge organizational incompetence.
- Communicate indebtedness and dependence on the organization.
- Rely heavily on organizational direction and reassurance.

A reflexive team will tend to improve how things are done and challenge behaviours that are not conducive to task performance and the betterment of team outcomes.

Team roles

One final but critical aspect of teams that we need to cover is the issue of team roles. In teams people are usually quick to take on specific roles in order to get things done. For example, consider a team designed to run a major event. A person will be in charge of budgeting and finance, another person in charge of operations management, another of marketing, another of catering, and so on. Each person has a specific role, and as each person performs their role in a synergistic way, the event is able to happen. Now let us say one person, the person doing budgeting, lets their role slip; then the project will probably fail as people lose track of costing and invoices do not get paid, and so on. Each role in the team is critical for success.

Not all roles are prescribed and often we can find ourselves taking on certain emergent roles. A team leader, for example, may not be formally identified, but one may emerge over time in order to lead the team (Ellis, 1988). Furthermore, different people have an orientation to different roles. A person may be a good people person and enjoy dealing with issues around relationships, or conversely they may not be comfortable dealing with people but have excellent ability to ensure jobs get done.

These person and task roles underpin some seminal work on team roles developed by Meredith Belbin. Belbin (1993; 2000) offered a model of team roles that identified typologies of the roles that individuals adopted as they worked as part of a team. He later developed an inventory, the Belbin Team Roles Self-Perception Inventory, which sought to measure and identify the types of roles people played in teams. Table 3.3 lists and describes Belbin's team roles and the weaknesses of each role. Can you identify yourself in any of these?

While Belbin's typology appears to provide an original and interesting way to establish and understand such roles, research has been quite varied in its support. Some researchers argue that the Belbin team roles have no validity or reliability and that it makes little sense to use these as explanations of team roles (Fisher, 1996). Others have provided research that supports Belbin's team roles and suggests that such team roles actually exist and vary across teams (Senior, 1997).

Despite the contention and contestations we believe the roles add value not because they are 'proven' as clear and distinct roles, but because they simply provide a frame from which we can make sense of team roles. For example, anecdotal experience tells us that each of these roles is important in getting things done. People have to generate ideas, others might be better at getting things done, and others may be good at playing devil's advocate and finding problems or pointing out limitations to the ideas. So rather than view these as real, measurable, and distinctive roles we use them more as a sensemaking tool.

Often problems occur due to role ambiguity and role conflict. Role ambiguity refers to the fact that people's roles have not been adequately established and understood. When people experience role ambiguity they experience anxiety and tension because they are uncertain as to what they should be doing. For example, if people in a team are all doing the same thing and some things are not getting done then we might assume that people are not clear about their roles. To avoid role ambiguity it is important we are clear about who does what, who is responsible for getting certain things done, and what happens and who is responsible when things do not get done.

Role ambiguity often leads to role conflict, especially when one person believes a team member is encroaching on their role and responsibilities. Indeed, role ambiguity can often make it very difficult for newcomers to teams and organizations to function properly (Slaughter and Zicker, 2006). Imagine you get a new job and think it is fantastic and on your first day you are placed in a team. Imagine your surprise when you join the team and you are uncertain about what it is that you are actually meant to be doing. Moreover, imagine that what you end up doing actually clashes with what another member is doing. What do you think the outcome may be? Would you or your new workmate be angry? As the new person how do you think you will be treated? Getting team role clarity is crucial in order to ensure team performance; this is irrespective of whether the team roles emerge, or whether they are prescribed.

The question of the roles people play has long been an area of research and theory. Role theory is derived from sociology and social psychology

TABLE 3.3   Examples of team roles

Role	Description	Weaknesses
The Plant	Creative, imaginative, unorthodox, and a problem solver	May be too preoccupied to communicate effectively with other people
The Resource Investigator	Extroverted, enthusiastic, communicative, explores opportunities and networks	Over-optimistic, loses interest easily once enthusiasm dies down
Coordinator	Mature, confident, and able to delegate well, clarifies goals, and promotes decision-making	Can be seen as manipulative, and can sometimes offload their work to others
Shaper	Challenging, dynamic, and thrives on high-pressure situations. Has drive and resilience to overcome obstacles	Prone to aggression, and can offend people, can lack emotional intelligence (ability to read people's emotions and empathize with others)
Monitor Evaluator	Strategic and discerning and makes rational decisions based on carefully weighed-up information. Tends to be an accurate judge	Can lack drive and passion, has problems in inspiring others
Teamworker	Cooperative in nature and is democratic, perceptive, and diplomatic. They are good listeners, good at developing people, and have the ability to disarm conflict and aggressive situations	May be prone to indecision at critical times
Implementer	Well disciplined, reliable, and dependable, usually quite conservative and efficient. Good at turning ideas into practical actions	Quite inflexible and resistant to change. Slow to respond to change
Completer/ Finisher	Conscientious and detail oriented. Searches out errors and omissions, and delivers on time	Anxious, inclined to worry too much, and uncomfortable in delegating responsibility
Specialist	Single-minded, self-motivated, and dedicated, provides knowledge and skills that are in rare supply	Contribution is specific and narrow, overly concerned with the technicalities

Text and Table 3.3 reprinted with permission, Belbin, R.M. (1993) *Team Roles at Work.* Oxford: Butterworth-Heinemann and Belbin, R.M. (2000) *Beyond the Team.* Oxford: Butterworth-Heinemann.

and is concerned with how people come to behave, think, and feel in relation to their socially sanctioned roles. Roles are complex and varied and are always socially defined and experienced. People expect others to fulfil certain roles in society and when they come into contact with people they will make a judgement as to the roles people will play in different contexts based upon certain individual and group characteristics. The implication of this is that the role that you are generally expected to play in society is a function of what social groupings you are believed to belong to. Notice

Check out the Companion Website www.sagepub.co.uk/managingandorganizations3 for free access to an interesting study on role conflict and role ambiguity by Slaughter and Zicker (2006), which considers how role ambiguity and role conflict affect the socialization of newcomers into existing groups.

here the parallels with the discussion on stereotyping and attribution error that we covered in Chapter 2. Let us consider gender roles.

Gender roles

Traditionally, occupations have been characterized as either masculine (male) or feminine (female). For example, certain job roles are seen to be feminine, such as nurses, child-care workers, seamstresses, and it is expected that these jobs will be occupied mainly by women. Other roles are perceived as masculine and tend to be dominated by men (construction and engineering, motor racing, and so on). After a while it becomes accepted that such gender roles are a social fact and we take it for granted that males and females tend towards certain jobs.

Of course, most of these gender roles are socially constructed to fit in with the strongly paternalistic and male-dominated institutions. Slowly but surely women are becoming better educated and increasingly entering the workforce and doing jobs that were traditionally the bastion of males, and many women have set up their own business. Men too are increasingly entering female-dominated careers such as nursing and child-care. As this becomes increasingly popular, perhaps one day there will not be the taken-for-granted assumption that certain jobs are for women and certain jobs are for men.

TEAM CONFLICT AND MANAGING TENSIONS IN TEAMS

It is a fact of life that at some point in our lives each and every one of us will participate, usually unwillingly, in an episode of conflict. Given that teamwork involves working closely with a number of people, the chances that we will experience conflict in such situations is more likely. There are a number of reasons why conflict can emerge in teams, many of which we have covered in chapters you have read or will read later on. Issues such as role ambiguity, social loafing, competing values, personality difference, differences in sensemaking, cultural and communication issues, power, globalization, diversity, and generational differences can all lead to conflict at work.

We cover issues of conflict throughout this book. It is appropriate here to define and discuss conflict more generally, identify some of its sources, and then focus directly on conflict in team contexts. Once we have done this, we will then focus on a fascinating area of workplace conflict – toxic emotions at work.

The term **conflict** is one of those words we all use, often without really thinking about its meaning. The *Collins English Dictionary* defines conflict as:

In organizational contexts we can define **conflict** as one or more people perceiving that their interests are or will be negatively affected by the interests of others. Such conflict occurs when people want the same thing (power, job, resources, land, space, etc.), and access to those things is limited. Conversely, conflict may occur because parties may actually want different things (such as different outcomes).

n. 1. a struggle or battle. 2. opposition between ideas or interests; controversy. ~vb 3. to be incompatible; clash.

IMAGE 3.3 Managing conflict is both an art and a skill. Artwork courtesy of Catherine Reinke (re-cycled artist) http://recycledartist.net/

Such definitions of conflict underpin the oppositional and combative nature of conflict. However, conflict is best understood by highlighting its philosophical underpinning. In the area of conflict theory there are many perspectives on conflict but we will consider two of the main ones here: the unitarist and the pluralist.

The unitarist approach argues for consensus and cohesion in organizations. In this approach conflict is abhorrent and avoidable and something that should be managed out of the organization. The unitarist perspective focuses on conflict at the individual, interpersonal level. Conflict occurs because an individual acts in a manner that is subversive to organizational performance and managerial prerogative. It is the role of management to ensure that employees understand their roles and position within the organizations. Conflict is a symptom of poor management and through control, the establishment of 'best practices', and people understanding their place in the organizational hierarchy, conflict can be avoided.

The pluralist approach argues that conflict is inevitable and, moreover, that it is necessary in balancing power in organizations (Dunlop, 1958). A balance of power means that the distribution of resources and power becomes more equitable (Hamilton and Sharma, 1997). In this sense conflict can be negative and positive, functional and dysfunctional, depending on whose perspective is taken. Table 3.4 provides some examples of functional and dysfunctional conflict.

Of course, how we come to understand positive or negative, functional or dysfunctional conflict is a question of experience. You and a workmate might both experience the same conflict situations yet one of you sees it as a positive in the long run, the other as a negative. For example, consider

TABLE 3.4 Examples of functional and dysfunctional conflict

Functional	Dysfunctional
The problem is solved	The problem continues to exist and fester
People experience growth and change as a result of the conflict	People are diverted from the team goals and task accomplishment
People actively become part of the solution to the problem	The team cohesion and morale are destroyed
People feel closer bonds after the conflict	Team members are polarized and divided into an 'us' and 'them'

Source: Adapted from Cappozzoli (1995: 28–30); Edelman and Crain (1993)

people who divorce or break up after a long-term relationship typified by arguments and conflict. Both parties may be aggrieved and saddened by the break up, but twelve months down the road one of the people has a wonderful new relationship and is about to go on a honeymoon to Hawaii, and the other continues to pine for his or her lost love. As such it is actually quite difficult to distinguish between functional and dysfunctional conflict until at least some time has passed (probably all the more reason why we should not overreact in times of conflict).

In their very entertaining book on conflict resolution Edelman and Crain (1993: 22–29) provide some key sources of conflict. While these sources are not explicitly linked to team conflict in the workplace, the sources are applicable, and so we provide some of them here, with our own examples of how they apply to teamwork:

- *Misunderstanding*: Occurs when the feelings and intentions of a party are translated in a way that is contrary to that which was intended. For example, one team member is ignored by a fellow team member when giving a presentation. However, the team member dislikes giving presentations, and is not intentionally ignoring the other person but rather is very nervous.

- *Dishonesty*: Dishonesty can be out and out lies, or even just half-truths, that eventually are found out. For example, a team member may often call in sick but one day is found healthy and enjoying a cool drink and sun-bathing on the beach.

- *Negligence*: Many conflicts occur due to simple negligence such as poor organizational skills, social loafing, leaking secrets told in confidence, and so on. For example, a team member may have told their team leader of an important holiday several months ago, and the team leader agreed to allow the employee some time off. However, when the time comes the team leader has forgotten this promise and expects the employee to change the date of their holiday.

- *Intention*: If we intentionally seek to create conflict and to provoke people then it is highly likely that we will succeed in creating conflict. For example, a handful of team members might gossip and utter personal insults at work towards one of their team members. Eventually the team member has enough and retaliates with anger.

- *Exclusive investment in one's own values and beliefs*: We are tied to our ideological belief systems. When we have opposing belief systems, and each of us is absolutely certain we are right, then conflict is inevitable. For example, team members may have extreme and differing views on religion, sexuality, politics, and even sports teams. Depending on how strong and immovable they are in these beliefs then conflict is always a real possibility.

- *Boundaries*: As with our discussion on team norms earlier, when limits to what is and is not acceptable are not set or clearly stated, then it will be likely that people will operate outside these boundaries. As such, step-ping outside of one's own boundaries sometimes means stepping over other people's boundaries. This has serious potential for conflict. For example, a team member may have worked long and hard on part of a project and comes back from lunch to find that another team member has started working on their section, overriding several days of work.

- *Mishandling conflict*: The avoidance of conflict and hoping it will go away is a serious source of conflict. More importantly, because many people are untrained in dealing with conflict, when they mishandle the situations the conflict can escalate beyond control. Often when we feel conflict between ourselves and another team member we may overreact and lose control. We might often say things we regret or did not mean, thus destroying our relationships and even ruining the team's cohesion.

- *Hidden agendas*: Sometimes people have a hidden reason as to why they want to see parties in conflict. Hidden agendas can be conscious – such as one team member seeking approval and favouritism from the team leader by constantly agreeing to work late, run errands, and do menial tasks for the team leader such as making coffee. Other times they can be unconscious in that one team member may lack social skills and often offend other team members due to insensitive remarks.

These are just some of the sources of conflict that might manifest them-selves in teams in addition to all the other issues of team conflict we have raised in this chapter, such as team roles, social loafing, and so on. We will now close this section by briefly discussing some approaches to conflict resolution in team contexts. The most common explanation of conflict management is the interpersonal conflict management styles model (Figure 3.2) offered by de Dreu and Van Vianen (2001).

The approach we use in resolving and managing conflict will have major implications for the strength and duration of the conflict. According to the model in Figure 3.2, certain kinds of orientations towards conflict manage-ment will result in certain outcomes. There are two factors that influence the approach to conflict resolution used: the level of assertiveness and the level of cooperation in resolving the conflict. The parties involved will vary in both these scales and will be highly assertive or submissive (the desire to

FIGURE 3.2
Strategies of conflict
management in the
workplace (adapted from
de Dreu and Van Vianen,
2001)

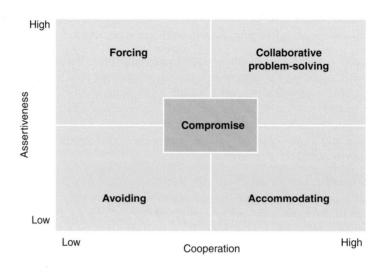

TABLE 3.5   Conflict management styles

Style	Characteristics
Collaborative problem-solving	This approach seeks a win/win solution. There tends to be a high concern for self and others. Emphasis is on being open, exchanging information, exploring and examining differences, and reaching an effective solution acceptable to both parties
Avoiding	This approach usually leads to a lose/lose position. There tends to be a low concern for self and others and so withdrawal, buck-passing, and sidestepping situations tends to be the norm in order to avoid the conflict situations
Forcing	This approach seeks a win/lose outcome. The needs of the other party are ignored or downplayed and one's own interests are central to the outcomes
Accommodating	This approach leads to a lose/win outcome. The others' interests are valued over one's own interests. Often cohesiveness is sought over conflict even if it means losing out
Compromise	In this orientation both parties win a little and lose a little. Both parties give up something in order to achieve an amicable solution

satisfy one's own interests), and with high or low cooperativeness (the desire to satisfy other people's interests). Table 3.5 describes each of the conflict management styles.

Of course, the style that we use will depend on the context. For some trivial things we may be more than willing to lose and allow others to win. For example, we may not be fussed about what colour chairs our team chooses for our office space, but we may be much more passionate about how work gets rewarded. Thus importance and relevance of the context is critical in determining whether a forcing, avoiding, compromising, accommodating, or collaborative style is used to conflict management.

More importantly, the notion of conflict we discuss here is somewhat simplistic because it is important that we understand the fundamentals of conflict. However, conflict is much more complex, especially when we consider the issues of power, politics, rationalities, and sensemaking. In this section we mainly focused on basic interpersonal psychology aspects of conflict. In other chapters we deal with much more complex notions. Finally, we will now discuss an innovative and interesting approach to understanding workplace conflict in the form of toxic emotions.

TOXIC HANDLING IN ORGANIZATIONAL CONFLICT

One certainty in life is that almost all of us must work for one reason or another, and for most of our lifetime. A fact of that certainty is that we are likely to spend more time with our work colleagues than with our own families. When we work as part of a close team, the emotions we feel and perceptions we have can be almost as intense as if it were a family relationship.

Fortunately, some of us will be lucky enough to work in jobs we love, working with people we get along with really well. Such jobs fill us with excitement and a sense of self-esteem, provide important social interaction, help build our sense of self-identity, and provide us with monetary and other forms of wealth.

Unfortunately, for many people this is less true – work can be a miserable, dangerous, unfulfilling, and even lethal place of existence. Moreover, we sometimes have to work with people that we find frustrating, challenging, and difficult. Frost and Robinson (1999) systematically reflected on the impact and coping strategies that emerge from such situations in an influential article in the *Harvard Business Review*. They were concerned with how to address what happens when organizations do bad things to good people. The article begins by discussing the impact that a new CEO had when brought in by the corporate board of a public utility. According to Michael, an employee in the utility, the CEO was authoritarian and insensitive to the needs of others:

> He walked all over people … He made fun of them; he intimidated them. He criticized work for no reason, and he changed his plans daily. Another project manager was hospitalized with ulcers and took early retirement. People throughout the organization felt scared and betrayed. Everyone was running around and whispering and the copy machine was going non-stop with resumes. No one was working. People could barely function. (Frost and Robinson, 1999: 96)

However, as we soon learn, Michael was not just a passive observer of these bullying behaviours – he played a vital role in helping the organization and its members to absorb and handle the stresses that were being created. Frost and Robinson termed these stresses 'toxins' and noted that Michael became a 'toxic handler' in the organization. According to Frost, toxic handlers are individuals within organizations:

who take on the emotional pain of others for the benefit of the whole system … like psychic sponges for a family or work system … they pick up all the toxicity in the system. (2003: 3–4)

The toxic handlers, therefore, play a very important role in organizations. Managers deal with toxic emotions at work every day in the role of toxic handlers, and can also be the source of toxicity (Anandakumar et al., 2007).

The following excerpt from Frost's book *Toxic Emotions at Work* provides a graphic sense of one particularly unpleasant way that a manager created toxic emotions at work:

Ryan was a senior manager who kept two fishbowls in the office. In one were goldfish, in the other, a piranha. Ryan asked each of his staff to pick out the goldfish that was most like themselves (the spotted one, the one with deeper color, and so forth). Then, when Ryan was displeased with someone, he would ask that person to take his or her goldfish out of the bowl and feed it to the piranha. (Frost, 2003: 35)

Think about the symbolism that Ryan is trying to communicate. You are as insignificant as a fish, swimming around in the fishbowl, and as long as I like you and you do what I expect of you, you will survive. The minute you do otherwise, you cease to be a survivor and will be eaten alive by the piranha. You are dispensable and will remain only while you are useful. What kind of working environment might such behaviour create and sustain? Employees might be productive, but the environment would be one based on fear and distrust. Many managers manage people in this way. They inadvertently, and sometimes purposefully, create toxic conditions at work by managing through fear and anger.

Frost characterizes the emotional pain that undermines hope and self-esteem in people at work as a toxin. To explain how managers create toxicity in the workplace, he identified seven deadly 'INs' of toxic emotions (Frost, 2003: 36). A description of these INs appears in Table 3.6.

TABLE 3.6 The seven deadly INs of toxic emotions

Ins	Description	Possible effect on groups
Intention	Managers who intentionally seek to cause others pain. They can be abusive and distrust staff. They manage through control, fear, and constant surveillance. They lead through punishment and fear	Reluctance of team members to question decisions that may not be in the best interests of the organization and team outcomes. Team members become socialized to believe teams should be managed in a similar way to the 'intentional' manager. Can promote aggression and conflict and push out people perceived as 'soft'

(Continued)

TABLE 3.6 *(Continued)*

Ins	Description	Possible effect on groups
Incompetence	Managers who lack the skills and abilities for effective people management. They may be excellent in technical skills but lack the necessary people skills. They are inconsistent in their decisions and lack integrity. Conversely, they may lack faith in their employees' abilities and skills, so they try to control every decision their employees make	The team may have direction in terms of tasks but lack cohesion due to poor people management skills. The team may display low levels of trust, and avoid responsibility and self-directions. Low levels of empowerment and autonomy make it extremely difficult for the team to operate as a team
Infidelity	Managers who do not value the trust and confidence of their employees and who betray any discussion made in confidence. Or, such bosses may make promises (e.g. a promotion) and never deliver, and some may take the credit for other people's work	High turnover of team members, low levels of motivation and desire to achieve outcomes. If outcomes are achieved it is in spite of the managers rather than because of them. Typified by high levels of resentment of management
Insensitivity	Managers may lack social intelligence. They have no idea, and do not care, how others feel. Such managers may also have no idea how others feel about them. They may be unable to regulate their own emotions and behave in inappropriate ways	Feelings of resentment, anger, pain, and disenchantment are rife. Team members are uncertain as to what mood a manager will be in
Intrusion	Managers who expect employees to forgo their own social or family lives for their work. They expect people to work long hours, weekends, and so on. They work long hours and expect everyone else to do the same – even if it is to the detriment of the person's family life	Burnout rates, stress, and anxiety will be high as people try to keep up with the workload. Feelings of guilt and resentment will be rife. Team members may be overly critical and judgemental of other team members if they are not putting in the same hours as others
Institutional forces	Toxicity can become embedded within the policies, procedures, and rules of the organization, especially when people are expected to act in ways antithetical to their own values and beliefs. Similarly, toxicity can be seen in organizations in employees that may not live by the organization's vision, mission, and policies. Imagine what it would be like to work in the police force and to blow the whistle on corruption when many of the police leaders are corrupt	Can promote unethical behaviour and collusion among team members, encourage groupthink and team cohesion at the expense of ethical behaviour
Inevitability	Some toxicity is inevitable and cannot be anticipated or controlled – for example, the death of a co-worker, a change in the world economy, or a terrorist flying a plane into a building. Sometimes, managers must cause pain in the short term to ensure growth in the long term. Inevitable toxicity can become a problem only in terms of how it is handled and managed in the context of the preceding INs of toxicity	Can devastate a team if a member dies or similarly if members are downsized. Sometimes a team may be under-resourced due to budgeting, which can cause high levels of anxiety and resentment.

Source: Adapted from Frost (2003: 36–50)

Looking at these toxic emotions, we can see that in most organizations some level of toxicity is unavoidable. However, the skills of toxic handlers ultimately make toxic emotions at work either disastrous or enabling. Think about situations in your life in which you have either handled toxic emotions or caused them.

Here is an example of a team situation that illustrates how toxic workplaces operate. Many of Frost's (2003) seven deadly INs are clearly evident in this case. When Tyrone was much younger, around 15 years old, he was employed as part of a team working in a kitchen. Two middle-aged brothers (whom we will call Nick and John) ran the café in a very unethical way. Many of the staff, including Tyrone, were working illegally because Nick and John had not registered their staff with the tax department. Knowing that Tyrone and the others were young and inexperienced, Nick and John would have them work extremely long hours without breaks, did not pay pension and other compulsory contributions, never logged overtime, and did not provide appropriate training – after all, they had no training themselves (to use Frost's terms, an example of *incompetence*). If employees questioned these conditions, they were either ridiculed or fired (*intention*). One day, Tyrone cut his finger very badly while working, slicing the tip off. John took him to the hospital but instructed Tyrone to say it happened while Tyrone was visiting John at home and that if he said otherwise, he would be fired (*insensitivity*). After about two weeks, Tyrone returned to the café, where he was told he was no longer needed. He received neither severance pay nor the previous two weeks' pay. Six months later Tyrone complained to the Industrial Relations Commission that he had been underpaid, unfairly dismissed, and exploited. Interestingly only two other team members supported Tyrone on the issue; the rest of the team decided to keep quiet and keep working. Eventually, however, Nick and John filed for bankruptcy, never paying a cent to anyone, and got away with behaving in unethical ways (*institutional*). In this situation the team's reluctance to respond to the toxicity ended badly for all involved.

WHAT'S THE POINT?

Each of the toxic emotions that Frost identifies can have devastating effects on people. The seventh deadly IN is inevitability and refers to the pain that comes from natural and human-made disasters. A team of al-Qaeda terrorists flew two airliners into the World Trade Center twin towers on 11 September 2001. The aim was to cause as much pain as possible to the US and its allies. However, out of that pain also emerged great bravery and teamwork. The bravery of the teams of men and women of the New York Fire Department is now legendary. However, the NYFD had to deal with immense organizational pain and managers had to be trained and skilled in dealing with high levels of emotional anxiety, depression, and post-traumatic stress disorders. So what is the point of toxic handling? The management of toxic emotions is a critical component of managing people. More importantly, we do not need disasters on a grand scale to cause toxicity at work because many managers, as Frost points out, are quite capable of creating a range of toxic environments.

Typically, toxic handlers fulfil vital, but often formally unrecognized, tasks for their organizations. Often, they burn out doing it. Think of them as filters that help remove the toxins that the organization or particular members in it can create. Although they may help to cleanse the organization, their doing so carries profound personal costs – they have to hear, share, and bear the misery and pain that the organization imposes on those it employs. Often, because the sources of the toxicity are people in formally authoritative and senior roles in the organization, there is little that they can actually do to rectify the situation. If organizations reward or are run by thugs, bullies, and the diplomatically challenged, expect toxicity to be pervasive. The best remedy is compassion, but this commodity is often a tender, precious, and vulnerable bloom, easily trampled by the foolhardy insensitivity of others, especially those in positions of formal authority.

Check out the Companion Website www.sagepub.co.uk/ managingandorganizations3 for free access to an excellent article by Peter Frost and colleagues (2006), which considers how we can practice compassion at work in order to alleviate many of the toxic emotions that organizations and managers create and which we have covered in this chapter.

SUMMARY AND REVIEW

Teams are increasingly a preferred form of mobilizing people at work. Teamwork plays an important role in ensuring human relations within organizations are productive, cohesive, and aligned to organizational outcomes while also balancing people's desire for meaning, autonomy, and social relations.

In this chapter we defined teamwork and considered why we form groups, as well as several aspects of team dynamics such as group size, cohesion and social facilitation, conformance and obedience. We then considered some of the problems we face in teamwork such as groupthink and social loafing and considered some ways of overcoming such obstacles. We then considered some issues around team development such as stages and processes of team development and argued that teamwork is complex and requires constant reflexivity of one's role in team tasks. We discussed and defined conflict and considered some orientations to understanding and dealing with team conflict that range from win/win, to lose/lose approaches. We finally closed the chapter with a discussion on the novel and fascinating work by Peter Frost on toxic emotions, and considered how the seven deadly INs affect our everyday working lives.

EXERCISES

1 Having read this chapter you should be able to say in your own words what each of the following

key terms means. Test yourself or ask a colleague to test you.

- Teams
- Groups
- Group dynamics
- Conflict
- Team roles
- Social facilitation
- Toxic handling
- Groupthink
- Virtual teams
- In-group bias
- Out-group
- Closed group
- Open group
- Formal group
- Informal group
- Role conflict
- Social loafing

2 **Conflict reactivity**. Imagine you are in a public space with a friend minding your own business. How would you respond to each of the following situations?

i A tall well-built man with dark sunglasses and several tattoos looks at you and says in a loud and angry voice, 'What are you looking at?' What do you do?

   a Do you try to explain calmly and in a friendly way that you were not looking at him?

   b Do you become confrontational and answer back in a forceful way?

   c Do you panic, and feel a sense of fear and quickly try to leave?

ii You and a friend are out having fun at a pub listening to music and you are continually bumped by another person even though there is plenty of room. How do you respond?

a Do you confront them and warn them of their behaviour?
b Do you ignore them and move?
c Do you say something to them and then move?

Think about your responses. What would happen if you say nothing and move in situation (i)? What about if you just up and leave in situation (ii)? How we react to conflict situations has important implications for what happens. Often just walking away is enough to disarm the conflict situation. However, often people do not want to lose face – add alcohol and drugs and the situations can become lethal.

3 Try to think of – and write down – a few scenarios in which either you were a toxic handler or you might have caused toxicity in a team context. They need not be work related: they might be in a social group, a party, at a sports match, or whatever you can think of and prefer to talk about. Thinking about your examples, which of the seven deadly INs of toxicity apply? Be sure to clearly identify which 'IN' applies.

ADDITIONAL RESOURCES

1 We recommend David Anspaugh's (1986) *Hosiers* as an excellent movie about teamwork and perseverance. The movie is about a basketball team in a small Indiana town and considers issues of social influence, teamwork, social norms, strength of character, and conflict. It provides insights into the emotional and passionate aspects of teamwork and team conflict.

2 Oliver Stone's (1986) *Platoon* is another excellent movie on the devastating effects of team conflict and social influence on behaviour. As two leaders start to fight a personal war during the Vietnam conflict, soldiers begin to pick sides and eventually the soldiers are fighting and killing no longer only the 'enemy' but also each other. The movie is a strong symbol of how individuals can subvert team goals in order to meet their own interests and how team members can easily find themselves in the in- and out-groups, and suffering from groupthink.

3 *The Band of Brothers* by Stephen Ambrose (2001) is a compelling and thought-provoking book about a group of young men who are transformed into a team of heroes during the Second World War as they fight in Normandy against the Nazis under appalling conditions. While we are against the glorifying of war, the book does provide several insights into the power of teamwork.

4 Two excellent, well-written, and informative books written by some of the world's leading experts on teamwork are by West et al. (2003), *International Handbook of Organizational Teamwork and Cooperative Working*, and West (2003), *Effective Teamwork: Practical Lessons from Organizational Research: Psychology of Work and Organizations*. Both books are excellent resources for understanding the psychology of teams, how teams are best designed and managed, the problems faced in teamwork, and how problems can be minimized and controlled.

WEB SECTION

1 Our Companion Website is the best first stop for you to find a great deal of extra resources, free PDF versions of leading articles published in Sage journals, exercises, video and pod casts, team case studies, and general questions and links to teamwork resources. Go to www.sage pub.co.uk/managingandorganizations3.

2 For state of the art briefings on how to manage organizations effectively, please visit the Henry Stewart Talks series of online audiovisual seminars on Managing Organizations, edited by Stewart Clegg: www.hstalks.com/r/managing-orgs, especially Micheal West's Talk #3 on *Managing teams and groups*.

3 If you are interested in reading more about Belbin's team roles, you can visit his website and read some articles on team roles and organizational performance at http://www.belbin.com/.

4 If you are looking for an excellent website with plenty of resources on teamwork, including links to a wide range of teamwork websites, resources, surveys, and advice, visit http://reviewing.co.uk/toolkit/teams-and-teamwork.htm.

5 The University of Colorado has some extensive online resources on conflict resolution at http://conflict.colorado.edu/. From the website you

can read and access articles and resources on conflict resolution. There are also some interesting surveys and exercises to try out.

6   Check out just how many social networking sites actually exists at: http://en.wikipedia.org/wiki/List_of_social_networking_websites.

7   Watch some great YouTube videos on teamwork, including:

- A short video on teamwork and sharing the workload, http://tinyurl.com/3ydu7x.
- A longer (four-minute) video with some nice quotes and proverbs on teams, http://tinyurl.com/36v96v.
- A humorous short film on teamwork and the importance of sharing and having fun to solve all kinds of problems, http://tinyurl.com/ 3b8h87.
- The amazing things a well-coordinated team from Turkey can achieve, http://tinyurl.com/365omq.

LOOKING FOR A HIGHER MARK?

Reading and digesting these articles that are available free on the Companion Website www.sagepub.co.uk/managingandorganizations3 can help you gain deeper understanding and, on the basis of that, a better grade in your studies:

1   Slaughter and Zicker (2006) present an interesting study on role conflict and role ambiguity in an academic context. They consider how role ambiguity and role conflict affect the socialization of newcomers into existing groups within academic departments in their paper titled, 'A new look at the role of insiders in the newcomer socialization process',

Group & Organization Management, 31 (2): 264–290.

2   For those of you seeking a very challenging read on teamwork, Frey (2004) has written a very good paper on how group members use symbols to relate and interact with each other. Indeed, Frey argues that symbols underpin group dynamics because it is through signs and symbols that rich interactions are generated. Frey's paper is titled 'The symbolic-interpretive perspective on group dynamics' and appears in *Small Group Research*, 35 (3): 277–306.

3   Practising compassion at work might seem a bit too soft and not really the role of managers. Kanov et al. (2004) show that doing the 'soft' stuff can actually be the hardest thing we can do as we relate and work with others in teams and organizations generally. They discuss how we can practice compassion at work in order to alleviate many of the toxic emotions that organizations and managers create and which we have dealt with throughout this chapter. Read their excellent and thought provoking paper titled 'Compassion in organizational life', *American Behavioral Scientist*, 47 (6): 808–827.

4   While groupthink often means people are trying to avoid conflict through cohesion, and that a lack of conflict can mean a team is in trouble, groupthink can also cause a team to spiral into depressive thoughts. At least that is what Granstrom and Stiwne (1998) say in their interesting paper that expands upon Janis's notion of groupthink. They consider how groupthink leads to depressive team behaviours and thinking and identify some symptoms and methods for overcoming depressive groupthink. Their paper is titled, 'A bipolar model of groupthink: an expansion of Janis's concept', *Small Group Research,* 29 (1): 32–56.

CASE STUDY

IS THERE 'HOPE' FOR A BRAND NEW AIRPLANE?

Introduction

In the summer of 2005 Boeing, the world's largest aircraft manufacturer, was in the midst of engineering the most advanced commercial jetliner in history. The Fortune 500 company, with over 100,000 employees, was adding a new jetliner (the 787) to its product line of twin-aisle jumbo jets. Not since 1993 had Boeing revealed a new product to the public, with its 777 aircraft. During the summer of 2005, a researcher from the Gallup Leadership Institute was examining the role of 'hope' (a component of psychological capital) in workplace teams. This case is told from his perspective.

The case

By the time I entered the series of daily meetings between the Electrical Design Engineering team (Electrical) and the supplier teams, frustration was really mounting. Boeing had already invested over 2 billion dollars (US) into the 787 with a radical new way to consider partnerships. Specifically, Boeing had made a strategic decision to partner with global suppliers to a much greater extent than with any other airplane before. Raw materials in Egypt were turned into parts in Russia. Parts were assembled in China and put into electrical systems in India. Those systems were joined to make sets of systems in Japan and then shipped to the US for final assembly. The Electrical designers needed to know the electrical properties of every part of the aircraft to create their design. Never had their job been so complicated in terms of data collection, data management, and maintenance.

After months of meetings the process went something like this. First, the Electrical design team would make a recommendation about how to receive data from suppliers. Next, the supplier teams would go back to all the related systems in their organization and see if that method would work. Simultaneously, Electrical would talk to all of its Boeing counterparts to see if the proposal would work. The next day Electrical would meet and determine that the proposal did not meet some constituency's requirements. That day, the series of actions would start over.

By late summer, because of the cumbersome process, conversations at the senior leadership level of the company included skepticism regarding the Electrical design team's ability to work with suppliers and achieve designs on time. Timing for such ambitious projects, of course, was critical. If Electrical were late, the delivery dates would be late, customers would drop orders, Boeing stock would heavily decline. Enter Bill Hamilton.

Bill was a 42-year-old senior manager who understood the concept of hope as a positive motivational state that consists of an interactively derived sense of *both* the agency ('will-power') and the pathways ('way-power'). He was the only senior manager without an engineering education and earned his position by tenacity and respect from his team. Before entering Boeing as a grunt labourer, Bill was an electrician on residential houses where he learned the value of pathways thinking. Pathways thinking, a critical component of hope, is when a person considers multiple paths to solve the same problem. This way, if one path is 'blocked' (e.g. the plan does not work) they can fall back on the contingency plan. Therefore, there is always *hope* for success because there are several paths to accomplish any goal. As an electrician, Bill would examine a house and determine several possibilities for an electrical design. This way, when a client changed the layout of the house, Bill would not have to reconfigure all of his plans but rather fall back on his contingency plans. He was also aware that while it was ideal if an individual employee had hope, when hope was evident in teams, there was a contagion effect where each team member's pathways thinking and motivation would transmit to other team members. Just as hopelessness was contagious, the positive side of hope could be cultivated at a team level for increased motivation and creative performance in challenging situations.

When Bill was asked to engage in the conversation with the suppliers he wasted no time implementing his approach. As the first meeting was coming to a close, people began to pick up their notebooks when Bill said softly, 'What do we do if that doesn't work?' Plan B was then generated. Then he asked, 'What are the obstacles in the way of achieving this plan?' and, 'What if this plan doesn't work?' At the end of the first meeting each group went to its constituencies with three different solutions. This was the first step in the team processes to start thinking in a hopeful way.

Within weeks, Bill had implemented a method whereby all major constituencies in Boeing and their suppliers attended the meetings (by face-to-face, phone or video), which had been increased to weekly. With each proposal, everyone was required to devise multiple contingencies. A method of working together was achieved that summer where data transmission, changes, and communication were established. Bill had not just 'hoped for the best' in turning around an important process that was heading for trouble. Instead, he drew from his psychological capital component of *hope* (the will *and* the way) to get the process on track and make a major contribution to the launching of the 787 airplane.

Questions

1 How did Bill effectively model *hope* for the Boeing and supplier teams?
2 Why is it that hope (and hopelessness) in teams can be contagious?
3 How can a team avoid running out of 'contingency plans' to attain an objective?
4 How can leaders help teams walk the fine line of maintaining creativity and improvisation while also planning for contingencies?

Case prepared by James B. Avey, Department of Management, Central Washington University; Brett C. Luthans, Department of Management, Missouri Western State University.

CHAPTER FOUR

MANAGING LEADING, COACHING, AND MOTIVATING

Transformation, Instruction, Inspiration

LEARNING OBJECTIVES

This chapter is designed to enable you to:

- Define what is meant by leadership and coaching
- Evaluate critically the main approaches to leadership theory
- Understand the changing role of the leader
- Understand the assumptions underlying motivation theories and their relevance to leadership and coaching
- Identify the emerging and alternative approaches to leadership and the value of self-leadership
- Evaluate the concepts of positive psychological capital and authentic leadership
- Understand the complex relationship between leadership and culture

BEFORE YOU GET STARTED . . .

A short story from Tyrone's childhood:

> When I was around eight years of age, I would follow my mother out into the front garden of our house and, every so often, our little old lady neighbour, called Pearl, would peer over the fence. I remember my mother would ask old Pearl, 'How are you today, Pearl?' and Pearl would usually answer in the same sad and tired voice, 'I'm managing, love; I'm managing.' By this, Pearl meant that she was just coping, just doing the bare minimum to survive. Because I was from a non-English-speaking background, I concluded that 'managing' must just mean 'coping'. Now, almost a quarter of a century later, I have come to realize that Pearl's notion of management is spot on: most managers I see or talk to today are just coping, and they are one day, one decision, one missed deadline, or one mis-communicated sentence away from failure or a disaster. In contrast, therefore, a leader might be someone who goes beyond just coping or just managing. The leader inspires, develops, and mentors people. Above all else, a leader is a humanist. We cannot afford our leaders to be anything else, can we?

INTRODUCTION

Literally, to lead or to exercise leadership is to be ahead of the others, to take them forward where they might not necessarily want to go, to make them go where they need to be, and to motivate them so that they overcome any fears or qualms that they might have about the process. Leadership describes a relation between people – one cannot lead a computer or a share portfolio. However, one could manage these inanimate objects. Hence, leadership necessarily involves social relations and social skills.

At face value, leadership appears to be a simple domain of interest. Almost anyone can think of a leader and can provide a definition of leadership or make feelgood statements about what a leader does or should do. However, after you go past leadership at a superficial level, it is one of the most complex, problematic, and time-consuming domains of management and organization theory. As an experiment, go to your favourite search engine, such as google.com or alltheweb.com, and enter the search term 'leadership'. If you had done this in June 2008 you would have returned over 160,000,000 hits for the term 'leadership', if you had done this in June, 2011 you would have returned over 418,000,000 hits. In just three years the number of websites concerned with leadership has tripled. It would take more than a lifetime for any one person to read, review, and critique each and every one of these web pages, articles, books, and book chapters. Arguably there is no other topic in management and organizations that has so much written and said about it, but still remains elusive and problematic as a concept.

IMAGE 4.1
Leadership

Leadership as a domain of interest has become an unnecessarily complex, confusing, and contradictory concept. Attempting to present old and new leadership theories in one chapter is challenging. First, there are the differences of opinion in terms of what leadership is. Is leadership, as the *trait* theorists argue, a question of unique traits that people are born with, like their height, weight, intelligence, and personality? Or is leadership, as the *behaviourist* school argues, specific ways of behaving that make you either an effective or ineffective leader? Or is leadership *situational*, where different situations create different leaders? Or is leadership *contingent* upon the interactions between leaders and the led? Or is leadership a *socially constructed* concept? Or is there no such thing as leadership per se, only what members of specific organizations make it in retrospect?

In this chapter, we introduce you to the current and central approaches to leadership. Rather than going into each and every theory in depth, we look at the main approaches to leadership. After we introduce the main approaches, we then explore some newer contributions to leadership. We look at substitutes for leadership and explore the possibility of life without leaders and the blurring of boundaries between leadership and followership. We then consider the changing role of leaders and leadership practice by discussing the role of coaching and of self-leadership. Also, because the task of both leaders and coaches is often expressed as being able to motivate people to achieve outcomes that benefit the individual, the team, the organization, and, in the case of leadership, more collective entities such as society, we think it is necessary to introduce you to the concept of motivation. We will focus on two very important aspects of motivation, intrinsic and extrinsic motivation. We close the chapter by discussing some positive psychological perspectives on leadership that argue that leadership should primarily be about inspiring and fostering positive change, corporate citizenry, and social, economic, and ecological sustainability.

WHAT IS LEADERSHIP?

In its simplest definition, **leadership** is the process of directing, controlling, motivating, and inspiring staff towards the realization of stated organizational goals.

A **leader**: (a) leads people as a ruler; (b) inspires people as a motivator; and (c) facilitates or guides them as a coach and mentor.

What is **leadership**? It is a term that gets tossed around promiscuously: almost every time a politician, business magnate, or football manager speaks on what is required to get results, the term occurs.

The *Collins English Dictionary* defines a **leader** as 'a person who rules, guides, or inspires others', and the process of leading as, 'to show the way by going with, or ahead … to serve as the means of reaching a place' (Hanks, 1986: 476). This simple definition falls a little short because it underplays the complexity inherent in the social relations and complex environments within which leadership, as a practice, happens.

Katz and Kahn (1978: 527–528) believed leadership is commonly viewed:

> as the attribute of a position, as the characteristic of a person, and as a character of behaviour … Moreover, leadership is a relational concept implying two terms: The influencing agent and the persons influenced … Leadership conceived of as an ability is a slippery concept, since it depends too much on properties of the situation and of the people to be 'led'.

Leadership may thus be seen as a product of one's position; as a set of personality traits; as a set of observable behaviours; as dependent upon the situation in which it is exercised; and as contingent upon how the leader and the people being led react and interact with each other. Obviously, leadership may be all of these many things, and so, not surprisingly, it is one of the most overtheorized, overresearched, and empirically messy areas of management and organization theory, with a clear lack of unity of perspectives or approaches. The problem is that people can come up with words to describe a leader, what a leader is or does, but few can say *why* these words describe a leader. Have a go at guessing the leader in the 'Who am I?' exercise.

The main aim of the 'Who am I?' exercise is to encourage you to reflect critically on the term leadership. In each clue are fundamental aspects of the leadership concept: character, behaviour, situation, and contingencies. Although we often see leadership as composed of factors that make us feel good, leaders are not always enlightened, humane, and oriented to personal growth; they are sometimes tyrants more concerned with their own egos than those of their followers, adept at practising domination, power, and delusional self-interest. Therefore, it is necessary to think beyond leadership as a simple construct and to reflect critically on what leadership might mean.

QUESTION TIME

Who am I?

To help students cope with the complexity of the topic of leadership, let us play a guessing game called 'Who am I?' The aims of the game are to help you think about (a) the qualities and life events that make someone a leader and (b) how no one theory or concept adequately accounts for leadership. Read the following series of facts about a famous leader and consider the leadership qualities inherent in these facts to come up with an answer.

- I was regarded as a good *artist* and had a flair for sketching and watercolours yet I was rejected from a prestigious art school.
- I then joined the armed forces and was awarded a prestigious medal for *bravery*, yet some of my officers claimed I would never be a suitable leader of men.
- After the war, unhappy with how my country was being run and eager to prove my detractors wrong, I joined a small political party and became a great orator able to *inspire* others.
- At the time that my ideas became popular, my country was plagued by *poverty and economic recession*.

- I was soon imprisoned as a political agitator but it was in prison that I helped grow my political party, and I wrote one of the most influential books in history.
- After leaving prison, I was given charge of my political party, and we went from a handful of members to hundreds and thousands of followers – many of whom abandoned senior positions in opposition parties to join me because they could see I was committed to changing how things were done in my country forever and they wanted to *follow* me.
- I eventually became *leader* of my country and one of the most influential figures in history. Indeed, all around the world I continue to *inspire* many followers even though I am long since dead.
- So, who am I?

Think about the clues and consider the qualities – artistic, brave, and ambitious. He was able to write books and change society from within a prison and to attract followers even from his opposition. For the answer see the end of this chapter.

Students often ask, 'What's the point of all this theory? Who cares if leaders are born or made?' Our answer is that leadership theory is critical for our understanding of the role individuals can play in shaping society and its organizations. More importantly, *leaders can and do change society*, so it is imperative that they do so in a socially responsible and ethical way (see also pp. 434–435). Only if we understand the theoretical underpinnings

Check out the Companion Website www.sagepub.co.uk/managingandorganizations3 for free access to an article by Susan Lynham and Thomas Chermack (2006), which discusses how complex the issue of leadership is, and seeks to address the underemphasis of whole system effects of leadership.

of those leadership perspectives in use by particular writers and leaders can we adequately reflect upon and answer appropriate questions about leadership. Moreover, the theory you subscribe to will underpin your own approach to leadership – after all, you may one day be a leader, and what you believe about leadership will influence your approach to what a leader is, what a leader does, and how a leader does it. Conversely, learning about different theories may cause you to reflect upon and to question your own beliefs.

Leadership as traits

> The clearest sign that a manager is doing an excellent job managing her team: she takes time off work and no one notices she is gone. (Anonymous)

> Great leaders plant trees whose shade they know they will never sit in. (Translated Greek Proverb)

The trait approach to leadership assumes people are born with qualities that are stable across time and situations, and which differentiate leaders from non-leaders. For a long time, trait theorists believed that leadership depended on certain physical features and personality characteristics. To investigate leadership, trait theorists would consider a wide range of demographic variables such as age, gender, height, weight, and ethnicity, to name a few. They also looked at certain personality characteristics similar to those found in the trait approach to personality (see also pp. 63–67). Such key demographic and personality variables were believed to differentiate truly exceptional leaders from mere mortals, which is why trait theory has also been known as the 'great person theory' (Barker, 2001). According to House et al. (1996), the difference between those of us who emerge as outstanding leaders and those of us who are always destined to follow is an undying drive for achievement, honesty, and integrity, and an ability to share and to motivate people towards common goals. Such people have confidence in their own abilities as well as intelligence, business savvy, creativity, and an ability to adapt to ever-changing environments (also see Kirkpatrick and Locke, 1991).

Doubtless many people believe in the great person theory. That is, they believe that certain physical features and personality characteristics will make you a leader. If this were true, the teaching of leadership would help only those with a predisposition towards leadership: the rest of us might as well either pack up immediately or perhaps enrol in a course teaching us how to be better subordinates.

In reality, however, there is little evidence to support the notion that leaders are born with special traits that non-leaders lack. In fact, those who argue for the great person approach tend to miss the point – that is, many characteristics they believe to be critical to successful leadership have been made important through social norms and culture. If we look at leadership in most organizations, leaders tend to be taller rather than shorter, and, more often than not, are male. To be consistent, these trait theorists would argue, because most leaders of major corporations are male, it must be an important trait in successful leadership. Also, in places such as the US, Australia, the UK and much of Europe most of them are also white, usually well educated in elite schools and institutions, and often from wealthy backgrounds. In fact, it makes a huge difference if you can choose your parents carefully! Of course, you cannot, but it is clear that a major factor that propelled leaders such as George W. Bush to their positions of leadership was that their fathers had already founded dynasties and substantial fortunes. Sure, if you are non-white or female, you can still make it, but it will be much harder for you, and you will have to expend more energy on the leadership attributes you have available or can cultivate – and that is on top of attribution errors made about you (i.e. the assumption that you got to where you did for certain reasons such as affirmative action – see pp. 184–191), or in the case of Barack Obama, that you are Muslim or not born in the US and so should not be president.

The trait theory of leadership, despite its shortcomings, has played a critical role in the evolution of leadership theory and research. Whether you agree or disagree with it, many have used it to critique and to reflect upon what it means to be a leader. Thus, even if the empirical evidence is weak, its strength has been to create some kind of discourse and scholarship in leadership as a concept.

To try to overcome the objection that many leadership traits that are assumed to be innate are actually based on norms and culture, newer theories have chosen to look at what leaders *do* rather than what traits they *have*. Some see leadership as situational or contingent upon many factors. Others see leadership as a socially constructed phenomenon – that is, what a leader is, and what a leader does, changes as society changes over time or as we move from one culture to another. Next, we visit these different perspectives of leadership, beginning with the behavioural school.

Leadership as behaviour

The behavioural theory of leadership is not concerned with the traits or characteristics that make someone a successful leader: it is concerned only with observable behaviour. Thus, for behaviourists, you either act like a leader or you do not. This is an important departure from trait theory because it implies that if we can observe how leaders act, we can codify and measure this behaviour, find out ways to teach it, and help to develop future leaders. A critical concept that is common to all behavioural theories of leadership is the notion that there are two underlying behavioural structures that characterize leadership – an orientation towards the following:

- Interacting and relating to other human beings.
- The task at hand, or the technical side of work.

You will find these two behavioural orientations in just about every theory you read about, even those outside the behavioural school. Though the terms used by these theories vary, they refer to the same fundamental

FIGURE 4.1

The managerial grid (adapted from Blake and Mouton's (1985) registered model) reprinted with permission from www.mindtools.com

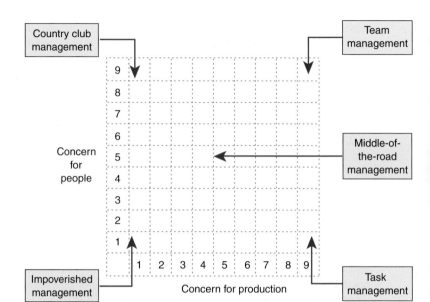

distinction. The terms used include: employee centred/task centred; relationship behaviour/task behaviour; concern for people/concern for production; and consideration/initiating structure.

The most recognized behavioural study of leadership was developed by Blake and Mouton (1985) at the University of Texas. The approach was later expanded upon by Blake and McCanse (1991) and is referred to as the *leadership grid* or the *managerial grid* (see Figure 4.1). The grid is divided into two dimensions. On one axis is the *concern for production* and on the other axis is the *concern for people*. Depending on their responses to standardized questions, a person is rated by an accredited psychologist on both dimensions on a scale from 1 to 9 (or low to high). The ideal position is to be high on concern for production and concern for people (9,9), or what Blake and Mouton (1985) refer to as *team management*. However, very few if any ever score 9,9 on their first try, so leaders are helped to develop their concern for people and their concern for production skills so that they reach the ideal position on the grid. Leaders that score 1,1 are said to practice *impoverished management* because they lack a concern for both people and production, so their ability to manage will be quite poor. Other styles include *country club management* (1,9), where there is a high concern for people while the concern for production is forgotten or ignored, so people being happy and having fun is more important than getting the job done. (These styles can be seen in action in the hit TV show *The Office*, if you have seen it, if not, do so as it is brilliant.) Conversely, a person may be concerned with only production, or what Blake and Mouton call *task management* (9,1), and then there is *middle-of-the-road management* (5,5).

As with the managerial grid, all major leadership theories seem to emphasize first, *consideration*, or the extent to which leaders take into consideration subordinates' feelings, needs, concerns, and ideas; and second, *initiating structure*, or the extent to which leaders are task oriented and more focused on ensuring that subordinates do what is required through autocratic direction, control, and surveillance. These two styles tend to be presented as being independent of each other, so a leader can be high or low on initiating structure and high or low on consideration, and it was long held that superior leadership was characterized by being high – high on both dimensions. However, there is little research to support the notion that effective leaders are only those high on both initiating structure and consideration (see e.g. Nystrom, 1978). As a result, researchers began to compare and contrast effective and ineffective leaders.

Again, in keeping with the theme of orientation towards person versus task, Likert (1979) argued that *employee-centred* leaders were more successful than *job-centred* leaders – mainly because job-centred leaders tended to be overly concerned with achieving efficiency, cost reduction, and deadlines, rather than with people's needs and goal achievement. However, common sense says that an overemphasis on people might compromise the completion of tasks and getting the job done, just as an overemphasis on tasks can alienate people and affect motivation and job satisfaction. It is therefore more likely that both dimensions are equally important, and this is the argument underlying the managerial grid. The managerial grid is more a behavioural training tool than a leadership theory: it emphasizes the need to *develop* a person's ability to manage both people and tasks.

WHAT DO YOU MEAN?

Weaknesses with behavioural and trait approaches to leadership

The behaviourist usually is interested only in observable behaviour and ignores often unobservable intentions. We can never know people's thoughts and intentions other than through social cues, and these can be masked behind observable behaviour that, on face value, appears to be exemplary.

If honesty and integrity are inherited traits necessary for elevation to leadership, then why do so many people reach leadership positions and attain enormous material wealth, power, influence, and control, only later to be revealed as crooks and charlatans who sometimes even use their 'leadership' to try to avoid the wrath of the law?

Why are the attributes that one group of people see as exemplary regarded as evil by others? For example, some compare Adolf Hitler, Benito Mussolini, Osama bin Laden, Saddam Hussein, and David Koresh to Satan, but presumably their many followers viewed them as great leaders – if not, then how did they attain such influential leadership positions?

At what point does observable behaviour tell us that people are no longer acting like leaders? After they murder people or corrupt organizations and steal millions of dollars? As an example, Enron, one of the largest energy companies in the world, was consistently heralded for its leadership, but in the end were the bosses at Enron really the corporate heroes they were often lionized as being before their malfeasance became evident and Enron collapsed?

The managerial grid appears to imply that all outstanding managers must have special skills for dealing both with the job and with people. Yet throughout history we have seen people reach the heights of leadership who are not always expert in tasks and others who are not always expert in managing people. Moreover, if you consider some of the people who have inspired you, we are sure that at least some of you will mention people who are no longer alive or people you have never met. It is a bit hard to manage people and tasks when you are dead or you never have face-to-face contact with your followers, so something else must make leaders be regarded as effective or ineffective besides merely what they do here and now.

The trait and behavioural approaches should not be totally discounted. Some situations, for example, call for high concern for people, whereas others call for high concern for production, and others call for both. However, leadership can also be thought of as being situational and contingent.

Situational and contingency theories

Some recent approaches to leadership argue that leadership emerges out of the situation. The same person who may emerge as a leader in one situation may find themselves unable to cope, let alone lead, in a different situation. Anecdotally evidence suggests there is some merit to the situational argument. For example, prior to the 9/11 attack on New York City, the former mayor of New York, Rudolph Giuliani, was known mainly for his strong stance on crime in New York. He implemented a 'three strikes and you're out' policy for repeat criminals. He had many critics, especially people who lived outside the New York area, who experienced escalating crime as a result of criminals moving away from the city. City crime rates were going down because the city was exporting rather than solving crime. Other than this policy, Mayor Giuliani had few things going for him.

However, during the 9/11 attacks, Mayor Giuliani took a strong leadership role – indeed, the moment made the man. The mayor's leadership was seen as so strong that he even eclipsed the then President George W. Bush, and the world watching the events that unfolded in New York could easily have been forgiven for believing that Mayor Giuliani was the leader of the US. Realizing the effect a situation can have upon a leader's success and popularity, former President Bush was also quick to try to leverage statesmanlike success out of the situation. He went from low legitimacy (because of the fiasco of the Florida vote recount during the presidential election in 2000) and relative political obscurity in the shadow of the charismatic Bill Clinton to record-high popularity ratings, at least until Americans began seriously to question the reason the country went to war with Iraq and the extraordinarily high number of American casualties involved. In many ways the situation and context can make and break the leader.

We have chosen to group together the situational and contingency approaches, even though some people like to separate the two. There are subtle differences between them, but we believe that these differences are not enough to make them distinct schools of thought. Underlying contingency theories is the notion that leadership is all about being able to adapt and be flexible to ever-changing situations and contexts. Contingency leadership theories have made one of the most important contributions to the evolution of leadership theory because leadership effectiveness is seen as being less dependent on innate traits or observable behavioural styles and more dependent on the context of leading, such as the nature of work, the internal working environment, and the external economic and social environment (Fiedler, 1964). Two main contingency leadership theories are discussed here: House's (1971) path–goal theory and Hersey et al.'s (1996) situational leadership model.

Path–goal theory of leadership   Perhaps the contingency theory that has been most studied and tested is Robert House's path–goal theory of leadership. According to House (1971; see also House and Mitchell, 1974), effective leaders motivate employees by helping them understand that their needs and expectations can be fulfilled through the performance of their jobs. The better an employee performs, the greater the need fulfilment. Moreover, the path–goal theory emphasizes that an ability and commitment to providing employees with the psychological and technical support, information, and other resources necessary to complete tasks is integral to the leader's effectiveness.

The path–goal theory has been extended, developed, and refined, and it is probably one of the most influential leadership theories around (House, 1996; Jermier, 1996). The path–goal theory is more advanced and complex than any of the theories we have looked at thus far because it lists four leadership styles and a number of contingencies that lead to leadership effectiveness. Table 4.1 lists and describes each of the four main leadership styles.

TABLE 4.1   Path–goal leadership styles and descriptions

Style	Description
Directive	The directive leader clarifies goals, what must be done to achieve them, and the outcomes of achieving the goals. They use rewards, discipline, and punishment and are mostly task oriented
Supportive	The supportive leader shows concern for the needs – especially psychological – and the aspirations of people at work. They provide a supportive and enjoyable working environment
Participative	The participative leader actively seeks and encourages the input and involvement of staff in decision-making and other work-related issues
Achievement-oriented	The achievement-oriented leader, as the name suggests, expects from people the highest commitment to excellence both at a personal and an organizational level. This type of leader believes that work should be challenging and that people will strive towards achieving these goals by assuming responsibility
Networking	The networking leader knows how to play the political power games to acquire resources, achieve goals, and to create and maintain positive relationships. (For more on power and politics, see also pp. 252–263.)
Values-based	The values-based leader is skilled in creating, sharing, and inspiring vision, and in ensuring that the organization and its people are guided by that vision and the values related to that vision

Source: Adapted from House (1996) and Jermier (1996)

However, you will notice that we have added networking and values-based leadership as two more issues that have emerged from House's (1996) and others' work (see e.g. Jermier, 1996; O'Toole, 1996: 101–108). We believe these will be increasingly important additions to House's original work because they move the leadership theory away from solely being interested in person-to-person relations to include relationships at team, organizational, and interorganizational or network levels.

An effective leader adjusts and adapts their style according to the situation and can use one or more styles as needed. However, the effectiveness of the leader ultimately depends upon two broad sets of contingencies. The first concerns employee-relevant contingencies, such as the employee's competencies, knowledge, skills, experience, and even their personality, such as whether they have an internal or external locus of control (see also pp. 64–67). The second concerns environmental-relevant contingencies, such as the nature of teams and the structure and nature of the task, just to name a few.

So, for example, let us assume you have completed your college education, you have been working for a leading bank for the last five years, and, over time, you have reached the position of head of corporate services. Up to this point, you have managed very junior staff in positions low on task structure that required little if any teamwork. Experience has shown you that a directive leadership style works best in this situation. However, last week, you were promoted, and now you manage a team of 15 people who value a high level of control over their work and their environment (i.e. high internal locus of control). They all have several years of experience in the department, have taken several training courses on implementing change, and enjoy working as part of a cohesive team that shares leadership duties.

How well would your directive leadership style work in your new position? It would be safe to assume that you and your team would not operate effectively, and, over time, you would experience friction because your staff would see you as unnecessarily controlling and directive. Your options for change would be: change the nature of the work and the type of staff so that they support your directive leadership style, change your leadership style, or cruise into crisis! Ideally, if people could change their leadership style, many problems could be overcome. However, more often than not, people avoid changing themselves and seek to change others and their environments instead.

Situational leadership model   Hersey et al.'s (1996) Situational Leadership Model's intellectual appeal resides in its emphasis on the subordinates' readiness and willingness to be led by others. As with path–goal theory, it is up to the leader to use the appropriate style after they have established what kind of people work for them. Figure 4.2 shows the four leadership roles – known as delegating (S4), participating (S3), selling (S2), and telling (S1) – together with the associated follower readiness (R4 to R1). The most appropriate leadership style depends on the amount of emotional support followers require in conjunction with the amount of guidance that they require to do their jobs – in other words, the follower's readiness.

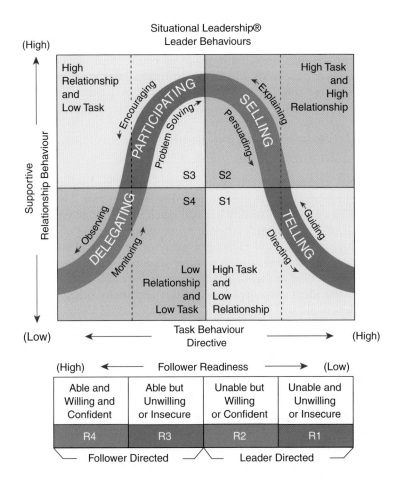

FIGURE 4.2
Situational Leadership
Model

Hersey et al.'s (1996) Situational Leadership Model is to contingency theory what the managerial grid is to behavioural theory: it is more a training and consulting tool than a theory per se. The Situational Leadership Model and other contingency theories depart from the trait perspective but share many elements of the behavioural approach. Where contingency approaches differ from the behavioural approach is in concentrating attention towards factors outside the actual person leading. Later, we discuss contingency-based views that argue that leaders may be substituted for processes, technology, policies, and can even be made obsolete in the workplace.

If a leader's competency is contingent upon factors outside their control, then there could be thousands of contingencies that affect leader performance. This raises the problem of where to start in the search for the contingent factors that might affect leadership performance. Obviously, there are changing and emergent contingencies: risk management, especially focused on the management of terror and security; sustainable management, focused on the environment and the political ecology of the material inputs and outputs that the organization is involved with, and gender management, managing in a gender-specific sensitive way. These are all contingencies that

Check out the Companion Website www.sagepub.co.uk/managingandorganizations3 for free access to an article by Richard Bolden and Jonathan Gosling (2006), which asks is leadership theory too rational and obsessed with competencies rather than relational; should it not be looking at issues such as emotions, fear, managing people, etc.? The paper argues that the competency approach is limited as a rational approach for selecting, measuring, and developing leaders.

Charismatic leadership is a leadership type that emphasizes the articulation of a vision and mission that promise a better life. Sometimes such leaders develop a cult following.

Transactional leadership epitomizes the initiating structure, concern for production, and task-oriented themes of the behavioural leadership literature.

Transformational leadership, as you probably could guess, epitomizes consideration and concern for people and similar relations-oriented themes.

leaders have to deal with today, but in each case they are the result of changes in the political agenda. Thus what counts as a contingency for management depends on what is made to count. And what is made to count depends in part on the changing institutional environment of regulation, opinion, and politics.

Transactional, transformational, and charismatic approaches

We now look at three relatively recent approaches to leadership that incorporate all the leadership theories we have discussed thus far. The leadership theories presented in this section are still much more in line with the trait, behavioural, and contingency schools. From the perspective of some views of leadership, neither Adolf Hitler nor many other political and organizational leaders would be viewed as positive leaders because they lack those humanist ideals that underpin positive psychology (see also pp. 72–79), whereas in the ideas presented here, Hitler and many other violent and brutal leaders could still be defined as leaders and listed along with Nelson Mandela, Mahatma Gandhi, and the Dalai Lama as examples of **charismatic** and other types of leaders, such as **transactional** and **transformational leaders**.

You could probably define each of these leaders yourself just by looking at the words charismatic, transactional, and transformational. See Table 4.2 on page 138 for a breakdown of each leadership approach.

Charismatic leaders can create the impetus for change. However, they can also be volatile and inconsistent and can be blinded by their own vision. Transformational leadership is an agent of change. Transformational leaders are the ideal people to have during major organizational change because they have the visionary component of the charismatic leader, but also have staying power and provide energy and support throughout the change process. If the transformational leader has a weakness, it is that organizational life is not always about constant change, so the effectiveness of a transformational leader can be short-lived. After the change occurs, another type of leadership style might be more appropriate. The transactional leader may be more useful during periods of homeostasis, when you want things to run smoothly.

WHAT'S THE POINT?

Might not good leadership also require an ability to be a good follower?

Reading through the multitude of textbooks on management, you could be forgiven for thinking that 'leadership' and 'followership' are distinct concepts: a leader is a person who provides direction and inspiration towards goals, whereas a follower is a person who does not ask why but only how; a leader says something, whereas a follower does that which is said.

What tends to be underemphasized is that inherent in many of the perspectives on leadership is a

(Continued)

(Continued)

lack of explanation about how exactly a good follower becomes a good leader and whether there actually is a difference between followers and leaders. A heart specialist is working in a large hospital under a management team, but would we say the specialist is subordinate to them? Just because you are in a leadership position does not make you a leader any more than being in a subordinate position necessarily makes you subordinate.

To become a leader in many fields, you are required to do your apprenticeship under a master, often for many years. So, might not good leadership also require an ability to be a good follower? More important, is there actually a difference between followers and leaders other than the labels attached? Perhaps leadership theorists and researchers should become more active in asking such questions. Such issues will become pertinent when we look at leadership substitutes and neutralizers, as well as the postmodern and dispersed leadership approaches, later in this chapter.

Perhaps theorists should view films more often: the dramatic quality of a good script, expert direction, and brilliant acting can often bring leadership issues to the fore – as, for example, in *Master and Commander: The Far Side of the World* (Weir, 2003),

where the relationship of the master and commander with his followers is a vital ingredient to his leadership. In one of the finest films about leadership, *Lawrence of Arabia* (Lean, 1962), T. E. Lawrence, a historical character, refuses the leadership position offered to him and exercises that leadership which he believes in inherently, from an ethical point of view. He is committed to the cause of the Bedouin with whom he associates rather than to the duplicitous policies of the British politicians and generals.

Typically, in the army, leadership is predicated on good followership, and it is the good follower who is given the opportunity to climb the ranks from private to corporal to sergeant, and so on. In this respect, Lawrence could be said not to have leadership qualities, despite the extraordinary charisma that is attached to him and his evident success in leading men into battle.

Perhaps it is best to think of the leadership–followership relation as a fluid one. On some occasions a skilful leader often serves people and organizations best by following the innovation, inspiration, or interpretation of one of the followers; on another occasion a leader may lead best by subordinating personal attitudes to those of superiors, peers, or subordinates in order to retain influence or carry a decision.

WHAT DO YOU MEAN?

Transformational?

Transactional leadership is effectively what good management is all about: the paperwork, the budgeting, the scheduling, with a bit of psychological support and motivation of people thrown in for good measure. However, transactional leaders do not cope well with major change and are not adept at managing the change process. Charismatic leaders can create the impetus for change, but they can be volatile and inconsistent and can be blinded by their own vision. (Our 'Who am I?' exercise earlier in this chapter shows that Hitler had many charismatic leadership qualities, but we do not think that you would want someone similar to Hitler to be your boss.) Indeed, there are not many business leaders who would be classified

as charismatic leaders; typically, such leaders tend to lead social or political movements rather than commercial organizations, although we did discuss Richard Branson earlier – is he an exception? Such leaders are seen to have sources of inspiration that deal with more fundamental human values than just the end of achieving profit. They are also concerned with the purposes to which such resources may be put. However, perhaps with the rise of new social movements and of the importance of corporate social responsibility and the emergence of new stakeholders, charismatic leadership will increasingly be sought in the corporate world as managers become more sensitive to the imperatives of ethical workplace and corporate practices.

TABLE 4.2 The transactional, charismatic, and transformational approaches to leadership

Approach	Description
Transactional	Transactional leaders do all the necessary and critical management functions such as role clarification and task requirements, and they know how to allocate and provide rewards and punishments. They adhere to organizational policies, values, and vision and are strong on planning, budgeting, and meeting schedules
Charismatic	Charismatic leaders are a bit more complex. They have a motivating effect upon people and are able to create grand visions about an idealized future. They are able to unify people towards that vision and to foster conditions of high trust
Transformational	Transformational leaders inspire change and innovation. They are the opposite of transactional leaders because they deal mainly with abstract and intangible concepts such as vision and change

Check out the Companion Website www.sagepub.co.uk/ managingandorganizations3 for free access to an article by B. W. Browning (2007) on a leader's expedition that went horribly wrong.

From the perspective of situational contingency arguments, in some situations you need a transactional leader to hold the ship steady, at other times you need a charismatic leader to create a vision and inspire the need for change, and sometimes you need a transformational leader to foster and manage the change process through to completion. Still, there are risks. Transformational leaders may end up believing too literally in their own hype; they might really think they are the heroes that their strategies seem to position them as being, effortlessly changing minds, actions, and paradigms.

More recently Bass and Avolio (2000; 2003) have developed the idea that leaders can be both transactional and transformational – or what is referred to as full-range leadership (Antonakis and House, 2002; 2004; Kirkbride, 2006). Full-range leadership includes transformational and transactional components, as well as passive-avoidant leadership characteristics – or non-leadership to be more precise. According to Bass and Avolio (2000), the ideal leader will be high on both transformational and transactional components, and low on the passive-avoidant ones. The next most favourable outcome is to be a high transformational leader, followed by a high transactional leader. The least attractive outcome would be to be low on transactional and transformational, and high on passive-avoidant. Table 4.3 provides an overview of each of the styles and their associated constructs.

There is a growing body of research supporting the idea of full-range leadership styles, and it has been shown that they are important in promoting knowledge management practices, such as sharing information, organizational learning, and knowledge transfer (Nguyen and Mohamed, 2011); are more likely to promote safety behaviours in the workplace (Martínez-Córcoles et al., 2011); are more ethical in decision-making and behaviours (Toor and Ofori, 2009). Female leaders who are perceived to display full-range leadership qualities are more likely to be promoted (Vinkenburg et al., 2011); and interestingly gender and level of educational tend to be important in leadership styles. The research suggests educated females tend to display more full-range leadership behaviours (Barbuto et al., 2007).

TABLE 4.3   The full-range leadership model

Transformational	
Idealized Influence (Attributes)	Perceived by others as transformational, optimistic, open, and energetic
Idealized Influence (Behaviours)	Risk-taking, leading from the front, leading by example with purpose, integrity, and consistent to values
Inspirational Motivation	Envisions change, highly symbolic, clear strategic vision and mission articulation and symbolism, articulation of visions, hopes, and desires
Intellectual Stimulation	Encourages innovative thinking, encourages people to question what they know and think, especially their reliance on outdated or overused methods and processes
Individualized Consideration	Supportive, sensitive to members' concerns, high EQ, mentors and develops others (even to the detriment of self)
Transactional	
Contingent Reward	Recognizes the contribution of others, is able to reward and motivate by linking into especially intrinsic, but also extrinsic motivations; clarifies expected outcomes and what will be delivered and how performance will be rewarded
Management-by-Exception (Active)	Monitors performance, solves problems as they arise to maintain performance
Passive-Avoidant	
Management-by-Exception (Passive)	Part of transactional leadership but tends to avoid monitoring performance; only reacts if problems become serious or problematic
Laissez-faire	Tends to let things pan out and sort themselves out. It really refers to non-leadership and the abdication of responsibility. Avoids decisions and defers judgement to others or to a later time in expectation that the problem will go away

Source: Adapted from Bass and Avolio (2000; 2003)

NEW PERSPECTIVES ON LEADERSHIP

A critical question and challenge for leadership theory and research is whether *leadership* is merely a term or, alternatively, something that actually exists. Will there come a time when leaders can be substituted, if not made obsolete, in organizations? Some contingency theorists argue that such a time is here. Others, such as the postmodernists, turn the term leadership on its head, painting a picture of leaders as servants. So let us look at both these perspectives a little closer, starting with the contingency view of *leadership substitutes* and *neutralizers*. Before we visit these approaches a quick word: leadership as a concept has come under constant bombardment – with statements such as, 'Leadership is dead' – even from the contingency theorists. However, we should remember one thing: many of these approaches, but especially contingency theory, fail to account for the fact that leaders can and do change the situation and the environment within which they operate – and they often do so intentionally. That is, leaders can sometimes control contingencies. In this way, they can actually use the contingent variable to control or to increase their effectiveness – and they do this in quite subtle and pervasive ways.

Substitutes and neutralizers

Some contingency theorists, such as Kerr and Jermier (1978), argued long ago that situational variables could act as substitutes for leaders, thus rendering the leader irrelevant. Let us look at an example to help illustrate how such a theory works. You might work as part of a self-managed work team (SMWT). In an SMWT, each team member might be involved in all decision-making about rostering, goal-setting, performance measurement and evaluation, setting of wages, and so on. There could be high levels of trust, shared responsibility, interdependence, and support. A leader, be it transactional or transformational, is not required. Similarly you may identify more with a profession (say psychology), and have high levels of autonomy, be motivated, capable, and high on self-efficacy (belief in one's ability and competence to complete tasks). For a team or individual equipped with the right resources, and knowledge of what needs to be done and by when, a leader can be a hindrance rather than a benefit.

Even people with low professional affiliations, skill level, and autonomy can be managed without leaders through carefully designed jobs high in formalized, routinized procedures and with training for employees to be able to identify and to rectify simple breakdowns in routinized tasks – really, not much different from monkeys flying multi-million-dollar rockets into space for NASA. (For more in-depth discussions of substitutes for leadership, see Podsakoff et al., 1993; Starke et al., 2011; Wu, 2010.).

WHAT DO YOU MEAN?

Forward together

In 1995 Sydney, Australia, was awarded the 2000 Olympic games. The triathlon and other water sports would be conducted in Sydney Harbour, but at the time the harbour was prone to severe contamination, especially from storm water runoff. Given that the Olympics would showcase Sydney to billions of people around the world, it was acknowledged that Sydney Harbour must be sparkling and clean.

Clegg et al. (2002) studied a major alliance involving five companies that were brought together to construct 20 km of tunnel under some of the world's most expensive real estate. The project was worth over A$0.5 billion and had to be completed in under three years (in time for the Sydney Olympics). The aim of the project was to construct a tunnel that would divert storm water away from Sydney Harbour towards a processing plant. By doing so Sydney Harbour would be clean, in time for the 2000 Olympics.

However, research conducted by the business partners had shown that a project with similar contingencies (such as ground conditions, size of project, tunnelling requirements), conducted in

(Continued)

(Continued)

California, took over seven years to complete. The leadership team decided that for the alliance to meet its ambitious objectives, it would have to develop some innovative approaches to dispersed leadership, including:

1 *KPIs*: The use of innovative key performance indicators (KPIs) that encouraged behaviour beyond business as usual. That is, the project would only be judged a success if the alliance excelled in all its KPIs. Thus, they had to be on budget, on schedule, improve the ecology of the areas within which they operated, do it all safely, and improve relationships and account for community stakeholders.
2 *Cultural alignment*: The use of an enculturation programme in which every member of the alliance underwent induction into the culture of the alliance, and was taught to be self-empowered. The training included the learning of specific cultural norms such as 'What Is Best for Project?', in which members would always act in the best interests of the project's completion, and 'No Blame Culture',

in which problems would be 'fixed', rather than wasting time apportioning blame when something went wrong. The culture programme included the learning and reinforcement of a number of alliancing principles, and these principles espoused values of self-leadership, team working, accountability, and responsibility for organizational outcomes.

3 *Psychological contracting*: Relationships were formed and bound via psychologically based contracts (i.e. understanding and agreement engrained and reinforced through culture). The traditional black and white letter legal contract was less important and restricted only to the most critical component. In this way the contractual document for the alliance was 28 pages long rather than the usual several hundred.

The result of the alliance was that it achieved all its stated KPIs, and did so beyond business as usual performance. In recognition of its innovative approach to project management, the alliance project team won several awards in North America, Europe, and Australasia.

Leaders as servants and the postmodern condition

As the boundaries between leaders and followers blur, the focus on 'the leader' in the more traditional theories highlighted earlier in this chapter become increasingly problematic. When leadership skills and responsibilities are dispersed or shared throughout an organization through empowerment, or leadership is substituted or neutralized, an emphasis is placed upon the process and practice of leadership and not upon the attributes or style of a unique person or set of persons – the 'leaders'. In short, *dispersed leadership theories* – theories that move leadership away from an individual person – may imply that leadership is something that many people can do, and actually do, and is therefore not a fruitful basis upon which to differentiate people at work. Furthermore, viewing leadership as a relational process suggests that the leader–follower relationship is no longer of central importance to the study of leadership (see e.g. Gordon, 2002), but rather the ability to be critically reflexive about one's own practices, and how these practices relate to and impact others are more important (Gambrell et al., 2011). Such views suggest that the boundaries that once differentiated 'the leader' from 'the follower' are becoming very grey – a follower is a leader is a follower is a leader, and so on, *ad infinitum*. This has opened the door to postmodern concepts, so it is appropriate to review at least one postmodern perspective on leadership – that of Boje and Dennehey (1999).

Postmodernism, postmodernity, empowerment, and neutralization

Postmodernism applied to organization studies has many critics. While some criticisms are valid many are based on incorrect assumptions, partly because postmodern theories can be somewhat confusing, and even convoluted. Postmodernism has its roots both in French philosophy and in architecture, but it was American cultural theorists Leslie Fiedler and Susan Sontag that did most to bring postmodernism into view and provide the impetus for its spread into art, cultural studies, history, philosophy, sociology, psychology, and most recently organization theory. Put simply, what is seen as true or false is a result of power relations and dominant discourses, which present 'truth or reality' in ways that are framed through systems of power. For example, for many profit is more important than environment, and this is reflected through policies, practices, the media, and so on.

Postmodernity is subtly different to the idea of postmodernism. Postmodernism is underpinned by the idea that reality is constructed, and that there are multiple realities, but what comes to be known as real or truth is talked into being. The critical idea in postmodernity, however, is that the idea of capitalism has spread into every area of society, and in every part of the globe, such as the media, education, health, sport, the arts, sciences, and so on. In this sense there is a pre-capitalist (premodernity) period prior to the industrial revolution, a capitalist (modernity) era that came about through industrialization and the growth of globalization, and a post-capitalist (postmodernity) era. In postmodernity, absolutely everything becomes about consumerism, even selling books like this. Many argue that we are now in the post-capitalist era – or in postmodernity (for an excellent account and discussion of this see Nicol, 2009).

WHAT DO YOU MEAN?

Postmodern leadership and empowerment?

Let us take a postmodern look at empowerment and leadership, and contrast this to contingency views of leadership. Empowerment addresses the power inequality inherent in subordination. We are subordinate because someone or something is in a relational position of power over us. Empowerment, therefore, concerns releasing the shackles placed on us by those who have power over us in the workplace. Employees are empowered when they are given control of organizational decision-making, as well as many other aspects of their work life, and by the use of self-managed work teams (SMWTs; these are teams that have full autonomy and control of all aspects for their work, including how the budget is spent, rostering, managing of human resources, etc.).

By empowering people, you are lowering their reliance on and need for leaders to rule over them and to be constantly monitoring them. Followers, through empowerment, start looking more like leaders.

However, what if you manage a small music store and you employ students who work on the

(Continued)

(Continued)

weekends while studying law or medicine? They come to work because it is fun, they like listening to music, and many of their friends come in on the weekends. (Maybe you have read Nick Hornby's novel *High Fidelity* (1995) – which was also made into a film (Frears, 2000) – in which the sales staff are interested in only those customers who are as cool and knowledgeable as the sales staff think themselves to be.) Such people do not mind working in low-status jobs because one day they know they will be wealthy doctors or lawyers. But although they are having fun, customers find they are extremely poor salespeople – they are rude and ignore customers in favour of their friends, and they take your business for granted. You know

they do not need the job, and the unemployment rate is so low that people can walk in and out of low-skilled jobs like these.

Because of all these contingencies, your ability to lead actually *neutralizes* your leadership ability. So rather than being able to substitute your leadership through contingent variables, such as empowerment of your friends, your leadership becomes impotent. Obviously, neutralizers can be viewed in a more negative light than substitutes. Indeed, substitutes can be very useful tools of empowerment and can free up your time for other duties, whereas neutralizers cancel out the benefit or effectiveness a leader might have.

WHAT DO YOU MEAN?

SERVANT model of leadership

S is for *servant*. The leader is the servant to the network. Leaders serve people and the people, in turn, serve customers. For a long time in the past, leadership was about differentiating oneself so that a leader would be different from a follower. In a postmodern perspective on leadership, leaders seek to rid the world of such differentiation; the leader articulates the servant conceptions of what the leader should be. Think of the CEO who dresses down and on Fridays works on the shop floor with the other workers.

E is for *empowers*. The leader empowers participation in social and economic democracy.

R is for *recounter of stories*. The leader tells stories about the organization's history, heroes, and future.

V represents being *visionary*. Leaders without vision, the reasoning goes, offer nothing, and people's hopes perish. At their best, visionary leaders should articulate a clear concept of what it is that followers already are committed to and believe in.

A is for being *androgynous*. Androgyny means no gender; the leader must be able to speak in both male and female voices.

N is for *networker*. The leader manages the transformation and configuration of the diverse network of teams spanning suppliers to customers.

T is for *team builder*. The leader mobilizes, leads, and dispatches a web of autonomous teams.

Postmodernism blurs the boundaries of how we understand and make sense of leadership, stressing that leaders are servants of the types of leadership that others recognize as leadership in discourse. Put simply, leaders become servant to the qualities that people characterize as leadership: they are therefore talked into leadership. Let us go through Boje and Dennehey's (1999) approach, in which each letter in the word SERVANT is given a special significance, to get some of the flavour of the postmodern approach from their analysis (see the What Do You Mean? box above).

TABLE 4.4   Premodern, modern, and postmodern leadership

Premodern leaders Leader as master	Modern leaders Leader as panoptic	Postmodern leaders Leader as servant
Master. Head of the work institution Owner of the slaves, serfs, and tools	**Panoptic.** Leader does the gaze on everyone, Big Brother style Bentham's principle of the Panopticon is central here: power should be visible and unverifiable (see also 271–272; 455–456)	**Servant.** The leader is the servant to the network. Leaders serve people who, in turn, serve customers Differentiates self from the people
Authoritarian. Enforces unquestioning obedience through authoritarian rule over subordinates	**Authoritarian.** Final evaluator of performance and quality	**Empowers.** The leader empowers participation in social and economic democracy
Slave driver. A leader oversees the work of others A real taskmaster	**Network of penal mechanisms.** Penal mechanisms are little courts for the investigation, monitoring, and correction of incorrect behaviour and then the application of punishments and rewards to sustain normalcy and reinforce leader's power	**Recounter of stories.** Tells the stories of company history, heroes, and futures **Visionary.** Without vision, we perish **Androgynous.** Male and female voices
Elite. Leaders are regarded as the finest or most privileged class and usually are drawn from such classes	**Organizational.** Lots of divisions, layers, specialties, and cubbyholes to cellularize people **Pyramid.** Leader sits at the top of the pyramid **Top.** The head boss, the top of the hill, and the highest-ranking person	**Networker.** Manages the transformation and configuration of the diverse network of teams spanning suppliers to customers
Ruler. Leaders govern and rule over other people	**Inspector.** In charge of surveillance, inspection, and rating of everyone else	**Team builder.** Mobilizes, leads, and detaches a web-work of autonomous teams
	Centralist. All information and decision flows up to the centre and back down to the periphery	

Source: Adapted from Boje and Dennehey (1999)

Boje and Dennehey provide a description and comparison of premodern, modern, and postmodern leaders, as shown in Table 4.4. They explain their model in terms of the stages of premodernity, modernity, and postmodernity: each typified by different forms of leadership. Their approach is novel and creative, but take a closer look at the table. Can you see any parallels with transformational, transactional, and charismatic leadership? Also, can you see some link to behavioural and contingency theory? Note how Boje and Dennehey conceive leadership almost from the perspective of a behavioural style.

Moreover, if leadership transforms through time, something must be accounting for that transformation from master to servant; are time and place the contingent factors? Also, are the nature and expectations of those of us who were once led changing as we access education, gain instant information through the Internet, and use the new technologies to receive greater exposure to contrasting views of political, social, and economic current affairs?

In a later paper Boje and Rhodes (2006) present a very innovative idea on the postmodern conception of transformational leadership. According to Boje and Rhodes, Ronald McDonald can be thought of as a transformational leader for McDonald's. Mr McDonald has been integral in transforming McDonald's from a restaurant that promotes the eating of fat- and sugar-laden meals, sold en masse to people at a very cheap price, to one that values the health, safety, and security of our families. Mr McDonald can now be seen eating healthy salads and low-fat meals at his restaurants; moreover, his name is synonymous with helping the families of kids with cancer and other serious diseases through Ronald McDonald House (Boje and Rhodes, 2006).

WHAT DO YOU MEAN?

Yes We Can! President Obama's historic win in 2008 heralded the dawning of a new era, not only for America, but for many people around the world. Obama's leadership represented hope for hundreds of millions of people, but the expectations on Obama, the human being, were unrealistic in many ways. Obama, irrespective of his obvious leadership qualities, has been subject to an unrelenting wave of criticism and political opposition, some fair, much of it not, and some of it plain lunacy. As President Obama campaigned for the 2012 election, he faced the prospect of a one-term presidency: how quickly things change in the world of leadership, even after getting Bin Laden.

Leaders as coaches

Great leaders create great leaders, not more followers. (Greek proverb)

Coaching is the process of developing and enhancing employees' job competencies and capabilities through constructive suggestions and encouragement.

Mentoring is the process of passing on the job expertise, skills, and knowledge in order to develop a protégé.

Check out the Companion Website www.sagepub.co.uk/ managingandorganizations3 for free access to Madsen and Gygi's (2005) very interesting interview with leadership guru John H. Zenger on his ideas about extraordinary leadership and its development through education and training.

Increasingly, an important function of leaders, particularly transformational leaders, is the ability to coach and mentor people at work. While leadership has long been of interest to organizational behaviourists, **coaching** and **mentoring** are more recent domains of research and theory. Coaching refers to the process of developing a person's own knowledge and skill sets in order to improve on-the-job performance. While coaching at work concentrates on achieving excellence in organizational outcomes and objectives, more recently life coaching has become an increasingly common 'profession'.

Coaching differs somewhat from leadership because a coach is not a person who directs people; rather a coach 'develops' the individual's knowledge and skills. Coaching psychology emphasizes the importance of psychological health, and so it has strong connotations with positive psychology. Even so, the ability to coach is now becoming a core challenge for good leadership.

Unlike coaching, mentoring is an ancient process of development that goes back at least to the ancient Greeks. It can be much more intensive than coaching, and often involves master and student, but mentoring can also include the mentoring of groups. In reality, everyone has a mentor at some stage in life. The mentoring relationship naturally occurs in our lives, even though we may not realize it – our parents, teachers, bosses, sports coach, and so on.

Dubrin (2005) identifies 12 key areas in which a person must be proficient in order to be an effective coach. By developing these skills in one's self, one will be able to develop and enhance other people's strengths and leadership capabilities. According to Dubrin, these critical areas include building trust, showing empathy, active listening, using influence, setting goals, monitoring performance, giving feedback, encouraging positive actions and discouraging negative ones, training team members, helping people solve problems, managing difficult people. Table 4.5 contains more detail about some of these approaches, and while these are important for effective coaching, they are just as critical for good leadership.

TABLE 4.5 Core competencies of coaches and mentors

Core Competency/ Capability	Description of a good coach
Trust building	Operate with integrity by modelling behaviour and acting with consistency; show honesty, and sincerity in communication; be open and communicative; be knowledgeable and seek out information and update knowledge; trust in people's ability and capabilities to get things done
Empathy	Demonstrate an ability to take the perspective of the other person and put yourself in their shoes; use the same figure of speech when you talk to people; provide and seek information that shows you understand what the other person is saying, feeling, or experiencing

(Continued)

TABLE 4.5   *(Continued)*

Core Competency/ Capability	Description of a good coach
Active listening	Ensure there are no distractions (noise, obstructions) when communicating; establish good eye contact; allow the person to speak freely – the good coach speaks 20% of the time and listens 80% of the time; learn from the people you coach; notice both the verbal and non-verbal communication, and manage your own body language (such as facial expressions, fidgeting, personal space, etc.); listen for understanding rather than agreement – this questioning is never confrontational but gentle and questions are well designed; the good coach will not directly tell a person what the problem is, nor what he or she should do about it, but will help them identify the solution to the problem themselves; the mentor, however, will offer his or her experience in dealing with an issue or problem
Influence tactics	Ethical influence tactics are important: act as a role model, shaping positive behaviours; be persuasive by knowing what you want, and what must be achieved, communicating the benefits – both personally for the coachee, and the organization – of achieving goals or behaving in certain ways; explore and understand why people may resist or object to decisions or changes; and use positive rather than negative language; be charismatic, assertive and use appropriate humour
Set goals	Help people develop and review a mission statement; establish specific and realistic goals, and set deadlines for those goals; develop a detailed action plan, and acknowledge that goals change over time so ensure you review them; support the goal setter through positive feedback and encouragement; and set individual, group and organizational goals as appropriate
Monitor performance	Develop a set of standards upon which people's performance will be assessed and involve people in setting these standards; measure actual performance as originally agreed, and compare the performance to the standards; take corrective action as needed
Feedback	Effective feedback, rather than efficient feedback, should be the key aim. Effective feedback involves careful communication about what is fed back and how it is fed back; feedback is provided frequently, and some interpretation on the part of the coach or mentor should be provided; ensure feedback is specific, and ensure the feedback conveys your feelings about the behaviour; seek feedback on your feedback and maintain rapport with the individual(s)
Encourage positive	Recognize and reward performance; compliment people on desired actions behaviours; be clear on what behaviour is rewarded; and choose appropriate rewards that fit the behaviour and desires of the person; provide rewards in a timely manner, but reward intermittently
Discouraging negative	Be clear about what will be punished and choose an appropriate actions punishment; supply ample feedback so that the person is clear on what he or she did wrong and how they can avoid it in the future; make sure punishment is timely and specific to the behaviour

Source: Adapted from Dubrin (2005)

Leaders as motivators

Part of the role of the leader as mentor or coach is the ability to motivate and inspire. There is not a single theory or approach to leadership that fails to recognize that a fundamental quality of leaders – irrespective of whether leadership is innate, learned, situational, or whatever – is an ability to inspire and motivate people.

Motivation is defined as the psychological processes that drive behaviour towards the attainment or avoidance of some object (be that object a person or relationship, an abstract concept such as love, or a material good such as money, an iPod, or a BMW).

While the psychological concept of **motivation** is over 100 years old, it has been applied to organizational and management contexts only since the 1950s. Motivation is necessary whether you are to lead yourself, to lead others, or to be led by others. It is therefore important to visit briefly some approaches to motivation and see how they are relevant to you as a leader. We discuss two key approaches to motivation – the process and content theories – and two key motivation concepts – intrinsic versus extrinsic motivation. Rather than talking about individual motivation theories, we explore the assumptions behind the theories and how such approaches might specifically relate to leadership. We introduce and discuss some basic assumptions underlying motivation concepts with the objective that it will help you to reflect critically upon what motivation means for you as a future leader and will help you think about and reflect upon the concept of motivation.

TABLE 4.6   Theory X and Theory Y motivation

Assumption	Theory X	Theory Y
Human nature	Inherently lazy and will seek to avoid work if able to. Behaviour based primarily on self-interest	Seeks fulfilment and meaning through work. Behaviour based mainly on society and community building
Wants and needs	Employees desire a sense of control, direction and clear instruction; avoid responsibility and autonomy	Employees desire autonomy and democratic leadership; avoid autocratic control and autocratic leadership
Motivational tools	Pay, bonus schemes and instrumental rewards, as well as punishment	Empowerment, opportunity for learning and career development, responsibility and self-leadership
Theoretical underpinnings	Scientific management (Taylorism), and Hard Human Resource Management. Management must assume control and the hierarchical relationship between manager and subordinate must be clear. Humans are important resources, but should be managed much as any other resource in order to achieve organizational objectives – thus if humans are a cost, then cost cutting involves downsizing	Human Relations, Soft Human Resource Management, Humanistic, and Positive Psychological approaches in which humans are perceived as the key assets in an organization. Humans are not a cost but a valuable source of capital and so downsizing should be avoided

Source: Adapted from Pitsis (2008a) *Theory X* and Pitsis (2008b) *Theory Y*

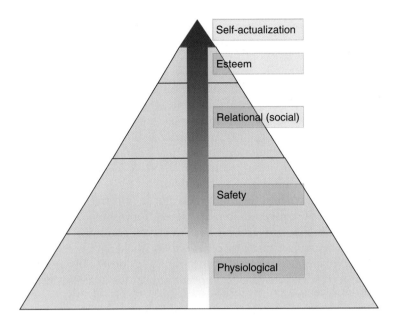

FIGURE 4.3
Maslow's Hierarchy of
Needs

One of the best-known perspectives on leadership and motivation is McGregor's Theory X and Theory Y. McGregor (1960) developed his work on Theory X and Theory Y after observing the main approaches used by people when managing and motivating people. According to McGregor, how we approach the way we motivate people is strongly influenced by our beliefs about human nature. McGregor argued that managers could be grouped in terms of their assumptions concerning the way people behave towards work (Table 4.6 presents a summary of the two approaches).

The concepts of **Theory X** and **Theory Y** are extreme opposites and it would be hard to find an organization that epitomises either theory in its extreme form. Moreover, McGregor developed these ideas in the 1960s when most corporate organizations approached a Theory X style of management. McGregor was a humanist psychologist (along with Maslow and others), and so he believed in an ideal world in which people come before profit. Much of motivation theory evolved out of the humanist school of psychology, and its main interest was to find those motivational processes that would lead to a psychologically healthy society.

Today we might say, if we take an overly cynical view, that much of motivation is about ensuring that people behave in the organization's best interest (Rousseau, 1996) – even if it is not in one's own interest. There has been a clear shift away from motivation theory's original objective, which was first and foremost about the psychological wellbeing and esteem of individuals, not about how much harder we can make them work.

For many centuries, philosophers have contemplated why we do the things we do. For instance, in the eighteenth century, Adam Smith held the view that we are motivated purely by self-interest. Smith (1961 [1776])

Theory X orientation assumes that people are lazy, require structure, direction and control, and want to be rewarded with money for a job well done.

Theory Y orientation assumes that people crave responsibility and autonomy, want to be treated with respect, and are driven towards self-actualization (Pitsis, 2008a; 2008b).

believed that self-interest was a central concept leading to the wealth of nations. As people set up companies to become wealthy, they created jobs, which provided income to people and tax revenue to government, which would be spent on health, education, security, and so on.

For Smith, this would even lead to innovation and technological change; because people would want more leisure time, they would innovate and change machinery to free up time for socializing. However, the perspective is seriously flawed because it cynically assumes that all action is motivated only by self-interest. Other philosophers such as John Stuart Mill suggest that we value only what is useful to us (Mill, 1962). Therefore, if other people cannot be useful, we will not value them.

Contemporary approaches to motivation focus on the satiation of needs – we all need food, love, shelter, and safety, for instance. When you do not have these things, you are 'pushed' to go out searching for them. There are many negative consequences if we do not satiate our needs – for example, starvation, loneliness, illness, injury, or death. In organizational behaviour, theories that focus on needs are known as **content theories of motivation**.

Content theories of motivation refer to those 'contents' within us that drive or push us.

One of the most famous content theories of motivation is Maslow's (1970) hierarchy of needs theory (see Figure 4.3). According to Maslow, there is a hierarchy of needs; as we meet the needs within each tier of the hierarchy, we can move on to meet the next level of needs. The hierarchy begins with typical physiological needs, such as the need to satiate hunger and thirst; second in the hierarchy are safety needs, such as shelter and security; third are the needs to belong, love, and be loved; fourth are esteem needs that are met by professional or other achievements, respect, and recognition. At the top of the hierarchy is the self-actualization need, or the need to live the happiest and most fulfilled life possible, the achievement of which usually requires us to realize our fullest potential.

The self-actualization component of Maslow's theory is its most critical part because it was embedded in his philosophy of life. Yet, if you look at almost any organizational behaviour textbook, you will find fleeting mentions of Maslow's theory as an early and outdated theory of motivation, criticized on the grounds that it assumes that motivation is hierarchical. Such thin criticisms and representations of Maslow's life work ignore his notion of *eupsychian management* (Maslow, 1965). Maslow coined the term 'eupsychia' for his vision of utopia, which, he argued, society should aspire to; with this vision, he attempted to refocus attention on motivation back to psychological wellbeing. Maslow believed that leadership should promote, support, and maintain psychological wellbeing at work by basing the structure of society and its organizations upon virtues, which, in turn, would filter into the broader society and the community. He saw leadership in organizations as integral in helping people self-actualize. Yet, if you look at Maslow's hierarchy of needs theory in any organizational behaviour textbook, it will not tell you that Maslow was driven to try to understand why some self-actualized people were what he called 'fully functioning' and how to capture and foster such positive virtues in society at large.

In essence, 50 years ago, Maslow thought about issues that still dominate much of leadership education and theory today. If people have to worry about where their next meal will come from, or where to sleep, or whether they have family support, how can they realize their full potential? The fundamentals of Maslow's arguments remain humanist despite their grounding in the early work that he conducted on primates.

Content theories do not sufficiently explain why people are motivated to behave in certain ways. To answer such questions, we need to consider **process theories of motivation**.

Proponents of process theories assume that you are more likely to behave in certain ways if: (a) your effort leads to your expected level of performance, (b) your level of performance gets the results you expect, and (c) you value such outcomes. Such assumptions are typical of a particular type of expectancy theory, known as expectancy theories of motivation (see e.g. Georgopoulos et al., 1957).

Process theories of motivation concern themselves with the processes that are involved in motivation. Some argue that the process is one of expecting that behaving in a certain way will realize certain outcomes.

To make the point about expectancy theory clear, let us assume that you take your OB final exam after having missed classes all semester long, you have fallen behind on your reading, and have rarely studied. In rational terms, you would expect that the lack of study would lead to failing the exam, and you find that you do actually fail. You thus learn that effort influences performance, and performance, in turn, influences outcomes. Let us also assume that the reason you have missed your studies is that your garage-band is becoming increasingly popular and you have started performing in pub gigs. So you have decided to concentrate your efforts on your band; you value the result in your management class much less than a successful rock career. In your sensemaking, it makes more sense to pursue something you value (a rock career), rather than something you do not value as much (a degree).

Another process theory, equity theory, extends the expectancy argument by adding that we also compare our inputs and outcomes to other people's inputs and outcomes (see Adams, 1963; Mowday, 1991). Equity theory – or social exchange theory – is by far one of the most dynamic and influential process theories. As an example, let us say that your rock band has been playing for ten years now but has never gained the recognition and rewards you believe it deserves, even while others become pop stars 'overnight' through *American Idol* or one of its many clones globally. You compare your effort, performance, and outcome to theirs and realize that the world is damn unfair. You believe that your inputs – your skills, experience, time, and effort – were well above those of the idol star, yet she is rewarded with fame, wealth, and a recording contract, whereas you end up playing after the 'Bingo' competition on Saturday nights. If only you had studied for that management exam. You give up being a musician or a model in disgust and start working in a music store, managing medical and law students who really do not need the job, money, or hassles, living out the alienated *High Fidelity* lifestyle.

TABLE 4.7   Examples of intrinsic and extrinsic motivation

Intrinsic	Extrinsic
Behaviour motivated by intrinsic factors such as self-expression, interest, and enjoyment	Behaviour motivated by extrinsic factors such as the promise of reward or threat of punishment
Motivated to finish reading because you are interested	Motivated to finish reading to meet a deadline
Working because you find the job stimulating and enjoyable	Working because you need the money
Changing jobs because you want the challenge	Changing jobs because you are certain you will be fired
Motivated to work in difficult jobs that challenge you	Motivated to work in difficult jobs to get the pay rise
Study to improve yourself	Study to get a high-paying job

Source: Adapted from Deci and Ryan (1987); Myers (2001: 451–452); Ryan and Deci (2000)

QUESTION TIME

Motivation or control?

Next time you are chatting to a friend, a work colleague, or a family member ask them this question: 'What is the difference between motivation and control?' Note how they answer this question and how they view the concept of motivation. As you listen to them think about the concept of motivation, and how it was originally linked to psychological wellbeing. Are their answers more in line with such approaches to motivation or are they more in line with the concept of motivation as a means of getting workers to do things they might not otherwise want to do? What are their

assumptions about people – Theory X or Theory Y? Jot your impressions down here.

_____

_____

_____

_____

_____

_____

_____

_____

_____

_____

Unlike many process theories, equity theory does not assume a rational process. If we were rational we would expend effort only when we think it will lead to an outcome that we value, and we would not expend effort when it leads to outcomes that we do not value. The theory acknowledges that sometimes our motives are hidden or subconscious (Adams, 1963). Why do people murder? Why do some leaders hide unethical and corrupt behaviours? Why do some people avoid effort? Why do some people put themselves in danger for other people? Why do some of us stay in a job or a relationship that makes us unhappy, sometimes for many years? Human behaviour is not always a rational and linear process. Often we find ourselves doing the very things that do not make us happy, and we, in turn, expect those working for us, or with us, to suffer the same existence. Perhaps a more fruitful way of thinking about motivation is to think about *extrinsic* and *intrinsic* motivation. Table 4.7 on page 152 lists descriptions and some examples of intrinsic and extrinsic motivation.

Obviously, you could think of more examples, but it should be clear by now that *intrinsic motivation* refers to those internal states that drive us towards behaviours that directly meet self-actualization and belongingness needs. On the other hand, *extrinsic motivation* refers to those internal states that drive us towards behaviours that directly meet esteem needs.

Theoretically, the two types of motivation are not mutually exclusive; however, notice that we used the word 'directly' in the previous sentence. In other words, sometimes money is important, even for an intrinsically motivated person, but it can be simply a means to an end – for example, to save enough money to realize your life dream of starting your own little restaurant. So, as a leader you have to know whether people – including yourself – are extrinsically or intrinsically motivated and not assume that all people are always intrinsically or extrinsically motivated by the same things. Moreover, much research suggests that the overuse of extrinsic motivation can kill or thwart intrinsic motivation (Deci and Ryan, 1985; 1987).

Ryan and Deci (2000: 70) argue that 'no single phenomenon reflects the positive potential of human nature as much as intrinsic motivation, the inherent tendency to seek out novelty and challenges, to extend and exercise one's capacities, to explore and to learn'. Imagine a wonderful world in which leaders manage and motivate people with an emphasis on self-actualization and the realization of intrinsic desires, and in which, in turn, organizations foster and promote self-actualization. Is this the hopeless dream of a handful of 'do-gooder' psychologists and rich celebrities? Ryan and Deci's (2000) *self-determination theory* may be something that allows us to take one step closer to achieving psychological wellbeing through work. In Chapter 2, we took a look at happiness, and essentially self-determination theory is concerned with psychological happiness.

Check out the Companion Website www.sagepub.co.uk/ managingandorganizations3 for free access to an article by Susan Herman (2007), which looks at how leaders sometimes do not motivate or inspire people because people do not value or consider the concept of leadership important.

Motivation: a question of self-determination

Ryan and Deci (2000) became increasingly dissatisfied with traditional conceptions of motivation theory – especially those theories with an emphasis on instrumental goal achievement. They therefore developed a comprehensive theory of motivation that is linked to personality and self-regulation. This theory is called **self-determination theory (SDT)**. SDT places great importance on the social context in thwarting or facilitating psychological wellbeing and health:

Self-determination theory (SDT) is a theory of motivation that emphasizes our intrinsic needs for being seen as competent, liked, and free from control of others.

> people's inherent growth tendencies and innate psychological needs that are the basis for their self-motivation and personality integration, as well as for the conditions that foster those positive processes. Inductively, using the empirical process, we have identified three such needs – the needs for competence (Harter, 1978; White, 1963), relatedness (Baumeister and Leary, 1995; Reis, 1994), and autonomy (deCharms, 1968; Deci, 1975) – that appear to be essential for facilitating optimal functioning of the natural propensities for growth and integration, as well as for constructive social development and personal well-being. (Ryan and Deci, 2000: 68)

A critical component of SDT is that emphasis is placed on social context. As is stated in the quote above, the need for competence, relatedness, and autonomy all occur in social contexts.

In many ways SDT is an exciting and promising field of motivation theory and research that we believe will make a significant contribution not only to leadership and organizational behaviour, but also to psychological health and wellbeing. SDT assumes we are active organisms, who inherently strive towards psychological growth and development, and seek to master ongoing challenges and to integrate our experiences into a coherent sense of self. All this requires a supportive social environment in order for us to function effectively, and ensure our active engagement in life and our psychological growth (see Deci and Ryan, 2000). When people feel they have achieved high levels of self-determination they are believed to be operating at high levels of psychological health and wellbeing because they feel more competent, social, and free (Thrash and Elliot, 2002; Vansteenkiste et al., 2004).

Try the self-determination scale in the Question Time box below developed by Kennon M. Sheldon (1995). It has been shown to be a reliable and valid predictor of psychological health and wellbeing (Sheldon et al., 1996). A higher score on the two constructs in the scale (less than 10 on both) indicates higher levels of self-determination.

QUESTION TIME

The Self-Determination Scale

Scale description

The Self-Determination Scale (SDS) was designed to assess individual differences in the extent to which people tend to function in a self-determined way. It is thus considered a relatively enduring aspect of people's personalities, which reflects (1) being more aware of their feelings and their sense of self, and (2) feeling a sense of choice with respect to their behaviour. The SDS is a short, 10-item scale, with two 5-item subscales. The first subscale is awareness of oneself, and the second is perceived choice in one's actions. The subscales can either be used separately or they can be combined into an overall SDS score.

Instructions: Please read the pairs of statements, one pair at a time, and think about which statement within the pair seems more true to you at this point in your life. Indicate the degree to which statement A feels true, relative to the degree that statement B feels true, on the 5-point scale shown after each pair of statements. If statement A feels completely true and statement B feels completely untrue, the appropriate response would be 1. If the two statements are equally true, the appropriate response would be 3. If only statement B feels true the appropriate response would be 5 and so on.

1   a. I always feel like I choose the things I do.
    b. I sometimes feel that it's not really me choosing the things I do.

Only A feels true   1   2   3   4   5   **Only B feels true**

(Continued)

(Continued)

2 a. My emotions sometimes seem alien to me.
   b. My emotions always seem to belong to me.

   Only A feels true   1   2   3   4   5   **Only B feels true**

3 a. I choose to do what I have to do.
   b. I do what I have to, but I don't feel like it is really my choice.

   Only A feels true   1   2   3   4   5   **Only B feels true**

4 a. I feel that I am rarely myself.
   b. I feel like I am always completely myself.

   Only A feels true   1   2   3   4   5   **Only B feels true**

5 a. I do what I do because it interests me.
   b. I do what I do because I have to.

   Only A feels true   1   2   3   4   5   **Only B feels true**

6 a. When I accomplish something, I often feel it wasn't really me who did it.
   b. When I accomplish something, I always feel it's me who did it.

   Only A feels true   1   2   3   4   5   **Only B feels true**

7 a. I am free to do whatever I decide to do.
   b. What I do is often not what I'd choose to do.

   Only A feels true   1   2   3   4   5   **Only B feels true**

8 a. My body sometimes feels like a stranger to me.
   b. My body always feels like me.

   Only A feels true   1   2   3   4   5   **Only B feels true**

9 a. I feel pretty free to do whatever I choose to.
   b. I often do things that I don't choose to do.

   Only A feels true   1   2   3   4   5   **Only B feels true**

10 a. Sometimes I look into the mirror and see a stranger.
   b. When I look into the mirror I see myself.

   Only A feels true   1   2   3   4   5   **Only B feels true**

Scoring information for the SDS. First, items 1, 3, 5, 7, 9 need to be reverse scored so that higher scores on every item will indicate a higher level of self-determination. To reverse score an item, subtract the item response from 6 and use that as the item score (so if you scored 5 for question 9, subtract this number from 6 and you get 1). Then, calculate the scores for the Awareness of Self subscale and the Perceived Choice subscale by averaging the item scores for the 5 items within each of subscale. The subscales are: Awareness of Self: Qs. 2, 4, 6, 8, 10; Perceived Choice: Qs. 1, 3, 5, 7, 9. Scores greater than 10 on both reflect a high level of self-determination.

This survey first appeared in Sheldon, K. M. (1995) 'Creativity and self-determination in personality', *Creativity Research Journal*, 8: 25–36.

The SDT is an important motivation theory underpinned by principles of positive psychology. It is therefore appropriate, and important, that we consider an increasingly popular aspect of the positive psychology of leadership: that of authentic leadership and positive psychological capital.

The positive psychology of leadership

Building positive psychological capital through authentic leadership
To be a leader is a huge moral responsibility because executive leadership can easily overwhelm reason. Hitler was able to lead men and women and influence them so strongly that they committed horrific acts. Indeed, his ability to read and use the situational contingencies, his vision, and his drive all came together, and he nearly achieved his ultimate goal. Because many researchers wanted to figure out how this type of blind loyalty to an evil leader could be avoided in the future, a large body of work is emerging that emphasizes and distinguishes leadership by behaviours and *cognitions* (or ways of thinking). Such approaches have emerged out of the traditions of positive psychology (see also pp. 72–75) and place virtues such as strength of character, wisdom, authenticity, and humanity before all else. Remember earlier that many of the traditional theories of leadership do not differentiate between leaders such as Hitler or Obama. As such, wisdom, authenticity and humanity are strong values that allow us to make sense of leadership as 'doing good'.

As the work of Milgram (1971) has shown, these values are extremely important. Milgram was intrigued as to why people would follow some leaders to the point where they would engage in atrocious behaviour. As a person of Jewish ancestry and as a social psychologist, Milgram was especially interested in why Germans, and many others, blindly followed the Nazi quest to exterminate all Jews. How could leaders have so much power and influence over people? Was there something specific about those Germans that made them obey the Nazi leader's orders? Or could any one of us become violent, murderous, blind followers given the right conditions? Milgram designed a study in which people were asked to give various levels of electric shocks to individuals (who unbeknown to the participants were actors in the experiment). The participants thought the experiment was about punishment and learning; however, after administering mild shocks to the actors, Milgram asked participants to give extremely high, lethal shocks to people. Over two thirds of respondents were willing to give the highest dose, even when the participants themselves appeared emotionally distressed (for a full description of the experiment see http://www.cnr.berkeley.edu/ucce50/ag-labour/7article/article35.htm).

As Milgram so eloquently noted a few years after his original study was published:

> ordinary people, simply doing their jobs, and without any particular hostility on their part, can become agents in a terrible destructive process. Moreover, even when the destructive effects of their work become patently clear, and they are asked to carry out actions incompatible with fundamental

standards of morality, relatively few people have the resources needed to resist authority. A variety of inhibitions against disobeying authority come into play and successfully keep the person in his place. Sitting back in one's armchair, it is easy to condemn the actions of the obedient subjects. But those who condemn the subjects measure them against the standard of their own ability to formulate high-minded moral prescriptions. That is hardly a fair standard. Many of the subjects, at the level of stated opinion, feel quite as strongly as any of us about the moral requirement of refraining from action against a helpless victim. They, too, in general terms know what ought to be done and can state their values when the occasion arises. This has little, if anything, to do with their actual behavior under the pressure of circumstances. (Milgram, 1974: 4–5)

Luthans and Avolio's (2003) concept of the **authentic leader** differs from the type of leader encountered in Nazi Germany and the Milgram experiment. Their authentic leadership development exemplifies many of the qualities espoused by positive psychology. According to Luthans and Avolio (2003: 242–243), authentic leaders are transparent. Their intentions seamlessly link espoused values, actions, and behaviours.

> **Authentic leaders** have the qualities of transformational leaders but also work on moral and ethical grounds; possess great self-awareness, integrity, confidence, and self-control; are positive and optimistic; are resilient (bouncing back from adversity); and are future oriented.

Authentic leaders inspire, transform, mentor, and develop (Gardner et al., 2005). The authentic leader might be the perfectly designed leader to achieve Maslow's eupsychian philosophy that we discussed earlier. Indeed, for many of his generation, John Lennon, with his commitment to peace, seemed to be such a leader, capable of taking his celebrity and parlaying it into consciousness-raising about profound and not just entertainment values. In this respect, Lennon was that unlikely iconic phenomenon: an authentic leader, writer, and musician, in the way that, more recently, others such as Bob Geldof and Bono have also sought to be.

The authentic leader, by definition, should be able to realize when she or he makes a mistake or inadvertently does wrong and will then take responsibility, accept accountability, and seek to amend the situation. In addition, a very important aspect of the model is that authentic leadership occurs within a context in which leaders are able to empathize with subordinates and to reflect cultural, moral, and ethical standards in their approach to management, so the authentic leader is not only a way of being and a way of seeing but is also situational. A critical aspect of the authentic leader is the ability to develop **positive psychological capital (PsyCap)** (Gardner et al., 2005; Luthans et al., 2002, Luthans et al., 2007).

> **Positive psychological capital (PsyCap)** refers to positive states such as hope, resilience, optimism, and self-efficacy through leadership and organizational behaviour that is oriented towards the positive psychological wellbeing and health of its members (Anandakumar et al., 2008).

Fred Luthans and his colleagues at the Gallup Leadership Institute in the University of Lincoln-Nebraksa have done most to develop and apply the concept of PsyCap. According to Luthans et al. (2007: 2), PsyCap refers to an individual's positive psychological state of development and includes (1) self-efficacy – or the confidence to take on and put in the necessary effort to succeed at challenging tasks; (2) optimism – making a positive attribution about succeeding now and in the future; (3) hope – or persevering towards goals and, when necessary, redirecting paths to goals in order to succeed; and (4) resilience – meaning the ability to bounce back and succeed in the face of problems and adversity.

Luthans and Youssef (2004) argue that the role of psychological capital leadership is to develop and enhance employees' psychological strengths. These strengths of self-efficacy, optimism, hope, and resiliency have been shown to be important in performance and satisfaction at work (Luthans et al., 2007). Leadership can play an important role in building psychological capital by acknowledging that everyone brings their life experiences with them to the workplace and that current workplace events shape an employee's confidence, hope, resiliency, and optimism (Bagozzi, 2003; Luthans, 2002; Luthans and Avolio, 2003; Luthans and Youssef, 2004). Stewart, Martin, and Tyrone have all worked for organizations where the building of PsyCap was the last thing on lists of priorities. Our anecdotal experience – that is evidence based on our own life experience – shows that such organizations are detrimental to happy, functional, productive, and healthy working lives, and they can stay dysfunctional for a very long time. PsyCap has been shown to reduce levels of workplace incivility, and also buffer people from the negative effects of incivility (Roberts et al., 2011); to promote servant leadership behaviours (Searle and Barbuto, 2011); and to improve performance (Peterson et al., 2011).

To believe that such positive ideals can be attained as absolutes (or universal truths) is not only idealistic, but in our opinion unrealistic and unattainable. Now, by no means should this imply that we should not try to strive for organizational and leadership behaviour that espouses positive psychological capital. However, to do so requires a change in the dominant sources of leadership wisdom.

Leadership wisdom

A concept closely related to authentic leadership is *leadership wisdom* (Dunphy and Pitsis, 2003). As with Gardner et al. (2005) and Luthans et al. (2002), the authors argue that leaders of the future will need to take stock of principles and concepts typified by positive psychology – but especially the notions of ecology, ecosystems, biospheres, diversity, and community. Leaders of the future will be authentic and will realize how interconnected everything is in the world. Our organizations are not free enterprises meant to consume all resources to produce products for all consumers. Rather, organizations are made up of you and me, our families, friends, and even our enemies, and what they do has an impact on all of us, both now and in the future. Leadership involves principles of social, economic, and ecological sustainability and ethical responsibility (see also Chapter 11, Managing Sustainably). Sustainability is not synonymous with keeping things the same: it still involves change and development, but it is about transforming society towards positive behaviour and cognition by avoiding overconsumption; addressing inequality; and using intelligent business methods, long-term vision and planning, and future-mindedness.

Pitsis and Clegg (2007) present a more challenging notion of leadership wisdom. In their paper they draw upon ancient Greek philosophy to argue that wisdom is the acknowledgement that one never truly knows. To search for knowledge and information before making or acting upon difficult decisions is analogous to acting ethically. Such an idea runs counter to management, for management is beholden to the need for action, and so patience and seeking out more information do not come naturally to many people. A wise leader will wait, actively listen, and search out more information in order to make a decision.

Pitsis and Clegg (2007) argue that there are several cognitive barriers that inhibit wise leadership behaviour. They draw upon the work of Ghoshal (2005), Mintzberg (2004), and Pfeffer (2005) to argue that much of the theory that underpins management education and training is based upon 'bad' theory, and outdated approaches. For example, many of the principles taught in business schools, and practiced by managers, are steeped in traditional forms of organizing, such as the quest for efficiency, the belief in perfect competition and the free hand of the market mechanism, and profit maximization as the core to organizational survival.

Imagine a world in which our leaders at least tried to live by ethical guidelines and values, and in which our organizations operate upon principles of authenticity and wisdom. This type of world would mean that many of the ways we do things at work today would have to change forever; it is a big challenge, but it is one that more and more people seem to believe in.

IS LEADERSHIP CULTURALLY VARIABLE? THE GLOBE PROJECT

One important discussion of leadership in the context of culture arises from the GLOBE leadership project. GLOBE refers to the Global Leadership and Organizational Behaviour Effectiveness research project. It involves over 170 researchers from over 61 cultures around the world using a range of quantitative (i.e. surveys) and qualitative (i.e. interviews) methods to examine the interrelationships between societal culture, organization culture, and organizational leadership. GLOBE is by far the most comprehensive research project on cross-cultural leadership.

In one of its earlier publications the GLOBE project sought to investigate how and if cultural differences affect and shape leadership behaviour and effectiveness (House et al., 2004). Given the globalization of society, a comprehensive and exhaustive study of leadership and its cross-cultural implications promises to be one of the most important areas of research and theory-building in leadership. Importantly, the GLOBE study has practical implications in terms of how leadership is applied across different cultural contexts. House et al. have identified six global leadership dimensions across 64 countries. These six styles include:

- Charismatic/value-based leadership, which refers to leadership that is perceived to be visionary, inspirational, self-sacrificing, and operates decisively and with integrity.

- Team-oriented leadership, which refers to leadership that is collaborative, diplomatic, cares for others, and is administratively competent.

- Humane leadership, which operates with modesty and humanely.

- Participative leadership, which is democratic and participative.

- Self-protective leadership, which is self-centred, status conscious, face-saving, and procedurally oriented.

- Autonomous leadership, which is highly individualistic, independent, autonomous, and unique.

According to House et al. (2004), charismatic/value-based leadership and team-oriented leadership are universally endorsed cross-culturally. Humane leadership and participative leadership tend to be universally endorsed, but self-protective and autonomous leadership are culturally specific. In other words, leadership styles that emulate many of the positive transformational approaches we discussed earlier in this chapter tend to be consistent across cultures. So, things like vision, inspiration, self-sacrifice, humaneness, diplomacy, competence, and decisiveness tend to be valued across cultures. However, the leadership style that values status, is self-centred, individualistic, autonomous, independent, and unique tends to be culturally specific. As such, it can be argued to an extent that leadership that resembles transformational or authentic leaders will tend to be valued irrespective of where leaders ply their trade. However, leaders who reinforce status, or value individualism and uniqueness, may not fit as well cross-culturally. That is, what the GLOBE project suggests is that the style of leadership used must take into account cultural differences and values.

SUMMARY AND REVIEW

What leaders do and what they say have profound effects upon the world. Leaders influence others and can make life fulfilling, enriched, and empowered (of course they can also make it empty, shallow, and powerless). Although some leaders provide others with the tools to become leaders themselves, other leaders abuse their power, authority, and trust to achieve and to realize their vision and mission of how they think society ought to be.

In this chapter, we have seen that leadership is an extremely complex and value-laden domain of theory and research. Is a leader, as the trait theory suggests, made up of inherent characteristics? The literature does not support such an argument. Behavioural theory sought to refocus leadership away from traits to how a person behaves – that is, one's behaviour makes one a leader or not.

Yet even the behaviourists could see that this was not the entire story, so theorists concluded that situational/contingent factors were influential in determining what made leaders and, more important, what made them effective. Leaders were then conceptualized as charismatic and transformational, with an ability to envision, to inspire, and to implement change. Others may be transactional in that they know how to be exemplary managers. Of course, if full-range leadership theory is correct, the best leaders are both transformational and transactional.

Some contingency theorists argued that the situational factors are so strong that contingencies could be used as substitutes for leadership, and some others even argue that leadership is null and void. The dispersed and postmodern approaches to leadership attempted to turn leadership around. The leader has changed over time, from premodern to modern to postmodern. The postmodern leader is a SERVANT.

No matter which leadership theory we look at, motivation emerges as a critical concept. Leaders must be motivated, but they must also motivate others by inspiring, envisioning, and empowering. We tied motivation into Maslow's hierarchy of needs by focusing on eupsychian management. We then discussed the importance of intrinsic and extrinsic motivation as a way of understanding motivation and leadership, and we emphasized the growing influence of Deci and Ryan's self-determination theory.

In light of Maslow, SDT, and from the perspective of positive psychology, we discussed what our roles and responsibilities might be as members of the human race and related this discussion to the positive psychological traditions of leadership, including the authentic leader and leadership wisdom.

Finally, we closed this chapter with a discussion of the exciting work being done in the GLOBE leadership project. In all, after studying this chapter we hope you have developed an appreciation of the main approaches to leadership, coaching, and motivating people.

Answer to 'Who am I?' exercise on p. 127: Adolf Hitler. A man with horrific intentions who gained the power to implement appalling practices ultimately responsible for the murder of millions of people, who inspired hundreds of thousands to carry out his dirty work, including many unspeakable acts against humanity as well as the barbarism of total war.

EXERCISES

1   Now that you have read this chapter you should be able to define in your own words each of the following key concepts:

- Leadership
- Coaching
- Self-leadership
- Leadership traits
- Leadership behaviour
- Leadership styles
- Transformational leadership
- Transactional leadership
- Charismatic leadership
- The GLOBE study and culture
- Servant leadership
- Authentic leadership
- Positive psychological capital
- Positive psychology
- Motivation
- Extrinsic motivation
- Intrinsic motivation
- Self-determination theory
- Maslow
- McGregor
- Theory X and Theory Y

2   What does it mean to say 'true leaders create more leaders, not more followers?' How far do you agree with this statement? Give reasons for your answer.

3   How practical is it to argue that leadership can be substituted or neutralized? Can we create leadership substitutes or neutralizers in any industry or organization? Why or why not?

4   Choose two perspectives or theories of leadership – the one you liked best and the one you liked least. Compare your choices with those of your peers and try to find out why you and your peers chose those theories or approaches. What was it about the theories that you liked or disliked? What were their strengths and weaknesses? Take note of how and why you and your peers differed or agreed.

5   Set up a class debate titled 'In the end, when you want to motivate people, all that matters is money – everyone has a price!' Have one team argue for the previous statement and one team against. Both groups should use current motivation research and theory to state their claims.

6   How might a leader be able to inspire people through the principles espoused by self-determination theory?

7   What is coaching and why is it a critical component of leadership?

8   Is it realistic to assume that the concept of positive psychology can be applied in the business world? Why or why not?

ADDITIONAL RESOURCES

1   There are many excellent resources on leadership. Two interesting approaches to leadership that paint a picture of the importance and influence of leadership upon organizations are Goleman et al.'s (2002) *The New Leaders: Transforming the Art of Leadership into the Science of Results*, and Kouzes and Posner's (1995) *The Leadership Challenge: How to Keep Getting Extraordinary Things Done in Organizations*.

2   Another excellent source is Den Hartog and Koopman's (2001) 'Leadership in organizations', in the *Handbook of Industrial, Work and Organizational Psychology*.

3 There are many good movies on leadership and motivation. One such movie is *Glengarry Glen Ross* (Foley, 1992), a film about a small organization made up of a dysfunctional sales team and a leader who (at the surface level) seems overly concerned about people. *Be warned that this movie contains extremely offensive language.*

4 Other films about leadership and inspiration include 'heroic quest' movies such as *Gladiator* (Scott, 2000) and *Master and Commander: The Far Side of the World*, as well as the *The Lord of the Rings* (Jackson, 2001–2003) trilogy. It is interesting to compare this form of account with that used by chief executives in their memoirs – they seem to be as seduced by the genre of the heroic quest as an archetype as are film-makers.

WEB SECTION

1 Visit the website of the GLOBE leadership project – there are some excellent resources, papers, and surveys on leadership (http://www.thunderbird.edu/sites/globe/).

2 For state of the art briefings on how to manage organizations effectively, please visit the Henry Stewart Talks series of online audiovisual seminars on Managing Organizations, edited by Stewart Clegg: www.hstalks.com/r/managing-orgs, especially Talk #5 by Ray Gordon on *Leading in organizations* and Talk #6 by Anthony Grant on *Understanding coaching*, as well as Talk #7 by Edward L. Deci on *The self-determination theory perspective on motivations in organizations.*

3 http://psych.rochester.edu/SDT/theory.html is a site that contains several resources on self-determination theory. You can download and complete a number of SDT questionnaires and inventories, and learn about how SDT is being developed and applied.

4 Some great clips on leadership are available from www.Youtube.com. See what you can find yourself, but here are some we recommend. Feel free to e-mail us your suggestions and we may add them to the next edition of this book.

    a Can you change your world? Leaders do. This short five-minute video provides several clips on the issues of leadership from a number of movies and also has a great soundtrack: http://tinyurl.com/2s8j4p. See if you can identify what kind of leadership each video represents.

    b What are the myths of leadership? Are you an eagle or a chicken? Here is a funny, if not a little bit creepy (creepy for Tyrone because he hates human-like puppets – but he likes Elmo), puppet show on leadership: http://tinyurl.com/2vzwv4.

LOOKING FOR A HIGHER MARK

Those of you looking to challenge yourself and write more advanced essay and exam answers might find reading and digesting the following papers can increase your ability to write higher quality responses. All these papers are available free on the Companion Website www.sagepub.co.uk/managingandorganizations3.

1 What do experts believe makes a good leader? Read a very interesting interview with leadership guru John H. Zenger on his ideas about extraordinary leadership and its development through education and training. Pay attention to the five core competencies or leadership tenets and see if you recognize them in other leadership models. Madsen, S. R. and Gygi, J. (2005) 'An interview with John H. Zenger on extraordinary leadership', *Journal of Leadership and Organization Studies*, 11 (3): 119–125.

2 What happens when leadership does not motivate people simply because they have lost respect for leaders? Susan Herman provides an engaging and wonderful account of a leadership conference in which a poet and hip-hop artist is the keynote speaker. The artist's speech was full of swearing, and almost entirely about how he did not know anything about leadership and was not interested in it, and in fact how he hates leaders, does not trust them at all. The response to his speech was dismay from the administration, astonishment from the faculty, and great enthusiasm from the majority of the students – including cheers, clapping, and celebrations. Herman uses this story to ask some important questions, most importantly the implications of

leadership at a time where faith and trust in and respect of many leaders is low among young people. Read it and see what you think. Herman, S. (2007) 'Leadership training in a 'not-leadership' society', *Journal of Management Education*, 31 (2): 151–155.

3 What does leadership behaviour, passion, commitment, and even obsession mean in desperate times? What if you were leading the first ever expedition across the Antarctic continent and your boat sank, and you were stuck in a frozen, foreign land with very limited supply. What would you do? How would you cope? Would you lead? Follow or get out of the way and give up? Blair Browning uses the diaries, pictures, archival data, and stories of Ernest Shackleton whose goals went from an exciting expedition to one of getting every man home alive. Browning writes a fascinating paper on how the story is a perfect way to teach and develop leadership, especially in the face of very bad odds. We think you will find this a very interesting read, so download it from our website. Read the article by Browning, B. W. (2007) 'Leadership in desperate times: an analysis of endurance: Shackleton's incredible voyage through the lens of leadership theory', *Advances in Developing Human Resources*, 9 (2): 183–198.

4 Leadership is a very difficult domain of research, but it is important that academics identify what kinds of leadership work, what theories make sense, and reflect what leaders do, how they do it, and why they do it. The paper by Susan Lynham and Thomas Chermack seeks to address the underemphasis of whole-system effects of leadership. Leaders are not free from their context, and no person, group, organization, or country is truly independent of other people, groups, organizations, and countries. Read the article by Lynham, S. A. and Chermack, T. J. (2006) 'Responsible leadership for performance: a theoretical model and hypotheses', *Journal of Leadership & Organizational Studies*, 12 (4): 73–88.

5 Can we specify a set of competencies (sets of identifiable skills and abilities) that underpin leadership? What might be the risks of obsessing with competencies that distinguish leaders from non-leaders? Richard Bolden and Jonathan Gosling argue that the competency approach is illusionary as a rational approach of selecting, measuring, and developing leaders. They believe that leadership is such a complex concept that identifying and developing leaders based on competencies is too simplistic. They find a substantial difference in the outcomes of leadership training when programmes take into consideration moral, emotional, and relationship dimensions of leadership. Bolden, R. and Gosling, R. (2006) 'Leadership competencies: time to change the tune?', *Leadership*, 2 (2): 147–163.

CASE STUDY

AUTHENTIC LEADERSHIP AT CLIF BAR ORGANIZATION

Introduction

This case is about the Clif Bar organization, and is presented from the perspective of the third person. It demonstrates authentic leadership which is a concept based in: (a) self-awareness; (b) balanced processing (i.e. seeking alternative, even contradictory, viewpoints); (c) transparency and disclosure of relevant information; and (d) morally based ethical actions. Authentic leadership is applying individual leader authenticity, which at the core represents being true to one's self, to the broader scope of leadership experiences that impact a leader's constituencies and organization. The case below will illustrate these points.

The story

In 2006, Clif Bar was a private company with estimated annual revenues of about $150 million and about 170 employees. Yet, there was a moment when it almost became another product line of a large mega corporation and another countless blip across the C-SPAN screen. It was a 'moment' that can be described as authentic leadership that changed the course of the future for the owner, employees, and customers of this unique company.

After two key competitors in the industry were bought by large corporations, an offer was made by a third large corporation to purchase the Clif Bar company in the year 2000. It was an outstanding offer that was sure to make both owners extremely wealthy to the extent that they would never have to work another day in their lives.

On the day of signing the contract, however, Gary Erickson, one of the owners, felt a sense of panic, so he decided to take a walk to consider his 'epiphany'. In that moment, being aware of his innermost thoughts, he realized he did not want to sell the company. He decided he was not going to give in to all the rational reasons that 'experts' gave him for selling the business, the primary one being the fact that key competitive products were recently bought by corporations with large marketing budgets; it was argued that Clif Bar would never be able to compete at that level and would wither away under the force of immense competition. But on this day, Gary listened to his conscience and made a decision that went against these experts, including the co-owner of Clif Bar, who would now have to be bought out. Gary defied the odds and decided to back out of the deal of a lifetime. He went on to buy out the other owner for over $60 million, even though he only had $10,000 in his bank account at the time.

In this case, his leadership paid off. The company has since grown from about $40 million in sales to $150 million, even while competing with mega corporations. Most recently Clif Bar became a leader in business sustainability by offering the nation's first incentive programme to pay cash to employees who purchase clean-burning bio-diesel cars, helping employees buy high-mileage hybrids, and offering a variety of rewards to those who leave their cars at home altogether.

Gary Erickson has demonstrated authentic leadership by aligning his actions with his conscience when he chose to back out of the sale at the last minute and follow his 'inner voice'. He trusted his own wisdom over the advice of the other highly experienced business people involved. Not only did he succeed in sustaining the revenue growth of the company over time, but Clif Bar continues to create innovative ways to be a company that values and takes actions towards sustaining the planet.

In retrospect, he could have been wrong about the future earning potential, but he would have still been right about himself. His level of self-awareness regarding his inner morals and values led him to maintain and grow one of the best-known outdoor food brands in the USA. Although authentic leadership in this example was clearly demonstrated by a major decision, that decision took years to carry through, and required a repeated focus on core values during that time. As a result, the company continues to thrive and lead other companies in social responsibility initiatives. Gary Erickson continues to lead the company in a way that is consistent with his core values system that places people and planet before personal profit.

Questions

1 What do you think the moral of the story is?
2 Would we still call it effective leadership or even authentic leadership if Clif Bar had gone bankrupt instead of increasing in revenues?
3 How did Gary use the concept of balanced processing and self-awareness when all experts were saying one thing yet he chose a different direction?
4 In this case, Gary was transparent about his intentions with his partner. What are the political and power-related circumstances that make it easy or difficult to be transparent at the upper levels of organizational leadership?
5 In an age of rational decision-making, how do authentic leaders stay true to themselves when the 'numbers' or evidence presented by respected advisors suggest a different choice?

Case prepared by Tara S. Wernsing, Gallup Leadership Institute, University of Nebraska–Lincoln; James B. Avey, Assistant Professor of Management, Central Washington University.

CHAPTER FIVE
MANAGING HUMAN RESOURCES

Diversity, Selection, Retention

LEARNING OBJECTIVES

By the end of this chapter, you will be able to:

- Describe the origins and meaning of human resource management
- Understand the key concepts in human resource management and how they affect organizational practice and performance
- Describe the 'hard' and 'soft' approaches to human resource practices and policies
- Understand the main methods and approaches to recruitment, selection, retention, and development used in human resource management
- Evaluate the human resource function and its role in shaping organizational behaviour
- Appreciate the role of government in influencing human resources policy

BEFORE YOU GET STARTED . . .

Some words from the Marx Bothers:

I don't care to belong to a club that accepts people like me as members. (Groucho Marx)

INTRODUCTION

'So, why do you want to work for us?' It is likely that almost all of us will be faced with this uninspiring question at least once in our working lives as we search for a job. Other typical questions include 'What are your strengths and weaknesses?', 'Tell us a little about yourself', 'Why did you leave your other job?', 'Can you work as part of a team?', and so on. These questions are not simply friendly banter: they are underpinned by specific intentions. Think for a moment: why would a possible future employer ask you these things? It is not because they want to date you (well, usually not!): it is because they want to determine if you are the right person for the job. **Human resource management (HRM)** concerns a broad range of practices and processes that include:

HRM is the process and practice of managing and advising management on the recruitment, selection, retention, and development of staff in an increasingly complex legal and social environment with the aim of achieving the organization's objectives as they are made sense of by its managers or consultants.

- Attracting and selecting employees in line with the strategic direction and intent of the organization.

- Managing and facilitating career development and advancement of employees.

- Dealing with and keeping abreast of current rules, laws, and legislation in industrial relations and other policy areas such as occupational health and safety legislation, equity and diversity, and anti-discrimination laws.

- Ensuring there are uniform procedures and company HR policy information available to staff and management on all aspects of employment.

Typically most large organizations will have a department dedicated to human resources. However, most people work in small to medium-sized organizations, many without a human resources department. The human resources manager in small organizations is usually also the business owner, manager, or supervisor, with typically a wider span of duties and responsibilities, and a much smaller HR budget. This is unfortunate because many of the HR challenges that large businesses face are the same as those that face small businesses. For example, it is just as important that a small business is able to attract and retain talented staff. More importantly, in the case of workplace accidents, where employer negligence is involved, it can often be easier for government departments and legal entities to pursue the small-business owner than large-company executives.

IMAGE 5.1   Shared meaning shared values?

Irrespective of business size, how HR managers approach their tasks is a function of their own and their organization's value systems. Do they value people? Is the most important aspect profit maximization and efficiency? What assumptions about human nature are dominant in the employer's mind? Do people simply want cash, or is a person's identity and self-esteem wrapped up in what they do for a living? All these questions are integral to the HR function. To explore such issues we need to consider the history of HR management and its origins and underpinning philosophies that drive different approaches in HRM. We will discuss the aims and objectives of HR and why it is important that HR policies are aligned to the organization's strategic vision and mission.

We will explore some of the contextual aspects of HRM that shape the way people are recruited, selected, retained, and treated once on board the organization. HRM is a complex and difficult part of organizational practice: HR managers and their teams must understand a plethora of government laws, rules, and regulations in areas such as equity and diversity (anti-discrimination and affirmative action), occupational health and safety, and industrial relations laws (both domestic and international). Not only must HR managers be knowledgeable about all these things, they must also have a strong awareness of what is happening in society – for example, generational differences are believed to have major influences on why and how people work. Knowing all these things, and transforming all this knowledge into understandable, easily accessible, and practical information is easier said than done.

We will focus on the areas of recruitment, selection, retention, and development of staff. If you were to ask any executive or business owner what they find most challenging in running their organization, it is likely that they would respond that finding and selecting the right staff is one of the most challenging. However, selection is only part of the HRM story; once you find people, you need to keep them. Herein lies one of our biggest challenges as managers – how do we actually keep people? A good HR manager will ensure practices, processes, and policies exist that maintain the interest of employees, and provide opportunities for staff development. First, let us delve a little deeper into the history and main themes in HR.

HR ORIGINS

Accounts of the origins of the theory and practice of HRM vary. HR practices have been studied implicitly by anthropologists for over two centuries as they investigated work practices in ancient times. For example, it has been found that many Anglo-Celtic people were named after what they did for a living – Smith, Cook, Miller, and Tailor are not simply surnames but also job titles: people were, quite literally, what they did for a living.

In ancient times people often did the same job for life: sometimes they were born into a trade, so a 'Carter' could, literally, be a carter, a 'Smith' literally a smith, and so on. They would follow in their father's footsteps. Some jobs required a lifetime of learning, practice, and experience before they could be mastered, and young people would enter apprenticeships where they would receive close mentoring. In many respects apprenticeships have changed very little over the centuries, and the model used to train people has remained strong. Young stonemasons, jewellers, glassmakers, chefs, and other craftspeople were bound to their masters through apprenticeships, often having to live with their employers until they mastered their trade. Today the apprenticeship system of staff training and development remains. Indeed, if you intend one day to be an academic you will find the apprenticeship model is alive and well in academia. Your research supervisors or advisors will be your coaches and mentors, guiding you through the process of designing and conducting research, writing and publishing your thesis, teaching, dealing with university policies and politics, and so on.

HRM grows up

While anything to do with finding and hiring a person for a job can be interpreted as HRM, the *theory* and *study* of HRM is quite new. They began with the introduction of HRM as an area of study as part of the Harvard University MBA and at the Michigan Business School in the 1980s. Often you will hear people refer to 'hard' and 'soft' HR models; in reality they are referring to the Michigan and the Harvard schools of HRM respectively. The notion of 'hard' and 'soft' approaches to HRM is an integral component of all HRM practices, so it is important we appreciate and understand what is meant by these two terms. To comprehend fully these two HRM schools of thought and to understand the meaning of the terms 'hard' and 'soft', let us look at two seminal approaches – Fredrick Taylor's scientific management and Elton Mayo's human relations approaches to management. (Both approaches are discussed in greater detail in Chapter 12). More so than most topics in this textbook, HRM is underpinned by variations of scientific management or human relations approaches – especially in regards to staff training and development, and on performance measurement and reward. While we cover these topics in greater detail shortly, they are important underlying concepts in HRM theory and practice. Table 5.1 summarizes the key points of both approaches to HR practice.

These two underlying themes of soft and hard HR practices can be seen in the Harvard and Michigan models. The models can also be matched to Douglas McGregor's conception of Theory X and Theory Y orientations to managing people (see Chapter 4 for more details). Theory X refers to managers who take a hard orientation towards managing and motivating people at work, and Theory Y refers to leaders who take a soft orientation (Pitsis, 2008a; 2008b).

In the **soft model of HRM** it is assumed that work is an integral part of life and should provide a fulfilling, empowering, and positive experience for people. People will be attracted to jobs that provide opportunity for growth and advancement; they will stay in jobs that invest in them as valuable assets.

In the **hard model of HRM** it is assumed that people do not want empowerment: they simply want to be told what is required of them, given the resources and training to achieve these requirements, and be remunerated if they go beyond those requirements. People will be attracted by good pay, clear objectives, and unambiguous job duties.

The **soft model of HRM** takes a humanistic approach to HRM; typically soft HR managers have a Theory Y orientation, which emphasizes that people are intrinsically motivated.

In the **hard model of HRM**, managers tend to have a Theory X orientation and believe most people would rather not be at work; for this reason management monitoring and control is integral, and typically extrinsic rewards such as pay raises and bonuses are used.

WHAT DO YOU MEAN?

Resources (n);

Backup supply – a reserve supply of something, such as money, personnel, or equipment

Corporate assets – any or all of the resources drawn on by a company for making profit, e.g. personnel, capital, machinery, or stock

Before considering the main functions of HRM, let us cover one very important concept underpinning HRM practice. This issue is central to HRM because it concerns the very name of human resource management – that is, 'humans' as 'resources'. The online encyclopedia, Encarta, describes resources in a number of ways. Two of the most interesting and most commonly shared are shown in the What Do You Mean? box above.

On the face of it, these definitions look benign. However, we need to deconstruct their meaning and etymology (that is, the origins of the words

Check out the Companion Website www.sagepub.co.uk/ managingandorganizations3 for free access to an article by E. C. A. Kaarsemar and E. Poutsma (2006) about how HR managers can implement and reinforce a true Theory Y philosophy in HRM.

TABLE 5.1 Hard and soft HRM practices and philosophies

HRM practices	Hard	Soft
Assumption about managing people	Staff will work to rule if not managed correctly. Emphasis is on the individual and on management control. People are a specific kind of resource and should be managed as such. Emphasis is on the strategic match of people to the organization's objectives	Staff are looking for self-fulfilment and meaning in work that comes from social relations. Emphasis is on teamwork and participative collaboration. Management should focus on creating fulfilling and meaningful workplaces that encourage autonomy and self-management. People are assets. Emphasis is on the value of viewing the organization as comprised of multiple stakeholders, staff being one of these interested stakeholders
Selection orientation	Selection should focus on the best people for the task. The emphasis is on the fit between person and task	Selection should focus on people who can enhance the organization and bring in new knowledge and expertise. More important than the fit between people and task is the fit between person and organization
Retention orientation	The retention of staff is less important than maintaining productivity and efficiency. Low-level jobs are easier to fill, so staff retention is not an underlying concern	Retention is achieved through building social networks in the organization. Commitment and identity with the organization is critical
Training and development orientation	People must receive the best training specifically for the task at hand, but all training and development must be specific to the task. The best training available should be used on the best people	Personal and organizational development is key. Using the knowledge and intellect of staff will benefit the organization. If people are not right for the task, design tasks, or find them jobs that are right for them
Performance orientation	Management ultimately drives and sets performance outcomes. Almost always measured at the individual level and always on the meeting of specific job-related outcomes. Poor performance is due to poor management control of employees	Performance outcomes are usually decided as a team. Performance evaluation is measured not only on task performance but on ability to work as a team player. Hence tasks that are not directly related to the specific job might also be part of measured performance outcomes – for example, social responsibility by volunteering time to charity events
Motivation orientation	Theory X orientation: mainly extrinsic rewards, such as monetary rewards in the form of bonuses paid for exceeding set targets. Time in lieu also used as a motivator (also see Chapter 4)	Theory Y orientation: mainly intrinsic rewards such as promotion, recognition, and opportunities for self-development, self-actualization, and self-management (also see Chapter 4)
HR model	Michigan model	Harvard model
Alignment to Management Philosophy	Scientific Management (i.e. Fredrick W. Taylor)	Human Relations (i.e. Elton Mayo)

Source: Adapted and extended from Price (2004)

and their meaning). When we take a closer look at the 'reserve supply of something', the 'something' refers to personnel. As a corporate asset, personnel are used 'by a company for making profit'. Personnel are of course humans, or more precisely human resources, yet it can sound as though they are merely an item on a corporate shopping list, along with other items such as money, equipment, capital, machinery, and stock. One could imagine a large warehouse somewhere, full of pencils, pens, envelopes, and boxes of copy paper, and just below that, perhaps some nicely packaged humans. Of course, we are only joking, sort of – most organizations do store people in offices for a large part of the day. However, the concept of humans as resources has very important implications for the notion of HRM because there are some very basic assumptions underpinning the notion of humans as resources.

Historically, some humans were thought of as resources that could be bought and sold as slaves – human bodies forcibly removed from Africa and made to work in the Americas – and for hundreds of years slavery was the most profitable trade in the world economy. Indeed, the British, French, and Dutch prospered greatly from the slave trade.

It was not only the slave trade that reinforced the treatment of humans as nothing more than resources. The wealthy industrialist classes in the UK, France, Germany, Spain, The Netherlands, and other colonialist nations helped to create a large working class. Economies were structured in terms of a division between the owners of capital and those whose only resource was the ability to provide their labour power by renting some of their time and labour to a capitalist for a wage.

At this time many nations saw an increase in the union movement, as unions were created to counter the increasing power of industrialists and owners of capital, and to ensure a fair wage for a fair day's work. Unionists believed the main aim of union organization was to ensure that humans were not treated simply as resources, but as human beings with lives, families, aspirations, and so on. For many in management, and some management theorists – including those within both the scientific management and the human relations schools – unions were seen as more of a source of disruption and conflict in organizational life.

One might be skeptical about the intentions of HRM and its role in people's – those human resources – working lives. You do not have to search far or wide to experience cases of people being treated as nothing other than a resource. Often companies pursue programmes of mass redundancies in order to influence stock market prices and every day there are cases of unfair dismissal, discrimination, and exploitation, even in some of the biggest and most successful companies.

Yet, while it is certainly true that the exploitation of people occurs on a day-to-day basis, it is also true that many organizations proclaim that their people are their greatest asset. Some of these companies have experienced phenomenal growth, even in times of great competition and challenge, and we will visit some of these throughout this chapter. The point to be made here is that the desire to treat humans as valuable 'assets' rather than as expendable 'resources' gives HRM a very important role within organizations – especially as unionism continues to decline, partly in the face of governments' aggressive neo-economic policies on industrial relations which privilege individual over collective contracts. So it is time now to visit the HRM functions that are central to the success and growth of organizations.

HRM IN CONTEXT

HRM and strategy

A key function of HRM is to assist the business to meet its strategic objectives. Earlier in this chapter we outlined the soft and hard approaches to HRM. While the Harvard and Michigan models are presented as the main HR models, in reality four general schools of thought evolved about HRM at around the same time. In addition to the Harvard and Michigan schools, Price (2004) lists two other important HRM schools of thought that have influenced the way in which HRM is understood, practiced, and taught: – these are the Warwick and the Schuler schools. Importantly, the Schuler school is named after Professor Randall S. Schuler who emphasized the critical role that HRM plays in strategic management. His work since the 1980s has sought to emphasize that, although the practice of HRM and the practice of strategic management are interrelated, most strategic management scholars underemphasize the role that HRM plays in business strategy (Schuler and Jackson, 2000; Schuler and MacMillan, 1984; Tarique and Schuler, 2010). From Schuler's work emerged the important but debated concept of strategic HRM.

Strategic management is a broad managerial function, usually formulated, implemented, and evaluated by the senior leaders within an organization. Strategy is more than just planning and executing, it is about change and leading from the front (Hamel, 2002; Hamel and Prahalad, 1996). According to Porter (1987; 1996), strategic management is what gives businesses competitive advantage because it differentiates them, and what they are doing, from other businesses. Traditional approaches to strategic management, such as those proffered by Porter and others, involve a vision of the future of an organization, then formulating, setting, and selling a clear plan, set of objectives, and measurement systems for the organization's future. The strategic plan is sold to staff, customers, and other stakeholders in order to help the business realize its vision.

According to Schuler and Jackson (2000), strategic management is comprised of five core practices that can be divided into strategy *formulation* and strategy *implementation*. They argue that these core activities can be directly transposed onto the key HRM functions of the business as **strategic HRM**. The strategic activities relating to formulation include: (a) deciding what business the company will be in, formulating a strategic vision, and generating a set of values and a general strategy; (b) identifying strategic business issues and setting strategic objectives; (c) crafting a set of strategic plans of action for meeting the objectives. The activities relating to

Strategic HRM: In the formulation stage strategic HRM can contribute to the organization's objectives by ensuring that all key HRM functions such as the recruitment, retention, and development of staff are consistent with the business strategy. In the implementation stage HRM can contribute by ensuring that people understand the key strategic intentions and objectives, and ensure that people are abiding by those strategic intentions through measurement of performance consistent with those objectives.

implementation include: (a) developing and implementing the strategic plans of action for functional units; and (b) evaluating, revising, and refocusing for the future. For Schuler and Jackson, strategic HRM is closely tied to strategic functions of strategy formulation and implementation.

In the formulation stage strategic HRM can contribute to the organization's objectives by ensuring that all key HRM functions such as the recruitment, retention, and development of staff are consistent with the business strategy. In the implementation stage HRM can contribute by ensuring that people understand the key strategic intentions and objectives, and ensuring that people are abiding by those strategic intentions through measurement of performance consistent with those objectives.

Much of the work on strategic management, and therefore strategic HRM, adopts a contingency theory perspective on the world. Contingency theory assumes that organizations constantly scan their environment, and that their response to certain variables, or contingencies, in their environment is what enables the organization to succeed. The strategic manager must always ensure that the organization is aligned with these contingencies, for if they are not, they must realign the organization to regain fit with its environment (Donaldson, 2002 [1987]; Schuler and Jackson, 2000).

Such conceptions of strategy assume that the business managers are in control and can alter and manage aspects of the organization as they see fit. In this sense the HR manager can help align the organization to fit better with the environment by selecting who is employed, how and why they are selected, how they are trained, and so on. The HR manager can formulate an HR strategy consistent with corporate strategy, and implement that strategy, and can then ensure that there is a performance measurement system in place to ensure staff are performing according to strategy. This assumes that management has control of where the organization is going and also control over the staff. That is, people in the organization are made to fit the overall strategic mission of the organization.

There is, of course, common sense in ensuring that HR and corporate strategy are well aligned. However, the notion that one can plan for and measure strategy, let alone design the entire HRM function around that strategy, is grandiose. The notion assumes (a) that the rational model of strategy is what actually gets implemented and (b) that external events are knowable, controllable, and manageable. In practice, however, the likelihood is that what is implemented is the various, contested, understandings of this model that people in different parts and levels of the organization possess. Specifically there is debate around the idea that one can plan for and measure performance on things that have not yet happened. That is, the contexts within which organizations operate are exemplified by uncertainty (unknowable events) and ambiguity (differences in understanding and perception about events and objects). Strategic management is therefore a process that 'happens' as it unfolds in real time and space (Carter et al., 2008; Clegg et al., 2011). That is, how can we plan for things that have not yet happened, but we simply think will happen? How can we plan

Check out the Companion Website www.sagepub.co.uk/ managingandorganizations3 for free access to an interesting and easy to read paper on strategic HRM by B. E. Becker and M. Huselid (2006).

for events that will only unfold as we think they will if everyone else shares our understanding and follows the rational plan perfectly? We know from a great deal of research that it is rarely the case that this happens (Brunsson, 2006).

The Strategy-As-Practice (SAP) movement attempts to reverse the trend towards viewing strategy as something that organizations have, and emphasizes the idea that strategy is something people do – or practice (Clegg et al., 2011; Golsorkhi et al., 2010; Johnson et al., 2007). As such, strategy is a fluid process that unfolds as people in organizations go about 'doing' strategy, and sometimes the outcome of the strategy is something which unfolds, or becomes, as a result of the practices rather than any pre-planned and carefully controlled and managed event (Bjorkeng et al., 2009; Clegg et al., 2011).

So, for many strategic management scholars, strategy is not so much what we plan as something we *do*. It is neither something that happens in isolation from everything else, nor something that is easily compart-mentalized into doable chunks that are 'plannable' and measurable. While we can say, 'Today I will strategize, tomorrow I will plan, on the next day I will implement', and so on, in reality the world does not operate in this way. To define and set up performance management systems for events that have not yet occurred is an activity that can be viewed with skepticism. Often what many employees find, as they negotiate how their performance will be assessed, is that over time the things they 'agree' to achieve and to be measured against end up becoming obsolete and irrelevant. Similarly, managers often believe in the myth that they can control all aspects of work as long as they can plan for it and thus will know what can be predicted in the future (Makridakis et al., 2010; Pitsis and Clegg, 2007). But the daily news suggests this is not so. Many staff and management in Bear Stearns, Goldman Sachs, Lehman Brothers, Merrill Lynch and Morgan Stanley, American International Group, Enron, WorldCom, One-Tel, Arthur Andersen, etc., all had their performance measurement and performance reviews in place, all in line with the strategic plans of the organizations. However, we wonder if these performance agreements and negotiation of salary and benefits included the potential and actual collapse of these companies? Informed by these stories, some management thinkers have called for a re-evaluation of the term strategic HRM, not so much because they oppose HRM but because they take issue with the concept that strategic management dealing with a specific list of contingencies can be exhaustive of the issues that might arise (you can read more about contingency theory in Chapter 14).

Those of you who go on to specialize in HRM will invariably study strategic HRM, and it is likely that you will then come across such debates about measurement of performance in line with strategic imperatives. Perhaps in some courses you will even debate whether HRM actually is strategic. In our experience, most HR departments simply implement what they are told to by company executives, and so it is the executives who are being strategic, something evident in the fact that relatively few boards include the HR director, nor do HR managers often present to the board and say, 'This is the strategy we believe the company must take, here is our ten-point plan to implement it, now let us go do it!' In most cases HR does not have a strategic role in an organization, which is not to say that it should not and cannot, especially in public organizations (Teo and Crawford, 2005). The debate on the role and effectiveness of strategic HRM in affecting organizational performance is young and inconclusive, but it promises to be a growing and interesting area of research and study (Brewster, 1995; Guest, 2011; Lawler, 2005; Schuler and Jackson, 2000), especially as alternative strategic management perspectives that challenge the dominant rational scientific approach to strategic management enter the fray (see Clegg et al., 2004; 2011).

HRM *and environmental complexity*

A complex and challenging aspect of the HR function is the need to remain up to date with the constantly changing legal, political, and social environment. In this section we will discuss a number of areas where HRM can provide critical knowledge and information regarding all aspects of managing people at work, specifically in areas that concern their employment.

Environmental complexity has a considerable impact on the core functions of HRM, such as recruitment, selection, and retention. However, what is often underplayed is the way in which organizations can alter and create the very environment they seek to adapt to. Here we will consider issues such as the changing nature of the workforce, issues of diversity and gender, equal employment and affirmative action or positive discrimination, and occupational safety and health.

All these things, either alone or in tandem, can significantly affect the ability of an organization, large or small, to function effectively. For this reason, the HR manager and their team – if fortunate enough to have one – have a key role to play in the organization. Whether those responsible for HR have their own department in a large organization, or whether they are a small-business owner with a handful of staff, understanding and accounting for the environmental complexity and uncertainty caused by social, economic, ecological, and political factors is crucial. The HR manager not only provides advice to other managers and staff on these issues, but also implements organization HR policies and procedures that reflect and help account for these complex issues.

Demographic changes: *'talking 'bout my generation'*

HRM requires management of the critical areas of employee recruitment, selection, and training and development in a way that is consistent with an organization's objectives. However, the organization does not exist in isolation from its context or the environment within which it operates. Because HR is fundamentally about people – irrespective of whether it is hard or soft oriented, or whether HR strategy can be planned or whether it evolves in response to events as they occur – everything to do with people has an impact on HR practices and processes. One of the most important concerns for organizations is the changing nature of the workforce. Here we will discuss selected key areas. The discussion will be by no means exhaustive; rather we cover these to ensure that we can all appreciate the complexity, challenges, and opportunities available in managing HR. The areas we will focus on are:

- Assumed generational differences between people that affect their attitudes, perceptions, and expectations about work.

- Knowledge, skills, and education levels of people currently in the workforce and on the job market.

- Types and levels of immigration and migration central to government immigration policy.

Let us begin with generational differences. One often hears people talk about Generation 'X', Generation 'Y', 'Baby boomers', 'Noughties', and so on. Some organizational theorists have asserted that generational differences will have profound effects upon organizations (Conger, 2000), but others argue the idea that generational differences have had a profound effect on organizational behaviour is still yet to be sufficiently proven (Parry and Urwin, 2011). Even so, many researchers have shown that generational differences not only exist, but also have important implications for HR practice (Benson and Brown, 2011; Burke, 1994; Lyons et al., 2005; Smola and Sutton, 2002). Benson and Brown (2011) show that one uniform HR policy cannot adequately account for the differences in work- and life-related values identified with each different generation. Hence, HR policy has to be sensitive and reflective of the values of the varied generations. So what does it mean to differentiate generations, to think of them as characterized by different types of behaviour, and why do they differ? Essentially every generation has claimed to have difficulty understanding the next.

   Different age groups experience events that shape their lives in different ways; these can be local or world events, and they occur as events in a specific period of people's lives. The Great Depression, the Second World War, the 1960s period of social experimentation and protest, the 1980s and the advent of economic rationalization, of corporate greed, downsizing and high unemployment, periods of rapid economic growth, the Internet, and, of course, 9/11 and the associated War on Terror, all these things leave an imprint on people's psyche. But smaller events also shape people – the proliferation of new technologies, changes in expectations about leisure time and work/life balance, improvements in education and health care, and so on. All these things transform people in implicit ways, and therefore also have an impact upon their attitudes and expectations around work. Table 5.2 lists some of the generations and some of their implications for HRM practice and policies.

TABLE 5.2   Managing the different generations from an HRM perspective

Generation?	Description	Implications for HR practice
Baby boomers	Born between 1946 and 1964. Almost all baby boomers will retire from full-time employment in the next 15 years. Typically, they grew up in times of post-war economic prosperity, and (except in the USA) most enjoyed free access to almost all services such as education, health, and so on. They are hard-working and committed and some have high incomes and savings – especially those whose children have left home. Many have families and mortgages and work hard to pay for these. They usually have strong relationship skills and drive. They can be resistant to change and to differences of opinions and between people. They also tend not to handle negative feedback very well, and they tend to avoid conflict	The implication for HR is the need for policies on retirement and redundancies. As they retire a knowledge/skills gap will be left that HR will need to address. Much work has to be done to ensure organizations are ready for the boomer retirement. Mentoring programmes and knowledge transfer can be used in positive ways to ensure boomers are involved in workforce transitions. Perks and benefits that will attract and retain boomers include help in financial planning for retirement; semi-retirement programmes where boomers' knowledge and skills continue to be utilized
Generation X (Baby busters)	Born between 1965 and 1980. There are fewer Generation X-ers than baby boomers. Typically, Gen-X grew up in times of economic downturn, high unemployment, and corporate collapse and greed. They tend to have low savings and prefer having a social life. Work/life balance is very important. They are usually quite self-sufficient and technologically savvy, quite adaptable to change, creative, and resist control and authority. They also tend to lack experience, have poor people skills, and can be overly cynical. Gen-X will fill the leadership and management gap left by baby boomers and will experience tensions of overtaking boomers, and handling Gen-Ys	Shortage of younger people poses serious problems in attracting and maintaining a competent, qualified workforce. Gen-X will be the leaders and managers of the future. They will place emphasis on family and so flexible scheduling will be an expectation; they are not 9–5 people and do not react well to monitoring and control because they believe in working smarter not longer. They thirst for development support, such as time off and financial support to study, not just in areas deemed relevant by the business. Both X and Y will prefer to work as part of projects rather than in specific positions in an organization. Thus project-based work will be used increasingly. Gen-X require technologies in their jobs, will use the Internet to help in decision-making and problem-solving, though are more skeptical about information than are Gen-Y

(Continued)

TABLE 5.2 *(Continued)*

Generation?	Description	Implications for HR practice
Generation Y (or Millenniums)	Born after 1981, Gen-Y will soon overtake both X and boomers. This generation is considered to have a much less serious attitude to work, preferring working to live, rather than living to work. They are believed to have little concern about jobs for life, and like Gen-X, will move jobs several times in their careers but at a much higher rate than Gen-X. They have grown up with technology, and so using it is second nature to them. They rely on family more so than Gen-X, and tend to be optimistic, positive, and prefer to work in groups or in collaboration with others. They lack experience, patience in learning, and can be naive in relating with others	Because of Gen-Y's ambition and reluctance to 'do time' in order to be promoted, they can be very difficult to manage and motivate if their career is perceived to be developing slowly. They are less independent than Gen-X and require closer supervision and attention. As the largest workforce of the future, they will need to be recognized as an important asset and so HR practices and policies that reflect Gen-Y values and expectations need to be formulated. This includes flexible working times, policies of work/life balance, group- and team-based work, and both extrinsic and intrinsic motivation such as free food and drinks. Policies will need to concentrate on attracting and retaining staff through a number of soft HR policies and practices. Both Gen-X and Gen-Y will expect cutting-edge communication technologies, but will also need assistance in developing their people management and communications skills. Gen-Y are especially open to technologies, especially the Internet, to locate information for problem-solving and decision-making – this can pose challenges to organizations given the high level of misinformation on the Internet

Sources: Nowecki and Summers (2007), and Proffet-Reese et al. (2007), and Wikipedia

WHAT DO YOU MEAN?

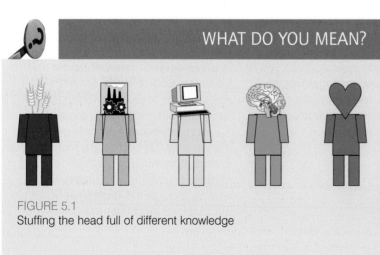

FIGURE 5.1
Stuffing the head full of different knowledge

The changing face of knowledge

Knowledge has transformed with time, as have the expectations of people's core skills sets and capabilities. Most of Western civilization has transformed from an agrarian, to an industrial, then a technological, and most recently a knowledge and emotions based society.

Changing face of knowledge

Let us now look at issues around knowledge, skills, and education levels of the workforce. It is not just generational differences that pose challenges to HRM practice and policy. The changing nature of the workforce in terms of education and skill is also a critical factor. A better educated workforce means people can be better informed about many issues relating to work and quality of working life. We have already seen (in Table 5.2) how Gen-X and Gen-Y are especially technologically savvy, though of course the use of technology is only a small part of what people do at work. The nature of knowledge and concomitant skills expected of people has transformed over time. Figure 5.1 represents the changing knowledge and skills of people in society over time. In Western civilizations most societies were structured around agriculture and artisan crafts such as tool-making, weapon-making, pottery, art, and so on. The demand for people with knowledge, skills, and abilities was concentrated around farming and artisan craftwork. However, as the Industrial Revolution gained impetus there was a change in the expectations of knowledge, skills, and abilities as there was a giant leap in economic growth. Industries based on mass pro-duction, heavy mining, heavy transport (such as trains and ships), and many other technological and scientific innovations, took the place of agricultural and artisan work. As we will discuss in Chapters 12 and 13, mass production brought with it standardized, routinized, and formalized work. Thus workers were no longer expected to be skilled artisans; rather they were trained to do specialized, repetitive tasks.

By the 1990s information technology (IT) professionals were being paid exorbitant amounts of money as the IT bubble kept expanding. University courses and degrees, and specialized IT colleges, appeared from every-where to meet the demand for people seeking IT qualifications. In many ways the IT rush was similar to the Gold Rush era of the US, Australia, and South Africa. Around the turn of the century, the Western world was said to have entered the stage of knowledge work and the growth of knowl-edge-intensive firms. It is likely, given that you are studying a management and organizational behaviour textbook, that you are or will be a knowl-edge worker yourself one day, as we are as the authors of this book, and that you will work in a **knowledge-intensive firm**.

Once knowledge-intensive firms included only consulting companies, legal firms, and other organizations where the outcomes were professional advice on organizational problems. Increasingly, however, even tradition-ally non-knowledge-intensive firms have moved to trading and promoting their knowledge. Most organizations in a variety of industries now involve at least some level of knowledge-based work, be it in banking and finance, tourism and travel, education, pharmaceuticals, food, and so on.

Mats Alvesson (2004: 139–141) argues knowledge-intensive organiza-tions, more than most, must acknowledge that people are critical to their growth and success. He offers two interesting concepts that he believes are critical concepts in HRM and how people are employed and treated at work. These are human capital advantage (HCA) and human process advantage (HPA), both of which are explained in the What Do You Mean? box below. According to Alvesson, effective HRM requires both HCA and

Check out the Companion Website www.sagepub.co.uk/ managingandorganizations3 for free access to an article by Ronald Paul Hill (2002), which provides an excellent overview and discussion of generational differences and their implications to management.

Knowledge-intensive firms create value by solving their clients' problems through the direct application of knowledge. Whereas knowledge plays a role in all firms, its role is distinctive in knowledge-intensive firms. Rather than being embodied in the process or product, knowledge resides in experts and its application is customized in real time based on clients' needs (Sheehan, 2005: 54).

HPA, but many companies prioritize these differently – not least because HCA is costly. Most try and design and implement work systems and processes that transform effort into specific, preordained outcomes.

Alvesson (2004: 137–139) argues that knowledge work and the growth of knowledge-intensive firms pose significant challenges to HRM practice and policy. He believes that most current HR practices are inappropriate for attracting and retaining knowledge workers and that the primary aim of HRM should be to enhance the appeal of the organization to talented staff. That is, the key to organizational excellence is to attract excellent employees, to retain them, and to develop and draw upon their talent. Indeed, research supports Alvesson's idea, showing that an emphasis on human capital advantage allows organizations to be more innovative (Camelo-Ordaz et al., 2011).

WHAT DO YOU MEAN?

Two types of advantage, according to Alvesson

Human capital advantage (HCA) – HCA refers to the employment of talent and the advantage that the organization derives from that talent. For this reason high levels of effort and expenditure should go into the recruitment, selection, and retention of exceptional and talented staff. The knowledge, skills, and qualities of these talented people lead to desirable organizational outcomes.

Human process advantage (HPA) – HPA refers to highly evolved processes that are difficult to imitate, such as systems of cross-departmental cooperation, executive development, and so on. The aim of HPA is to set up the preconditions for organizational functioning and synergy between people and processes. This can include job design, policies, and so on. The emphasis is on process delivering outcomes rather than specific knowledge of employees delivering outcomes.

Another transition in knowledge and skills can be seen in Figure 5.1, where it is represented by the symbol of the heart. The heart represents the growing emphasis on the ability of people to practice empathy and compassion at work, to exhibit high levels of emotional intelligence, communicate effectively, and work closely with other people (Cooney, 2011). In many ways, knowledge workers will also require an ability to relate from the heart. One of the leaders in this area was the late Professor Peter Frost. We have an excellent interview with Professor Frost on the Companion Website (www.sagepub.co.uk/managingandorganizations3), in which he discusses how matters of the heart are the essential skills and attributes required of leaders and employees for the future.

Often you will hear arguments that women will be better suited to such new 'emotional roles' at work because caring, empathy, and relationship-building are all feminine-type roles. How often have you heard people say women are better listeners and communicators than men? Often research supports such findings; for example, there has long been a strong correlation between gender and helping behaviours and altruism (Mesch et al., 2006; Piliavin and Unger, 1985), and overt claims about women's superior communication skills over men:

> there is some evidence that many women are exceptional global people for the following reasons. One, they tend to approach relationships and negotiations from a win-win strategy that results in success for both sides ... Two, women tend to be more formal, show more respect, and take care in establishing relationships than men. Three, women tend to be better listeners and more sympathetic than men. (Abbott and Moran, 2002: 78)

Such claims should be viewed with some skepticism because often there is a role expectation that women and men will behave in certain ways. Moreover, much of the research conducted on gender difference involves people rating men and women on different variables. The ratings attract a halo effect in that women are often rated as being more helpful and altruistic than men simply because they fulfil a specific gender role such as mother, wife, or girlfriend (see Hendrickson-Eagley, 1987). We are not saying that these attributes are not important in the workplace, or that being emotionally sensitive, an excellent communicator and listener, and so on, are not critical skills and knowledge to possess. They are, and employers will increasingly demand such knowledge, skills, and abilities as businesses emphasize relationships and collaboration more and more. Our point is that too much emphasis is placed on the idea that men and women are fundamentally different and naturally inclined towards one form of employment than another – rather people fill specific roles in life, and act and are perceived to act in accordance with these roles (Fletcher and Sydnor Clarke, 2003; Rees and Spreecher, 2009). It is not that they are really differences in sex, but rather socialized differences – and so it is no less important that men should be expected to develop and possess emotional skills and knowledge (see also the discussion of gender roles in Chapter 2, Managing Individuals).

INSTITUTIONAL SHAPING OF HRM

The picture we have painted so far is that HRM is a difficult and challenging endeavour, in which generational changes and the transition towards knowledge work have increasingly complicated its role. However, in many ways these changes are what give life to the growth and interest in HRM as a domain of research and practice. One more area that we will now discuss has far-reaching and significant implications for the practices and policies enacted by HR managers. Through public policy, government shapes society, and therefore the workforce, in a wide range of areas. Here we consider only three: diversity and equal opportunity, occupational safety and health, and industrial relations law. We begin with diversity and equal opportunity. The demographic transformations that we described earlier in this chapter directly and indirectly implicate organization policy on issues of workplace safety, and gender, equity, and diversity. Let us take a look at gender, equity, and diversity first.

IMAGE 5.2   Diversity – as DJ Mitch sees it (you can find DJ Mitch's page at www.veneziablog.com/deepindub/diversity)

Equity and diversity

One of the most important and politically charged aspects of HRM practice is dealing with issues of gender, equity, and diversity. Let us start with **diversity**.

In an organizational context, **diversity** can most simply be defined as variety in geography, culture, gender, spirituality, language, disability, sexuality, and age.

The most common form of diversity is cultural diversity, and given that organizations are more or less comprised of members of society, one would expect that they would reflect the diversity in that society – or so the theory goes. Most industrialized countries in the world have relied heavily upon immigration in order to grow prosperous. Some new countries, established on the traditional lands of an indigenous population, such as the USA, Canada, and Australia, are almost entirely comprised of migrants.

The sources of the migrant population have transformed with time, which has provided such countries with a culturally diverse society.

The most significant wave of new migrants occurred immediately after the desolation of Europe in the Second World War. Many of the Jewish people who survived the horrors of Hitler's Nazi regime fled Europe for the USA, Australia, or to join the new state of Israel, on land previously controlled by the British as protectors of the Palestine Mandate and settled by several different peoples, predominantly Palestinian. Post-war Europe saw Italians, Greeks, and Yugoslavians (as they were called then) also flee Europe for the relative wealth, safety, and opportunities available to them in relatively free and democratic countries such as the USA, Canada, Australia, and New Zealand. Later, war and despotic regimes in Vietnam and Cambodia respectively saw a large intake of South-East Asian refugees, and the war in Lebanon also saw a flow of Middle Eastern migration. Interspersed between them all came migration from Third World nations, and nations experiencing civil unrest, such as China, India, Pakistan, the West Indies, Sudan, as well as South Africa and Zimbabwe (for excellent accounts of international migration see Castles and Miller, 2003; Jupp, 2002; Kupiszewski and Kupiszewska, 2011).

Diversity is not restricted to cultural diversity. Take a moment to study Table 5.3. Clearly diversity poses great challenges for HRM. On the one hand, it is a complex, emotionally charged, and legally and socially explosive area of organizational behaviour. On the other hand, it can be a source of growth, competitive advantage, and creativity. Indeed, if there is one thing that organizations cannot afford to get wrong it is their approach to HR processes and practices concerning diversity.

TABLE 5.3   The key diversity categories: their descriptors and HR implications

Category	Descriptors	HRM practice implications
Geography	Affinity to or identification with a particular geographic location, which may include, but is not limited to, the following: country, region, state, county, vicinity, rural, urban, suburban	• Some organizations offer travel allowances and other reimbursements • Some organizations, either voluntarily or by law, must employ people from specific geographic locations – sometimes this is done via negotiation in order to operate on private or public land. (For example, diamond mining giant Argyle Diamonds actively employed and trained indigenous residents from Western Australia)
Culture	Cultural diversity refers to an individual's affinity, or identification with, a particular cultural dimension – such as race, ethnicity, nationality, colour, and so on	• Organizations must have policies on cultural diversity such as anti-discrimination policies and conflict resolution and complaints handling, equal employment opportunity. Some organizations are required by law to enact positive discrimination and affirmative action
Gender	Gender diversity is usually limited to male or female gender	• In theory there must be equal employment opportunities for both males and females. Organizations are not allowed to discriminate on gender grounds • Some organizations include maternity leave, and the expectation is that the organization will not discriminate against employment and promotion of women based on the fact that they have children – remember we did say, in theory • Many organizations also have sexual harassment training and clear policies on sexual harassment

(Continued)

TABLE 5.3 *(Continued)*

Category	Descriptors	HRM practice implications
Spirituality	This refers to religious and or spiritual affiliations which include Christian, Muslim, Jewish, agnostic, atheist, denominational, and non-denominational	• Most larger organizations must not discriminate, nor allow their staff to discriminate or exclude people based on spiritual beliefs
Language	This refers to an individual's linguistic identity, which can be monolingual (speaks only one language), bilingual or multilingual (speaks two or more languages)	• Some organizations with a high number of immigrant staff have a policy of translating HR material, signs, and so on into the dominant non-English language • In fact some organizations actively seek out bilingual and multilingual people due to increasing globalization and cultural diversity in society
Disability	Disability identity refers to an individual's identification with some type of visible and/or invisible impairment, which can include physical, mental, visual, and hearing	• An organization, except where certain abilities are absolutely necessary to perform the task, such as eyesight for an airline pilot, should not discriminate against people with a disability • Where a person acquires a disability while in employment, some organizations actively seek out alternative roles and tasks for the individual (e.g. as the police do when they place an officer on 'light' or 'desk' duties after the officer has been injured)
Sexuality	This refers to sexual orientation which includes heterosexual, homosexual, lesbian, bisexual, transsexual (sex change), and transvestism	• As with gender, it is often unlawful to discriminate against people based on their sexuality; however, this protection is limited, as policies and laws vary from state to state and country to country
Age	This refers to a person's identification with a particular age category, generation, and so on, such as twenty-something, thirty-something, baby boomers, Generation X, Y, etc	• In many countries, in theory, employers cannot discriminate based on age

Source: Adapted and extended from Hopkins (1997: 5)

In Western Democracies there is an assumption that notions such as equity and diversity are highly valued. Aristotle, the Ancient Greek philosopher, defined democracy as 'rule by the people, for the people', and over time democracy became about the pursuit of religious freedom, separation of powers between church and state, basic human and civil rights. Of course that is in a perfect world; in reality there are a number of challenges facing democracy as a form of government. From this perspective some human resource policies are designed to reinforce the ideas we take for granted about living in a democracy. While our discussions here are almost exclusively

TABLE 5.4   Average yearly earnings, by industry and gender ($US in 2005)

Position/industry	Female	Male
Accountants	85,375	119,314
Accountants (1–5 years' experience)	72,534	94,314
Advertising account executive	49,000	56,000
Allergists or immunologists	190,983	254,289
CEO, health care	152,673	195,783
Lawyer	73,476	84,188
Government/lobbying, non-profit	73,907	96,655
Managing editor	55,983	62,574
Neurological surgeons	337,031	487,000
Reference librarian (0–5 years' experience)	38,399	39,958
Retail store sales	19,864	31,148
Teachers	42,848	46,956
Web infrastructure	69,850	87,750
Average full-time employee	97,071	127,379

Source: Susan Van Dorsten, NAFE Magazine and the National Association for Female Executives (2004, Fourth Quarter)

about equity in industrialized democracies, we fully acknowledge that there are other forms of government that have very little interest in freedom, equality, and human rights. We also recognize that the global flows of monetary policy and commodity prices have a profound effect on equality around the world. What is clear, however, is that if you live in an egalitarian regime (such as a democracy), there are lower levels of inequality than in other regimes (Galbraith, 2011). Indeed, inequality can be thought of as counter to democracy, and so organizations can play a critical role in promoting equality; that is the theory, but the reality is quite different.

Gender inequity is a highly emotive issue typified by a variety of arguments and perspectives. Consider pay inequity between the genders – Table 5.4 lists the pay rates for males and females in a number of professions. In the five years since these statistics the USA has yet to see any real changes in terms of equal pay for women (*New York Times*, 13 July 2010), and even as recent as 2012, the gender inequity gap in pay seems to still not have been addressed. The story is the same for most other countries, especially for Australia and the UK, where women are paid less than 85 per cent of what males earn for the same job, qualifications, and experience (*The Sydney Morning Herald*, 2 March 2010; *The Guardian*, 7 September 2009; see also http://www.eoc.org.uk and http://www.equalityhumanrights.com). Even in Germany and Sweden women face an array of stereotypes that reinforce pay inequity (Lilja and Luddeckens, 2006).

Such inequity continues today and while several initiatives are being implemented to counter inequity, it is clear that change is extremely slow.

Check out the Companion Website www.sagepub.co.uk/ managingandorganizations3 for free access to an article by E. C. A. Kaarsemaker and E. Poutsma (2006) about how HR managers can implement and reinforce a true Theory Y philosophy in HRM.

Often people may rationalize pay inequity as being the result of women's choices, such as choosing not to advance their careers or to work full time because of family commitments, or that, because women bear children, their employment is a financial risk which should be accounted for in wage levels (Lilja and Luddeckens, 2006). A related defence of the gender pay gap is that people in positions of power tend to be men, and so bonuses and pay are based on the individual's effect on organizational performance: if women are not in positions where they are measured on performance they will not receive bonuses, and hence will have a lower income (Roth, 2006). While publicly many people and organizations deplore such inequity, the reality is that the inequity continues to exist. Of course, migrant women are doubly disadvantaged when it comes to pay because migrant workers who do not speak the language of the country they have migrated to are paid significantly less than other workers – irrespective of gender (Boyd and Pikkov, 2005; Kung and Wang, 2006).

When considering the diversity categories, descriptions, and HR implications we presented earlier, we need to attend to one very important fact. The nature of HR policy on diversity cannot be separated from government policy and ideology. For example, if a government favours 'cultural integration' and assimilation, it expects that migrants will forgo their cultural past and integrate fully within the dominant culture. If a government values multicultural diversity then it will ensure diversity is preserved. Some countries, such as Canada (see the case study at the end of this chapter), take the 'perfect neutrality' approach, in which the aim is to ensure that all forms of diversity are fully protected and all discrimination is eradicated. Most governments, however, will ebb and flow between cultural diversity and cultural assimilation – depending on the mood of the constituents, on the country, the prospect of an election (if one is allowed) and, ironically, the spiritual disposition of those in charge (such as Christian fundamentalists, Islamists, or Zionists) with their specific views on homosexuality, gender roles, and disability.

Fortunately many developed-nation governments in the OECD appear to value almost all the categories of diversity we covered earlier. However, there are many more governments around the world that have scant regard for human rights of all kinds. Many governments, especially those in the industrialized world, have a range of laws, acts, and regulations upholding and reinforcing the principles of equity and diversity and equal employment opportunities. Moreover, global organizations such as Amnesty International, United Nations Human Rights Council, and GlobalVision also oversee the policies and practices of governments and organizations in terms of issues of equity and diversity. In the web section of this chapter you will find some outstanding government links to equity and diversity in the USA, UK, Sweden, Australia, and other countries.

In the workplace context, equity means that people will be treated fairly. As a general rule, governments that value equity and diversity all have certain elements in common; these include protection against discrimination based on gender, sexuality, culture, language, religion, disability, and age in the workplace. These include, but are not limited to, protecting people from:

- Being denied an interview or employment based upon any one or more of the above.

- Being denied promotion or advancement due to one or all of the above.

- Experiencing persecution, ridicule, and harassment based on one or all of the above.

MINI CASE

Wal-Mart up against the wall – taking diversity seriously?

Almost every few days in early 2007 a new magazine article or news story emerged concerning the HRM practices of the massive US-based company Wal-Mart. As an example, read this article, edited from the New York Times online (www. nytimes.com).

COURT APPROVES CLASS-ACTION SUIT AGAINST WAL-MART
By Steven Greenhouse
Published: New York Times Online – 7 February 2007

Wal-Mart's efforts to block the nation's largest sex discrimination lawsuit suffered a big setback yesterday when a federal appeals court in San Francisco ruled that the case should proceed as a class action. Legal specialists said the ruling would increase pressure on Wal-Mart Stores to settle the case, in which the retailer is accused of discrimination in pay and promotions. Wal-Mart executives said they would appeal, voicing confidence that the decision would be overturned.

The court ruled yesterday that the lawsuit should proceed as a class action – the largest such civil rights case in history – because it raised common questions of law and fact, because the six named plaintiffs were typical of the class and because there were so many women that it was impractical to handle the matter in individual cases.

The majority wrote, 'Plaintiffs' expert opinions, factual evidence, statistical evidence, and anecdotal evidence present significant proof of a corporate policy of discrimination and support plaintiffs' contention that female employees nationwide were subject to a common pattern and practice of discrimination.'

Wal-Mart's lead lawyer, Theodore J. Boutrous Jr., said that yesterday's decision was not based on the merits of the case. 'Wal-Mart has a strong antidiscrimination policy,' he said. Arguing that the ruling contained factual and legal errors, Mr. Boutrous said Wal-Mart would ask the three-judge panel to reconsider the case and would also ask a full panel of 15 Ninth Circuit judges to consider it. Mr. Boutrous asserted that yesterday's decision conflicts with Supreme Court rulings and other Circuit Court rulings.

A lawyer for the plaintiffs, Joseph Sellers, hailed yesterday's decision. 'This ruling confirms that no company, no matter how big, is exempt from the civil rights law, no matter what Wal-Mart claimed,' he said. Brad Seligman, the plaintiffs' lead lawyer, estimated that the class – which includes all women who have worked at Wal-Mart at any time since Dec. 21, 1998 – encompasses more than two million. 'Simple math, given the size of the class and the types of disparities we've shown, indicate that the losses to women are in the billions,' Mr. Seligman said.

He said the ruling showed that 'it is time for Wal-Mart to face the music.

- Knowing what you now know about HR and equity, what HRM policies and procedures might have avoided such outcomes for Wal-Mart?
- What advice would you give Wal-Mart in relation to HRM practices for the future?

Affirmative action attempts to address long-standing and institutionalized discrimination against people of diverse backgrounds – such as gender, race, etc. – by discriminating in favour of people perceived as belonging to categories that are disadvantaged.

One of the most controversial HR policies enacted by governments is **affirmative action**. Affirmative action (or positive discrimination) originated in the US, specifically in the Thirteenth, Fourteenth and Fifteenth Amendments and in the 1966 Civil Rights Act. The main aim was to address the damage done as a result of slavery and racism against African-Americans, and by gender stereotypes to women. Today affirmative action applies to all categories of diversity in order to reinforce the American ideals of fairness (Crosby et al., 2003). In Australia affirmative action was applied especially to reverse the bias against indigenous people, as well as women, and is enacted in a number of laws and acts. Many of these are administered by the Affirmative Action Agency and include the Affirmative Action (Equal Employment Opportunity for Women) Act, 1986. While Australia and New Zealand were the first countries to allow women to vote, indigenous people in Australia, similarly to African-Americans, had very few rights until the 1960s.

Many people, for no other reason than race, gender, colour, ethnicity and so on, were, and continue to be, excluded from many jobs in favour of white males (in the West that is; there is similar discrimination against white people in some Asian and African nations). The main application of affirmative action is aimed at influencing organizations to review employment policies for discriminatory practices. The next most commonly reported policies relate to companies' efforts to assist employees to balance the competing roles of work and family. Very few affirmative action policies seek to challenge traditional patterns of employment, and policies that seek to 'fix' people into certain positions are even less commonly reported by organizations (Sheridan, 1998).

According to the National Organization for Women (http://tinyurl.com/svqc7), affirmative action is often opposed because it is seen to promote reverse discrimination, in that, if a white person or a man and a black person or a woman apply for a job, the black person or woman must get it. Such an understanding, which is quite prevalent, is somewhat of a myth because both the black person and woman must possess the relevant skills and qualification. Despite negative perceptions in some parts of society, research has found that affirmative action is generally positive and is predominantly based on merit (Crosby et al., 2003). Moreover, when explained in a way that connects with people's values of fairness, equality, and opportunity, positive discrimination policies tend to be supported by the broader public (Does et al., 2011).

Overall, equity and diversity are important, we believe, and the principles espoused by proponents of equity and diversity are the cornerstone of a free, open, progressive, and democratic society, the practical test of which is how any society treats not only its own citizens but also those who seek citizenship. Whether you become an executive officer, a supervisor, or an HR manager, these things should feature in any and all aspects of your organization's HRM decisions, practices, and processes.

Check out the Companion Website www.sagepub.co.uk/managingandorganizations3 for free access to an article by Barry Goldman and his colleagues (2006), which considers perceptions towards discrimination in the workplace, as well as their legal and social ramifications.

Occupational safety and health

Death and injury have a variety of causes, including chemicals, gases, equipment failure, risks associated with the nature of the work (mining,

IMAGE 5.3   Danger at work

police and fire officers, soldiers, etc.), employee or employer negligence, incompetence or mental illness, violence (by colleagues or customers), and ergonomic design flaws (Collins and Schneid, 2001; Tehrani and Haworth, 2004). These are issues of **occupational health and safety (OHS)**. As with equity and diversity, OHS is also legislated. Its simplest expression is found in the many safety notices that abound in the workplace.

Violation of OHS legislation has two extremely negative impacts: first, it results in death or injury; and second, it can result in criminal proceedings, fines, and even imprisonment for management, including the HR manager. In the event of a death or injury, management can be personally liable if it can be shown not to have implemented and understood relevant health and safety legislation in the workplace – irrespective of whether the business is large, medium, or small. The HR manager, along with management in general, must design and implement OHS management systems, processes, and training in accordance with OHS legislation.

All OHS acts and legislations are framed around the following:

> Preventing death and injury at work.

> Dealing with events that can or have caused death or injury.

> Dealing with compensation paid to the family or next of kin of the deceased, or paid to the injured person(s).

> Dealing with the occupational rehabilitation of the injured person(s).

Any management system must adequately account for each of the areas listed.

OHS laws, acts, and legislation are complex, and can be confusing. Fortunately governments provide excellent resources and training that HR

Occupational health and safety (OHS) refers to legislation, policies, acts, practices, and processes that are aimed at protecting all workers from injury and death in the workplace.

managers can use to help design, implement, and enforce their OHS management systems. (See e.g. Australia: The Australian Safety and Compensation Council, http://www.ascc.gov.au/ascc/; UK: The Health and Safety Commission, http://www.hse.gov.uk/aboutus/index.htm; USA: Department of Labour: OHS Administration, http://www. osha.gov/)

HRM IN PRACTICE: THE CORE FUNCTIONS

The core HRM functions have, without a doubt, the potential to influence significantly the performance and outcomes of organizations (Becker and Gerhart, 1996). We have reviewed a number of texts with chapters on HRM and some seem to favour an emphasis on quantity of content over quality. We do not expect you to become a professional HR manager after doing an OB course – especially given that most OB courses either do not cover HRM or, if they do, usually cover it in one or, if you are lucky, two lectures. Thus, rather than present you with a detailed step-by-step manual of the core HR functions, we prefer to provide you with an overview of each of these functions with some practical examples and illustrations. In this way we provide you with an easy to read and understand introduction to the core HR functions. Understanding these functions, as a manager, is very important because it provides you with knowledge that will complement the people and organizational management skills and knowledge that you are acquiring as you study. So, it is time to look at the recruitment, selection, retention, and development of people in organizations.

Recruiting people

As we discussed earlier in this chapter, demographic changes associated with migration and generational changes have critical implications for the ability of employers to attract talented, qualified staff to their organizations. To complicate matters further, the demand for talented and qualified staff has gone global. No longer are organizations competing against only their local competitors for staff, they are competing against large international corporations and international governments offering the promise of higher standards of living, higher wages, career prospects, and so on. As jobs are going global, so too is recruitment. In addition, sustained global economic growth has created staff shortages in several countries' sectors. This applies in the case of white-collar knowledge workers and blue-collar (trades) workers, which includes plumbers, electricians, chefs, firefighters, and police officers. Furthermore, as with the selection stage, one should pay particular attention to relevant equity and diversity acts, laws, and legislation when recruiting. As such, one of the critical aspects of effective HRM is the ability to design appropriate recruitment methodologies.

Recruitment refers to the processes and practices used to attract suitable employees to the organization.

Recruitment involves searching for and obtaining potential job candidates in sufficient numbers and quality so that the organization can select the

IMAGE 5.4   We want you as a new recruit!

most appropriate people to fill its job needs (Shen and Edwards, 2004: 816). The process of recruitment requires that the organization and the HR manager know what they are looking for in terms of skills, knowledge, and capabilities and that these things match what is required for the job. Importantly, effective recruitment should be targeted appropriately. As a case in point, when Tyrone was an executive chef in Sydney he advertised for a pastry-chef on an international website. Two weeks later he received approximately twenty résumés; by the end of the week he had 198 applications, of which only 1 per cent were from Sydney, Australia, and two came from Iraq. Knowing what you need and targeting your recruitment appropriately is critical.

The Uncle Sam poster is one of the most recognizable images, if not all over the world, then definitely in the English-speaking world. Indeed, every nation has its version of Uncle Sam, such as the old COO-EE! posters used in Australia and the 'Empire Needs Men' posters from the UK for the First World War. These posters were integral to the recruitment of men into the army at a time when many young people were being killed in the war, and many more were needed to wage a 'total' war, thus recruitment was crucial.

Today HR managers and departments have a variety of tried and trusted recruitment strategies at their disposal. These include job ads in local, city, suburban, national, and even international newspapers, recruitment and employment agencies, government employment agencies, the Internet and e-recruitment websites, internal communications, specialized industry publications and associations, through to networks, word of mouth, and even via serendipity (that is, by good fortune). In the recruitment stage the applicant is provided with a realistic job preview (RJP). This specifies critical essential and desirable job criteria. The unique aspect of the RJP is that the employer lists both positive and negative aspects of the job. More recently innovative multimedia approaches are used such as video or YouTube presentations to provide a realistic sense of what working in the target job would be like. Incumbents present both the positives and negatives about the job; and the applicant is provided with firsthand experience of the ins and outs of the working environment(s). The RJP provides the applicant with detailed glimpses into the job and so it is likely that being transparent about the virtues and less virtuous aspects of the job ensures that the successful applicant knows what to expect (Adler, 2011). In other words, the RJP creates a stronger psychological contract between the new employer and employee because it is based on reality rather than on false information (Adler, 2011; Guest, 2004; Robinson et al., 1994). Realistic job previews have been shown to correlate with low staff turnover, and to increase productivity compared with other methods of recruitment (Phillips, 1998; Weiss and Rupp, 2011).

Selecting people

Selection refers to the tools, methods, and criteria upon which people will be, and are, selected for a given position, and includes job applications, interviews, tests, and measurement. Selection is related to the recruitment stage of the HRM function.

In reality **selection** and recruitment are not entirely distinct functions. Both require high levels of synthesis between: (a) the nature of the job(s) being filled; (b) the skills, qualifications, capabilities, and attributes required of the prospective employee(s); and (c) the skills, qualifications, capabilities, and attributes of the people available in the job market. Where recruitment concentrates on attracting the right person for the job, selection concentrates on choosing the right person based upon a range of selection techniques and methodologies.

In order to aid selection the HR manager will ensure that a clear job–duty statement has been written. Typically, job–duty statements should include a list of essential criteria and desirable criteria required or expected of the applicant. The essential criteria are those aspects of the job – the knowledge, skills, expertise, abilities, and capabilities – critical to the job's performance. The desirable criteria are those extra aspects that, while not critical, are looked upon favourably by potential employers.

WHAT'S THE POINT?

An example of a job–duty statement with key selection criteria

KEY SELECTION CRITERIA – ACADEMIC STAFF
UTS: HUMAN RESOURCES
Senior Lecturer in Organizational Behaviour

Skills and attributes

- Ability to work in a team.
- Good oral and written communication skills.
- An enthusiasm for research and teaching.
- Good rapport with students, staff, and the members of the community.

- Flexibility as regards patterns and location of teaching (days, evenings, block release at either or both campuses or in off-campus settings).
- Capacity to develop industry links and obtain research funding.

Knowledge

- Demonstrated knowledge of management and organizational behaviour theory and practice.
- Practical knowledge of management and the principles of organizational behaviour.

(Continued)

(Continued)

- An understanding of and ability to apply the principles and practices of effective teaching.
- An understanding of and ability to apply equal opportunity in the workplace.

Qualifications

- Doctoral degree in management or related discipline.

Experience required

- Teaching experience with evidence of good teaching performance.

- Evidence (such as research papers) of a capacity to undertake high-quality research that will lead to journal publications in the field of management and organizational behaviour.
- Demonstrated capacity to contribute collaboratively to at least one of the research strengths of the School of Management.
- Experience in teaching in the area of leadership and/or management consulting is desirable.
- Well-established research and publication record in the field of management/organizational behaviour including evidence of publications in high-quality refereed international journals.

The job–duty statement in the What's The Point? box above is the actual one that Tyrone responded to when he applied for a job as a Senior Lecturer in Organizational Behaviour at the University of Technology, Sydney, in 2007. The Head of the School of Management, along with a committee, determined that the school required more staff in OB; however, the changing nature of the academic environment also required a potential staff member with an ability not only to teach, but also to conduct and publish research in OB and management, to attract research funding and have industry links, among other things. The HR department then advertised the position and handled the applications, and sent the applications to the Head of the School and her committee of internal and external interview panel members.

With well-designed job–duty statements, applicants are able to ascertain whether they would be appropriate for the position. They then have to demonstrate that they are the ideal candidate by writing a job application in which they address each and every criterion specifically and with practical examples – in this example, not just by saying 'I do lots of research, and I enjoy it so I am a really good researcher'. Rather the applicant would write something like:

> As demonstrated by my publications in journals such as *Organization Science*, *Organization Studies*, my best research paper awards at the Academy of Management, as well as my papers under current or second review in journals such as *Academy of Management Review*, *Human Relations*, and *Journal of Organizational Behavior*, I am able to publish research in reputable journals of significant impact. My first publication in *Organization Science* investigates … blah blah blah.

Indeed, applicants must address each and every essential and desirable criterion in detail in order to demonstrate that they clearly meet the criteria. Obviously Tyrone was able to do this because he got the job at UTS.

The essential and desirable criteria are designed for a specific reason. It helps the potential employer to develop a set of measures, or weights, in order to rate and rank a potential employee. The better the applicant is able to articulate how they meet those criteria, the more 'ticks' they get. For jobs where several candidates apply with similar qualifications, experience, and performance outcomes, the task of selection becomes more difficult. A number of selection tools and techniques are available that aid the process of selecting appropriate candidates. These tools include:

- *The job application*: Unless the job applicant is applying from within the organization, the job application is usually the very first contact a prospective employee will have with their potential employers. The good job application usually includes: (a) a letter covering the applicant's key strengths and highlighting achievements; and (b) a curriculum vitae addressing the essential and desirable criteria, and including relevant biographical data such as educational and work history, membership of professional associations, as well as extracurricular activities such as volunteering, sports, and so on. Of course, there is the possibility that people will exaggerate their successes in résumés. As a result, security and information checks are now becoming a big business, which adds to the cost of the selection process.

- *The job interview*: Successful applicants usually receive a telephone call, a letter, or e-mail stating that they have been shortlisted for the position, and are invited to attend an interview. Some organizations also let applicants know if they were unsuccessful, but some do not. The job interview is almost always formal, with prepared questions, and usually includes an interview panel. The questions will always centre on the core aspects of the job. For example, assume we own a marketing company and we are interviewing two people for the position of marketing manager. After reviewing our essential criteria, we developed a range of questions aiming to highlight the applicant's knowledge, experience, and abilities in both marketing and managing projects. Let us say a critical criterion of success in marketing management is the ability to meet tight deadlines. We would ask these people for concrete examples about how they meet deadlines under pressure, and how they prioritize deadlines. Now let us say the first person answered, 'Well, I was at university and I always handed in my assignments pretty much on time', and the second person said, 'Well, last year I was handed two major accounts by my boss, both were scheduled for completion on the same week. So I met with both clients over lunch and we discussed their expected outcomes. I used reverse planning and carefully implemented a number of contingency plans along the way.' Who would you employ? (Hint – it is not the first person!)

- *Tests and measurement*: Increasingly, organizations are using more advanced and some would say invasive tests. Most of us will be expected to do one test or another at some stage in our professional careers. Tests include personality tests such as the Big Five Personality

Factors (see Chapter 2), intelligence tests, tests of general aptitude and cognitive abilities, psychometric tests, even mental health tests. In some organizations, mainly in the US, people undergo bio-feedback, lie-detection tests, even DNA and drug tests, and today a number of knowledge-intensive companies (i.e. consultancies) have emerged that conduct a whole range of selection methods (see http://www.employee select.com/).

Research suggests that the use of such selection tools is a good predictor of performance of staff (Borman et al., 1997), especially so when multiple selection tools – what is now increasingly called multiple hurdles – are used appropriately (Mendoza et al., 2004). Moreover, both qualitative and quantitative techniques are useful in selecting staff, as long as the tools are well designed and appropriately used (Ehigie and Ehigie, 2005). Some organizations now use a range of innovative selection techniques such as 'role plays' and other simulation exercises to select. One extreme example is the approach used in the popular television show *The Apprentice*, where Donald Trump or Lord Alan Sugar place a number of young 'talented' people through a series of gruelling situations until they are left with the successful candidate.

Now we cannot leave this topic without raising some serious questions about selection tools. The first concerns equity and diversity. Organizations have been successfully sued because their selection techniques were judged to be discriminatory against certain people (Holly, 2003; Landy, 2005). For example, intelligence tests have been shown to have a cultural bias, and there are also issues of English-language skills, education levels, and so on. If a person can show they were discriminated against because of the selection tools used, this can be very expensive for the company (Gardiner and Armstrong-Wright, 2000; Landy, 2005). Second, measurement and testing explicitly involve the total subjugation of the individual to strangers – sensitive and powerful information is collected on people, and this is before they are even members of the organization. In this sense there are some serious ethical questions that need to be asked about how personal information is used, shared, stored, and destroyed. While the topic is becoming of increasing interest, there is still a dearth of research and literature, which should be a general concern to all people (Gardiner and Armstrong-Wright, 2000; Gilliland, 1993; Landy, 2005; Ryan and Ployhart, 2000).

Retaining and developing people

If the right people have been appointed by the HRM process, then it is crucial that they should be **retained** and allowed opportunities for **staff development**.

This final HRM function addresses the processes and practices of retaining and developing an organization's best assets – its people. In most industrialized countries it is now generally well recognized that employers can no longer offer job security and so a range of retention and development methods will prove the key not only to retaining and developing talent, but also

Retained retention refers to the practices and process used to retain staff, and often includes **staff development**, which refers to the processes, procedures, and policies designed and implemented to enhance and update the skills, knowledge, and capabilities of staff in relation to their career and their job.

to attracting talent to the organization (Lawler, 2005). Indeed, staff will actively seek out and participate in training and development when jobs are challenging and the organization values career progression (Tharenou, 1997).

There are two interrelated aspects to retention and development: retention consists of the methods and approaches used to keep talented people in the organization in some way – such as awards, promotions, and remuneration; development concerns the methods and approaches used to enhance, transform, and better utilize staff knowledge, skills, and capabilities – such as training, mentoring, and education.

In an organizational context, developing people most often means providing them with training and education that assists them in entering and finding their way around the organization and familiarizing them with the job (*orientation*); skills training that aids in learning and updating skills required for the technical aspects of a job, and management or leadership development programmes that help develop employees' managerial and leadership skills. Such forms of development can be via on-the-job training, which includes coaching, apprenticeship, and mentoring programmes; off-the-job training, which includes formal courses and programmes, delivered in-house or by independent training and education institutions, and also online; as well as other training and development methods such as role plays, scenarios, and so on.

WHAT DO YOU MEAN?

The question to ask is not what if I spend all this time and money training and developing a person and they leave? Rather it should be what if I don't spend any money on their training and development and they stay? (A quote from a change consultant)

Distinguished Professor Edward E. Lawler III argues that organizations should forget about loyalty contracts and instead move towards 'value propositions' that are tailored to the types of employees being sought and also promote continued development and improvement in order to sustain one's edge. Through the use of value propositions, Lawler believes organizations should strive towards virtuous spirals in their HRM practices and processes:

> Organizations need to offer a skills and performance-based substitute for the loyalty contract that motivates selective retention and high performance. It needs to stress that continued employment is based on performance and having the right skill set for the organization's business strategy. It also needs to stress that people are rewarded for performance and skill development. When this is translated into the right combination of reward

IMAGE 5.5   Relaxing at CBS

system practices, people will be motivated to excel and those who excel will be motivated to stay because they will be highly rewarded. This is the foundation of the virtuous spiral, in which both sides win and create success for each other. (2005: 14–15)

Lawler identifies some organizations that have promoted the virtuous spiral. These include Microsoft and Procter & Gamble in which large stock options are provided to employees, as well as generous professional and self-development programmes. Southwest Airlines has long been a preferred employer. Southwest was one of the only airline companies in the USA to thrive in the face of a downturn in air travel and chaos post 9/11, a time that saw major airlines file for bankruptcy – including United Airlines and American Airlines.

Many organizations realize the importance of play at work and space in which to relax. An example is CBS (Copenhagen Business School) as shown in Image 5.5. Another organization that takes the retention and development of staff seriously is Google. Google is renowned for attracting some of the brightest minds from all over the world from a range of professions such as computer programmers, designers, marketers, and even philosophers. It retains the best staff by offering them work that is challenging, fun, and also is in line with values of sustainability. Imagine working somewhere where you can take your pets, eat for free, play during work times, and even have a nap when you want, as Google's corporate website demonstrates.

Of course, one has to be extremely careful regarding the type of value propositions that companies such as Google try to create and reinforce through 'virtuous' spirals. By way of experiment, look at images of Google on their website, what kinds of people do you think they would attract? What sorts of people do you think it is looking for? In 2004 Google had an age discrimination suit filed against it, and the suit focused on the 'youthful' corporate culture branded by the organization and reinforced through its HR practices. A former Google executive claimed wrongful termination because he did not fit in with Google's youthful culture (Shah and Kleiner, 2005). Google won the case in 2006, but the man appealed and the case still continues today. Thus, those very things that are designed to attract and retain talent can sometimes result in litigation (Hurley-Hanson and Giannantonio, 2006). According to Lawler:

> organizations that link skill development with continued employment – and rewards with performance – handle change more effectively than others. In a sense, you might say that they create 'mobile' human capital; people who realize that they must continue to learn, develop, and perform in order to maintain their positions and careers. Today, organizations need mobile capital. Getting stuck with obsolete human capital is just as big a negative as getting stuck with outdated equipment and materials. (2005: 15)

Such claims are all well and good, but one should be extremely careful in referring to humans as obsolete capital – perhaps the former Google executive felt he was deemed obsolete capital because of his age? Fortunately Google, in many ways and with very few exceptions, is an exemplary organization with excellent working conditions, training and development programmes, and employee benefits and remuneration (Effron et al., 2003; Menefee et al., 2006).

Much of Lawler's arguments concerning HR were underpinned by the economics of Milton Friedman, in particular that an organization must ensure that making money is its first and most critical objective; employees should only be retained if they fit such a value proposition. More recently, however, Lawler and his colleagues have moved entirely away from the arguments that organizations should be driven by performance at the expense of sustainability and corporate social responsibility, and go as far as to argue that there needs to be a complete 'reset' in management thinking in relation to what constitutes performance (Lawler et al., 2011: Ch. 1). Of course, many of us in the Critical Management Studies and Positive Organizational Studies fields have been arguing this for years (so we thank Professor Lawler for his 'reset').

Inherent in arguments about training and retaining staff is the principle that the organization should only seek to retain staff that are deemed talented and worth the effort (no obsolete human capital allowed here!), and develop staff that will be willing to increase effort and performance. Of course, this begs the question of the measurement of performance. Performance measurement and evaluation is one of the most difficult things to do because there is no consensus on defining performance. Moreover, as many jobs move away from manufacturing or producing goods, in favour of knowledge work and service provision, it becomes increasingly difficult to conceptualize and operationalize performance, and much work still has to go into considerations of the validity and, especially, the ethicality of performance appraisal. To be sure, we are not saying that performance measurement and appraisal will not work: indeed, there is evidence to suggest it can (Smither et al., 2005). Rather, we are saying that how it works may not be a reliable measure and basis upon which to reward and retain staff (Atkin and Conlon, 1978). Table 5.5

TABLE 5.5   Common performance appraisals, their use and their limitations

Performance appraisal system	Its use	Its limitations
Performance appraisal interview	Very common. This is used as a formal session where the employee meets with their supervisor or manager to discuss the employee's work plans for the next reporting period and their performance over the previous reporting period. In this session they will agree upon certain performance outcomes on given tasks and duties, the employee's weaknesses and strengths, and desires and intentions for development and training, and will often include a question on perceptions about management and supervisors. An appraisal will be given in terms of whether the employee is progressing well or has certain limitations and weaknesses, as well as recommendations for development and growth	• Evaluations can be open to halo effects where evaluations are tainted by emphasis on one or two talented individuals rather than on the specific performance of the individual being appraised • Errors and bias can occur if the person evaluated is attractive, or a member of the in-group (friends) or out-group (foes) • Can be used as a political tool for pushing problem or difficult people out of the organizations rather than as a true appraisal of performance • Supervisor may not have sufficient knowledge and training to conduct interviews, nor possess sufficient knowledge about the employee's job and tasks
360° and 180° feedback	The least common approach. It involves a survey completed by the employee and a range of people, including peers, direct reports (180°), and subordinates (360°) and can also include customers and other stakeholders. The survey provides multiple ratings and multiple evaluations on the target person's performance at work. Often these measure ability to manage and deal with people, job knowledge, competence, strengths and weaknesses, and so on	• Can be biased towards overtly positive ratings or overtly negative ratings • Can sometimes cause conflict and resentment as, while 360° feedback is anonymous, the target often guesses or thinks they can guess who provided the ratings. Can sometimes even lead to a 'witch hunt' to identify the negative raters • Often 360° feedback surveys are generic, off the shelf, and not tailored specifically to the organization's needs • Raters might be inexperienced in rating people and using such surveys • Can be expensive and require data input, low-level statistics, and analysis

(Continued)

TABLE 5.5 *(Continued)*

Performance appraisal system	Its use	Its limitations
Behaviourally Anchored Rating Scale (BARS)	The BARS, like the GRS below, is a behavioural appraisal. The BARS involves a range of critical incidents centred on specific aspects of a job. The incidents are presented as behavioural statements concerning performance on each task. A person is rated in accordance with the behavioural statement that most closely describes that person's performance on each job-related task on a scale that provides options on opposite extremes. (E.g. 1 = details person, who checks over the most minute details... 9 = big picture person, with very little or no eye for details)	• Underplays or ignores cognitive aspects, especially of the rater, and there is no significant evidence that BARS is better or worse than any other rating system
Graphic Rating Scales (GRS)	The employee will be rated on a number of behavioural variables: these can include attendance, job knowledge, and customer service, quality of work, corporate citizenship behaviours, presentation and personal appearance, and so on. The person will be rated or ranked, and measured against a baseline score. Bonuses, promotions, and other benefits are usually tied to performance appraisal scores	• Evaluation criteria may become obsolete or redundant between the time performance targets were set and when they are evaluated • Similar issues to BARS and performance appraisal interview

Sources: Tziner et al. (2000); Nathan and Alexander (1985)

outlines some of the more common appraisal systems used, and some of their more common shortcomings.

Overall, we may say that, while there are many limitations to performance management, measurement, and appraisal, they do have a role in assisting HRM decisions. Indeed, we would be the first ones to say that there is nothing worse than staff effort and hard work going unrecognized and unappreciated by employers. However, many performance measurement systems are poorly designed and inappropriately used and applied. Error and bias in ratings have commonly been reported. There can be legal ramifications when performance measurement systems fail to accommodate diversity (Arvey and Murphy, 1998; Atkin and Conlon,

1978; Olson and Hulin, 1992; Spector, 1994; Watkins and Johnston, 2000), and the systems are often used more as a tool of managerial control and subjugation than as a system that benefits the employee in any real way.

THE INDUSTRIAL RELATIONS CLIMATE

The issues most commonly dealt with under the banner of **industrial relations (IR)** include: claims for improved working conditions (occupational safety and health, working hours, and so on); claims for better pay and reward systems; the nature of notification of redundancies, and discrimination or unfair dismissals and disagreement on promotion of employees. However, the definition we have provided in the margin may be a little too broad since not everything associated with the employer/employee relationship comes within the scope of IR. Most countries have an IR commission or government department that deals with a number of issues pertaining to employer/employee relationships and the IR climate.

> Industrial relations (IR) refer to the relationship between employers and employees.

Table 5.6 provides links to the relevant government departments and commissions that deal with IR issues. This list is not comprehensive, as individual jurisdictions – states, local councils, counties, and boroughs – might also have IR powers and responsibilities. We list the main federal and commonwealth bodies that include resources and material on IR laws, acts, and other relevant issues. We are certain that you will find these links will enable you to access some very interesting reading. (If you are not from one of the countries listed, we welcome an e-mail from you telling us where you are from, and a link to the equivalent government body that deals with IR in your country.)

TABLE 5.6   Government organizations that deal with IR (all sites last accessed 14 July 2011)

Country	Organization	Weblink
UK	Department of Trade and Industry	http://www.dti.gov.uk/employment/index.html
Australia	Department of Education, Employment and Workplace Relations	http://www.dewr.gov.au/
US	The Department of Labor	http://www.dol.gov/
New Zealand	The Department of Labour	http://www.dol.govt.nz/
Sweden	Ministry of Employment	http://www.sweden.gov.se/sb/d/8281

Note: Most of these countries also have independent IR commissions to handle IR matters and disputes between employees/unions and employers/employer associations

Our aim is not to deal with specific acts and pieces of legislation because IR legislation varies between countries. Rather, in this section we will deal with three broad but interrelated themes integral to the IR climate: unions, wage-setting and conditions, and OHS. Though these may vary across different national boundaries, there are certain issues that are shared irrespective of the nation where you reside.

Unions

Unions can be defined as an association of wage-earning employees mobilized and organized in order to represent their constituents' interests. These interests can often be counter to the interests of employers, but not always necessarily so.

Unions are closely associated with IR and employer/employee relations. They tend to be politically charged organizations and are often perceived, sometimes correctly, as being in direct opposition to the interests of employers and employer associations. However, many organizations achieve excellent performance results when they work with unions (Appelbaum and Hunter, 2005; Kochan et al., 2009; Reardon, 2006). Unions have had to transform their activities and the way they relate to organizations, governments, and non-unionized labour. The old hard-line adversarial approach that once typified unions has mellowed out. This has occurred mainly because of a decline in union membership around the industrialized world (Bronfenbrenner, 1998), but also because of aggressive government policies implemented by political parties such as the Republicans in the US, Conservatives in the UK, and the Liberal Party in Australia. (It should be noted, however, that the relationship between social democratic parties and trade unions has also changed in recent years, with policies of economic labour market deregulation also pursued by nominally social democratic parties). In the US union membership has declined from a peak of 35 per cent in 1954 to 12.9 per cent today (Reardon, 2006: 171). The decline is similar in Australia (Burchielli, 2006) and throughout the UK and much of Europe (European Industrial Relations Observatory On-line, 2004).

The issues on which unions represent their members include wage negotiations, conditions of employment, penalty rates, and working hours, as well as OHS pension, and superannuation. Unions also assist members in a range of other employment-related areas such as unfair dismissal and advice on corporate HR practices and policies. Today many smaller unions have amalgamated or been consumed by large unions and are represented by mega trade union organizations such as the AFL-CIO in the US, ACTU in Australia, and UNISON in the UK. Because unions were traditionally associated with programmes such as that outlined in Marx and Engel's *Communist Manifesto*, organized labour has always been treated with suspicion, if not contempt, by many businesspeople and conservative governments. In view of the decline in union numbers around the world, it may be that the general population also finds unions irrelevant and overconfrontational in orientation. However, the unions' decline has coincided with a remarkably long boom in these economies. Unfortunately, most people do not realize what the unions have achieved in their long, and often acrimonious, opposition to business owners. Wins have included overtime pay and reduced working hours (Trejo, 1993), paid holiday leave (Green, 1997), paid maternity and paternity leave (Baird, 2004). In the US, unions have influenced policies that have transformed societies – for example, the Public Accommodation Act of 1964, the Voting Rights Act of 1965, equal employment opportunity legislation, anti-poverty legislation, and the Occupational Safety and Health Act of 1971 (Freedom and Medoff, 1984).

Despite the decline in union membership, some organizations have found that cooperating with unions can actually improve performance and commitment of employees to the organization's cause. This may apply even when open book management is used (see e.g. Clegg et al., 2002). 'Open book management' means that the finances of the organization are transparent to all stakeholders, including the union. This is not a new approach: Brazilian millionaire businessman, Ricardo Semler, between 1980 and 1990 turned his organization around with soft HR approaches (he was a Harvard MBA graduate); at Semler's business the unions were actively involved in the running of the business, and open book management was also used (Semler, 1993). Evidently finding ways to work with unions can actually benefit the organization.

Semler's idea to involve unions in a proactive way in his business has gained considerable attention over the last few years, but the idea is quite old. It dates from the Scanlon Plan of the 1940s (also known as Gainsharing). Joseph Scanlon was a former steelworker and union leader, and later Massachusetts Institute of Technology graduate, who believed union/employer cooperation was the key to growth and prosperity for society. A large body of work has supported the Scanlon Plan and its overall beneficial environment of cooperation between key stakeholders (Collins, 1998; Hatcher and Ross, 1991; Schuster, 1983; 1984). Joseph Scanlon became increasingly interested in how unions, employees, and employers could participate for win–win outcomes. He advocated that the best way to do this was to involve unions and employees in key decision-making. It should not be forgotten that at the time that Scanlon was doing this, the dominant management model was the Theory X orientation to employee/employer relations.

More recently, the literature and research on participatory approaches to OB have downplayed the role of unions. However, those true to the original Scanlon Plan ensure that unions are incorporated. Indeed, such approaches might provide an excellent way for unions to regain some lost ground. However, many critical management scholars who subscribe to the neo-Marxist models of management/employee relations in terms of labour process analysis would argue that even participatory management should be viewed with great skepticism. They argue that words such as 'empowerment', 'gainsharing', and 'participatory management' are nothing more than new managerial words of control and subjugation (Hancock and Tyler, 2001; Howcroft and Wilson, 2003; Voronov and Coleman,

TABLE 5.7   Types of negotiated contract; their strengths and weaknesses

	Individual agreement	Collective agreement
Details	Contract of employment, wages, and conditions that are negotiated between the employee directly with the employer	Contract of employment, wages, and conditions that are negotiated collectively. Usually between union and industry or company representatives
Strengths	1 The individual agreement is believed to provide employees with greater power to negotiate for higher wages and other conditions. Employees are given flexibility in sacrificing unused benefits in favour of more desirable ones (e.g. sacrifice holiday or sick pay for pay rises). An employee can choose to use a bargaining agent to represent them; the agent can be a family member, a union representative, and so on 2 Employers are less bound to cumbersome legalities around termination based on poor performance and other work-related discipline matters. Employer's risk is reduced because they are able to deal with employees on a case-by-case basis, allowing the employer to downsize or lay off staff (temporarily or permanently), during economic downturns or for other financial matters	1 The individual can rely upon the knowledge, skills, and expertise of union delegates to negotiate wage levels and conditions. The employee knows the conditions and wages are fair because they usually are applied across the industry 2 Employer is able to deal with issues at a broader collective level; because agreements are collective, wages and conditions will be standard across the board
Weaknesses	1 Individual agreements override any collective agreement and once an individual agreement is set, collective bargaining gains no longer apply to the employee who signed an individual agreement. Can be highly inequitable because those with the knowledge, education, experience, and disposition to negotiate effectively do well in the employer/employee negotiation. Those who lack such attributes, skills, knowledge, and experience can be taken advantage of 2 Union power and influence becomes eroded, and employee legal protection is significantly reduced with the onus of proof placed on the individual employee	1 Collective agreements can be legal and managerial nightmares for employers, especially when they employ both unionized and non-unionized labour 2 The individual has little negotiating power outside accepting the award, wages, and conditions for their job and their industry

Sources: The information in this table is derived from the various government websites listed in Table 5.6, specifically the Department of Employment and Workplace Relations (Australia), the Department of Labor (USA), and the Department of Trade and Industry (UK)

2003). It seems that in some ways people can sometimes feel that they are damned if they do, damned if they don't, when they attempt to address quality of working life.

Employment relations

In this final section on the IR climate we will look briefly at a specific HRM issue that we believe is critical in the current economic climate: the nature of employment contracts. As we said earlier, we will not go into specific IR labour laws here. Rather, we provide a general theme that underpins all labour contracts between employees and employers – collective or individual contracts. Table 5.7 on page 206 indicates the main features, strengths, and weaknesses of each type of negotiated contract.

As the table indicates, there are both positives and negatives in the individual and collective agreements. In reality, presenting a table like this underplays the serious implications and ideologies underlying these two approaches. The argument for and against **individual agreements** versus **collective agreements** is a war of political and economic ideologies about the nature of work and employment. We will leave it up to you to decide whether you agree with one or the other, or neither of these.

The movement towards individual contracts, while being advocated as positive and in the interests of talented employees, raises some serious issues that need to be addressed. First, the individual contract is, as Lawler (2005) believes contracts should be, one based on the objective of getting rid of 'obsolete capital'. Over time the USA and Australia have watered down the ability of unions to seek collective agreements on the members' behalf. Part of the reason for this is obviously to ensure employers are not committed to maintaining employment levels when they experience downturns. Downsizing, outsourcing, permanent and temporary layoffs typify both the US, Australian and to a lesser extent the UK markets. In Sweden, as with many other North European and more social democratic countries, 90 per cent of employees are protected by collective agreements, many of which include job security (*Landsorganisationen I Sveirge*, 2006). Indeed, recent research shows that countries that actively avoid policies of downsizing and layoffs, but are typified by companies that value and actively seek to create job security, are actually outperforming countries that do not (Eichengreen, 2007; *New York Times*, 25 February 2007).

Individual agreements, as the term suggests, refers to the process of individuals negotiating the terms and conditions of their work, including pay, rewards and remuneration and so on.

A **collective agreement** is a written agreement, made between the employer and the employees, which sets out terms and conditions of employment. Usually it is made between a union, as a body representing employees, and an employer. Collective agreements are typical of social democratic approaches to industrial relations.

SUMMARY AND REVIEW

From the day we decide to go out to work to the day we cease working, human resource management (HRM) processes and practices will have an effect on all aspects of our working life. HRM can be a complex task: it deals with how people are recruited to the organization, how they are selected, retained, and developed. While at face value recruitment, selection, retention, and development seem like straightforward tasks, they are in fact extremely complex and sometimes controversial processes. HR and HRM do not occur in a vacuum; the HR manager cannot simply assume that anything goes, because HR occurs in specific contexts undergoing constant change: government policy, industrial relations, unionization, social attitudes, globalization, demographic changes, immigration, technological changes, and so on, all affect the ability to perform and implement the major HR functions.

In a democratic and free society certain core human rights issues are taken seriously: they include equity, diversity, and justice. Such values should not be forgotten when performing the core HR functions we covered in this chapter because to do so would be not only unethical but often unlawful. Of course, in practice they often are forgotten: sometimes organizations get away with it, and sometimes they do not and end up in tribunals or the courts. However, in a world that is undergoing such rapid transitions, where the Internet provides endless sources of information (some of which, at least, is valid!), people are more knowledgeable and inquisitive about how they should be treated at work. If people are going to expend effort, apply their talents, capabilities, knowledge, and a skill for an employer, money is no longer the main motivator. Organizations must be thoughtful and reflexive in how they attract and retain talent, and we would expect that those organizations that do so will prosper.

EXERCISES

1   After having read this chapter you should now be able to define or describe each of the key concepts below. Try and use your memory and your own words before looking back through the chapter for the description of each word.

- Human resource management (HRM)
- Hard and soft HR
- Recruitment
- Performance review and assessment
- Equity and diversity
- Realistic job preview
- Benefits and remuneration
- Human process advantage
- Human capital advantage
- Affirmative action (positive discrimination)
- Selection
- Training and development
- Humans as resources
- Workplace regulations and legislation
- Strategic HRM
- Knowledge workers
- Occupational health and safety
- Unions
- Industrial and employment relations
- Collective bargaining
- Enterprise bargaining

2   What are some of the main contextual issues that HR managers must account for in their everyday practices?

3   What are the core HRM functions and how might they have an impact on different aspects of organizational performance?

4   This exercise assists in writing realistic job previews. Draw a table with two columns and in one column write 'good' and in the other write 'not so good'. Now, if you work, think about your job; if you don't work, think about the task of being a student. Assume you want to leave work or university and you have been told you can leave as long as you find a replacement. List all the positives and negatives of the job by using the appropriate good and not so good columns. Once you have listed all these, write a job ad using the realistic job preview. Compare your realistic job preview with others in your class. What differences and similarities do you find?

5   With your peers discuss critically the following statements:

    a   'Maternity leave makes it too easy for women to opt for getting pregnant at the expense of the organization.'

    b   'Should women and men have equal pay? Why and under what conditions would inequity in pay be justified?'

    c   'Does affirmative action and positive discrimination work? Why or why not?'

6   In groups, discuss the performance appraisals used at work or university. How well do these systems work? Are they fair? How would you design a performance appraisal system for students studying this subject at university or college?

7   Divide into two teams; team 1 will follow the scientific management model of HRM and team 2 will follow the human relations model. Assume you are the co-owner of a medium-sized company that deals in the production and export of electrical components for plasma HDT TV sets. You have a staff of 25, and you are seeking to hire another five people. Read through your team's allocated column (i.e. scientific management or human relations) in Table 5.1, and then, as a team, design your HR policies in terms of each area of the HRM practice orientations. Once you have completed this, both teams present their models and compare and contrast the differences in approaches.

8   Debate: Unions are a waste of time and money! Choose two teams of three, plus one moderator and one timekeeper, with the rest of the class to act as the audience and judges. Organize a debate between two groups with one group for the affirmative (unions are a waste of time) and one group for the negative (unions are not a waste of time). It is best to have a week to prepare, do some research on unions, and bring along facts and figures. Perhaps your teacher may even purchase a reward of some sort for the winning team!

ADDITIONAL RESOURCES

1   There are some great movies on issues about work and employment: Kevin Smith's (1994) *Clerks*, Colin Higgins' (1980) *Nine to Five*, and Mike Judge's (1999) *Office Space*.

2   A classic IR movie is the John Ford classic, *How Green Was My Valley* (1941), which traces 50 years in the lives of a close-knit clan of Welsh coal miners. As the years pass, the Morgans try to survive unionization, a lengthy strike, and a mining accident; meanwhile, their hometown and its venerable traditions slowly disintegrate.

3   There are also some fantastic situation comedies on TV, such as *The Office*, and some all-time classic episodes concerning work in *The Simpsons* and *Futurama*.

WEB SECTION

1   A company's HR practices can have the potential to send the company broke. For example, accusation about Wal-Mart's treatment of women has seen a phenomenal growth in numbers of women seeking to be represented in a class action against the company. See http://www.walmartclass.com/public_home.html. (Note that we do not verify or endorse this site as a legitimate source for legal representation; it is provided merely as a practical example of what happens when HR practices of companies are not well designed and thought out.)

2   For state of the art briefings on how to manage organizations effectively, please visit the Henry Stewart Talks series of online audiovisual seminars on Managing Organizations, edited by Stewart Clegg: www.hstalks.com/r/managing-orgs, especially Talk #2 by Tyrone Pitsis on *An introduction to managing people in organizations*. There is also another complete set of Henry Stewart talks on Human Resource Management.

3   http://www.hrmguide.net/ is an excellent resource for students and practitioners of HRM. The site is full of the latest information and ideas in HRM, and provides some excellent links to a number of valuable and interesting sites.

4   To read an interesting article on the knowledge revolution and its impact on work, visit http://www.dallasgroup.com/future.asp.

5   For our American readers, the US government's Equal Employment Opportunity Commission is an excellent resource, go to http://www.eeoc.gov/.

6   For our Australian and New Zealand readers, there is an excellent equity and diversity tool-kit with lots of great links and resources, http://tinyurl.com/2ktj5b.

7   For our UK readers there are some very excellent resources on the government websites: http://tinyurl.com/3bu7kr, http://www.opsi.gov.uk/, and http://www.direct.gov.uk/en/Employment/index.htm.

8   For our Swedish readers the International Labour Organization has some great resources, go to http://tinyurl.com/2jxjyd.

9   This article debunks some of the myths associated with affirmative action in Australia, and is written by an engineer: http://www.wisenet australia.org/ISSUE41/myth.htm.

10 This YouTube video of President Obama talking about CEO pay inequity shows how important the problem is: http://www.youtube.com/watch?v=oJtB6V5wVGY.

11 This is an award winning essay on affirmative action that appeared in the prestigious *Medical Journal of Australia*, 183 (5): 269–270, written by a doctor practising medicine in an indigenous community: http:// tinyurl.com/35u2rj.

12 This is an interesting take on union/organization relationships from an HR manager in the pharmaceuticals industry: http://tinyurl.com/3awsdx.

13 See an interview with the HR maverick, Ricardo Semler: http://www.youtube.com/watch?v=gJkOPxJCN1w.

LOOKING FOR A HIGHER MARK?

By reading and digesting the following articles you can gain a deeper understanding of some of the concepts we have covered in this chapter. A deeper understanding might mean that you can write a more thorough and detailed paper, report, or essay and thus gain a higher grade. Each of the articles below is available for free from the Companion Website www.sagepub.co.uk/managing andorganizations3.

1   What can we learn about management from Mr Burns and the way he treats his 'human resources' in his nuclear power plant? A very entertaining and critical look at management using Montgomery Burns' leadership style and his attitudes to human capital can be found in an article by Professor Carl Rhodes. The paper has some classic quotes and stories from *The Simpsons* and links these to making sense of human relations in organizations. Download and enjoy the article from the Companion Website: Rhodes, C. (2001) 'D'Oh: *The Simpsons*, popular culture, and the organizational carnival', *Journal of Management Inquiry* 10 (4): 374–383.

2   How can a Theory Y orientation be realized in HRM strategies? Eric C. A. Kaarsemaker and Erik Poutsma consider this issue through employee ownership. They argue that organizations should propagate the idea that employees deserve to be co-owners and take employees seriously as such, and that the HRM system should reinforce this Theory Y philosophy as a reality, not just rhetoric. The article is ready to be downloaded from the Companion Website: Kaarsemaker, E. C. A. and Poutsma, E. (2006) 'The fit of employee ownership with other human resource management practices: theoretical and empirical suggestions regarding the existence of an ownership high-performance work system', *Economic and Industrial Democracy*, 27 (4): 669–685.

3   What are the human resource implications of the generational difference? Ronald Paul Hill considers the generational differences and expectations of Boomers versus Gen-Y, and provides managers, as well as educators, with some insights into how they might better deal with these differences. Read about Hill's insights by downloading the paper, Hill, R. P. (2002) 'Managing across generations in the 21st century: important lessons from the ivory trenches', *Journal of Management Inquiry*, 11 (1): 60–66, from the Companion Website.

4   Why do organizations discriminate against certain people, what leads to this discrimination, and what are the consequences of it? These are important questions with strong implications for you as future managers. Barry Goldman and his colleagues deal with these questions in the hope of organizations better

dealing with, understanding, and identifying discriminatory practices, their antecedents, and consequences. The article is download-able from the Companion Website: Goldman, B. M., Gutek, B. A., Stein, J. H. and Lewis, K. (2006) 'Employment discrimination in organi-zations: antecedents and consequences', *Journal of Management*, 32 (6): 786–830.

5 The future shape and nature of strategic HRM promises to be an exciting area of research, theory, and practice. The paper by Brian Becker and Mark Huselid considers not only the current state of strategic HRM but also its future directions in a complex and changing globalized world. This is a very interesting and easy to read paper on strategic HRM and is available from the Companion Website: Becker, B. E. and Huselid, M. (2006) 'Strategic human resources management: where do we

go from here?', *Journal of Management*, 32 (6): 898–925.

6 How do you feel about genetic testing in employee selection, and retention of people being based on genetic qualities? What might a future hold in which the process of selection involves genetic testing? Does that prospect scare you or excite you? What if it was you being genetically tested for a job? Lizabeth Barclay and Karen Markel tackle this issue head on in a worrying but fascinating article on the issue of genetic testing in selection. The paper is free to download from the Companion Website: Barclay, L. A. and Markel, K. S. (2007) 'Discrimination and stigmatization in work organizations: a multiple level framework for research on genetic testing', *Human Relations*, 60 (6): 953–980.

CASE STUDY

MIDWESTERN HEALTH SYSTEM (MHS) AND CISCO AS EXEMPLARS OF COMPASSIONATE HUMAN RESOURCE PRACTICES AND POLICIES

Suffering is fundamental to human experience. Often it is triggered by such events as illness, accidents, death, or the breakdown of relationships. As organizations are places of human engagement, they are invariably places that harbour feelings of joy and pain and reactions of callousness or compassion in response to another's suffering (Dutton et al., 2002). The emotional and social cost of human suffering in organizations includes loss of work confidence, self-esteem, and health; as well as toxic relations involving reduced employee cooperation (Frost, 1999; 2003). The financial and social cost is astronomical, even in the wealthiest nations on earth (Margolis and Walsh, 2003).

Awareness of the power of compassion to lessen and alleviate human pain (Kanov et al., 2004; Lilius et al., 2008) has lead to growing interest in compassion in organizations under the banner of Positive Organizational Scholarship (POS). Compassion is defined by POS scholars as a three-fold process of noticing another person's suffering, feeling empathy, and responding in some way to alleviate the pain (Dutton et al., 2006; Frost et al., 2006).

Human resource departments in organizations that strive to be compassionate actively promote compassion both by encouraging compassionate co-worker relations, establishing systems and policies to ensure that employees' pain is recognized, acknowledged, and responded to with compassion, and by developing compassionate leadership.

Compassionate co-worker relations

Human resource departments can promote compassionate co-worker relations by encouraging co-workers to recognize, feel, and respond to each other's pain through kind words, providing comfort with flowers and cards, hospital visits, open listening, help with home and office work, and financial support (Frost et al., 2006). Examples of such supportive employee relations are found among the employees at MHS.

Several years ago at MHS, an employee with seven children required bypass surgery but didn't have enough money to take leave from work for the period of operation and recovery. Neither did he have insurance coverage to provide this support. In a show of support, a co-worker set up a tax trust fund and other co-workers from among the 75 who worked in the lab submitted donations (Frost et al., 2006). In less than a week, $5800 was collected, more than enough to cover the employee's time off work. Afterwards co-workers expressed feelings of pride to be working among people who care. This example demonstrates the provision of tangible support in compassionate co-worker relations. Yet, support does not have to be tangible. Just knowing that someone cares is often all that matters. When another MHS employee struggled to work while attending to her critically ill mother, her co-workers daily asked after her welfare and enquired if they could do anything to help (Dutton et al., 2007). She later explained that most of the time there was nothing they could do, but knowing they cared and were eager to help boosted her spirit. She further stated that it enhanced her relationships with her co-workers, which she described as irreplaceable.

Compassion can be expressed towards others at all levels of social relations – colleagues of equal hierarchical status, junior employees, as well as senior supervisors. When the dog of a senior supervisor at MHS was diagnosed with cancer, her staff showed great compassion by enquiring about her pet's welfare and listening each day as she revealed greater detail of the illness as well as 'happy' stories from her healthy days (Dutton et al., 2007). When the supervisor called in one day to say she would be late as her dog had just passed away, the staff made a collection and sent flowers. Sharing such a moving experience brought them all closer together as friends beyond their professional roles.

Compassionate policies and systems

Human resource departments can further promote compassion within the organization by establishing policies and systems that legitimate, reflect and ensure the enactment of a culture that underscores and supports values of dignity, commitment to others, respect, equality, importance of members, etc. (Frost, 1999). It further supports beliefs that people are more than their professional identity, that humanity should be displayed, and that members are like family (Dutton et al., 2006). Finally, it is reinforced by outcomes of the practices of compassion such as trust, quality connections, and positive emotions, creating social resources based upon the conceptualization of the organization as one that cares (Dutton et al., 2007).

The fulfilment of compassionate organizational values and policies is executed through the development of compassion supporting systems. When a Cisco employee visiting Japan had a medical emergency and couldn't find an English speaking health care support, Cisco designed a network system to provide medical assistance to Cisco employees travelling abroad (Dutton et al., 2002). The objective was to ensure that no Cisco employee would again feel so forsaken and alone in a frightening situation. This system has proven invaluable on many occasions. During a period of civil unrest in Jakarta, Indonesia in 1998, employees found themselves in the middle of the conflict zone. Cisco used its networks to organize an ambulance that could travel unimpaired through the city streets, to collect employees, and drive them hidden under blankets to a waiting airplane at a deserted army airstrip and fly them to safety.

Systems can also be established to build the organization's capability for compassion by recognizing and rewarding compassionate acts (Dutton et al., 2007; Frost et al., 2006). The MHS had in place such a system by way of a monthly newsletter entitled 'Caring Times', which was distributed to the entire hospital staff (Dutton et al., 2007). The newsletter contained stories of HMS staff performing compassionate caring behaviours.

Questions

1 Describe the HR approach used by MHS and Cisco.
2 How was compassion embedded within MHS and Cisco?
3 What might be the result, in terms of positive psychological capital, of the HR approaches used in this case?

Case prepared by Ace Simpson, UTS School of Business, University of Technology, Sydney.

CHAPTER SIX
MANAGING CULTURES

Values, Practice, Everyday Organizational Life

LEARNING OBJECTIVES

This chapter is designed to enable you to:

- Recognize that organization culture is a more complex phenomenon than is often thought

- Understand why managing culture within organizations can be a challenge

- Understand why organizations typically have multiple cultures and subcultures, and that these are not easily managed by managers

- Distinguish between integration, differentiation, and fragmentation accounts of organization culture

- Describe how official conceptions of organization culture often function as a resource for managing, rather than a literal description of the state of affairs

- Explain why the influential work of Geert Hofstede is subject to serious criticism

BEFORE YOU GET STARTED . . .

Unfortunately, it takes just a bit longer for organizational members to change their organization than it takes the organization to change its members.
(Joschka Fischer, recent German Foreign Minister)

INTRODUCTION

Culture represents the totality of everyday knowledge that people use habitually to make sense of the world around them through patterns of shared meanings and understandings passed down through language, symbols, and artifacts.

Norms represent the tacit and unspoken assumptions and informal rules, the meaning of which people negotiate in their everyday interactions.

Managing the **culture** of an organization is sometimes presented as an easy task. This chapter will show, among other things, why that is by no means always the case. For one thing, there often is not a singular organization culture. For another, whatever cultures exist are often not easily amenable to being managed.

Culture largely comprises the habits, values, mores, and ways of acting – often referred to as **norms** – by which people identify themselves and others, both those whom they see as alike and those whom they see as different, as members of distinct groups. One way to establish clearly what the norms are is by breaking them; breaching the norm draws it to attention so that it becomes remarked upon. In other words, you are more likely to know when you are breaking cultural norms, than when you are practising them.

THE CONCEPTS OF CULTURE

High culture and the cultures of everyday life

What do you think of when you hear the word *culture*? Beethoven, Picasso, Shakespeare's *Hamlet*, and Tchaikovsky's *Swan Lake*, or Eminem's rhymes, Damien Hirst's dead animals, *Harry Potter* novels, and *The Lord of the Rings* movies (Jackson, 2001–2003)? Well, of course, these are all *culture* – not just because of where they are performed or exhibited but because they are resources that some people use and relate to in their everyday lives. Culture does include the formally approved pieces that are a part of the established order of that which is deemed to be tasteful. However, culture is not just 'high art'. Culture also includes the pop and the transient. In fact, everything that is constructed according to some underlying rule, even if the rule is one of randomness, forms a part of culture – no matter whether it is gangsta rap, Shakespearean sonnets, or the ancient Chinese book/oracle *I Ching*. Everything that marks out the way that we relate to our habitats, offices, nature, and each other is a part of culture. To put it in other words, our everyday existence and the ways that we relate to it are embedded in cultural norms, cultural artifacts, and cultural practices.

WHAT DO YOU MEAN?

The idea that organizations with good leaders will have a strong culture is at least 2,000 years old. In the Bible, you can find accounts of the 'good shepherd', whose goodness resided in tending his flock. For many management writers, leaders should be good shepherds. In this view, managers are perceived to use culture to secure consent to their projects; they tend those in their charge, cultivate them. McNay (1994) points out that, under Christianity, the relation between the shepherd (or the king or the leader) and his flock underwent a subtle transformation from a relation of obedience to one of dependence. Culture was thought of as being similar to a farmer cultivating his plants 'to ennoble the seeds and enrich the crop' (Bauman, 1992: 8). Culture as human tending conjures up the metaphor of a gardener weeding out unruly crops or the gamekeeper ferreting out rats and rabbits from burrows to eliminate those rivals who might also reap or harvest the game. The good gamekeeper, farmer, and shepherd were closely related in that all were good managers. The contemporary manager, rather like a gamekeeper, tends an organizational arena wherein the employees may be vicariously treated as the crop – that which is to be cultivated. Or, if you were a cynic, most of us are like sheep, and there is certainly some suggestion of the tendency to follow blindly in strongly normative views of culture.

IMAGE 6.1 All the rules of golf are subject to final interpretation by the gentlemen of the Royal and Ancient Golf Club, St Andrews ('St. Andrews' by H. G. Gawthorn)

Of course, art objects, paintings, popular music, poetry, and other **artifacts** are not the only things that are constituted according to rules – so are societies and organizations. All societies have rules about who can do what to whom and under what circumstances, or what you can and cannot wear on particular occasions, or which people are allowed access to specific

Artifacts are those things with which we mark out territory: the decorations and art in a building; the furnishings and fittings; the styles of clothes that people wear; the types of desks, offices, and computers that they use – these are all artifacts that tell us, subtly, about the environments we occupy or are in.

places and under what circumstances. Given that we all need to eat to live, it is particularly interesting to consider the rules that surround food. All societies have rules about what is edible and what is not. How do *you* feel about chicken's feet, a delicacy in Hong Kong; Witchety grubs, an Australian Koori treat; dog, a perennial favourite in Korea and some other parts of Asia; rats, sometimes on the menu in China; or cow's stomach lining (tripe) popular both in the north of England and in many parts of Continental Europe?

Sports make the importance of rules for defining a specific culture clear. Organizations such as the Royal and Ancient Golf Club of St Andrews are repositories of elaborate rules about membership and members' duties, and enforce and interpret the rules of the game of golf. The rules of a sport may be more or less formal. Golf is very formal, but what about skating? Skaters can have a fairly organized sense about the rules of the game they play. The two Images (6.2a and 6.2b) of skaters show an informal skate competition in Paris that was set up on the Pont Louis, a bridge that is closed to traffic, which goes over the River Seine from the Ile de la Cité. The apparatus was composed of found materials (notably street barriers, which the participants picked up on the street as they sped to the venue on their skates). All the participants understand the rules: the aim, as can be seen from the subsequent pictures, was to clear an obstacle set as high as possible, as stylishly as possible.

Culture is a concept with its own complex history that stretches back long before organization theorists began to study it. Consider Image 6.3, showing Traitor's Gate at the Tower of London – the place where traitors, having been transported by barge up the River Thames, entered the tower to await their execution (or, if they were lucky, imprisonment). Traitor's Gate stands as a stark reminder of what might be the consequences of breaking the organization culture rules in an organization ruled by an absolute authority, such as the Tudor monarchy of Henry VIII. Many of the king's courtiers and two of his wives – Anne Boleyn and Catherine Howard – saw that gate close behind them.

Today, there are still a few CEOs who seem to imagine that they can behave like Tudor monarchs. Many examples were provided at the trial of Lord Conrad Black, the ex-newspaper magnate, accused of using organizational finances as if they were his personal property, and convicted on charges of fraud. Referring to the 'greed of Conrad Black and his complete disregard for his shareholders', Hugh Totten (a partner for the New York law firm Perkins Coie) commented, 'It makes him look like some English Tudor monarch rather than the CEO of a public company with responsibility to shareholders' (Bone, 2007: 45). As we write this chapter, during July 2011, the unfolding scandal in the UK concerning phone hacking, bribery, and the destruction of evidence sanctioned by the actions of senior News International executives (quite how senior is not yet proven) seems to suggest a belief on the part of such executives that they were above the law. Indeed, comparisons are being drawn with the Watergate scandal that occurred during the Nixon presidency in the US, while comparisons have also been made in the non-News International

IMAGE 6.2A and 6.2B
Even informal street games
have clearly improvised
rules

press between the regime of Rupert Murdoch as head of News Corp (the parent company of News International) and that of an absolutist sovereign. For example, in the politically conservative UK newspaper *The Telegraph*, the chief political commentator, Peter Osborne, states that News International had run 'a flourishing criminal concern that took an evil pleasure in destroying people's lives' in the way it managed the *News of the World* newspaper. Rupert Murdoch, chief executive of News Corp, 'used his power to immense effect, undermining and attacking our greatest public institutions – above all the monarchy and the judiciary. His employees believed they were above the law and could act with impunity. And this was indeed the case, thanks to the connivance of police, politicians and the press' (Osborne, 2011). The effect of these actions was severe: billions of dollars were wiped off the value of News Corp's stock; the bid by News Corp to take over the 61 per cent ownership it did not have in BSkyB was withdrawn as a result of censure by the House of Commons, and the wider operations of News Corp in both the United States and Australia were brought into question and became subject to further investigation. Meanwhile, an influential social movement began mobilizing against the Murdoch empire globally (https://secure.avaaz.org/en/stop_rupert_murdoch_donate/?cl=1161774853&v=9589).

In fact, few organizations today have the power of absolute authority. Most modern CEOs, outside of 'Press Barons' such as Black and Murdoch, find it difficult to be absolutist rulers because they do not have the powers of an absolutist monarch, but are enmeshed in the rules of complex bureaucratic regulation. Nonetheless, their organizations are just as full of complex culture as any Tudor court. And, like a Tudor court, the cultural rules can often be very implicit, subtle, and highly political in their interpretation.

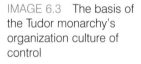

IMAGE 6.3 The basis of the Tudor monarchy's organization culture of control

Organization theory discovered the importance of culture quite early in its development. Parker (2000: 128) notes perceptively that F. W. Taylor sought to create a single utilitarian culture to minimize employee resistance and to maximize productivity – and, of course, to increase profits. However, Taylor in 1911 did not focus explicitly on culture. The earliest explicit research into culture as an object of specific study arose when Roethlisberger and Dickson (1939) realized that the most significant variables governing the output at the Hawthorne plant appeared to be not physical but social (see also pp. 464). As Mouzelis (1967: 99) pointed out, such factors defined the 'culture of the group'.

Managers can draw on various types of expert knowledge (psycho-technological and managerial) to manage culture by using comprehensible prescriptions to regulate actions (Kono and Clegg, 1998; Mayo, 1946): job descriptions, manuals of procedures, and mission and vision statements all serve to shape, subtly, the members' sense of their organization's culture. Increasingly, managers seek to secure compliance through shaping employees' attitudes and sentiments (Senge, 1990).

Views that link an organization's culture with its performance seek to do so by creating a common frame of understanding (Kotter and Heskett, 1992): the assumption is that if you can create harmony in terms of expectations and behaviours that flow from the organization culture, the organization will perform better. The earliest approaches to organization culture actually referred to it using a term from the psychological literature, *organizational climate*. Schein (2002) argues that this term was a precursor to the concept of organization culture. As Ashkenasy (2003) demonstrates, these roots are pervasive in discussions of organization culture. However, while some writers have seen culture as the great unifier in organizations, others see it as the great divider.

Levels of culture

Organization culture comprises the deep, basic assumptions and beliefs, as well as the shared values, that define organizational membership, as well as the members' habitual ways of making decisions, and presenting themselves and their organization to those who come into contact with it.

Level 1 consists of artifacts, including visible organizational features such as the physical structure of buildings and their architecture, uniforms, and interior design. This level is easily observable but does not reveal everything about an organization's culture. Sometimes researchers use the term organizational climate to refer to the more evident and malleable aspects of the organization's environment. For instance, the rich and powerful often use architecture to impress the less fortunate with the magnificence of their wealth. The ways in which these artifacts of power are manifested vary enormously from society to society (see Images 6.4 and 6.5).

Level 2 comprises **espoused values**. Values represent a non-visible facet of culture that encompasses the norms and beliefs that employees express

Schein (1997) defines **organization culture** as the deep, basic assumptions and beliefs that are shared by organizational members. Culture is not displayed on the surface; instead, it is hidden and often unconscious. It represents the taken-for-granted way an organization perceives its environment and itself. To clarify the various components of culture in organizations, Schein differentiates between three levels of culture (Figure 6.1).

Espoused values are a person's or social group's consistent beliefs about something in which they have an emotional investment as they express them; they are articulated in speeches, writings, or other media.

FIGURE 6.1
The levels of culture,
according to Schein

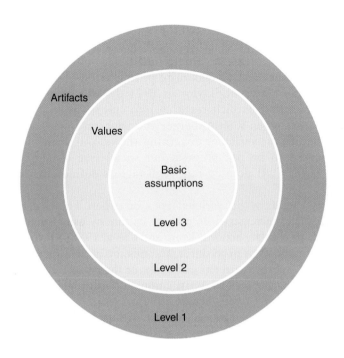

Basic assumptions are defined by Schein as the core, or essence, of culture, represented in difficult to discern, largely unconscious, and tacit frames that subconsciously shape values and artifacts, formed around deep dimensions of human existence such as the nature of humans, human relationships and activity, reality and truth.

when they discuss organizational issues. A mission statement or a commitment to equal employment opportunities is part of this level.

The deepest culture – the **basic assumptions** hidden beneath artifacts and expressed values – is found in level 3. This bull's eye in the dartboard of culture is the most important level. It includes the basic assumptions that shape organizational members' worldviews, beliefs, and norms, which guide their behaviour without being explicitly expressed. It is the most influential level because it works surreptitiously and shapes decision-making processes almost invisibly. It is hard to observe and even harder to change. Nonetheless, it is the level that carries the most potential for transformation. (Notice the Freudian influence on these conceptions of culture in terms of unconsciousness and hidden depths; see also pp. 67–70.)

STORIES OF STRONG CULTURES

Stories are an important part of organizations; often they circulate as gossip, sometimes as part of the informal legends, sagas, and mythologies of the organization and characters deemed important in its history. The key point about stories is that they are transmitted orally through story-telling, although they can be recorded and become a part of the official story – think of how Silicon Valley companies such as Apple and Hewlett-Packard started off in garages and grew to become global corporations. Research on corporate cultures has used stories as data about top leadership that circulated

IMAGE 6.4 and 6.5 Buildings as artefacts of power designed to awe the populace

widely in the organization. These tales captured something special and unique about the organization and often showed the exemplary qualities of the leadership in some way. Phenomena such as myths and legends became important objects for research. The culture became identified with everything from common behavioural patterns to espoused new corporate values that senior management wished to inculcate (Schein, 2002). The researchers who did most to popularize the story-telling approach initially were Peters and Waterman (1982).

Peters and Waterman: McKinsey changing the world of organizations

Tom Peters and Robert Waterman, two consultants from McKinsey & Company (the multinational consulting firm) who had, with links to Stanford's Graduate School of Business, offered an account of culture based on an instrumental view of the relation between managerial practice and management knowledge. They promoted the concept that culture that is strong and unifying – which is shared by everyone in an organization – is what makes companies great.

Peters and Waterman's *In Search of Excellence: Lessons From America's Best-Run Companies* was published in 1982. Previously, the central concern that had characterized much of management and organization theory had been organization *structure*. This changed markedly as a result of *In Search of Excellence*, which propelled culture to centre stage in corporate analysis, resulting in related research that we will refer to as *excellence studies*. The message was simple: great companies have excellent cultures. Excellent cultures deliver outstanding financial success. What makes culture excellent are core values and presuppositions that are widely shared and acted on.

Books such as *In Search of Excellence, Corporate Cultures: The Rites and Rituals of Corporate Life* (Deal and Kennedy, 1982) and *Organizational Culture and Leadership* (Schein, 1997) helped make culture a popular and acceptable topic in business. Excellence studies stressed how a pattern of learned and shared basic assumptions framed organization members' perceptions, thoughts, and feelings. Put simply, culture encompassed the following questions:

- How were things done in particular organizations?

- What was acceptable behaviour?

- What norms were imparted to new members?

- What norms were members expected to use to solve problems of external adaptation and internal integration, and which ones did they actually use?

Theorists presumed that if you forged a strong culture that incorporated all organization members in shared beliefs and commitments, everything else – good morale, performance, and results – should follow. Having such a widely shared and integrative culture in organizations is often viewed as a panacea for management and a sure-fire recipe for corporate success.

Few management books have been as popular as Peters and Waterman's *In Search of Excellence*. Its appeal is apparent, packed as it is with anecdotes, lively stories, and lists. According to Peters and Waterman, top management's job was to show leadership through culture building by making values clear, transmitting them widely, reinforcing them in practice, and backing them up. Formal policies, informal stories, rituals as well as rules, and constantly practising what you preach should ensure a strong culture. Effective cultures were also unambiguous, unitary, harmonious, and managerially integrative. On the other hand, pluralistic cultures that accommodated dissent and conflict were regarded as dysfunctional and were a sure sign that the culture was unproductive. Strong leadership that articulated clear values should overcome opposition.

Top managers embraced these arguments, as did many scholars who produced studies on the keys to excellence in organizations (e.g. Deal and Kennedy, 1982; Kanter, 1984; 1990; Pascale and Athos, 1981). They argued that improvements in productivity and quality would accrue when corporate cultures systematically align individuals with formal organizational goals. Culture was understood as the glue that should hold organizational objectives and individual needs together.

In Search of Excellence and subsequent excellence studies shaped the world of practice through the authors' consultancy work with McKinsey & Company (Colville et al., 1999). In fact, Peters and Waterman's work translated ideas from quite subtle and complex organization theories to apply them to practical exigencies. The origins of these theories were the sensemaking perspective of Weick (1969; 1979; 1995). As Colville et al. (1999: 135) argue, these origins were reflected in *In Search of Excellence* through the insights that 'fundamentally … meanings matter' and that 'mundaneity is more scarce than people realize' (1999: 136). *In Search of Excellence* was not simply a publication 'offering advice for addressing pragmatic problems thought to be relevant to managers, consultants, and other individuals who work in or with organizations' (Barley et al., 1988: 34). Peters and Waterman produced a work that translated unfashionable and highly abstract organization theory into a form that a wider audience was able to appreciate (Colville et al., 1999).

Peters and Waterman have a nice story to tell. Integrate everyone into one managerially designed and approved culture of excellence and superior performance will be the outcome. Subsequent researchers supported this idea (Denison, 1990). However, as critics are not too unkind to point out, many of the so-called excellent companies had in fact become far less successful within eighteen months of *In Search of Excellence* being published. The change in their circumstances did not slow the rollout of the rhetoric of excellence in management-speak, however. It proliferated rapidly. Soon, nearly every manager and wannabe manager could be heard talking about how important searching for excellence was, and many management consultants were only too happy to help design a culture to make this happen.

Despite *In Search of Excellence* being a huge commercial success, there are problems with it: it was too one-dimensional, too focused on culture as just one aspect of organization life and too focused on the stories only of top managers, almost as propaganda for the managerial elite and their views of the way culture should be. But millions read it.

Check out the Companion Website www.sagepub.co.uk/ managingandorganizations3 for free access to an article by Ian Colville, Robert Waterman, and Karl Weick (1999) about how *In Search of Excellence* was conceptualized and researched.

Strong cultures, homogeneity, and disaster

Research on the demise of England's Barings Bank has shown (Stein, 2000) that too much consensus and homogeneity in an organization can easily lead to blind spots that can be fatal. Barings was the world's first merchant bank, but its proud tradition ceased suddenly in 1995 when it collapsed because of the activities of a 27-year-old trader in its Singapore office, Nick Leeson. Of course, one could blame Leeson personally for the disaster because he was acting unethically (trading speculatively without telling anyone what he was doing, and covering up his tracks as he did so), but this would not explain why Barings collapsed. Rather, it collapsed because he was able to do these things due to a lethal mix of elements in its organization culture. As Stein argues, 'Barings' problem [is located] squarely with the institution rather than with Leeson … the conditions for Leeson's fraud were set in place substantially prior to his arrival at Barings' (2000: 1227). They were deeply embedded in the culture of Barings as an organization.

Barings was a very conservative and established bank that recruited its board members from the English aristocracy. Indeed, previous generations of Barings had been governor-generals in colonial Egypt and Kenya. It was the bank of the British monarch's mother. It was just about as Establishment as it was possible for a bank to be.

In the 1980s, the UK government deregulated the banking industry. One consequence was that banks faced more challenges in a more turbulent environment than they had previously. Barings decided to employ a risk-taker who was expected to make sense of the new situation: Nick Leeson. He was known as a maverick, someone who told stories about himself that were not always exactly true, as well as someone who liked to drink and gamble. At its worst, these predilections occasionally resulted in unseemly behaviour; as Stein writes, 'in a drunken stupor one night, Leeson had exposed his buttocks to several local women in a bar' (2000: 1219). In short, he was not the publicly acceptable face that young men drawn from the English aristocracy would have preferred to present. But the bank's management agreed that it needed someone different than they were used to hiring if they were to master the challenges ahead. Barings promoted Leeson, and soon he was trading in Singapore with the bank's money – and lost it.

Normally, there are many control mechanisms in place that should ensure that an individual employee cannot lose all the company's assets by gambling on the stock market (in the case of Barings, it was £860 million). But Barings management ignored all the signs that Leeson was losing the bank's money. The organization culture at Barings was strongly homogeneous among the gentlemen of the top management team, which made them blind to seeing what was really going on in the accounts that Leeson managed. Moreover, their bonuses depended on his gains as he reported them. They had hired an entrepreneurial type of person, and they left him to do the job, with very hands-off control because, in the past, class and breeding had made strong discipline by management unnecessary. As the Bank of England subsequently reported, there was no clear explanation as to why Barings management did not question why the bank should be apparently lending more than £300 million to its clients to trade on the Singapore Exchange when it had collected only £31 million from clients for those trades. Barings had a strong culture – one in which no one dared to point out that all was not quite what it might seem – which had disastrous outcomes. Leeson described the culture as one in which employees never asked questions because they did not want to appear ignorant. The dominant unofficial culture was one of no questions, despite whatever may have been maintained officially.

The case of Barings shows we should not assume that a dominant culture is always the official one. In some organizations, such as various police services or firms such as Enron and WorldCom, a dominant culture of corruption has become widespread. Although such cultures are not 'officially official', their proliferation suggests that formal tolerance enabled them to flourish and to become established as the local norm. To illustrate this point, we refer to a study of hospitals and the way that they dealt with terminally ill patients; it shows that there was a well-established 'officially unofficial' culture that shaped the organization's treatment of those of its 'members', i.e. patients, who departed the organization by dying.

Sudnow's *Passing On: The Sociology of Dying* (1967) compares the culture of two hospitals, one private and one public. One characteristic of both was that most deaths in the hospitals seemed to occur in the mornings. Although Sudnow initially could not figure out why this was the case, he eventually discovered that when death occurred on the night shift, the staff would try not to recognize the fact because of the attendant duties associated with it. Dead bodies are a bureaucratic nightmare; heaps of paperwork and a lot of physical and cleanup work are associated with them. Thus, the shift culture regarded dead bodies as a nuisance best left for the new morning shift to attend to. Hence, deaths peak in the morning, when the new shift clocks on and has to register, statistically, the fact of death.

Check out the Companion Website www.sagepub.co.uk/ managingandorganizations3 for free access to articles by Ian Greener (2006) and Andrew D. Brown (2005) if you want to learn more about the collapse of Barings Bank, as seen by management and organization theorists.

The culture of management

In principle, managers who have a capacity to understand management theoretically should be better able to manage than inspired amateurs. However, we should bear in mind a point made by Mintzberg (1973): in practice, managers change tack every ten minutes or so. One consequence is that managers are more likely to steer with intuitive judgements because managing means doing many things under tight pressure rather than having leisurely opportunities to consult the latest research. Hence, an intuitive ability to understand the different elements of organization culture that they are working with is an essential prerequisite for the job.

WHAT'S THE POINT?

How should practical managers relate to organization and management research?

Donaldson (1992) would have managers follow the findings of management science. He would want them to be skeptical about popular management recipes, such as the excellence studies promoted. What managers actually do, what management science says they should do, are sometimes significantly different.

There is a great deal of anecdotal evidence suggesting that managers – even very important ones – are not necessarily as rational as they might seem to be. Our favourite example is one of the most popular of US presidents, Ronald Reagan. A former actor, Reagan used the scripts of films that he knew, such as *Star Wars* (Lucas, 1977–2002), when communicating the sense that he made of the world that he sought to manage. Meanwhile, his wife, Nancy, consulted her astrologer. Do not laugh: for many decision-makers in some economies, such as Hong Kong, the predictions of astrologers or feng shui practitioners are at least as important as those of econometricians or management consultants – and are sometimes as effective.

Nancy was not the only politician's wife to consult New-Age-Type guru's – Cherie Blair was well known for her penchant for receiving advice from her 'lifestyle coach', Carole Caplin. The *Daily Telegraph* (3 July 2007) contained an interesting story about 'When Asia's rich and powerful need advice' they call on 'a tiny, hunched deaf-mute' soothsayer in her mid-forties called E. Thi, universally known by the nickname ET in Asia. She numbers Thaksin Shinawatra, ex-Prime Minister of Thailand and present owner of Manchester City Football Club, the Burmese Junta, the Indonesian Foreign Ministry, and the Nepalese monarch among her clients (see http://tinyurl.com/29jxtb).

Some other managers, trained in business schools, may seek to apply some rational models that they dimly remember from their MBA, when they were taught that a culture of 'excellence' was the way to go. They thus replicate lessons from their youth, repeatedly, even though the truths of that time may have become the errors of today. Still others manage their organization culture by thinking of the most recent columns they read in the press or that last book they bought at the airport on a business trip, or how their mother or father brought them up, or how a winning sports team is managed. Managers in various contexts have different relevancies guiding their culture of managing, and not all are guided by management theories.

Practising managers' conceptions of culture are important. They shape what they regard as 'best practice'. If managers think that a unitary culture will be less troublesome and more supportive of their projects they will apply it as a kind of recipe knowledge. For a while, *In Search of Excellence* seemed to provide a good recipe. The trouble with recipes is that if everybody cooks according to the same script, the lack of variety becomes bland and boring, and there is no innovation in the diet. The lack of innovation applies not only to the competition between organizations but also to organizations in which everyone subscribes to the same culture, enacting the same realities. The more recipes we have to work from, from different approaches, the more skilled we will be in blending experience and ingredients, theory and practice, management and managing.

Thus, we would argue for polyphony in preference to strong cultures. Managers are better off with pluralism, better with dissonance, because it offers more space for innovation. If everyone agrees on the direction being steered and the underlying values, such a situation is foolish if they are wrong and their common agreement does not enable them to see the dangers ahead. The *Titanic* was not just a ship; it serves as a metaphor for all those who are secure in the belief that they are unsinkable.

Academics and their students should be skeptics – those who are prepared to suggest that the recipe may not necessarily be all that it is cracked up to be. Sometimes skeptics might suggest alternative recipes, whereas other times they might ask whether you really want to use *that* recipe if you want to achieve *that* outcome. Sometimes, they scoff at the recipe. We think that management academics, at their best, should be able to speak out about organizational power without suffering adverse consequences. Some of them are well-paid people, engaged in secure positions, with a privileged access to potentially influential people – their students. As such, they should not be afraid of speaking or writing in ways that represent views that, to paraphrase the economist J. K. Galbraith, challenge the conventional wisdom (Galbraith, 1969).

Experienced managers will rarely know as much about the theory of management as you do as a student. Some may belittle theory. We think they should, if that theory is prescriptive and tells them what they should do. No theory can operate without regard for context. That is why we stress the need always to relate managing – what managers actually do – to the theories, artifacts and other resources that they manage with. The point of theory in management is not its 'truth' but its use.

Culture in Disneyland

For cultural anthropology the enthusiasm for unitary cultures as a source of excellence in organizations might have been surprising.

Cultural anthropologists stress that it is usually societies whose belief systems are in trouble that seek to re-emphasize symbols and rituals to stress that there are unitary beliefs (Alvesson and Berg, 1992). In doing so, their elites are making a conscious effort to impose value consensus. An example from twentieth-century history is the post-Prague Spring Soviet-backed Husak regime in Czechoslovakia (as it then existed), which was imposed by Soviet tanks in 1968 along with martial law and the overthrow of the Dubcek government. The new policy of the Husak government was actually termed 'normalization'! The process of normalization meant reasserting a state of repression and limited freedoms on the aspirations of the Czech and Slovak peoples for self-rule on a more liberal model. What is ironic is that it took foreign intervention, tanks, troops, and the overthrow of a government – all pretty extraordinary interventions – to create this highly contrived and forcefully imposed 'normalcy'. What was regarded by the Soviet authorities and their emissaries as 'normal' was seen by the protestors of the Prague Spring as an authoritarian imposition. Organizations that demand fealty to corporate cultures against the skepticism of their members echo this authoritarian behaviour in demonstrating that the authorities believe that they know what is best for ordinary people and will impose it, if necessary, even if against their will. Think of the actions of organizations such as Wal-Mart in opposing trade union representation among their workforce.

Like prisms, organizations have many facets that are seen and refracted through different perspectives. Managers are sometimes strongly committed

Cultural anthropology is the study of specific societies and cultures, using the methods, concepts, and data of field-based research in its descriptions and analyses of the diverse peoples of the world. Sometimes called social anthropology, it developed as an adjunct of imperialism in the nineteenth century, mapping largely small-scale (or 'primitive'), non-Western societies, but in the twentieth century has developed its fieldwork methods of inquiry into areas as diverse as youth cultures and corporate cultures.

to the official version of the organization culture. On this basis they may thus assume that other managers and members will be also. However, such assumptions of cultural homogeneity may well be simplifying complex realities by concentrating only on officially endorsed accounts of what the organization is. Sometimes there is more than one dimension to a situation.

Highly developed value integration may be seen as a way of emphasizing underlying basic assumptions – especially when they are under threat. Anthropologically oriented organization researchers are attuned to the politics of symbolic action (Smircich, 2002 [1983]). Sometimes, from this perspective, one implication is that people might, on occasion, mean more than they say. It would not be surprising if this were the case; the world of organizations usually includes different types of actors, opinions, and conceptions of culture that quite often come into conflict with each other. Organizations are arenas within which many things might happen that put a big smile on top management's faces, but there is also much going on that will just as surely wipe it off.

Organizations with friendly public images are often revealed to have elaborate facades. For example, Van Maanen (1991) revealed that Disneyland at that time was not the fun place its marketing promoted; instead, it was an environment with many stressed-out workers, often obnoxious customers, and generally hassled supervisors, all seeking an advantage over others, and using organization resources to do so. Despite this reality, in the 'smile factory' (as Van Maanen calls it), a strong corporate culture sought to make sure that every employee behaved according to Disney's philosophy. Uniforms, education through the University of Disneyland, and an employee handbook embodied this spirit. However, the stressed-out staff found their own way of dealing with the masses of visitors. For especially nasty customers, employees developed informal mechanisms to discipline them. For instance, the 'seatbelt squeeze' on amusement rides was but a 'small token of appreciation given to a deviant customer consisting of the rapid cinching-up of a required seatbelt such that the passenger is doubled-over at the point of departure and left gasping for the duration of the trip' (Van Maanen, 1991: 71). Or bothersome pairs could be separated into different units so that they had to enjoy a ride without each other (the so-called 'break-up-the-party' gambit; Van Maanen, 1991: 72). These and many other unofficial and informal rules and practices were learned and developed on the job and formed a part of the culture of Disneyland. Probably not quite what Walt had in mind, though!

Culture is not just the formally approved ways of doing things; it is also the sly games, informal rules, and deviant subcultures of lower level employees against supervisors and supervisors against lower level employees, women against men and men against women, and creatives against management types as well as management types against creatives (Burawoy, 1979; Rosen, 2002 [1985]; Young, 1989).

Organization culture and George Orwell's Nineteen Eighty-Four

As we have seen, strong cultures do not necessarily equal good cultures. One of the strongest critiques of the dominant orthodoxy that strong cultures are good cultures came in a scathing article by a British academic, Hugh Willmott, who drew inspiration from Orwell's most celebrated book, *Nineteen Eighty-Four* (1949), to make sense of corporate culture programmes (Willmott, 2002). In the book, Orwell imagined Oceania, a totalitarian state set in the future. It maintained coercive control through, among other things, making the official parlance of Oceania Newspeak, a perversion of the English language. Although Newspeak is based on English, all contentious political words are removed, and, more generally, the vocabulary is much reduced. The purpose of the language is to limit that which can be said and thought. The ultimate aim of Newspeak is to produce a mode of communication that requires no thought on the part of the speakers. This ideal is achieved, in part, through the use of abbreviations that serve to conceal the true meanings of terms. For instance, the Oceania Ministry of Law and Order, where torture occurs, is known as Miniluv. One of the important features of Newspeak is doublethink, which refers to the capacity to hold mutually contradictory views at the same time.

So what does the dystopian fiction of a writer who has been dead for half a century have to do with corporate culture? Willmott (2002) argues that Orwell can help us understand what he characterizes as the dark side of the corporate culture project. Willmott contends that corporate culture is best regarded as a form of Newspeak. The words, terms, and artifacts that describe the culture can be regarded by corporate elites as a gift bestowed on organization members through cultural design. The assumption, however, that organization members will want to receive these gifts uncritically and reproduce them unreflectedly in a perfect echo of corporatespeak may well be too much. Most of us retain degrees of skepticism about the latest change projects and initiatives that our organizational masters impose on us. One of us works in a Business School whose philosophy is expressed in the phrase 'Forward-thinking, Work-ready'. To be forward thinking and simultaneously work ready seems to be a contradiction in terms, given the practices of organizations in the wider world, such as News Corp, that embrace criminality and corruption. Other senior managers of organizations seem to think being 'work ready' means being ready to accept levels of sexual and other forms of harassment that are punishable by law, given the frequency of such law suits and their reporting in the press. With Willmott, the language of corporate culture programmes should be seen as a means of attempting to control the choices and identities open to employees that is plagued by doublethink, in which the values of community and autonomy can be simultaneously celebrated and contradicted, as in the slogan 'Forward-thinking, Work-ready'. Much as the Party member in Orwell's Oceania, the well-socialized, self-disciplined corporate employee is 'expected to have no private emotions and no respite from enthusiasm … The speculations which might possibly induce a skeptical or rebellious attitude are killed in advance by his early-acquired inner discipline' (Orwell, 1949: 220). Under the guise of giving more autonomy to the individual than would be the case in organizations governed by bureaucratic rules, corporate culture threatens to promote a new, hypermodern neo-authoritarianism. No longer governed by clear rules, organization members know that as long as they can parrot the corporate line, they can claim to be acting responsibly.

Willmott finds this potentially more insidious and sinister than bureaucracy, with its clear formal rules and limits, because it leaves no space for an autonomous professional ethos. The notion of the classical public servant as a person who works according to the dictates of conscience embedded in a professional ethos disappears in favour of a vision of the loyal employee. Loyalty is seen to be expressed in the ability to reproduce various corporate lines in appropriate contexts and to keep any reservations or misquiet to one's self. In such a situation there would be nothing guiding organization members' actions other than the appearance of conformism. Everything is supposed to be subordinated to the greater good of the corporate culture. Only within this frame can organization members find freedom and value.

Making up culture

Much contemporary organization culture discourse represents a desire by management to enlist workers' cooperation, compliance, and commitment to create an *esprit de corps* with which to limit human recalcitrance at work (Barker, 1998). The rhetoric of control, coupled with a new vocabulary of teamwork, quality, flexibility, and learning organizations, constitutes culture management projects that seek to create culture as a mechanism of soft domination (see also pp. 265–267).

Management writing on culture increasingly came to focus on how it could be used to constitute and enthuse members' commitment to the organization. Programmes of cultural change are often designed to make the culture more explicit and better understood. (Casey, 1995; du Gay, 2000a; Jacques, 1996). At the furthest point, what such thinking about the relation of organization members and organization culture sought to construct was 'designer employees' (Casey, 1995) – people made up in such a way that they were organizationally most functional.

MINI CASE

Recruiting at Cathay Pacific

The ultimate designer employee is depicted in a Cathay Pacific recruitment advertisement from 1997. The employee is a specific category of organizational subject imbued with an obvious, natural, or acquired demeanour, comportment, and specifications:

Who am I?
I travel the world but I'm not a tourist.
I serve 5-star cuisine but I'm not a chef.
I walk the aisle but I'm not a fashion model.

I care for people but I am not a nurse.
And I do it all from the heart.
Who am I?
I am …

… a flight attendant with Cathay Pacific and you could be one too! (Cathay Pacific Airways, 1997)

- To what extent has Cathay Pacific generated a strong culture among its flight attendants and other staff? (Hint – start from http://tinyurl.com/3xvsox.)

Management practitioners seek to use culture and control to try and frame the subjectivity of their employees – to try and get them to see things with the same set of relevancies that they have as managers. We see this most readily in some post-excellence accounts of quality management, such as the Six-Sigma movement popular in Japan and much of East Asia (Kono and Clegg, 2001). Principles such as *seiri* (putting-in-order), *seiton* (arrange properly), *seiketsu* (cleanliness), *seiso* (cleaning), and *shitsuke* (good behaviour), seen in many plants of Japanese corporations, seek to govern not only the workplace but also the comportment of employees in the workplace (March, 1996). Organization culture prescribes norm-defined management techniques and habit-inducing routines that culminate in a new consciousness and a new set of beliefs and values that promise a new personhood, a new subjectivity, and even a new embodiment. Think of highly designed conceptions of organization culture that frame what it means to be an organization member, such as those associated with the advertisement for Cathay Pacific that we saw previously. The employee has to work from the heart; this is what it means to be designed for work as a Cathay flight attendant.

For Casey (1995), a designer culture has the following characteristics:

1   Individual enthusiasm manifested in the values of dedication, loyalty, self-sacrifice, and passion. These values translate into the use of the organizationally approved forms of language, including buzz-terms, as well as a willingness to be part of the team at work, in play and recreation (joining in at the pub, for instance), and putting in long hours at work – where you earn your salary from 9 to 5 and your promotion from 5 to 9.

2   A strong customer focus, where customers are not just the end-users but employees and other significant stakeholders are thought of as customers.

3   Management discourse characterized by a language of team and family, which is inclusive of everyone – even if they would prefer not to be a part of the team or family.

4   Finally, public display of the designer culture. There will be many artifacts, such as websites, that display images of the culture, such as team photos, team awards, employee of the month, and such like.

Owners and senior managers who have a paternalistic relation to their employees will urge them to be part of the organization family. The use of family metaphors – we're all one big happy family here – is particularly inappropriate. The family metaphor is widely used to try and represent an organization culture, as for instance when people talk of disloyalty when an employee criticizes the firm or approaches another organization for a position – almost as if they were having an affair! Of course, the whole notion of the organization being metaphorically aligned with a family is suspect, as we should recognize. Are managers then parents and employees children? Not all families are a haven from a heartless world; some are awful places, with institutionalized abuse, violence, and cruelty, which are hard to escape. But an idealized notion of family is the one that is usually at work in designer cultures, never the one that takes the sad facts of the family law courts as its empirical compass. Actually, although we cannot choose our families, we can, in principle, choose our organizations. Therefore, we can choose to escape a perverse organization and go elsewhere, but membership in many families does not allow such choice. We suspect that most of you would prefer being exploited by an organization that you can leave easily rather than being held captive in a family (or a family business) that is relatively inescapable. Family bonds are much harder to escape than an employment contract, so here is our advice: beware of employers claiming family ties or suggesting that the organization in which you work is like a family!

DIFFERENT PERSPECTIVES ON CULTURE

The politics of managing culture

Integration perspectives   Cultural practices enable managing to happen by binding entities together, and sometimes there is friction. Managing creates a nexus of peoples, ideas, materials, and technologies that can act semi-autonomously in pursuit of strategies. Culture is the shorthand term that captures the ways in which people are able to make sense of their managing and being managed. Modern managing involves the creative destruction of existing recipes and practices embedded in cultures. Such managing means disorganizing and deconstructing past routines, retaining some while changing others. Culture is always in process, never static – it is constantly evolving, deconstructing, reconstructing, and resurrecting itself.

Practising managers need to find solutions to new problems every ten minutes or so (Mintzberg, 1973). Not surprisingly, they have little time for reflection or for reading the latest research knowledge other than that which is immediately available, local, contextual, working knowledge. In such a situation, the excellence studies made perfect sense because they provided generic solutions that seemed to be capable of being applied to many problems that could be now reclassified as culture issues. The great strength of the culture perspective was that it seemed to promise the dissolution of all that friction and resistance that managers know they often produce routinely, as a normal part of their work. In the place of conflict it offered integration. Indeed, some analysts refer to the strong cultures model as an **integration perspective.**

Integration theorists define culture as 'organization-wide agreement with values espoused by top management' (Martin and Frost, 1996: 608). Often, they suggest, such agreement was assumed by researchers only after the views of top management had been sampled! When decisions were not overtly biased by sampling decisions to exclude likely sources of dissenting views, they were often made to exclude any data that seemed to suggest a

According to Martin and Frost (1996), adherents of the **integration perspective** define culture as a phenomenon that is consistent and clear. Because they define organization culture in terms of unitary and shared assumptions they include in their evidence only manifestations of it that accord with this definition, thus excising all the plural and non-integrative aspects of the culture.

weak or fragmented culture as an inconsequential margin to the central cultural values. Martin and Frost are scathing:

> each 'strong' culture was a monolith where every manifestation reinforced the values of top management, employees complied with managerial directives, and preferences were assumed to share these values, and there was, apparently, only one interpretation of the meaning of events shared by all. These studies were designed so integration research would find what it was looking for. (1996: 608)

Critiques of the integration perspectives   Many anthropologically inclined researchers were critical of integrationist findings because they systematically excluded resistance, subcultures, and countercultures from their analysis. These critics saw the concept of dominant cultures as unitarist. Rather as a religion might proclaim itself to be the one true faith and develop protocols for ensuring congregational compliance with its precepts, more secular organizations can privilege the views of managers of the organization against those other members or stakeholders for whom a subculture, or even subcultures, might be more important (Willmott, 2002). Subcultures may form around the status attributes of the workforce (such as ethnicity, gender, class, and skill) or on the basis of spatial markers (such as where people work and the conditions under which their work is performed). Sometimes, there may be a well-organized counterculture centred on a union or an ethnic subculture, reinforced by a strong sense of community among co-workers. Often this is the case among those who do blue-collar, dangerous work, including dockers, miners, and construction workers.

The integration theorists countered that if you went looking long enough and hard enough for such things as subcultures, you would be sure to find them, especially, the critics continued, if the research consisted of 'focused, non-random samples of lower level employees' and if the process involved 'ignoring (or not searching for) evidence of values shared on an organization-wide basis' (Martin and Frost, 1996: 608). They went on to say that, if properly conducted with appropriate skill, even ethnographers could come to see that deep fundamental values might be shared by a majority of organization members (Schein, 1997).

Predictably, with such disagreement between researchers surfacing in the public arena, the idea that culture might be a quick fix for corporate ills became harder to market. The committed ethnographic researchers were never very interested in the market, anyway. They saw themselves as more akin to anthropologists who practiced long-term participant observation and brought tales from the field to the public arena (Van Maanen, 1988).

The anthropologists resonated somewhat more with those who felt outside the approved cultures of excellence. Organizationally, if, for whatever reasons, you felt unable to bond with the strong cultural values being stressed, you were likely to feel some degree of unease. For instance, many women in organizations felt excluded from implicitly masculinist strong cultures. If work was to become even more of a boy's club as a result of its having a strong culture, these women were not going to be happy with this outcome. Linda Smircich and Joanne Martin, both major American feminist organization theorists, know a thing or two about dominant (masculine) cultures – and about how to resist them. And what they saw in the strong-culture literature raised their feminist hackles; they thought that it seemed to privilege an exclusive club to which leaders could aspire – but the implicit message was that they could succeed only if they were male. Being on the team meant joining in with a world that was masculinized, centred on sports talk, drinking, and blokey inclusiveness. While that was fine for 'the boys' it tended to marginalize 'the girls'. Knowing what it was like to be a female in a world dominated by men, they tried to create a theoretical space within which to make sense of why resistance to dominant masculine culture projects might occur – and not just as a result of poor socialization. They argued that if resistance was an attribute of insufficient socialization, the culture literature was ideological in the extreme. If you opposed the dominant culture, you were automatically a deviant and needed more socialization and training. There was no space from which it might be legitimate and justified to resist.

Smircich (2002 [1983]) began with methodological criticisms of data based on survey findings. She was particularly critical of the approach to data collection by functionalist researchers. Typically, they had little deep knowledge of the culture that they wrote about, knowledge gained from **ethnography** and the use of anthropological methods (e.g. living in and mingling intimately with the community being researched). Usually they just administered a questionnaire with a series of questions and Likert-scale response sets. One consequence was that the studies of excellence often ended up being accounts of the espoused values of the top management as if they were the values characterized throughout the organization, rather than being a study of the values actually used by all managers in practice. Thus, these 'excellent' cultures were more often than not top managerial wishes, the fulfilment of which was empirically questionable because the ethnographically rich data that might address it had often not been collected.

Differentiation perspective Martin (1992) became particularly concerned with the lack of concordance between researchers from two different perspectives using different methodologies. In the perspective that she classified as 'integration research', the a priori assumptions were that culture was the vehicle of integration for organizations; consequently, that was what was researched. A contrasting perspective is known as the **differentiation perspective.**

Researchers inclined to a differentiation perspective start with a predisposition to see plural cultures rooted in different experiences within organizations.

Various studies demonstrate that organizations are often unstable and characterized by conflict (Calás and McGuire, 1990; Gregory, 1983; Martin, 1992; Meyerson, 1991; Riley, 1983). Organizations may have members who share strong values about basic beliefs with some, but not all, of the other members of the organization. There will be cliques and cabals, relatively separate lunch networks, and distinct coffee circles.

Ethnography is an approach to research that attempts to understand social phenomena, such as organizational life, as it happens and in its own terms. It involves in-depth interviews, participant observation, and detailed case study, and generally approaches research from the point of view of understanding what the subjects themselves think. It starts from the premise that meanings and understandings are socially constructed.

The **differentiation perspective** stresses that the normal divisions to be found in organizations – of departments and disciplines, of spatial locations, of gender, religiosity, ethnicity, age, and other attributes of human beings – will all tend to be potential bases for specific local cultural formation. The assumption is that experience of more than one culture is likely to be the organizational norm.

When these groups are sufficiently clearly articulated in terms of cultures, we refer to them as *subcultures*, which are occupational and professional groups that reflect different interests, tastes, and habits; such subcultures develop alongside whatever may be the formally acknowledged organization culture (Gagliardi, 1990). Subcultures coexist with other cultures and can become dominant if they can unify adherents through the use of resources, symbols, and other forms of meaning (Clarke et al., 1976). If a subculture reflects a cohesive group and defends plausible ideas, it may become dominant and legitimate (Gagliardi, 1990). If it challenges legitimate values, it becomes a counterculture. Countercultures engage in oppositional political activities (de Certeau, 1988; Scott, 1990).

Culture: integrated, differentiated ... and fragmented   Martin (1992) suggests that cultures are always simultaneously somewhat integrated and somewhat differentiated: they are rarely totally coherent or totally differentiated. An organization culture might be *integrated* when it reflects a wide consensus, *differentiated* when it is confined to separate subcultures. However, an organizational culture may be best seen through a **fragmentation perspective** when there is little consensus and the situation is essentially ambiguous.

The fragmentation approach shares very little with the normative integration theorists, who argue for the benefits of a strong culture, and the differentiation proponents, who say that a strong culture equals a dominant culture, and a dominant culture is one that subordinates differentiated subcultures.

The picture represented by fragmentation perspectives is more likely to be one that represents contradictory and confusing cultures battling for the soul of the organization as well as those of its employees. Individuals are more likely to exist in a state of competing cultural commitments, where they are constantly under competing pressures to identify themselves and their organization with rival conceptions of an appropriate cultural identity. In such a situation, 'consensus is transient and issue specific, producing short-lived affinities among individuals that are quickly replaced by a different pattern of affinities, as a different issue draws the attention of cultural members' (Martin and Frost, 1996: 609, citing the work of Kreiner and Schultz (1993) on emergent culture in R&D networks as an example).

Although Martin suggests that any of these different conditions for organization culture formation can be found simultaneously at any given time, they can also provide a framework for depicting changes in organizational culture over time, such as in Gouldner's (1954) study of a gypsum plant (see pp. 490–492). We could easily describe the study's events in terms of a shift from an integrated culture of community to one that became differentiated and then fragmented by the unexpected strike action.

From any perspective that sees organization culture as more akin to fluid processes than stable value systems, measuring culture would be meaningless. We can understand its fluent and changing nature better through ethnographic case studies. Chan (2003: 313) argues that the 'treatment of culture as a fixed, unitary, bounded entity has to give way to a sense of

The **fragmentation perspective** is suspicious of the desire to make culture clear. According to the fragmentation view, culture is neither *clearly* consistent nor *clearly* contested, but likely to be muddled and fragmentary. A fragmented organizational culture is one that forms around specific issues and then dissolves as these fade or are resolved. The nature of fragmentation is that specific and opportunistic cultural coherencies form at different times around different issues.

fluidity and permeability'. He suggests that earlier studies of organizations as essentially 'negotiated orders' (Strauss et al., 1963) are better guides to managerial behaviour. Rather than seeing the organization as a fixed pattern, managers should instead look at the ways that the members of the organization use its resources (including conceptions of its values and culture) constantly to negotiate the sense of what it is that they are doing in and as an organization. In this view, the members of the organization create culture from the mundane, everyday aspects of their work and often use the managerially approved dominant culture as a resource in doing so, but not always in ways that would be approved within its rhetoric (Linstead and Grafton-Small, 2002).

Chan (2003) suggests that culture should be thought of as a way of accounting for what has been done in and around an organization, as a way of making sense of what has been experienced. Thought of in this way, culture is far harder to engineer than the strong-culture perspective suggests. Rather than being just a matter of replacing one set of normative assumptions with an alternative set, producing yet another mission and vision statement, culture consists of loosely negotiated, tacit ways of making sense that are embedded in specific situations in the organization rather than an all-enveloping structure that somehow contains all who are members. Because culture is overwhelmingly situational, culture is usually quite fragmentary, forming around certain emergent issues and then dissolving. Often, managers take different sides on these issues and are thus divided among themselves.

Organization cultures can make organizations confusing, because different cultural constituencies overlap and are only partially understood in terms of common sensemaking. Culture is rarely a clear, sharp image of corporate and individual identity; it is more likely to represent different or fragmented forms of ambiguity. Confusion about what is really going on is normal in many organizations; asking questions about clarity is not. Culture is an artifact of the methods used to investigate it and the assumptions that make such an investigation possible. Realistically, if you cannot define culture clearly, and the people whose culture it is supposed to be do not know what it is, it can hardly be the cure for corporate ills.

The fragmentation perspective in its research reports a world in which ambiguity provides a protective shroud from the meaninglessness of everyday organizational life. Meyerson (1991) discovered in her study of social workers that:

> ambiguity pervaded an occupation whose practitioners had to operate in a world where the objectives of social work were unclear, the means to these goals were not specified, and sometimes it wasn't even clear when an intervention had been successful or even what success in this context might have meant. (Martin and Frost, 1996: 609)

Cynics might say that this is not surprising, given that the example is social work, an area that is usually under-resourced and that is one in which people have to deal with the many complex problems of often severely dysfunctional clients. However, there are studies of other cultural contexts, which are certainly not resource poor and that have a premium on clarity and detail, in which fragmentary cultures were normal. For example, Weick (1991) discusses a case involving air-traffic controllers in which normal fragmentation produced tragic effects. They were working at Tenerife Airport one foggy night as two jumbo jets manoeuvred in their airspace. Pilots, controllers, and cockpit crews struggled to communicate but failed. The barriers of status and task assignment, not to mention the more general problems of languages spoken, all conspired to produce an organization culture that was mired in fatal ambiguity. When a foggy day met a fragmented culture in the airspace of Tenerife Airport, a disastrous impact occurred. The two jets collided, and hundreds of lives were lost in the atmospheric and cultural fog. As we mentioned in the introduction, cultural cues become particularly acute in organizational handovers.

The texts of culture

Culture is less like a family and more like an unfolding and indeterminate text – something that we can all read or watch at the cinema and understand but not necessarily make the same sense of (e.g. Chan, 2003). Think of movies that are hard to decipher, that have enigmatic stories, characters, or endings. Often we interpret these differently from our friends.

At the simplest level, the way we come to know organization cultures is through textual accounts. We look at websites; we read accounts of organizations in magazines and newspapers; or we look at PR material that the company produces. All of these accounts are either literal texts or discourses that are text-like. These texts might be those of researchers or consultants, or they may be managers' artifacts, such as company reports. They could even be the texts of everyday life embedded in the discourses of people at work: what people ordinarily say about the organizations that they work for and know. Sometimes familiarity breeds contempt and the everyday accounts will be very different from the well-turned PR prose!

Carefully constructed textual artifacts, say some contemporary theorists, mirror the practices that they address. The social realities of everyday working life in organizations are much like texts as well. They consist of actors attached to various accounts and stories with which they seek to enrol and influence others who are trying to influence them at the same time. There are official accounts, but there are also unofficial and downright scurrilous accounts as well, and only a fool would ever believe just the official story. All of these stories circulate as either literal texts or discourses that are text-like. Such stories are all social constructions whose social constructionists are positioned within them – on whom the texts reflect, and who reflect on the texts in various ways. These texts – whether formal or informal in their production – are elaborate constructs fabricated out of the bricolage that organizations provide. With these resources we are always doing cultural construction as we talk some sense into being and deny the sense of other accounts or ideas.

Fragmentation in culture is to be expected when we are trying to capture a certain reality. Social realities are always already textual – the words and deeds of the subjects concerned – before they are reworked into the texts of culture. All texts of culture suppress, silence, and marginalize some elements of discursive reality that some other account of the same underlying texts might instead privilege. That is, culture acts as a structure around individual behaviour: it constrains what actions one might take, and encourages particular actions over others – as a result cultural texts are powerful forces within organizations. People seek to find a sense of their self within the cultural texts that the organization makes available for them to use and there is no reason to expect that they will only find these in the officially approved texts.

The view that organizations should be thought of as complex cultures that can be read in fragments, like incomplete and multifaceted texts, has become widely associated with postmodernist accounts of culture. Rather than join what Martin and Frost (1996) call the culture war games, postmodern theorists seek to demonstrate the strategies that make moves in these games possible and the reflexive edge of thinking about those debates that occupy centre stage (Clegg and Kornberger, 2003). Typical postmodern accounts include reflexive analysis by analysts of their ordering of the data that constitutes what they take to be the culture, and sometimes it also includes the voices of research subjects, which are usually omitted by others (Clegg and Hardy, 1996; Jeffcutt, 1994). Methodologically, postmodern analysis seeks to deconstruct the assumptions that underpin particular accounts of culture and to show that the account is an artifact of these assumptions (Smircich, 2002 [1983]).

MEASURING NATIONAL CULTURES

If it is a big assumption to think that organizations have a singular culture, how much bigger is the assumption that countries have a singular national culture? And that it can be measured? Some researchers argue that we *can* measure an organization's culture and its effects on performance (see Gordon and DiTomaso, 1992). One prominent researcher along these lines is Ashkenasy (2003), for whom values are the core component of organization cultures. He says that conceptions of organization culture are more reliable when they can be measured rather than just described and argues that the concept of a value system allows you to do this. Hofstede (1980) goes one step further: he says that you can measure the values of a national culture.

Geert Hofstede, the writer best known for having measured national culture, in terms of values, studied only one organization – but he studied it in over 40 countries! It is now widely known that the unidentified organization that Hofstede (1980) reported on in his book *Culture's Consequences: International Differences in Work-Related Values* was the multinational company IBM. He describes culture as 'mental programming', as 'software of the mind', as 'subjective'. Hofstede is a cultural determinist: for him the national culture will determine the shape of the organization culture. While the population of a nation can be differentiated on many grounds, Hofstede claims that, nonetheless, a national population shares a unique culture. His empirical basis for this claim, however, is a statistical averaging of the principal data – questionnaire responses from IBM employees. It is as a statistical average based on individuals' views, which he calls a 'central tendency' (1991: 253), or 'an average tendency' (1991: 253). In other words, it is a statistical artifact.

Hofstede's data drew on a data bank of 75,000 employee attitude surveys undertaken around 1967 and 1973 within IBM subsidiaries in 66 countries, which he analysed statistically. He found that the data demonstrated that there were four central dimensions of a national culture, such that 40 out of the 66 countries in which the IBM subsidiaries were located could be given a comparative score on each of these four dimensions (1980). Hofstede defines these dimensions as follows:

- *Power distance*: 'the extent to which the less powerful members of organizations and institutions (like the family) expect and accept that power is distributed unequally' (Hofstede and Peterson, 2000: 401).

- *Uncertainty avoidance*: 'intolerance for uncertainty and ambiguity' (Hofstede and Peterson, 2000: 401).

- *Individualism versus collectivism*: 'the extent to which individuals are integrated into groups' (Hofstede and Peterson, 2000: 401).

- *Masculinity versus femininity*: 'assertiveness and competitiveness versus modesty and caring' (Hofstede and Peterson, 2000: 401).

Hofstede arrived at the national patterns by averaging the means of the distribution of the data collected on individuals in terms of the national samples. Consistent patterns were established in terms of national variation – variation according to the means, which were, of course, statistical devices for representing the sum of individual variance. The upshot would be similar to saying that the average Dutch person is taller than the average Chinese person; the statement accepts that the average is a summary device. The average tells you nothing about what any particular Dutch or Chinese person's height may be any more than it informs you about the values they hold. An average of values, although it is economical, is about as meaningful as an average of height. Just as there would be wide variance in the height of any given population so there would be wide variance in the values of that population, a point that is well established in McSweeney's (2002) critique. As he says, Hofstede assumes that it is national cultures that produce the variance in his data but provides no evidence to support the assumption; any other classification made on the basis of another assumption would have done just as well – or as badly – as an explanatory device.

To accept Hofstede's analysis is to assume the cultural homogeneity of nations – that lines on a map inscribe a unitary, patterned, and consistent common culture. In the vast majority of cases in the contemporary world, this is hardly feasible. There are few singularly ethnically, linguistically, and culturally homogeneous countries among the major nations in the world

Check out the Companion Website www.sagepub.co.uk/ managingandorganizations3 for free access to an article by Brendan McSweeney (2002) if you want to learn more about what's wrong with the assumptions that Hofstede makes and what the implications are for management.

today. Indeed, one of the countries that Hofstede (1980) treated as a unitary cultural space in his study, Yugoslavia, no longer exists as such – precisely because it was not a unitary cultural space in the first place, as indicated by the horrors of the 'ethnic cleansing' and associated mass murders in the early 1990s that were its major contribution to world affairs. In many countries, modern identities are much more likely to be plural than singular, as shown in hybrid, hyphenated identities such as Anglo-Indian, Viet-Australian, and so on. Will the diversity that the organization's members display in their everyday life not be reflected as diversity in the organization as well?

You could argue that it is precisely because organizations are able to pick and choose who joins them – through human resource management practices – that they may be said to have cultures (but the countries they operate in also have equal employment and anti-discrimination laws!). In other words, they select people to fit the culture. Contrary to this viewpoint, however, many organizations have been torn apart by bitter internal conflicts, even when professionally managed, which make the idea of their having only one culture seem questionable.

SUMMARY AND REVIEW

In this chapter we have introduced some key ideas about organization culture and its discussion in management and organization theory:

- The notion that we can make others do what we want them to do by persuading them to want to do it is one that has a long pedigree. It eventually became formalized as an integrative view of organization culture, spurred by the remarkable commercial success of *In Search of Excellence* (Peters and Waterman, 1982).
- The 'strong-culture' perspective, even though it is the most popular, is not the only well-developed view of organization culture.
- Other views see strong cultures as the problem, not the solution, and think of them as dominant rather than empowering.
- More recently, ethnographers have suggested that it may be quite normal for some organizations to have neither a strong nor a dominant culture. On the contrary, culture may be characterized by fragmentation.
- Finally, postmodern theorists suggest that all representations of culture are characterized by such a complex intertextuality – the texts of the subjects, the texts of the organization, and the

texts of the authors – that they are better thought of as occasions for further analysis than as in any sense a definitive account of what really happens.

- Managers who are familiar with postmodern thought are at least less likely to be duped into believing that culture is a panacea and might be more sophisticated in the ways that they seek to understand and possibly to use it.

EXERCISES

1 Having read this chapter you should be able to say in your own words what the following key terms mean:

- Culture
- Organization culture
- National culture
- Subculture
- Counterculture
- Levels of culture
- Dimensions of culture
- Cultures' consequences
- Espoused Value
- Artifacts
- Basic values and assumption

2 What are the three levels of culture, and how do they operate?

3 What are the management arguments for a strong culture?

4 What is the difference between seeing a culture as strong or dominant?

5 What are the differences between integration, differentiation, and fragmentation accounts of culture?

6 What would postmodernists make of organization culture?

7 In what ways are contemporary managers the pastoralists of the modern age?

8 Should management academics prescribe organization cultures?

9 How useful is the construct of national cultures?

10 Think of culture as a multilevel concept, with sub-cultures, counter-cultures and so on: how easy is it to design an organization culture in such circumstances?

11 Can culture be managed, or is it just something that is there? Look at the students around you; think of your conversations with them, and discussions in class. To what extent can the variance between their value statements be considered reflective of a 'national culture'?

   a What might it mean to say that an individual has a national culture?

   b How might it affect the way that you do your work?

   c In what ways is your work, organizationally, shaped by what your national culture is?

ADDITIONAL RESOURCES

1 Probably the best way to come to terms with organization culture is to consult some exemplary studies of it. Peters and Waterman's *In Search of Excellence: Lessons from America's Best-Run Companies* (1982) is the obvious point to start.

2 From a more anthropological and ethnographic perspective, Martin et al.'s (1988) study, 'An alternative to bureaucratic impersonality and emotional labour: bounded emotionality at The Body Shop', is of considerable interest because it demonstrates how the distinctive culture of The Body Shop, a cosmetics chain, produces highly committed employees. Many of you have probably been in a Body Shop at some time; now you can read all about what it means in terms of an integrationist organization culture. Another easily accessible and good narrative account can be found in Van Maanen's (1991) 'The smile factory'. He provides an entertaining account of the corporate culture at Disneyland.

3 An excellent account of organization culture from a detailed ethnographic perspective is Kondo's *Crafting Selves* (1990), which does a really nice job of unpicking the assumption that Japan has a national culture that easily creates effective and harmonious organizations.

4 There is a very thorough analysis of the literature on national cultures in *The Sage International Encyclopedia of Organization Studies* entry by d'Iribarne (2008).

5 Films often provide a detailed insight into organization cultures. Think of the stress on family values as an integration metaphor in *The Godfather* movies (Coppola, 1972, 1974, 1990) or the emphasis on the sources of gender differentiation in the otherwise seemingly integrated 'organization man' world of the movie *Down With Love* (Reed, 2003) or the *Legally Blonde* movies (Luketic, 2001; Herman-Wurmfeld, 2003).

6 Interesting examples of strong organization cultures and their effects are provided by military/war movies, especially *A Few Good Men* (Reiner, 1992), starring Jack Nicholson, Demi Moore, and Tom Cruise.

7 Perhaps one of the most interesting movies ever made about organization culture is one based on a true story: *Colonel Redl* (Szabo, 1985). Colonel Redl is an outsider in the Austro-Hungarian court at the turn of the nineteenth century. He is part Jewish, part Catholic, part Ukrainian, part Hungarian, and gay. Within this sociopolitical context, he does not fit anywhere into the culture. He manages to pass himself off as a member of the dominant culture; however, he ends up being blackmailed and disgraced, and the culture leaves him with only one organizational option, which occupies the closing reels of the film.

8 Both the late Peter Frost and Joanne Martin, whom we have discussed in this chapter, can be seen in short interviews on the Companion Website www.sagepub.co.uk/managingand organizations3.

9 There is also a film of the Barings Bank disaster caused by Nick Leeson, *Rogue Trader* (Deardon, 1999). This makes particularly interesting viewing, if seen in conjunction with the classic business movie *Wall Street* (Stone, 1987), as an illustration of an organization culture premised on absolute selfishness and ruthlessness.

WEB SECTION

1 Our Companion Website is the best first stop for you to find a great deal of extra resources, free PDF versions of leading articles published in Sage journals, exercises, video and pod casts, team case studies and general questions, and links to teamwork resources. Go to www.sage pub.co.uk/managingandorganizations3.

2 For state of the art briefings on how to manage organizations effectively, please visit the Henry Stewart Talks series of online audiovisual seminars on Managing Organizations, edited by Stewart Clegg: www.hstalks.com/r/managing-orgs, especially Talk #9 by Stephen Linstead on *Managing cultures*.

3 Much of the best work on organization culture consists of organizational ethnographies. There is a very good website run by Randy Hodson at http://tinyurl.com/378p83. It has a great many references to many different ethnographic studies of work and organizations as well as being a really useful guide to doing ethnographies.

4 The work of Geert Hofstede in *Culture's Consequences* (1980) is well represented in controversies on the web. For instance, there is the site http://tinyurl.com/2ndzbj, which includes summaries of Hofstede's work and critiques of it, the most useful of which is McSweeney's (2002) paper from *Human Relations*, which called 'Hofstede's model of national cultural differences and their consequences: a triumph of faith – a failure of analysis'. You can find this paper on the Companion Website www.sagepub.co.uk/managingand organizations3. Geert Hofstede's official website can be found at http://tinyurl.com/ 2rcsa7, in which, at http://tinyurl.com/2o2egs, you will find a vexed tale about the relationship between the two Geert Hofstede websites. The first mentioned is an 'official' and 'authorized'

Geert Hofstede site; the second mentioned is not.

5 At http://leo.oise.utoronto.ca/~vsvede/culture.htm you will find an amusing exercise for assessing an organization culture.

6 There is an insightful essay available at http://tinyurl.com/2s96re on organization culture and symbolism by Rafaeli and Worline, from the *Sage Handbook of Organizational Culture and Climate* (2000), an invaluable resource in its own right.

7 The 'grandfather' of organization culture, Ed Schein, has a website at http://web.mit.edu/scheine/www/home.html. For a good idea of a more consulting take on organization culture take a look at the web pages of any of the big consulting firms, and key in 'culture', or look at http://www.managementhelp.org/trng_dev/basics/reasons.htm, for a more specialist appraisal. Another interesting page from a consulting perspective is http://tinyurl.com/2syu3m, which is oriented to changing organization culture.

8 As is often the case, Wikipedia has a good basic entry – see http://en.wikipedia.org/wiki/Organizational_culture.

LOOKING FOR A HIGHER MARK?

Reading and digesting these articles that are available free on the Companion Website www.sagepub.co.uk/managingandorganizations3 can help you gain deeper understanding and, on the basis of that, a better grade:

1 The best-selling management book, *In Search of Excellence*, which shaped a great deal of debate about organization culture in management circles, *had a scholarly genesis, as argued by* Colville, I., Waterman, R. and Weick, K. (1999) 'Organizing and the search for excellence: making sense of the times in theory and practice', *Organization*, 6 (1): 129–148. While many critics have suggested that *In Search of Excellence* was unalloyed managerialism these authors argue that it was, in fact, a clever blending of sophisticated organization theory packaged for a mass market.

2 Greener, I. (2006) 'Nick Leeson and the collapse of Barings Bank: socio-technical networks and the "Rogue Trader"', *Organization,* 13 (3): 421–441, and Brown, A. D. (2005) 'Making sense of the collapse of Barings Bank', *Human Relations,* 58 (12): 1579–1604, are excellent to read in conjunction with watching the film, Rogue Trader (Deardon, 1999). These papers demonstrate organization theory in action – understanding and explaining a significant social event that we can all learn about by watching the film.

3 McSweeney, B. (2002) 'Hofstede's model of national cultural differences and their consequences: a triumph of faith – a failure of analysis', *Human Relations*, 55 (1): 89–118, is a scathing analysis of what has been an important set of research findings. The importance of Hofstede's work has been not only that it has been widely used for executive training and MBA teaching but also it has been a prime foundation for research in international business. McSweeney, quite rightly, we would argue, demolishes these foundations. It is notable that even though Hofstede is widely recognized as an expert on culture he trained as an engineer not an anthropologist or sociologist. Had he done so, he might have been familiar with Emile Durkheim's (1982 [1895]) classic *The Rules of Sociological Method*, which, if followed, would never have allowed such a dodgy construction to be built on such rotten foundations.

CASE STUDY

Enacting organization culture

In the 1980s 'culture' operated as a kind of 'open sesame' concept in management theory. Subsequently it has been heavily criticized. Despite the critics, the concept of culture continues to be widely used by managers and consultants. It signifies processes of importance in organizations that other concepts do not capture so well. A project of 'managing culture' was devised in the year 2000 in collaboration with the Scandinavian engineering consultant company SEC.

Cultural merging

SEC was in a heavy growth period, after mergers and acquisitions of a number of firms. The reasoning behind the mergers was to position the company for the purpose of delivering complete solutions to large engineering projects, which were getting increasingly higher shares of the total project market. The challenges of creating and realizing practical synergies after mergers and acquisitions are all too familiar from the literature. Since 1997 corporations have globally spent well above $5 trillion on mergers and acquisitions, yet in 83 per cent of 700 large mergers the stock price of the combined organization did not rise above those of the single entities.

SEC identified challenges with diverse organization cultures and work practices in the different companies it had acquired for realizing its ambitions. For example, some of the companies comprised highly specialized, mono-disciplinary engineers with a much sought-after expert status, and which subsequently had a wide geographical area as their 'field' of work. On the other hand, some companies comprised highly trans-disciplinary engineers with work practices targeted towards complex and often local projects where they had responsibilities for more or less the totality of the project. Thus the project was initiated with the slogan of 'accelerated cultural integration'. In a collaboration between key members of the company and our team of researchers we defined the

work tasks implied in the slogan in terms of barriers and enablers for knowledge exchange. The project subsequently focused on methods, concepts, and approaches for accelerated cultural integration after and during the new company mergers and acquisitions.

Rituals of cultural exchange and dissemination

The underlying premise was that faster (than the natural cadence of time would have achieved 'left to its own' social evolution) cultural integration would enable conditions for improving, and lowering the costs of, knowledge sharing. A guiding principle in the project was that culture cannot be dictated through directives and decisions, but rather is enabled through communal practices of everyday work. The basic methods of the project were twofold; first, to facilitate process meetings where top management and local project workers met in all the locations where SEC had offices; and second, to follow closely through interviews two specific projects that SEC was accomplishing at the time, and on the basis of them make two so-called 'learning histories'. We had about 15 process meetings and 20 interviews with top management, middle management, project leaders, and project members. Both in the real-life gatherings and in the learning histories we focused on what we called 'fruitful dilemmas' that SEC employees were facing in daily work activities. Through the 'dilemma doorway' the process meetings provided arenas for people to meet, get to know each other, and exchange different perspectives on significant phenomena and challenging themes. The learning histories, with their intimate project practice focus, provided a possibility to lay down traces and 'sedimentations' in the company from the discussions, perspectives, and practices that the process meetings and the two project cases spurred. Through this work two critical 'sets of oppositional stories' displaying core dilemmas in the company surfaced. We conceived these two sets of oppositional stories as two of the most important myths that were guiding different practices and thus constituting key cultural knowledge in the company.

'Heart surgery – the cheaper the better?'

One of the most important activities in project-based companies such as SEC is undoubtedly the process of acquiring and initiating new projects. SEC, like similar companies, lives on project acquisitions, accomplishment, and satisfactory deliverances, and stories of project creations have naturally a significant place in story-telling practices and thus in the reproduction of culture in the company. The learning histories from SEC focused to a large extent on what might be called the myth of 'project initiation', which in the specific case of SEC was labelled 'Heart surgery – the cheaper the better?' Basically, the dilemma of project initiation as unfolded in the myth and displayed in the learning histories, stretches along an axis from an understanding of project acquisitions as highly formalized procedures answering 'invitations for tenders' from potential customers, on the one side, to an understanding of acquiring projects through a history of reputation and trust with 'good customers' and intimate personal relationships on the other.

'The flying engineers'

Much of the focus in the SEC project meeting discussions (which we considered as enacting rituals enabling cultural exchanges) evolved around aspects of 'the ideal organizational structure' of the company, and practical consequences of the form chosen. Again dilemmas were at the core, not surprising, given the challenges of knowledge sharing after mergers and acquisitions had taken place in a distributed environment creating a singular entity out of several large and small former companies, 'inhabited' by engineering experts of different disciplines. For example, the leader of one of the divisions in SEC on several occasions when discussing priorities, strategies, or challenges said, 'We cannot make the flying of engineers a business idea!' The contention received mixed applause. Some groups and individuals consented to it, notably the specialized high-status experts, while others expressed their absolute disagreement. The saying pinpointed some of the dilemmas pertaining to the myth concerning the existence of 'the ideal organizational form'. In the joint dialogic unfolding of this myth during the project, company members increasingly realized that whatever organizational form you chose to realize, you gain some and you lose some. And like cultural practices that never can be reduced to static structures, you move on.

Questions

1 Is it possible to 'manage culture' at all, or is this a contradiction in terms?
2 Based on your own experience, discuss possible approaches to 'managing culture'.
3 What does culture consist of in this case?

Case prepared by Emil A. Røyrvik, SINTEF Technology and Society, emil.royrvik@sintef.no.

PART TWO

MANAGING ORGANIZATIONAL PRACTICES

CHAPTER SEVEN

MANAGING POWER, POLITICS, AND DECISION-MAKING IN ORGANIZATIONS

Resistance, Empowerment, Ethics

LEARNING OBJECTIVES

By the end of this chapter, you will be able to:

■ List the main resources proposed as bases of power

■ Understand how power and legitimacy are related

■ Know what power relations are

■ Recognize that power conflicts are normal and acceptable in organizations

■ Understand how management of power may form a normal part of management practice

■ Describe the 'soft' ways in which power operates

■ Use power positively

■ Discuss decision-making in organizations

BEFORE YOU GET STARTED . . .

A consultant's experiential viewpoint:

I always thought politics was a dirty word at work, but it's reality, it's reality and it's not ... being sneaky, it's just making sure that, you know, your people that are going to help you go where you need to go, are aware of you and know what you do, so it's... talking about what you've done, your achievements, to the right people. (Young consultant in a global company)

INTRODUCTION

Organizational politics, broadly speaking, refers to the network of social relations between people in and around organizations, between employees and their managers, customers, suppliers, competitors, etc., all of whom can be involved in organizational politics, insofar as they are involved, whether wittingly or not, in practices of power.

The most common definition of **power** is that it is the chance of an actor to realize their own will in a social action, even against the resistance of others. The actor may be an individual or a collective entity. At its most mechanical, power means forcing others to do things against their will. However, power can be far more positive and less mechanical when it shapes and frames what others want to do – seemingly of their own volition.

Understanding office and **organizational politics** is an important skill for all managers, which underlies and shapes the formal structures of rationality and authority in which organizational life is situated.

We have seen that organizations are made up of formal and informal rules that coordinate actions of different people. But how can organizations make sure that people – who have diverse backgrounds, particular interests, and different understandings – comply with these rules? **Power** is the concept that encompasses the mechanisms, processes, and dispositions that try, not always successfully, to ensure that people act according to the rules of the game. Hence, power should be one of the central concepts in both management practice and theory.

Max Weber is recognized as the 'founding voice' on power in organization studies. He distinguished between key terms such as authority, which requires the consent of those being managed, and domination, which does not. He saw power as a pervasive aspect of organizational life, as people in management sought to execute actions through imperative commands – orders – that may or may not be resisted. The imprimatur of authority attaching to management was a great asset in securing compliance from subordinates.

The definition of power is routinely explained as A doing something to B to cause B to do something that B would not otherwise do. However, power is more complex than just the push and pull of attraction and repulsion, command and control. It also involves the structuring of dispositions and capacities for action, as well as action itself.

We explore power themes in this chapter, looking at the good, the bad, and the ugly in power relations. We take care not only to concentrate on the negatives but also to accentuate the positives. After all, if power is inescapable, we might as well learn how to use it wisely.

Organizations operate within complex internal and external networks of interests and opportunities, which make 'social and political skills vital to managerial success' (Douglas and Ammeter, 2004: 537). Yet, most studies of organizational behaviour make little or no reference to politics and political behaviour. Politics is seen as something done either to resist managerial authority or it is an example of maverick management: where self-interested action by individual managers prevails, acting with the sole objective of advancing their own career interests. Any organizational benefit may be coincidental or secondary. 'Politics' is frequently conflated with 'politicking' (Mintzberg, 1985), which is seen as something disreputable. Perhaps for this reason, as organization theorists began to think and write about power they did so in terms that often saw it as illegitimate.

Researchers in organization theory and management in the era after the Second World War developed a set of expectations about the exercise of power in organizations that they had derived from the formal structure of bureaucratic authority (Bennis et al., 1958). However, a number of case studies contradicted these expectations. Surprisingly, these case studies discovered bases of power outside the formal structure of authority and described the resulting power games and the rules that made them possible. More recently, interest in discussions of power has shifted to issues of resistance – how people in organizations resist formal organizational authorities.

SOURCES OF POWER

We spend at least one-third of our adult lives working in organizations in which we enter into complex relations of power that range from some other people getting us to do things we would not otherwise do, to us doing the same to other people. We will spend that third of our lives in different organizations. At best, these will be warm, friendly, welcoming, open places in which we can do our jobs with pride, growth, and achievement. At worst, however, they may be akin to places of concentrated power that frame and shape our hours therein as a heavy and unhappy time.

As organization theorists began studying the empirical workings of organizations, they noticed that some members of organizations were able to exploit seemingly impersonal rules for their own ends. The prevalent conception identified organization hierarchy with legitimacy: thus, when actions were identified that seemed to subvert or bypass the official hierarchy of authority, they were labelled 'illegitimate' – they were not authorized. In this way, power came to be seen as illegitimate, whereas authority was legitimate.

At various times, several key assets have been promoted as the basis for expert power in organizations. The most pervasive of these has been seen to be the ability to control uncertainty in bureaucratic organizations. More recently, there has been a shift in focus from bureaucracy to consideration of more empowered alternatives. But, as we will see, **empowerment** is not necessarily all it is cracked up to be – it can mean even tighter control.

If an organization makes people do things they normally would not do, power must be the central issue. Many potential sources or bases of power

Empowerment means giving someone more power than they had previously. Transferring power to the individual by promoting self-regulating and self-motivating behaviour through innovative human resource policies and practices, such as self-managing work teams, enhanced individual autonomy, and so on.

have been listed, including: information; expertise; credibility; stature and prestige (Pettigrew, 1973); uncertainty (Crozier, 1964); access to top-level managers and the control of money, sanctions, and rewards (Benfari et al., 1986; French and Raven, 1968); and control over resources (Pfeffer and Salancik, 2002 [1974]). We consider some of the more important of these bases of power in this section.

Legitimacy

Legitimacy attaches to something, whether a particular action or social structure, when there is a widespread belief that it is just and valid.

Power works best when it is seen least. If people already want to do what is expected of them, there is no need to exercise overt power. If **legitimacy** can be created for individual actions, it greatly reduces the chance of opposition to them because it creates a meaningful context in which these actions can be accepted and justified (Edelman, 1964; 1971).

In managing and organizations the arbiters of legitimacy are always significant others rather than the actor the status of whose action is in question. Such significant others can be subordinates or superordinates, customers, suppliers, government, and so on. Legitimation lowers the probability of resistance, as Blau (1964: 199) recognized when he noted that 'stable organizing power requires legitimation … The coercive use of power engenders resistance and sometimes active opposition'. Legitimation is achieved through what Pettigrew (2002 [1977]) called the 'management of meaning' – a double action because it seeks both to create legitimacy for one's initiatives as it simultaneously seeks to delegitimize those it opposes.

Some of the main sources of legitimacy are symbolic. Images can represent a great deal of power in simple ways. For example, the law is often portrayed as an institution that impartially weighs justice in its

IMAGE 7.1   A skyline of symbolic power

scales. That the common symbol of this power is blindfolded while holding the scales of justice is meant to represent it as a legitimate authority; it shows that an impartial judiciary resides over a mass population that is weighed equally in the scales. Cathedrals were among the most symbolically important buildings in many European cities until relatively recent times; they were often the largest, tallest, most richly decorated, and most symbolically laden buildings that people would ever see. They represented the condensed and local power of the church as an institution. In Muslim countries, the mosque has fulfilled a similar function, with its high minarets from which the faithful might be called to prayer, and an inspiring dome under which those in prayer might gather.

When spiritual power had to jostle for space with increasing commercial power the boards of the various banks would compete with each other to build imposing temples of commerce, often demonstrating visually that their bank had a solid, classical presence (with lots of Corinthian columns, high vaulted ceilings, and solid timbering). Banks needed their customers to trust in them and the material and symbolic presentation that bank buildings and location made was important in securing this trust. Today, of course, the skylines of famous cities are crowded with the towers and skyscrapers of the major corporations that now far outreach the spires of the cathedrals in their thrust into the sky. The skyline is an ever-changing record of shifting symbolic power.

Uncertainty

At a fundamental level, churches, banks, and other organizations seek to impress those who worship and invest in them, use their services, buy their products, and serve in their employ, that they are bastions of certainty and security in an uncertain world.

Step inside organizations and what happens? Is **uncertainty** banished? To some extent it is: all those rules that define a bureaucracy are in part intended to take the uncertainty out of everyday work and organization. However, Weber himself pointed out ways in which uncertainty could creep back in. Weber (1978) used the example of the uncertainty that the elected members of a legislative assembly experienced, in terms of parliamentary, budgetary, and other procedures of rule, compared with the far more detailed and certain knowledge of their senior permanent public servants. He saw the uncertainty – a lack of knowledge of the precise rules of the bureaucracy – of elected politicians as their undoing in power terms when compared with permanent civil servants. However, the generation of empirical researchers in organization theory after the Second World War reversed this analysis. For them, uncertainty increasingly became seen as a *source* of power rather than a constraint on its exercise.

Uncertainty and power are not strange bedfellows, and their proximity has been much explored in organization theory. The view for the last 50 years has been that when an organization experiences uncertainty in areas

We can define **uncertainty** as the inability to know how to continue some action, a lack of a rule or undecidability about which rule to apply.

of organizational action, if a person has organizational skills that can reduce that uncertainty, they will derive power from such expertise. In other words, this view states that despite formal hierarchies, prescribed organizational communications, and the relations that they specify, people will be able to exercise power when they control or have the necessary knowledge to master zones of uncertainty in the organizational arena.

One of the earliest proponents of these views conducted research in one of the most clearly prescribed of organizations: a military bureaucracy. Thompson (1956) researched two US Air Force bomber wing commands, comprising both flight and ground crew personnel. The flight crew had greater formal authority, but the role of the ground crew was central for the safety of the flight crew. Their need for safety conferred a degree of power on the ground crew that was not evident in formal authority relations. Their technical competency vis-à-vis safety issues put them in a strategic position to secure their own interests – to exercise 'unauthorized or illegitimate power' (Thompson, 1956: 290), which they rationalized in terms of a need for safety. Hence, the maintenance workers controlled the key source of uncertainty in an otherwise routinized system.

In a study conducted by Crozier (1964) in a French state-owned tobacco factory, uncertainty also proved to be a central resource. The female production workers, at the technical core of the organization, were highly central to its workflow-centred bureaucracy. The male maintenance workers were marginal, at least in the formal representation of the organizational design. The production workers were paid on a piece-rate system in a bureaucracy designed on scientific management principles. Most workers were, in effect, de-skilled. The bureaucracy was a highly formal, highly prescribed organization, except for the propensity of the machines to break down. The effect of them doing so was to diminish the bonus that the production workers could earn. To maintain earnings, the production workers needed functional machines.

Work stoppages made the production workers extremely dependent on the maintenance workers, whose expertise could rectify breakdowns. Consequently, the maintenance workers possessed a high degree of power over the other workers in the bureaucracy because they controlled the remaining source of uncertainty in the system. Management and the production workers were aware of the situation, and they had made attempts to try to remedy it. Management had introduced planned preventive maintenance to be done by the production workers, but manuals disappeared and sabotage occurred. Maintenance workers were indefatigable in defence of their relative autonomy, privilege, and power. Through their technical knowledge, they could render the uncertain certain and the non-routine routine. The benefit of maintaining routine was a degree of autonomy and relative power for the maintenance workers in excess of that formally designed. There was also an issue of gender; the male maintenance workers used their expert knowledge as a masculine device over and against the female production workers.

Crozier's (1964) study was a major landmark. He had taken an under-explained concept – power – and attached it to the central concept of uncertainty. After this study, the field developed rapidly. A theory called the 'strategic contingencies theory of intra-organizational power' (Hickson et al., 2002 [1971]) emerged. It sought to build a theory from existing ideas, particularly that power was related to the control of uncertainty and that, following Tannenbaum (1968), it could be measured. Tannenbaum had developed a measurement of power, the control graph. The graph maps the means of the perceived power of each level in the formal hierarchy of an organization by averaging the sum of the perceptions of people in the organization of the amount of power vested at various levels within it. In this way, intersubjective measures of power may be achieved. It became apparent that power was not something that was fixed – it could be increased. Organizations that were quite similar structurally could design power quite differently.

Strategic contingencies

Hickson et al. (2002 [1971]) sought to measure power in organizations. One of their theoretical innovations was to use a formal model. The organization was conceptualized as comprising four functional subsystems or subunits dealing with production, marketing, maintenance and finance (Figure 7.1). The subunits were seen as interdependent. Some were more or less dependent and produced more or less uncertainty for other subunits. What connected them was the major task of the organization, coping with uncertainty. The theory ascribes the differing power of subunits to imbalances in the way in which these interdependent subunits cope with and handle uncertainty. The most powerful are the least dependent subunits that cope with the greatest systemic uncertainty, although there are certain qualifications – namely, that the subunit is not easily substitutable with any other subunit and that it is central to the organization system. Note the absence of a vertical dimension and the assumption that each subunit is quite contained and unitary.

To conceptualize an organization as composed of subunits is to flatten out the normal hierarchical representation of it as a 'structure of dominancy', to use Weber's (1978) terms. This new perspective views the organization on a horizontal rather than vertical axis. Viewing organizations as more horizontal than vertical structures is to make a number of assumptions about the unitary and functionally cohesive nature of subunits. In reality, each subunit is typically a hierarchy with a more or less problematic culture of consent or dissent. For it to be treated as if it were unitary, there needs to exist some internal mechanisms of power that would allow for such a representation. In other words, there must be a hierarchy of order that is effectively reinforced through everyday organizational actions.

Inputs   Outputs

FIGURE 7.1
An organization conceived
as made up of subunits

Strategic contingencies theory assumes that management's definitions prevail and that each subunit is a perfectly unitary form of organization, one capable of being glossed as a single actor. For this to be the case a great deal of power has to have been exerted. Indeed, sometimes they are a perfectly unitary form of organization, in which case management has exercised power. When they are not, management is outmanoeuvred. Being intermittently outmanoeuvred is a fate that most managers are familiar with. Later empirical analysis to test the theory deliberately sought out a simple and tightly regulated bureaucracy (Hinings et al., 1974). The theory worked.

Resources

Open systems: In an open systems approach, organizations were viewed as systems that were open to inputs from their environments and that sent outputs to their environments as a result of their internal transformation processes.

Similar to strategic contingencies theory is the resource dependency view. This derives from the work of social psychologists such as Emerson (1962) and related work by French and Raven (1968). All resource dependency theorists view a certain resource as key in organizations, but they differ in which resource is regarded as key. Resource dependency theory was formulated in the 1970s as an **open systems** model that examined how environmental contexts affect organizational behaviours and decisions. The focus is on how managers in organizations secure the flow of resources essential for organizational survival. 'As such, the theory recognizes that organizations act not only in response to, but also upon, their contexts. Specifically, organizations strive to influence organizations upon which they are dependent for scarce and critical resources. These actions are frequently political' (Greenwood, 2008: 1383).

Pfeffer and Salancik (2002 [1974]) hypothesized that power would be used in organizations to try to influence decisions about the allocation of resources. Resources may be raw materials, capital, information, authority, or any other essential resource. Most resource dependency theory emphasizes material resources, such as labour, capital, and information. Resources have to be procured and secured from a network of other organizations. While the organization is thus *dependent* on other organizations, rationally it will strive not to be overdependent. To be so places it at risk, as a hostage to the actions that these other organizations might undertake or fail to undertake: banks may not advance loans, for instance, because the organization is perceived as being already overindebted. Organizations respond to resource contexts by *adaptation* (i.e. through internal changes to strategies or operations) and/or by *domination* (i.e. through efforts to control the environment).

Using archival data on decision-making in the University of Illinois, they confirmed their hypotheses, suggesting that power is a positive-sum game for those that have control of critical resources – using the power these resources bestow, they can acquire yet more resources, to leverage more power. Those that have resources attract more resources and thus more power. From this perspective, power is often conceptualized as if it were a zero-sum game in which, rather like being on a seesaw, more resources on the part of one party outweigh those of another party because they can be gained

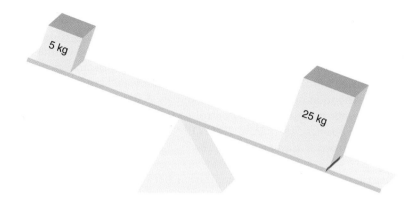

FIGURE 7.2
A zero-sum conception of power

only at the expense of the other party. It is assumed that there is a fixed amount of power to go around (Figure 7.2).

Michel Crozier subsequently revisited the links between power and uncertainty as a critical resource (Crozier and Friedberg, 1980). Members of an organization meet each other in spaces that offer relatively open opportunities for control of rules and resources. People do not adapt passively to the circumstances that they meet; they use these circumstances creatively to enhance the scope of their own discretion, through shaping and bending rules and colonizing resources. Power is still seen in terms of the control of uncertainty as it is played out in daily struggles over the rules of an uncertain game.

There is no doubt that uncertainty – as well as the other contenders for strategic resource status – can be a source of power, but not in a context-independent way. What counts as a resource can be made to count only in specific contexts. For instance, box cutters, which are used for cutting paper and cardboard, are not usually thought of as powerful resources – or at least they were not until 9/11. Then, in the hands of determined terrorists, they were responsible for what has now passed into history. So, if information, uncertainty – or box cutters – are to count as resources for power, they will do so only in specific contexts.

To the extent that specific resources are related to power in a general way, without regard for context, they are not very helpful. Anything can be a resource in the right context – the context is what is important. Thus, possessing scarce resources is not enough to deliver power over and above that formally authorized; one also needs to have an explicit knowledge of context (Hickson et al., 1986; Pettigrew, 1973; 2002 [1977]) and how to use resources accordingly.

POLITICS

The process of mobilizing (or demobilizing) power is the process of politics. Given the stress on authority and formal organization in the literature, politics are often seen as what happens when members of organizations behave in ways that are potentially authoritatively illegitimate. Pettigrew (2002 [1977]: 45) sees the mobilization of power as what happens when either individuals or sub-groupings within organizations make a claim against the extant resource-sharing system of the organization. As Pettigrew suggests, power is central to the strategy process in organizations because decisions about what strategy to maintain or innovate will always be political. Such decisions are 'likely to threaten the existing distribution of organizational resources as represented in salaries, in promoting opportunities, and in control of tasks, people, information, and new areas of business' (Pettigrew, 2002 [1977]: 45). What do organizational politics arise from, according to Pettigrew?

1 Structural divisions in the organization between different component elements and identities, and the different values, affective, cognitive and discursive styles associated with these. Think of the differences between the creative types in an organization and the accountants.
2 The complexity and the degree of uncertainty attached to a central dilemma (as we have seen from previous theory). Being able to control uncertainty that is hardly of much significance will not deliver power.
3 The salience of issues for different actors and identities in the organization. If the issue isn't one that concerns the top management team it is probably a poor basis for a power claim.
4 The external pressure coming from stakeholders or other actors or organizations in the environment. If important people externally are pushing an issue those within who can resolve it will become more empowered.
5 The history of past politics in the organizations in question.

Consequently, power and organizational politics are central to much of what normally goes on in organizations, as Buchanan and Badham (1999) argue in very convincing terms. Organizations are often lived and experienced as a series of 'turf wars' between different branches, divisions, departments, occupations, and cultures located within these. Thus, organizations should be conceived as arenas in which many and varied war games will be in play, with the rules of the game constantly shifting and frequently unclear, and always overlapping. Talk to anyone with long experience of organizational life and they will be able to recount many examples of war games.

According to Pettigrew (2002 [1977]: 47), organizational politics are fundamentally concerned with the management of meaning. Actors in these political relations seek to legitimate the ideas, values, and demands that they espouse while simultaneously denying or decrying those that they seek to oppose. Thus, power is ultimately deployed in games of organizational symbolism. It is wrapped up in myths, beliefs, language, and legend – the stuff of organization culture.

In a realists' guide to organizational politics, Buchanan and Badham (1999) noted that those managers in organizations who are not politically skilled will fail. In their terms, managers have to be good at 'power steering'. From a similar perspective, politics may be defined as the mobilization of support for a position, decision, or action (Crick, 1962: 67). The underlying purpose of politics involves mobilizing support for particular actions by reconciling different interests and values. Thus, power steering means using skills to influence decisions, agendas, and participation in organizational politics. Political competence means being the kind of manager who can get things done, despite resistance, because they are skilled at political games (Bacharach, 2005: 93).

Organizations as political arenas

In Mintzberg's (1983a; 1984; 2002 [1985]) terms, the organization is a political arena, one in which the system of politics comes into play whenever the systems of authority, ideology, or expertise may be contested in various political games – that is to say, almost always. Mintzberg identifies various commonly occurring political games, including those depicted in Table 7.1.

In organizations, politics are normal and serve many orderly functions. They can be the harbinger of a need for realignment (Donaldson, 1999), the midwife to change (Pettigrew et al., 1992), the source of renewing innovation (Frost and Egri, 2002) or, sometimes, the instrument of death (Havemann, 1993). Thus, political games are to be expected – they are neither aberrant nor deviant. The types that Mintzberg specifies are not mutually exclusive, of course, and may often overlap and interlink, but they typically find expression in several major forms in the political arena, which vary with the duration and intensity of conflict (Table 7.1).

TABLE 7.1   Political games in organizations

Insurgency games	Played by lower status participants against the dominant elites
Counter-insurgency games	Played by the dominant elites against the insurgents
Sponsorship games	Played by patrons and clients
Alliance-building games	Played among peers who implicitly seek reciprocal support
Empire-building games	A political actor or subsystem seeks to capture others and enrol them as subordinate to its interests
Budgeting games	The objective is to secure resources
Expertise games	The games of strategic contingency
Lording games	Relatively powerless players seek to 'lord it' through using what they claim to be their legitimate power over those who are supplicant or lower in status: think of family politics between elder and younger siblings
Line vs staff games	Each side uses legitimate power in illegitimate ways in games of rivalry
Rival camps games	Alliance or empire-building games develop into rival blocks that face each other in zero-sum games similar to those witnessed in international relations between competitive countries or blocks of nations
Strategic candidate games	Those in power seek to ensure the succession of preferred candidates as vacancies arise
Whistle-blowing games	Participants, usually lower status ones, seek to expose malfeasance or illegitimacy outside the organization to effect internal policy or strategy changes
Young Turks games	Organizational authority is preserved, but a coup unseats its present incumbents to institute a regime change

Episodic confrontations are fairly normal: for example, a takeover attempt occurs, of a whole organization or a part thereof by another part. An episode of intense conflict occurs from which victors emerge. Sometimes the combatants, often uneasily, enter into a treaty. Uneasy treaties can often lead to shaky alliances as political forces regroup, perhaps to fight another day. Often, however, the struggles are so vicious that the losers exit or are forced from the organization, such as when the top management team that resisted the victors is 'let go'. People in organizations that cannot manage their power relations, because they cleave around fundamentally opposed worldviews, will end up spending more time fighting each other than seeking to find common purpose against competitor organizations. Only very large organizations or those with no competition can survive sustained complex politics for long.

Power and the politics of resistance

Resistance to change consists of those organizational activities and attitudes that aim to thwart, undermine, and impede change initiatives. It is a widely observed phenomenon in organizations. The resistance can be overt, in the form of wildcat strikes, campaigns, or other forms of collective action, or it can be covert, through attempts at undermining change programmes through widespread adoption of cynicism, irony, and ambivalence.

Dialectics refers to the contradiction between two conflicting forces, where each shapes the other, often against the pressure that is being exerted.

Resistance is a term that has long been a part of the vocabulary of students of organization. Coch and French (1948) noted that **resistance to change** is normal.

It is because of the nature of turf wars, uneasy treaties, and thwarted ambitions that power in organizations rarely if ever flows effortlessly as pure authority; because its legitimacy is often contested, power is typically not free of friction. And where there is friction, there must be resistance. To use these metaphors betrays the origins of the terms – they derive, of course, from physics. They are rather mechanical terms, as is so much of the vocabulary in organization and management theory. However, resistance need not be simply a question of physics – it can be more organic and dialectical.

The **dialectics** of power and resistance have recently been addressed in a very good book, *Contesting the Corporation* (Fleming and Spicer, 2007), which offers a window on the corporate world that is too rarely viewed. Behind those many facades of contemporary corporate life – the visions, missions, websites, spin doctors, consultants, coaches, culture, corporate scripts ('have a nice day'), the uniforms, the corporate attitude and attire – stand real people, sometimes feeling trapped by their roles and the necessities of life that demand they be filled appropriately, sometimes playing – ironically, cynically, creatively – with the demands that are made, sometimes exercising the right to be men and women able to voice that which makes them different, unique, and existentially free. The reality of life contained and constrained by the corporation contains many corporate and contested strategies of power, resistance, and struggle. These are normal states of affairs.

Resistance is 'a reactive process' whereby people embedded in power relations actively oppose initiatives enacted by others (Jermier et al., 1994: 90). Often, resistance has been researched in terms of industrial relations conflicts at work between management and workers, especially where the latter are collectively organized in unions (Clawson, 1980). More recent researchers focus on subjectivities of resistance. These may be constituted in many ways: through memories of a fairer time or better work, perhaps, or through local social organization, such as familial or community networks, as well as solidaristic organizations, including trade unions (Clegg, 1994; Knights, 1990).

A number of studies provide graphic examples of how resistance may be variably organized. In the next section, we highlight one study in particular because it demonstrates the ways in which power and resistance, culture and meaning, are densely interconnected.

Resistance by distance

Collinson (1994) presents a case study of a factory in northwest England in which the management had traditionally treated the workers as if they were commodities, easily hired and fired. The workers were marked by decidedly second-class terms and conditions of employment. The organization had recently been taken over by an American firm. In its dealings with the men (there were no women) on the shop floor, the firm applied some current management ideas, such as a corporate culture campaign and a collective bonus scheme. The workers resisted these moves because what management said symbolically did not tie in with what the workers experienced in day-to-day practice. The corporate culture campaign was resisted as 'Yankee bullshit' and 'propaganda'. The bonus scheme made the workers more economically oriented towards work, more closely tied to the cash nexus than to a corporate culture.

The workers, regarding themselves as objects of contempt by management, found an alternative system of values in the camaraderie of their masculinity that was expressed in hard, dirty shop-floor work. Securing themselves in this identity, they distanced themselves as much as possible from what, in terms of their values, was the culturally strange – and comparatively 'soft' – foreign world of (Yankee) management.

In fact, what they did was turn the world of work as seen from the heights of management on its head. They resisted promotion from the shop floor as selling out to the other side. They devalued the clean, white-collar world of the office in favour of the harder edged and 'blokey' masculinity of the shop floor as an authentic sphere of real knowledge grounded in experience rather than theory.

Collinson termed this phenomenon 'resistance through distance'. The workers distanced themselves from management by asserting that it was 'management's right to manage' and something they wanted no part of. They resisted through keeping their distance.

The use by management of collective bonus schemes meant that when faced with layoffs, the shop stewards in the union argued for wage cuts rather than layoffs, which many of the men, in need of the higher wages, resisted. So although the resistance strategies might have appeared to be based on a collective identity, it was one that was fragile and easily ruptured. It was also highly reactive; it resisted through reacting to the authority attempts of management. Like many studies of resistance, Collinson shows both how resistance creates space for employees in organizations and how those spaces serve to secure further their incorporation within the organizations. Resistance is a two-edged sword.

IMAGE 7.2
Resistance in Oaxaca, Mexico, against violent and confrontational anti-labour tactics by the authorities

Check out the Companion Website www.sagepub.co.uk/ managingandorganizations3 for free access to an article by Peter Fleming and André Spicer (2003) if you want to learn more about power, resistance, and its relation to subjectivity at work.

Resistance, whatever form it takes, is always *against* something. Organizationally, those resisted against usually seek to construct or construe the resistance that they encounter as illegitimate, as something outside authority. To the extent that initiatives and actions are given sanction by organizational authorities, then, by definition, resistance to them *must be* illegitimate. In cases in which whatever is being resisted is represented as being normal, rational, and desirable (e.g. 'we need to change periodically to regain market share'), any opposition can easily be regarded as lacking legitimacy.

Resistance is undoubtedly part of politics. The definition of political activity offered by one of its foremost students is that it is 'activity ... undertaken to overcome some resistance or opposition' (Pfeffer, 1981: 7). The vocabulary makes it clear: when there is opposition, there is politics – or, as we might as well say, the presence of politics points to the absence of tyranny, for if there were no opposition or resistance, there would be no politics. Looked at this way, organizational politics seem better than the alternative.

DOMINATION AND AUTHORITY

Authority attaches to forms of domination over others that are viewed as legitimate.

Hardy and Clegg suggest 'organizational structures and systems are not neutral or apolitical but structurally sedimented phenomena. There is a history of struggles already embedded in the organization' (1999: 375). The paradox of power seems to be that you have power only if you are in a superior position in the organization and are opposed in what you want to do by others who are at the same or a lower level; when you want to do something against the resistance of these others, it is termed **authority**.

When people seek to do something against superordinate will, it is usually considered to be resistance to authority. Authority is seen as legitimate; resistance is seen as illegitimate. In management and organization theory, organizational politics increasingly become defined as the unsanctioned or illegitimate use of power to achieve unsanctioned or illegitimate ends, as Mintzberg (1983a; 1984), Mayes and Allen (1977), Gandz and Murray (1980), and Enz (1988) all argue. From this perspective, organizational life reduces to a morality play about efficiency: either members do what they are scripted to do in their formal organization roles in the terms that authorities determine for them, or, if they do not, they are behaving illegitimately. Being moral and being efficient become identical actions in a well-designed system.

Organizations should never be seen just as systems, as engineering that is more efficient when there is less resistance, in the analogies of physics. Organizations always have vested within them traces of the past, as something recurrent, shifting, taking on new meanings, shaping the future. In Weber's terms, organizations already incorporate a 'structure of dominancy' in their functioning. The relations that they encompass are invariably saturated and imbued with power. It is distilled deep in the structure, culture, and history of the organization, which often 'normalizes' power relations so that they hardly seem like power at all.

One of the major strategies of normalization is to practice empowerment. Thus, much recent management theory has been written in praise of teamwork and against bureaucratic hierarchies, because it is believed that this is the way to minimize the expression of power. In the next section, we show that neither the presence of teams nor the absence of hierarchy means an end to power. First, we look at power structured through soft domination, where hierarchies seem to be blurred by project teams, and then consider the role power plays in teams.

Soft domination

The central tension in organizations, when viewed through a power lens, is between resistance and obedience (Courpasson, 2002). On the whole, from the perspective of management control, the latter is a far more productive result of policies than the former. Excessive use of coercion and force invites resistance; therefore, power as a hard instrumentality, a presence as unsubtle as a billiard ball ricocheting around the table, will, on the whole, be declined in favour of more subtle mechanisms.

One theorist who has explored such methods is Steven Lukes, who built on debates in political science to analyse power not only in terms of its mechanics but also its underlying dimensions. His main insight was that power could be used to prevent conflict by shaping:

> perceptions, cognitions, and preferences in such a way that [people] accept their role in the existing order of things, either because they can see or imagine no alternative to it, or because they view it as natural and unchangeable, or because they value it as divinely ordained and beneficial. (Lukes, 1974: 24)

Power is able to achieve these effects to the extent that it is effectively subsumed through legitimation within an integrated system of cultural and normative assumptions. Given the integrated system of cultural and normative assumptions and an efficient organizational apparatus, goals can be achieved. Authorities create legitimated rules that are reinforced by clear and credible threats to career, rewards, status, employment, and so on. Hence, analysis of power in organizations needs also to focus on the subtle mechanisms through which obedience is produced – **soft domination**.

Soft domination is based on the appearance of equality in the organization among peers and the reality of a pervasive system of controls. Chief among these are instrumentally legitimate techniques used by the entire management community, such as human resource management, auditing, and holding managers accountable to plans. These are modern modes of making people responsible, of rendering them surveyable, and of exercising surveillance over them. What sustains senior management and limits organizational members, ultimately, is the political concentration of the power of control over the deployment of human resources in the hands of a minority combined with the regular use of credible sticks (e.g. formal warnings) and carrots (e.g. performance-related pay) deployed within clear rules.

More often than not, these forms of accountability and surveillance become the basis for the games people play at work (Burawoy, 1979). People today often conceive of the workplace as a game in which they are 'survivors'. There are many things to survive – for example, a performance appraisal, not losing face over a policy or procedural conflict, not being downsized and made redundant, and not getting a promotion. Above all, people in organizations have to become skilled game players – they have to know the rites and the rules of the games inside out and constantly use the spaces that they can create from these to exercise whatever discretion they can produce and to rationalize that which they cannot.

Soft domination is characterized by the administration of rules that give managerial discretion to managers while reinforcing the strength of centralized authorities, because those who are delegates know that their obligation is to act creatively but to do so within the systems of authority (Courpasson, 2002).

Electronic and team surveillance

A number of writers, including Poster (1990), Lyon (1994), Bogard (1996), and Sewell (2002), see modern electronic forms of surveillance as replacing the apparatus of power laboriously constructed by bureaucracy. Extended electronic surveillance has been seen as the hallmark of high modernity, of a world in which surveillance is insidious, making the majority of people increasingly transparent to others who may not be transparent to them (Robins and Webster, 1985).

Zuboff (1988) introduced the **Information Panopticon** as a key term. The electronic eyes of the Information Panopticon are numerous. They are aimed at us all as generalized bodies caught in their eye. We are aware of their existence in creating a normative environment – but it becomes a matter of choice as to whether we allow them to target us specifically. Our deviance defines their acuity, unless we are in total institutions, where their acuity defines our deviance.

The Information Panopticon privileges organizational elites by making it possible to consolidate various sources of electronic information about

Increasingly, people in organizations and everyday life generally are subject to electronic surveillance, through instruments such as closed-circuit TV (CCTV), speed cameras, security cameras, and so on. These forms of surveillance have been referred to as the **Information Panopticon**.

IMAGE 7.3   The eye in the sky … in the UK the average citizen is captured on CCTV 22 times a day

the many who serve the organization (Robey, 1981). Sewell (2002) argues that electronic surveillance supplements, rather than replaces, earlier forms of surveillance. Its basic thrust is to make people in organizations more accountable and less autonomous.

The Information Panopticon is often used in conjunction with policies whose avowed purpose is quite opposite to these intentions. Sewell concentrates on teamwork. Teams operate with two dimensions of surveillance: vertical and horizontal. Vertical surveillance focuses on the aberrant: aberrant waste, time, quality, and so on. To define the aberrant, you must first define the normal, which is usually done by establishing performance norms on a statistical basis that enables the aberrant to be immediately transparent – it stands out as a deviation from the norm of time taken, quality produced, or waste accumulated. Electronic forms of monitoring of performance make the norms more transparent and are supported by peer review through horizontal surveillance. Although electronic and traditional forms of surveillance reinforce the vertical dimension, which seeks to make the subject of surveillance their own monitor, the horizontal dimension causes us to monitor each other. Panopticism explains only some vertical aspects of this group scrutiny (Hetrick and Boje, 1992).

Empowerment

Teamwork is not usually thought of as a mechanism of power, but recent theory has suggested that it is (Barker, 2002; Sewell, 2002). Indeed, as

Sewell notes, teamwork is usually associated with the rhetoric of empowerment, trust, and enhanced discretion. Sometimes it is even referred to as 'giving away' power. There has been a flood of popular management books whose message is cast in terms of this normative rhetoric, as an analysis by Barley and Kunda (1992) has demonstrated. These books often espouse single-answer solutions for harried managers; TQM (Total Quality Management), organizational learning, lean production, and BPR (Business Process Re-engineering) are among the recipes that Sewell notes. What all of these methods have in common, he suggests, is a reversal of the highly individualistic approach to the employee that earlier perspectives such as scientific management had championed. Rather than isolate, observe, and individually measure the times taken by individuals for doing standardized tasks and discouraging them from communicating with others while doing so, the new approach encourages communication and sociability. No longer are employees to be set competitively against each other; instead, they work together as members of teams that have been designed to cope better with more flexible manufacturing methods and to provide opportunities for more intelligent organization of work (Clarke and Clegg, 1998), where there is greater distributed intelligence of systems and discretion.

However, teamwork does not abolish politics. Rather, it relies on what Barker (2002) terms 'concertive control' as its horizontal mode of surveillance. The forms of power at work help create the types of subjects that work there (Foucault, 1983; Knights and Vurdubakis, 1994; Townley, 1993; 1994).

Concertive control

Barker begins his account with a brief snatch of interview data with an employee called Ronald, who is reported as saying that he is more closely watched under a new team-based work design than when he was closely supervised by a manager. The team is a stricter supervisor than his supervisor had been! Barker calls this situation one of **concertive control**, something that occurs where there is 'a substantial consensus about values, high-level coordination, and a degree of self-management by members or workers in an organization' (2002: 180). The team shares a common commitment to do or plan something in cooperation or in harmony with each other. Organizations that use such teams lower the costs of surveillance and control because the team mentality becomes the apparatus through which control is governed.

> **Concertive control** is exercised in teamwork situations where the sense of responsibility that you have to the immediate members of the team impels you to work intensively and to not let them down.

Concertive control, argues Barker, is what occurs when organizations become post-bureaucratic, when they adopt decentralized, participative, and more democratic designs, a strategy that has long been promoted by more liberal management theorists such as Follett (1941) and Lewin (1951). Recently, the trickle of liberal management writing has become a flood, as theorists increasingly have sought an alternative to bureaucratic models (see also pp. 540–547; 583–584). These arguments are characterized by a stress on a new age of post-bureaucratic liberation, in which organization members abandon hierarchy and control by formal rules in favour of consensual and values-based action. Popular writers such as

Kanter (1990), Peters (1988), and Drucker (1998) promote the benefits of 'unimpeded, agile authority structures that grow out of a company's consensual, normative ideology, not from its system of formal rules' (Barker, 2002: 183). The argument is that 'cutting out bureaucratic offices and rules' will 'flatten hierarchies, cut costs, boost productivity, and increase the speed with which they respond to the changing business worlds' (Barker, 2002: 183). Employees collaborate to develop the means of their own control. The Information Panopticon sought to make each worker the governor of what they did at work, aware as they were of the supervisory gaze. Concertive control reinforces this awareness through the discipline of teams (see also pp. 89–112).

Under the new forms of concertive control and soft domination, power is refined into evermore subtle techniques using instrumental means to make employees accountable and transparent. For example, there may be a vision statement that states, 'We are a principled organization that values teamwork' (Barker, 2002: 183). On this basis, team members agree that being principled means that they all arrive at work on time – and they ensure that they do, using norms that they have enacted from the agreed-upon value statement to structure the systems of their own control. Authority shifts from the hierarchy and formal rules to the team and socially created and generated rules.

Teamwork is now seen to have a much wider utility. It is not just a means of producing collaboration between distinct organizational units; it is also a way to enhance the effectiveness of members of the same organizational unit. The researcher who has looked most closely at power relations in teams that have been designed to be self-managing is James Barker. He charts the shifts in management style from more hierarchical to self-managing teams; see Table 7.2.

TABLE 7.2   Barker's self-managing teams

Hierarchical management: hierarchically ordered supervision	Team management: shift to self-management
The supervisor has precise supervisory responsibilities	The supervisor is replaced by a team of 10–15 people, who take over the responsibilities of their former supervisor
The supervisor gives instructions	Self-managing employees gather and synthesize information, act on it, and take collective responsibility for their actions
Management relies on formal rules and authority expressed in terms of disciplines that seek to reinforce this authority	Management provides a value-based corporate vision that guides day-to-day actions by being a reference point from which employees infer appropriate action
The supervisor checks that instructions have been followed	The self-managing team guides its own work and coordinates with other areas of the company
The supervisor ensures that each employee fulfils their job description	The self-managing team is responsible for completing a specific well-defined job function for which all members are cross-trained. All members of the team have the authority and responsibility to make essential decisions, set work schedules, order materials, and coordinate with other teams

One reason that many organizations are designed in terms of self-managing teams is that such teams are supposed to cut costs by laying off front-line supervisors and gaining productivity benefits from better motivated and more committed employees (Mumby and Stohl, 1991; Orsburn et al., 1990; Wellins et al., 1991). In Barker's case study of ISE Communications, he observed that a shift away from hierarchy and formal rules led to a tighter form of control based on peer surveillance. Empowered organizations not only provide new means for control, as Barker (2002) suggests, but also make opportunities for the everyday negotiations and games of power more difficult. It is more difficult to negotiate when the people that you work with, rather than a supervisor, impose the limits. It is much easier to steal some time from a supervisor or manager with whom you do not share any obvious interest, other than a necessity to work, than it is from colleagues. You all depend on each other – and that is the subtlety of concertive control. Everyone is empowered to speak – but with the same agreed-upon voice.

Institutional entrepreneurs and hegemony

Institutional theory is an approach that tries to explain why the managers of organizations seem to make a very restricted set of choices about organizational design. The top management teams that are able to shape organizations are often referred to as **institutional entrepreneurs**, although institutional entrepreneurs may arise anywhere.

Institutional entrepreneurs engage in political processes that both reflect and shape the values of the stakeholders that they deal with, strategically. It is this set of values that are dominant, and the strategies that maintain them, that Italian political theorist Antonio Gramsci (1971) characterized as 'hegemony'. Where there is **hegemony**, it is the active consent of those subject to it that constitutes their subordination. Dominant values are taken to be those of the general interest and are articulated as such. Thus, under conditions of hegemony people are unable to specify their interests except in terms of the concepts that subordinate them; thus they cannot achieve autonomy. Hegemony theorists assume that objective interests can be identified. In other words, it is assumed that for workers or women (or whatever category of social identity one is focusing on) there are some real interests that, *if* members of that group could just see things clearly, *they would* articulate. The problem is that how these interests are defined is always affected by the theory of implicit interests involved. Thus, for example, feminists see gender as the key issue, whereas for Marxists it is class.

The crucial point is that if there is widespread agreement on values – or at least if widespread agreement can be represented or produced – there may be little necessity to exercise overt power. Shrewd institutional entrepreneurs realize this and rather than fight battles over particular issues seek to create coalitions of interest that broadly agree on the basic values. They construct networks of power relations that articulate and shape basic values. So, institutional theory, on this reading, is a form of power theory: the reason that so many organizations share similar practices and designs is not simply that they are culturally valued, but that the values in question are those held by elite alliances. Institutional entrepreneurs who want to challenge these values in a radical way will find it very difficult to build the

Institutional entrepreneurs are those people who occupy key positions with wide legitimacy attached to them, who are capable of bridging between the interests of diverse stakeholders, and have the capacity to introduce new practices and persuade stakeholders of the good fit of these practices with the routines and values that they embrace (Phillips et al., 2004).

Hegemony signifies a system of rule or domination where those who are being dominated, or ruled, consent to that rule. It is a state of ideological conformance said to have been imposed on a subordinated group of people because of the concepts through which they think – concepts that do not enable them to assert a point of view that reflects a better understanding of their interests and the situation.

necessary alliances and will tend to be outflanked and overwhelmed by those institutional values that comprise the current hegemony. Only, perhaps, when there is some acute crisis, which shakes general beliefs in the efficacy of these values, will there be a tournament in which alternative ideas might emerge. This is certainly the case in organizations that have undergone crisis: the crisis is typically used as a rationale for building new values and coalitions of interest around them, and discrediting the previous regime.

If organizations can continue without crisis then organizational hegemony – where one point of view is predominant – will be easier to maintain. It will be marked by a strong organization culture and an absence of countervailing points of view, because almost everyone has come to accept the dominant views (Lukes, 1974). In the next Mini Case box, we consider a case in which organizational hegemony had been crucial for a very significant global organization, which was written about by the ex-chief economist of the World Bank and Nobel Prizewinner, Joseph Stiglitz.

Check out the Companion Website www.sagepub.co.uk/managingandorganizations3 for free access to an **article by** Christine Räisänen and Anneli Linde (2004) about how hegemony can occur in the context of managing projects.

Check out the Companion Website www.sagepub.co.uk/managingandorganizations3 for free access to an article by Thomas B. Lawrence and Nelson Phillips (2004) about how the tourist activity of whale-watching resulted from and developed institutional entrepreneurship.

THE EXTREMES OF POWER

Total institutions

Organizations always place constraints on individuals' freedom of action, which people sometimes resist. However, a more important question about power in organizations is not why people sometimes resist but why, much of the time, they do not. Obedience, in fact, is a far more fundamental question than resistance. One way of researching the mechanism of obedience is to look at some extreme cases in **total institutions**. The rationale for doing this is that, in extreme cases, the normal tendencies of everyday organizational life are more obvious because they are more concentrated.

Total institutions are those organizations that share the essential feature of controlling almost the totality of the individual member's day-to-day life. Boarding schools, barracks, prisons, and asylums can be categorized as total institutions.

MINI CASE

Organizational hegemony in the International Monetary Fund

Stiglitz (2002) provides an account of the International Monetary Fund (IMF). (Stiglitz, a Nobel Economics Prizewinner and ex-World Bank economist, is someone both well-enough placed to make a diagnosis and hardly likely to be dangerously radical in doing so.) The IMF is an organization that was established in the late stages of the Second World War with the express purpose of minimizing the harm from – and, if

possible, preventing – global depressions. Its mandate was to maintain international liquidity through loans to economically distressed countries that had insufficient economic resources to stimulate aggregate economic demand domestically.

It is a global organization funded by taxpayers around the world. Yet it is not responsible to them, nor does it have their views represented to it. Instead, it hears, represents, and reflects the views of national finance ministries and central bankers, over which one country – the USA – has effective veto in its deliberations.

(Continued)

(Continued)

Its contemporary policies champion 'market supremacy with ideological fervour ... the IMF typically provides funds only if countries engage in policies like cutting deficits, raising taxes or raising interest rates that lead to a contraction of the economy' (Stiglitz, 2002: 12–13). These policy positions were the outcome of a hard-fought battle in the IMF that occurred in the early 1980s, when it became dominated by free-market economists who were under the thrall of the fashionable prescriptions associated with the governments of President Ronald Reagan in the USA and Prime Minister Margaret Thatcher in the UK.

Stiglitz (2002: 15) argues that the IMF has functioned in what is sometimes called, after a medical metaphor, an 'iatrogenic' manner – its policies have exacerbated the very problems that they were supposed to solve, rather as a surgical procedure might complicate an underlying condition it was designed to cure. Rather than contributing to global stability, they have made the international economy less stable, more crisis-ridden, and indebted countries poorer. Why and how has that been possible?

Stiglitz sees two main factors contributing to the absence of debate between opposing viewpoints: first, a problem of *governance*; and second, a problem of *representation*. Governance addresses the question of who decides. Commercial and financial interests from the wealthiest countries in the world dominate the IMF. Its policies reflect these interests – hence the market emphasis – because why would the suppliers of capital let the state do something that they believe markets can do better and more profitably? These suppliers are the dominant commercial and financial interests in the wealthiest countries. Institutions such as the IMF, as well as the World Bank and the World Trade Organization (WTO), intervene in the economic management of poorer countries. But those intervening are always representatives of the most developed countries, are chosen by those developed countries behind closed doors, and do not necessarily have any experience of the developing world. As Stiglitz (2002: 19) says of these institutions, they are 'not representative of the nations they serve'.

Raising the problem of representation addresses the issue of who speaks for the countries in need of assistance. The answer is simple: 'At the IMF it is the finance ministers and the central bank governors' who 'typically are closely tied to the financial community; they come from financial firms, and after their period of government service, that is where they return' (Stiglitz, 2002: 19). Such people 'naturally see the world through the eyes of the financial community' in the advanced economies. It is not surprising that the IMF policies have been addressed more to the interests of commercial and financial power rather than those of poor peasants or hard-pressed local businessmen trying to pay off the taxes that the IMF imposes.

Stiglitz argues this is a situation of taxation without representation. When people are taxed without political representation, they tend to resist through non-representational means – they take to the streets, riot, and rebel. Ever since the WTO met in Seattle in 1999, the rebellions in the developing world have been echoed in the heartlands of the global institutions, as idealistic and impassioned opponents of the dominant consensus about globalization have rioted to try to have their alternative views broadcast. In organizations that were less hegemonically constrained through having more inclusive governance and representation, there would be less need for illegitimate means of resistance.

IMF policies, according to Ambrose (2007), have been most adept at reproducing the necessity for IMF intervention. From an organizational point of view, the IMF needs client states that are indebted: they are its *raison d'être*. Its structural adjustment loans, he suggests, lead to more poverty and debt, thus creating the need for more structural adjustment loans. This is predictable, given the infiltration of finance ministries with former IMF and World Bank employees.

Not only does hegemony operate through reproduction of the organization mission but it also works through organizational resistance to changing it. For instance, in April 2006, the president of the IMF suggested a new role for the institution in managing the world economy: that it should convene bilateral and multilateral meetings among major economies to address serious imbalances (implying, in particular, China with its controversial 'managed' exchange rate and huge trade surplus, and the USA with its massive deficit). The idea of a new mandate with which to mediate global economic frictions, while welcomed by some member representatives, has made little headway against US representations. Meanwhile, surprisingly, the IMF is losing money as an increasing number of countries, following in Brazil's 2005 wake, settle their debts with the IMF, and loan-repayment income diminishes as a consequence.

- Why is the IMF an internationally hegemonic organization?

The Canadian sociologist Erving Goffman used anthropological research to investigate how authority was configured in extreme contexts. He chose extremes because the everyday mechanisms of authority and power were much more evident there than in the world of the corporate 'organization man' (Whyte, 1960). Goffman (1961) initiated the discussion of extreme organizations when he coined the term total institution.

People within total institutions are cut off from the wider society for a relatively long time, leading an enclosed and formally administered existence. In such contexts, the organization has more or less monopoly control of its members' everyday lives. Goffman's argument is that total institutions demonstrate in heightened and condensed form the underlying organizational processes that can be found, albeit in much less extreme cases, in more normal organizations.

Total institutions are often parts of a broader apparatus, such as a prison or detention centre. Total institutions do not just include organizations that make people inmates against their will, however. They can also include organizations founded on membership contracted on voluntary inclusion – for instance, a professional army, a boarding school, a residential college, or a religious retreat such as a monastery or convent (Table 7.3).

What these very different types of organizations have in common that make them total institutions are that each member's daily life is carried out in the immediate presence of a large number of others. The members are very visible; there is no place to hide from the surveillance of others. The members tend to be strictly regimented and often wear institutional clothing such as uniforms. Life in a total institution is governed by strict, formal, rational planning of time. (Think of school bells for lesson endings and beginnings, factory whistles, timetables, schedules, bugle calls in the barracks, and so on.) Hence, members of total institutions are not free to choose how they spend their time; instead, it is strictly prescribed for them. It is because of this that the members lose a degree of autonomy because of an all-encompassing demand for conformity to the authoritative interpretation of rules.

TABLE 7.3   Different types of total institution

Characteristics	Types
Places to put people that the state deems incapable of looking after themselves (these people, who vary historically and comparatively, have included the 'feeble', the 'lunatic', or the 'disabled')	Long-stay hospitals for people with chronic disabilities. These used to be called 'asylums'
Restrictive organizations that institutionalize people who pose a threat to others, such as people with communicable disease of contagion who are legislatively contained for the duration of their disease	Sanatoria or isolation wards
Punitive organization in which people are confined	Prisons, 'gulags', concentration camps, prisoner-of-war camps, or detention centres for asylum seekers
Organizations dedicated to a specific work task spatially separated from other organizations	Boarding schools, military barracks, and vessels at sea, or remote company towns
Retreats from the world	Monasteries, abbeys, convents, or growth and learning centres

WHAT'S THE POINT?

Full Metal Jacket

The depiction of life in the US Marines boot camp in the 1987 Stanley Kubrick film *Full Metal Jacket* is a good cinematic representation of one type of total institution. In the film, identities are stripped through organizational means: the arbitrary assignment of nicknames and numbers; the loss of personal characteristics, such as haircuts, under the Marine razor; total conformance demanded with instructions that are almost always shouted at recruits, often at close range, sometimes associated with physical violence to the person so that they are intimidated into obedience; deconstruction of the person as an individual who is then 'remade' as an element of an institution, whose new identity exists only with reference to institutional symbols and structures, through rigorous discipline and physical exercise. An *esprit de corps*, based on the new identity as Marines, is developed.

Full Metal Jacket depicts an extreme example of a common phenomenon: organization socialization, the processes through which members of an organization learn what it means to be a member. Sometimes this is done formally, through induction or training programmes, but much of the learning that occurs is informal and not subject to authoritative control.

If we accept Goffman's analysis, it becomes evident that the essential core of organization is power – organizations exert power over their members by making them do things that they would not otherwise do. Organization members may have to dress up in uncool uniforms, have haircuts that are not trendy, and pretend to be interested while doing stupid things. Of course, the uniforms can vary from an explicit uniform to one that is implicit: the black suits, white shirts, black ties of the earnest Mormon; the almost *de rigueur* trouser suit and contrasting shirt of the corporate woman worldwide; or the pinstripe suit of London businessmen. Even the boys from a neighbourhood skater gang have a dress code, and becoming a part of their gang means learning their ways of behaving, doing, and thinking, and often speaking (using certain slang words and listening to certain music).

Uniforms and other symbols of membership grant you access to those organizations which embrace the symbols you adopt; however, they also exclude you from membership of those organizations with differing dress codes, therefore they define your place in society. A person dressed as a skater would have trouble gaining acceptance in the corporate financial world as would a 'suit' in most gangs and youth subcultures.

If organizations necessarily exercise power over their members, what are the ethical implications of the ways in which they do so? A short trip into history can help answer this question by looking at one of the twentieth century's most extreme cases of systematic abuse of power and ethics on a large-scale, organizational basis.

The ethics of organizational obedience

Adolf Eichmann was one of Hitler's deputies, the Head of the Department for Jewish Affairs. He led the Reich's effort for the Final Solution, efficiently organizing the roundup and transportation of millions of Jews to their deaths at infamous camps such as Auschwitz, Treblinka, and Bergen-Belsen. After the Second World War, Eichmann escaped capture and lived in Germany for five years before moving to Argentina, where he lived under an alias for another ten years. Israeli agents finally captured him in 1960, and he was tried for crimes against humanity.

Eichmann's defence was that he was just a bureaucrat who had to obey because he was simply following orders. (Hannah Arendt wrote an account of his trial, in which she coined the memorable phrase 'the banality of evil' (Arendt, 1994) to register her interpretation of the events she reported, in which evil was delivered through mechanisms such as a punctual and efficient railway timetable.) Although Eichmann was subsequently found guilty and executed, his defence was important because it posed the question of the extent to which a person who is obedient to organizationally legitimate authority can be held accountable as an individual for their actions.

In the context of an inquiry into the nature of the Holocaust, the renowned sociologist Zygmunt Bauman extensively addressed such questions (Bauman, 1989). Bauman's answer is interesting for management students; essentially, he notes how central aspects of organizations contribute to the ease with which organizational malfeasance can occur. At the heart of the moral question is the interpenetration of power and ethics. Why do ordinary people in organizations do morally bad things when asked to do so? What aspects of an organization make unquestioning obedience feasible? Kelman (1973) suggested that three organizational attributes, at a minimum, make this phenomenon more probable. Subsequent analysis has extended the list greatly to include 20 characteristic ways of constructing total institutional power relations (Clegg et al., 2006a).

Techniques of power

When we master a technique, our skill has its own charm, aesthetics, and beauty, and we can take sheer delight in using it, irrespective of its moral effects:

> Technical responsibility differs from moral responsibility in that it forgets that the action is a means to something other than itself ... *the result is the irrelevance of moral standards for the technical success of the bureaucratic operation.* (Bauman, 1989: 101; emphasis in original)

When technique is paramount, action becomes purely a question of technical power – the use of means to achieve given ends. For instance, as a master of logistics, Eichmann was enormously proud of his achievements in the complex scheduling of trains, camps, and death.

Organizational power that makes you technically accountable and responsible for results expressed in a purely quantitative form has two profound effects. First, it makes you *utterly transparent* – either you achieve your targets or you do not. Second, it relieves you of *moral indeterminacy* – and, as we will shortly see, *moral responsibility*: if you are authorized to do something and given targets to achieve by superordinates' guiding strategies and plans, obedience surely is appropriate, and authority should be served.

Organization work is a ceaseless round of activity. Most organizational members are in the middle of organizational chains whose links are not always clear. People are not always aware of the consequences of what they do and do not do – after all, most of the time, they are just doing what they are told (shred those files, write those cheques, dispatch those troops, or maintain those train schedules). Divisions of labour in the complex chains enable us to keep a distance from effects; we can represent them in terms of intermediary forms of data (kill rates, efficiency statistics, and so on). Our labour moves minute cogs in a bureaucratic machine necessarily intermeshed with so many others that we are just one small element in the overall scheme of things. We do not even have to try to understand the totality. The system of which we are a part is responsible, not us.

Especially when actions are performed at a distance on people defined as administrative categories, the people are effectively *dehumanized* (Kelman, 1973). The more dehumanized they are, the easier becomes the application of pure technique to their cases. When whatever is being worked on can be represented quantitatively, as a bottom-line calculation, it is so much easier to make rational decisions (cut costs, trim fat, speed throughput, increase efficiency, defeat the competition) without concern for the human, environmental, or social effects of these decisions.

How ordinary people can use authority to do extraordinary things

We have already discussed the Milgram experiments in Chapter 4 in the context of leadership. Now we want to consider their implications for ordinary members as power subjects. Ordinary people do extraordinary things, as the experiment by Milgram (1971) shows. Milgram's research question was quite simple, as you will recall: he asked to what extent individuals are inclined to follow the commands of figures perceived to be in authority. His answer demonstrated that the kind of situation in which people are embedded determines, in part, how they will act. He designed an experiment in which white-coated scientists instructed ordinary people (whom we call the subjects) to do cruel and unusual things to other people (whom we call the participants) as part of an experiment in a laboratory.

In a nutshell, the subjects were instructed to administer increasing levels of electric shocks to the participants as part of a behavioural learning programme. They did so under a range of circumstances. When participants gave incorrect answers to test questions, they were to be administered a shock, with each one to be higher than the one before. (No shock was actually administered – the participants, unbeknownst to the subjects, were actually actors who performed the responses that, physiologically, would be the normal reaction to the levels of shock being administered.) When the subjects were face to face with the participants and told to administer the electric shock directly to their hands, using force if necessary, only 30 per cent of the experimental subjects did so. When the subjects could still see the participants but used a control lever that administered the shock instead of having to force the hands of the participants onto the plates administering the shock, 40 per cent did so. When the subjects could no longer see the participants but could only hear their distress as the current surged, 62.5 per cent were able to apply the current. Moving the others out of earshot marginally improved the rate to 65 per cent.

The more distance – both physically and psychologically – there was between the controllers and the controlled, the easier it seemed to be to do inhumane and cruel things. The closer the relation between the controller and the supervisor, and the more removed the subject, the easier it became to continue. Obedience flows more easily when the subjects of action are at a distance. When these subjects can be transformed into objects in the controller's mind, obedience flows even more easily.

Another factor facilitating the application of current was its incremental thresholds – once someone had committed to the action, each increase in the threshold was just a small step, just another slight increase in pain to be endured. It is not as if they started out to kill another person or cause them irretrievable injury. They just did what they were instructed to do, only they did a little bit more of it each time. Where such action should stop, once started, is not at all clear. After someone has committed to the action, especially if others are complicit, what Milgram (1971) termed 'situational obligations' arise. In other words, people felt obliged to do what they were asked to do in a specific situation, which tended to override more general and abstract moral principles that they might also hold. In organizations, with complex divisions of labour, sequential action invariably makes us complicit with many others, in many interactions.

Milgram (1971) made one crucial change to the experiments to test out a further hypothesis: that plurality produces space for reflection and pause for consideration. In the experiments reported thus far, there was only one expert giving instructions. He introduced another expert and instructed them to disagree with each other about the command being given. The disagreement between authorities paralysed the capacity for obedience of the research subjects: out of 20 subjects in this experiment, one refused to go further before the staged disagreement; 18 broke off after it; and the remaining subject opted out just one stage further.

Polyphony – the presence of competing and conflicting voices – increases the probability that people will think for themselves rather than just do what they are told. Thus, strong organization cultures that suppress value difference are more likely to produce unreflective and sometimes inappropriate organizational action than more democratic and pluralistic settings.

This discussion leads us back to total institutions. It is in these, precisely, that we would least expect to find polyphony and difference. As Bauman suggests, *'the readiness to act against one's own better judgement and against the voice of one's conscience is not just the function of authoritative command, but the result of exposure to a single-minded, unequivocal and*

Check out the Companion Website www.sagepub.co.uk/ managingandorganizations3 for free access to an article by Nestar Russell and Robert Gregory (2005) about how organizations can make the undoable doable, which discusses the cases about which you have just read.

monopolistic source of authority' (1989: 165; emphasis in original). Total institutions – organizations that presume to exercise strong cultural control over their members, to the extent that they diminish pluralism – squeeze the space in which civility, reflection, and responsibility can thrive. As Bauman urges, 'The voice of individual moral conscience is best heard in the tumult of political and social discord' (1989: 166).

Even in times and circumstances that are considered normal, you might find powerful total institutions at work, which the following case demonstrates. Again, the absence of polyphony is one of the preconditions for the establishment of total institutions. Haney et al. (1973) designed an experiment that resonates with government practices that are accepted as normal and routine in many societies. The researchers divided a group of male American college students into two types of people: guards and inmates. They created a mock prison in a laboratory basement, using as subjects 21 healthy male undergraduate volunteers. Each person was to receive $15 a day for two weeks. Nine were randomly selected to be 'prisoners', with the remainder designated as 'guards' who were to supervise the prisoners in a rotating three-shift system. Each wore the symbolic garb of the role. Prisoners were given unflattering uniform clothing and tight caps to simulate shaven heads. Guards were put in a militaristic-type uniform and given LA cop sunglasses. Names were suppressed with norms of impersonality, and complex rules and penalties for their infraction were promulgated. Then the experiment began.

The experiment had to be aborted after less than a week. No sense of solidarity developed between the two groups, and almost all of their conversation centred on the roles assumed in the experiment. An escalatory chain of events occurred; the construed authority of the guards was enforced by the submissiveness of the prisoners, tempting the guards to further and increasingly illegitimate displays of the power that their authority allowed them to exercise, leading to further humiliation of the prisoners (Bauman, 1989: 167). Bear in mind that the subjects were all normal, well-adjusted people before the experiment began, but that after one week they were playing their roles with such conviction that the experiment had to be abandoned because of the real possibility of harm to the 'prisoners'.

Positive power

By contrast to these experiments in perverse power, consider some alternative experiments in what appears to be positive power. We will, in Chapter 14, encounter virtual organizations and knowledge workers, the kinds of people one finds concentrated in areas such as Silicon Valley in California, USA, Fortitude Valley in Queensland, Australia, and Sophia-Antopolis, in Provence, near Antibes, in France. Here highly qualified employees, often with PhDs, cluster in high-tech, bio-tech, and creative industries, networking, working online, and working virtually, seemingly without concerns about power. They are highly paid, work in informal environments, and love the work they do. It was the science park of Sophia-Antopolis that formed the inspiration for the novelist J. G. Ballard's *Super-Cannes* (2001), in which he reflects on the ethics of the relations of power, freedom, and control in these new forms of organizations.

QUESTION TIME

Super-Cannes and The Organization Man

Super-Cannes

This is an excerpt from a novel by J. G. Ballard where a central character is explaining his philosophy of life and organizations to a skeptical listener.

A giant multinational like Fuji or General Motors sets its own morality. The company defines the rules that govern how you treat your spouse, where you educate your children, the sensible limits to stock-market investment. The bank decides how big a mortgage you can handle, the right amount of health insurance to buy. There are no more moral decisions than there are on a new superhighway. Unless you own a Ferrari, pressing the accelerator is not a moral decision. Ford and Fiat and Toyota have engineered a sensible response curve. We can rely on their judgment, and that leaves us free to get on with the rest of our lives. We've achieved real freedom, the freedom from morality.

Unconvinced by his case, I said: 'It sounds like a ticket to 1984, this time by the scenic route. I thought that organization man died out in the 1960s.'

He did, our worried friend in the grey-flannel suit. He was an early office-dwelling hominid, corporate version of Dawn Man who assumed a sedentary posture in order to survive. He was locked in a low-tech bureaucratic cave, little more than a human punch card. Today's professional men and women are self-motivated. The corporate pyramid is a virtual hierarchy that endlessly reassembles itself around them. They enjoy enormous mobility. While you're mooning around here, Paul, they're patenting another gene, or designing the next generation of drugs that will cure cancer and double your life span.

The Organization Man

This is the title of a famous 1960 book by William F. Whyte. Here is how he identifies the species:

The organization man: If the term is vague, it is because I can think of no other way to describe the people I am talking about. They are not the workers, nor are they the white-collar people in the usual, clerk sense of the word. These people only work for The Organization. The ones I am talking about belong to it as well. They are the ones of our middle class who have left home, spiritually as well as physically, to take the vows of organization life, and it is they who are the mind and soul of our great self-perpetuating institutions. Only a few are top managers or ever will be. In a system that makes such hazy terminology as 'junior executive' psychologically necessary, they are of the staff as much as the line, and most are destined to live poised in a middle area that still awaits a satisfactory euphemism. But they are the dominant members of our society nonetheless. They have not joined together into a recognizable elite – our country does not stand still long enough for that – but it is from their ranks that are coming most of the first and second echelons of our leadership, and it is their values which will set the American temper.

The corporation man is the most conspicuous example, but he is only one, for the

(Continued)

(Continued)

collectivization so visible in the corporation has affected almost every field of work. Blood brother to the business trainee off to join Du Pont is the seminary student who will end up in the church hierarchy, the doctor headed for the corporate clinic, the physics Ph.D. in a government laboratory, the intellectual on the foundation-sponsored team project, the engineering graduate in the huge drafting room at Lockheed, the young apprentice in a Wall Street law factory.

They are all, as they so often put it, in the same boat. Listen to them talk to each other over the front lawns of their suburbia and you cannot help but be struck by how well they grasp the common denominators which bind them. Whatever the differences in their organization ties, it is the common problems of collective work that dominate their attentions, and when the Du Pont man talks to the research chemist or the chemist

to the army man, it is these problems that are uppermost. The word collective most of them can't bring themselves to use – except to describe foreign countries or organizations they don't work for – but they are keenly aware of how much more deeply beholden they are to organization than were their elders. They are wry about it, to be sure; they talk of the 'treadmill,' the 'rat race,' of the inability to control one's direction. But they have no great sense of plight; between themselves and organization they believe they see an ultimate harmony and, more than most elders recognize, they are building an ideology that will vouchsafe this trust.

- Compare and contrast the employees in Ballard's novel with those in Whyte's account: why do you think they might be similar or different?

Source: Ballard (2001: 95–96), Whyte (1960: 1) available at http://tinyurl.com/ 2cvyua, accessed 27 February 2007.

POWER, POLITICS, AND DECISION-MAKING

Think of everyday language – it is in *head*quarters where decisions are made, by *heads* of departments, which the organization is supposed to follow. Decision-making is understood as management's task *par excellence* – the bureaucratic *cogito* (the thinking brain) whose decisions the corporate body should follow. Management makes decisions on strategic directions, action plans to implement them, and forms of control to evaluate their effect.

Usually, the model of decision-making is described as a perfectly well-organized, rational, and logical process. First, the problem is defined. Second, all the relevant information that leads to an optimal solution is collected. Third, reviewing the data, management (perhaps with the help of technocratic 'experts') develops several possible solutions. Fourth, evaluating the possible solutions carefully, management makes a decision regarding the optimal solution. Fifth, this solution is implemented in a top-down approach and evaluated constantly by management. Such constant processes of rational decision-making, supported by the latest IT equipment and an army of analysts and consultants, are meant constantly and incrementally to refine and improve an organization's processes and products. The problem of recalcitrant hands is solved by turning them into disciplined and reflexive extensions of the corporate body, able to exercise discretion, but in corporately prescribed ways.

Thus, decision-making has often been discussed as if it were a highly rational activity: a decision is seen as a rational choice based on a logical connection between cause and effect, made in the context of a rational search for solutions to something defined as a problem, for which the options can be rationally weighted and compared and the optimum decision chosen. Unfortunately, such 'rational actors' are rarely to be found outside of introductory textbooks, especially of economics; real life is a bit more complicated.

One of the earliest writers to recognize this complexity was the Nobel Economics Laureate, Herbert Simon. He recognized that few if any decisions are made under conditions of perfect rationality (Simon, 1957). Issues are frequently ambiguous; information about alternatives will often be incomplete, and the choice criteria unclear. In addition, others may see the issues, alternatives, and choices in utterly different – sometimes antagonistic – terms. And the time, energy, and political will to reconcile different positions may well be lacking. Consequently, most decision-making uses criteria that aim for 'satisfactory' outcomes rather than 'maximal' utility: satisficing. Thus, most decisions are not ideal but make do with what is seen to be available and relevant. Managers operate with bounded rationality rather than complete rationality. Decision-makers can only review a limited range of factors and possibilities in making decisions because of the limitations both of the information available to them and their cognitive and temporal ability to handle its complexity. Hence, they can only ever exercise what is known as bounded rationality – that is a rationality that makes do within these cognitive and temporal limits rather than searching ceaselessly for all information and data that is available.

Simon (1960) makes a contrast between two types of decision that managers may have to deal with: programmed decisions can be made by reference to existing rubrics. The programmed decisions are fairly easy and can be categorized as operational questions that admit of solution by applying organizational rules that subordinates can be trained to do. Non-programmed decisions have no precedents, are unfamiliar, novel, and complex, and cannot be left to subordinates: they are what are sometimes referred to as messy or intractable problems.

As Miller and Wilson (2006: 470) put it, topics for decision may be complex; definitions problematic; information unavailable and/or difficult to collect; solutions hard to recognize; and the process generative not so much of solutions as headaches from further problems. Most significant organizational issues involving major commitments of resources that top management teams have to deal with usually fall into this category. Problemistic search, incremental solution, and dynamic non-linear reiteration and redefinition of almost all the terms in the decision mix will characterize these types of activity (Braybrooke and Lindblom, 1963; Lindblom, 1959; Quinn, 1978; 1980).

Incremental decision search and solution means many small steps, which are easier to retrace if things do not go as hoped for. 'Once each small step has been taken it gives a clearer picture of what has to be done and the future becomes more focused', as Miller and Wilson (2006: 470) put it. Also, small steps are more likely to cool out resistance than big sweeping changes which will always seem obviously threatening to existing interests in a way that a smaller change – as a part of a larger iterative, emergent, and unfolding design – will not. Muddling through, as Lindblom calls it, is less scary. Common processes in muddling through include finding an initial simple impasse and further investigating it to reveal more complex political issues, from which a basic search for a solution ensues. The search is modified as the complexity and politicality of the issue start to become more apparent. Next, a basic design for a solution is advanced and then, typically, the basic design is subject to blocking moves from other interests. Finally, a dynamic design process is developed as changes are made, opponents brought on side, isolated, or otherwise neutralized (Mintzberg et al., 1976; Nutt, 1984).

QUESTION TIME

What makes your rationality bounded?

You have an assignment to do and it is due in 48 hours. Obviously time will be a bounded constraint on your rationality – but, thinking about how you usually go about doing assignments, what are the other elements of your own bounded rationality that you can think of? Jot them down below and then compare notes with your friends.

_____
_____
_____
_____
_____

Is your rationality bounded in the same ways as your friends' or differently? Why do you think this might be? Can any theories that you have learned already from this book help explain this finding?

The **garbage can** refers to situations characterized by 'problematic preferences', 'unclear technology', and 'fluid participation'.

Cohen et al. (1972) pushed March and Simon's (1958) critique one step further, announcing that the decision-making process in organizations is organized according to the logic of what they call the garbage can. The **garbage can**, of course, is a metaphor. Problems, solutions, and decision-makers, unlike in traditional decision theory, are seen to be disconnected. Specific decisions do not follow an orderly process from problem to solution, but are outcomes of several relatively independent streams of events within the organization. Decisions are made when solutions, problems, participants, and choices flow around and coincide at a certain point. There is a large element of randomness in where they come to rest. Like garbage in a can, what gets placed next to what is often purely random. Yesterday's papers end up stuck to today's dirty diapers just as downsizing attaches itself to profit forecasts.

Starbuck (1983) similarly argued that organizations are not so much problem solvers as action generators. Instead of analyzing and deciding rationally how to solve problems, organizations spend most of their time generating problems to which they already have the solutions. It is much more economical that way. They know how to do what they will do, so all they have to do is work out why they will do it. Just think of any consulting business – its solutions to whatever problems occur will be what it currently offers. Products such as TQM, BPR, and so on, are solutions to almost every problem, and thus it is not so much the problem that drives the solution but the solution already at hand that is waiting to be applied to a variety of different issues.

When decisions begin and end, as well as where they begin and the steps they go through, are not at all as clear as rational models might suggest (Hickson et al., 1986). Hickson and his colleagues looked at 150 decisions in 30 organizations; some decisions that the organizations' top managers defined as strategic were found to be resolved within a month while others dragged out over four years, with the mean time for strategic decision-making proving to be just over 12 months. Nonetheless, how the decisions were arrived at varied between three predominant processual paths, characterized by *sporadic, fluid,* and *constricted decision-making* (Table 7.4). The more political the matter for decision, the more stakeholders tend to be engaged; the more complex the problems are, the more fluid the processes tend to be. The key stakeholders are usually intraorganizational, typically production, sales and marketing, and accounting in the organizations that were studied.

With regard to the implementation of decisions made, subsequent research by the Bradford team of Hickson and colleagues (2003) has found that there are two typical ways of managing implementation. Where the management team has a pretty clear idea of what it is doing, and the likely reactions of others to it, a more planned mode of implementation occurs, based on experience. Where the management team doing the implementation has less experience and is not so sure what it is doing, the receptivity of the context in which the decision is being implemented is crucial. In other words, it matters a great deal if the team can succeed in getting key people 'on-side' (Hickson et al., 2003; Miller and Wilson, 2006).

TABLE 7.4   The Bradford studies of decision-making

Sporadic processes	Fluid processes	Constricted processes
Many disruptive delays	Little informal interaction	Revolve around a central identity or figure, such as a finance or production director
Uneven quality of information	More formal meetings	Widespread consultation across a range of expertise
Many sources of information	Fewer delays	Neither as fluid nor as sporadic as the other two types
Scope for negotiation	Shorter cycle of decision-making	More authoritatively structured
Informally spasmodic and protracted process	Process steadily paced, formally channelled, and speedy	Process carefully and narrowly channelled by the identity directing it

WHAT DO YOU MEAN?

The politics of decision-making as sensemaking

A famous case study of decision-making was made of the 1962 Cuban missile crisis by Allison (1971). The Soviet Union had installed missiles on Cuba, which were aimed at the USA, just 44 miles (70 km) away. Many people thought that the outbreak of a nuclear war was imminent as the respective leaders of the USSR and USA faced each other off, neither willing to compromise: US President Kennedy demanded the missiles be dismantled and USSR President Kruschev argued that if NATO could ring the Soviet Union with missile bases, what was the problem with bases in Cuba? Allison suggested that the crisis looked very different depending on the type of model through which one looks at it. The trouble is that if one party is looking through one model and another party is using another model – say a rational as opposed to a political model – then the opportunities for miscalculation and misunderstanding are enormous. One side will define the matter in terms of one set of issues; the other side will define it in terms of a different set of issues. Each side will be busy organizing some issues into politics while others will be organized out, or as Schattschneider (1960: 71) put it, there will be mobilization of bias occurring, with different sides mobilizing different biases and excluding other biases. Thus, as agendas form some issues will be suppressed or poorly represented, and fall into the space of 'non-decision-making' that Bachrach and Baratz (1962; 1970) wrote about.

Non-decisions are the unspeakables of local politics, the covert issues on which it has already been decided that no action will be taken. Their existence may not even be registered as they are sidestepped, suppressed, or dropped. Within organizations, the differential resources, expertise, and access that attach to players in complex power relations mean that the strategy of making some issues 'non-decisions' – perhaps by controlling who is given voice, or whose voice is noted, or seen as rational, sensible, and useful – serves to constrain agendas in the interests of those who already occupy dominant relations of power. Like the tip of the iceberg, only those matters already acceded to be legitimate and rational make an appearance on the agenda. At its most subtle this occurs when there is an apparent consensus about what issues are and are not, such that there is no conflict about issue definition. An apparent hegemony, as we saw in the IMF, is created. The official view is the only view registered. Of course, this assumes that there are few opportunities for actors to create awareness about non-issues and non-decisions.

The best case of how non-issues can become issues is probably the shift from a perspective on global warming that once consigned it to an issue not worth taking seriously, the preserve just of hippies, eco-freaks, and maverick scientists, to a situation where its reality and the need to deal with it preoccupies many boardrooms around the world and most, but not all, significant politicians. Social movements such as Greenpeace and Friends of the Earth have created an agenda where issues of climate change are now taken very seriously indeed. With the relational power that they have achieved by their lobbying, demonstrating, and documenting, they have been able to change what is taken for granted as rationality. Their increasing social power has shaped the social construction of knowledge, and the definition of rationality. As Flyvbjerg (1998: 369) argues, power produces knowledge and knowledge produces power – whatever is taken for granted as rationality will be an effect of the existing relations of power and knowledge. Thus, decision-making occurs in a complex web of political relations that are constantly shifting the shape of what counts as knowledge, rationality, and truth.

- An important part of organizational politics is shaping the agenda, getting some issues on to it, making sure that they remain there, and keeping other issues off. But remember, everyone is probably playing the same game!

It is one thing to make a decision and quite another to see it through into successful implementation. There are three different ways of connecting decision-making and implementation:

1 *Continuous connectedness* is provided by the key involvement of personnel usually drawn from production, finance, and marketing, throughout the processes of decision-making and implementation. They see the whole phased process through, provide a memory, and retain commitment as other interested parties drop out of the loop.

2 *Causal connectedness* is more complex. Three elements are crucial: the degree of contention, seriousness, and endurance of the processes of decision and implementation. High degrees of contention tend to limit familiar solutions – these are clearly not working if the contention is high – and they also indicate a context less receptive to whatever solution is proposed. Contentious decisions tend to be faster – perhaps because under these circumstances management decides to crash through or crash. Decisions characterized by a high degree of consensus take longer to make and implement, but there may well be a lot less firefighting afterwards (Dooley et al., 2000). The more serious the importance of the decision being made, in terms of the top management team's opinion, the more specific steps will be taken to implement it in an experience-based approach, while, from a readiness-based approach, the more priority will be given to implementation. There is also a relationship between how long the consequences of the decision are expected to endure – endurance – and acceptability. The longer lasting the implications of the decision will be, the more the top management team should care about the acceptability of what is being implemented. Crashing through under these circumstances will more likely lead to a crash rather than a successful decision, especially where the key buy-in of production, finance, and marketing has not been achieved – where the process has low acceptability.

3 *Anticipatory connectedness* involving thinking forward in terms of the future perfect tense – what we will have achieved when we have implemented the decisions we will have made – is important for decision-makers; if we do implement this decision what will be the effect? Thinking in an anticipatory way about the impact of the decision can feed back on the decision itself. If implementation of the posited and projected decision seems unlikely to be smooth, because implementation will be intricate, then the decision-making process probably needs revisiting, thus dragging out the process further. There is a form of feedback from imagined implementation to possible decision, making the decision process more protracted.

Check out the Companion Website www.sagepub.co.uk/ managingandorganizations3 for free access to an article by David Buchanan and Andrzej Huczynski (2004) about how films, in this case *12 Angry Men* (Lumet, 1957) and *Thirteen Days* (Donaldson, 2000), can be used to illuminate the politics of interpersonal influence in decision-making as a multilayered phenomenon, shaped by contextual, temporal, processual, social, political, and emotional factors.

THE ETHICS OF DECISION-MAKING RATIONALITY

In order for a decision to be named as such it must involve some form of choice. If a decision is made simply by applying a system of rules to a set of data, then there is no real decision – only the following of a particular pro-gramme (see Jones, 2004). Thus, regardless of the possible rational calcula-tions, the instant that a decision is made 'must be heterogeneous to the accumulation of knowledge ... not only must the person taking the decision not know everything ... the decision, if there is to be one, must advance towards a future which is not known, which cannot be anticipated' (Derrida, 1994: 37). The implication is that 'ethics and responsibility do not involve perfect and clear knowledge and absence of ... decision-making difficulties, but are themselves emergent in and even defined by the experi-ence of double-binds ... For Derrida, responsibility and ethics necessarily involve working with 'undecidability' (Jones, 2004: 53).

If organizational power and decision-making consist of configuring social relations such that others will likely do what has been decided else-where, then the successful achievement of the exercise of such power would render those others only technically accountable and responsible for their actions, and without ethical responsibility to other people. It would have the profound effect of relieving them of moral doubt – if they are authorized to do something and given targets to achieve by superordinates working to guiding strategies and plans, then, surely, obedience is appro-priate and authority should be served? It is this doubt, this undecidability, which is the very condition of ethically responsible decision-making. Stressing undecidability and attesting to the limits of calculability opens the field of decision-making to ethico-political considerations, says Derrida (1988: 116). Indeed, if a decision did not undergo the ordeal of undecidabil-ity there would be no space for ethical or political responsibility (Derrida, 1996). In relation to organizations the implications are significant – the authoritative application of rules and calculations, when seen as the pri-mary site of responsible decision-making, must render those decisions as irresponsible.

In the era of 'post-bureaucratization' many organizations stress 'auton-omy, responsibility and freedom/obligation of individuals to actively make choices for themselves' (du Gay, 2004: 41). A post-bureaucratic notion of responsibility is closely circumscribed by notions of enterprise, economic rationality, free-market principles, and individuality conceiving of indi-vidual responsibility primarily in terms of 'financial accountability' (du Gay, 2004: 176). Insofar as one is 'free', one's liberty to make decisions is confined within these bounds. Approaches to management that seek to critique and replace bureaucratic rationality with one that is entrepreneur-ial result in the domination of a set of values in which market economics are the basis of moral and social normalcy. Hence, while market norms and culture may replace the formal habits of bureaucratic rules and policies, organizational control of ethics through preordained codifications remains unchanged – it is just that the code has changed. A shift from formal rules to market norms still suggests that a pre-calculated rationality ought to govern decision-making.

Some theorists have proposed 'corporate governance', in a series of analogies with the political process (Clarke, 2004), instead of a concern with ethics. Good governance is typically seen as being held accountable.

The executive board is regarded as the government, with shareholders being seen as analogous to the electors. But, the analogies are not apt. Electorates are based on citizenship rights; shareholder meetings are based on proprietary rights. The citizen's privileges as a member of a state are clearly different from the shareholder's privileges as an owner of an in-principle entitlement to receive a dividend from a corporation.

Being in organizations and doing things according to the conventional rule – such as shareholder value, profit maximization, party loyalty, or discipline – is not a sufficient account in justification of ethical responsibility to those who will, at some time, hold the organization responsible, irrespective of the organization's preferences in the matter. Holding the organization accountable to dominant interests, such as the party, the nation, or the Führer (as in the extreme case of Eichmann), and thus working according to rule, as the singular interest so constituted defines it, is not a sufficient account to justify ethical responsibility. Principles of concordance with legitimate authority as a rule for action, as either intuited or formally expressed, are an insufficient basis to ensure ethical outcomes. In a world of social relations increasingly dominated by organizations there is urgent necessity for democratic principles of stakeholder representation to be more widespread, organizationally, and less ritualistic, politically. And this means that managers have to be able to manage with power positively in terms of both their internal and external dealings.

WHAT'S THE POINT?

Managing with power: seven steps to its effective use

1 Decide what your goals should be and what you are trying to accomplish in consultation with direct stakeholders in your organization.

2 Diagnose patterns of dependence and interdependence; which individuals both inside and outside the organization are influential and important to achieving these goals?

3 What are the points of view of the important people likely to be? How will they feel about what you are trying to do?

4 What are the power bases of the important people? Which of them is the most influential in the decision?

5 What are your bases of power and influence? What bases of influence can you develop to gain more positive control over the situation?

6 Which of the various strategies and tactics for exercising power seem most appropriate and are likely to be effective, given the situation you confront?

7 Based on steps 1–6, choose an ethical course of action to get something done.

MANAGING WITH POSITIVE POWER

How can we build positive, ethical power? To be a good manager means knowing how and when to use what kind of power wisely. When using power to manage others, always remember that those you are seeking to manage probably also will be trying to manage you with power. Thus the old adage 'do unto others as you would have others do unto you' is worth recalling. Although you may think of their response as resistance, to do so presumes a value legitimacy that may not be justified on your part. They are trying to manage your management of power through their management of the power that they can enact in the situations in which they find themselves or that they can create. Power is nothing if not creative.

Crucially, your managing with power means achieving common definition, a genuine accord, on which to base strategies, tactics, and actions. Positive uses of power make things happen that would not otherwise have happened – not by stopping some things from occurring, but by bringing new things into creation, involving less force and more listening, working with, rather than against, others.

Managing with power does not always mean seeking to impose a specific meaning on an uncertain context because it entails arbitrary structuring of others' realities. In contrast, the alternative model is often seen as one where people advocate bottom-up decision-making, seeking to listen to what others in the organization have to say. Organizations that use empowerment seek to enhance the overall systemic powers of the organization, to mobilize everyone's resources to get things done. Such use of power frequently means giving way in the organization conversation, not claiming a special privilege because of title or experience, and not being selectively inattentive to others, but listening and attending to them.

The challenge for future power theory, as Pfeffer (1992: 340) suggests, is 'to manage with power', where you recognize, diagnose, and respect the diversity of interests and seek to translate and enrol members within organizational courses of action, while at the same time listening to what others are saying, modifying your position accordingly, and choosing the appropriate strategies and tactics to accomplish whatever is chosen.

Sometimes, after taking all that into consideration, it still means making others do what they would not otherwise have done, against their resistance. Power can be like that. Yet, it does not have to be so. Coercive power should be the refuge of last resort for the diplomatically challenged and structurally secure, not the hallmark of management's right to manage.

Organizations may listen or may not, may work with the creativity and diversity of people's identities or work against them. The politics of power and decision-making can be based on active listening rather than assertive denial through the instrumentality and ritual of established power. To build such organizations – ones that seek to extend the organization conversation rather than to exploit its lapses – would seem to be one of the more pressing aspects of the agenda for future managers.

SUMMARY AND REVIEW

The pervasiveness of power is the most central aspect of organizational life. Much of the time, power is wrapped up in the velvet glove of authority, but inside that velvet glove is an iron fist. This fist has control of the levers of power that authority confers – the power, essentially, to determine policies and practices within the organization, most fundamentally expressed as whom the organization chooses to employ and whom it chooses not to employ.

Many organizations shape whether we work and how we are employed if we do; thus, these types of organizations have power over most of our life chances as wage earners. For this reason, it is important to understand the limits of power and authority, resistance, and obedience. In organizations, we have to put up with people and situations while doing the work we have to do or choose to do. It is important that our choices in how we discharge these duties can be defended ethically.

Fundamentally, power is shaped by what we know and how we know what to do. Organizationally, it is easy for this knowledge to be applied questionably, which is why it is important that organizations always be polyphonic rather than totalitarian spaces. Being able to articulate organizational dissent should be a normal and essential bulwark of civil liberty and individual freedom.

EXERCISES

1 Having read this chapter you should be able to say in your own words what the following key terms mean:

- Power
- Legitimacy
- Strategic contingencies
- Uncertainty
- Context
- Politics
- Resistance
- Domination
- Hegemony
- Total institutions
- Decision-making
- Non-decision-making

2 What power games characterize what types of organizations?

3 In what way is managing with power positive?
4 Are power and resistance inseparable?
5 Who gets empowered through empowerment strategies?
6 What common features do total institutions and (seemingly) normal organizations share?
7 Where is the border between use and abuse of power in management?
8 Why is there more to understanding power than listing its most common bases?
9 Think back to your school days: what were the main forms of discipline – in an everyday, routine sense – that you experienced? Now, think about any jobs that you have done – what were the major forms of discipline there?

ADDITIONAL RESOURCES

1 Our Companion Website is the best first stop for you to find a great deal of extra resources, free PDF versions of leading articles published in Sage journals, exercises, video and pod casts, team case studies and general questions, and links to teamwork resources. Go to www.sagepub.co.uk/managingand organizations3.

2 Many people have written about the topic of managing power in organizations, and finding just a few suggestions for further reading is hard. One place to start would be Lukes' (1974) slim volume, *Power: A Radical View*, if only because of its brevity – 50 pages – as well as its elegance and lucidity.

3 If you find the previous resource interesting, you might want to try Clegg's (1989) *Frameworks of Power* and another book that he wrote with Courpasson and Phillips (2006), *Power and Organizations*, although neither is written for the introductory student.

4 The work of Michel Foucault is important and notoriously difficult. A good introduction is Barker's (1998) *Michel Foucault: An Introduction*.

5 Probably the most interesting case study of power in and around organizations in recent years is Flyvbjerg's (1998) *Rationality and Power: Democracy in Practice*, researched in the arena of urban planning in the town of Aalborg in Denmark.

6 A good introduction from a managerial point of view is Pfeffer's (1992) *Managing With*

Power: Politics and Influence in Organizations. There is a discussion of this – and many other perspectives – in Cynthia Hardy's and Stewart Clegg's chapter, 'Some dare call it power' in the *Handbook of Organization Studies* (edited by Clegg et al., 2006b).

7 An example of the power of distance can be found in Ian McEwan's novel *Atonement* (2002: 202), where a character involved in the British retreat to Dunkirk reflects on the 'indifference with which men could lob shells into a landscape. Or empty their bomb bays over a sleeping cottage by a railway, without knowing or caring who was there. It was an industrial process. He had seen their own RA units at work, tightly knit groups, working all hours, proud of their discipline, drills, training, teamwork. They need never see the end result.'

8 The classic film about a total institution and organizational power is Milos Forman's *One Flew Over the Cuckoo's Nest* (1975). McMurphy is a prisoner who has been assigned to a mental institution because of his persistent rebelliousness in prison. After he gets there, he is assigned to Nurse Ratched's ward, where a series of power games occur. The most memorable are the group therapy scenes, with Nurse Ratched practising what she calls 'therapy' on the group of patients. McMurphy (played by Jack Nicholson) sets out to undermine her domination of the ward. The ward is organized and controlled through a rigid set of rules and regulations, which McMurphy questions.

The contest of wills with the nurse is played out as a struggle, with McMurphy trying to win over the other inmates to a spontaneous and independent style of thinking rather than one stuck in the routines that the nurse reinforces because they make the ward more manageable. In the first of the two group therapy scenes, McMurphy butts in and tries to get the nurse to switch on the TV set so they can watch the World Series. This suggestion is put to the vote – she clearly disapproves, and her domination is such that only three inmates vote. During the next therapy session, Nurse Ratched determinedly presses one member with questions he does not want to answer. Another member proposes another vote about watching the second game of the World Series. McMurphy encourages the patients with the great lines, 'I wanna see the hands. Come on. Which one of you nuts has got the guts?' Nine votes are cast in favour, and McMurphy senses victory – but Nurse Ratched changes the rules to defeat the proposal: 'There are eighteen patients on this ward, Mr McMurphy. And you have to have a majority to change ward policy. So you gentlemen can put your hands down now.' McMurphy turns and gestures to the patients of the ward who are uninvolved in the therapy group, most of whom are seemingly in their own private worlds. 'You're tryin' to tell me that you're gonna count these, these poor son-of-a-bitches, they don't know what we're talkin' about.' Nurse Ratched replies: 'Well, I have to disagree with you, Mr McMurphy. These men are members of the ward just as you are.' Nurse Ratched adjourns the meeting and closes the voting session. One of the outer group members not in the therapy session, a pivotal character called Chief, slowly raises his hand, so McMurphy says, 'The Chief voted. Now will you please turn on the television set?' The Nurse replies, 'Mr McMurphy, the meeting was adjourned and the vote was closed.' 'But the vote was 10 to 8. The Chief, he's got his hand up! Look!' 'No, Mr McMurphy. When the meeting was adjourned, the vote was 9 to 9.' Democracy in action in organizations often involves the highly undemocratic manipulation of the numbers. The film also illustrates the ways in which ordinary people can do quite extraordinary things as well after they have a uniform and are dealing not with people but with institutionally defined inmates: McMurphy ends up being lobotomized to 'cure' him, although there is palpably nothing wrong with him other than a strong and stubborn streak of individualism and anti-authoritarianism.

9 We also suggest watching the German movie *Das Experiment* (Hirschbiegel, 2001). It is very similar to the Haney et al. (1973) experiment, which we described in this chapter. It shows, impressively, how the abuse of power can shape human relations and create a fatal dynamic.

10 The Stephen Spielberg (1993) film of *Schindler's List*, adapted from the 1982 Thomas Keneally novel, *Schindler's Ark*, is a classic account of the ways in which the Holocaust was organized and resisted.

11 Organizations frequently enact routine deeds that, at the end of the functional chain of action, have appalling consequences. Have you seen the film *The Insider*, starring Russell Crowe (Mann, 1999)? It is a good example of this point. Tobacco companies knew that their products were killing people, but they kept on making those products because the fact that people died was an externality of their business model, and it had no immediate causal consequences in terms of legal responsibility. Besides, people smoking made profits for the tobacco companies, and they needed to recruit new smokers to replace those who died, or they would lose market share.

found at http://www.geocities.com/Athens/Forum/1650/htmlpower.html. It should be noted that the author of this chapter, Stewart, has fairly severe reservations about this approach to power. It seems to neglect the formal structures within which power relations get played out and seems to suggest that power consists of having resources. Think about it: if it is just the case of resources why could the USA not pacify Iraq with its overwhelming force after winning the Second Gulf War?

5 There is a good lexicon of decision-making terms at http://faculty.fuqua.duke.edu/daweb/lexicon.htm.

6 At http://dieoff.org/page163.htm you can find a classical contribution by Nobel Laureate Herbert Simon.

7 The US National Defense University has a nice page linking organizational power and politics at http://tinyurl.com/ysv9zv.

WEB SECTION

1 In addition to these suggested additional resources, do not forget to look at what is also available on the Companion Website www.sagepub.co.uk/managingandorganizations3, including free PDF files of recent papers related to this chapter, which you can download; video interviews with famous academics talking about related themes; as well as many other resources, such as connections to interesting websites.

2 For state of the art briefings on how to manage organizations effectively, please visit the Henry Stewart Talks series of online audiovisual seminars on Managing Organizations, edited by Prof. Stewart Clegg: www.hstalks.com/r/managing-orgs, in particular, Talk #10: *Organizational politics*, Richard Badham and Talk #11: *Managing organizational decision making*, Susan Miller.

3 A great resource site is www.criticalmanagement.org/. It is packed with useful and searchable bibliographic references and links as well as pod casts.

4 A useful online introduction to an organizational behaviour account of power can be

LOOKING FOR A HIGHER MARK?

Reading and digesting these articles that are available free on the Companion Website www.sagepub.co.uk/managingandorganizations3 can help you gain deeper understanding and, on the basis of that, a better grade:

1 Peter Fleming and André Spicer (2003) 'Working at a cynical distance: implications for power, subjectivity and resistance', *Organization*, 10 (1): 157–179, is a really good analysis of the contemporary politics of resistance in these post-Marxist times. It retains the essence of a critical stance but updates it to see resistance as a more personal, although organizational, phenomenon that is still rooted in the experience of exploitation at work, rather than seeing it in terms of collective action.

2 Thomas B. Lawrence and Nelson Phillips (2004) 'From *Moby Dick* to *Free Willy*: macro-cultural discourse and institutional entrepreneurship in emerging institutional fields', *Organization*, 11 (5): 689–711. A really interesting and fun paper on how whale-watching was institutionalized. It serves as a practical demonstration of the importance that Schumpeter

(2006 [1942]) attributed to new markets, new products, new methods of production, new sources of supply, and new ways of organizing for innovation to occur.

3 Christine Räisänen and Anneli Linde (2004) 'Technologizing discourse to standardize projects in multi-project organizations: hegemony by consensus?', *Organization*, 11 (1): 101–121. This article traces redesign processes in a major telecom organization and shows how the 'new' practices are disseminated within organizations. It provides a good account of how hegemony can be constructed in practice by organizations.

4 Nestar Russell and Robert Gregory (2005) 'Making the undoable doable: Milgram, the Holocaust, and modern government', *American Review of Public Administration*, 35 (4): 327–349. This is another look at the classic experiment by Milgram, relating it to events today. Just because a study is a classic it does not mean that it is no longer relevant!

5 David Buchanan and Andrzej Huczynski (2004) 'Images of influence: *12 Angry Men* and *Thirteen Days*', *Journal of Management Inquiry*, 13 (4): 312–323. How some great films can be used to make some good points about decision-making. This article is best used by instructors in the classroom in conjunction with the films – or at extracts from them.

CASE STUDY

APPOINTING A CEO

Here is a story told from my own perspective and with the benefit of a lot of hindsight. In 1980 I led the small team that founded Celltech, the UK's first research-based biopharmaceutical company. The formation of the company was widely recognized as novel and important. The UK was a world leader in biological science but the USA was the place where new biotechnology companies were being formed. It was hoped Celltech would reverse this trend. Celltech did turn out to be highly innovative, not only in science and technology, but also in its relations with academic research and in the openness and trust within the company, an environment right for a knowledge-based business.

By the end of the 1980s the company had been successful financially, had several key patents, and a pipeline of promising projects, and it had a workforce of some 300 people, nearly half of who were PhD scientists. Nevertheless, I found the job of CEO a demanding one and after ten years I said it was time to retire. I thought I was acting responsibly when I decided to leave. There was an obvious person to take over: my deputy, whom we will call Peter, who was very keen to get the job.

Most members of the board of directors knew little about knowledge-based businesses. Probably they were pleased to be presented with a task they found more familiar – that of appointing my successor.

The board must have had reservations about Peter as CEO, but they were not open about them. Probably they feared he would quit if he did not get the job and that this would damage the business. Whatever their reasons, the board organized a formal and lengthy search process. The process failed to produce anyone suitable and the board then announced that the search would continue for more months. Peter resigned in disgust and I said I was leaving anyway. Things looked bleak for Celltech. Then, unexpectedly, a senior person from the industry expressed interest and the board had little choice but to appoint

him. In the end he did a great job. The company continued to prosper as an independent business for ten years until acquired by a Belgian company for US$ 2.5 billion. The new owners showed their confidence in the Celltech team by putting it in charge of their whole pharmaceutical R&D.

Why did the succession process go wrong? It is clear that the board were at fault in giving Peter false hopes and in asking me to go along with a phoney recruitment process. Perhaps board members had found themselves uncomfortable with their responsibility for a knowledge-based business and were too keen to demonstrate power. Perhaps Peter was too ambitious. Although I thought I was behaving responsibly, I later realized I was at fault too. I thought I was avoiding the classic mistake of the proud founder of an organization who cannot let go. But I now realize I concealed from myself that Peter was a psychological surrogate, who could continue the traditions I had established in the company. If he had become CEO, I would have felt I still had my baby.

What are the lessons from this story? First, everyone was motivated by power, however well it was concealed or however pure people thought their motives were. The company claimed (rightly) that it was extraordinarily open and free from politics. But on this key issue, openness was not practiced and deviousness took over. With a deeper understanding of power, everything could have been done more honestly. This would have been much less risky and would have caused much less grief to those involved, including me.

Questions

1   Using what you have learned in the chapter on power, how would a deeper understanding of power lead to more positive outcomes?
2   'Everyone was motivated by power', says Fairtlough. Analyse the power moves and how they played out, using the theories discussed in this chapter.

Case prepared by Gerard Fairtlough, Triarchy Press, Axminster, Devon.

CHAPTER EIGHT
MANAGING COMMUNICATIONS

Meaning, Sensemaking, Polyphony

LEARNING OBJECTIVES

By the end of this chapter, you will be able to:

- Explain the different concepts of communication
- Understand the importance of communication processes at different levels
- Appreciate the different levels of, and audiences for, communication in organizations
- Discuss the benefits and shortcomings of different communications approaches
- Evaluate critically the power of communication
- Appreciate why polyphony is important in organizations

BEFORE YOU GET STARTED . . .

You cannot not communicate. (Paul Watzlawick)

INTRODUCTION

Organizations, first and foremost, are communicating entities; they are composed of people who are able to speak to each other and who want to speak to others. They have products to sell, news to distribute, clients to reach. Plans, change programmes, and strategies all need to be communicated. Gossip, PR strategies, informal chats and jokes, as well as marketing campaigns, branding exercises, and websites communicate what an organization is all about. If you have a great business idea and a really smart plan with which to realize it but no one knows, you will not achieve anything. You need to communicate your ideas to others. For instance, you might need a bank to lend you money to kick off your project and help you through cash flow problems, or you might have to convince an investor to finance your project or recruit reliable suppliers to ensure the quality of your product. No wonder that one of the earliest treatises in organizational communication was Dale Carnegie's best selling *How to Win Friends and Influence People* (1944). In short, **communication** connects all organizational activities with each other. It is a game that we all learn to play.

The process of exchanging information between two or more people or entities defines communication. Organizational communication is what occurs when an organization seeks to communicate with various audiences. These audiences may be employees, customers, investors, regulatory bodies and so on.

Fascination with communication reaches back to the ancient Greek philosophers, who emphasized the importance of rhetoric. Aristotle analysed the role and power of rhetoric in public speeches and events. Following this tradition, it was 'studies of propaganda and the flow of information and mass media effects (in the first half of the twentieth century) that would lay the foundations of what is now commonly thought of as the beginning of a communication science' (Bordow and Moore, 1991: 7). The old study of rhetoric transformed into that of opinion-making, propaganda, and the strategic use of information to ensure or create 'suitable' narratives that would explain and legitimize the order of things.

In most accounts, communication is understood as a direct cause–effect relation, as an act in which information is passed from a sender to a receiver. However, in the 1950s the emerging discipline of **cybernetics** changed the field dramatically.

The concept of feedback stressed that communication was not only a one-way effort from a sender to a receiver but a reciprocal undertaking. Person A sends some information (message) to B, and this information is transported through channels (media) that might affect and change it.

Communication can be defined as exchange of ideas, emotions, messages, stories, and information through different means including writing, speech, signals, objects, or actions. It may be intentional, such as a carefully phrased letter, or unintentional, such as the inferences another person may make about one's body language.

Cybernetics can be defined as studying feedback and other communication mechanisms in machines, living organisms, and organizations.

IMAGE 8.1   Like games, communication is based on feedback loops: your next sentence depends on the reaction of your opponent, whose reaction depends on your action, etc.

The message does not simply inform B but might change B's behaviour. B's change in behaviour is noticed (received) by A, influencing future action. Put simply, communication is an interactive circle that involves sender and receiver, messages, media, and feedback loops.

Early communications research used cybernetics to focus on the relationship between superior and subordinate in terms of (a) flows of information, (b) their impact on efficiency, and (c) the possible distortion of communication as it moved up and down various channels in the organizational hierarchy (Bordow and Moore, 1991). Nowadays, communication is understood not just as merely passing on information but as an active way of creating, shaping, and maintaining relationships and enacting shared values, common cultures, agreed goals, and means for their achievement.

Normally, different disciplines within management explore the relations between organizations and the diverse groups created, maintained, and nurtured through distinct patterns of communication. These disciplines are marketing (communication with customers), public relations (communication with shareholders and stakeholders such as local communities or environmentalists), and human relations (communication with internal audiences). Bypassing this division of labour, we synthesize aspects of each discipline in this chapter to produce insight into the fascinating ways in which organizations communicate.

THEORIES OF COMMUNICATION

Organizations can be seen as multiheaded hydra (the mythical beast of Greek mythology), with many mouths speaking to different internal and external audiences. Of course, with many mouths speaking simultaneously, it is sometimes difficult to gain agreement, understand what is being said, or to remain consistently 'on message'. Organizations often suffer from these problems. Communication from one part of an organization is contradicted by a message from one of its other parts. Additionally, the giant hydra does not live in a vacuum, where no other messages circulate. Instead, the environment is full of other, sometimes competing, and sometimes conflicting, stories: someone's got it in for the organization; they are planting stories in the press. Maybe the unions are agitating, or employees are gossiping, and the markets chatter about the stories that circulate as the hydra tries to chill out the stories it does not like or want.

QUESTION TIME

Take the 2010 oil spill in the Gulf of Mexico as a case study. Research the official response from BP and compare it to the voices of other organizations such as the US government, activist organizations, and the *Financial Times*. In how far do these voices differ? What do they identify as cause of the disaster? What arguments do they put forward to claim relevance and plausibility for their stories?

Different theories try to map this terrain. In organizational behaviour theory, the flow of instructions from the top to the bottom of an organization is supposed to ensure that employees do what management decides they should do. Within an OB perspective, there are several different emphases (Frank and Brownell, 1989). First, there is a cultural emphasis, in which communicating produces and shares common meanings and interpretations (see also pp. 216–222). Theorists who stress the primacy of human relations emphasize the importance of communication for a climate of openness, trust, commitment, and collaboration (see also Chapter 2 and 3). Those who view OB from a power perspective understand communication as a medium through which conflicts and struggles will be played out as a means to influence and recruit others to preferred views and interests

(Frank and Brownell, 1989). They do not assume that your preferences and those of others will necessarily align; in fact, they are more inclined to think they will not (see also Chapter 7).

A recent school of critical thought is referred to as *discourse theory*. From this perspective, discursive communication (including writing, speaking, etc.) informs our actions and decision-making processes. For instance, the discourse of human resource management allows you to ask certain questions, make assumptions about employees, and so on, that are entirely different from those that would be triggered by Frederick Taylor's scientific management (see pp. 453–457). Think of Taylor's description of factory workers as 'hands' in the early 1900s. Thinking of them as 'hands' evokes implicit meanings including an image of a headless and heartless worker who is easily replaceable, because all they contribute is manual dexterity, which is tightly trained and controlled. This changed during the human relations movement and Elton Mayo's emphasis on emotions and feelings at work. In the 1980s the focus shifted to workers as being human resources that can be systematically managed, trained, and exploited. In each case, the particular way of speaking about workers influences the way we think about and try to manage them: in the world of an HR manager employees are resources that should be developed, managed, and harnessed. On the other hand, in Taylor's scientific management employees were nothing but a pair of hands that were replaceable. Other contemporaries such as Henry Ford wrote over the entrance to his factory 'hands' entrance'. The two cases show how different labels (employees as hands or as human resource) reflect different ways of organizing and managing them. Discourse analysis argues that the differences and inequalities of the social world are directly connected to the world of language: because we use certain metaphors to make sense of the world, and often do not reflect on the implications of these metaphors, they frame our way of thinking about the world and restrict our imagination. Language is the map that guides us through the world; the map does not neutrally describe the territory but actively shapes it through highlighting certain points (tourist attraction, scenic drive, etc). In other words, language frames, and sometimes even shapes, reality.

Sounds complicated? It isn't. Gareth Morgan made a similar point in his classic book *Images of Organizations* (1986): if you think of organizations as machines, instead of cultures, or as living organisms, for example, it makes a big difference when you try to understand them and devise a plan of action based on that understanding.

Analysis of organization discourse suggests that the language employed in the communication within organizations shapes organizational reality. Gordon Shaw, formerly executive director of planning and international business within 3M, describes the importance of discourse in organization by using the concept of story-telling:

> Storytelling is the single most powerful form of human communication. Stories allow a person to feel and see information, as well as factually understand it. The events come alive for the listeners so that they 'see' with you and become physically and mentally involved in the story. Storytelling allows

Check out the Companion Website www.sagepub.co.uk/ managingandorganizations3 for free access to an article by Steve Maguire and Cynthia Hardy (2006), and one by Islam Gazi and Michael Zyphur (2007), if you are interested in discourse theory.

you to create a shared vision of the future ... The potential leverage in conceptualising, communicating, and motivating through the use of strategic stories (both inside and outside the enterprise) will define superior management in the future. (Shaw, 2000: 194)

Check out the Companion Website www.sagepub.co.uk/ managingandorganizations3 for free access to an article by David Barry, Brigid Carroll, and Hans Hansen (2006), if you want to find out more about text, context, and story-telling.

Corporate stories differentiate a company from its competitors (just as your personal story – your history – distinguishes you from anybody else) and create a shared sense of community and belonging among internal and external audiences. As organizational boundaries blur more and more, external and internal are concepts that lose their descriptive importance: employees also watch TV ads and read external messages intended for stakeholders, and internal communication shapes how employees represent the organization to outsiders (Cheney and Christensen, 2001). Everything an organization does communicates meaning, both verbally and non-verbally (whether the organization intends or desires it to or not). It is not only glossy brochures that tell you what an organization stands for but also, much more important, the actual behaviour of its management and employees. In our social world we use clothing and other artifacts to communicate who we are. Take the example of the hill tribe from northern Vietnam in Image 8.2: what does the image communicate?

The well-known saying that 'one cannot not communicate' means that even non-interaction is a form of interaction. Think of your mum who is angry with you because you did not spend time with her on Mother's Day and therefore will not speak to you. This non-communication expresses something more than words. Or think of that text message you never wrote to your boyfriend about something else that you did other than be

IMAGE 8.2 Look at the image of a hill tribe from northern Vietnam: although the image does not speak, the dresses, the colours, the facial expressions, the posture, the fact that only women pose for photos for visitors, etc. – almost everything in the image communicates a great deal about the life of these people

IMAGE 8.3   Underground

with him. That can bring you trouble. When the girl you dated the other day does not answer your calls, she is also communicating something. It is almost impossible not to communicate.

What is true of people is also true of organizations: they communicate even when they think they do not. Consider the messages communicated by the essentially similar subway signs shown in Images 8.3 and 8.4 on pages 301 and 302. What do they suggest to you about the organization that each represents?

Levels of communication

A conventional way of making sense of communication in organizations is to distinguish the different levels of communication. Communication can be

IMAGE 8.4   Metro

analysed by looking at the level of personal and social involvement. Littlejohn (1989) differentiates between four levels of communication, shown in Figure 8.1.

Whereas the first three types of communication are mainly situated in an interpersonal context (face to face, with exceptions such as a phone call or e-mail), the fourth type is mediated through channels of mass communication (again, there are exceptions, such as 'word of mouth'). **Dyadic communication** occurs between an employee and manager; small-group and team communication happens in meetings, brainstorming sessions, and workshops; and finally, mass communication is at work in marketing and PR campaigns. Wherever it occurs, through whatever modes, organizational communication is a culturally driven process of sensemaking. People communicate to make sense for themselves and others; sometimes they communicate to mislead, other times they do so

Dyadic communication means two-party communications. Dyadic communication can be impersonal when two people interact without direct personal contact as well as face to face and unmediated.

FIGURE 8.1
Levels of communication
(after Littlejohn, 1989)

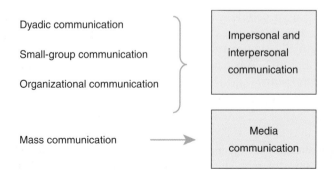

to be understood clearly. No wonder there is ample opportunity for messages to become mixed and for the wrong audience to receive or interpret an incorrect message (Watzlawick et al., 1967). Sometimes signs that communicate the same message can differ markedly: attractive communication is pretty easy to spot: compare the Underground and Metro signs.

Dyadic communication: interpersonal When the manager from production and the newcomer in the marketing department go for lunch together, or meet while smoking outside the building, they might build some understanding of each other's task that will be helpful when their company launches its next product. Sure, they may be doing other things, such as flirting, chatting about sport, or fashion, but they also get to know each other's work. They are communicating interpersonally, face to face.

Interpersonal communication is based on interdependence, where each person's behaviour is a consequence of the other's. Such behaviour can be expressed both verbally and non-verbally and have either a formally framed or informal character. A selection interview, for instance, is a formally framed organizational procedure, whereas a chat over lunch may be informal.

Every communication has an informational aspect and simultaneously tells you something about the relationship of the people involved. The manager saying to his subordinate, 'You have until Monday to write this report', or 'Would it be possible to have your report by Monday?' communicates almost the same information, but the two sentences define the relationship quite differently. Communication always has a meta-communication aspect, and organization managers should be well aware of this – the way the message is projected and received is as important as the content it contains.

Communication involves multiple meanings, interpretations, distortions, and omissions. It is not so much the smooth processing of information but rather the complex, interactive emergence of knowledge, meaning, and narratives that drive communication. And in this process, the transitions are neither additive nor linear; what you learn now may change everything you thought you knew before or will know in the future. This theme is often played out in movies such as *Sliding Doors* (Howitt, 1998), a film that showed how an accident can change the whole foundation of a relationship and a life.

Communication comprises a series of interactions seen differently by the participants (Figure 8.2). For instance, a leader with a need for control can generate resistance from employees. If the leader responds with tighter control, this is likely to generate further resistance, which may be interpreted as a lack of motivation. But the increased control produces even more resistance and less motivation! We will encounter further examples of these dynamics in Chapter 13, when we discuss bureaucracy. When a vicious circle is in play, it is quite tricky to resolve. Both parties have good reason for their behaviour. They are part of the same interaction, but they differ fundamentally in punctuating what is happening. Whereas the

Interpersonal communication refers to direct interaction between two or more people.

IMAGE 8.5 Dyadic communication is key to human relationships. Often it is overshadowed by multiple meanings, interpretations, distortions, and omissions

FIGURE 8.2
Vicious circles at work

subordinate might argue that they are demotivated *because* of a lack of trust, the superior might stress that *due* to a lack of motivation only strictly enforced controls can guarantee a minimum of engagement. Both parties are weaving the same story, participating in the same dialogue, but punctuate it differently and thus create different realities in which causes and effects are reversed. The amplification of misunderstanding escalates in such circumstances.

QUESTION TIME

Communicative double interacts

According to Weick (1979), organizations consist of processes that he calls a double interact. Weick defines the double interact as an *act* followed by a *response* that leads to a *reaction* changing the initial act followed by a response, in an ongoing loop. Think of a typical work situation: a supervisor says that he has to control employees because they do not seem to be motivated; the employees are not motivated because they are tightly supervised and feel demotivated by the lack of trust. You can see how a vicious circle is produced and sustained. The interesting thing is that both parties live in the same world but attribute cause and effect differently. For the supervisor, tighter control is the effect, caused by low motivation levels; for the workers, tight supervision is the cause for low morale. In such a situation both parties are right and wrong at the same time. Trapped in the ongoing loop they can argue forever without finding a solution.

An example demonstrating the double impact, would be the case of a manager who tells an employee that the employee must increase productivity and quality and will be monitored more closely in the future (act). Demotivated through this lack of trust,

the employee responds by taking more sick days and taking less care of quality standards (response). The manager understands this behaviour as proof of the necessity to tighten the control mechanism and reacts by increasing pressure on the employee (re-adjusted action), which leads to a drop in employee motivation, resulting in even more sick days and poorer quality! It is important to see that this vicious circle is played out in daily communication. As you already know by now, such fatal dynamics result from the complexity of communication processes (Watzlawick et al., 1967).

- Can you think of any double interacts that you have experienced? How and in what ways were they double interacts? Jot them down below and compare notes with your friends.

_____

_____

_____

_____

_____

_____

_____

_____

Dyadic communication: impersonal   A letter or e-mail between you and an officer from the Taxation Office is dyadic but impersonal.

Think of a call centre that is, by definition, an interface between customer and organization. When it puts you on hold and bombards you with uninteresting new offers while you are waiting, it is communicating how the organization that you are seeking to gain information from takes care of customer needs. Directing you through a complicated number system to the 'right' person, call centres assume that digital communication is the appropriate level of involvement. However, it is not necessarily the appropriate frame for establishing a relationship. Companies miss out on the chance to express and actively shape their relationship with consumers when they restrict themselves to such forms of communication. Also, the relationship is purely complementary: if the customer has a problem, the call centre resolves it as long as it is a standard problem – one for which it has a standard solution. But, as we will see shortly, organizations can learn

Check out the Companion Website www.sagepub.co.uk/ managingandorganizations3 for free access to an article, by Dennis Gioia (2006) about Karl Weick, someone whose work on sensemaking has had a major impact in management theory.

a great deal from their customers about what they want, how they actually use their products, and what improvements they wish. A more dialogical style would involve customers more interactively and create stronger relationships (see also Chapter 9).

Small-group communication   Group-level dynamics differ from those in dyadic communication. Think of a team with nine members. Communication is not only face-to-face, but roles are established, sub-groups formed, and a different dynamic is created. A group is formed by dynamics beyond the influence of its individual members. The culture, as well as the quality of problem solving within a group, depends on the interaction between its members. Group pressures influence their members' ways of thinking as the phenomenon of groupthink demonstrates (Littlejohn, 1983: 237).

WHAT'S THE POINT?

When groups comprise teams that are too like-minded we get Groupthink

Groupthink occurs when a group of people used to working together end up thinking the same way (see also pp. 99–100). There are six negative impacts of groupthink:

1 Groups limit the discussion of alternatives to only a few and do not consider the whole range of possible solutions.
2 Those options favoured by the majority are often taken without being revisited.
3 The group does not re-examine disfavoured alternatives.
4 Expert opinions are generally not valued more.
5 Groups are highly selective in collecting and valuing information.
6 Once a decision is made, the group is so confident that it does not think of alternatives for plan B scenarios.

Groupthink is often marked by several symptoms:

- Groups have an illusion of invulnerability.
- Groups undertake joint efforts to (post-)rationalize the actions they undertake.
- Groups tend to see themselves as inherently moral.
- Persons outside the group are branded not only as outsiders but also as less worthy in some ways – they are stupid or bad, for instance.
- Self-appointed 'mind-guards' protect the group.
- The group exercises self-censorship, which ensures both uniformity and homogeneity. Thus, the negative outcomes of groupthink are enacted, reinforced, and exercised in communication.

Taken that organizations rely more and more on teamwork, these tendencies to groupthink are frightening. They indicate that organizations actively have to manage communication in teams if they are to overcome these problems.

Shared meanings   Organizational communication comprises a series of recurring communication patterns that occur throughout the entire organization. In a rather awkward formula, Weick (1979) argued that organizing is a consensually validated grammar used to reduce equivocality by means of what organization members constitute as sensible interlocking behaviours. Now, this is rather a mouthful, but what we think Weick means is the following: communication takes place on the basis of shared understandings and implicit rules, which function as if they were a grammar. They produce predictable communication patterns, which organization members use to reduce the time spent worrying about the huge amount of things they do not know in order to make their tasks more manageable by focusing on the predictable. That is, they seek to reduce equivocality. The way they do this is through developing shared routines with others in the organization. These shared routines produce the interlocked behaviour expressed in and through the double interacts – different ways of sensemaking.

Placing an emphasis on consensual validation helps you understand that shared meanings form one fundamental aspect of organizations. These shared meanings are 'agreements concerning what is real and what is illusory' (Weick, 1979: 62). But meanings are not always shared. Think of organizations where the newly merged partners turn out to be sharing the same bed but not the same dreams. The merger between two companies that appeared synergistic but shared totally different cultures, styles of communication, and ways of making sense – such as the Time Warner/AOL merger or Citibank and Travelers – is a case in point.

WHAT DO YOU MEAN?

The grammar of organizing

Think of a restaurant like McDonald's: what holds it together is a complex set of rules that allows all people that work and eat there to interact. When you walk into a typical McDonald's the menu gives you several options. Ordering at the counter, you have to translate your craving into the McDonald's products and meal combinations. That is important, otherwise the person behind the counter could not tell the kitchen what to prepare next. And the kitchen could not tell the many suppliers which products to drop in next Monday. In order to make such complex chains function, every organization has particular forms, routines,

practices, and processes. The rules involved may be thought of as a grammar that reduces all possible combinations to a handful of legitimate ones. They all ensure that outcomes can be achieved by interlocking different behaviours and actions. Again, think of McDonald's: it could offer you an endless variety of burgers but in order to create predictability it reduces the number to a dozen or so, throwing in a special or new choice every now and then. Of course, sometimes this grammar ossifies the organization: for instance, when McDonald's decided to add coffee and healthier meals to its product offer it had to change the way customers, employees, and suppliers interacted.

All organizational reality is constituted and constructed through communication *and* miscommunication. Although formal communication programmes try to facilitate shared meaning, there will always be stories, myths, and gossip circulating as well. It is important not to assume that organizations are some privileged space of shared meaning; though they may strive hard to achieve this, there are often countervailing tendencies.

Besides this internally focused communication, organizations also constantly talk to their environments and diverse stakeholders (such as suppliers, network partners, investors, etc.). Basically, organizations communicate their identity, their values, and their reason for being to these audiences. Corporations seek to express a sense of what they are and, in doing so, they build strong relationships with key stakeholders. Mass communication is one (preferred) way of achieving this.

Mass communication Since McLuhan (1964) coined the phrase the 'global village', the importance of mass communication has constantly increased. **Mass communication** has four characteristics: (a) it is communication to a large, anonymous, and heterogeneous audience; (b) it is primarily one-way communication, meaning that feedback from the audience is restricted; (c) it is transmitted through different channels that work fast; and (d) the sender is usually a big organization rather than individuals (Littlejohn, 1983). Billboard advertisements were an early form of commercial mass communication but by no means the earliest or the most pervasive in Western experience (see Image 8.6).

In contrast to the three other levels of communication, **mass communication** goes from one point to many receivers.

One of the earliest forms of explicit mass communication developed in the Christian church. In an age when literacy was not widespread, the church controlled the most powerful means of mass communication. Because the majority of the church's congregational members were non-literate, they were able to relate to iconic symbols much more easily than to sophisticated literary sources such as the Bible. The church realized this, and, as well as through the words spoken by priests to the masses as they interpreted the Bible and papal edicts, it communicated through religious art as its central representational form. The most sophisticated representational forms were the paintings and stained-glass windows of religious art, still to be seen in the churches and cathedrals of Europe. However, much more numerous and available to the populace at a local level, in their homes and everyday observances, far from the cathedrals and churches, were representations of Christ on the cross and the Virgin Mary, objects that could as easily fill a niche in the home as play a role in a procession. These were the core icons and, as such, examples of one of the earliest and best developed forms of mass communication (see Image 8.7). These symbols played an important function. In Weick's (1969) terms, we might say that they helped to reduce equivocality about belief. Pieces of inert wood, when appropriately rendered and painted, could become holy icons, calling forth attendant rituals and behaviours.

The church was particularly effective at mass communication when there were few other organizations offering competing messages. Today, of course, most large organizations have marketing and PR

IMAGE 8.6   Parisian billboards add grace and style to civic space

departments or agencies that seek to find appropriate channels to help them reach relevant audiences and get their message across. Advertisements on TV, billboards, websites, and newspapers remain organizations' preferred ways to tell the rest of the world who they are and what they have to offer. While mass advertising can be costly and, as specialists argue, ineffective and inefficient, other means of interactive mass communication are therefore explored. Of course, the Internet and the Web 2.0 explosion have paved the way to new forms of communication.

IMAGE 8.7   Christ on the cross, communicating that he died to save us from our sins

WHAT DO YOU MEAN?

Add as Friend: Barack Obama, President of USA

Information and communication technology (ICT) changes fundamentally how we organize every aspect of life, including politics. The 2008 US elections that saw Barack Obama winning against the conservative John McCain are a good example in case. Analysts have suggested that Obama's victory is partly due to his clever use of the Internet. Arianna Huffington, editor in chief of *The Huffington Post*, goes as far as to claim 'were it not for the Internet, Barack Obama would not be president. Were it not for the Internet, Barack Obama would not have been the nominee'. Obama used Web 2.0 tools effectively and managed to mobilize supporters, communicate his vision, and reply to criticisms. He used Facebook, Linkedin, and YouTube (see http://www.youtube.com/user/BarackObamadotcom) to broadcast his

(Continued)

(Continued)

messages at low cost to an audience that was thought to be tired of politics. Of course YouTube is much cheaper than paid TV ads: campaign manager Mr Trippi calculated that Obama's YouTube messages where watched for 14.5 million hours in total, which equates to a value of $47 million of paid TV ads. New media are not only more cost-effective but they are also trustworthier when friends send links to each other and news spreads by word of mouse. Mr Trippi speculates, 'Just like Kennedy brought in the television

presidency, I think we're about to see the first wired, connected, networked presidency'. Indeed, if you check out Linkedin or Facebook you can become friends with the president of America – if there was not that limit of 5,000 friends. With the next president, be fast and build up your social capital.

Source: Claire Cain Miller, 'How Obama's Internet campaign changed politics', *New York Times*, 7 November 2008.

MINI CASE

Communicating without a budget: ambush marketing

The 2010 soccer world championship in South Africa was a prime opportunity for big brands to communicate what they are all about by associating themselves with the best that soccer has to offer. They pay millions to have the privilege of exclusivity, hoping their sponsorship dollars will push them ahead of their rivals. For FIFA, sponsorship is lifeblood: 30 per cent of its revenue derives from Budweiser, McDonald's, Coke, Visa, and other major sponsors.

Clever communication strategists see opportunities in ambushing the official sponsors and gain if not fame then at least notoriety for their stunts. At the 2010 soccer world cup, the Dutch beer brewer Bavaria ambushed the game Denmark vs Holland. Bavaria hired some 35 women wearing bright orange mini dresses during the match,

advertising the brewery. Although the dresses did not feature the logo of the company, FIFA reacted swiftly and ejected 'beer babes' from the stadium. Later, two women allegedly in charge of the ambush were arrested under the Contravention of Merchandise Marks Act, which states that companies may not benefit from an event without paying for advertising. The law is meant to protect the official beer sponsor of the event, Budweiser, and ensure that it can reap the fruits of its sponsorship investment.

- Conduct some online research to find other examples of ambush marketing. Use communication theory to explain how ambush marketing works. Finally, discuss whether ambush marketing is ethical or not.

Source: *The Guardian*, 16 June 2010; we'd like to thank Chris Carter for alerting us to the case study.

Organizational communication and organizational design

In a large and strictly hierarchically organized company, it is unlikely that the CEO will speak to people from the bottom, or that people from the bottom will be able to communicate their ideas directly to top management. Also, it is hard for different departments that are not directly linked to each other to interact. Put simply, the organizational design decides who communicates with whom directly. The more specialization, formalization, and centralization, the more restricted is communication (see also Chapter 12).

Open-space offices, shared photocopiers where people intermingle and chat, and corporate events where the usual sense of hierarchy is relaxed (usually when everybody is a little drunk and people may forget themselves, taking risks that only become evident when the hierarchy reinstates itself) all produce the internal flow communication and ensure the necessary exchange that is inhibited by the formal structure. To undo these structures is the necessary precondition of rich communication processes. Following Bordow and Moore (1991), such processes have four major functions:

1 *Informative function*: Communication transports information about facts and figures that are the basis for informed action. Thus, communication generates action.
2 *Systemic function*: Communication is the glue between organizational members. It establishes efficiencies for social interaction.
3 *Literal function*: Communication does not merely transport facts from sender to receiver but also connotes meaning and sense. In fact, communication is sensemaking.
4 *Figurative function*: Communication links an organization to its wider environment. It represents an organization's identity, its mission, and its purpose. Put simply, it legitimizes an organization.

Christensen and Cheney (2000) argue that the distinction between different communication disciplines such as marketing, PR, and advertising is no longer easy to draw. PR functions were once specialized in their focus on an organization's contact with the public, whereas marketing tried to manage relations with customers. But when Shell, for instance, tried to sink the Brent Spar oil platform in the North Sea, it was the public who reacted quickly, loudly, and impulsively. Unfortunately, this public was simultaneously its customers, so who should have reacted for Shell – the PR or the marketing department? Or take another disaster that BP is responsible for – the oil spill in the Gulf of Mexico. The difference between the public, consumers, employees, and other stakeholders is increasingly blurred. Hence different functions including PR, marketing, HR, and others manage an organization's communication with its environment, seeking to get relevant information from the environment and respond to it adequately. In addition, well-informed and briefed employees can serve as employee-ambassadors spreading the message an organization seeks to promote. General Motors, for instance, integrated internal and external communication in the 1980s as it relied on its employees (who received both commercials on TV at home and memos at the workplace) to promote the emphasis on safety (Christensen and Cheney, 2000: 248).

Audiences

Communication is not just sending messages; it also involves receiving them, and different audiences are involved in the reception of meaning – which may not always be that intended. Three main audiences receive organizational communication: internal audiences (employees) targeted through **intraorganizational communication**; other organizations (partners, suppliers, etc.), who receive **interorganizational communication**; and the wider society (markets, society, press, etc.).

Intraorganizational communication   Communication can be downward, upward, or horizontal, and comprises both formal and informal messages. Downward communication means the flow of communication from superior to subordinate. Such communication has several functions. It instructs employees, provides them with goals, explains how they can achieve them, gives feedback concerning their performance, and seeks to build commitment.

Upward communication means the flow of communication from subordinates to superiors. It includes employees' feedback concerning rules, strategies, implementations, and so on. Employees often know most about customers, services, and products, as they are in daily contact with them. Naturally, management lacks this knowledge, even though it forms the basis for strategic decision-making. So to be good strategists at the macro level, they need to be good communicators at the micro level. A famous study conducted by MIT focused on the difference between Japanese and American ways of producing cars, and it revealed that Japanese employees were more actively involved in the definition and refinement of car manufacturing process improvements (Womack et al., 1990). US industry, however, was still mainly organized according to concepts derived from Taylor, making such communications difficult. This difference in the management of communication was one of the determinants of the success of Japanese corporations during the 1980s.

Finally, horizontal communication describes communication that takes place between different departments. Marketing, for instance, might need to know planned product innovation for the next few years in order to align its campaign with the long-term image.

A good deal of managerial work involves providing information and facilitating communication (Mintzberg, 1973). Managers spend most of their time gathering information from other people, by talking, listening, and negotiating in meetings, by informal conversation, and through other media. Peters and Waterman (1982) took this idea one step further and defined a leadership style called 'management by walking around'. In essence, the manager must not only be seen around the place but also be seen to be aware of what is going on and acting on it.

An example of the power and importance of such intraorganizational communication is given by Ginger Graham, CEO of ACS, a $300 million US company. Newly appointed, she found the company in denial of the real roots of its recent failures. She wrote a plea for open and honest communication within the company (Graham, 2002). And she started to practice what she preached when, at an annual meeting, instead of saying the usual friendly things, she said, 'I've always heard about what a wonderful company ACS is, but frankly, that's not what I see'. After saying straightforwardly

Intraorganizational communication occurs inside an organization and typically engages organizational members.

Interorganizational communication takes place between members of different organizations.

what everyone knew but nobody openly dared to admit, there was a huge relief in the audience and among employees that – finally – someone from top management could see and address the hot issues. What Graham did from this moment on was, in her own words, to

> create a culture that would allow everyone in the company to feel free to tell the truth, from top managers to the people on the loading dock. Only by arming ourselves with the truth, I felt, by owning up to it, and by acting according to it, could deep-rooted problems be identified, understood, and ultimately solved. (Graham, 2002: 43)

An atmosphere of openness and honesty can be a trigger for change. All communication is important internally, even when it is addressed externally. For instance, branding and marketing communication is usually directed towards external stakeholders, but it also affects employees. Mitchell (2002) argues for the importance of 'selling the brand inside'; when done, it creates a powerful link between the services the company sells and the employees who actually sell it. If employees do not know what an organization is promising its clients, how can they live up to what is being preached? In fact, it becomes important that external and internal marketing are connected. All internally focused information is important externally: if the markets get negative reports from within a company, it will be reflected in their valuation of the firm.

Mitchell (2002) provides an instance of a financial services institution that announced it was shifting from being a financial retailer to becoming a financial advisor. A year and a marketing budget later, nothing had happened. Customers did not feel that the announced shift had occurred and still seemed to see the institution in retail terms. The reason was simply that employees were not convinced by the new strategy. Marketing had targeted only customers and forgotten that there was an important internal market to convince – its own employees.

Interorganizational communication for collaboration Interorganizational collaboration and networks have become increasingly important for organizations.

Like humans, organizations build relationships that sometimes end up happily ever after but other times end in acrimony. Oliver (1990: 104) distinguished six reasons why organizations might collaborate with other organizations:

1 *Necessity*: Collaboration might be based on the fact that an organization is working together with another organization in order to meet legal or regulatory requirements.
2 *Asymmetry*: Collaboration can be driven by the wish to control relevant environments. A clothes manufacturer might work closely with its suppliers in order to exercise control and power over them.
3 *Reciprocity*: The interests of two organizations might be better pursued when they join forces and form an alliance from which both benefit, such as occurs in a trade association.

4 *Efficiency*: Obviously, this motivation to collaborate is based on the idea of improving organizational performance through collaboration.

5 *Stability*: Organizations might collaborate in order to maintain a level of stability otherwise unreachable.

6 *Legitimacy*: Organizations seek collaboration in order to legitimize their own business. Shell, for instance, works together with Greenpeace, which obviously helps Shell to produce the image of a caring and responsible company.

For the growth of networks, mutual trust and consensus are decisive. This can only be achieved by communication. Two organizations working together need lots of coordination, cooperation, and bargaining, which sometimes inevitably produce conflict and coercion, all of which will be played out in communication and non-communication (Irwin and More, 1994).

Successful networks rely on managed communication in which two roles are especially important, the boundary spanner and the interlocker. The boundary spanner represents and communicates an organization's goals to its environments and acquires information from the outside, which is necessary for the organization. He or she has the ability to bridge the gap between inside and outside, ensuring the flow of information across boundaries. The interlocker is a member of two organizations (say a senior manager in company A and board member of company B) and knows things that the boundary spanner, as an outsider, would not be able to decode. Gossip, rumours, or industry trends can be examples of information that the interlocker can communicate because of his or her position (see also Chapter 8).

Communication with stakeholders In **communication with stakeholders** organizations use different distribution channels (TV, print, radio, Internet, and specially organized events) to communicate what they offer. As products and services become increasingly refined and simultaneously more similar and exchangeable, organizations seek unique ways to position themselves in the marketplace. PR, marketing communication, reputation management, and branding are the organizational means for differentiation. They communicate what an organization stands for – promoting not only its products but also its core values and its identity.

As products and services change quickly, and the difference between original and generic products increasingly blurs (think of the cola market with all its cheap generic brands), companies try to establish a unique identity. They create this through communications, including mission statements, corporate design (business cards, stationery, etc.), retail outlets, logos, and other activities, such as sponsorship. The soft drink producer Red Bull, for instance, the biggest global energy drink manufacturer, selling more than a billion cans a year, promotes its soft drink heavily through promoting extreme sports events (www.redbull.com). The goal is to establish an image of the organization that goes beyond the characteristics of its products. Rather, the products should be promoted through this image.

> **Communication with stakeholders** describes communication between an organization and other relevant parties (stakeholders) such as media, community groups, labour unions, politicians, etc.

MINI CASE

Communicating Nike

Consider the example of Nike. People buy Nike shoes not only because of their qualities but also because of the fitness aesthetic these products promote, the lifestyle people associate with them, and the hardly tangible but tremendously valuable identity that Nike provides to its customers; that is, if Shaq O'Neal or Michael Jordan uses Nike, would you not want to as well?

There is, however, a dark side to the Nike story – a story not of excellence but of exploitation, of sweated labour, and maggots in the canteen food. Sometimes what is communicated corporately is not what is communicated organizationally. The short version of the story, as reported by David Boje on his website, is as follows:

> While consumers and sports-spectators associate Nike with fast and powerful athletes, it's no surprise that not everyone associated with the company is a Marion Jones or Tiger Woods. In fact, some Nike factory workers find everyday activities, let alone sports, to be daunting challenges. When you work sixty hours a week making sneakers in an Asian or Latin American factory and your friends disappear when they ask for a raise, it is not so easy to be a sports-spectator. Two prime examples: At Kukdong, Nike's partner factory in Mexico, women ... asked for fair wages, no worms in their food, and their own union. These women were physically beaten and given bruises and black eyes for asking for basic human rights you and I take for granted. It's a familiar story: young girls set out on a magical journey of adventure, seduced by Nike partner ads for better jobs, only to find that things they value most are living without terror.

When stories like this one became public Nike acted quickly to ensure that its image would not be damaged too much. Today, many companies that have factories in developing countries collaborate with NGOs and have inspectors to ensure that their partner organizations behave ethically.

- How effective have Nike's communications strategies been? Use the web to check out the pros and the cons of Nike's communications strategies.

Communication as marketing

The shortest definition of **marketing** is meeting customer needs profitably.

Because it is a well-developed discipline in its own right, people in marketing would not necessarily agree that their subject is a part of organizational communication. However, the core activity of **marketing** – promoting products, services, and, by extension, an organization's identity – is, in fact, a communication exercise.

Behind these words, 'meeting customer needs profitably', however, lurks a complex task and libraries filled with research. EasyJet, for instance, discovered that people were willing to fly more cheaply by doing without on-board service. The Body Shop found that cosmetics produced in an ethically and environmentally responsible and sustainable way, which were not animal tested, met a broad-based consumer need.

Once identified, such needs become the starting point for strategy making. The next step is to communicate this strategy to customers and stakeholders. This means making people understand why you offer what you offer and why they should buy your services or products. You have to communicate your unique selling proposition to potential customers. Marketing is all about this communication.

According to Kotler, marketing communication develops in five steps (Kotler, 2000: 552):

1 *Identifying the target audience*: If you want to sell clothing you have to identify who you would like to sell it to. You could target men, women, or children. But these categories are not precise enough by far. If you decide to target women you have to consider different sub-groups such as fashionable 14–18 year olds, 18–24 year olds that are more independent, 25–35-year-old businesswomen, etc. Each audience is a target market in itself.

2 *Defining communication objectives*: Once you know your audience you have to define the objective of your communication: do you want your audience to learn about your brand? Or do you want them to come to your sale next Saturday?

3 *Designing the message*: Depending on the audience and the objective, the message would differ significantly. If you want to establish a strong brand image among sport-loving men you might decide to sponsor football. But if you want people to come to your Saturday sale you will send a different message!

4 *Selecting communication channels*: Channels of communication include traditionally TV, radio, and print advertising; additionally, there are new channels such as online e-mail, SMS, blogs, etc.

5 *Measuring the communication process's results*: Finally, once you have decided how to communicate your message you should measure the effectiveness of your campaign. Online-based campaigns are very popular because it is very easy to measure how many unique users visited a site. Other communication activities such as sponsorship are very hard to quantify: the extent to which sponsoring a big sports event changes the brand image of a sponsor is a very tricky question to answer.

Marketing is one part of organizational communication. It includes advertising, sales promotion, PR, personal selling, and direct marketing. Typically, it communicates through distribution channels used to display the products (the strongest message of organizations in areas such as retail) and selling channels (e.g. banks that facilitate transactions).

The marketing mix is the combination of marketing tools an organization uses to accomplish its goals. McCarthy (see Kotler, 2000) differentiated between four main categories: products, price, promotion, and place. These form the tool kit for both marketing and communication tools. As the marketing guru Philip Kotler suggests:

> Company communication goes beyond the specific communication platforms … The product's styling and price, the package's shape and color, the salesperson's manner and dress, the place's décor, the company's stationery – all communicate something to the buyers. Every brand contact delivers something, an impression that can strengthen or weaken a customer's view of the company. The whole marketing mix must be integrated to deliver a consistent message and strategic positioning. (2000: 550)

The concept of integrated marketing becomes increasingly important as organizations become more customer oriented. For instance, cheap air-fares, friendly staff, no delays, and clean cabins describe a service designed around customer needs. But in order to deliver on these, firms strive to integrate finance, human resources, cleaning staff, and airport management. Instead of communicating the benefits of a certain product in a market crowded with similar messages, organizations increasingly try to build a strong, lasting, and powerful image in the minds of their potential customers. This allows organizations to decouple their products from their image and establish themselves as a strong brand. For instance, although you might not know all the services Google currently offers, you certainly know what Google means in terms of its values: Google is a brand.

Communication as branding

A simple definition describes a **brand** as the image of an organization that is created through design (e.g. its name, ads, logo, etc.), its behaviour (e.g. employees), and its products and services.

Olins (2000) and Hatch and Schultz (2001) identified several reasons why branding is so influential and a key to success. First, a **brand** makes choice easier. You probably know the feeling of standing in front of a packed supermarket shelf and being completely overloaded by the information and choices you face. Market economies create choices that are paralysing when you are confronted by many interchangeable products with slight variations in packaging and product information. Powerful brands shortcut the need for you to make comparisons, thus making choice easy – if somewhat redundant. Thus, branding is the conscious projection of a consistent image of itself that an organization seeks to communicate.

Second, brands bring consistency and continuity to your consumer life. Think of those thousands of products in a supermarket: rather than checking out all 50 different toothpastes, you might choose the one that you are familiar with. Put simply, brands help us save time and effort by making choices easier. Third, brands help us to make up our own identity and provide us with devices to tell others who we are (or at least, what we try to be). Just think of clothes. Wearing a Hugo Boss suit, sunglasses designed by Porsche, and a Rolex instantly says a great deal about who you want to be (or be taken to be). The same goes for street-level fashions and design; they provide a source of identity. However, the icons can be quite different. For instance, see if you can identify in Image 8.8 some of the images being marketed in the selection of T-shirts hanging in the market and imagine the kind of identity construction that would accompany wearing them.

Fourth, brands reduce costs. Instead of marketing every single product separately, promoting the brand saves money. Take Sony. Regardless of whether it is a TV, a stereo, or a game, people associate the Sony brand name with quality.

Finally, having a strong brand means being vulnerable; people look extremely closely at what Nike and Shell are doing, and, due to their visibility, any negative message about them travels quickly through newspapers or

IMAGE 8.8   Faces on T-shirts

websites. At best, brands become universal signs, such as Coca-Cola, the world's most recognizable brand (see Image 8.9).

Branding expresses what and who an organization is. It is not just a matter of cosmetics – where stylish packaging promotes a product whose real costs are a fraction of the asking price, or packaging old ideas in new boxes – but a way of communicating the identity of the company. Think of Absolut Vodka. Its image as a company that is young, sophisticated, and chic does not derive from its product, but rather its products are incubated by its style. Vodka is vodka, one might say, but Absolut managed to transform its product into a unique, recognizable, and successful brand, as an icon that inspires people. It is witty, droll, iconoclastic, and cool.

Icons, as Holt (2003) argues, are encapsulated myths that bring products alive. Nike, for instance, is not just in the business of selling sneakers – which are merely a vehicle for a story – because its products embody the myth of individual achievement through perseverance. In this game,

IMAGE 8.9 Do you want a Coke with that?

products are but one way to tell the corporate myth and to provide a story that customers appreciate.

Branding is about interacting with the public and communicating your organization, its values, and its contribution to society. Benetton, apart from launching campaigns that made it one of the most recognized (but also most contested) companies worldwide, also features a magazine called *Color* dedicated to issues such as slavery, prisons, and refugees. *Color* is translated into many languages and sold in over 60 countries. It analyses topics and makes people aware of marginalized problems. Doing so, Benetton positions itself not just as a clothes manufacturer but also as a highly socially responsible organization that is concerned with social issues.

QUESTION TIME

Successful branding involves customers and creates a relationship between them and the company

The Body Shop is an excellent example of branding. Anita Roddick, founder of The Body Shop, created a strong brand identity around the notion of a profit-with-principles philosophy. The company protests against animal testing, supports developing countries, plays an active role in women's and equality movements, to name but a few of its many activities (Joachimsthaler and Aaker, 1997). These express the company's values clearly and consistently and simultaneously motivate staff members. Benetton, on the other hand, got into trouble with its brand strategy. When Benetton started advertising using images of HIV-positive people on its billboards and picked

(Continued)

(Continued)

up similar hot issues, it doubtless created brand awareness, but it failed to link this awareness back to its business – selling clothes. Rather, it alienated both target market and retailers (Joachimsthaler and Aaker, 1997).

Think of a brand that you have bought and enjoyed. What were the reasons? Jot them down.

_____

_____

_____

_____

_____

_____

Now, think of a brand that you have bought and not enjoyed. What were the reasons? Jot them down.

_____

_____

_____

_____

_____

_____

_____

Compare notes with your friends. Do you have similar positive and negative brand identifiers?

COMMUNICATION AT WORK

Given the variety of approaches, channels, audiences, and levels of communication, it is critical for organizations to coordinate their communication activities. One way of managing the multiheaded hydra is explored through the concept of the expressive organization (Hatch and Schultz, 2001).

Creating the expressive organization

In an interesting contribution to management and organization theory, Schultz et al. (2000) developed the concept of the **expressive organization.**

The key task of an expressive organization is to communicate its identity to its internal and external audiences. It integrates the levels of communication and the different audiences and aligns corporate communication accordingly.

If a company manages to communicate an identity associated with values such as being innovative, fresh, and creative, it will attract top-level employees and simultaneously motivate its staff members. It will also attract new customers and build strong ties to existing customers. Furthermore, it will be easier for such a company to get financial investors on board as well as build strong relations to key suppliers.

In an increasingly competitive environment, advertising and branding will not be sufficient tools to differentiate a company from its competitors. Increasingly, organizations will compete on the basis of what they are and their ability to express a core identity and values. Managing symbolic and emotional capital through communication thus becomes the core business of management. Even the symbol of manufacturing and production that invented the assembly line, Ford, announced a shift in its orientation towards, and understanding of, its core business. As one of its executives stated, 'The manufacture of cars will be a declining part of Ford's business. They will concentrate in the future on design, branding, marketing, sales and service operation' (quoted in Olins, 2000: 51). A car company's move from tangible cars to more intangible assets implies that understanding

In a nutshell, the concept of the **expressive organization** captures different levels of organizational expressions and their impact on processes such as strategy making, human resources, marketing, and others.

communication is its prime task. Brands such as Skoda, VW, Audi, and Seat all belong to the same company and share a body platform with each other: evidently, the difference between these products is not so much the physical characteristics of the car but more the different look, feel, and intangible values associated with them. Thus, managing a car manufacturer means, more and more, managing meaning. And this management of meanings relies heavily on communication.

It is important to understand that an organization expresses itself through various activities: its employees' behaviour, its physical design (including uniforms, retail outlets, buildings, etc.), its corporate identity (logo, web page, etc.), its advertisements, its strategic intent, its involvement in community activities, and so on. Put simply, everything speaks. Organizations always communicate and cannot avoid doing so. Thus, the expressive organization focuses on the communications that constantly (consciously or not) enact any organization.

As Hatch and Schultz (2001) argue elsewhere, in order to compete successfully with its competitors, an organization has to create a strong corporate identity reflected in the corporate brand. Such an expressive organization aligns three major organizational features that are normally separately analysed: vision (strategy), culture (employees), and image (brand). In order to align these 'strategic stars', the authors suggest analysing the three possible gaps between them:

1   *The vision–culture gap* emerges when management moves away from its employees, developing a vision that is not shared, understood, or supported by the rest of the organization. The vision does not inspire the whole organization sufficiently.
2   *The image–culture gap* derives from a misalignment between employees' behaviour and expressed image. The company does not practice what it preaches.
3   *The image–vision gap* results from a conflict between an organization's vision and the environment's image of the organization. If management wants the company to go in a direction in which its customers and other stakeholders are not going, the best strategic plan is in vain and will eventually fail.

The key to success is to analyse the gaps and, through careful research, close them by understanding the stakeholders' point(s) of view and needs, the employees' perspective, and the strategic intent of top management.

Managing with words?

Understanding the power of communication and language enables you to utilize words to manage organizations. Take the example of employees. As a manager, you might refer to them generically as employees, but you could also call specific people, on different occasions or in different contexts, 'hands', 'human resources', 'team players', 'stars', 'deadbeats', 'losers', and so on. Different metaphors not only affect people differently but also trigger different thoughts. Resources can be exploited and developed, whereas hands are only utilized and, symbolically, come independent of minds, brains, and bodies. By using different metaphors and communicating through them, managers create different realities (see also Chapter 1).

Through telling stories, organizational members shape the organization. Deal and Kennedy (1982) identify three roles that stories play in organizations. First, they anchor the present in the past. They locate an organization's history and its background, which makes it possible for people to understand the current situation. Second, they maintain cohesiveness. By sharing the same stories, they provide members with a sense of community and common values. Finally, they explain why things are the way they are. Stories explain a good deal of the practices and behaviour that are displayed in organizational life. To this we might add also that they define normalcy and its range; they locate the deviant both as extraordinarily good as well as extraordinarily bad.

WHAT'S THE POINT?

Listening

Communication for an expressive organization starts not with speaking but with listening. As Carl R. Rogers found in his experience as a psychotherapist in counselling, the main obstacle to communication is people's tendency to evaluate (Rogers, 1991). This phenomenon can be overcome by strengthening another skill – listening. Especially when people talk about emotionally charged issues, they stick to their own frame of reference and forget to understand the other's point of view. But as Rogers suggests, change can only be accomplished by understanding *with* someone, not by understanding *about* someone.

- A simple technique can help you grasp the importance of listening: before you start to argue with people, summarize their points so accurately that they agree and are satisfied. This means you have actually fully understood what they want to say.

MINI CASE

Communication as a strategy

An example drawn from the Navistar Company illustrates the linkage of communication to strategy (Argenti and Forman, 2000). John Horne, CEO of the heavy truck manufacturer Navistar, joined it in 1993 and found the organization in a less than ideal situation. Key stakeholders (employees, unions, senior management, the financial community, media) had lost trust in the company, and the overall situation was not very pleasant. Horne decided that the way to change this was through bringing his employees on board (again) – and this happened through a well-developed communication initiative.

The first step was to visit the plants in order to engage all employees in a discussion of how to beat competition. Soon this became a formal

(Continued)

(Continued)

management task, and every month a member of senior management visited a plant. At meetings that involved some 30 workers, who talked to their colleagues about their needs beforehand, they spoke about the good things and things that could be improved. After the meeting, management published a report that included answers to the issues raised. Furthermore, assembly plant workers were invited to visit the headquarters and discuss workers' needs with the decision-makers informally and directly. Such communication practice develops joint processes of strategy making and implementing, where workers and managers learned mutually from each other.

Second, Horne started a survey of employees focusing on their specific work situations. The results of the survey were published, and an action plan was developed, including deadlines and deliverables, involving, especially, union leaders, making them participants in the change process. Through these efforts and a couple of related exercises (such as a PR campaign, introduction of leadership conferences to improve leadership, etc.), Horne brought Navistar back on the road to success. He started communication processes with different audiences. Through creating a shared communicative basis, the organization enacted a common future in and through these communications (see Argenti and Forman, 2000).

- Think about either where you work or where you study. How effectively does the organization communicate with you and what ways are most effective, from your point of view?

Power and communication

Every way of managing involves power. Communication is no exception; it is never a neutral device to express reality. In fact, it is a powerful means to establish and reinforce organizational reality. The following story illustrates the power of communication. Thomas Watson Jr, chairman of the board of IBM, was challenged by a supervisor, described as

> [a] twenty-two-year-old bride weighing ninety pounds whose husband had been sent overseas and who, in consequence, had been given a job until his return. The young woman, Lucille Burger, was obliged to make certain that people entering security areas wore the correct clear identification. Surrounded by his usual entourage of white-shirted men, Watson approached the doorway to an area where she was on guard, wearing not a green badge, which alone permitted entrance at her door, but an orange badge acceptable elsewhere in the plant. 'I was trembling in my uniform, which was far too big,' she recalled. 'It hid my shakes, but not my voice. "I am sorry," I said to him. I knew who he was alright. "You cannot enter. Your admittance is not recognized." That's what we were supposed to say.' The men accompanying Watson were stricken; the moment held unpredictable possibilities. 'Don't you know who he is?' someone hissed. Watson raised his hand for silence, while one of the party strode off and returned with the appropriate badge. (Peters and Waterman, 1982, quoted in Mumby, 1987: 121)

The story makes clear that regardless of power and the status within the organizational hierarchy, all members have to obey the rules equally strictly. Both Watson and the supervisor set an example of correct behaviour: Watson by organizing the right badge and the supervisor by acting strictly according to the rules. But the story also functions as a reference point for organizational members (especially for newcomers who do not yet know how the organization works in reality) and has some more subtle meanings. As the story demonstrates, everybody at IBM has to accept the rules equally. What the story does not say, however, is that these rules are established by management and people like Watson and not by the supervisor.

Mumby (1987) argues that the story has several hidden meanings that powerfully influence organizational reality. If Watson was really just another employee who has to follow rules, the story would not be worth retelling. Simultaneously, Watson is introduced as an 'ordinary' employee who can be spoken to much as any other member of the organization, but at the same time he appears as a godlike figure in the story. Just look at the description of the two actors. The supervisor is described as a 'twenty-two-year-old bride weighing ninety pounds whose husband had been sent overseas'; her clothes do not fit her, and she is nervously facing Watson. While the story paints a poor picture of her, only working because her husband is overseas, Watson appears as a mythical figure, surrounded by the kind of entourage that normally accompanies a king. Whereas the supervisor speaks, Watson, again godlike, does not speak at all – other people speak for him. And even at the point in the story when he might have spoken, he simply raises his hand and things happen. Using this ostensibly innocent story as an example, you can see the power of communication at work. It tells organizational members how they have to behave (follow rules strictly) and simultaneously it promotes and reinforces organizational power relations (Watson as a godlike figure, Burger as a woman who struggles with her job).

Communication is more powerful when it uses images instead of words and concepts. Looking at how leaders spark people through communication, a team of researchers analysed the communication style of US presidents and the inspiration felt by citizens (Roche, 2001). The results of their study were interesting. Presidents who were described as charismatic and great used image-based words to communicate their vision. They painted verbal pictures that truly inspired their fellow citizen. John F. Kennedy said in his inaugural address, 'Together let us explore the stars, conquer the desert, eradicate disease, tap the ocean depths, and encourage the arts and commerce'. Compare this with Jimmy Carter's address in which he said, 'Let our recent mistakes bring a resurgent commitment to the basic principles of our nation, for we know that if we despise our own government, we have no future'. Whereas Kennedy used lively pictures, Carter used abstract concepts that seem to remain empty and fail to create commitment. Barack Obama represents the latest example of a president that successfully deployed ornate language featuring visions and images of the future. Put simply, image-based communication is more powerful than conceptually driven language. Instead of talking just about sustainability, for example, talking about how we can stay in touch with our children and with nature is likely to move more people.

WHAT DO YOU MEAN?

When the announcement of a fact creates that very fact

An example from sport that you can find in Weick's book (1979) illustrates the power of prerogative humorously: 'The story goes that three umpires disagreed about the task of calling balls and strikes. The first one said, "I calls them as they is." The second one said, "I calls them as I sees them." The third and cleverest umpire said, "They ain't nothin' till I calls them."' As the third umpire argues, balls and strikes do not exist independently of judgement; rather, they become real only when they are pronounced as such. But most managers are involved in games that are far more complicated than baseball and have far more ambiguous and inherently problematic rules, and under these circumstances it would be a foolish manager who believed their own pronouncements without first securing feedback.

Polyphonic communication

In a metaphor often used by writers and artists, organizations may be said to be similar to the Tower of Babel,[1] imperfect and diverse buildings, the product of people speaking many tongues. Different cultures and subcultures, each having their own voice, enacted messy organization reality. Instead of forcing all people to speak one language, homogenizing the organization in monotonic communication, which would lead ultimately to the death of creativity (see also pp. 388–395), management must recognize the value of **polyphony**.

Boje (2002) has a metaphor for understanding organizations that makes use of *Tamaraland*, a theatrical production. *Tamaraland* is a play in which different acts take place simultaneously in different rooms, which the audience is free to move between. What a member of the audience encounters, as well as the sense they make of it, will vary markedly according to the route they take around the rooms. The production makes problematic notions of what it is to be a member of the audience. More important, however, the play disrupts notions of linearity, especially through the way in which the audience may have infinite experiences of the play by virtue of the order in which they have entered particular rooms. For Boje, *Tamaraland*, as multiplicities of meaning, outcome, and experience, is a projection of contemporary organizations. His suggestion is that although organizations may well be scripted through missions, strategies, and so forth, there are too many directors (i.e. finance, marketing, human resources) for only one script to be followed.

Boje suggests that we regard organizations as a meta-theatre, as a multiplicity of simultaneous/discontinuous dramas, whose sense you make as you go along. Multiple people make multiple senses, and successful processes of sensemaking listen democratically to voices normally silenced. People from the periphery (newcomers and outsiders) will think more creatively because they are 'exposed to ideas and developments that do not conform to the company's orthodoxies' (Hamel, 1996: 77). Thus, rather than provide

Polyphony means literally the presence of many voices and hence different ideas and perspectives.

strong leadership that silences dissent, organizations should use the polyphony they have available in their narratives. 'Narratives', as Mumby suggests, 'provide members with accounts of the process of organizing. Such accounts potentially legitimate dominant forms of organizational reality, and lead to discursive closure in the sense of restricting the interpretations and meanings that can be attached to organizational activity' (1987: 113). Thus, narratives are not only devices of sensemaking but also a 'politically motivated production of a certain way of perceiving the world' (Mumby, 1987: 114). As we have argued using the IBM example above, stories told can also have powerful effects. Stories enact and reinforce a certain image of an organization that can influence its members almost subliminally, beneath the threshold of their awareness. Those narratives that provide the matrix for normal organizational talk, action, and decision-making can, therefore, be productive or counterproductive, functional or dysfunctional. If the images are monotonic, have been conceived remotely, and imposed downwards onto organization members, there is more probability of a lesser sense of ownership, commitment, and responsibility, because few opportunities for participating in sensemaking or sharing have been created. By contrast, seeking to manage organizations polyphonically means engaging in different stories that are communicated through different channels with different means at the same time. Doing so, we reduce the risk of groupthink and increase our ability to think creatively.

SUMMARY AND REVIEW

Organizational communication is absolutely central to managing. It ranges across many approaches to analysis, as we have seen. Key theories come from the areas of organizational behaviour and discourse theory. Whereas the former focus on shared meanings and interpretations, the latter focuses on the constitution of reality through communication.

We have discussed different levels of communication including interpersonal communication (direct communication between you and your friend in a pub); impersonal communication (between you and a call centre operative); small-group communication (within a team); and finally mass communication (e.g. an Apple ad in a magazine that tells you about the latest product).

It is important to keep different levels of communication separate because they all follow different rules. What works well in mass communication would not go down well when you apply it to your discussion with a friend in a pub. In order to communicate effectively you have to differentiate between the audiences of communication: you can communicate within an organization, with another organization, or with other stakeholders such as media, a local community group, or labour unions.

The chapter has taken you through organizational behaviour, communication theory, and marketing, helping you to grasp fully the significance of communication. Although you will hear more about these concepts in other courses it is important to see how they relate to communication in organizations. Schultz and Hatch's concept of the expressive organization provides a synthesis of these strands of research, which is an important development for understanding the way that contemporary organizations are developing into largely communicative entities that subcontract almost everything other than control over the brand. It is this path that major corporate organizations such as Nike and Zara follow.

Managing communication means managing with power. We will also encounter this issue in

Chapter 13 when we discuss Gouldner's analysis of vicious circles. In the context of managing communication, the positive aspects of power are particularly evident. Communication, involving speaking, listening, and meaning making from and across many different identities, necessarily involves polyphony. Managing polyphony requires rethinking of monotonic meaning, singular cultures, and one-way communication organized in a top-down authoritative model.

EXERCISES

1 Having read this chapter you should be able to say in your own words what each of the following key terms means. Test yourself or ask a colleague to test you:

- Communication
- Sensemaking
- Identity
- Polyphony
- Branding
- Groupthink
- Expressive organization
- Deconstruction
- Marketing
- Public relations

2 What are the main approaches to communication theory?
3 How do organizations communicate through marketing and branding?
4 What, in the context of management and communication, are vicious circles and how do they happen?
5 What are the main media for organizational communication?
6 What needs to be aligned in an expressive organization?
7 How do words socially construct organization realities?
8 What is the power of silence in the IBM story?
9 How would you manage in a polyphonic organization?

ADDITIONAL RESOURCES

1 It is probably just as well that you be familiar with some of the popular accounts of the importance of organizational communication – as they have been so influential – and none has been more influential than Carnegie's (1944) *How to Win Friends and Influence People*.
2 A classic text for understanding the mass media of communication is McLuhan's (1964) *Understanding Media*. It would be interesting to take his ideas about what constitutes 'hot' and 'cool' media and apply them to some of the media that have developed since he wrote.
3 In terms of critical perspectives on communication, including the nature of organizational communication as gendered discourse, the volume edited by Corman and Poole (2000) called *Perspectives on Organizational Communication: Finding Common Ground* is a useful, if advanced, text.
4 The most innovative contribution in this area in recent years is *The Expressive Organization: Linking Identity, Reputation and the Corporate Brand*, edited by Schultz et al. (2000).
5 The classic film about organizational communication is the superb early Francis Ford Coppola film *The Conversation* (1974). The context of *The Conversation* was Watergate and the fascination with the Nixon tapes and Nixon's surveillance tactics on his colleagues as well as his enemies. We see it as an organizational allegory on the centrality and difficulty of really understanding communication when the message is opaque, the intent mysterious, and the effects can be deadly. It is also an allegory on how we can use communication strategies to conceal rather than reveal.

WEB SECTION

1 Our Companion Website is the best first stop for you to find a great deal of extra resources, free PDF versions of leading articles published in Sage journals, exercises, video and pod casts, team case studies and general questions, and links to teamwork resources. Go to www.sagepub.co.uk/managingand organizations3.
2 For state of the art briefings on how to manage organizations effectively, please visit the Henry Stewart Talks series of

online audiovisual seminars on Managing Organizations, edited by Stewart Clegg: www.hstalks.com/r/managing-orgs, especially Talk #14 by James Barker on *Managing communication*.

3 Check out http://www.stlukes.co.uk/ if you want to find out more about the world of ad agencies and brand experts.

4 To see the world of glamorous advertisement and some outstanding ads see the home page of the International Advertisement Festival in Cannes: http://www.canneslions.com/.

5 For a critical perspective on multinational brands see http://multinationalmonitor.org.

6 To find out more about the trouble a global brand – Nike – has to deal with, see the radical site http://www.blackspotsneaker.org.

7 Another entertaining (though radical) site that celebrates the rejection of global brands and advertising is http://www.adbusters.org/ home/.

8 A more moderate view on the world of advertisement can be found at http://www.adforum.com.

9 Powered by global branding expert Interbrand, this weekly online magazine gives you valuable insights into the world of branding: http://www.brandchannel.com.

10 Check out Richard Branson's Ted Talk on www.ted.com. The godfather of branding provides interesting insights into management, leadership, and the art of turning oneself into a mega-brand.

LOOKING FOR A HIGHER MARK?

Reading and digesting these articles that are available free on the Companion Website www.sagepub.co.uk/managingandorganizations3 can help you gain deeper understanding and, on the basis of that, a better grade:

1 Gioia, D. A. (2006) 'On Weick: an appreciation', *Organization Studies*, 27 (11): 1709–1721, which is a good introduction to and appreciation of Weick's work.

2 Barry, D., Carroll, B. and Hansen, H. (2006) 'To text or context? Endotextual, exotextual, and multi-textual approaches to narrative and discursive organizational studies', *Organization Studies*, 27 (8): 1091–1110, a sophisticated textual analysis of narrative.

3 Maguire, S. and Hardy, C. (2006) 'The emergence of new global institutions: a discursive perspective', *Organization Studies*, 27 (1): 7–29, as their title suggests, takes a discursive look at how a new discourse shapes the emergence of new global regulatory institutions, specifically the roles played by actors and the texts they author during the institution-building process of the Stockholm Convention on Persistent Organic Pollutants (POPs).

4 Gazi, I. and Zyphur, M. (2007) 'Ways of interacting: the standardization of communication in medical training', *Human Relations*, 60 (5): 769–972, draws on Weberian, Habermasian, and Foucauldian perspectives to explain the ways that occupational rationalities are embodied in doctor–patient encounters, and how these rationalities structure and are structured by occupational conceptions of medical clients.

5 Kärreman, D. and Rylander, A. (2008) 'Managing meaning through branding – the case of a consulting firm', *Organization Studies*, 29 (1): 103–125. The authors provide an illustrative case study of a consulting firm and how it uses the tools of branding to manage the symbolic dimension of work. Their focus on internal branding illustrates that branding is not only a marketing practice but also a question of leadership and organization.

CASE STUDY

MANAGING COMMUNICATION

Data is an ICT communication agency. Data started out developing tailor-made applications based on inspiration from artificial intelligence computing. Within ten years Data grew from a small core of 12 developers to more than 130 employees. As the company grew, the projects it performed got bigger and its services slightly more product oriented. With a continuously growing portfolio of projects, and continuously growing size of these projects, Data needed to enhance project management skills in the organization. These skills included formal project management procedures, such as budgeting and contract negotiation, as well as softer skills, such as management of client expectations, team motivation, and so on. A wide range of project management skills proved hard to nail down. These skills were typically tacit practices lacking clear-cut definitions, involving emotions and people skills, and drawing on collages composed from a wide range of experiences. Communicating these skills, the experiences of the employees and managers, across the time and space barriers that project work placed on them, became a central issue.

One of the tools developed for this cause was Scheherazade's Divan. According to the ancient Persian tale, Scheherazade is the story-teller in the *1001 Arabian Nights*. Each night for 1001 days she tells the King of Persia a story, and his waiting for the next story is what keeps her alive. Like Scheherazade, Data figured that it needed stories to stay alive, or at least to keep on growing, thus it created Scheherazade's Divan. Scheherazade's Divan is a virtual story mediator, designed as computer software that presents stories. It presents a large sample, all of them created by employees and managers in Data. These stories are comprised of different formats, such as text, cartoons, movie cuts, sound files, and so on. All employees in Data can contribute stories, and there are no predefined notions of style or content. In other words, Scheherazade's Divan is an attempt to articulate and capture some of the informal practices in the organization, nourish them, and spread them throughout the organization.

One day a programmer chose to video-tape himself telling a story from a project he had just entered. The project was fairly large, the customer had recently criticized the mid-project deliveries, and there had been internal friction concerning the staffing of the project. In the video the programmer criticizes the project, identifies project members, describes the contribution of some of them quite harshly, and portrays himself as a knight in shining armour, saving the project. As he does this, he sits, laid back, by his computer, with an ironically twisted grin on his face. Less than two hours after the videotape was presented on Scheherazade's Divan, the management team removed it. Within minutes the whole organization knew not only that the story had been withdrawn but also that it was there in the first place. The whole organization was in a buzz; some resented the idea of censorship, some thought that the story as it was told should not have been presented in that way, and others again thought that it was correct that the story as they thought it occurred should be told.

Questions

1 The creation of Scheherazade's Divan can be explained as an authorizing of employees' knowledge and voices. Discuss the pros and cons of enabling, and authorizing, informal communication in a public space.

2 Censorship of communication is found in any workplace. Discuss the different formal and informal forms that it might take.

3 Communication such as Scheherazade's Divan was intended only for internal dissemination: is it realistic to think that what is designed for inside stays inside?

Case prepared by Kjersti Bjørkeng, KUNNE, SINTEF, Norway.

NOTE

1 According to Genesis 11 the Tower of Babel was a tower built to reach the heavens by a united humanity to reach their God. God, observing the arrogance of humanity in the construction, resolves to confuse them to prevent any further attempts. He does this by making the previously uniform language of humanity one of multiple languages, immutable each to the other, thereby preventing any such future efforts. The story is an origin-myth about the multiplicity of languages.

CHAPTER NINE
MANAGING KNOWLEDGE AND LEARNING

Communities, Collaboration, Boundaries

LEARNING OBJECTIVES

This chapter will enable you to:

- Explain the basic theories of knowledge management and learning
- Understand the importance of these theories for organizations
- Examine the benefits and shortcomings of these approaches
- Understand the challenge that learning and managing knowledge poses for management
- Identify organizational practices that encourage learning

BEFORE YOU GET STARTED . . .

Francis Bacon said in 1597 that 'knowledge is power'; we think that 'knowledge is good, but critique is better'.

INTRODUCTION

Knowledge: That which is a part of the stock of ideas, meanings, and more or less explicit understandings and explanations of how phenomena of interest actually work or are structured or designed and relate to other phenomena: facts, information, and skills acquired by a person through experience or education.

Knowledge management is the process of managing knowledge to meet existing and future needs. Put simply, knowledge management is all about know-how and know-why.

Organizational learning: Argyris (1960) defines organizational learning as the process of detection and correction of errors. In many respects, organizational learning is similar to individual learning. The idea is that organizations learn when the *knowledge* that their members have is explicitly known and codified by the organization. Organizations should seek to make as much of what their members do as explicit as possible. If members leave, the *explicit knowledge* that they developed in their jobs should stay.

Learning is the process of acquiring knowledge and capabilities in addition to those already known. Usually thought of as something that individuals do, it is often associated with specific institutions, such as a school or a university. However, recently there has been a shift of emphasis to informal and work-based learning that occurs outside these specific institutional areas and in employing organizations.

In 1988, Arie de Geus, Senior Manager at Royal Dutch/Shell, wrote a paper in which he stated 'the only competitive advantage the company of the future will have is its managers' ability to learn faster than their competitors' (1988: 74). Since then, **knowledge, knowledge management,** and **organizational learning** have become buzzwords of our age. Not only should students and adults learn, but whole organizations and even societies are supposed to learn constantly. Lifelong **learning** seems to be the most valuable asset in an age in which information is everything and knowledge is the key to success. According to management guru Peter Senge, the distinctive feature of successful companies is their ability to learn (Senge, 1990). Companies such as General Electric, Coca-Cola, and Shell use learning concepts in their organization and claim that they are the key to success. In short, knowledge seems to be the most important strategic asset of organizations.

The concepts of learning and knowledge management have many parents, as Easterby-Smith (1997) pointed out. Two distinct streams – one from psychology and one from more technical approaches to management information – come together in this literature. The older tradition of information management emerged from library studies because, once upon a time, if you sought knowledge, it could most readily be found in books and libraries.

What previously was scarce and zealously guarded is now freely available. Knowledge in the modern world is everywhere; it is no longer under strict control by monastic authorities. Books are just one medium used to process and store technical information; information processing now includes databases and, of course, the Internet. There are many places where we can acquire and learn different approaches to knowledge. Today, you are more likely to find out what you need to know from a laptop than a book.

When one investigates the ways in which management researchers have addressed knowledge, some distinctly different approaches are discernible. Psychologically oriented researchers have focused on different learning styles: how knowledge is acquired, how people learn, and how knowledge is transferred. Sociologists have looked at learning from the more general perspective of social structures and interaction, emphasizing the influence of power, politics, and ideologies. From the 1980s, with the rise of a cultural perspective on management, the importance of norms, values, and rituals is more obvious.

However, knowledge really sprang into prominence when change management became linked with organizational learning. In particular, Peter Senge's best-seller, *The Fifth Discipline* (1990), made knowledge a hot topic. We live in a knowledge society, in which information is paradoxically both the most valuable resource and one that constantly overloads us to such an extent that we neglect its richness and depth. In such a world, the management of this knowledge and its development (i.e. learning) becomes one of the most important concepts in management practice. Hence, almost every major consultancy has a knowledge management practice these days, in which it seeks to exploit present knowledge to develop opportunities for further knowledge. We investigate, first, where know-how might come from, and then we consider the types of knowledge that might be the sources of know-how.

WHAT DO YOU MEAN?

Knowledge management and organizational learning

Most management theorists differentiate between knowledge management and organizational learning. For us, knowledge and learning are closely interlinked concepts, or two sides of the same coin. On the one side, knowledge management focuses on the actual creation, dissemination, and transformation of knowledge; on the other, learning involves change in the existing state of knowledge. Thus, we argue that knowledge management focuses on the existing resources within an organization, and learning focuses on the dynamic development of these resources.

KNOWLEDGE MANAGEMENT

Sources of knowledge

Knowledge can take many different forms and can derive from many sources: figures, information, written instructions, stories, rumours, gossip, beliefs, and so on. Think about where people at work – in particular, decision-makers – get their knowledge. In the modern world, much of what people know comes from formal bodies of knowledge, especially science. Universities educate tomorrow's managers and, through imparting information about management research, these educational institutions seek to provide knowledge about how current issues might be resolved. Of course, universities are not the sole providers of knowledge. Fulop and Rifkin (1999) argue that the following three particularly influential sources of knowledge are far more important than scientific treatises and management textbooks:

▪ *Learning by doing*: The complexity and variety of managerial tasks make it hard to formalize what managers do when they manage. Thus, to obtain most of their knowledge, they learn when they are actually in the middle of managing. Common sense, reflection, and informal conversations with their colleagues tell them how to react and what to do in certain situations. Such action-oriented behaviour is not always the best, however. Consider how often things get broken when you learn while you do, compared with an approach where you think before you do, and then learn. The classic example of the difficulties of learning while doing is the story of the Apollo 13 space mission, which introduced the phrase 'Houston, we have a problem' to the wider world. Here the mission, seemingly routine, was underway, when the crew and ground-based flight command had to learn and improvise their way from disaster to triumph.

Hearing stories: Managers learn what their job is all about through stories that are told in the organization. Stories are good formats because they relate the core of an experience (and take the freedom to embellish it a little to make it more interesting). Accounts of how a tricky problem was solved, an important deadline was met, or a disobedient employee was disciplined, communicate the message of how things are done in the organization. Regardless of whether these stories are true or not, they form a template for managers' own experiences and help them make narrative sense of messy situations.

Being exposed to popular accounts: Fulop and Rifkin (1999) refer to stories that are printed and communicated through management seminars as exemplary cases drawn from a great organization culture. These accounts often tell how great CEOs managed to turn around large organizations and how their practices can be applied by almost everybody, everywhere, anytime. These popular accounts, sometimes communicated through the quality popular business press (such as the *Harvard Business Review*) as well as the general media, provide a clear focus on how to do things, summarizing them in case studies. Equipped with the success story of how other managers developed outstanding practice and gained standing ovations, it is intended that manager readers will be impressed.

QUESTION TIME

You will already have a certain image of what managing means and what managers do when they manage an organization. Where does your knowledge about organizations and management come from? Is it based on your own experience when you were working? Is it fuelled by stories from your friends or relatives? Or does it derive from books about Richard Branson or TV shows such as *The Apprentice* with Donald Trump or Lord Alan Sugar or *The Office*? Jot down your ideas below.

_____
_____
_____
_____
_____

Ask your friends (who are *not* doing a management subject) what they think managing involves and what organizations do. Why do they think what they do? What is the main source of their ideas?

Types of knowledge

Ironically, what we know about the concept of knowledge itself is actually limited. Polanyi (1962; 1983) came up with a distinction that still dominates the debate. His basic idea was that we know more than we can tell. At first this may sound paradoxical, but think of the example of riding a bicycle: you might be able to do it, but you cannot describe this complex process in all its aspects and facets. Another example would be the rules of grammar: you must use them to communicate clearly, but you probably could not spell out all the rules that you were using at any particular time. Thus, Polanyi differentiated between two types of knowledge: **tacit knowledge** and **explicit knowledge**.

Nonaka (1991) and his colleague Takeuchi (Nonaka and Takeuchi, 1995) adapted the notion of tacit knowledge for management practice. For Nonaka and Takeuchi, explicit knowledge is the formalized, accessible knowledge that can be consciously thought, communicated, and shared. Tacit knowledge, on the other hand, consists of personal beliefs, values, and perspectives that individuals take for granted; they are not easily accessible and thus are hard to communicate. Tacit knowledge is a personal cognitive map that helps you navigate – consciously or not – through routines, practices, and processes. Organizationally, it enables you to fill in the gaps between what is formally stipulated and what you actually do.

Nonaka (1991) differentiates between four basic patterns of knowledge creation, as shown in Figure 9.1. Looking at the fourfold table that he creates, we can see that, as the grid suggests, there are four major movements during which knowledge is created.

Tacit knowledge is the knowledge you actually use when you do things but you cannot necessarily articulate it. An example is the knowledge required to ride a bike.

Explicit knowledge is the knowledge you can consciously talk about and reflect on, usually elaborated and recorded in such a way that others can easily learn it.

WHAT DO YOU MEAN?

The difference between tacit and explicit knowledge

The difference between the two types of knowledge is easy to understand when you look at artificial intelligence programs. For example, the information needed to play chess is highly explicit knowledge that you can program into a computer; indeed, the computer can calculate faster than a human brain what would be the best move in any given situation. On the other hand, if you instruct a computer to make small talk, it cannot do so; the rules for what you are supposed to say, when you are supposed to laugh (even if it is just to be kind), or when something is meant to be ironic, cynical, or offensive are deeply embedded social behaviours that are almost impossible to turn into explicit knowledge. If you ask a friend why they behaved in a certain way during a conversation, and the friend says, 'Well, simply because that is what you do', then you know that your friend is referring to tacit, not explicit, knowledge.

FIGURE 9.1

Nonaka's tacit and explicit knowledge dimensions

	Tacit	Explicit
Tacit	Socialization	Internalization
Explicit	Articulation	Combination

- *Socialization (the move from tacit to tacit)*: People learn codes of conduct and rules of behaviour implicitly from other people without ever thinking about their meaning. Think of how you have learnt basic behavioural patterns: rarely you will have acquired them through reading a book and reflecting on them. Rather, you probably absorbed them through mimicking how others behave. Hence, your knowledge guides your actions but you have little awareness why and how it does so. Often we become aware of our own set ways of thinking and doing things when we visit other cultures: suddenly even the simplest things that we take for granted are done differently; when we ask why this is the case, more often than not the answer will be a shrug with the shoulders rather than an explicit explanation. A good example is rules of behaviour in traffic: while the explicit traffic regulations in Ho Chi Min and Hamburg are rather similar, the tacit knowledge you need to master traffic could not be more different.

- *Combination (the move from explicit to explicit)*: People combine ideas they are already well aware of. You tell me the latest news in microbiology, and I tell you what is happening in microphysics. One organization allies with another and knowledges are combined (Badaracco, 1991). Such a combination can be decisive; when Sony collaborated with Apple, they produced much more elegant microcomputers than Apple could have achieved on its own. Similarly, Sony learned a great deal from Apple, which led to the production of Sony's own array of portable computers, such as the VAIO. Open source platforms such as www.innocentive.com formulate problem briefs and seek solutions from outsiders who receive a reward if they manage to solve the problem. Such collaboration is based on knowledge sharing rather than the creation of new knowledge within an organization (see also Chapter 8).

- *Internalization (the move from explicit to tacit)*: Things that you learned once become a pattern in your repertoire; you begin to take them for granted, and you forget that you learned them in the first place. If you start working in a new job in a different country, you might at first wonder why things are done the way they are done, but after a while you accept them as a social fact of that society. Therefore newcomers are often a valuable source of insights as they have not (yet) become accustomed to the culture of an organization; they might be able to see things that could be done differently.

Articulation (the move from tacit to explicit): Through articulating and sharing within the organization, new knowledge becomes accessible and part of official processes. For instance, the US-based product design firm IDEO developed a sophisticated research methodology that it uses to discover customer needs. One technique is simply asking the question 'Why?' several times until customers can articulate the real reason why they want to buy a certain product. For instance, you might say that you want an iPod because you like listening to music. Asked why you like listening to music you might say, 'Because I like music'; again, when asked 'Why?' you might answer, 'Because all my friends listen to music' – which reveals that iPods are as much a symbol of being part of a community as they are devices to play music.

In the last decade, management theorists have increasingly suggested that tacit knowledge contributes significantly to innovation processes (see also pp. 372–373). Thus, it is very important for management to attempt to organize and manage tacit knowledge, and try to transform elements of tacit knowledge into organizationally explicit knowledge – an idea that marks the birth of the concept of knowledge management.

No wonder management tries to dip into the pot of tacit knowledge; whereas explicit knowledge encompasses all you can talk about, tacit knowledge is a much deeper and richer source, and knowledge management is the instrument that is supposed to allow managers to savour this rich stew. Developing this resource and aligning it effectively with change became the domain of what is known as organizational learning.

Check out the Companion Website www.sagepub.co.uk/managingandorganizations3 for free access to an article by Boris Ewenstein and Jennifer Whyte (2007) if you want to find a new take on different types of knowledge.

Organizational learning

Obviously, talking about learning touches on a rather broad field: for example, you can learn to drive a car, you can learn a mathematical formula by heart, you can learn how to play the drums, and so on. Each of these processes requires different skills, timing, and involvement. Although learning something by heart goes rather quickly (and is in fact forgotten quickly because it involves repetition and lodges in short-term memory), learning to play an instrument can take years and requires that you have *talent* (an inherent potential which you either have or do not). Learning to drive a car is an entirely different kind of process from the others; it involves not only cognitive but also complex bodily skills. To be a good driver, your feet must touch the clutch and accelerator, your hands must act according to what you see and the information you are processing (about the road conditions, traffic, and so on), and you must factor in your experience of similar situations. Organizations accomplish far more complex

Organizational learning: Argyris (1960) defines organizational learning as the process of detection and correction of errors. In many respects, organizational learning is similar to individual learning. The idea is that organizations learn when the *knowledge* that their members have is explicitly known and codified by the organization.

processes than driving a car. How do they learn to fly to the moon (as the NASA did), organize peace-keeping missions (as the UN does) or coordinate the activities of several 100,000 employees (such as German industrial giant Siemens, which employs 400,000 people globally).

Let us start with a simple question: what is organizational learning? In the past, managers valued only what was explicit, codified, and routine, but gradually throughout the systematic development of management they began to realize that organizational learning – similar to the skills mentioned in the previous paragraph – involves far more than meets the eye. Whereas Taylor (1967 [1911]) sought to establish the one best way to do things as management's way, elsewhere, especially in Japan, the emphasis shifted to one of continuous improvement (Kono and Clegg, 1998). The premise was that it was not only managers who should know what was happening – other members of the organization might also know and might even be able to think of better ways of doing things. The organization could learn from the tacit knowledge, shortcuts, experience, and improvements introduced by its members. If all of these were captured and implemented then they could be a powerful source of competitive advantage. That management might not, a priori, know best was a significant retreat from the position of scientific management.

Taylor's scientific management in 1911 was basically an attempt to find out what workers were actually doing so that it could be codified. Before Taylor, managers set the agenda and the objectives of what was to be done, but they did not know how workers actually achieved what they did. Taylor wanted to change this situation; the lack of knowledge on management's side made it hard for managers to tell realistically how much time workers should take to do a certain task. Moreover, when problems suddenly occurred, management could not react because it lacked the know-how of workers. Taylor set out to change this state of affairs, trying to get the knowledge out of the workers' heads and into management's prescriptions to make it an accessible and objective phenomenon for managerial control. Taylor was convinced that knowledge was power and managers should own it; more contemporary managers, exposed to the philosophies of continuous improvement and quality management, might agree with the sentiment but not have the same expectation of monopoly rights. Knowledge is generated anywhere in the organization: often, the hierarchy of power is the exact reverse image of the hierarchy of ideas. Employees that meet customers on a daily basis and learn about their feedback often know more about potential new innovations than management which spends time in internal meetings and planning processes.

Can organizations learn?   Although you might agree that learning is an important concept for individuals and even for classes, can entire organizations learn? Is it only the members who learn how to do things? How do organizations learn? Think of old and established organizations, such as the Catholic Church. Its liturgy has changed entirely over the centuries, but the organization goes on, seemingly forever. In the Church as well as in secular organizations, what persists are the routines, practices, and stories that embody and enact the organization's individual character. The specific

Check out the Companion Website www.sagepub.co.uk/ managingandorganizations3 for free access to an article by Emmanuelle Vaast (2007) if you are interested in exploring the relations between power, bureaucracy, and knowledge.

character of an organization is formed through its routines, processes, practices, and stories – put simply, those cultural facets – that constitute where organizational knowledge is 'stored'. To change organization culture – the store of knowledge – organizations must both relinquish old habits and learn new ways (see also Chapter 6).

Knowledge as a barrier to learning   The biggest enemy of learning (besides the usual suspects, such as lack of interest) is, ironically, knowledge itself. Whenever we assume that we know something, this implies that we can stop learning about it. In fact, often we think that when we know, we do not have to learn any more. We know how to ride that bike, drive that car, or chant that liturgy.

WHAT DO YOU MEAN?

How do organizations learn?

There is a simple way of imaging how organizations learn. Think of your university: there is a certain way students have to enrol: courses are described online and in brochures; electives and majors are communicated through the website; assessments consist of multiple choice tests, group work, essays, etc. The point is that universities have established this way of doing things over centuries. If your lecturer leaves, the university will continue to do the same thing. In fact, after about 30 years the entire staff of your university will either be retired or work elsewhere. Still the university will work with the same processes and routines that are now played out by other staff. In this perspective it matters very little what individuals learn; organizations have their own way of doing things that has grown historically. In order to change this way of doing things it is not enough to educate employees; rather, practices have to be changed and turned into new routines. If this happens, we speak of organizational learning.

The problem is that we do not know how to know otherwise. Starbuck (1983) offers a good example: Facit, the assumed name of an organization in the 1960s that produced better mechanical calculators at lower costs than any other company in the world, failed exactly because it thought it knew what to do:

The engineers within Facit itself concentrated on technologies having clear relevance for mechanical calculators, and Facit understood these technologies well. Top, middle and lower managers agreed about how a mechanical-calculator factory should look and operate, what mechanical-calculator customers wanted, what was key to success, and what was unimportant or silly … No resources were wasted gathering irrelevant information or analyzing tangential issues. Costs were low, service fast, glitches rare, understanding high, expertise great! … Relying on the company's information-gathering programs, the top managers surmised that Facit's mechanical-calculator customers would switch to electronics very slowly because they liked mechanical calculators. Of course, Facit had no programs for gathering information from people who were buying electronic calculators. (Starbuck, 1983: 92)

Facit's problem was exactly that it already knew a lot, which made learning more seem like a waste of time. However, after the market and technology had changed, it was already too late to learn the lessons that the competition had learned already. Facit failed because it knew too much about what it did and had insufficient knowledge about competitors, technologies, and customers.

Learning as adaptation

Levitt and March (1988) as well as Argyris and Schön (1978) tackled the kinds of problems that led to Facit's failure when they thought about how organizations can learn and change. Their theories still provide the template for most accounts of organizational learning, so we explore them in detail. Levitt and March (1988) understand learning as a process of adapting to the environment that an organization is dealing with. Organizations turn past experiences into routines and learn in this way. Learning is played out as adaptation to environmental changes; think of new technologies that force organizations to explore the new opportunities they make possible. Speaking generally, such learning processes increase an organization's competence and thus are beneficial. However, Levitt and March identified what they call the 'competency trap'. It occurs when an organization does something well and learns more about it until it becomes such an expert organization that it does not see the limits of its achievements. It cannot change in response to the changes in its environment because it has become so focused on doing things its way, even when it becomes evident that the old routines are no longer working.

QUESTION TIME

Imagine you are a CD manufacturer, a book publisher, or a video rental business. What lessons would you learn from the story of Facit? What new knowledge will be critical for the future of these businesses? And what old knowledge should you forget in order to manage future challenges?

The example of the failure of Facit makes the point. Although Facit learned to build the best calculators in the world, it failed because it relied on its competencies. Its competencies made it blind to what it did not know. What it did not know was that electronic innovations were outflanking the knowledge basis of what it was that they knew so well. In common parlance, they were about to expire, and the future would consign their technology to the junkyard. It was this phenomenon that Argyris and Schön (1978) tackled from an inter-organizational perspective when they distinguished between single- and double-loop learning – which sounds a bit knotty but is not difficult to grasp.

Single- and double-loop learning

Argyris and Schön (1978) were among the first researchers to focus on the phenomenon of organizational learning. In contrast to Levitt and March (1988), they researched organizationally internal preconditions and implications of learning processes. To understand ways of learning, they differentiated between two types of learning: **single-loop learning** and **double-loop learning** (or learning I and II).

If you attend a training seminar where you learn to use PowerPoint and related programs, you will obviously learn something (even if you only learn that you do not want to learn how to use PowerPoint!) Such learning happens within a given frame of reference: the parameters are given and clearly defined, and the learning experience focuses on how to optimize (or maximize or increase) your capacity within this frame. This is an example of single-loop learning.

Double-loop learning is not the acquisition of knowledge that you need to accomplish a given task; rather, it involves rethinking the task and considering whether its accomplishment is beneficial or not. Managers in a weekend seminar discussion of the company's mission and core values are engaged in double-loop learning processes when they redefine the market for their products or the products themselves.

To put this distinction metaphorically, single-loop learning involves learning the competencies necessary to play a certain game successfully, whereas double-loop learning requires thinking and learning about what is the most valuable game to play. Single-loop learning concerns acting according to the rules of a certain game; in contrast, double-loop learning involves learning what the actual rules of the game are and how they could be changed to make another game. Single-loop learning focuses on optimizing problem-solving behaviour in a given context, whereas double-loop learning challenges the core assumptions, beliefs, and values that frame the context. In the words of Argyris and Schön:

> When the error detected and corrected permits the organization to carry on its present policies or achieve its present objectives, then that error-and-correction process is *single-loop* learning. Single-loop learning is like a thermostat that learns when it is too hot or too cold and turns the heat on or off. The thermostat can perform this task because it can receive information (the temperature of the room) and take corrective action. *Double-loop* learning occurs when error is detected and corrected in ways that involve the modification of an organization's underlying norms, policies and objectives. (Argyris and Schön, 1978: 2)

For organizations, these distinctions have important implications. Whereas single-loop learning is important to improve performance incrementally, double-loop learning questions the business an organization is in, its culture, and its strategic vision. Double-loop learning represents an ability to reflect on the single-loop learning processes and to understand when fundamental change is required.

Single-loop learning means optimizing skills, refining abilities, and acquiring knowledge necessary to achieve resolution of a problem that requires solving.

Double-loop learning means changing the frame of reference that normally guides behaviour.

IMAGE 9.1 Nike Air Force 1 Low White/Red. Nike learnt that customers wanted classic shoes as worn by sports heroes, even if they were overengineered for everyday use. The Nike Air is such a classic. KixandtheCity.com

WHAT'S THE POINT?

Learning at Nike

To make these concepts more concrete, think of the example of Nike. When Nike learned how to produce shoes more cheaply through outsourcing to Asia or learned to improve the quality of its shoes by engaging athletes in their design, it was engaged in a single-loop learning process. But when Nike, thinking that its shoes were completely overengineered for everyday use, stripped the design out of them, it began a process of double-loop learning. The result of Nike's action was that customers no longer wanted to buy the shoes because they no longer embodied the Nike spirit. Customers wanted to wear the shoes their idols wore. In facing and resolving this challenge,

Nike was engaged in a double-loop learning process. In such a situation, Nike had to find out which business it was in, what its mission was, and what its core value proposition was. Learning that normal customers loved overengineered sports shoes because such shoes communicated something that customers could not get anywhere else, fundamentally changed Nike's understanding of its identity and how the company should do and be what its identity entailed (Hatch and Schultz, 2001). Put simply, to improve how you do things you engage in single-loop learning. In order to question what you do and change it more fundamentally you will have to engage in double-loop learning.

Single-loop learning is fine as long as everything stays in place so that what you are doing has a market and customers keep returning. But it is risky. It only needs some innovation elsewhere – through double-loop learning – and your customers might vanish and the market disappear. Your organization, if it is not double-loop learning, could soon be in trouble.

Learning through exploitation and exploration

March (2002) writes about the **exploitation of knowledge** and **knowledge exploration**. The exploitation of knowledge focuses on repetition, precision, discipline, and control of existing capabilities. The hallmark is process improvement, deepening and refining existing knowledge about ways of doing things, which is risk averse and measurement oriented; it seeks measurable improvement in performance as a result of systematically identifiable causal factors. Exploitation is aided by strongly legitimated and uncontested organization cultures where people know and perform in highly institutionalized appropriate ways.

March contrasts knowledge exploitation with knowledge exploration. Knowledge exploration requires more relaxed attitudes to controls and institutional norms. Evolving and adaptive organizations need to be able to exploit and explore simultaneously. If they are only good at exploitation, they will tend to become better and better in increasingly obsolescent ways of doing things; they will find themselves outflanked. And if they are only specialists in star trekking, in exploration, they are unlikely to realize the advantages of their discoveries, as they lack the exploitative capacities to be able to do so. Organizations have to learn to balance search and action, variation and selection, and change and stability (March, 2002: 271). Organizations will most often attempt risky exploratory behaviour when they are failing to meet targets rather than when they are achieving them; however, risks are best taken when there is sufficient slack or surplus resources that the organization can afford to risk different ways of doing things.

The **exploitation of knowledge** occurs through routinization, standardization, and formalization of what is already known and done: doing it more cheaply, quickly, efficiently.

Knowledge exploration involves serendipity, accident, randomness, chance, and risk-taking, not knowing what one will find.

 WHAT'S THE POINT?

The success trap

Paradoxically, success can breed failure. The phenomenon has been described as the success trap. It arises from being too good at exploitation. Imagine an organization that keeps on repeating actions that mimic what was successful previously, and consequently develops highly specific capabilities that new ideas do not match in action, thus encouraging aversion to exploration. A good example would be General Motors, Chrysler, or Ford, the giants of the US auto industry. They developed tremendous know-how in building big cars that US consumers liked – before petrol prices soared, and consumers developed a sense of environmental responsibility.

Asian car manufacturers were quick to respond and offered more suitable alternatives while the former US giants failed to explore new green technologies and innovative car designs fit for the twenty-first century. Consequently, in 2009 General Motors, formerly the biggest US company, had to file for bankruptcy. Or think of the story of the calculator manufacturer Facit: it also became a victim of its own success. The moral of this story is that organizations cannot rely only on their past experience and know-how: being in too deep a groove is dangerous. Organizations need both exploration *and* exploitation, but not too much of either. But how can we design them to achieve this?

(Continued)

(Continued)

In a series of papers, Michael L. Tuschman and Charles O'Reilly (2004; 2008) developed the idea of the ambidextrous organization. Ambidextrous organizations create specialist subunits with unique processes, structures, and cultures that are specifically intended to support early stage exploration within the larger parent organization, which is focused on exploitation of existing knowledge. In other words, the ambidextrous organization characterizes an entity that is capable of simultaneous exploring and exploiting. By being ambidextrous, say Tuschman and O'Reilly, achieved through growing many small, autonomous units instead of one monstrous organization, a firm can have it both ways: exploiting what it knows while simultaneously exploring new knowledge.

In many respects it is least likely that risks will be taken at this time because the grooves of success are already directing the organization. March offers a good diagnosis of why efficient forms of exploitation are likely to continue to be reproduced as the dominant organization form. A successful organization will resource activities and promote people that contribute to that success; however, at the same time tomorrow's winning ideas might question past recipes for success and hence implicitly undermine the organization's hierarchy and culture. Where innovation does occur, then it is likely to be rewarded only where its exploration rapidly becomes exploited.

March states that '[i]maginations of possible organizations are justified by their potential not for predicting the future (which is almost certainly small) but for nurturing the uncritical commitment and persevering madness required for sustained organizational and individual rigidity in a selective environment' (2002: 275). Many organizations must fail so that the few models of difference may survive 'in a system that sustains imaginative madness at the individual organizational level in order to allow a larger system to choose among alternative insanities' (March, 2002: 276). Empirical research thus far suggests that the majority of new organization practices remain incorporated within traditional organizational forms, that organizations may embrace new technologies and practices but do not necessarily change their forms in consequence (Palmer and Dunford, 2001).

QUESTION TIME

Research the dot-com boom that collapsed in 2001, using the web. Find businesses that focused on the exploration of new ideas without paying attention to the exploitation.

- To what extent did the development of these companies exemplify a system that sustained 'imaginative madness' at the individual level and to what extent did it allow the larger system to choose among 'alternative insanities'?

March (2002) thinks that the framework of increasingly rapid organizational change will be more likely to create rapid incremental turnover in organization forms than radical discontinuities. In an environment demanding greater flexibility and change of organizations, these changes will tend to play out not just in individual organizations but also in terms of the population of organizations. Some organizations will be selected as efficient, adaptive, and legitimate, whereas others will not survive because they do not match what the environment requires. He foresees a future of short-term organizations that are effectively disposable. These organizations will efficiently exploit what they know how to do until some other organizations emerge to do this better. Then they will die. Adaptability will occur at the population level rather than necessarily at the specific organizational level. Overall, efficiency will be served, although specific organizations may not survive.

For March's scenario to be realized, however, there has to be a pool of organizations that are discontinuously exploring learning through active imagining. Of course, without the pioneering of new forms and structures, there would be no new and more efficient mutations of organization forms to succeed those that already exist. Now, if March is right, what this probably means is a double-edged movement: McDonaldization of the efficient but relatively disposable exploiters of knowledge, with the exercise of imagination reserved for those organizations that seek to explore new forms of knowledge. What is foreseen is a type of *Blade Runner* scenario: highly innovative science-based knowledge organizations in gleaming towers for the highly paid, skilled, and educated, on the one hand, and, on the other hand, lots of street-level organizations that are exploitive and relatively impoverished, providing a poor working environment.

WHAT'S THE POINT?

Exploration and exploitation

- If organizations cannot exploit what they know efficiently they wither and atrophy.
- If organizations cannot explore so that they know how to do different things (double-loop learning) or the same things differently (single-loop learning) they wither and atrophy.

- Organizing successfully involves managing both exploration and exploitation.
- Organizations must be balanced and structurally include exploitation and exploration in the form of the ambidextrous organization, for example.
- Too much of either pursued single-mindedly leads to atrophy.

DRIVING FORCES BEHIND KNOWLEDGE AND LEARNING

In summary of the chapter so far, we can understand organizational learning as being 'best applied to organizations which are able regularly to monitor and reflect on the assumptions by which they operate, so that they can quickly learn about themselves and their working environment, and change' (Gabriel et al., 2000: 323). As we saw with Levitt and March's (1988) and Argyris and Schön's (1978) analyses, learning is about self-reflection, which triggers insights into organizational routines, beliefs, and values. After these facets of an organization are understood, they are open to being changed – theoretically. But how is such learning actually accomplished, and what are the driving forces behind learning? In this section, we focus on two major arenas that drive learning: communities of practice and collaborations. Whereas the first concept focuses on learning within an organization, the second explores the learning that occurs when organizations collaborate.

Learning in and through communities of practice

According to Etienne Wenger, a **community of practice** represents a social learning system that develops when people who have a common interest in a problem, collaborate to share ideas and find solutions.

With his concept of a **community of practice**, Wenger (1998; 2002), a consultant and researcher, understands learning as a process deeply embedded in what he calls a 'social learning system'.

Wenger argues that learning does not happen just in the individual mind, departmental routines, or organizations; rather, learning is a process that occurs in social learning systems. Consider your own experience as a student of management; of course, learning takes place (we hope!) while you are reading the lines we have written. But, equally important, you learn in the classroom when interacting with colleagues and teachers. Perhaps you might talk to a friend who is working, or think of the experiences you had in casual jobs you took during summer vacations, or maybe you already have a job – these are the resources that you use to make sense of what you hear. Or maybe you watch movies or read newspapers and link what you see and read back to what you are learning in the higher education context. When you speak to a friend who decided to study law instead of management, maybe you try to explain why you enjoy studying management and why it is important. Combined, it is all these interactions that make up what Wenger calls a 'social learning system'.

When such a system is established, it often blurs the boundaries of single organizational contexts. It creates learning alliances (between a university and an organization, perhaps), regional clusters (maybe a group of organizations in a high-tech industry, such as in Silicon Valley), and global networks (think of all those Linux users, unknown to each other, who, through cyberspace, are making the Linux system evermore robust and challenging Microsoft). Learning often takes place through the almost imperceptible networks that bind us together with others, both inside and outside the organizations in which we work. Translucent and like a spider's web, the objective of networks is to capture knowledge.

For organizations, Wenger's (1998; 2002) ideas have important implications; learning does not occur in isolated activities such as training weekends or know-how seminars offered every six months. Rather, it happens within the normal contexts that span organizational boundaries and processes and that bring many different activities together. As Wenger puts it, the interplay between the competence that an individual's institutional environment represents and an individual's own experience is what triggers learning.

Communities   Wenger's (1998; 2002) notion of communities of practice captures the actions that take place in social learning systems. Regardless of whether you look at a group of students who work together on a project, the R&D team of an organization, or a street gang, they are all communities of practice because they are the social building blocks of learning systems. It is within these communities that we define what counts as competence, whether it involves designing a successful project answer, developing breakthrough innovations, or solving a problem.

Take the example of a design firm: organizational members are dressed casually and wearing a 'cool' T-shirt with interesting prints from foreign cultures is seen as appropriate clothing. Ideas are developed in brainstorming sessions and by looking at design work from artists and other creatives. The development of products such as a new logo takes place through a playful trial and error process in which the individual designer needs creativity, passion, and courage to develop something new that will not only please the client but also other fellow designers. Now compare this with a large accounting firm such as PricewaterhouseCoopers: organizational members are dressed formally and values of professionalism are held in high esteem. Rather than brainstorming ideas, solutions most often come from diligent study of similar cases, scrutinizing of books, and decisions from the high court. A good solution is one that not only respects the law but also saves the client money. In the two cases, each community of

IMAGE 9.2   Informal learning in progress

practice defines what constitutes competencies: in the case of the design firm it is creativity, thinking outside the box, and experimentation; in the case of the accounting firm it is detailed legal knowledge, sound understanding of the client's business, and reliable advice that has to hold (sometimes) all the way up the high court. According to Wenger (2002), different competencies are defined by three elements.

- *Sense of joint enterprise*: Members need to understand and share what their particular community is about and how they can contribute to their community. Put simply, if you work for PricewaterhouseCoopers you need to understand the core values or professionalism and respect the organizational model of the partnership. If you work for a design firm, creativity and knowledge about trends are key to becoming a successful employee.

- *Relationships of mutuality*: Communities are built and sustained through interaction between their members. Through interaction with each other, they establish relationships of mutuality. To be a member, you must be trusted as a member of this community. Put simply, if you are a member of the Mafia, or want to pass for one, you have to be prepared to live outside the law that everyone else follows. Diego Gambetta's fascinating book *Codes of the Underworld: How Criminals Communicate* (2009) provides some great examples of how undercover police agents had to commit minor crimes in order to be accepted by the members of the organizations they attempted to infiltrate. Gambetta recounts that some criminal syndicates challenge potential new members to commit a random murder – something an undercover police agent clearly could never do. The movie *Donnie Brasco* with Johnny Depp tells the story of an undercover agent who lives through the dilemmas of mutuality in order to be accepted as part of the New York Mafia.

- *Shared repertoire*: Over time, communities of practice produce a common history. They establish a shared repertoire of stories, languages, artifacts, routines, rituals, processes – put simply, a culture (see also pp. 216–221). Being a member of a community means having access to this repertoire and the knowledge of how to use it accordingly. Think of the scene in the movie *Gladiator* (Scott, 2000) in which the character Maximus, played by Russell Crowe, finally gains the acceptance of his peers by behaving, fighting, and talking like a gladiator.

The social learning system encompasses many smaller communities of practice. These communities, equipped with a sense of joint enterprise, relationships of mutuality, and a shared repertoire, are the building blocks of learning. Obviously, these building blocks are not good per se – just think of the shared repertoire of stories that can often be organizationally quite scathing. Shared understanding and trust is the basis for communicating about change; but, as we have seen – theoretically, with Argyris and Schön (1978), and practically, with the example of Facit – these shared assumptions can lead to homogeneity, blindness, and groupthink (see also pp. 99–100).

Boundaries   Communities of practice must interact with other communities, which shifts the focus to the boundaries around communities. On one hand, boundaries are important because they trigger the establishment of a community. However, on the other hand, they need to be spanned and transgressed to facilitate the flow of information. The boundaries around communities of practice are less clearly defined than organizational boundaries. For instance, a community of practice can involve not only parts of an organization but also an important supplier who works closely with the organization.

WHAT'S THE POINT?

Wal-Mart

A good example of close collaboration between an organization and its suppliers is the US-based retailer Wal-Mart. Being the largest organization in the world with about 1.6 million employees and a turnover of more than US$250 billion, Wal-Mart can make or break the business of its suppliers. If your company produces toothpaste and Wal-Mart decides to stock it in its almost 4,000 stores you can be almost 100 per cent certain that your sales will increase manifold. Wal-Mart will also help you to develop and refine your product: through access to its massive database you can learn in which stores customers buy your product, when they buy it, and what else they put in the shopping cart. Wal-Mart will also help you to figure out the best way to package your product and how to deliver it to the Wal-Mart supercentres from where products are delivered to the stores. Often, this collaboration becomes so close that suppliers open up offices next to the Wal-Mart headquarters in Bentonville, Arkansas. Procter & Gamble for instance has several hundred employees working in Bentonville who liaise every day with their largest customer and work on improving their collaboration.

Communities can evolve across organizational boundaries and can include non-organizational members. Boundary-spanning activity is important because it offers unique and rich learning opportunities. Being confronted with an outsider's perspective or challenged by someone with a different social and cultural background can trigger new insights. The clash between what you take for granted and what someone else might see in a different light can become the starting point of an innovative and creative process (see also pp. 388–395).

Wenger (2002) argues that communities of practice can become hostage to their own history, and an outsider or newcomer might challenge the repertoire that makes them inert and reactive (see also p. 389). Managing the boundaries of interaction between the communities of practice that form a social learning system is thus an important managerial task. As Wenger (2002) suggests, there are three ways of managing boundaries – through people, artifacts, and interaction:

- *People*: People can act as brokers between communities of practice and span their boundaries. Think of a woman who is a board member of an organization and who also works as senior manager in another company. She lives in two worlds simultaneously and can infuse one community of practice with knowledge from the other. By doing so, she creates learning opportunities for both. Of course, brokers run the danger of being marginalized, overlooked, and becoming invisible in communities because they do not exclusively and fully belong to only one community. Thus, managing their needs, expectations, and experiences is an important task. Sometimes organizations explicitly seek such members – for instance, when they want to have *interlocking directors* (people who already hold a directorship in another company and can bring to bear their experience from that firm and industry to a different type of organization).

- *Artifacts*: Objects such as tools, documents, models, discourses, and processes can act as boundary spanners as well. Think of a bar in which people from different backgrounds meet and chat. In this case, a bar's preferred beer brand, the type of music it plays, or the sports it broadcasts can function as a broker between different groups. As another example, some groups – such as surfies, skaters, or homeboys – might be linked to each other through their preference for specific clothes and fashion items. In this case, a common interest of all three groups in Nike products – even though they might use them quite differently – creates a potential bridge that could minimize the gaps between them.

- *Interaction*: Interaction can be a direct boundary-spanning activity because it exposes the beliefs and perspectives of one community to another. Think of an exchange programme between your university and a university in another country; through the exchange programme, you are exposed to another culture. By comparing your own culture to the other one, you might learn new perspectives and change established ideas. Organizationally, this interaction happens between customers and sales staff; salespeople that form one community of practice talk to the community of users about their products and services, and complaints from customers are used to improve existing services and products or even to develop completely new ideas.

In complex interdisciplinary project teams, such as the collaboration between Swatch and Mercedes that resulted in the Smart Car, different communities of practice combine and challenge the knowledge and competencies of the others. When this is done well, it provides a rich learning opportunity for organizations, given that they accept that they cannot fully own or control these processes. As Wenger (2002) notes, organizations can participate in such opportunities, leverage them, and learn. However, the precondition for such learning is the willingness to open up the organizational boundaries and increase transparency. Hence trust becomes an important ingredient in successful learning partnerships.

Learning in and through collaborations

Arguably, many companies are skeptical when it comes to working across boundaries in **collaborative relations**. They arc scared that their competitors could gain access to their know-how and run off with the fruits of the valuable learning they have acquired over the years. Growth is to be achieved through mergers and acquisitions rather than through networking and collaborating.

> **Collaborative relations** involve the process of sharing resources including ideas, know-how, technologies, and staff between two or more different organizations in order to create a solution to a given problem.

WHAT'S THE POINT?

Alliances and collaboration

Negotiating alliances and collaboration have become new ways of growing and expanding. Take the example of the airline industry. Instead of competing and pushing each other out of the market, there are two major alliances: One World and Star Alliance. Through a clever network, the companies in each alliance build on their respective strengths and compensate for each other's weaknesses. Without each airline having to fly to every destination in the world, the alliances are able to offer flights just about everywhere through their networks. And through a smart reward system (frequent flyer points), they retain customers within their network and create loyalty.

Collaborations can trigger knowledge creation and organizational learning when organizations work closely together with suppliers, retailers, customers, universities, or consultants. Or they might focus on collaboration internally among different divisions, teams, and experts. The electronics company Philips and the sportswear giant Nike, for instance, announced in March 2002 that they were collaborating (see von Stamm, 2003: 164). The rationale behind the deal was simple. Nike is a world leader in marketing, sports, innovation, and material technology, Philips is a leading innovator in the field of 'wearable electronics' technologies and has considerable knowledge about consumers and digital technology. Thus, their collaboration brings together different expertise and should enable them to combine and transform their knowledge into new products. It is important that both companies learn from each other and, through broadening their knowledge base, trigger innovation and change (see also pp. 379–386).

From a learning perspective, collaboration is an important means to access new knowledge and transfer skills that an organization lacks. Moreover, facing the challenge of creating more and more complex products, it is hard for any organization to stay at the cutting edge in every single detail. Just think of the automobile industry; almost every part of a new car is a complex mini-project in itself, from the stereo system to the computer-controlled engine, the light aluminium subframe, and even the tyres. Thus, car companies are forced to work closely with their suppliers and, in collaboration, they learn from each other. Obviously, this is a dangerous game because no one wants to give away too much information or divulge secret knowledge that competitors could use. However, without trusting and sharing, collaborations are hard to keep alive. As in every learning situation, collaboration needs an open environment in which ideas can grow and spread.

Drawing on extensive research, Tidd et al. (2001) identified three major issues that determine successful learning through collaboration. First, an organization must have the intent to learn through collaboration. Instead of trying to steal its partner's assets, it needs to see the opportunity to learn mutually. Second, it requires transparency. If cultural barriers block the flow of knowledge between companies, or if one partner refuses openness, learning cannot take place. Also, if the knowledge is more tacit than explicit, it will be harder for a partner organization to acquire it. Finally, absorptiveness, referring to the capacity to actually learn, is important.

Learning often happens through a trial and error process in which mistakes and failure provide the richest source of learning. However, normally, organizations do not embrace mistakes as opportunities for learning but as mechanism to allocate blame: usually a scapegoat needs to be found to blame when a failure occurs. Management that sees in mistakes only the negative is likely to block organizational learning processes because it excludes mistakes from its agenda and brands as 'losers' those people who make mistakes.

David Kelley, managing director of the product design firm IDEO, has identified the blame-game as the biggest hurdle in the learning process. Therefore, at IDEO employees are encouraged to make mistakes quickly and learn from them fast. As the management guru Tom Peters (who admires IDEO for its innovativeness) has put it, the only difference between successful and unsuccessful organizations is that the successful ones make their mistakes more quickly.

ORGANIZATIONAL LEARNING AS PARADOX?

The paradox of organizational learning

WHAT'S THE POINT?

9/11 – what should we learn?

It is not always clear what we should learn from a certain experience. Although we share the same experience, we might disagree completely on the consequences of the event. Take the terrorist attacks on the USA on 11 September 2001. What happened is clear, but the learning that different people and factions draw from this event could not vary more fundamentally. Should we fight state sponsored terrorism and declare the 'axis of evil' as state enemy # 1 as George W. Bush did? Or should we intervene in selected countries with the aim to install democracy and freedom? On the other hand, attempts from the West to implement change might radicalize fundamentalists and increase their popularity in Muslim countries. In other words, whereas some suggest fighting fire with fire, others argue that doing so will simply lead to more of the same problems. The action of one party is the occasion for reaction from the other party, and what one side identifies as cause is seen by the other as effect. Thus, learning is based on the interpretation of a particular situation, and this is always contested terrain.

In mainstream texts on learning and knowledge management, learning is depicted as a more or less straightforward process. Weick and Westley (1999) would not necessarily agree with this dominant view; rather, they challenge the concept of organizational learning in its fundamentals, arguing that the term *organizational learning* is, in fact, a paradox (or, as they put it, an **oxymoron**). Just like the members of a dysfunctional family, organization and learning are things that do not seem to fit together well. As Weick and Westley argue, learning and organizing are 'essentially antithetical processes, which means the phrase "organizational learning" qualifies as oxymoron' (1999: 190). Organizing is all about ordering and controlling – or, as the authors put it, about decreasing variety – whereas learning is about disorganizing and increasing variety. If learning is about exploring new terrain and understanding the unknown, and organizing is about exploiting routines and the already known, organizational learning is a paradox. Weick and Westley suggest not that we should simply forget the concept but that we should be careful that, in using it, we make sense of its ambivalence. Put simply, learning happens when the old and the new clash and create a tension.

> An **oxymoron** is a figure of speech that combines two normally contradicting terms (such as deafening silence or military intelligence).

WHAT DO YOU MEAN?

A learning organization is a paradox

As the old proverb goes, knowledge is power. Learning means changing knowledge and therefore it also means questioning those who have power. Take the example of an employee questioning their manager: more often than not the manager will understand this as questioning their authority and react negatively. Learning – and especially double-loop learning – implies questioning the rules of the game. Of course, those who are comfortable with the current rules and those who have established these rules will be critical of attempts to change the status quo. Also, we have seen that learning implies a trial and error process that can be messy. Organizations are made up of rules and routines that try to make the world stable and predictable. Learning challenges these rules and those who have established them. Therefore, one can argue critically that learning and organization have a paradoxical relationship!

A practical guide to organizational learning

As we have seen with March's provocative ideas of learning, learning happens somewhere between organizations exploring what they do not know and exploiting what they do not know. Or, to put it another way, profound learning happens when single-loop learning (exploitation, evolution, adaptation, and habit) intersects with double-loop learning (exploration, revolution, and thinking outside the box). Weick and Westley (1999) analyse three ways of dealing with the complexities of exploring and exploiting. Their ideas are framed by the metaphors of humour, improvisation, and small wins as moments of learning.

Humour: Jokes and funny situations provide opportunities for learning because they play with the meanings we normally associate with specific words and deeds, turning them upside down. Almost every joke pulls together things that are normally separated and, in doing so, creates a surprising element that makes us laugh. In addition, the normal social order is suspended for a moment when we are telling a joke; you might say 'just joking ...' when you are telling a joke and you say something that might be true but that is not socially acceptable. (Remember, in the ancient feudal kingdoms, the only one allowed to tell the truth was the fool or the jester!) Finally, humour happens spontaneously; it cannot be planned or forecast. The funniest situations happen out of the blue. Humour carries the flexibility and richness of quick and creative response to the environment and represents a way of exploring new ideas.

Improvisation: Improvisation is another concept of learning that deals productively with the tension between learning and organizing. Actors and jazz musicians improvise, and so do employees; rather than sending people to seminars where they learn things they cannot apply back in the organization, learning on the job – improvisation – encourages people to play around with everyday patterns and to change them slightly, not necessarily radically, but *in situ*. Improvisation is always based on an interplay between past, present, and future; by carefully listening and changing past rhythms, something new emerges. Also, errors play an important role within improvisation. To enable learning and development, errors are tolerated and used as starting points for future improvisation. Finally, improvisational learning is a team event, not a one-person show. It relies on the feedback of others, their feelings (rather than their rational capacity alone), and their contribution to change.

Small wins: Small wins, according to Weick and Westley (1999), are not the big revolutionary changes promised by consultants or management gurus but rather the learning opportunities that happen when you *almost* do business as usual. The researchers give the example of feminists, who sought to change laws and regulations, which turned out to be quite a successful learning strategy. However, while working to achieve their overriding goal of equality for women, the feminists scored a small win by showing that language itself was deeply gendered (chair*man*, post*man*, and so on). This seemingly small win had a big impact, making our society learn much more about the ways in which gender is deeply embedded in how we normally do what we do and become who we are. Thus, small wins might look small, but their effect can be quite big. Again, they are moments of learning because they juxtapose order (common language) and a sense of disorder (new language), creating the space in which learning happens.

Learning, unlearning, non-learning?

As we have seen, learning is a process that is in tension with the core processes of managing and organizing. Because learning happens only when there is some freedom to experiment with actions and ideas, it challenges management practices that focus on order, predictability, and control. Given this problematic relationship between learning and organizing, you might wonder whether learning is always good for organizations. If learning challenges organizations, why should they learn at all? This is exactly the question that Brunsson (1998) asks in a thought-provoking and ironic paper introducing the idea of the non-learning organization. He argues that non-learning organizations are healthier than learning ones, which is an idea directly in opposition to the commonly accepted view that there is a positive relationship between learning and organizational performance. In fact, most scholars and management gurus argue that learning leads to greater efficiency and better performance.

Brunsson (1998) looks at public sector organizations and wonders whether their non-learning – the way that they keep making the same errors – is simply pathological (something bad) or whether their persistence with routines (their non-learning) is something more fundamentally positive. He starts by suggesting that if learning is as extremely positive as theorists suggest, non-learning must be dysfunctional and negative for organizations. Instead of following the mainstream argument (learning is good, therefore non-learning must be bad), Brunsson (1998) turns the order upside down and argues that non-learning can result in the following unexpected benefits for the organization:

- *Tolerance of contradictions*: When learning organizations face contradictions, challenges, or problems in their environments, they have to adjust either their behaviour or their objectives. They have to act consistently over time and constantly align their behaviour with their objectives. Non-learning organizations, on the other hand, are much more flexible. If they face an environment in which contradictions and uncertainties are the norm rather than the exception, they can still operate normally. The budget agencies, for instance, were confronted with unsatisfactory reports and asked for better reports next time. However, despite the incomplete reports, they accomplished their tasks. Non-learning organizations manage contradictions well because they accomplish what they have to do, even though they hope that things will be better next time.

- *Organizational discretion*: Non-learning organizations are capable of benefiting from the gap between talk, action, and decisions. Although they kept asking for better reports, they did their job based on the same unsatisfactory reports that they had always received. Facing this situation, a learning organization would probably become unsatisfied, and its employees would be frustrated enough to seek better sources of information, whereas the non-learning organization is able to differentiate between what it would like to have (better reports) and what it actually has (incomplete reports). Again, this makes the non-learning organization flexible, and it provides a certain kind of freedom – such organizations can be realistic in their task accomplishment and remain idealistic about the future.

In light of these positive aspects of non-learning, Brunsson argues that the non-learning organization is in fact an emancipated organization. Learning organizations have to change, adjust, and align all the time, whereas non-learning organizations can deal with contradictions, inconsistent demands, and gaps between ideal worlds and actual reality. They are emancipated because they can disregard the (ostensible) need for change that drives learning organizations.

The power of learning

Knowledge management and scientific management Knowledge management practitioners like to think of themselves as conceptually new and innovative. However, as we have seen above with the example of Taylor, the focus of knowledge management is quite old; transforming tacit knowledge from employees into explicit knowledge that is owned by the company was the driving force behind the idea of scientific management in 1911. Taylor disliked the fact that the workers knew more about the actual process than he or the managers did. Workers could tell stories about why things are the way they are, and others had to accept these stories. Management lacked any better, alternative knowledge because it did not have a basic understanding of the tasks that the workers accomplished. Without such objective knowledge, how could management coordinate and control effectively? Taylor's initiative in getting the knowledge out of workers' heads and making it an object of managerial manipulation in Bethlehem Steel was a harsh way of transforming tacit into explicit knowledge. It sought to destroy the craft basis of existing know-how from the situation in prior generations, where knowledge and status were coterminous – that is, one did not become a master without having acquired the knowledge of a journeyman and apprentice – so this separation of power and knowledge was unthinkable (see also Chapter 7).

Lifelong learning equals lifelong examinations In organizational terms, we have already talked about Taylor's approach and the way he empowered management: he simply gained knowledge that had been the workers' domain. Scientific management changed the power relations, made the worker an object of study, formalized the worker's task, and made any worker exchangeable with another. The difference between Taylor's scientific management and modern knowledge management is that Taylor thought you have to codify knowledge only once, whereas knowledge management realizes that you can never stop learning or codifying – it is a lifelong process.

Given the enthusiasm for the concept of lifelong learning, it is interesting to consider one of Foucault's (1979) core arguments, which sheds some light on the dark side of lifelong learning – that lifelong learning might very well imply lifelong examination. Foucault focused especially on the examination as a common practice integrating knowledge and power. Once, the integration was institutionally fairly specific: it occurred mostly at school and university. Thus, Western societies that praise continuous learning are simultaneously paving the path of lifelong learning with exams that assess the learners, given the centrality of performance measurement to contemporary management culture. As you know from your own experience, exams are powerful instruments that shape your behaviour and, by extension, your personality. Or think of the assessment centres that are widely used tools of human resource management. They are almost perfect examples of the knowledge/power link because they have the power to assess someone (using their knowledge dimension) and change them (using their power dimension).

For Foucault, the examination is such a powerful tool because it combines both a hierarchical observation and a normalizing judgement. These are the two functions of examinations. First, they make individuals visible (who is clever, who is not?) and allow the supervisor to categorize them and establish a hierarchical relation among students. Exams enable supervisors to find out who are their potential 'stars' and who is the 'deadwood'. Second, examinations make it possible to judge people and to compare them with each other. They establish a norm that enables the supervisor to categorize some as normal and those who do not comply as abnormal. Think of your class. You and your classmates might have different strengths and skills that are not easily comparable. The exam ignores these individual differences and judges everybody by the same template; it normalizes people as it ignores their differences and subjects them all to the same metric. The process of scrutiny transforms ordinary individuals into cases who are obliged to compete with each other in relation to one common standard.

Foucault analyses three mechanisms that form the heart of the examination:

- *Visibility*: During examinations, the learning subjects are fully visible, whereas the examiners are almost absent. We see this power working through surveillance; transforming the individual into an object that is visible and that can be assessed ensures discipline. For instance, many organizations routinely test their employees and link promotion back to successful results.

- *Individuality*: Examinations transform a group of people into individuals by making individual features comparable. Exams establish a hierarchy within a group and put each individual in their place within the hierarchy. Organizations that test their employees can create tables where they rank all employees and categorize the top 10 per cent as 'high potential'. This means that employees constantly compete among each other for the top 10 per cent.

- *Case*: Exams transform individual characters into cases that are documented and objectified. Every individual has a history in this system that can be compared with others. Individual development can be assessed and, if necessary, corrected. Yearly or even six-monthly performance reviews mean that each employee is turned into a case recorded in a file where their supervisor can track progress of learning and development and, if necessary, correct the career path.

Examinations combine the hierarchical surveillance of people with the normalizing judgement of the supervisor. This makes individuals visible, transforms each into a case, and renders them open to powerful intervention. A society that understands itself as continuously learning must see its shadow as well in a never-ending series of examinations that shape individuals.

SUMMARY AND REVIEW

In this chapter we have explored key issues of organizational learning and knowledge management. We started our journey by arguing that 'the only competitive advantage the company of the future will have is its managers' ability to learn faster than their competitors' (de Geus, 1988: 74). In this perspective the capability to learn and manage knowledge is one of the most important aspects of organizations. Knowledge management is the process of managing knowledge to meet existing and future needs, and to exploit present knowledge to develop opportunities for further knowledge.

We have explored different sources of knowledge (learning by doing; hearing stories, popular accounts). We have also discussed tact and explicit types of knowledge, and how they can be transformed from one to the other. Learning as changing knowledge is a key concept in management. Levitt and March (1988) understand learning as a process of adapting to the environment an organization is dealing with.

A second key theory we have discussed is single-loop learning. It basically means optimizing skills, refining abilities, and acquiring knowledge necessary to achieve resolution of a problem that requires solving. Double-loop learning describes learning as changing the frame of reference that normally guides behaviour. The dialectic between exploring new ideas and exploiting old ones (March) frames the dilemma of organizational learning.

With the concept of 'communities of practice' (Wenger) we have analysed learning as a social process that occurs within social learning systems. These communities are characterized by

three key features: a sense of joint enterprise; relationships of mutuality; and a shared repertoire. We have explored how learning happens through collaboration between organizations and across organizational boundaries.

Critically, we have stressed that organizational learning is no guarantee that what organizations will learn will benefit them. Organization theorists interested in knowledge management seek to ensure that organizations learn the appropriate lessons and retain what is good while avoiding or discarding what is bad. That seems pretty straightforward, but, as this chapter has repeatedly suggested, the process is not quite as simple as it seems.

Sometimes, non-learning organizations may have an advantage over learning organizations. Learning organizations can place their members under a fearsome audit and sap their vitality; they can also codify what is unimportant and inconsequential while missing that which is profound because it is so deeply embedded in the normal ways of doing things. These issues often come to haunt organizations that downsize; thinking that they have routinized and learned everything that they need to know from their members, organizations find out too late that downsizing results in not only live bodies walking out the door but also the departure of some deeply embedded and important knowledge that managers did not know would be missed because they did not know what they had until they lost it.

Still, as the chapter has covered, there are many ways of seeking to ensure that knowledge is managed appropriately. Most importantly openness to error, improvisation, humour, and a strategy of small wins are key in creating a learning organization.

EXERCISES

1 Having read this chapter you should be able to say in your own words what each of the following key terms means. Test yourself or ask a colleague to test you.

- Organizational learning
- Knowledge management
- Tacit knowledge
- Implicit knowledge
- Learning as adaption
- Exploring and exploiting

- Single- and double-loop learning
- Communities of practice
- Collaboration
- Unlearning
- Lifelong learning
- Organizational learning as paradox

2 Why is learning important for organizations?
3 Where does knowledge come from?
4 What does Nonaka think is the most important knowledge to manage and why?
5 What differentiates single-loop learning from double-loop learning?
6 How would you describe the paradox of organizational learning that results from exploring and exploiting?
7 To what extent does the concept of the ambidextrous organization provide a solution to the paradox of organizational learning?
8 What do communities of practice do in terms of learning?
9 Why should organizations collaborate across boundaries?
10 Why might the term organizational learning be a paradox?

ADDITIONAL RESOURCES

1 The formative work of Nonaka and Takeuchi (1995), drawing on ideas from Polanyi (1962), has been very influential. The concept of tacit knowledge as Polanyi develops it is not quite as easily tamed and domesticated by management as Nonaka and Takeuchi suggest (see Ray and Clegg, 2007).
2 The missing dimension from most treatments of knowledge management is the way that knowledge always implicates power and is always implicated in power. The classic text is Foucault's (1979) *Discipline and Punish*, especially the graphic opening pages, in which he contrasts a gruesome execution with the rules of a model prison established in France just 60 years later. To the former belongs a fearsome vengeance, to the latter a reforming zeal – but neither vengeance on the body nor zeal towards the mind of the criminal is a practice of knowledge that we can easily understand unless we consider the regimes of power associated with them.
3 In terms of films, *Terminator 3: Rise of the Machines* (Mostow, 2003) is one that comes to mind. In this movie, a machine, played by Arnold Schwarzenegger, knows what the future holds for the hero and heroine, and he has to ensure that they meet their fate. If only organizations were able to have such prescience!
4 *The Right Stuff* (Kaufman, 1983), about the NASA space programme, is a good resource for organizational learning. The movie is based on Tom Wolfe's bestselling 1979 book of the same name. The film dramatically depicts the way that an organization – in this case, NASA – learned and did not learn. In a similar vein, the film *Apollo 13* (Howard, 1995) is also required viewing.
5 We also suggest watching *Bowling for Columbine* (Moore, 2002), which is an absolutely surreal journey through American society. The movie explores why and how American gun culture emerged and is learned anew with each generation.

WEB SECTION

1 Our Companion Website is the best first stop for you to find a great deal of extra resources, free PDF versions of leading articles published in Sage journals, exercises, video and pod casts, team case studies and general questions, and links to teamwork resources. Go to www.sage pub.co.uk/managingandorganizations3.
2 For state of the art briefings on how to manage organizations effectively, please visit the Henry Stewart Talks series of online audiovisual seminars on Managing Organizations, edited by Stewart Clegg: www.hstalks.com/r/managing-orgs, especially Talk #16 by Tim Ray on *What does knowledge work do*?, and Talk #17 by Elena Antonacopoulou on *Mastering business action: implications for management learning in business schools*.

3   An extremely rich source of themes related to knowledge management and learning is http://www.brint.com/km/.

4   For a rather interesting site with many links to the world of collaboration and knowledge, see http://www.lgu.ac.uk/deliberations/collab.learning.

5   Highly professional and updated news is provided by the Society of Organizational Learning: http://www.solonline.org.

6   For a nice and simple introduction to the theme of communities of practice, see http://www.ewenger.com.

7   A website that set itself the goal of sparking critical thinking and triggering learning for students and organizations is http://www.critical-thinking.org.

8   Check out the fascinating Ted talk by Sir Ken Robinson on learning and creativity. It is not only informative but also good fun! See http://www.ted.com.

LOOKING FOR A HIGHER MARK?

Reading and digesting these articles that are available free on the Companion Website www.sagepub.co.uk/managingandorganizations3 can help you gain deeper understanding and, on the basis of that, a better grade:

1   Ewenstein, B. and Whyte, J. (2007) 'Beyond words: aesthetic knowledge and knowing in organizations', *Organization Studies*, 28 (5): 689–708. In this paper the authors investigate aesthetic ways of knowing in organizations through detailed observation of design work in architectural practice.

2   Vaast, E. (2007) 'What goes online comes offline: knowledge management system use in a soft bureaucracy', *Organization Studies*, 28 (3): 282–306. This paper investigates when and how online practices (i.e. practices of management and use of web-based IT) impact offline practices (i.e. regular work practices and communication patterns) within a bureaucratic environment.

3   Mir, R. and Mir, A. (2009) 'From the colony to the corporation', *Group and Organization Management*, 34 (1): 90–113. Building on a case study of a multinational corporation (MNC) and its local Indian contractor, the authors study knowledge transfer and learning across international boundaries.

CASE STUDY

MANAGING KNOWLEDGE

Let us introduce Athena, a medium sized consultancy company, employing around 100 consultants. Athena delivers custom-made software applications for their customers, primarily knowledge management and work flow support tools. The consultants work in client projects and often work from the customer's site for several weeks, sometimes months, in a row. This makes it difficult for the employees as well as the managers to share knowledge and experience across their different projects, and to keep track on the latest solutions developed. To enable the consultants to work together, and work as a team, the consultants themselves have developed a wide range of well functioning software applications, or knowledge management tools: they have designed their own intranet and extranet, and applications for sharing project specifics like best practices exemplars and project management procedures.

The tools the consultants have developed are primarily dedicated to the articulation and spreading of codified knowledge. In addition to these efforts, Athena has made the not so common decision to invest in knowledge sharing practices that cannot easily be accounted for. At Athena the management decided to extend the lunch break, sponsor free lunch for all employees, and hire a chef with the work instruction 'spoil them'. The lunch area is now in the centre of the Athena building. Entering the lunch room in the morning, the first thing greeting you is the smell of freshly brewed espresso, the second is the smile of the chef, and the third is a couple of employees in the corner playing darts. If you pause for a moment you can get a glimpse of your lunch being prepared; if you take the time to stop, which one often does, you might get the recipe.

The reasoning behind the lunch initiative was that it would encourage the employees to eat together, to talk together, to socialize. By making the lunch attractive, they wanted to tempt their consultants to come to head office more often. In other words, believing that knowledge sharing is primarily a social enterprise, a natural extension of spending time together, extending lunch and making spending time together attractive was seen as a perfect way of enhancing knowledge sharing and creating practices.

The investment has turned out to be a big success. Around noon the lunch area gets crowded. You hear a buzz of talk about projects, slick computer designs, programming codes as well as Saturday's pub round and the lack of kindergarten availabilities. There is no obvious hierarchy among the luncher's, no scheduled seating, employees, managers, and customers all line up for their food. There is just a big smorgasbord of hot and cold meals, the promise of a good meal, and potential for good company. On Fridays it is more crowded than ever, as Fridays are labelled 'lunch with all', and consultants working off site are encouraged to come 'home'. The Friday lunches are used for presenting important announcements and project achievements.

Questions

1 (How) Can you justify calling free lunch a knowledge management tool?
2 What types of knowledge, if any, can be said to be shared and possibly created in such an initiative?
3 Discuss what types of knowledge management efforts you would invest in if you were a senior manager.

Case prepared by Kjersti Bjorkeng KUNNE, SINTEF, Norway; Arne Carlsen KUNNE, SINTEF, Norway.

CHAPTER TEN
MANAGING INNOVATION AND CHANGE

Creativity, Chaos, Foolishness

LEARNING OBJECTIVES

This chapter is designed to enable you to:

- Explain the basic assumptions of innovation management
- Grasp the role of change in organizations
- Understand the role of creativity in business
- Analyse different approaches to change and creativity
- Discuss the benefits and shortcomings of these approaches
- Appreciate these approaches' challenges for management
- Discuss organizational practices that trigger innovation and change

BEFORE YOU GET STARTED . . .

If I had asked people what they wanted, they would have said faster horses.
(Henry Ford)

INTRODUCTION

When did you last do something for the first time? Ask many organization managers this question, and the answer would probably be that it was quite a long time ago because, like bad habits, organizations are hard to change. Changing processes, practices, routines, products, or services and coming up with new ones is neither easy nor always enjoyable; doing something new can be quite painful and difficult. Thus, organizations tend to stick to the format they are used to and the things they already know. They find **innovation** difficult.

When we think of innovation, it is customary to make the following distinction: a company can (a) change the products and services it offers (product innovation) or (b) change the way it delivers them (process innovation). Let us use a concrete example. Henry Ford, founder of the Ford Motor Company and the assembly line, was one of the greatest inventors in the history of management, according to Wren and Greenwood (1998: 41). However, his way to success was anything but smooth. Born in 1863 as the son of a farmer in Michigan, he fiddled around with engines on his father's farm. In those days, cars were seen as a curiosity, and the majority of people did not believe that they would have a bright future; most cars were based on experiments with electric- or steam-powered engines. In fact, there were not many cars around in 1900; of the 4,192 cars that were built in 1900, not even 1,000 were gasoline or petrol powered. After the failure of his first business venture, Ford raised more money and developed his models N and T, which became big successes. In 1908, he sold more than 10,000 cars. Ford's assembly line, the idea for which he got from the methods used for butchering steers in the Chicago slaughterhouses, was a process innovation that made changes in management style, production, marketing, and strategy possible. The assembly line innovation allowed for massive growth. In 1909, Ford produced 13,840 cars; seven years later, in 1916, the company produced 585,388 cars! Simultaneously, the cost of producing each car decreased from $950 in 1909 to $360 in 1916.

The Ford success story illustrates how technology innovation (engine), change in payment of employees ($5 per day for workers, which was a lot of money back then), and production (assembly line) all led to something new and revolutionary. However, at the beginning, he was struggling with the common-sense notions of his time, and probably not many of his contemporaries would have had much trust or confidence in his adventures. For example, his high wages were called 'industrial suicide'

Innovation can be defined as the creation of either a new process (process innovation) or a new product or service (product/service innovation) that has an impact on the way the organization operates.

and 'socialism' by Ford's critics. Even more famously, Henry Ford argued that if he had listened to the market and what people wanted he would have built a faster horse.

WHAT DO YOU MEAN?

Innovation and change

Innovation and change are important for organizations. Speaking organizationally, innovation (either of practice or of products) leads to change that allows a company to position itself differently from its competitors. It does things differently (practices) or it offers different things (products/ services). Either way, it establishes itself strategically in the market. The competitive advantages of organizations are built on this core concept.

Because innovation and change are interrelated (see Tidd et al., 2001), we have put them together in this chapter. For instance, you might invent a new way of cooking a burger or a vegetarian meal; this turns into an innovation if you manage to monetize your invention and turn your idea into a business proposition. In other words, while we invent a lot of things (often commercially useless things, such as a new way of tying shoelaces or cutting cucumbers) only a few turn into innovations that have commercial value.

To use a more up-to-date example of how change and innovation are interlinked, think about the technological innovation of the Motion Picture Experts Group level three protocol. If you think you have never heard of it, maybe you know it better as MP3. It allows you to compress large music files and transfer them fast through the Internet. This product innovation is changing an entire industry and forcing it to rethink its business practices of handling music – recording, distributing, and so on. The initial success of Napster (see Tidd et al., 2001), Kazaa (www.kazaa.com/ us/index.htm), Apple's iTunes stores, and new gimmicks such as the iPad and the iPhone tell the story of an industry whose business model is under technological siege. Learning from these examples, we see innovation forces organizations to change and rethink their business models: Apple, for instance, is not any longer a computer manufacturer but a leading lifestyle company that makes a significant amount of its revenue through music sales.

PLATFORM INNOVATION

The automobile is the classic example of the platform innovation: Henry Ford's story of the genius innovator is only half of the truth. Rather, Ford benefited and exploited a social movement that paved the way for a society in which the car would take on the status of a cultural object – sometimes even a cult object. When the first car-like vehicles were invented towards the end of the nineteenth century, people could not agree whether they were a blessing or a curse. Some called them a 'devilish contraption' while others argued that 'you can't get people to sit on an explosion' (quoted in Rao, 2009: 20). Cars were deemed expensive, dangerous, noisy, slow, and unreliable. People could not even agree on a name for them – some called them locomobile, others quadricycle, and so on (Rao, 2009: 19). While it was hard to imagine a name for those new monsters, it was even harder to imagine how they could be used.

Rao argues that one key element that made the car a culturally accepted object was reliability tests. In these tests cars competed against each other to demonstrate that they were trustworthy: 'Reliability contests were credible because each race was an event that could be interpreted as evidence of the dependability of cars by the public. Since reliability contests were public spectacles, they were emotionally charged events. Finally, reliability contests had "narrative fidelity" because they combined the logic of testing with the practice of racing and created a compelling story' (2009: 32). In other words, these contests made the advantages of cars tangible and visible to a large audience; they created familiarity with a new technology and produced stories people could relate to. Henry Ford had won one of those reliability contests in 1901 against the established producer, Alexander Winton, which helped to legitimize the start-up of the Ford Motor Company two years later (Rao, 2009: 32). Rao's point is that market rebels, including those who organized reliability competitions, those who attended them, and those who wrote about them extensively, created an atmosphere in which either car critics could be convinced that the car was a symbol of progress or they could be successfully marginalized.

The ecology in which the invention of the car could become a commercial success did not stop with reliability contests. John Urry (2007) argues that the car marked a radical departure from the train, which was the great nineteenth-century transport invention. While the train was public and followed a time regime set by the railway companies, the car embodied the opposite: it created and meant *freedom* (I can go where I want), *privacy* (the car as living room on wheels), and *individuality* (from choice of model to tuning or 'pimping' up the car).

As well as cultural legitimacy, the car required a huge infrastructure to become useful: roads, highway networks, petrol stations, repair workshops, public licensing authorities, police, legal framework, insurance, and so on. In the twentieth century, entire cities have been modelled to accommodate the car – think of Los Angeles as the most often quoted example. Once such a system takes shape, innovations against the grain of the established ecology are hard to implement because so many players benefit from the status quo. The politics of the present situation prevail: in Los Angeles they were enough to stymie any public transport rapid transit ideas for decades because of the entrenched power of the petroleum and related products lobby.

Even when we know that cars have a negative impact on the environment and make our cities dysfunctional, and that each and every year roads produce 1.2 million dead and more than 20–50 million injured people, at an estimated cost of $518 billion, the car is still *the* preferred means of transportation. The power and diffusion of the car involved a whole network of actors who had to collaborate to create the cultural and physical conditions to turn the 'devilish contraption' into a desired object and a cultural icon. Hence, the moral of the story is that successful innovation is more than just developing an idea: it needs the active shaping of a **platform** in which the idea can grow and create traction.

> A **platform** is defined as an evolving eco-system that is created from many interconnected pieces.

This is the point that Cusumano and Gawer (2002) make. They argue that successful firms do not simply develop new products and services and compete with others in open markets. Rather, leading firms establish a platform on which new products emerge.

Importantly, innovations have to build on other pieces to make sense to customers. Think of a new application for your iPhone or computer software: these complex new products have to be able to communicate with existing technology. Platform leaders are those companies who control or at least shape the structure of overarching systems architecture. In other words, platform leaders define the rules of the game, the size of the playing field, and the entry conditions for players. Of course, to be able to control the platform is a powerful position that leads to a significant competitive advantage. A good example for a platform leader is Microsoft Windows: its ubiquitous operating system forces friends and foes to engage with its technology (Cusumano and Gawer, 2002).

CENTRAL APPROACHES AND MAIN THEORIES

Opinions about **change** vary between researchers: some argue that change is the exception and stability is the norm, whereas others support a process-based view according to which almost everything is in flux and transformation. Speaking generally, there are four types of change that can be separated analytically: (a) life cycle; (b) dialectical (struggle-based); (c) evolutionary; and (d) teleological (vision-based) (Van de Ven and Poole, 1995). Life cycle change can be thought of in terms of stages of maturation and growth or aging. Dialectical changes occur through the interplay, tensions, and contradictions of social relations. Such change can be observed in two-party-dominated political systems such as those in the USA or the UK. Change often occurs in moves from the left to the right of the political arena. Evolutionary changes, such as developing sustainability strategies to deal with environmental regulations, are essentially adaptive. For instance, an organization that decides to develop a new online-based product because its major competitor is working on one is responding to environmental change. Finally, teleological change is driven by strategic vision, such as when a city government aims to host a future Olympics and creates an organization to oversee the bid.

> Fundamentally **change** refers to a transition that occurs from one state to another.

WHAT DO YOU MEAN?

Innovation phases

The history of innovation in management and organization theory can be delineated in three steps (Clark, 2003): from after the Second World War up to the 1980s; the 1980s; and the last decade or so. During the post-war era up to the 1980s, innovation was conceptualized in terms of technological progress. Advances in technology – new machines, refined technologies, or new products such as the ambitious, often government subsidized, projects of the two main airline manufacturers, Boeing's Dreamliner (US) or Airbus' A380 (EU) – were created as a result of national investments in big science – expensive, prestigious mega-projects – undertaken by major research centres. Organizations had to adapt incrementally to the changes that the stream of modern technologies produced if they were to keep up with their competitors. Hence, developments in technology were seen as the driving force behind organizational change, a view that can be characterized as 'technological determinism' (Clark, 2003). Technologies are seen to change autonomously and have necessary causal consequences.

Between 1980 and 1990, the emphasis shifted from technology as the driving force towards a conception of technology and organization as interactive systems. The success of Japanese companies in the 1980s showed that technological innovation and change were deeply embedded and, in fact, depended on a national, cultural, and social context. By analysing the innovation process, researchers found that forces beyond management's rational planning tools (and, hence, beyond their control) shaped the process significantly. Suppliers, users, and employees translated change processes and innovation into their own context and made sense of it in ways that confused management. The notion of the rationally developed and executed plan as the core device of change and innovation began to be questioned, which ultimately challenged notions of predictability and control.

More recently, managers and theorists have started to recognize that the driving force behind innovation is not always the same. Whereas in the past, changes in the environment have been viewed as responsible for change and innovation, lately two considerations have been highlighted: the roles of different stakeholders, especially customers; and the fact that innovation does not happen in a vacuum. An infrastructure is required to provide a platform for innovation to grow. There are many levels to this infrastructure, including scientific knowledge, institutional norms, competent human resources, curious financial investors, educated consumers, and stable legal, political, and economic cornerstones. These parameters of innovation can only be controlled by an organization to a limited extent because most of them are out of an organization's reach. Think of the example of Henry Ford above. Or think of a biotechnology company that experiments with genetically modified food. It not only needs highly trained staff from universities but also relies heavily on public opinion and the favourable resolution of legal and ethical issues that dominate the debate. None of these are implicit in the science or the organization of innovation, yet they are fundamental to its potential success.

Some writers see innovation as very specifically a matter of science and R&D, whereas others view it as part of a broader picture. Nelson and Rosenberg (1993) suggest restricting the concept of innovation solely to new knowledge or new combinations of existing knowledge of technical innovations as measured outputs. Others suggest inclusion of organizational, institutional, and social innovation (see Edquist, 2000). This chapter follows the broader conception of innovation as a social process.

Planned change

Recall the concept of rational management, which we encountered in Chapter 1. As we shall see in Chapter 12, Taylor argued for a complete rational reorganization of the entire shop-floor base of the enterprise. Taylor's change initiatives were built upon two principles that have been remarkably resilient: (a) that change is accomplished through rational plans developed, implemented, and monitored by management; and (b) that these change programmes are put in place to minimize future changes. Put simply, the promise is that if you adapt change ideas (from scientific management, for instance) and change your organization accordingly, you will never need to change again. This approach views change as something that is unfortunately necessary; change is undesirable because it is an interruption to the natural state of organizations, which is a stable equilibrium. The expectation is that stability will be interrupted by short periods of change, forced upon an organization either by technological progress or by new organizational processes. In any case, the environment induces change externally, and the organization has to adapt as quickly as possible to achieve equilibrium again. Business as usual is the ideal, with everything else being a disturbance.

WHAT DO YOU MEAN?

Unfreezing, moving, refreezing

Kurt Lewin packaged this philosophy of change theoretically. In his model of change (Lewin, 1951), he identified three steps that are involved in changing organizations and people: first, you have to unfreeze the current state of affairs; second, you move things to where you want them to be; third, after you have succeeded, you refreeze again. This simple chain of unfreeze, move, refreeze became the template for most change programmes. Some differ in terms of how many steps they assign to each phase, but few question the underlying rationale and logic of Lewin's model (see Cummings, 2002: 265).

A typical example of a rational approach to change is business process re-engineering (BPR), which was developed, disseminated, and successfully marketed by Hammer and Champy (1993). BPR encompasses a radical rethinking and redesigning of core organizational activities to achieve higher efficiency and performance. It is based on two simple assumptions. First, BPR analyses organizational activities step by step so it can develop suggestions for improvements (such as time saving, cost cutting, and so on) on a micro level and reassemble the whole process in the most efficient way. Second, it redesigns the entire organization in accordance with these findings without paying attention to its past history or its cultural and social context.

If you think this sounds a lot like an overly rationalist approach to management, you would be correct. Even the name gives it away as an engineering rationality. However, the engineering is not very robust – roughly 70 per cent of the change initiatives made as BPR fail, which explains why BPR has been less successful in colonizing the change market than its proponents had hoped.

Theories of processual change

Most contemporary approaches to the analysis of organizational change reject Lewin's type of approach. The root metaphor of unfreezing/freezing is profoundly problematic because organizations are always in motion; they never respond solely to singular design imperatives but usually emerge from many pressures and directions, even though management change agents may be able to exercise a steering capacity (Buchanan and Badham, 1999).

The processual perspective emerged from the work of a number of writers, but there is no doubt that it was Pettigrew who had the single greatest impact. His magnum opus, *Awakening Giant: Continuity and Change in ICI* (1985), was a careful case study that challenged many of the dominant assumptions about how organizations change. The plans of change agents equipped with formal schemas were not reflected in what actually occurred. Instead, change appeared to be both incremental and evolutionary, as well as being punctuated by revolutionary and radically discontinuous periods. He saw 'change and continuity, process and structure' as 'inextricably linked' (Pettigrew, 1985: 24). Rather than stages of change being observed, processes could be seen changing in patterns produced by the interplay between the contextual variables of history, culture, and political processes (Pettigrew, 1990).

ICI (Imperial Chemical Industries) went through a crisis in its traditional way of organizing. It made the decision to change its organization structure and processes. A large organization such as ICI often initiates major programmes of change, but there are also changes introduced by snipers and ambushes as well as those that are planned; symbols are used to advance change as much as to retard it, and rumours about boardroom manoeuverings and executive succession, in both the organization and the wider business community, are rife. Organizational change is not unlike a long and contested campaign in which successfully positioning and maintaining the dominant myths and symbols is of vital importance. And it is the task of leadership to achieve such positioning (see also Chapter 4). In doing so, as Buchanan and Badham (1999: 231) remind us, management is a contact sport, one in which 'if you don't want to get bruised, don't play'. In the game of organizational change, it is directed and strategic change that retains the central focus, so there is little room for gifted amateurs, although many participants may well try to press sectional or local advantages in the opportunities that widespread change presents.

Taking Pettigrew (1997) as our cue, what does the process perspective require for a theory of organizational change? It has a strong emphasis on process and temporality rather than seeing change as a sequence of linear events that occur and are then frozen. This implies that anyone seeking to change organizations must exhibit mastery of power and politics (See Figure 10.1). Managers usually seek to manage as if organizations were rational, even when

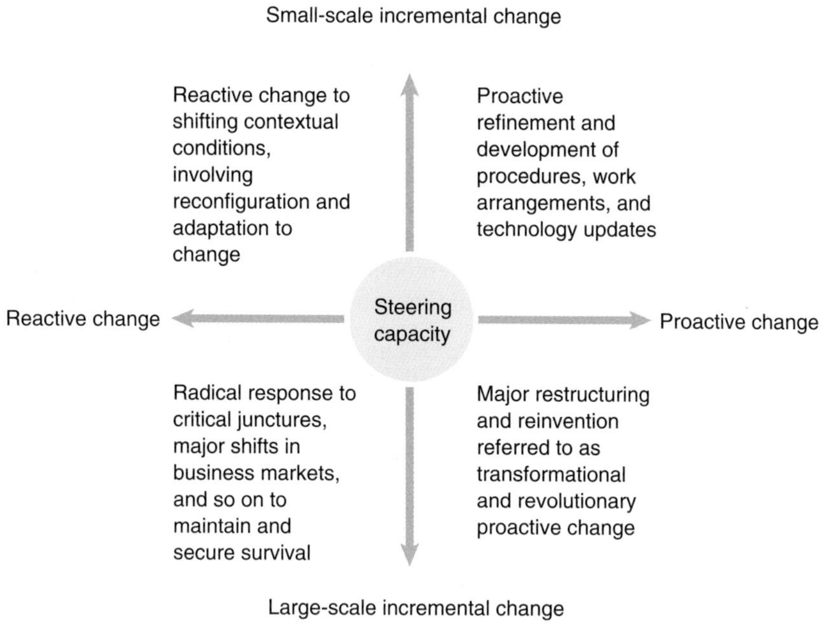

Small-scale incremental change

FIGURE 10.1
The capston steering
change model (adapted
from Dawson, 2003: 23)

Reactive change to shifting contextual conditions, involving reconfiguration and adaptation to change

Proactive refinement and development of procedures, work arrangements, and technology updates

Reactive change ← **Steering capacity** → Proactive change

Radical response to critical junctures, major shifts in business markets, and so on to maintain and secure survival

Major restructuring and reinvention referred to as transformational and revolutionary proactive change

Large-scale incremental change

rationality is a mere facade or veneer for mobilizing resources, allies, and opponents in a political struggle for change. More often than not, organizations feature messy and ambiguous problems that stop short of drifting into chaos.

Innovation and change at the edge of chaos

Current approaches to innovation do not put very much emphasis on rational planning. Instead, they stress the politics of innovation and the balance that is necessary between freedom and the responsibility required for autonomous and disciplined creativity. Change cannot be prescribed through one-best-way or prescriptive practices but instead there are many different ways of achieving innovative outcomes. In fact, innovation sometimes happens while management is busy making other plans.

Chaos   Some writers suggest that, rather than planning and order being the normal conditions for organizations, management needs to become accustomed to **chaos**.

Innovation challenges established management practices and beliefs, especially planning and controlling functions. Pascale (1999) introduced four new principles derived from complexity theory that can frame the innovation process differently:

- *Equilibrium equals death*: Remember when you first learned to ride a bike? The idea that those narrow wheels could stay balanced might have struck you as crazy until you learned that, when riding a bicycle, you can stay balanced only when you move. Organizations are not that

Check out the Companion Website www.sagepub.co.uk/ managingandorganizations3 for free access to two papers by E. Schein (2006) and by I. Stensaker and J. Falkenberg (2007) that will help you dive deeper into processual theories of change.

Chaos is a Greek word that is in opposition to cosmos (an orderly and harmonious system). Normally chaos is related to the unpredictability of a system.

different; as long as they move, they gain stability, but after they cease to move, they do not retain their balance, and being an unbalanced organization in the fast-moving corporate world (like being an unsteady bicycle rider steering through fast-moving traffic) is a recipe for death. Innovation and creative breakthroughs push an organization away from equilibrium and increase the necessary variety it has to deal with. As Tim Mannon, the president of Hewlett-Packard's (HP) Printer Division, said, 'The biggest single threat to our business today is staying with a previously successful business model one year too long' (quoted in Pascale, 1999: 90). Hence stability can be dangerous.

Self-organization is important: Organizations are capable of organizing themselves according to internally evolving principles. In managing complex unforeseeable tasks or events such as disasters, people organize themselves, and an order evolves that is not imposed by a mastermind. Instead of acting according to a purposefully designed plan, people interact spontaneously, and patterns of collaboration emerge. A good example is a soccer game: there is no hierarchal relationship between individual players, rather they are self-organized around the attractor of the ball, and bound by the rules of the game. From the perspective of the innovation process, this means that management should give up fantasies of control and rather focus on supporting self-organizing powers of a system.

Complex tasks need more complex problem-solving processes: To maintain a complex system, many apparently chaotic and unstable processes work together. Think of a high-wire performer for whom many small, ostensibly chaotic movements maintain balance on the high wire. The same goes for innovation; lots of trial and error steps may finally come into balance and lead to successful innovation. During the initial process of innovation, a chaotic patchwork of actions and outcomes seems to prevail, whereas in the final stages, more orderly patterns emerge. We know what sense we make only after we have made it. As Weick (1995) says, all sensemaking – even that projected into the future – has a retrospective quality about it. The fact that we did not achieve a certain plan by the due date turns into a great step in the innovation process because it helped us realize that we were doing the wrong thing, going in a foolish direction. Without some foolishness, we would never find our way to what we can later determine is wisdom. All the mistakes on the way can be represented retrospectively as learning that will eventually be rewarded in the final successful innovation outcome (see also Chapter 9).

Complex organizations can only be disturbed, not directed: Small causes might have huge effects, and vice versa. In a complex organizational environment, changing one pattern might transform the entire company. In innovation processes, calculations about invested resources and predicted outcome are meaningless because what innovation will produce may simply not be calculable. Think of ideas that were truly new, such as the telephone, the Internet, or simple things such as Post-it notes; their potential for changing organizational practices and consumer behaviour could not be forecast simply because no one could imagine the impact they would make on everyday life. Thus, all that can be done is to make sure that the system does not come too close to equilibrium and that it keeps on moving, experiencing new ideas as opportunities and not as threats.

The way these four principles conceptualize innovation and change is radically different from the rational approach outlined previously in this chapter. They take into account the limited capacity of management to order and to prescribe, and argue for a more complex, chaotic, and emergent understanding of the process of innovation. Innovation that is supposed to lead to truly new outcomes and change cannot be detailed, prescriptively, in advance. The future is uncertain and the end is always near, shifting in and out of our grasp.

The changing innovation agenda

In 1983 the Minnesota Innovation Research Program started a longitudinal study of service, product, technology, and programme innovation. The goal of the programme, which was conducted by more than 14 teams, was to analyse the processes of innovation, from concept development to implementation. This huge research effort resulted in the book *The Innovation Journey* by Van de Ven et al. (1999). It describes the journey from an initial idea to its development and realization. What the authors

IMAGE 10.1 The London Eye (or Millennium Wheel) – an innovation that succeeded!

found, however, did not confirm mainstream opinion that innovation is a stage-wise, linear, clear-cut process of trial and error learning that unfolds in a stable environment. Rather, innovation is a more complex adventure that is inherently uncertain and far from equilibrium. At the same time, they were critical of conceptions of innovation that see it as a random process or as merely an accidental event that is fundamentally unplanned, unpredictable, and unmanageable. Such an approach, they suggest, implies that you should somehow 'turn the organization off to invent and develop innovations, and turn it on to implement and diffuse innovations when they emerge' (Van de Ven et al., 1999: 5). Such a view leaves no option for managing innovation; instead, it suggests that 'innovation management' is an oxymoron and that innovation happens not because, but in spite, of management. Take the London Eye – it was only supposed to be a temporary exhibit but proved so successful it became permanent.

MANAGING CHANGE AND INNOVATION

Peter Drucker defines innovation as the 'specific tool of entrepreneurs, the means by which they exploit change as an opportunity for a different business or service. It is capable of being presented, as a discipline, capable of being learned, capable of being practiced' (Drucker, quoted in Tidd et al., 2001: 38). Innovation is an entrepreneurial tool; it should be exploited, and it is a discipline that can be learned and practised, in other words. Although this is a nice easy definition it misses a few important things:

- The probability of resistance.
- The likelihood of organizational politics shaping the unfolding innovation process as much as any rational plan.
- That innovation will always be a blend of rational planning and anticipation, and unanticipated as well as predictable political actions.

Managing the politics of change and innovation

Innovation changes organizational power relations: 'Accomplishing innovation and change in organizations requires more than the ability to solve technical or analytical problems. Innovation almost invariably threatens the status quo, and consequently, innovation is an inherently political activity' (Pfeffer, 1992: 7).

Innovation is inherently political. As Van de Ven and his colleagues (1999: 65) found, 'managers cannot control innovation success, only its odds. This principle implies that a fundamental change is needed in the control philosophy of conventional management practices'. At its core, innovation is a journey into the unknown and thus is inherently unpredictable and uncontrollable. Most change initiatives fail (recall those BPR programmes with a failure rate of more than two-thirds) not because the ideas or concepts were not refined or smart enough, but because the actual implementation was not understood and executed perfectly – which it never will be.

QUESTION TIME

Changing

Hirschhorn (2002) discusses in the *Harvard Business Review* the idea that change can be conceptualized as consisting of three different, though closely interlinked, initiatives. First, there will be a political campaign, which should create strong and lasting support for the desired change (see also Chapter 7). A second initiative will be a communication campaign, ensuring that all major stakeholders understand and share the idea of change and are committed to the principles and consequences behind it (see also Chapter 8). Finally, there will be a rationally planned campaign that makes sure that the human and material resources necessary for a successful change are available. Without paying

attention to these political implications, innovative ideas cannot be turned into actionable and tangible outcomes.

* Can you think of any campaign that has been oriented to you as a consumer, whether from government, business, or an NGO, that follows this three-stage model? Jot down your thoughts on it below and share them with others in your study group.

_____

_____

_____

_____

_____

Hirschhorn's focus is intraorganizational, which makes sense managerially because the organizational arena is the one most subject to managerial control. However, innovation is not something that occurs just within the firm, because the firm itself is embedded within a broader innovation system.

Recent studies of innovation demonstrate the interdependence of economic, political, social, and cultural factors. Some of these factors are external to the organizations involved, as a part of the broad institutional setting, whereas others are internal, such as those that Hirschhorn focuses on. The relative degree of success enjoyed by organizations and networks of organizations in nations and regions in the global knowledge-based economy depends on the effective management of these factors. Therefore, there is a need to understand better the complex interdependencies between internal firm dynamics around the innovation process and the broader institutional settings in which the firms operate.

Institutional settings have been identified in terms of local contexts that interact with the system of innovation – including networks of organizations in the public and private sectors – to initiate, import, modify, and diffuse new technologies. The concept of the system of innovation shifts the focus from an isolated firm so that it may be seen as part of a network of organizations embedded within specific contexts. The type of context may not only be identified at a regional or a local level but also include deliberately constructed virtual networks that seek to eclipse contextual specificity.

WHAT DO YOU MEAN?

Social innovation

Innovation is not contained within the boundaries of the corporate world. The great challenges of our time – such as climate change, radicalization of cultural identities, poverty, an aging population, and rapidly rising health care costs – need innovative answers if we want to solve them. But who could work on holistic, complex solutions for large-scale challenges? Governments and the public sector in general seem to be too thinly resourced and organized too much in silos to tackle these challenges. On the other hand, corporations, the drivers of much of innovation in the past two centuries, seem to be more concerned with ensuring the survival of their existing business models and annual (if not quarterly) returns for their shareholders. Neither markets nor government planning provides a satisfying answer. How, then, can we tackle the big challenges of our time? Who will be the innovators to solve these problems?

The answer that is mentioned in the corridors of power and community movements alike is: social innovation. Robin Murray, Julie Caulier-Grice, and Geoff Mulgan define social innovation in *The Open Book of Social Innovation* 'as new ideas (products, services and models) that simultaneously meet social needs and create new social relationships or collaborations. In other words, they are innovations that are both good for society *and* enhance society's capacity to act' (Murray et al., 2010: 3). A good example for social innovation is micro-finance: in poor regions development is often stifled through the lack of access to finance. In these regions, a small amount of money could go a long way. For big banks it is not an attractive business though: they prefer customers with big incomes who use their credit cards and pay back their mortgage on time. The Grameen Bank Project founded by Muhammad Yunus, who was awarded the Nobel Peace Prize in 2006, is a good example of micro-finance. For more details see the good overview at http://en.wikipedia.org/wiki/Grameen_Bank.

Two emerging forces shape social innovation: first, technology as enabler of social networking where people share ideas and solutions. Second, a growing concern with what Robin Murray, Julie Caulier-Grice, and Geoff Mulgan call the human dimension, which becomes more important than systems and structures. How does social innovation work? Murray and his colleagues have devised a six-step process:

1 *Prompts, inspirations, and diagnoses*: Every new idea starts with the perception of a problem or a crisis. In the first stage of social innovation, the problem is experienced, framed, and turned into a question that tackles the root of the problem.
2 *Proposals and ideas generation*: Initial ideas are developed and proposal discussed. Importantly a wide range of ideas is taken into account.

3 *Prototyping and pilots*: Talk is cheap – so ideas need to be tested in practice. Trial and error, prototyping, and testing are means of refining ideas that cannot be substituted by armchair research. The motto is: fail often, learn quickly!

4 *Sustaining*: This step includes the development of structures and sustainable income streams to ensure that the best ideas have a useful vehicle to travel. Resources, networks, and practices need to be organized so that innovation can be carried forward.

5 *Scaling and diffusion*: Good ideas have to spread – hence the scaling up of solutions is key. This can happen formally, through franchising or licensing, or more informally, through inspiration and imitation.

6 *Systemic change*: The ultimate goal of social innovation. This involves change on a big scale driven by social movements, fuelled by new business models, structured by new organizational forms, and regulated by new public institutions and laws.

Innovating through significant stakeholders

There are many driving forces and many stakeholders behind innovation. In the last decade or so, managers and theorists started to recognize that the driving force behind innovation is not always the same. Whereas in the past, changes in the environment have been held responsible for innovation, more recently, the roles of different stakeholders, especially customers, have been highlighted.

Check out the Companion Website www.sagepub.co.uk/ managingandorganizations3 for free access to an excellent article by M. Lounsbury and E. T. Crumley (2007) on institutional forces and innovative practices.

Market–technology linkages

The process of bringing innovation from conception through design and implementation is referred to as **market–technology linking** (Burgelman, 1983). Innovative Japanese organizations have been recognized for completing this process particularly well (Kono and Clegg, 1998; 2001).

Various techniques have been used for innovation success. These include cultivating 'lead users' (Von Hippel, 1986) who work with professionals to create innovative product features. Another approach is to design multifunctional project teams. These can overcome tensions that arise because technology and market knowledge are separate areas in the organization, rarely communicating with each other. Incorporating competencies that are not necessarily a part of the innovation team (e.g. external lead users, such as in the case of the LEGO example from the Mini Case below) can create a potential tension between *control* and *innovation*. Many complex organizations concentrate best on what they can control through routines and standard operating procedures. However, concentration on control minimizes learning from innovation by filtering out new information, reinforcing past routines, and focusing on foreseeable and manageable issues. It also tends to reinforce existing circuits of power within the firm, based on existing resource control (Clegg, 1989; Pfeffer and Salancik, 1978), thus reinforcing conventional sensemaking (Weick, 1995). Innovation may require organizations to rethink their business in ways that operational controls do not easily allow (Workman, 1993). LEGO provides a good example.

Market–technology linking involves integrating the firm's unique competencies with customer needs, market structure, and technologies, together with its manufacturing, sales, and distribution capabilities.

MINI CASE

Co-creation through lead users: innovation at LEGO (Antorini, 2007; Kornberger, 2010)

In 1998, LEGO released a new product, called LEGO Mindstorm. At the heart of it was a yellow micro-chip that made all sorts of movements and behaviours possible. The product became an instant hit – within three months 80,000 sets had changed hands. There was just one small problem: the buyers were not children, but adults. And that was despite the fact that LEGO marketed the product to children, not adults. Worse, these adults did not consume the product as the LEGO Masterminds had anticipated. Within weeks, hackers from all over the world had cracked the code of the new toy and created all sorts of new applications: Mindstorm users built everything from soda machines to blackjack dealers. The new programs spread quickly over the Internet and were far more sophisticated than those LEGO had developed. More than 40 guidebooks advised how to get maximum fun out of your 727-part LEGO Mindstorm set. How did LEGO react? First, negatively: consumers were meant to consume, not produce their own versions. They were not meant to challenge LEGO's in-house product developers. Confusion set in. Inaction followed. Then, after a year, LEGO started to listen to those unruly users and attempted to understand what they were doing with the product and, more importantly, the LEGO brand.

After lengthy discussions, LEGO came to understand that the community around its products was doing something interesting, and that just because it was not included in the LEGO business strategy planning did not mean it was not important. First, LEGO learnt that the boisterous creators were actually not a homogenous group. While part of the LEGO community was into outer space, there was a second group who shared a love for trains and real-life modelling. The two groups could not be more different. The former was about fantasy, science fiction, humour, and free building; the latter was about real-world models, suburban life, no-nonsense and precisely scaled modelling. Despite these differences, they formed a community around the LEGO brand that shared a passion

for innovation. LEGO users produced physical and aesthetic add-ons such as batteries for cars and trains, or clothes for figures. Other users developed new play themes such as LEGO Harry Potter or LEGO Life on Mars, which explored new experiences for users. Finally, some LEGO fans developed new building techniques, such as new styles of buildings, models, or colour effects that can be achieved through the combination of existing bricks. Of course community members toying around with ideas do not develop automatically marketable new products. Most of their new ideas were incremental improvements that left basic product ideas unchallenged. But about 12 per cent of all user innovations represented more radical explorations of new functionalities and new experiences. These included strategy games with multiplayer features and role-play elements, such as BrickWars. Or mosaic building techniques: rather than copying existing images with LEGO bricks, an image is translated into pixels (LEGO bricks) and then assembled digitally. Software called PixeLego has been developed and distributed for free by users to translate images into LEGO Syntax. Another example is LDraw (www. ldraw.org), an open source software program that allows users to create virtual LEGO models and scenes; or www.brickfilms.com, where animators create short films using LEGO figures.

The moral of the story? The LEGO brand facilitates a new connectivity between consumers and producers, allowing them to interact and co-create. Be sure, LEGO isn't a singular example: Procter & Gamble's *Connect + Develop*, innovation-exchanges such as www.yet2.com, www.inno-centive.com or www.yourencore.com, and open source movements (think Linux or Wikipedia) allow global interaction between restless consumers, freelance researchers, retired scientists, inventive students, and large corporations.

• Imagine you are LEGO's chief innovation manager. What organizational challenges do you think could result from co-creative, open innovation? How does LEGO have to change in order to benefit from the changing rules of the game?

There is much we can learn from the LEGO case. As the LEGO example has shown, the brand community is a crucial part of the organization's innovation engine. Having an active and innovative user community helps LEGO keep an eye on trends for new products. Maybe more importantly, it helps to develop marketable product innovations. The long list of user-based innovations that have found their way onto the shelves include LEGO Studies, based on brickfilms.com; LEGO Factory, based on LDraw; LEGO Mosaic, based on PixeLego, and LEGO Vikings, based on a user-developed play theme. Traditionally, innovation is meant to occur deep inside organizations: product managers, R&D experts, and scientists represent the 'mind' of the firm in search for the next 'big thing'. Marketing provides sporadic feedback from (potential) customers through survey data, needs analyses, focus groups, and so on. Information from these groups is taken in-house, digested, analysed, and fed into the product development process. However, the flow of information is slow and distorted through noise in the channels. The interpretation of the data by product managers, R&D experts, and marketeers results in solutions that are at best approximations of what matters to the customer. These approximations are exacerbated by the limitations of the sources of feedback. For example, a focus group of consumers sitting in a room cannot adequately represent the lived experience of the product consumption. At best it is an approximation. Of course, in a relatively stable world, this trickle of information provided by traditional tools is, more often than not, enough to innovate. In more competitive environments – fragmented and rapidly evolving markets – co-creation offers an intensified communication mechanism between producers and consumers that fuels the innovation process. Co-creation upsets the established division of labour between organizations producing new ideas and passive consumers who are waiting to be spoon-fed with new products – a division that has become firmly entrenched as part of corporate culture. The brand plays a crucial role in the co-creation process: especially in the non-mediated medium of the Internet, where the brand offers the only recognizable interface that frames the conversation between producers and consumers.

The brand transformation also radically changes the sociocultural make-up of the organization. External communities that crystallize around the brand form a quasi-extension of internal cultures. In fact, culture cannot be confined within the bounds of the organization. The LEGO brand community co-constitutes the culture of LEGO through sharing of ideas and practices with employees. Empowered by new information and communication technology, users become actively engaged in previously internal organizational production processes. In other words, culture extends beyond the boundaries of the firm through those consumers who form brand communities and engage in creative, unruly, and co-producing practices. Creative consumption does not occur in a vacuum, though: rather, user communities crystallize around brands. These brand communities describe a new form of social organization, mediated by brands. Following more than a 100 years of mourning the decline of social organization, in everything from Tönnies' *Community and Civil Society* (2001) to David Riesman, Nathan Glazer and

Reuel Denney's *The Lonely Crowd* (2001 [1950]) brand communities provide a new form of social cohesion. The brand of LEGO is used by literally tens of thousands of people to express who they are and to relate to other like-minded individuals. This new form of social organization is far from leading towards a harmonious new society. Rather, the communities that form on- and offline are testimony to the tribalization of society. The defining characteristic of a tribe is its unique lifestyle; its defining currency is not formed from the pros and cons of rational discourse but from what's 'in' and what's 'out'. Being part of a tribe, individuals play roles and use brands as plots and props to stage convincing performances. But while the cohesion within a tribe is high, its tolerance to change is low. In fact, those tribes organized around brands might turn out to be particularly conservative and reactionary when the brand changes. At LEGO, the community thwarted innovation at various junctures. For instance, LEGO introduced a colour change of its bricks because it felt that new colours would be more appealing to children. However, the LEGO User Group sparked controversy about that: for collectors, new colours posed a challenge in regards to integration of new and old bricks. The corollary of this insight is that open does not automatically equal good, progressive, or democratic. Rather, co-creation redraws the fields of the chessboard, redefines the moves players can make, and the power they wield.

The control that organizations enjoy over production and distribution vanishes as users short cut these circuits of power and relate to each other more directly. Multiple authorship implies the loss of a single authority that is usually represented by management. The new distribution of authority puts a lot at stake – including an organization's deep-seated identity. At LEGO, the identity of the organization emerges out of the brand-facilitated conversation between external communities and employees. While a brand manager might project a certain organizational identity, the brand inevitably escapes management's control. A brand represents a socially constructed meaning system; yet meaning is an accomplishment that requires understanding, interpretation, and evaluation – all deeply subjective processes. Put simply, like beauty, a brand exists in the eye of the beholder. And there it is hard to control: the sensemaking processes of the reader (consumer) co-constitute, and sometimes override, the text of the author (brand manager). The challenges for management are formidable: managing identity in the context of co-creation requires an organization to develop high tolerance for ambiguity, uncertainty, and paradox. Brands provide the arena in which an organization's identity emerges out of the interactions between consumers and producers. A stable identity remains illusive: rather than searching for an enduring essence, organizations continuously oscillate between self-definition and definition by outsiders. The brand provides the space for this dialogue to unfold: it enables an organization to focus narcissistically on its uniqueness, and, at the same time, forces it to keep an eye on outsiders' visions. Rather than dreaming of a unified hierarchy, brands transform organization into a form of organized heresy: the search for differences becomes the core of their identity. The brand manifests itself as the interface where those different, competing, and contradictory narratives clash and are, temporarily, reconciled. Rather than being the sole author of an organization's identity, the brand manager becomes the editor of a polyphonic, sometimes even dissonant, narrative.

MINI CASE

Customer scenarios

So-called 'customer scenarios' (Seybold, 2001) map the needs of different customers and use them as input for new ideas. This approach harnesses both rational planned initiatives (technologically driven change) as well as creative and lateral thinking.

Let us look at how this actually works. Tesco, a UK-based supermarket chain with £39 billion of revenue yearly, decided to let its customers do the innovative thinking when the company started Tesco Direct in 2001 as an online shopping window. Most Internet grocers assumed that online shopping would attract customers because it would be a way for customers to save time because they could avoid being physically present in the supermarket. However, these grocers failed in their venture. Tesco Direct listened to its customers and found out that they actually loved shopping in stores, seeing new and fresh products. In other words, shopping was not a chore that they wanted to avoid. Tesco Direct also found out that, when customers purchased online to save time, they wanted to do so from the grocery stores where they usually shopped rather than from some remote location they did not know. Thus, Tesco Direct changed its online service and came up with an innovative system that made both Tesco Direct successful and the customers happy. Customers shop online from their own store, the one with which they are familiar, where they have confidence in the fresh quality of the produce.

Tesco Direct then changed its organization to centre on this innovative concept and came up with a whole set of new practices. The in-store order pickers employed by Tesco for the Internet shoppers have special shopping carts with online displays. The display shows them their route through the supermarket, including data on peak traffic areas (such as the fresh bread section between 8.30 a.m. and 9 a.m.). As the order picker walks down the aisle, the display tells them which product to pick. After it is dropped into the shopping cart, it is automatically scanned. If a product is not available, the display suggests a similar product, which was recently bought by the specific customer whose order is being met.

Listening to and observing the customers closely and imagining how technology could deliver what they wanted triggered these innovative concepts. Changing routines and practices then refined these concepts. The system now has 750,000 customers who place 20,000 weekly orders online, generating profits of more than £6.2 million. Tesco learnt from its customers.

- What could the educational institution that you are enrolled in learn from the students as its customers? Conduct a small survey of customer satisfaction among your friends.

It pays to empower your customers so that they can do the innovative thinking for you because they might know what they want, and what they do not want, better than do experts in a remote lab. But there is more to be learned from the LEGO and Tesco Direct cases (see above). Innovation and change are just one side of the same coin, and creativity is closely linked to often technology-facilitated interaction. The source of creativity and innovative concepts is not captured within the company but found in the community.

Innovating through employees Of course, innovation does proceed only from the outside in; often, creative companies employ creative people to come up with new ideas. However, the practices needed to manage creative staff differ fundamentally from traditional management practices. Chris Bangle, global chief of design for BMW in Munich, manages creative staff; his job is to mediate between financial and technological constraints and innovative and creative design ideas. Thus, he has to balance creativity and the commercial side of BMW. In his view it is the leadership's tasks to foster innovation and simultaneously achieve commercial goals (Bangle, 2001). Simply, because innovators are usually not accountants, the logic of commerce often sounds odd to them. On the other hand, finance departments often understand the latest innovation as a fancy of the design team and regard it as a cost rather than an investment in a valuable asset. Bangle decided to protect his creative resources and make sure that they could work without being interrupted by people who did not understand what they were doing. In this way, innovative products could emerge – regardless of whether they were financially feasible or not. At BMW, Bangle sent his design team away from its normal work environment so that it could develop its ideas without being interrupted by criticism: 'To make certain that no one could possibly trample on the seeds they were planting, I instructed the group to keep their whereabouts a secret – even from me' (Bangle, 2001: 50). In such safe spaces, away from business-as-usual constraints, creativity and innovation are born.

Similar to the findings of Van de Ven and his colleagues (1999), Bangle views the type of innovation process a company uses as a crucial component in its success. Shifting the focus from design (innovation) to engineering (implementation) too quickly kills creativity. Therefore, designers must have the space and the time to play around with ideas and act outside the usual constraints. By protecting the process of innovation, managers are kept from overstepping creative boundaries. To make sure that creative people do not fool around forever, deadlines are imposed to ensure that playfulness and exploration find an end rather than becoming an end. These deadlines also assure managers and engineers that these processes, which to them may appear to be uncontrollable, will result in tangible outcomes.

Managing innovation requires extraordinary communication skills (see also Chapter 8). The various groups must understand each other's language: innovators must understand corporate requirements, budgets, and deadlines, whereas managers must let go and trust in the people involved in a process with unknown output. The art of managing innovation is to bridge this gap and create a mutual understanding. As Bangle (2001) concludes, business and creativity are not the same, but they can be directed towards the same ends. Think of the glue that created the Post-it notes that the guy at 3M developed against the orders of his boss. His boss could not see the value in this tool because he could not relate to it at all. The same point applied to the chairman of IBM when he claimed in the 1950s that there was a world market for only about five mainframe computers. Again, he simply did not understand the new concept because he could not relate to it. Or think of groundbreaking artists; how many of them had the same fate as Van Gogh, who died poor and lonely, because everybody thought his art was nothing but madness? Years later, we know better. Innovation means taking risks – and sometimes the risks may be very obvious and the destination unclear.

Innovation is much more demanding than is routine. Routine can be managed mechanistically, whereas innovation needs to be managed organically. Mechanisms require only routine action (Burns and Stalker, 1961). Organic structures require members not only to enact innovation but also to make sense of the plurality of organization and network members that may be involved in many indeterminate aspects of innovation. Organicism implies commitment of psychic energy and attention. It embodies the tension between responsibility and freedom. In innovation, people have to be free to follow the lead of the TV series *Star Trek*, going boldly where no one has gone before, but they also have to be organizationally responsible in terms of timelines, budgets, and goals. Organizations tend to be much better at framing these responsibilities than they are at empowering creativity. Organizations must manage the tension between freedom and responsibility to balance commitment with accountability.

Innovating through collaborators   Collaboration between organizations is usually temporary but often produces long-lasting relationships. Collaboration has intended purposes but its emergent benefits may be more important. Collaborations are dialectical systems, and their stability is determined by balancing multiple tensions within systems of accountability (Das and Teng, 2000). Certain large-scale, complex, project-based tasks are rarely completed by a single organization; instead, they involve many project partners, each of which brings specialized skills and competencies to the task at hand, such as constructing a tunnel.

The global economy is marked by the increasing importance of knowledge and creativity, which, paradoxically, places a premium on innovation facilitated by proximity. Although the modern economy is global, it is also resolutely regional; Silicon Valley is the best example. Innovative capabilities are frequently sustained through sharing of a common knowledge base, interaction through common institutions, and proximal location. Local, socially embedded institutions play an important role in supporting innovation (Leonard and Sensiper, 1998). Organizations that are able to relate to one another in a proximate geographical or regional space seem better able to collaborate.

Collaborations link people and knowledge, simultaneously tying them to multiple external contacts. Knowledge circulates through internal and external networks at various levels. Achieving sustainable competitive advantage means being faster and better at innovation, which often comes down to being better connected and having more effective collaborations. Swann et al. (1999) suggest that what is important is how networks interact with knowledge: what knowledge, who has it, and how it can be accessed. National and regional institutions – such as universities and research centres, as well as firms, government policies, and programmes – frame regional innovation capabilities (Bartholomew, 1998; Dodgson, 2000: 25–26) because they define the availability and quality of the *what*, *who*, and *how* of innovation and its knowledge networks.

WHAT'S THE POINT?

Innovation is a risky business – but so is failure to innovate!

Failure is the norm for approximately 50 per cent of innovation projects, according to research by Cozijnsen et al. (2000). Hence, feedback on failure is essential to achieve successful innovation because it revises present understandings and shifts stakeholder projections. Innovation is highly complex, uncertain, and creative, thus regular feedback is essential (Romme, 2002). Indeed, the success of feedback processes may be related to the frequent failure of the projects being managed (Morin, 1984).

If innovation is risky, not innovating is even riskier!

Mapping innovation

Although innovation challenges management's urge for planning and controlling, it is not a purely random process. Van de Ven et al. (1999) delineated a road map to innovation that encompasses major steps on your way towards the new. It provides a rough outline of the complex, ambiguous, and dynamic terrain from where discovery and creation emerge. According to Van de Ven et al., the innovation journey can be differentiated in three main periods: initiation, development, and implementation. These periods are covered in the following subsections.

The initiation period   Innovations usually involve a gestation period of several years in which apparently coincidental events happen that, looking back, set the stage for innovation. This period levels the playing field for innovation to emerge. Then, internal or external shocks (such as a new manager, a loss in market share, and so on) trigger concentrated efforts to initiate innovation. These shocks lead to a concentration of attention from diverse stakeholders. Plans are developed to gain resources internally and to create legitimacy externally. However, these plans are marketing tools more than project descriptions.

The development period   As soon as development begins, the initial idea splits up into multiple ideas that proceed in different directions. Because it is unclear which path will be paved with gold and glamour, innovators have to explore many of them only to discover that they were not glittering highways. Innovations also depend on other innovations – think of innovations in the mobile phone industry that are highly dependent on developments in other fields. In this stage, setbacks and mistakes are common as unexpected changes erode the basic assumption the innovation was built on. Also, criteria to assess the achievements of the project differ between resource controllers and innovation managers. People who are committed to the idea tend to see progress and new opportunities where external agents see only hesitation and dead ends. Moreover, staff changes frequently occur in the development period. Motivation and euphoria are often high at the beginning, whereas setbacks and mistakes breed more and more frustration and closure towards the end of the innovation journey.

Top managers and powerful key stakeholders (such as investors) act in contrasting ways and serve as checks and balances on each other. It is at this stage that network building with other organizations is necessary, and top management should be involved in this process to gain political support, which can sometimes lead to unintended consequences. A partner today may well be a competitor tomorrow. Close partnerships may lead to groupthink (see also pp. 99; 306). In addition, drivers of the innovation project are often engaged with external stakeholders (such as competitors, state authorities, and so on) to generate an infrastructure that supports (rather than undermines) their innovation, creating the paradoxical danger of simultaneous cooperation and competition.

To innovate means to build multifunctional communities of practice (Wenger, 2002), where the disparate views of various and often incoherent disciplinary knowledge can be integrated and the politics managed (see also Chapter 6). In addition, project responsibility has to be maintained in terms of emergent criteria that allow for both exploratory and exploitative learning. Techniques such as phase reviews and budgetary accountability help achieve project milestones that assist exploitative learning. *Exploratory learning* involves a critical tension between strategic emergence and strategic determination because top-down plans do not easily allow new opportunities for learning to emerge. Bottom-up emergence does not easily allow innovation to be integrated and incrementally cumulated.

Research shows that project teams sometimes punctuate projects through a mid-term transition in which progress is reviewed and a new sense of urgency and a new agenda created. This finding suggests that surprise and interruption are devices that can be used to raise levels of arousal or tension (Gersick, 1988; 1989; 1994). A consciously generated sense of crisis can interrupt inertia (Kim, 1998). The alternation between inertia and crisis can be seen as a means for a system to remain in a state of continuous change, neither settling into equilibrium (equating with low tension or emotional closure) nor falling into chaos (equating with high tension, Brown and Eisenhardt, 1997). Management evaluation requires great subtlety if it is to capture these elements of the innovation process.

The implementation period The implementation and adoption of the innovation are achieved by integrating the new with that which is old, established, and already known, fostering a fit within a local context and situation. Politically, the radically new and different will probably not be embraced by everybody because people have committed time and emotions to the status quo. Evolution and integration, not revolution and transformation, seem to be the keys to success.

Finally, innovations reach the end of their organizational careers – they are either released or dumped as top management and investors assess whether the innovation was a failure or a success. However, the criteria against which management assesses the innovation are often inappropriately loaded in terms of short-term financial indicators. Thus, it is important to focus on monitoring and evaluating the innovation process. This process challenges usual management evaluation, which rarely incorporates all the organizational competencies that successful appraisal of innovation would require. Management generally involves abstract and generalized calculations. With such calculations, it is difficult to capture novelty and uniqueness. Standard budgets, deadlines, and reporting protocols can all sabotage innovative efforts. Members can be transferred or let go, and crucial tacit learning can be lost from the innovation process. Formalization can be demanded and the critical detail missed. Managing innovation successfully means that organizations must manage the tension between determination and emergence to link innovation with the firm's resources and strategy.

Being innovative or producing innovations is not automatically useful or profitable. Rather, usefulness can be assessed only at the end of the innovation journey, and what the destination seems to be is always subject to redefinition and renegotiation as the journey unfolds because during the journey the criteria of judgement change.

Leading the innovation journey   Managing innovations requires leadership skills and involvement from the top of an organization. Van de Ven et al. (1999) established that many managers are usually involved in innovation processes, shifting among four roles: sponsors, mentors, critics, and leaders. Each understands and acts from different perspectives, providing a checks-and-balances function. Their decision-making is influenced by the pragmatics of innovation more than by long-term strategic orientations. For simple and trivial tasks, a hierarchical power and leadership structure might be appropriate, but for the complex and ambiguous innovation journey, it would be highly inappropriate: 'Directing the innovation journey calls for a pluralistic power structure of leadership that incorporates the requisite variety of diverse perspectives necessary to make uncertain and ambiguous innovation decisions' (Van de Ven et al., 1999: 15). Thus, leadership in innovation processes differs from business-as-usual management tasks. Given the ambiguous nature of the innovation journey, we should recognize that it is highly unlikely that the innovation process will be smooth, rationally unfolding, and bereft of politics and contestation. On the contrary, the production of consensus and a single strategic intent unifying the heterogeneous opportunities of innovation would seem to be rather more a part of the problem than the solution.

CREATIVITY, FOOLISHNESS, AND MANAGEMENT FASHION

The innovator's dilemma

In his influential book, Clayton M. Christensen analysed why successful organizations (such as Apple, IBM, and Xerox) sometimes fail when they face change and innovation. Describing this failure as the *innovator's dilemma*, his provocative thesis is that not poor but good management is the reason:

> Precisely *because* these firms listened to their customers, invested aggressively in new technologies that would provide their customers more and better products of the sort they wanted, and because they carefully studied market trends and systematically allocated investment capital to innovations that promised the best returns, they lost their position of leadership. (Christensen, 1997: xii)

Check out the Companion Website www.sagepub.co.uk/ managingandorganizations3 for free access to a very interesting and general paper by T. R. Schatzki (2006) on organizational practices.

Christensen regards good management as the reason for failure, which he explains in the following way. Disruptive technologies are the key to innovation. However, most technologies are *sustaining technologies*, meaning that they improve the performance of existing products rather than replace them. Disruptive technologies, on the other hand, result in worse product performance (at least in the short term) for existing products. Compared with established products, new disruptive technologies often perform at a lower level of perfection. For instance, top-end decks, tone arms, and immaculate quality vinyl beat early CDs hands down for tonal warmth and resonance, though CDs did not scratch as easily and were easier to use, played more music, and were portable. The CDs had characteristics valued by markets: they were smaller, and they were also easier and more convenient to use. Another example of disruptive technologies was the off-road motorbike manufactured by Honda and Kawasaki. Compared with sleek BMW and Harley Davidson machines, these models were primitive, though they could go places that the big bikes, with their smooth finish, could not. The desktop computer was a disruptive technology relative to the mainframe computers developed by IBM.

The problem for established companies is that they generally do not invest in disruptive technologies because they are simpler and cheaper and thus promise less profit, or they develop in fringe markets that are not important to big players. After the market is big enough to create serious profits, it may be too costly or too late to join. Often, the established firm's best customers do not want, and cannot use, the new, disruptive technologies, and the potential customers of the new technology are unknown. Proven marketing tools and planning skills do not necessarily work under these conditions.

MINI CASE

Search, organizing dissonance and entrepreneurship

When shipwrecked Robinson Crusoe walked on the beach he knew what was valuable and what not – and he knew instantly that he had to act when he saw those footprints in the sand. Unfortunately, our world is more complex. When do we have to act? What is valuable? How can we decipher those signs showing us as much of the future as they hide? Where should we search? And how should we organize search?

(Continued)

(Continued)

Search becomes a major challenge to navigate the world. A new economy is evolving around the central concept of the search engine, replacing the steam engine, the dynamo of the industrial revolution. In an information society, the capacity to produce is eclipsed by the ability to find, edit and connect information and new ideas.

The world of business is struggling with search. Typically, search is outsourced to the entrepreneur. In a Darwinian struggle, so the story goes, thousands of entrepreneurs worldwide explore niches and new ideas. Most fail. But some make it. Once they have made it, their search has come to an end. They stop exploring and switch to exploiting their ideas – until younger entrepreneurs make them obsolete and the process starts all over. Schumpeter (2006 [1942]) has termed this transformation creative destruction. IBM gave way to Microsoft, and Microsoft to Google, and Google to Facebook, and Facebook to Twitter, and so on. Each of those firms emerged out of entrepreneurial drive and acumen, grew into a formidable corporation, and lost sight of new ideas because it focused on exploiting its capital.

In his book *The Sense of Dissonance: Accounts of Worth in Economic Life* David Stark defines the entrepreneur as the person who is able to exploit uncertainty. Stark describes entrepreneurship as the ability to keep multiple principles of evaluation at play simultaneously and benefit from the friction between them. Rather than deciding what is valuable and what not, the entrepreneur keeps on collecting items with different (maybe even contradicting) values and defers judgement about their usefulness. In the words of Stark, 'entrepreneurship exploits the indeterminate situation by keeping open diverse performance criteria rather than by creating consensus about one set of rules.' (Stark, 2009: 16).

While it might be possible for an entrepreneur to chase several different ideas at the same time, organizations usually put a premium on efficiency and alignment. This results in a singular value system that drives the organization and enforces consensus. Remember that search requires the opposite mindset: if you search you have to be open-minded and look at each item you find from a different perspective – especially if you're not sure what you are looking for! Stark argues that organizations should actively seek different principles of evaluation, different regimes of what counts as valuable, and different mechanisms to determine what is potentially interesting and worthy for future exploration. Strategically speaking, the dilemma is obvious: in an organization that is perfectly well aligned with an environment that demands typewriters, the PC could only be perceived as negligible noise. After a long tradition of building big cars that would be filled with cheap petrol, GM, Chrysler, and Ford did not value small cars built by their Japanese competitors.

Stark's question is: how to marry organization and the entrepreneur? He refers to heterarchy as the organizational form that allows diverse principles of evaluation to flourish at the same time. While hierarchy reflects a heavenly order, heterarchy is a pattern or relations between elements that are in respect to power and authority equal. While hierarchy relies on a singular rationality informing the organization, heterarchy accepts that there are several bounded rationalities each of them having their own evaluation principles.

For Stark, heterarchy resembles organized dissonance. He argues that organizations with 'greater diversity in ways of doing things are more likely to have the capacity to adapt when the environment changes' (2009: 179). While dissonance might be something to be avoided, it might emerge as an organizational form that can cope best with the problem of search. Accepting polyphony (Kornberger et al., 2006) as the reality of organizational life, heterarchy is the form that allows for multiple entrepreneurial strategies that have their own evaluation principles.

- What are the potential problems of a heterarchical organization that embraces dissonance? How could you manage these potential problems?

Being foolish and creative   It should be clear by this point in the chapter that innovation and change cannot be entirely planned and will unfold in largely unpredictable and uncontrollable ways. These facts might be scary and challenging for the world of management, which is used to control (see also Chapter 12). As the senior vice president of research and development at 3M puts it:

> innovation … is anything but orderly … We are managing in chaos, and this is the right way to manage if you want innovation. It's been said that the competition never knows what we are going to come up with next. The fact is, neither do we. (Van de Ven et al., 1999: 181)

The statement of the 3M manager is echoed, and somehow anticipated, by James March, one of the most thought-provoking minds in the field of management and organization theory. In his playful paper, 'The technology of foolishness' (March, 1988), he criticizes two major building blocks of common-sense thinking that are both closely linked to the concept of rationality (see also pp. 460–464). First, he tackles the idea of pre-existing purposes that inform our actions generally and change initiatives especially, and, second, he questions the principle of consistency that should link our purposes, decisions, and actions so that they are aligned. March says that innovation happens not because of but despite these two principles; the problem is that goals are not given beforehand but are developed in context and are thus subject to change. He argues that sometimes we have to do things for which we have no good reasons to come up with a new objective.

Think of the team at Sony who came up with the idea of the Walkman. At the beginning, the Sony team did not have the image of a portable little music-playing gadget in their minds; rather, they bounced ideas around without having a clear purpose (du Gay et al., 1997). It was exactly this freedom, this lack of clear-cut objectives, which made it possible to come up with something innovative.

The call for consistent rational behaviour is counterintuitive when it comes to innovation. March (1988) juxtaposes playfulness with rationality and argues that playfulness unleashes creativity and innovation because it emphasizes improvisation, trial and error, and the general openness to try out new things. The urge for consistency would not allow us to act in different, maybe even contradictory, ways because this course of action seems to be irrational and hence undesired. As March argues, 'we need to find some ways of helping individuals and organizations to experiment with doing things *for which they have no good reason*, to be playful with the conception of themselves' (1988: 262, our emphasis). He delineates this as the technology of foolishness, an approach that 'might help … in a small way to develop the unusual combinations of attitudes and behaviors that describe the interesting people, interesting organizations, and interesting societies of the world' (1988: 265).

In summary, March (1988) suggests that a narrowly defined notion of rationality that is obsessed with order and control might be counterproductive when it comes to the question of innovation, change, and creativity. Rather, he suggests that a technology of foolishness that allows us to do playful things for which we have no good reasons might be more appropriate to explore new terrain. This technology of foolishness happened at 3M, where a chemist discovered the not overly sticky adhesive that formed the basis of the Post-it note. Playfully exploring where new ideas lead, without a purpose in mind, can lead to great outcomes; at 3M, management learned this lesson, and asks employees to devote 15 per cent of their time to working on things they fancy – a practice adopted by many innovative firms, including Google.

MINI CASE

The paradox of innovation and change

To paraphrase the Greek philosopher Plato (1968), innovation is a paradoxical concept: if things are really new and innovative, we would not understand them at all because they would embody a radical break with all we know. What we usually call new is not really new – it will resemble phenomena we are used to. Take a new car. Is it new because of its styling and engineering? Does it not resemble all the other cars so much that it is hardly justified to speak about innovation in this case? Thus, the paradox is that the new is either already known and established, but disguised in new clothes, or, if it is really new, it is unrecognizable and beyond the ken of our understanding.

The perfect example is the invention of the telephone. Alexander Bell presented his idea to senior managers at Western Union. They listened

patiently to him and, after a couple of days, Bell got a letter from them saying, 'after careful consideration of your invention, which is a very interesting novelty, we have come to the conclusion that it has no commercial possibilities ... we see no future for an electrical toy'.

Obviously, the guys at Western Union were not exactly right; within four years, there were more than 50,000 phones in the USA, and after 20 years, there were 5 million, and the patent became the single most valuable patent in history (see Tidd et al., 2001). Innovation requires the creativity of foolishness to stick with an idea beyond the stage where most people would dismiss it entirely.

- What are the contemporary equivalents to the phone as innovative ideas initially not understood? Can you think of any and what were the reasons for initial non-acceptance and ultimate acceptance?

How to kill creativity   It is hard to tell how one can actually nurture creativity, but it is quite clear how one can kill it quickly. We have compiled with the help of others' research a practical guide for managers who want to avoid innovation and creativity (Amabile, 1998; Kanter, 1984: 204; Morgan, 1989: 54; Ordiorne, 1981: 79). Think of it as ten easy steps for sustaining routines to the point that they will eventually destroy your organization:

1   Always pretend to know more than anybody around you. Especially be suspicious when people from below come up with ideas. You know better!
2   Police your employees by every procedural means that you can devise. Insist that they stick to the rules of good old bureaucracy and fill in many forms that need to be signed by almost every senior manager in the organization.

3 Run daily checks on the progress of everyone's work. Be critical (they love it!), and withhold positive feedback, which would only encourage them to do things that are potentially dangerous.

4 Make sure that creative people do a lot of technical and detailed work. Make sure that they do their own bookkeeping, and count everything you can count as often as possible.

5 Create boundaries between decision-makers, technical staff, and creative minds. Make sure that they speak different languages.

6 Never talk to employees on a personal level, except for annual meetings at which you praise your social and communicative leadership skills.

7 Be the exclusive spokesperson for every new idea, regardless of whether it is your own or not.

8 Embrace new ideas when you talk, but do not do anything about them.

9 When the proposed idea is too radical, you can always argue that no one has done it before and that there might be reasons for this.

10 When the proposed idea is not radical enough, just say that the idea is not really new and that someone else already did it.

Of course, this list is far from being complete; there are many small practices that can be built into organizational routines that may help you effectively avoid unnecessary creativity, such as organizing endless meetings in which you discuss and rehash every new idea without actually developing them; sticking to the protocols of ways that have been successful in doing things so far; throwing lots of detailed questions on the table (cash flow in the next couple of weeks, uncertainties in your business environment, and so on); insisting that everything needs to be planned carefully before steps of action can be taken; nurturing the not-invented-here syndrome – the list is endless, sadly. Although the vast majority of organizations seem to follow the ten rules, some more creative organizations try to work with a structure that actually triggers innovation and change.

Being monstrous!

Innovation is meant to be something good and useful per se. However, what is useful and what is not is seen only at the end of the innovation journey; it cannot be assessed at the beginning. As Van de Ven et al. suggest:

> the usefulness of an idea can only be determined after the innovation process is completed and implemented. In this sense, it is not possible to determine whether work on new ideas will turn out to be 'innovations' or 'mistakes' until a summary evaluation occurs after the innovation journey is completed. (1999: 11)

Or, to put it more philosophically, according to Nietzsche:

> Indeed, we have not any organ at all for *knowing*, or for 'truth': we 'know' (or believe, or fancy) just as much as may be *of use* in the interest of the human herd, the species; and even what is here called 'usefulness' is

ultimately only a belief, a fancy, and perhaps *the most fatal stupidity by which we shall one day be ruined.* (Nietzsche, 1974: 301; emphasis in original)

Weick (1979) puts it more bluntly when he advises us to stamp out utility. Similar to the innovator's dilemma, this question of usefulness forms quite a big challenge to ordinary management thinking. The whole task of management seems to be ordering, planning, and calculating; usefulness seems to be the benchmark of everything managers do – if it is useful for growth, it is good, and, if not, it should be abandoned. However, innovation challenges this thinking and thus questions the underlying core fundamentals of management theory. Innovation brings up the possibility of monstrous creations – strange and threatening phenomena not previously seen. As the French philosopher Jacques Derrida suggests:

> A future that would not be monstrous would not be a future; it would already be a predictable, calculable, and programmable tomorrow. All experience open to the future is prepared or prepares itself to welcome the monstrous. All of history has shown that each time an event has been produced, for example in philosophy or in poetry, it took the form of the unacceptable, or even of the intolerable, of the incomprehensible, that is, of a certain monstrosity. (Derrida, 1995: 387)

Think of new products and processes in the history of management; they were monstrous to the extent that they seemed to be unacceptable and incomprehensible for their time. Innovation that is not monstrous but tamed and takes the form of well-known pet animals is incremental at best. Radical innovation that co-evolves with new behaviours and platforms always has monstrous characteristics when compared to the status quo. Thus, truly innovative undertakings always have something monstrous about them, something that scares and frightens many people, including management.

Creative structures?

The creative process can be illustrated by using the example of Frank Heart, one of the core team members of the group that developed early hard- and software for the Internet. He remembers how the members of the group worked together:

> Everyone knew everything that was going on, and there was very little structure ... There were people, who specifically saw their role as software, and they knew a lot about hardware anyway; and the hardware people all could program. (Quoted in Brown and Duguid, 2001: 93)

These highly creative people were working in a relatively small team, driven by highly motivated people, built around self-organizing and flexible principles. Creativity, defined as the ability to combine previously unrelated dimensions of experience, flourishes in such an environment. However, this communication-intensive practice challenges companies when they start to grow; professional management structures are put in place to manage new ideas – their design, development, sales, marketing, and so forth. Brown and Duguid (2001: 94) observe that 'once separated, groups develop their own vocabularies; organizational discourse sounds like the Tower of Babel'. At Xerox, for instance, what had been intuitive to scientists turned out to be unintelligible to the engineers who were supposed to transform the idea into a marketable product. As each group told its tales, 'the scientists dismissed the engineers as copier-obsessed "toner heads," whereas the engineers found the scientists arrogant and unrealistic' (Brown and Duguid, 2001: 94).

Thus as Brown and Duguid go on to say, one of the greatest challenges that innovative companies face is the step from initial innovation to sustainable growth, a challenge that can be managed only by carefully balancing structure and creativity. Creativity without structure tends to grow out of touch with reality, whereas structure without creativity results in a loss of innovation. This conundrum brings us back to the exploration/exploitation dialectics that we have discussed in Chapter 9 (March, 2002).

One strategy to overcome this problem is to use structures as shelters – that is, to create sheltered workshops in which innovation can occur undisturbed by routine. As the BMW example illustrated, establishing safe 'playgrounds' in which innovators can explore without being constrained by a business-as-usual philosophy can help to create new ideas and trigger innovation. The risk, however, is that sheltered workshops can become ivory towers. Disseminating and integrating new knowledge into everyday organizational structures and practices from a position of remoteness seems to be almost impossible.

Turning creative ideas into successful products takes more than business-as-usual concepts; the process must combine elements of structure with elements of process by building project teams that include both R&D people and process improvers, together with end-user representatives and those who will have manufacturing and delivery responsibilities for the design that is implemented. There is no point in having a great design that cannot be made, improved, sold, or used. Thus creativity becomes a major asset in the conceptualization of innovation and change. The ability to think outside the box, however, is something organizations find hard because their efforts are focused on order, control, and predictability. Stacey argues that creativity is linked to instability:

> Organizations with the potential for creativity are those that are tensed by the presence of efficient formal hierarchical systems that are continually being subverted by informal network systems in which political and learning activity takes place. Creative systems are systems in tension and the price paid for creative potential is an unknowable long-term future. (1999: 75)

Management fashion

Certain organization innovations might be trendy, but what if they were a mere fashion? Recently, management scholars have put emphasis on the role of fashion in the dissemination and application of new ideas and practices. As Abrahamson (1996) argues, fashions are set by gurus and adopted quickly by consultants and the media. They are nicely packaged collective beliefs sold and communicated through highly symbolic labels such as BPR or lean management. Using a highly seductive rhetoric, these fashions promise simple solutions to complex problems. The power of fashion derives less from the actual message (after all, BPR was in many ways merely a restatement of Taylor's (1967 [1911]) scientific management) than from the symbolic power it conveys. Managers and companies who do not adopt the latest trends are seen to be inert, reactive, and past-oriented instead of dynamic, proactive, and future-oriented. Thus fashions create considerable pressure on organizations.

The problem, however, is that fashion offers lots of rhetoric but little substance. Although it claims to offer innovative solutions, they are often no more than superficial one-best-way recipes that ignore the complexity of the actual situation. The task for management lies in the tricky job of differentiating mere fashion from effective innovation. Just imagine a company that went with every fashion; it would have to change every couple of years, and it would never be able to form a unique character. Instead of learning, it would change its practices like fashion victims change their clothes.

MINI CASE

St Luke's

A good example of how creativity can be harnessed in a business environment (and turned into money) is St Luke's, a London-based design and ad agency. It includes on its client list some big names, such as British Telecom and The Body Shop. St Luke's is an organization that succeeds in the creative industry through carefully managing a key paradox: how do you push employees to their limits and provide a safe and flourishing environment for them at the same time?

The *Harvard Business Review* (Coutu, 2000: 143) called St Luke's 'the most frightening company on earth'. The unique structure of the company enables it to master the paradox; it is entirely owned by its employees and, as the founder, Andy Law, says, they are Star Trekkers:

Our employees must take nothing for granted; they must peel away all the levels of their personalities to become who they really are. That's frightening. It's terrifying to have no

pretences about yourself, yet that's what gives you the psychological resources to question all the rules ... What accounts for our creativity is that we constantly go deeper into ourselves than other people do. (Coutu, 2000: 145)

The whole company keeps moving constantly. For instance, it opened an office in Stockholm:

Why Stockholm? We didn't analyse the market to see whether there was an opportunity there. But we analysed ourselves and saw that we needed a bigger canvas for people to experiment on, and we needed a more diverse group of employees to produce more creative work. So we are going to Stockholm to set the creative process on fire by doing some intercultural experimentation. We are going to learn from people who were taught to think differently than we were and whose culture requires them to communicate in a different way. We are mixing the creative gene pool. (Coutu, 2000: 146)

(Continued)

(Continued)

In their work practice, people at St Luke's do unusual things as well. They intentionally destabilize the workplace to keep habit at arm's length. If you were an employee there, when you started working in the morning you would not know where you would be sitting, and your contract and actual job might change without any notice. At St Luke's, everything is in constant flux, which keeps the employees creative.

St Luke's practices are similar to the essence of jazz improvisation. For example, when Miles Davis formed his various quintets, he liked to keep them underrehearsed so that they would not lapse into routine. When he recorded his bestselling album *Kind of Blue* (Davis, 1959), he took the musicians into the studio with no rehearsal, no charts, and just told them to play the tunes that he had prepared loose arrangements for. This kind of improvisation has been held up as a model for how creative organizations should operate, and St Luke's seems to have learned these lessons well (Barrett, 2002; Kamoche et al., 2002).

St Luke's might prove to be the exception to the rule that businesses are boring and the opposite of creative. Thus this approach, much like the movement from chaos that we considered earlier, challenges the assumptions of the innovation-as-technology and the change-as-rationally-planned schools of thought. However, as we have seen, innovation does not rely on chaos; structures can help maintain the balance between routine and random.

• Analyse any organization that you can identify as exceptionally creative. How does it manage its creativity?

SUMMARY AND REVIEW

In this chapter we have discussed the main theories of innovation and change.

Planned change and its model of unfreeze–change–refreeze offer a simple way of understanding change. Processual theories argue that change is more complex and has to be studied as it unfolds over time. Recent theories explore the importance of chaos and unpredictability for the innovation process and argue that innovation cannot be planned. Implicitly this challenges management practice that focuses on planning and controlling. However, it is doubtful if change and innovation can be successfully and continuously achieved in a planned, rational manner.

Clark (2003: 137) argues that most innovation in organizations occurs through alterations to the population of organizations. Firms that do not innovate die, and new firms will replace them. Change and innovation happen through replacement, mergers, or acquisition of organizations more than through the reorganization of companies.

Managing innovation implies focus on the politics of change. Change always means changing the status quo, and some people might be very comfortable with the current status or very uncomfortable with the prospect of instability. Hence, change is an inherently political activity. It is also crucial to stress the role of stakeholders in the innovation process. Customers, employees, and collaborators can help you to innovate. Understanding the innovation journey, we differentiated separate periods including an initiation period, a development period, and an implementation period.

We discussed some of the 'dark sides' of innovation, including the innovator's dilemma, the paradox of innovation, and management fashions with its (organizational) fashion victims. In conclusion, it is important to recognize that innovation is one of the hottest topics in contemporary management. Rather than view innovation, creativity, and change as a rationally planned process, we concentrated on its emergent, processual, and political aspects. Central to this process are what we have identified as the key tensions of innovation in organizations, which centre on making innovations happen in terms of the organization changes and creativity that are required.

EXERCISES

1   Having read this chapter you should be able to say in your own words what each of the following key terms means. Test yourself or ask a colleague to test you.

- Innovation
- Change
- Planning
- Social innovation
- Order
- Chaos
- Paradox
- Co-creation
- Creativity
- Management fashion

2   What are the assumptions behind planned change?
3   Why is change a process?
4   Why does innovation occur between chaos and order?
5   How do politics frame change processes?
6   Who are the main stakeholders in change, and how do they shape the processes?
7   What does the innovation journey look like?
8   What is the innovator's dilemma?
9   How do foolishness, fashion, and structure shape change?
10 What role can customers play in the innovation process?
11 What is the significance of social innovation? How far does it differ from organizational innovation?

ADDITIONAL RESOURCES

1   There are so many books about innovation, change, and creativity that it is rather hard to know where to begin, but we will keep it brief. A good sourcebook on change is the text by Hardy (1995), *Managing Strategic Action: Mobilizing Change: Concepts, Readings, and Cases*. It is especially useful because it looks at not just success stories but some failures as well. A good starting point for innovation is Christensen's (1997) book, *The Innovator's Dilemma: When New Technologies Cause Great Firms to Fail*, or the more narrative account by Wren and Greenwood (1998), *Management Innovators: The People and Ideas That Shaped Modern Business*, which tells stories about inventive managers.

2   March's (1988) paper, 'The technology of foolishness', is a must read.
3   The best article on the politics of innovation is the rather demanding but extremely excellent article by Frost and Egri (2002), 'The political process of innovation'.
4   There are many useful films on the topic of innovation, change, and creativity. Perhaps the best is *Apollo 13* (Howard, 1995), especially its emphasis on the creative processes that brought the astronauts of the Apollo mission back, even in the midst of chaotic problems. It illustrates organizational learning as improvisation in action.
5   As an example of how *not* to innovate, consider the film *Titanic* (Cameron, 1997), about an innovation that failed because of some of the assumptions of the designers about basic aspects of the ship and the environment in which it operated.

WEB SECTION

1   Our Companion Website is the best first stop for you to find a great deal of extra resources, free PDF versions of leading articles published in Sage journals, exercises, video and pod casts, team case studies and general questions, and links to teamwork resources. Go to www.sagepub.co.uk/managingandorganizations3.
2   For state of the art briefings on how to manage organizations effectively, please visit the Henry Stewart Talks series of online audiovisual seminars on Managing Organizations, edited by Stewart Clegg: www.hstalks.com/r/managingorgs, in particular, Talk #12: *Improvising improvisational change*, by Miguel Pinha e Cunh and Joao Vieira da Cunha, as well as Johannes Pennings' Talk #5 in the series on The Origins and Development of Management, called *Innovation: the paradox of back to the future*.
3   To become familiar with the lingo of change managers visit this site: http://www.change-management.org.
4   Another useful site with many links is http://www.odportal.com/change/index.htm.
5   For a site full of ideas and how to make them work see http://www.innovationtools. com.
6   Find out how you can turn your ideas into money at http://www.inventioncity.com/.

7 A reliable guide to the world of innovation is to be found on the Harvard site: http://hbswk.hbs.edu/topic.jhtml?t=innovation.

8 To see the best inventions of each year visit the web page of *Time* magazine, where you will also find an interesting guide to current innovative entrepreneurs: http://tinyurl.com/ ykfv7m.

9 A really innovative company's website can be found at http://www.mmm.com/.

10 A nice and entertaining website featuring links and quite good quotes by celebrities is to be found at http://www.rewardingideas.com.

11 A funny little exercise to find out how creative you really are is at http://areyoucreative.com/.

12 In 2010 the Danish and Finnish governments released a report with the promising title *The New Nature of Innovation*. Check out the accompanying website at http://blogs.denmark.dk/jesperpagh/2010/05/04/the-new-nature-of-innovation/ and watch the video with C. K. Prahalad. In your view, what is new about the 'new nature' of innovation?

13 The site www.ideo.com introduces you to IDEO, one of the most innovative firms in the world. Check out the news section where you will find links to inspiring books by and about IDEO.

14 Check out www.creativeinnovation.com.au, which is Australia's virtual portal for entrepreneurs in the creative industries. It is informative with lots of links and practical tools.

15 If you are interested in social innovation you can download *The Open Book of Social Innovation* for free at http://www.nesta.org.uk/publications/reports/assets/features/the_open_book_of_social_innovation. You can find more information on www.socialinnovator.info.

LOOKING FOR A HIGHER MARK?

Reading and digesting these articles that are available free on the Companion Website www.

sagepub.co.uk/managingandorganizations3 can help you gain deeper understanding and, on the basis of that, a better grade:

1 Lounsbury, M. and Crumley, E. T. (2007) 'New practice creation: an institutional perspective on innovation', *Organization Studies*, 28 (7): 993–1012. This paper examines the case of the creation of active money management practice in the US mutual fund industry, drawing on both institutional and practice scholarship, to develop a process model of new practice creation that redirects attention towards the multiplicity of actors that interactively produce change.

2 Schatzki, T. R. (2006) 'On organizations as they happen', *Organization Studies*, 27 (12): 1863–1873. This essay examines what organizations are as they happen. It first argues that the happening of an organization has two basic components: the performance of its constituent actions and practices and the occurrence of events whereby its material arrangements causally support these activities.

3 Schein, E. H. (2006) 'From brainwashing to organizational therapy: a conceptual and empirical journey in search of "systemic" health and a general model of change dynamics. A drama in five acts', *Organization Studies*, 27 (2): 287–301. This paper presents a set of concepts about the nature of the organization, the nature of the individual, and the nature of the career – the set of events that tie the individual and the organization together.

4 Stensaker, I. and Falkenberg, J. (2007) 'Making sense of different responses to corporate change', *Human Relations*, 60 (1): 137–177. This paper argues that organizational-level responses, and how these develop over time, can be explained by examining individuals' interpretative responses.

CASE STUDY

EXPLORING EXPLORATION CREATIVITY

Oil exploration is a high-risk, high-outcome endeavour. A single offshore well drilled on a geo-logical prospect can cost over A$100 million. A single discovery can amount to over A$100 bil-lion. All wells are based on very qualified guess-work; some may have an estimated discovery probability as low as 20 per cent. We will present three sets of empirical observations on creativity in oil exploration, all taken from a multi-year action-learning project with the exploration teams in a major oil corporation. The puzzle is this. Creativity is typically regarded as an exception, associated with stable dispositions of gifted indi-viduals, peak experiences, and intense bouts of more or less deliberate innovative efforts. What if creativity is not an exception, but a quality of forms of work, *embedded* in everyday practice? And can one address creativity at work in settings where key personnel question the usefulness of the very concept of creativity?

'We don't call it creativity'

He was one of the first persons we interviewed, a respected manager of an exploration team and a person who had participated in many successful exploration efforts. 'I associate creativity with something that persons in fluffy garments are doing when they are painting doodles and call it art,' he snuffs. 'I don't see how that kind of creativ-ity has a place in my work. Exploration operates within basic physical laws and is about putting together data in a large puzzle, basically knowing your field and doing long term science based knowledge accumulation.' There is laughter. An interlude follows where we partly agree on not looking for the exploration equivalent of pottery making, partly try to qualify how creativity is not contrary to science-based work. Then the explo-ration manager starts to talk passionately about the importance of seeing the big picture in small-scale prospect analysis, about seeing regional wholes, not only singular blocks or licences or prospects or wells, about being able to imagine geological processes that took place hundreds of millions of years ago, about the importance of conjuring alternative interpretations of the same data, about tectonic movements, thinking in four dimensions, seeing opportunities rather than problems, the use of sketches for zooming out, and the eternal need for persistence and pas-sion in exploration. Creativity as science-based imagination? We still think of this as one of our best interviews.

'Why are you not using any creativity techniques?'

We had just been rounding off a two-day work-shop with exploration teams. The agenda was to develop and rank hydrocarbon prospect ideas in selected geological regions, staged as an 'explo-ration creativity workshop'. The workshop was led by the chief geologist, while we as external researchers had assisted in design and some of the facilitation. It was the third workshop of its kind, and the corporate word of mouth on the two preceding ones was quite good. One of the participants – an experienced facilitator of many development processes in the corporation and well versed in creativity techniques – had asked to join the workshop to see what was going on. At the end of day two he popped a good ques-tion: 'Why are you not using any creativity tech-niques?' Indeed – why had we not? Part of the answer may seem straightforward. Geologists use a highly specialized vocabulary that will typically leave outsiders in the wild after 5–10 seconds. External facilitating of, for example, a brainstorming session on geological prospects would be very likely to slow down the process, as the many complicated combinations of ideas would have to pass the filter of an (at least par-tially) ignorant mind. Could this have been over-come with the use of a trained geologist as facilitator? Perhaps – the problem here seems to be that many creativity techniques presuppose distinctness of ideas at an early stage of concep-tion and carry the implicit assumption of the value of *steering* idea generation and combina-tion, *and* the assumption that such techniques are more or less valid across widely different domains of activity. These are hefty assumptions. The kinds of discussions we have witnessed in exploration teams seem more like the jamming of jazz musicians than developing new dishwashers. Fragments of ideas, data, viewpoints, and alternative interpretations are connected, unconnected, enriched, stripped, negated, and saluted in a stream of collective efforts where no single individual has more than a temporary lead. One may try to specify the overall output of the jamming sessions and prepare the ground with communicative tools and resources. But detailed facilitation? Probably not.

'The key was understanding why the previous wells did not work'

After having interviewed more than two-dozen oil finders about their successful exploration efforts, a clear pattern began to emerge. It seems that many success stories in exploration share a plot, with a breakthrough interpretation in the wake of many years of data gathering, painstaking analysis, and, typically, a series of costly dry wells based on geological interpretations later found invalid. Successful exploration, then, is often based on the ability to come up with an *alternative* geological model based on the data from dry wells. What does this implicate? A cynical explanation would be that prolonged exploration efforts in a region where there is oil are bound to result in a discovery, sooner or later, and that all discoveries are retrospectively justified as being based on a genius analysis rather than mere luck. More optimistically, the breakthroughs result from novel combinations of interpretations, emerging from a succession of analytical and interpretive efforts with many people and teams involved. Maybe dry wells sometimes are *necessary* as precursors to breakthrough interpretations. Maybe we should talk of *slow* creativity?

Questions

1 Starting from your own experiences, what do you think constitutes creativity at work? Can we do with one creativity concept for all kinds of work?
2 What do you think are the motivational drivers of creativity at work?
3 To what degree would you say that creativity is an individual versus a collective phenomenon, and can activities that lead to breakthrough innovations be 'routinized'?

Case prepared by Arne Carlsen, Tord F. Mortensen, and Reidar Gjersvik, SINTEF Technology and Society, KUNNE.

CHAPTER ELEVEN

MANAGING SUSTAINABLY: ETHICS AND CORPORATE SOCIAL RESPONSIBILITY

Morals, Conduct, Responsibility

LEARNING OBJECTIVES

This chapter is designed to enable you to:

▪ Understand the importance of ethics for organizations

▪ Outline current approaches to ethics

▪ Debate ethical dilemmas concerning money and morals, and profits and principles

▪ Grasp how ethics works in practice

▪ Know what is corporate social responsibility (CSR)

▪ Understand how to improve sustainability

Economics does not account for the cost of consumption. (Al Gore, An Inconvenient Truth)

INTRODUCTION

Usually, **ethics** is understood as reflecting on and recommending concepts of right and wrong behaviour.

The concept of **ethics** has a long history in Western philosophy.

It follows from our definition of ethics, that *business* ethics is the reflection on the ethical behaviour of business organizations. Much discussion of business ethics focuses on the ethical consequences of individual and organizational behaviour. On the one hand, some argue that 'good ethics is good business'. They suggest that the pursuit of economic interests within the given restrictions of the law will automatically lead to ethical behaviour. In this perspective, being ethical means simply following rules for doing good business. On the other hand, most critical ethicists argue that the pursuit of economic self-interest by firms is fundamentally opposed to ethical conduct. In their perspective, financial profit and moral principles cannot be aligned; profits and principles, morals and money, are fundamentally opposed forces that cannot be aligned. According to this view, either the pursuit of profits or the pursuit of ethical behaviour must be compromised.

THE CHALLENGE OF MANAGING ETHICS

Think of fast food chains that sell sugary drinks and fatty food to young children contributing to a nation-wide obesity epidemic – are they acting ethically when doing so? Think of large multinational energy corporations that might exploit and pollute the environment they are working in (just remember the BP oil spill in the Gulf of Mexico in 2010) and cut deals with governments that do not respect human rights – are they acting responsibly? Or think of fashion brands that produce cheap shoes and clothes in developing countries, often employing children working in miserable conditions – are these companies doing the right thing? Many firms maximize profits through outsourcing production to developing countries. The unethical results of this strategy are that they employ workers who, by the standards of most of its customers, are poorly paid and oppressed. Moreover, some of them are under the age of 14 and work in 'sweatshops'. Though in the developing countries in which they work there might be considerable competition for these jobs, the cost of the labour used in production hardly compares with the millions that firms such as Nike spend on marketing their products, especially through promotional tie-ups with leading sportspeople such as tennis champion Rafael Nadal.

Speared by these inequities, a critical audience picked up these practices of Nike and protested against Nike management, successfully lobbying it to change practices. Nike was successful in terms of business goals but as the goals were achieved in ways that liberals in the developed countries could question, the strategy turned out to be counterproductive in marketing terms.

Of course, ethical issues are rarely clear-cut: the picture is much harder to calibrate from the perspective of the developing world's workers themselves. Yes, they are exploited in global terms, and the work is demanding and detailed – but, in terms of comparable wages in their domestic economies, they are privileged. A young woman working in a factory sweatshop for a few dollars a day looks like exploitation; indeed, it is – but in the developing world such employment might mean the difference between starvation and survival for her family. In the light of these arguments it is not easy to answer the question whether Nike acted unethically or not. You might say 'yes' because it exploited workers; or you might say 'no' because it allowed workers to have a job in the first place.

Recent scandals in the corporate world – think again of the BP oil spill or the behaviour of investment banks such as Goldman Sachs that contributed to the global financial crisis – have made ethics central to public debate over the sustainability of business success. Other trends reinforce this centrality; for instance, the growing interest in **corporate social responsibility (CSR)** demonstrates that **stakeholders** expect more from organizations than just financially successful performance.

Often this is reflected in the shift to triple bottom-line reporting – reporting on People–Planet–Profit – in which the impacts that are measured are not only financial but also those registered on employees and the natural environment. Put simply, rather than reporting the financial profit or loss of a firm, the impact of the firm's doings on the planet and on people should be reported too. In this sense firms are not only responsible for financial success but also for human wellbeing and the environment. Accountability extends beyond narrow criteria and focuses on the link between business and society. While we have looked at the impact of organizations on people in the chapter on human resource management (Chapter 5), here we will also look at the impact that business has on the planet. Increasingly, the **sustainability** of an organization is becoming seen in terms of not just getting the financial side right but also minimizing the effect that the organization has on the ecology that sustains it and its people. The practical implications of these recent shifts are that organizations are increasingly under pressure to rethink the ethical consequences of their behaviour and readjust their actions accordingly: external stakeholders and the environment have become key influencers of organizational practices and processes.

The theories explored in this chapter will help you to understand the tensions and dynamics underlying the debate about what is ethical conduct. As we will argue in this chapter, there are no simple guidelines for prescribing right and wrong behaviour. What is ethically sound in one

Corporate social responsibility (CSR) occurs when an organization seeks to meet or exceed legal and normatively mandated standards, by considering the greater good of the widest possible community within which it exists, both in local and global terms, with regard to the environmental, social, economic, legal, ethical, and philanthropic impact of the organization's way of conducting business and the activities it undertakes.

Stakeholders are key individuals or *groups* of individuals with vested interests or 'stakes' in a given decision or project. The stakeholder can be a direct or an indirect stakeholder. A direct stakeholder is a customer, a supplier, a government body, or anyone else formally linked to the organization. An indirect stakeholder is a member of the community who is not directly involved in the organization but who is affected by its behaviour, such as a resident in its immediate community.

Sustainability: Literally, ensuring that resources are renewed. A sustainable use of resources would leave the world short of nothing that was depleted in any process – that resource would be renewed – and would ensure that nothing deleterious to the world's natural systems resulted from whatever processes were being undertaken.

IMAGE 11.1 Highly unethical small business in Bangkok, Thailand. The business is selling false English-language proficiency certificates for students who want to gain admission to overseas English-language degree programs as well as false driving licences

context might be seen as unethical in another. For instance, most of us would agree that torturing a person is unethical. However, what if this person is suspected of knowing about a planned terrorist attack and torture is the only way to get the vital information from them? In this case, would torture still be unethical? Or would it be unethical to let many potential victims die as a result of the planned attack? Questions such as this are not easy to answer: certainly governments in different countries do not agree on the answer to such questions, so some of their organizations torture or condone torture, while others do not. Hence, the objective of this chapter is not to argue for one or the other side but to develop your sensitivity for and interest in ethics. Our aim is to encourage you to understand business activities and decisions not only as economic 'facts' but also as ethical issues.

A rapidly growing body of academic literature reflects the importance of business ethics. Although ethics has its antecedents in both ancient philosophy and religion, business ethics is an emerging discipline. Further, while a consideration of the ethics of business can be traced back to the seminal work of Adam Smith, whose focus was as much moral as economic, the explicit development of business ethics as a field of research and study is more recent.

Ethics research is a broad field. In recent years a key ethical issue concerns sustainability in the broadest sense – what is the impact of the business on the ecology, habitat, and species of Planet Earth? These are big ethical questions that are sometimes referred to in terms of corporate social responsibility. So, in this chapter we will look at ethics in general, and approaches to analysing the ethics of a business, as well as the broader issues of corporate social responsibility, especially in terms of sustainability.

APPROACHES TO BUSINESS ETHICS

Thinking about ethics

The core issue in business ethics is how businesses ought to act. What is an ethically sound way for business to behave? However, as we will see there are no simple answers to this question. Friedman (1982) argues that businesses are neutral instruments that have been created for the pursuit of goals that they do not control. In this perspective an organization can only fulfil its function; it cannot be judged ethical or unethical.

Think of a small *boulangerie* bakery: it exists to fulfil a function, which is baking good bread. One could argue that this is its only purpose; the question of an ethical or unethical bakery would not make sense since it can only fulfil its function. If it performs this function well it will be rewarded by loyal costumers who support the business and help it to grow; if not, the business will ultimately go broke as customers cease purchasing bread from that particular bakery. However, if in the process of selling its bread the bakery were to use non-biodegradable plastic bags which then get dumped in landfill, would it still be a good bakery, as one whose rubbish can end up in landfill for infinity?

One influential view is that of Milton Friedman (see What's the Point box below). He argues that businesses should stay within the rules of the game and must not engage in illegal or criminal activities. That is about the only limitation he imposes on business: as long as they respect the law they should, according to Friedman, be free to do whatever they want to increase their profits.

It is easy to argue that this simple rule does not ensure ethical behaviour. Think of a global sports brand that manufactures its products in a developing country paying minimal wages to children: according to the law of the developing countries, the sports brand may act legally. However, from an ethical perspective the behaviour of the company might be unacceptable. It can be argued that Friedman's position relies too much on a belief in the self-regulating forces of capitalism.

In fact many consumers agreed with these views and put companies such as Nike or Gap under immense pressure to change their work practices in developing countries (see Chapter 8 on communication). Further, such a view overlooks the power dynamics that contribute to the creation of laws. In many developing and developed nations corporations and corporate interest have a disproportionate influence in the creation of laws – especially those directly relating to their costs of production such as the cost of labour or public utilities. This influence has increased, albeit in a complicated fashion, with the increase in multinational corporations the world has recently seen.

WHAT'S THE POINT?

The only responsibility of a business is to make profit

The following quote by Friedman gained worldwide notoriety – to either condemn capitalism's laissez-faire approach or justify capitalists' operations:

> The view has been gaining widespread acceptance that corporate officials and labor leaders have a 'social responsibility' that goes beyond serving the interest of their stockholders or their members. This view shows a fundamental misconception of the character and nature of a free economy. In such an economy, there is one and only one social responsibility of business – to use its resources and engage in activities designed to increase its profits so long as it stays within the rules of the game, which is to say, engages in open and free competition,

without deception or fraud. (Friedman, 1982: 133–134)

Not everything that is legally allowed is ethically sound: just because something is not illegal does not make it automatically ethical. Think of your own social network: would your friends find it acceptable if you cheated on your partner and covered it up with lies? How about if you cheat in an ethics exam?

The main theories in business ethics address ethically problematic issues. How should a business behave? What is the right thing to do? Who is ultimately responsible for the actions of an organization: the individual or the organization? And how can ethics be 'managed' and ethical behaviour ensured throughout a company? We will attend to these questions in the next section.

Normative and descriptive ethics

Normative ethics seeks to establish means of judging whether business practices are right or wrong.

Broadly speaking there are two different schools of thought in the business ethics community. For some, business ethics is conceived of as a **normative ethics**.

Normative ethics can assist managers in dealing with moral dilemmas or to enable past actions to be judged in terms of their ethicality. Business ethics uses normative models in order to investigate the ethical nature and consequences of particular events or practices in business. In this normative approach, business ethics is generally understood as being related to the rules and/or cultural norms that govern, or should govern, organizational conduct. In organizations this commonly means that managing ethics is done through formalized codes of conduct that should govern everyday actions and decisions. Indeed, it is reported that 78 per cent of the US top 1,000 companies have a code of conduct (Nijhof et al., 2003). This approach is also used in theories of business ethics which develop normative models for passing ethical judgement on business practices (e.g. Brass et al., 1998; Gatewood and Carroll, 1991) or propose the development of ethical rules for organizations (e.g. Beyer and Nino, 1999).

The **descriptive approach** to business ethics would not seek for normative guidelines that ought to be applied in practice, but rather monitor and describe what actually happens.

The study of business ethics has also been pursued through a **descriptive approach**, which uses scientific analysis to describe the actual behaviour of organizations and their members.

The key question in both approaches is whether ethics is *relative* to history and tradition or whether there is a set of *absolute* norms that are valid at any time anywhere in the world. For instance, although gift-giving to facilitate business might be an established part of one country's business culture, it might be considered unethical in other countries: giving and receiving gifts might be seen as normal in certain countries, whereas it might be understood as bribery in others. In this example, values are relative. Whether an action is ethical or not depends on the cultural context with which you are dealing as well as the cultural norms of your own business culture. Where the two do not coincide then there is always the possibility of behaviour being construed as unethical by one or other party. For instance, it is evident that, depending on the culture, giving or not giving gifts to facilitate business could both equally be construed as unethical.

MINI CASE

Is there a set of absolute values that are not negotiable?

We could argue that men and women should be treated equally regardless of religious belief or the culture in which they live. The Universal Declaration of Human Rights from the United Nations, written in 1948, has as Article 1 the following:

> Article 1: All human beings are born free and equal in dignity and rights. They are endowed with reason and conscience and should act towards one another in a spirit of brotherhood.

- How consistent is Article 1 with cultures in which women's sexuality is celebrated either in representations of them in scanty dress that makes them attractive to men, or where their whole body and face are totally covered while men's are not? When some societies embrace sexual display of parts of the body as the norm and others insist on total coverage – but only for women – is this treating everyone as free and equal in dignity? What should international businesses do about this in their employment practices?

Well, Article 1 might be problematic if we think about it enough – but what about Article 5?

> Article 5: No one shall be subjected to torture or to cruel, inhuman or degrading treatment or punishment.

Certain countries, including the US, engage in practices that are very close to cruel, inhuman, or degrading treatment. Pictures from Abu Ghraib Prison and reports from Guantánamo Bay Prison provided evidence that the US interprets Article 5 differently.

During George W. Bush's War on Terror the US administration argued that certain techniques such as water boarding are acceptable if they make suspects speak and hence contribute to saving the lives of innocent people. If not everybody agrees on such basic values, one can imagine how hard it would be to agree on other ethical values universally. For instance, we might all agree that workers should receive a fair wage for their input. However, what constitutes a fair wage in a developing country? If it is two times more than an average local salary could one argue it is fair? It may still be only a fraction of the market value at which the products are sold for in developed economies – so is it fair that the organization's shareholders increase their value by diminishing that which is paid in wages to their employees by moving production to a cheap-wage economy? It could be argued, for instance, that it is only inward investment from more developed economies that will raise wage levels in the less developed ones. From this point of view, the relativities are not so important. As you can see, it would be very hard to develop universal rules around such issues: they very much depend on personal values and beliefs that differ from person to person.

Ethics pays: good business equals good ethics

One prominent argument is that ethics and business are, or at least can be, aligned in order to create competitive advantage. The core argument here is that ethics does not contradict the driving forces behind business organization and that there is no conflict of interest between profits and principles. Francis and Armstrong (2003), for instance, argue that an ethically informed risk management strategy increases commercial outcomes, prevents fraud, and lifts corporate reputation.

In this argument, an organization's ethical commitment is driven by its self-interest: because it wants to make profits, the company will behave ethically, or in short: ethics pays. Such a perspective dates back to Adam Smith's argument that maximizing personal advantage will lead, through self-interested actors competing in the market, to a maximum of collectively beneficial outcomes. In sum, this suggests that 'good ethics is good business'. Thus, profits and principles are mutually inclusive rather than mutually exclusive frames (see *The Shell Report* (2003) for a business example).

Does ethics pay? 'Ethics pays' is the argument behind 'strategic philanthropy' (Seifert et al., 2003), as 'intangible resource for competitive advantage' (Hall, 1993), as 'marketing instruments' (Maignan and Ferrell, 2004), or as means to increase organizational commitment (Cullen et al., 2003). For instance, Porter and Kramer (2002) argue that companies should use their philanthropic budget only to improve their 'competitive context' – that is, philanthropy should enhance the quality of the business environment in those locations in which businesses' operate (2002: 58). The education of the workforce, the availability of economic infrastructure, and the promotion of business aims would all fit the bill. Such investments are proposed as simultaneously good both for business and for the various stakeholders involved. So, for instance, McDonald's may support neighbourhood schools or provide Ronald McDonald houses for sick children, and this may benefit both McDonald's and children in the community.

Such examples raise questions, however. How disinterested is this as philanthropy or how much is it a marketing exercise? And does it matter? You could argue that if it is doing good and putting resources where they would not otherwise go, if it is also marketing, so what? But on the other hand, is it marketing food that is basically unhealthy and contributes to childhood obesity, excessive waste from the packaging, and provides a McDonaldized model for business that is uncreative and inimical to innovation? What might appear to be ethical behaviour in one dimension of an organization's remit may be counterbalanced by equally unethical action elsewhere.

Porter and Kramer argue, 'the more closely a company's philanthropy is linked to its competitive context, the greater the company's contribution to society will be' (2002: 68; see also Handy, 2002). For example, doing something good and improving the organization's prospects are aligned. Providing good education to people is not only an altruistic act; it also ensures that the organization will have a pool of educated people that it can employ when needed. In this case smart business thinking equals ethical behaviour. The ethical rules and the rules for organizing efficiently and profitably are positioned as being the same. Just following the rules will produce just and profitable outcomes. In sum, behaving ethically means rigorously applying the rules of good management. According to this view, there is no need to be concerned about ethics for, in the long run, good management will by definition be a harbinger of both profits and ethical outcomes: the two will be conjoined like Siamese twins.

Ethics as an individual responsibility

An alternative approach argues that ethical conduct is more a matter for individuals as opposed to businesses or organizations (Soares, 2003). Following this approach, it is ultimately the individual human being (manager or employee) who has to defend ethical values and make ethical choices, often in spite of their organization. Unethical organizational behaviour results from the individual actions of 'bad apples' that are either amoral or guided by immoral principles. For instance, the humiliation and irregular treatment of Iraqi detainees in Abu Ghraib would be seen as an example of a few bad apples, such as Private Lyndie England.

The 'individualization' of ethics suggests that the individual manager is ultimately responsible for ethical behaviour and that the organizational requirement is for 'empowering ethics', which supports moral learning and development, instead of restricting ethics through codes (Kjonstad and Willmott, 1995). The heroic individual, so the argument goes, needs to listen to their inner voice or 'moral impulse' (Bauman, 1993; 1995). Such organizational members are 'morally assertive' and use their personal ethics to mediate corporate priorities (Watson, 2003). Ethics here is understood as a moral task for managers, who have personal responsibility for ethics.

If ethics is essentially a matter of individual behaviour, then organizational ethics would reside solely in the free will of the individual. In this scenario, the organization (and its rules) is a powerful framework within which an individual should act ethically. Conceived this way, an organization is an ethically questionable entity based on rules that individual members respond to according to their own personal ethics.

Ethics and bureaucracy

In sharp contrast to the above view, some have argued that the shape of the organization is more important than the individuals in it. This argument is often expressed in terms of the reform of public bureaucracies in the image of market-driven organizations (du Gay, 2000a). Changing bureaucracies into more entrepreneurial organizations that are 'post-bureaucratic' (Heckscher, 1994) will, it is argued, shape the ability of members to behave ethically. In principle, making these organizations more flexible will allow their members to exercise more discretion. Think of a service such as a hospital. These are complex professional bureaucracies, with an extensive division of labour. Within each profession there are strong ethical codes and a sense of the right thing to do – usually expressed in terms of an ethic of patient care. What happens if the hospital becomes a 'Trust Fund', with a budget that has to be managed by the professionals within it? It will certainly become more market-oriented, because the managers have to think about alternative uses of scarce resources. However, this may mean that they will have less time for a patient-centred ethic. They may also be urged by hospital administrators to respond more to the health issues of their wealthy and privately insured patients, rather than poorer people. In this case, bureaucracy guarantees a more patient-centred ethic of care, though this may involve more waiting or queuing. Thus, the argument for bureaucracy is that it preserves 'a certain ethical dignity … in the face of … persistent populist, philosophical and entrepreneurial critiques' (du Gay, 2000a: 9) coming from arguments for the superiority of markets. Against markets an 'ethic of personhood' is argued for. Such an ethic would stress 'autonomy, responsibility and freedom/obligation of individuals to actively make choices for themselves' (du Gay, 2004: 41).

When choice is associated with markets, the focus on individuality suggests that ethical people should be enterprising and individualistic and, above all, steadfast in their privileging of economic rationality. Markets that empower individual choice see no place for trust, mutual dependence, social bonds, and honourable commitment (Sennett, 1998).

The liberal ethical argument for bureaucracy   Some thinkers have argued that bureaucracy may well act as a guardian of ethics. They argue that the formal rationality found in bureaucracy ensures that everybody is treated as a 'case', regardless of their status, religion, ethnic or class background (du Gay, 2000a). A formally rational bureaucracy would be one in which every case is treated the same. If this formal rationality was replaced with what Max Weber called substantive rationality, where the way that a case is treated is determined by the substantive status of the people involved, then, for instance, capacity to pay, religion, gender, class, or another (substantive) reason would determine the treatment that you receive. The core argument for bureaucracy is that such a substantive rationality would lead to the domination of a set of values in which market economics become the ethical basis of society (du Gay and Salaman, 1992). Such ethical values are dominated by notions of enterprise, economic rationality, free-market principles, and individuality, conceiving of individual responsibility primarily in terms of 'financial accountability' (du Gay, 2004: 176).

The argument against the market is that bureaucracy's ethicality derives from the training that it provides in 'the rules' for bureaucrats, in terms of technical expertise. Through a clearly defined hierarchy members understand everybody's responsibilities, duty, and rights. They are conditioned to think of the office that they hold in terms of a 'vocation', something detached from personal privileges, passions, and emotions (du Gay, 2000a: 44). Bureaucratic modes of organizing provide an institutional framework for responsible governance (du Gay, 2004) in which individual responsibility and ethical conduct can be framed. According to this view, if we want ethical behaviour we should have more old-style Weberian bureaucrats who stick to their rulebook. In this view it is not that humans would, by birth or definition, be ethically sound beings who are led astray by bureaucratic routines; rather, it is bureaucracy that provides the possibility for ethics by providing a framework beyond personal desires, needs, and fantasies.

Business ethics as a paradox: critical perspectives

More critical approaches to ethics in organizations question the convenience of the 'ethics pays' arguments outlined above. They are skeptical about the possibility of profit-seeking organizations, premised on the exploitation of the people that they employ, being ethical (Jones, 2004). The critical approach suggests that the core assumptions of classic management and organization theory do not position moral principles as 'a higher priority than firm profits' (Quinn and Jones, 1995: 22). Therefore, if profits are paramount, ethics will inevitably suffer: that is, if ethics potentially compromised profits, it is the former that will be sacrificed. Ethics is seen to be opposed to business rationality: their values are incompatible.

This critical approach asks whether business ethics is possible in a system that is driven by the pursuit of profits. The attempts by writers such as Porter and Kramer (2002) to align profits and principles, responsibility and performance, philanthropy and strategic advantage, would be ridiculed by critics such as Jones (2004). The critical argument suggests that business ethics is a paradoxical concept: businesses are there to make profits; and making profits means maximizing one's own advantage, which more often than not will imply damaging someone else's. Take for instance a furniture manufacturer: if it wants to maximize its profits it will pay minimum wages to its employees, buy the cheapest raw materials available (which might mean, say, wood from rainforests in Brazil), and only implement those environmental filters that it is forced to use by law. All three practices will definitely contribute to increased profits; however, all three practices might be seen as unethical.

MINI CASE

How ethical should advertising be? Look at the three images that follow. The first one looks like it might be an advert for lipstick. The second one seems to suggest that the lipstick is sensual, exotic, sexy. Only when we get to the third image do we realize that this is an advert for a car – the Suzuki Swift. There are several ways of interpreting the advert; maybe it is trying to position the car as the kind of car a sexy young woman who wears bold lipstick might drive. Or, maybe it is trying to suggest that if you drive the car then you will be sexy and attract such lips to kiss you. Is it (always) unethical to sell products using sex?

(Continued)

(Continued)

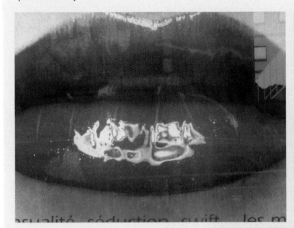

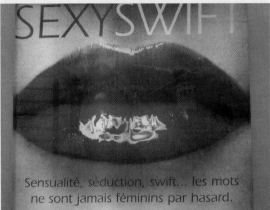

IMAGE 11.2, 11.3 AND
11.4 Luscious lips; sexy
words; red car

Ethics as Catch-22

From the critical perspective, the essential principles of capitalist society do not value ethical behaviour. That is, commercial success and good behaviour are seen as mutually exclusive. Even where companies choose ethically sound practices, this does not mean that the companies themselves are necessarily ethically sound. For instance, The Body Shop does not rely on animal testing for its products. Whereas some might argue that this is an ethically sound decision, radical ethicists argue that The Body Shop engages in these practices only so it can promote itself. Put simply, being ethical becomes a marketing slogan that is adopted because it contributes to the bottom line. From a critical perspective, no action based on such a motivation can be called ethical. Business is by definition selfish, hence there can be no such thing as business ethics. So, this is a Catch-22 for business. If you do nothing to be seen to be ethical, then the business will be judged unethical. If, on the other hand, you do something that *is* seen to be ethical, you will be rebuked for 'being ethical' as a marketing ploy. Business cannot win this argument. The case study of Google explains the dilemma – what would you do? Whose ethics do you have in mind? Your shareholders' money (as Friedman would define your responsibility) or the freedom of the Chinese people?

Check out the Companion Website www.sagepub.co.uk/ managingandorganizations3 for free access to a paper by D. J. Moberg (2006), which will help you understand how organizations and managers develop ethical blind spots.

MINI CASE

Corporate diplomacy – or how to behave responsibly?

On 29 March 2010 the *Jerusalem Post* featured an article entitled 'Google searches for a foreign policy'. The accompanying illustration showed three statesmen (no women, I am afraid) from Iran, the US, and China plus one corporate statesman from Google.

Of course, governments develop foreign policies to protect their citizens. And citizens can check on their governments through elections and other institutions of democracy such as parliamentary inquiries. But in our globalized world, organizations increasingly face challenges that used to be the business of states. As the *Jerusalem Post* article argues, Google and other high-tech firms have to develop foreign policies, as national governments are unclear on what to do and how to act in the face of change. Google and its China business are a good example in case. In 2006 Google entered the rapidly growing Chinese market. Google came under pressure because it offered in accordance with the Chinese government a censored search

engine to the Chinese public. For a company whose mantra is Don't Do Evil it seemed pretty close to evil to collaborate with an autocratic system that does not believe in freedom of speech or search. In its defence Google argued that it is better to have a censored search engine than none at all. However, over the years, tensions mounted and Google reported that the Chinese government had hacked into human rights activists' G-Mail accounts and its network had been infiltrated. In 2010 Google decided that the trade off did not work and decided to re-direct Chinese Google users to its Hong Kong site. The Chinese government was not impressed with Google's evasive strategy and threatened not to renew Google's operating license, which means Google would go dark in China. Google would lose access to 400 million users, representing the world's largest Internet population. The long-term economic consequences of such a move for Google are hard to imagine as Chinese competitors including the search engine Baidu are increasing their market presence in China.

(Continued)

(Continued)

The question cannot be reduced to an economic calculation, however. Clay Shirky, an academic from New York University, argues that Google does not export a simple product or service – but freedom. Hence Google needs to think about the impact it has on the democratic and institutional settings in the countries where it operates. In other words, Google has to balance its own values with the values of the countries it operates in. Other high-tech providers such as Twitter or Facebook share a similar challenge: when Iranians demonstrated against their regime after elections in 2010, Twitter became the medium of choice to organize protests. Deliberately or not, technology companies become entangled in politics and questions of what's right and wrong.

- Imagine you are head of the corporate social responsibility department at Google. What arguments for and against doing business in China can you think of? How would you make a decision? How do you explain to your shareholders that the decision to leave China was the right thing to do – despite the rapidly developing billion people market it represents? Prepare a short press statement that explains your reasoning and anticipate some of the points of critique that others might raise.

CORPORATE SOCIAL RESPONSIBILITY

Corporate social responsibility has been adopted as a formal policy goal by many advanced society governments and businesses. Organizations that commit to CSR typically adopt sustainable development goals that take account of economic, social, and environmental impacts in the way they operate. Why should business bother with CSR? After all, neo-classical economists have long argued that business owes abstractions such as 'society' nothing: shareholders are the owners of business and business's obligation is to do everything (within the law) to advance shareholder value – not to squander it on well-meaning but irrelevant CSR projects. On the other hand, the stakeholder model of the firm would insist that shareholders are but one set of stakeholders; that there are plenty of other significant stakeholders, ranging from customers, NGOs, communities, and civil society more generally, as well as activist groups claiming to articulate the interests of the environment, animals, disadvantaged people(s), or other 'mute' or muted stakeholders.

MINI CASE

CSR in Austria: from implicit to explicit, by Markus A. Höllerer (2010)

During its impressive career, the concept of CSR has not only conquered Anglo-American parts of the world but also entered fields where it encountered existing, strongly institutionalized, and taken-for-granted ideas of good entrepreneurship. For many reasons, Austria is a unique setting to study the dis-semination of CSR in managerial discourse. First and foremost, and as a common feature of the majority of continental European countries and their governance system, social responsibility of business is nothing new per se. To the contrary: the implicit notion of CSR has been firmly anchored in their institutional context – as an 'indigenous', taken-for-granted idea that already had been in existence before CSR was 'discovered' as a strategic instrument

(Continued)

(Continued)

used to maintain corporations' licence to operate. What is, indeed, new is that corporations have started to pick up the rhetoric and explicit vocabulary of CSR during the last decade.

Such a deeply ingrained understanding expresses a consensus of powerful societal agents and is materialized in various ways from legal regulation to informal practices of political decision-making (the so-called 'social partnership', built upon a tacit and informal agreement between the government, the major employers' associations, and various employee interest groups). Austria has, thus, been portrayed as *the* country of corporatism – as an icon of corporatist and stakeholder governance in post-war Europe opposed to, for instance, the United States. It was especially the business elite that felt responsible for the socioeconomic architecture of the nation – an idea that frequently came with a flavour of paternalism that is due to the important role of small and family-owned businesses in Austria, and which involved the balancing of different stakeholders' interests due to the claim, and also obligation, to know better what is good for stakeholders – perhaps better than themselves – and for society as a whole. While not labelled and explicitly referred to as CSR, 'good Austrian entrepreneurship with responsibility' has left its imprint in public discourse and has been firmly anchored in Austrian society.

Nonetheless, especially with growing pressure from international financial markets, and also as a reaction to the fierce public debate on the rise of shareholder value in Austria throughout the 1990s, the global victory march of Anglo-American-style CSR did not stop at Austria's doorstep. Despite considerable skepticism, the formerly implicit understanding has been increasingly replaced by explicit CSR policies and rhetoric since the turn of the millennium. However, this also resulted in a more fragmented and less clear understanding of what social responsibility of business actually encompasses. Recent research (Höllerer, 2010), thoroughly examining the CSR discourse in Austrian corporate annual reports since the early 1990s, shows that the CSR discourse provides several strategic fields for the corporate world to engage with. A first option of strategically employing CSR focuses on topics in the area of *sustainability* (e.g. the holistic perspective of the triple bottom line) and, thus, also connects with the debate around environmental issues. A second option revolves around *good corporate governance* and enhanced transparency, both of increased relevance since a global wave of financial scandals and corporate fraud in the 2000s. A third line within explicit CSR addresses a number of central and

powerful stakeholders and, consequently, grasps CSR as focused *stakeholder management* implying the balancing of divergent interests. Fourth, corporations use explicit CSR terminology to talk about corporate values and their sociopolitical role within society; here, they think of CSR mainly as *philanthropy* and support of societal groups in need that do not have power or voice in corporate decision-making. This means that the *responsibility* of corporations for less privileged members of society remains – to some extent, and at least on the rhetorical level – decoupled from *accountability* towards powerful stakeholders.

So, what does this mean for an organization? Above all, the increasing necessity to talk about and communicate certain issues (i.e. issues of social responsibility) points to their decreasing taken-for-grantedness. Obviously, the long-established societal consensus and tacit understanding in Austria – with corporate leaders embracing sociopolitical tasks by virtue of their elitist position – came to an end when facing new challenges in a globalized world of business. Explicit CSR provides an umbrella as well as the conceptual tools and vocabulary to tackle a broad range of 'problems' at the business-society interface. However, unclear content and scope of CSR feed into its perception as an ill-defined concept; on the practical side, societal expectations and 'threats' are diffuse – and so are responses from the corporate world. On the other hand, while the shift from implicit to explicit CSR led to considerable challenges for organizations and management, it also created novel opportunities. Organizations are now able to proactively utilize their CSR standing as a strategic resource in order to strive for legitimacy ('license to operate') and competitive advantage. This obviously requires a managerial approach towards CSR and its integration within the corporate strategic agenda. Empirical evidence indicates that little is known how to best position an organization when it comes to social responsibility; CSR is currently still perceived as an all-inclusive notion used by corporations to address an entire bundle of societal demands. It remains, however, unclear if such a 'generalist' strategy (as opposed to a 'specialist' strategy and a clearly focused CSR identity) yields best results in terms of organizational legitimacy.

- Investigate the CSR policy of a firm from your home country. How far does the CSR policy reflect (like in the case of Austria) a global language game? What older, more local traditions and approaches does CSR replace? What are the consequences of this shift?

IMAGE 11.5 Don't bite
from the apple of corruption

Looked at in this broader way, the question becomes one of time periods:
if businesses serve only shareholder value interests in the short term and do
so in such a way as to jeopardize other interests that might claim representation or be represented, these may then in the long term boomerang back
on the business by attacking its legitimacy or reputation. Thus it becomes
a matter of shareholder value to attend to broader stakeholder interests. As
Vogel (2005) suggested, it may well be the standard business case that the
primary responsibility of companies is to create wealth for their shareholders. But the emergence of CSR and activists associated with it adds a twist:
in order for companies to do well, financially, they must also act virtuously.

Taking CSR seriously

Cynics might say that it becomes a matter of shareholder value for business
to *appear* to be concerned about CSR issues. A common critique, therefore,

is that CSR is often no more than a tool of corporate 'greenwash' – a rhetorical device employed by corporations to legitimize the corporate form and accommodate the social consciences of its consumers.

However, CSR, if monitored by civil society organizations or other independent external auditors, can operate as civil regulations which limit the range of acceptable behaviours open to firms and institutionalize new responsibilities. Among the common range of auditors are *AccountAbility*'s AA1000 standard, based on notions of triple bottom-line (3BL) reporting; the Global Reporting Initiative's Sustainability Reporting Guidelines; Social Accountability International's SA8000 standard; and the ISO 14000 environmental management standard. Additionally, NGOs, such as Oxfam, often monitor closely the activities of transnational corporations in industries such as mining and the local impact that they have on communities, politics, and the environment.

If a firm projects itself as being socially responsible, and avoids embarrassing exposures of malpractice, it can deepen and strengthen its reputational capital and pre-empt two forms of risk, suggests Utting (2003). First, it can help avoid short-term reputational risk related to exposure of a firm's malpractice, which often carries financial sanctions (Hamann et al., 2003). For instance, after the 1999 WTO protests those firms listed on the *Fortune 500* that were perceived as socially irresponsible suffered a 2.7 per cent loss (Spar and La Mure, 2003). CSR can help accommodate consumer preferences for socially responsible products.

Green stakeholders – from concerned individuals, activist stakeholders, through to green organizations in civil society or non-market-based organizations such as Greenpeace – can play a key role in shaping the green agenda for organizations. Civil society organizations have increased the energy they devote to directly lobbying and exposing the malpractice of corporations, which has helped to change consumer preferences and citizen's attitudes towards human rights, the environment, and exploitative relationships. Just as civil society activists can change the broader public perception of what business should be doing, they also shape managerial preferences through developing new concepts of social responsibility, taught in business education and propagated by industry organizations and civil society. While rational actor models assume management's decisions are premised on primarily narrowly defined cost–benefit analysis, this is not always the case.

MINI CASE

BP – beyond petroleum?

BP's 1998 installation of solar power cells at 200 of its pumping stations looks like an example of commitment to green values. However, BP invested only 0.1 per cent of its portfolio in solar panels while simultaneously expanding its fossil fuel extraction and exploration programme. In effect, one could argue that BP has conducted a public relations campaign designed to accommodate its consumers' concerns about the effect of

(Continued)

(Continued)

carbon emissions upon the world, while also expanding its fossil fuel extraction process. BP has also adopted 'socially responsible' positions on global warming to mitigate regulatory risk and legitimize its operations. By defecting from the Global Climate Coalition, an association that denies global warming, it was able to take part in debates over policy prescriptions, voicing a preference for market-based and voluntary solutions. Greenwash is the term that has been coined for espousing the rhetoric of CSR while minimizing its practice.

- How ethical is BP? Use the web to research arguments 'for' and 'against' the position that BP is an ethical corporation, paying particular attention to the high-profile industrial accidents that it has been involved in, especially the Deep Water Horizon disaster in the Gulf of Mexico. Is there a clear answer?

Interorganizational relations between civil society organizations and corporations, stretching from the confrontational to the collaborative, have developed and implemented rules in a multilayered and diffused fashion, forming a dense institutional field of 'civil regulations'. For instance, these regulations can serve to constrain firms by changing internal/employee norms and practices, embarrassing firms that commit malpractice despite having built reputational capital around social responsibility and can bind firms through voluntary, yet external, audits.

Discourses of CSR were initially placed on the business agendas by civil society movements and they continue to be influenced heavily by civil society movements. Consider the case of Nike again: analysis of NGO campaigns against Nike shows that firms may be able occasionally to direct CSR discourse by pre-empting or exceeding civil society or consumer expectations. However, firms are generally responsive if they fear that shareholder value will be affected. Media discussion that is adverse, or criticism from government or submissions to public hearings, such as Senate Committees, influence CSR discourses. NGOs will, no doubt, continue to use their position and resources to push progressive CSR agendas, although business has not been slow to react in setting up its own fronts in civil society, such as the World Business Council on Development.

Highly concentrated, heavily capitalized, and diversified corporations are the easiest target for CSR activism. They have more reputation to protect and face a greater risk of backlash from consumers in sophisticated societies. Regionally based firms, which have far less diversification and capitalization levels, and undercapitalized firms, trading close to financial failure, are far harder to affect.

As supply chains become ever more global, there is the risk that the top-tier firms simply outsource more unethical practices to less capitalized enterprises for cost cutting and, because they are at arm's length, denial, if socially irresponsible actions are uncovered there. They can always cover their legitimacy by adopting codes of practice, which they can then claim these other firms, unbeknown to them, flouted. Moreover, if the actions of the industry leaders create a general impression of social responsibility, those firms that have poor records of CSR will be able to free-ride on their efforts, enjoying the benefits of mitigated regulation risk without the costs of social responsibility. If industrial leaders are not differentiated from poor practitioners of social responsibility, the benefits of their positive activities will be reduced: as a result they may put less resources into socially responsible practices or reap less benefits, as consumers fail to articulate between those industry members who are, and are not, responsible practitioners.

What role do NGOs play in spreading CSR?

NGOs encourage firm-level action to avoid CSR problems. Typically, they advise firms to consistently communicate messages regarding CSR in a firm-level fashion, rather than in terms of an industry as a whole.

NGOs should lobby those dominant firms that have shown a commitment to CSR policies to use their global supply chains and contractual relationships to enforce socially responsible practices on junior industry partners. This would require major companies clearly to articulate socially responsible practices (which provide a further opportunity for civil society to critique and influence them) and ensure governance controls are appropriate for promoting site-level compliance.

Furthermore, NGOs should lobby socially conscientious investment funds as well as industry- and trade-union-based superannuation funds, to restrict capital flows to those firms with low levels of capitalization and poor CSR records. In addition, where industry bodies are dominated by firms that are among the most socially responsible, companies that do not practice CSR may be de-listed.

Small and medium-sized enterprises (SMEs) sometimes complain that compliance with CSR is beyond their technical expertise or level of surplus capital. NGOs can help overcome this by showcasing SMEs that have achieved improvements in their CSR practice and suggesting cost-effective ways of being socially responsible.

While the CSR movement contains implicit dangers of corporate accommodation and of acting as a legitimization device, corporate organizations, and civil society NGOs can guard against their co-option. CSR rhetoric offers important opportunities for civil society to further development objectives and effect meaningful improvements. It also provides opportunities to educate top management teams in corporations about social responsibility as an ongoing, developmental, and deepening process.

CSR is now a part of the normal polyphony that management has to deal with. As Brown and Coupland (2004) suggested, organizations are constituted by those conversations, and fragments of conversations, that occur in and around them, in which many voices strive to be heard, and where what was once a distant echo from outside the chambers of power can become a glorious noise once it gains access. CSR is neither necessarily good nor bad from any particular ethical viewpoint; what matters is how it works in practice – and practice is a constantly evolving phenomenon, as the website of the International Centre for Corporate Social Responsibility at Nottingham University demonstrates through its publications.

QUESTION TIME

What are the positive CSR actions of the educational institution you are studying at? Jot them down below as a reminder of what organizations can do.

....

....

....

....

....

....

....

What are the negative CSR actions of the educational institution you are studying at? Jot them down below as a reminder of what organizations should not do.

....

....

....

....

....

....

....

ETHICAL RULES FOR CORPORATE SOCIAL RESPONSIBILITY

As discussed above, ethics is often packaged in the form of codes of conduct. Codes of conduct are a set of rules that organizations adopt; adhering to this set of rules should then ensure ethical conduct. As we have said, 78 per cent of the US top 1,000 companies have a code of conduct (Nijhof et al., 2003). These codes are often referred to as statements of CSR. For instance, health care products manufacturer Johnson & Johnson published a much-cited code of ethics on its website (see Mini Case below).

MINI CASE

Johnson & Johnson's Ethical Code for the Conduct of Pharmaceutical Medicine

Preamble

Our Ethical Code for the Conduct of Pharmaceutical Medicine is intended to complement our Credo by providing more specific standards of conduct and behavior for physicians, clinical research scientists and others who are responsible for medical aspects of pharmaceutical research and development.

Our Ethical Code is intended to describe the principles that guide ethical decision-making to ensure the safe use of our products, and the best interests of our patients and their families, doctors, nurses and health care providers.

It is envisioned to be the standard for addressing all ethical dilemmas regarding pharmaceutical research and its applications.

Our Ethical Code

It is our fundamental responsibility to place the wellbeing of the patient first by appropriately

(Continued)

(Continued)

balancing risks and benefits and to ensure that the best interests of patients and physicians who use our products receive utmost consideration.

It is our responsibility to apply Credo-based values and judgment regarding the design, conduct, analysis and interpretation of clinical studies and results.

It is our responsibility to adhere to the principles of good clinical practice.

It is our responsibility to ensure all Company-based, medically relevant product information is fair and balanced, accurate and comprehensive,

to enable well-informed risk-benefit assessments about our products.

It is our responsibility to understand differences in values across cultures and to appropriately adapt our behaviors without relaxing our ethical principles.

It is our responsibility to appropriately challenge each other regarding medical and ethical concerns.

- Research Johnson & Johnson's handling of the Tylenol incident, using the web. How and in what ways did the company live up to its ethical code?

CSR codes state the principles that guide ethical decision-making. They set out rules that are supposed to ensure ethical behaviour. However, the implications and effects of different rule-based approaches to ethics can be expected to vary according to their context. We will identify a number of dilemmas that codes of conduct create.

When rules work to effect compliance

One possible effect of working with rules as a framework for ethics and responsible behaviour is that they alienate individuals from exercising moral responsibility. An extreme example of this bureaucratization of ethics might be found in Bauman's (1989) seminal discussion of the organization of concentration camps in the Third Reich. Bauman argues that the people who organized and executed the Holocaust did so by following precisely defined rules. By breaking complex chains of actions into small, calculable tasks and prescribing their execution through rules, individual responsibilities were made opaque and led, ultimately, to inhuman and absolutely unethical results. Thus, simply following ostensibly neutral rules can lead to the worst ethical outcomes (Bauman, 1993; 1995).

When codes are seen as an iron law, then trouble is at hand. How can one prescribe ethicality for responsible subjects by denying them opportunities to learn (follow the rules and you will not make a mistake)? How can the application of external rules legislate for responsible autonomy, irrespective of individuals' interpretations of these rules? The rule might be that as a railway employee the trains should run on time. What their cargo might be is not a concern for the individual. However, when the 'cargo' is people who are being sent to their deaths, can one be so sanguine about following the rules? Rossouw and van Vuuren (2003: 397) suggest that a 'compliance mode' of ethics can result in disempowerment, bureaucratization, feelings of individual irresponsibility, and a mentality that implies that 'what is not forbidden is allowed'.

Implicitly, code-based ethics suggests that if organizational members do not exercise discretion and just follow rules, then they will be behaving ethically. Remember, from Chapter 7, this was the Eichmann defence. In this sense the rules are designed to anaesthetize individuals from moral obligations by locating responsibilities only within an institutional domain. However, this view is based on the assumption that what is organizationally prescribed is ethically appropriate and that ethicality equates with routine behaviour. Neither seems plausible: keeping the trains on time to the death camps was organizationally correct but ethically repugnant, and the failure to resist the organizational routines that made the trains run on time assisted the slaughter of over 6 million people. While being a good bureaucrat with a proper regard for timetables was a form of automatic behaviour, it was hardly ethical. Therefore, organization members cannot easily separate what is ethical from the exercise of responsible autonomy. Codes of conduct do not support such responsible autonomy because they promote compliance with rules set by someone else. Bauman's argument exemplifies the worst possible case of what might happen when rules actually work.

Strictly following the rules may not be the best guarantee of good organizational outcomes, in other circumstances, anyway. Codes of conduct rarely assure that stated goals are achieved. If they did, working to rule would not be such an effective industrial relations tactic. Codes merely guide what free and autonomous subjects will choose to do. For instance, equal employment opportunity (EEO) legislation has not been sufficient to gain women equal status in organizations, despite being based on the belief that law and rules, implemented properly, will bring about more ethical circumstances. In practice, discrimination is enacted through the hardly tangible cultural micro-practices of everyday organizational life (see Martin, 2000; Meyerson and Kolb, 2000). For instance, although promotions are supposed to be based on performance and potential, women often have diminished career options. This is because they are less 'visible' and network less with the powerful – less likely to be invited to the bar with the 'lads' after work or invited to the golf course on the weekend. A legal framework of rules as the basis for ethical practice insufficiently stresses the relation between rules, their enactment, and the actual practices of organizing. Rules always have to be made sense of. They do not make their own sense. And they always have to be interpreted in the context of other rules. For instance, in a consulting company we know, the informal rule is that you earn your pay between 9 and 5 and your promotion between 5 and 9 – when you stay behind in the office to put in extra time. For people who have the responsibility for picking up the children from school or the crèche, more often than not the mother rather than the father, then such an informal rule cuts across any formal commitment to equal opportunity.

MINI CASE

Gender at work

The context of the flexibility initiative: 'functioning in a hostile environment'

One of the authors of this book studied a large professional services firm's gender programme that was designed to create the best possible professional workplace for women. In a public presentation, the CEO of the firm articulated his approach to helping women succeed in business as follows:

> my agreement with the women was that if we continued to have meetings and to complain about the men's behaviour, I am kind of walking out of the place, because my past experience and track record is proving that that is not necessarily the most productive use of my time. But if anybody was interested in helping women to succeed in business, then I am happy to stay ... our whole idea is to say, who are our most talented women? How can we fast-track them? And what do we have to do for them to make sure that they outperform their male counterparts? And how can they function in an environment that is pretty hostile? (CEO, Public Speech)

We found the quote in several respects puzzling. Although there was clear intention to change things and create a more equitable workplace there was something wrong. Let us explore what. The CEO made very clear that he is not acting on complaints because it is not a productive use of his time. Consequently gender issues were only deemed important if they were linked to business success. Thus the gender initiative was framed in terms of the business case; the women who opted into it accepted they would be contributing to the firm's business success and would, as a result of doing so, be able to progress their careers within the organization. Moreover, the CEO's focus was not on helping women in general but on helping 'talented women'. One could argue that this is problematic because 'talent' is of itself a social category negotiated and defined within a patriarchal system. Moreover, why is it necessary for women to 'outperform' men in order to make their careers? Finally, the CEO asked how can women function in 'an environment that is pretty hostile'? Again, the message here is that it is not about changing the environment but about learning to function and (out)perform (others) in such an environment. The environment is depicted as a given, unchangeable reality in which people have to fit in.

- How would you analyse the CEO's approach to ethics? Do you agree with his views? How could you formulate a different narrative that might be more inclusive?

When rules work as ceremonial facades

An ethics formulated on the basis of explicit rules will operate like other institutionalized rule-based systems (see Chapter 13). Following Meyer and Rowan (1977), such systems can function as ceremonially adopted myths used to gain legitimacy, resources, stability, and to enhance survival prospects. Thus, to maintain ceremonial conformity, 'organizations that reflect institutional rules tend to buffer their formal structures from the uncertainties of technical activities by becoming loosely coupled, building gaps between their formal structures and actual work activities' (Meyer and Rowan, 1977: 340). In their search for legitimacy, organizations use codes of conduct as standards to justify what they do (Brunsson and Jacobsen, 2000). In this sense, having codes of conduct becomes a 'public relation exercise' (Munro, 1992: 98).

When ethical rules are at odds with other types of rules

Warren (2003) has shown that deviance (breaking rules) in organizations can in fact be constructive. Confronted with management realities and specific organizational practices such as human resource management, marketing, production, or accounting, a clash of logic, language, and basic assumptions that drive the perfect world of prescriptive ethics and the imperfect world of business reality seems unavoidable. Imagine a marketing officer wanting to avoid a product recall because it would damage the image of the company, which might lead to a decrease in sales and a loss of jobs. However, the production manager might find this attitude unethical because a faulty product could potentially hurt customers. Both could argue that their suggestions were ethical. Following their own logic they might each make good arguments that are, unfortunately, mutually exclusive.

WHAT DO YOU MEAN?

Which rule is right?

Two different rules, each ethical in its own context of application, may clash when enacted together. In strict Islamic societies women have burned to death in female institutions as the male fire-crew wait for the male guardians to allow them access to the women's space. Each rule that is applied, saving lives, putting out fires, and respecting the purity of women, might in itself make sense within an Islamic context, but in the context of a fire in a school or maternity ward the fact that one rule is embedded in strict interpretations of the Koran while the others are not means that there is a clash between the rules.

Rules cannot account for these ethical dilemmas, since it is two or more rules that, looked at separately, create the dilemma. To take a business example: a company that produces pharmaceuticals may be committed to environmental values as well as to helping Third World countries. Each rule seems ethical and 'good' in itself but what if they clash? Management has at least two options: either producing at lower cost in less environmentally friendly ways and thus being able to distribute a new medicine much less expensively in Third World countries, or manufacturing according to high environmental standards and selling the medication at a higher price. In the second option, the environment is respected but the limited economic resources of poor patients are not, meaning that many people who need the medicine will be excluded from using it. Ethics is *at stake* when these two rules clash – and no third meta-rule can be applied to resolve the dilemma. As Munro concludes, 'codes are almost useless to individual employees who are faced with their particular dilemmas' (1992: 105).

Ethical decisions emerge out of dilemmas that cannot be managed in advance through rules.

When a member of an organization faces a novel and ethically charged situation they do more than merely apply a formulaic rule in order to decide on a course of action. Rather, ruling is an activity, as the gerund demonstrates: the member has to apply the rule (interpret it) in the specific situation that can lead to a situation where two ethical rules compete with each other. As Munro (1992) has shown, it is exactly this competition between two ethical rules that characterizes ethical situations as dilemmas. As he argues, the 'very nature of moral dilemmas is that they arise from the existing norms of behaviour, which sometimes demand contradictory things of a person' (1992: 102).

Where people enact one rule they must do so in the context of their knowledge of other rules. Think of a 'No Standing' sign. Such a sign, as seen in many Western cities, means that cars are not allowed to stop or park in the area designated by the sign. 'No Standing' does not mean that one must fall down, be prone, or seated. Nor does it mean that one must be mobile. Of course, this context is not supplied by the sign itself, but by its socially skilled interpretation. It is feasible that someone unused to Western cities seeing such a sign and having the skills to read it might get it wrong – possible, but not likely because only a cursory reference to context would provide plenty of counterfactual clues to interpretation.

When the rules are ambiguous in their application

Some approaches to ethics suggest that analysing the consequences of that behaviour can assess the ethicality of behaviour. Thus, behaviour is said to be 'good' if the consequences of this behaviour are seen to be useful or valuable. This utilitarian logic is problematic, however, because it fails to account for situations where different people can interpret the consequences of actions differently. Indeed, what are good consequences for one party can be awful for other parties. As Willmott (1998) puts it eloquently, one party's freedom fighter is another party's terrorist. Or, as in the case below, one culture's gift is another culture's bribe.

WHAT'S THE POINT?

No gifts, we are ethical!

Shell tried to implement a code of conduct that stated (as principle number 5) that employees are not allowed to receive or give any gifts from clients, suppliers, etc. (see *The Shell Report*, 2003). Such a rule should prevent the corruption and bribery that ostensibly occurred in some of Shell's activities in developing and other economies.

However, as Shell found out, in some countries giving and receiving gifts is simply a normal practice of business. Acting strictly according to the 'no-gift' rule would mean, in these cases, losing business opportunities. The general and universally defined rule 'no gifts' needs to be set in context, interpreted, and sometimes broken – in order to do business according to ethically local habits and traditions.

In terms of ethics, rules do nothing by themselves – the concern is with how people interact with and use the rules according to local culture-specific and industry-specific practices.

Can an individual truly assess and predict the consequences of their behaviour? In a complex and fast-changing world in which multiple cause and effect relations form a dense web, calculation of the consequences of one's behaviour will often fail. Moreover, in organizations that are 'garbage

(Continued)

(Continued)

cans', where processes are messy and rationality a scarce good, the consequences of one's behaviour are likely to be unpredictable (see Chapter 7). In such an environment, the best of intentions is often not good enough; worse, as the proverb goes, the road to hell is paved with good intentions.

Paradoxically, on the other hand, sometimes ostensibly bad practices can lead to surprisingly ethical outcomes: take Oskar Schindler, for instance, well known since the 1993 film, *Schindler's List*, based on Thomas Keneally's (1982) novel *Schindler's Ark*. Schindler was a womanizer, a money-hungry man who understood the war of Nazi Germany as a business opportunity rather than as a threat. He followed

the SS into Poland and became heavily involved in the black-market and the underworld and became friendly with the local Gestapo. He procured women, alcohol, and other favours for them. With these newfound connections he managed to acquire a factory, which he worked with Jewish labour. Despite this seemingly selfish behaviour, he managed to rescue 1,200 Jews – as Thomas Keneally wrote. The implication of this story is that ethically dubious practices can have ethically good outcomes, and good practices bad outcomes. Rules that simply state what is good and bad provide simplifying templates for complex ethical problems and dilemmas and cannot account for Schindler's dynamics.

When rules assign responsibilities

Rules can be employed to assess organizational responsibilities and thus to ascribe blame to individual managers when responsibilities are interpreted as having gone awry. This use of rules is problematic in several respects. By excluding emotions, personal responsibility, and by considering humans as neutral personnel, organizations fail to understand and act according to ethical values, suggests du Gay (2000b). Implicitly, the argument is that only good individuals, trained in ethics and equipped with sound moral principles, can ensure that the organizational machine works ethically. It all depends on the people. If the organization does not act according to rule, then a decision-maker should be identified and be held personally responsible. Sometimes this can lead to sacrificial victims – when it is systems that are responsible.

WHAT DO YOU MEAN?

Sacrificing a victim when a system was responsible

We have looked at the collapse of Barings Bank in 1995 in earlier chapters. We want to return to this case again because it focuses so many issues so well. In this case the problems faced by the bank were ascribed to the unethical behaviour of a single 'rogue trader' – Nick Leeson. Allocating responsibility

to this one person is insufficient to explain why Barings collapsed, however (Drummond, 2002; Stein, 2000). Rather, it was a lethal mix of structural, cultural, and historical rules that prefigured the end of Barings. As Stein (2000: 1227) argues, 'Barings' problem [is located] squarely with the institution rather than with Leeson ... the conditions for Leeson's fraud were set in place substantially prior to his arrival at Barings'. Blaming Leeson personally

(Continued)

(Continued)

means neglecting to account for local contexts, organization cultures, and the history of decision-making at Barings.

It is too easy to personalize problems rather than see them as embedded in a complex interrelation of contingencies. Such simple views echo the popular management and sporting press, where the success (and failure) of organizations is attributed to the one person at the top – say business success in the case of Jack Welch or Bill Gates or political failure in the case of George W. Bush or Tony Blair.

ETHICS AS PRACTICE

Doing ethics, being ethical

Perhaps we should consider ethics in the context of situated practice – what we do when we are being ethical – rather than from the perspective of generalized pronouncements on the effects of rules. Take the example of (business) bluffing (Carr, 1968; Carson, 1993): bluffing is not ethically conspicuous when one plays poker or wants to buy a car; however, bluffing in a courtroom or in a marriage might be unethical because the context of the situation does not allow for bluffing. Thus, in looking at when and how ethics is enacted the context is decisive. If we examine how ethics is differentially embedded in practices that operate in an active and contextualized manner we can understand that ethics inhabits the spaces between rules, between subjects interacting with rules, and the different ways that these spaces, rules, and actors can be understood and enacted.

A concern with ethics as practice asks how are rules translated into practices and how are they enacted in everyday organizational contexts? Empirically, what needs to be investigated is the adhering, violating, ignoring, or creative interpreting of rules and how these actions frame rule users, shapers, enforcers, defenders, critics, and interpreters. As shown above, pure rule following can lead to ethically questionable outcomes just as the ethics of the rules themselves is not guaranteed. Therefore, interpreting and adapting rules according to local circumstances, including sometimes even breaking rules, might be ethically sound. Ethics as practice addresses the gap between rule following and other possible responses to them. Understanding the enactment of rules, or ruling as a practice, makes visible the dilemmas as well as possibilities of ethical conduct – aligned or opposed to the official code of conduct.

Where current approaches consider ruling as a means of governing (or trying to govern) ethical activity by prescribing to other people what they should and should not do, considering ethics as a practice shifts focus to how rules are enacted, how they are implemented and made practical. While rules are resources used to legitimize and to negotiate organizational realities, ethics conceived as practices focuses on the potentially unethical use of these resources.

Just as any other form of practice, ethics is enacted through specific discourses. As discourse we understand the written or spoken, verbally or non-verbally communicated texts constitutive of organizational realities, including codes of conduct, stories, and interaction between people. It is in the everyday use of language that moral and ethical judgements are made – often in passing, embedded in the 'natural' categories of language use.

Ethics expressed in and through the categories used in everyday language

Take for example the value seen in being an 'organization man' as an ideal type of worker (Whyte, 1960) in the 1950s. And he was a man – this was a time when women often retired from the workforce after marriage and most women aspired to be married to an organization man who could provide for them and their children through the security of their employment and pension. The organization man was a man who was loyal to one organization and built his whole career there. By the 1980s the organization man was rarely referred to. As we have seen in the market critique of bureaucracy, the focus has now shifted to entrepreneurial selves who exercise initiative rather than just follow the rules (du Gay, 1996).

In each case a different discourse creates different categories for being a 'good' employee: one sees the employee as a rule-follower; the other sees the employee as a person who can be trusted to show initiative. In both contexts, the meaning of 'being ethical' might differ.

Understanding ethics as practice implies analysing those discourses that enact particular ethical attributions. For instance, ISO 14000, introduced by the International Standards Organization, opened up new ethical possibilities for organizations. They could choose to adapt or to ignore the standard – but in doing so they had to respond to and use the discourse triggered by ISO (see Bansal and Hunter, 2003; Brunsson and Jacobsen, 2000). As Karl Weick puts it, they have to make sense of the new situation: sensemaking is 'less about discovery than it is about invention. To engage in sensemaking is to construct, filter, frame, create facticity ... and render the subjective into something more tangible' (1995: 13–14). Ethical problems and unethical action do not exist per se – they only exist as they are talked into being by the ways in which people make sense.

In judging whether a given behaviour is ethical or not, therefore, we need to understand the discourse that nurtures the ethical sensemaking process. Thus, for instance, rules that forbid smoking inside offices are embedded in a discourse about the ill effects of secondary inhalation of matter known to be cancerous. These ethics could not be applied at a time when the link between smoking and cancer was not known or accepted. Hence, in many old movies, we see smoke-filled rooms as the normal kind of habitat of hard-bitten reporters and detectives. Specific discourses create the conditions of possibility for notions of ethics to be applied; their application constitutes particular types of social action as either ethical or not ethical: think of smoking again.

There is a relation between subjectivity and power (Foucault, 2003). The practices employed in an asylum, for instance, constitute certain historically formulated and specific identities associated with being mentally ill (see Foucault, 1965; Goffman, 1961). For instance, people who were regarded as 'village idiots' in the Middle Ages were venerated as having a particular wisdom and insight, and had a special role in the community. By the nineteenth century such people were confined in 'lunatic asylums', and a popular entertainment consisted of going to watch the lunatics in the asylum. In the twentieth century they were often released to 'care in the community', which, too often in practice, meant homelessness, exploitation, and a lack of any therapeutic framework.

Similarly, when Phillips and Hardy (1997) researched the UK refugee system they found that refugee identity was conceptually constructed discursively. 'What is a refugee?' becomes a key question. For instance, refugees are not usually allowed to be 'economic migrants' seeking a better life. They must be able to demonstrate persecution that is unequivocal. Also, there is the question asked at an individual level of 'Who actually is a refugee?' That is, given the categorical meaning, does this particular person fit the category?

Thus ethics not only shapes the subjectivity of organizational members, but also provides resources through which organizations can shape the identity of both employees and others (Styhre, 2001). Such shaping never occurs on a level playing field, to use a popular metaphor. It has political heights and gullies, deeply overshadowed spaces, others that bask in the light of what is taken to be pure reason, and underground roots that spread under the terrain, shaping it in unseen and thus radical ways. As du Gay (2000b) suggests, liberal forms of managing and governing create social actors as subjects of responsibility, autonomy, and choice upon whom political institutions seek to act by shaping and utilizing their freedom.

Check out the Companion Website www.sagepub.co.uk/ managingandorganizations3 for free access to a paper by M. Kornberger and A. D. Brown (2007), which provides a more detailed empirical study of ethics as practice, co-written by one of the co-authors of this book.

Practices at work: designing ethical behavioural change

In his 2007 book, Gordon lifts the lid on one such set of circumstances. He was able to research a specific organization where it was evident that unethical conduct flourished. The organization was the New South Wales Police Service. The NSW Police Service is one of the largest police organizations in the world with more than 17,000 employees serving a population of 7 million in the state of New South Wales, an area of more than 800,000 square kilometres, equivalent in size to the US state of Texas. In 1997 the results of a Royal Commission, a statutory inquiry authorized by the state government with all the powers of a judicial body, revealed the reality of policing in NSW to be very different from the ethical values that the Service espoused: the Service was rife with unethical and corrupt behaviour. Examples of such behaviour included the abuse of authority, the taking of bribes, providing false evidence, drug dealing, commissioning criminals to commit crimes, fixing internal promotions so that corrupted members were promoted, and the use of intimidation and stand-over tactics as well as murder (Wood, 1997).

The Royal Commission's findings illustrate how strong discipline and a strict adherence to authoritarian principles of management constituted a culture of obedience and fear in the Service: even if one was not corrupt, one did not question the authority of superiors. Dubious practices went unchecked; over time, the sense of dubiousness was lost to the point where practices that violated almost every element of the Service's ethics became part of the everyday routine.

Acting in response to the Royal Commission's findings and recommendations, the NSW government appointed Mr Peter Ryan, from the UK, as the new Commissioner of Police, who initiated a reform programme aimed at achieving 'ethical and cost efficient policing' (Ryan, 2002). Commissioner Ryan understood modern management concepts (empowerment, teams, and flatter structures) to be the solution to the problems highlighted by Wood (1997). He initiated a departure from a traditional hierarchical and military structure and, over the next five years, diligently implemented a reform process employing contemporary theories of organizational design to create a frame within which to combat unethical behaviour.

Chief among the new instruments was the Operations Control and Review (OCR) meeting, introduced by Ryan and his team with the intention of changing the ethics of the service. The OCR was designed as a formal meeting in which the senior management team of the Service coordinated and discussed the operational performance of each local area. Officers testified that the OCR had a pervasive impact. The meeting functioned as a form of Electronic Panopticon in reverse: it did not exercise surveillance over all members but all members exercised surveillance over it as it was broadcast throughout the Service, transmitted via police television to local area commanders across the state.

While the OCR was designed to coordinate the operational performance of the different local area commands, according to the comments of numerous officers it appeared to be more of an arena in which senior executives reinforced their superiority by attacking and punishing local area commanders. The focus on individuals rather than operations was reflected in the pervasive use of metaphors such as people appearing before it placing their 'heads on the block', portraying the OCR as a setting for an execution. Other officer's commented that 'it is just a big magnifying glass', indicating that the OCR should be seen in terms of a very public mechanism for framing 'normal' expectations.

The OCR meeting was a prime medium through which officers in management positions throughout the Service were made aware of how management is done in the Service. Rather than leave space for dialogue, the OCR enforced an unambiguous and fact-driven question and answer discussion that simply did not allow for ethically charged situations to be discussed.

In fact, the OCR marginalized interpretive problems that officers might experience with ethics in practice and installed a 'fact-driven' discourse that, in its focus on results, did not allow discussing how these results were achieved ethically. The OCR focused on tangible results that each local area commander had to present. For instance, they had to report on how many drug dealers they arrested in their area. Of course, an ethically responsible and modern approach to policing might not count the number of small dealers that are arrested but focus on preventive measures. Hence, a commander who arrested fewer people for drug possession was, according to the OCR, less effective than one who arrested many.

You can see that the OCR, introduced to change ethics, in fact added to the ethical dilemmas of the police. They had to report their ethically complex reality in a black and white, figures-driven format. However, reality is more complex than a set of rules. Rather than being a catalyst for learning, the discursive practice of the OCR meetings turned the new initiative into a mechanism for non-learning that was achieved through putting potential problems into a specific temporal, spatial, personal, and structural context, introducing a strict procedure that distributes responsibilities in a particular way.

Ethics in practice requires an openness to accept and discuss ethical dilemmas: ethics is at stake not only when we have no rules at hand but also when rules clash. Thus, the acceptance and discussion of ethical dilemmas is one step towards more ethical management. Instead of reducing practice to simple wrong–right answers, we suggest making ethical problems visible and discussing them as complex problems rather than ones that can be managed according to an economic calculus. In practice, organizations typically wrestle with ethical difficulties rather than using rules to avoid them. Nowhere is this more evident than in the area of what has come to be called corporate social responsibility.

Check out the Companion Website www.sagepub.co.uk/ managingandorganizations3 for free access to an article by Ray Gordon, and two of the authors of this book, Stewart Clegg and Martin Kornberger (2009), which provides more details on the New South Wales police case.

CORPORATE SOCIAL RESPONSIBILITY AND SUSTAINABILITY

How responsible are managers?

According to Handy (2002), 90 per cent of all Americans do not trust managers to look after the interests of their employees and only 18 per cent think that they look after their shareholders properly. He argues that 'these countries that boast most stridently about their democratic principles derive their wealth from institutions that are deficiently undemocratic, in which all serious power is held by outsiders and power inside is wielded by a dictatorship or, at best, an oligarchy' (Handy, 2002: 52). And, as the surveys demonstrate, oligarchic elites do not generate trust in the institutions that sustain them. Thus, ethics is an important issue for organizations facing environments in which their customers, clients, employees, patients, students, etc. are clearly ethically sensitive. At best, codes of conduct are insufficient to ensure ethical behaviour, at worst they provide quick-fix answers that prevent ethical dilemmas from being debated.

The task of ethics permeates up, down, and across an organization, as the example of sustainability suggests. Since the publication of the report of the Intergovernmental Panel on Climate Change, by UNESCO on 2 February 2007, the reality of global warming is now widely accepted. Almost as widely accepted is the realization that corporate and business activity is contributing significantly to this warming. Many business leaders are now well aware of this fact and are seeking to do something about it.

Increasingly, ecologists are not alone in changing the way that business is done. There is a growing realization that although we have created a hugely successful business system for generating needs and satisfying them, one of its side effects has been a huge growth in environmental degradation, toxic wastes, and species risk. This is especially the case in those industries that comprise the petrochemical complex, which supply so many modern essentials, from familiar things made of plastics, nylon, and other artificial fibres, to complex compounds we have probably never heard of. Many of these chemicals are highly toxic.

MINI CASE

Ray Anderson's story of sustainability

Ray Anderson is the chairman of Interface Inc., the world's largest manufacturer of carpets. Interface makes an enormous number of carpets. It also used to cause huge pollution: every year its factories produced hundreds of gallons of wastewater and nearly 900 pollutants.

After reading Hawken's (1993) *The Ecology of Commerce: A Declaration of Sustainability*, Anderson was converted to a sustainable point of view that he vowed to implement in his own business.

First, Anderson reduced waste and conserved energy by recycling. Of course, this makes great business sense. Less waste can equal more profit as you use all that you pay for rather than throw a lot of it away. Before Anderson read Hawken, 6 tons of carpet trimming was sent to the landfill by his company each day. By 1997 that waste was

reduced to zero. New computer controls were installed on boilers to reduce carbon monoxide emissions (by 99.7 per cent), which also improved the boilers' efficiency, resulting in further decreased waste and increased profits.

Anderson has written about his conversion in a 1999 book, *Mid Course Correction: Toward a Sustainable Enterprise: The Interface Model*. What is this model? It is one that aims for complete sustainability, using solar and wind power in the place of fossil fuels, planting trees to offset carbon pollution caused by trucks transporting carpets, making carpets out of organic materials such as corn.

- Look at http://www.myhero.com/myhero/ hero. asp?hero=r_anderson and Anderson's book, if you have it locally available. What could the organization you work or study in do to be more sustainable, following Anderson's ideas?

A **risk society** is one in which the life-threatening disasters that it might be subject to cannot be controlled within a specific territory: Chernobyl or global warming are good examples.

Toxic chemicals are one component of what German sociologist Ulrich Beck calls the **risk society** (Beck, 2002). They cannot be contained within any one plant or nation; if they escape into the ecology they spread through the air, rivers, and rain into the environment of people unaware of the risks they face and unable to do much about them.

Clearly, in complex chains of interorganizational relations, especially at the far end of the chain, especially when the end of the chain is perhaps selected because standards there are laxer than at the beginning of the chain, there is ample opportunity for things to go wrong. A global trade in toxic waste is a trade based on unequal standards. How can businesses and societies seek to minimize risk?

There are a number of ways that concerned people are seeking to limit the risks of ecological disaster and create more sustainable modes of business, giving rise to what Jermier et al. (2006: 618) term the 'new corporate environmentalism'. At the centre of this movement is the attempt by businesses and business leaders to play a leadership role in reforming the way business does business, by making it more sustainable, and to use the tools and approaches of rational management to improve ecological behaviour. Thus, the new corporate environmentalism seeks not only to comply with whatever governmental or industry regulations may be in place, but also to develop more proactive sustainability approaches. This places sustainability, or as it is sometimes referred to, **corporate greening**, at the core of a firm's strategic agenda.

> **Corporate greening** is a process that involves trying to adopt green principles and practices in as many facets of the business as it is possible to do so.

What is corporate greening?

Corporate greening involves the espousal of 'green' values, which are becoming increasingly mainstream in the wake of the Kyoto Treaty and the realization that sustainable production is equivalent to more efficient production. Inputs that are not wasted and processes that do not provide outputs that have to be scrapped are both ecologically and economically rational. Waste is irrational and inefficient.

Corporate greening could involve green production that uses less energy, green materials that recycle and aim for zero waste, green transportation (for instance, using bicycles or pedal-powered scooters to get around the workplace or between organizations), green facilities that are designed to minimize energy waste and use, green products that use less non-renewable resources, and a continuing programme of educating employees and spreading learning about being green employees as widely as possible.

Marketing could point to the green benefits of the product and the processes taken to produce it, and not be wasteful of paper or other resources (Buckholz, 1998). It could report, for instance, the widespread use of environmental management systems and standards to structure organizational processes and behaviour, and the use of green accounting standards that as a part of their 'triple bottom line' report on the environmental impact of the company or organization (Kolk, 2000).

The company may form green partnerships with NGOs or community organizations to extend green practices in the broader society (e.g. Gordon, 2001; Wasik, 1996). The organization might join bodies such as the World Business Council for Sustainable Development, or align itself with something such as the United Nations Global Compact. Above all, it will seek to outdo whatever is constituted as regulatory best practice, seeking to make itself greener than it is obliged to be.

What are the consequences of going green?

One consequence of saving materials, wastage, resources, is that less money is wasted. Another consequence of a tight regulatory regime limiting the opportunities for businesses simply to dump their 'externalities' in a local – or distant – environment is that they have to become more innovative in devising systems and practices that limit waste and harmful side effects. In principle a green business should be a more profitable business, as Porter and van der Linde (1995) argued: it gets a double dividend of greater social responsibility and greater profit. Of course, once the easy wins have been achieved then it becomes harder to keep gaining double dividends.

Other ways of gaining further dividends from corporately sustainable behaviour may come from using a corporate leading role to force best standards throughout an industry by making suppliers standard compliant if they want to continue doing business. International standards such as the ISO 1401 standard have been used in this way by firms such as the Ford Motor Company and General Motors – all their suppliers have to be ISO 1401 compliant.

Of course, as the critics have been quick to point out, ISO 1401 does not necessarily create better ecological performance, as Jermier et al. (2006: 634–635) argue. A great deal depends on how rigorously and independently the business is audited to the standard, and what the sanctions are for non-conformance. Again, the effectiveness of any social contract is contextually specific – while some forms of civil regulation will be very effective, others will be markedly less so.

WHAT'S THE POINT?

A brick in time

Stewart once went to a meeting of members of a Scottish Chamber of Commerce, held in a large multinational company headquarters near Edinburgh. The speaker for the day asked a rhetorical question: 'What would you say if I told you that in a business such as this I could save you over 10,000 pounds a year?' The consensus was that this was a good thing. Then he reached into his briefcase and pulled something out of it, while at the same time asking, 'What would you say if I told you that you could save that money with this?' People looked puzzled – how could a common or garden building brick save money? He proceeded to tell them: 'Put one of these in every toilet cistern and you will save 10,000 pounds a year in water that would otherwise get flushed away.' Well, everyone agreed this was a great idea and went away committed to introducing bricks into their organizations. But it is a very simple and easy win – continuing to gain double dividends may be a little harder.

Small wins: learning to be green   Organizations cannot be green if those within them do not adopt green behaviours across the board. Turning off the lights, turning down the heater or the air-conditioning, using the windows to cool a room rather than the air-conditioning unit, walking or cycling to work, or using public transport, rather than driving – all these small things can make a big difference. These are the small wins, though.

Learning to be green   We can learn to be green and the organizations we work for can be crucibles for green learning. Jermier and his colleagues (2006) suggest that several factors characterize a successful green learning organization:

- *Lifelong learning*: Ensuring that the organization really is a learning organization, constantly trying to find not only new ways of doing the same things better (single-loop learning) but also new things to do in innovative ways (double-loop learning).

- *Developing critical thinking skills*: Helping organization members gain confidence in critical reflection on existing ways of doing things and encouraging them to voice their opinions as to how things might be done better, developing future-oriented scenarios that are more sustainable.

- *Building citizenship capabilities*: Encouraging employees to think not just as employees – in terms of the firm benefit – but as concerned citizens desirous of reducing the overall ecological footprint of not only the organizations they work for and with, but also the impact that they make in their daily lives.

- *Fostering environmental literacy*: Encouraging people to learn about specific environmental problems and solutions, their causes, consequences, and connectedness.

- *Nurturing ecological wisdom*: Sharing an eco-centred understanding of the web of life, the centrality of responsible, ethical and sustainable behaviour to a good life.

Three things need to come together to build green learning in organizations: the creation of a public sphere; the development of communicative rationality, and discursive design. A public sphere is a space in which the 'public reason of private citizens' predominates. Organizations can become actively involved in educating their members for participation in green debates in the broader society as concerned citizens and parents rather than just as employees of Corporation X. Here they should be able to develop communicative rationality – a commitment to frank and open debate – as well as the capability of assessing and evaluating evidence, and reaching evidence-based ethical decisions independent of specific interests. They will learn to speak the language of the environment as a form of non-instrumental rationality, which is shaped not by the instrumentality of their or their organizations' interest, but the public, ecological, and ethical good.

Such a model of social responsibility may seem idealistic. But recall where we started this section – that the world's scientists have now accepted that global warming is a reality and that a major contributing factor is the industrial systems that we have designed. It will not be possible to solve this problem with a narrowly instrumental attitude. If these prevail then there will always be some firms, some industries, and some countries that are prepared to tolerate standards that are irresponsible. We are all on the Earth together and if we are to leave it in good shape for the future generations then we need to accept responsibility for its stewardship as a collective necessity.

Check out the Companion Website www.sagepub.co.uk/ managingandorganizations3 for free access to a paper by G. Moore and R. Beadle (2006), which summarizes some of the topics that have been discussed in this chapter.

SUMMARY AND REVIEW

In this chapter we have reviewed contemporary approaches to ethics, corporate social responsibility (CSR), and sustainability.

Ethics, CSR, and sustainability are sometimes seen as 'soft' topics but they have become more and more important for businesses in the twenty-first century. Ethically related issues have become both much more central and diverse, with the environment now being at the core of contemporary concerns. The triple bottom line is now the reporting standard of choice for organizations that seek to demonstrate that they are being ethical in a broad sense. The shift to a concern to be seen to be ethical means that organizations and their managers now have to relate to a much wider set of stakeholders, concerns, and interests in a meaningful way. There are no simple or easy recipes telling managers how to manage ethically – they have to be acutely aware of the necessity to manage ethics in practice. Managing ethics implies dealing with paradoxes, ambiguities, and trade-offs rather than being a simple and easy matter of applying clear rules to identifiable cases.

EXERCISES

1 Having read this chapter you should be able to say in your own words what each of the following key terms means. Test yourself or ask a colleague to test you.

   - Values
   - Business ethics
   - Corporate social responsibility
   - Sustainability
   - Stakeholders
   - Corporate greening
   - New corporate environmentalism
   - Non-governmental organizations (NGOs)
   - Codes of conduct

2 How would you define business ethics?
3 What are the different approaches to ethics?
4 Why are rules a problematic way of ensuring good governance?
5 What are the key elements of the 'ethics as practice' approach?

6 Why did the ethical behavioural training in the New South Wales Police Service fail? From your perspective, how could the failure have been avoided?
7 What is corporate social responsibility?
8 What sorts of things must organizations do if they wish to become more sustainable and lessen their ecological footprint?
9 To what extent is the term 'business ethics' a paradox?

ADDITIONAL RESOURCES

1 There are many interesting texts on business ethics that give you a deeper understanding of the topic. For a critical perspective we would recommend *For Business Ethics: A Critical Approach* by Campbell Jones, Martin Parker, and Rene ten Bos (2005). A more upbeat look at ethics is Andy Crane and Dirk Matten's book (2004) *Business Ethics: A European Perspective: Managing Corporate Citizenship and Sustainability in the Age of Globalization*. Both offer good introductions to key topics discussed in this chapter.

2 For further research we can recommend the two edited volumes on business ethics that have been put together by the authors of this book. The first is Clegg and Rhodes' *Management Ethics: Contemporary Contexts*, published in 2006; the other is Carter et al. (2007) *Business Ethics as Practice: Representation, Discourse and Performance*. Here you will find more specialized contributions that might be helpful if you have to write a thesis or an essay.

3 As noted in the introduction to this chapter, there are several journals that deal with business ethics including *Journal of Business Ethics*, *Business & Professional Ethics Journal*, *Journal of Business and Professional Ethics*, *Journal of Business Ethics*, and *Business Ethics Quarterly*. They all offer valuable insights into business ethics.

4 Further, we can recommend several excellent movies; most notably, we think, Al Gore's movie, *An Inconvenient Truth* (Guggenheim, 2006), a timely and interesting film that helps to understand the pressing needs to change (corporate) behaviour.

5 Less famous, but nonetheless very powerful, we would recommend the movie *Thank you for Smoking* (Reitman, 2005). It tells the story of a PR guy who works for the cigarette industry and follows his attempts to cover up the truth about the health risks of smoking. It shows in a humorous way how corporate spin works and how 'truth' is manufactured by PR departments.

6 *The Fog of War* (Morris, 2003) is a documentary that tells the story of Robert McNamara, former US Defense Secretary. The film documents how horrible events such as the burning down of Tokyo and the dropping of the two atom bombs in the Second World War and later on the Vietnam War were rationalized by the US administration. It also shows that ethical decisions are not easy to make and that what is ethically right and what is wrong are often established after ethical decisions have been made.

7 We think it is worth looking at Alex Gibney's (2005) *Enron: The Smartest Guys in the Room*, a film that tells the story of the collapse of Enron and Arthur Andersen. The movie shows brilliantly how a total lack of ethics contributed to one of the biggest corporate collapses in history.

8 This brings us to our last movie that we think is worth your while: *The Corporation* by M. Achbar (2003) explores the psychopathic nature of corporations and includes interviews with people such as Noam Chomsky, Naomi Klein, Milton Friedman, and Michael Moore.

WEB SECTION

1 Our Companion Website is the best first stop for you to find a great deal of extra resources, free PDF versions of leading articles published in Sage journals, exercises, video and pod casts, team case studies and general questions, and links to teamwork resources. Go to www.sagepub.co.uk/managing andorganizations3.

2 For state of the art briefings on how to manage organizations effectively, please visit the Henry Stewart Talks series of online audiovisual seminars on Managing Organizations, edited by Stewart Clegg: www.hstalks.com/r/managing-orgs,

in particular, Talk #16: *Managing sustainably*, Suzanne Benn and Talk #17: *Managing ethically*, René ten Bos.

3 The website www.business-ethics.org is the International Business Ethics Institute's home page. The Institute's goal is to 'promote equitable economic development resource sustainability and just forms of government'. You will find interesting articles on the value and importance of business ethics for practice, a bibliography, as well as many useful links.

4 The Business for Social Responsibility in the USA can be found at www.bsr.org. It is a global organization that aims to help its members be successful in a sustainable way and respect ethical values of stakeholders and the environment.

5 www.ethicalcorp.com is a portal for CSR and ethics; feature articles, events, news, and other sections help you to keep up to date with the debate on ethics and CSR.

6 Another useful CSR resource is CSR Europe, which you can find at www.csreurope.org. This European-based forum features many reports, events, and other interesting sections related to CSR and ethics.

7 http://www.gcmonitor.org is a website that monitors multinationals and reports critically about their deeds. It is an interesting site for exploring some of the dark side of business.

8 www.globalethicsmonitor.com reports on latest issues related to ethics. It is a very informative site where you can find the latest trends and company strategies in regard to business ethics.

9 A more radical site directed against one company – Shell – can be found at www.schnews. org.uk. The organization behind the site presents itself as (s)hell's angels.

LOOKING FOR A HIGHER MARK?

Reading and digesting these articles that are available free on the Companion Website www. sagepub.co.uk/managingandorganizations3 can help you gain deeper understanding and, on the basis of that, a better grade:

1 Moore, G. and Beadle, R. (2006) 'In search of organizational virtue in business: agents, goods, practices, institutions and environments',

Organization Studies, 27 (3): 369–389. An intriguing look at virtue ethics in practice.

2 Moberg, D. J. (2006) 'Ethics blind spots in organizations: how systematic errors in persons' perception undermine moral agency', *Organization Studies*, 27 (3): 413–428. This paper looks at how common perceptual frames create ethics blind spots that undermine moral agency.

3 Kornberger, M. and Brown, A. D. (2007) '"Ethics" as a discursive resource for identity work', *Human Relations*, 60 (3): 497–518. This article analyses how participants in a not-for-profit service organization (the 'Incubator') drew on understandings of 'ethics' in order to make sense of their individual and collective selves.

4 Gordon, R., Clegg, S. and Kornberger, M. (2009) 'Embedded ethics: discourse and power in the New South Wales Police Service', *Organization Studies*, 30 (1): 73–99; reprinted in Clegg, S. R. (2010) *SAGE Directions in Organization Studies (Volume II)*, London: Sage, pp. 301–333. In this article two of the authors of this book, together with Ray Gordon, demonstrate how change programmes with good ethical intentions can produce results that were unanticipated and that embed further the issues they were trying to change.

5 Stubbs, W. and Cocklin, C. (2008) 'Conceptualizing a "sustainability business model"', *Organization and Environment*, 21 (2): 103–127. There are many different ways of thinking about sustainability. Given the dependence of traditional management paradigms on the neoclassical model and industrial society, they are inherently limited in their ability to address ecological issues. The authors argue that new models of business need to be developed in which sustainability is intrinsic.

CASE STUDY

GRANBY ZOO

Emerging from the private menageries of royal families in Europe during the eighteenth century, public zoos remained primarily focused on entertainment until the second half of the twentieth century. Costumed chimpanzee performances, elephant rides, orang-utan tea parties, and displays of human 'savages' were common spectacles in various zoos around the world during this period. From the 1960s, leading zoos increasingly concentrated on animal conservation, breeding endangered species in more natural habitats (as their enclosures began to be called), and on eco-efficiency. Granby Zoo, one of the most popular zoos in Canada and a major economic driver in its region, is an example of the metamorphosis that such institutions have undergone.

Granby Zoo began as a private menagerie of the humanitarian, industrialist, animal lover, and charismatic Mayor of Granby for 25 years, Horace Boivin. Wanting to create a beautiful city where all would feel happy, he established several parks including the celebrated Granby Zoo that officially opened in 1955. It immediately became a major tourist attraction, receiving nearly 300,000 visitors in its first season and supporting many local businesses in the process. Despite its popularity, it was a financially strapped small and medium-sized enterprise (SME) that employed a skeleton staff with a few retired farmers as zookeepers. These zookeepers fed the restaurant scraps to the animals and allowed visitors to interact with them like they were domestic species. They were unable to recognize the animals' stress signals and unaware of how inappropriate the animal care was or how prematurely these animals deceased. By the 1970s, with increased habitat destruction, species extinctions, the emerging environmental and animal rights movements, new conservation networks, and growing knowledge in fields such as zoology, zoo conservation efforts at Granby Zoo began. Despite several attempts by the vet to improve animal care, most calls were not heeded. Zookeepers repeatedly blocked her efforts and management was focused solely on survival following several years of financial losses

(blamed on poor weather, union strikes, and subsequent negative publicity, as well as several pay rises). This vet left in the early 1980s and expressed her frustration with the lack of progress being made to improve animal care by publishing a scathing book.

Granby Zoo had returned to profit by this time, largely assisted by a new attraction that saw visitor numbers increase by 35 per cent in 1984. When the management staff left in 1985, the president hired a new vet who was also given two new responsibilities previously held by the director of infrastructure: animal curator and zookeeper manager. With this new power, the vet was able to replace rapidly half the zookeepers with trained specialists who supported his efforts to improve animal care. The vet's vision was inspired by a best-practice zoo conference he attended in his first year, where he learned about the potential of exchanging or breeding animals with other zoos rather than purchasing them from dealers (which was increasingly difficult and expensive as wild species numbers diminished). This required good animal records and healthy specimens, so the vet began improving animal diets, care, and habitats. With financial resources available and management behind him, the vet applied for accreditation from the network of leading American zoos that focus on conservation. While certification was not initially awarded, the recommendations stemming from the evaluation assisted the vet in pushing through a series of improvements, which saw Granby Zoo accepted into the prestigious Association of American Zoos and Aquariums by the end of the 1980s. During this period Granby Zoo began focusing on housing and breeding endangered species in international networks, supporting conservation efforts worldwide, reintroducing certain almost extinct species back into the wild, and educating thousands of visitors each year about such issues. By the 1990s, animal conservation and education were firmly anchored in the zoo's mission.

The early 1990s saw Granby Zoo enter another period of financial difficulty. Facing repeated poor weather, increased competition, union problems, bad press, and aging infrastructure, the zoo made one loss after another. No longer able to care adequately for several charismatic species, Granby Zoo decided to part with them and visitor numbers further diminished. During this period certain employees began environmental initiatives such as recycling cans, an environmental club, and saving energy. While some assisted in raising revenues or decreasing costs, the lack of follow-up and coordination meant that they were often short-lived. With the zoo facing closure in 1996, the board members decided to recruit a new CEO who had a reputation for saving enterprises in difficulty. This individual immediately began installing a culture of 'wow' service, which saw visitor satisfaction and union relations improve considerably. Then he began championing an idea that would end the zoo's financial insecurity: an aquatic centre. While many employees were concerned that it would dilute the zoo's conservation role, they were quickly won over. When the aquatic park opened in 1999, visitor numbers and visit time increased by 39 per cent and 60 per cent, respectively, where they have remained ever since, making new investments in animal habitats, infrastructures, and conservation efforts possible.

By 2003 Granby Zoo had paid back its debts and began planning a major modernization project to celebrate its 50-year anniversary. The board chose a new CEO with a background in communication and the environment. She saw the potential to create a 'greener' zoo and immediately established green principles to guide all those involved in the modernization project. Early in 2004 she hired an environmental coordinator to organize, evaluate, and follow up several projects collectively referred to as the 'Green Zoo'. By 2006 Granby Zoo had: decreased its water consumption by 70 per cent; become one of Canada's largest users of geothermal energy; built 72 per cent more energy-efficient ecological constructions; banned all non-organic cleaning products; and increased recycling substantially. While this process continues, Granby Zoo has already won several prestigious prizes, received much positive publicity, and set new profit records.

Questions

1 How have criteria for measuring zoos as 'good' or 'ethical' evolved? How and why did Granby Zoo's *raison d'être* evolve?
2 When did Granby Zoo become an ethical organization? What made it so?
3 Which factors contributed to the success of ethical initiatives in Granby Zoo? Which factors limited such progress?
4 How did certain individuals (the vets, zookeepers, environmental coordinator, or upper management) facilitate or hinder such change?

Case prepared by Annelies Hodge and Marie-France Turcotte, School of Management, University of Quebec at Montreal (UQAM).

PART THREE

MANAGING ORGANIZATIONAL STRUCTURES AND PROCESSES

CHAPTER TWELVE
MANAGING ONE BEST WAY?

Thinkers, Principles, Models

LEARNING OBJECTIVES

This chapter is designed to enable you to:

- See that modern management is what makes possible much of what we take for granted today

- Understand the relation between surveillance and management control

- Appreciate why an increase in scale led to innovations in management

- Describe the main approaches that developed in early management theory and continue to inform management today

- Know how management ideas spread globally

- Understand McDonaldization as the major force shaping much of the way we live

BEFORE YOU GET STARTED . . .

Improvising on a statement by the English landscape painter John Constable:

> *Remember that management is a science of which organizations are but the experiments!*

INTRODUCTION

In this chapter we look at some of the most influential ideas about management, ideas that have travelled widely, perhaps because they are all fairly simple. These ideas reduce management to simple principles or one-best-way models. In this chapter we will encounter ideas of management embedded in control of slavery; in the design of buildings; in the application of engineering to management; in the structuring of both the formal and the informal in human relations. These ideas include the views that management means moral leadership, or that management should be seen in terms of relations of democracy and autocracy; that management at its core consists of the systematic exploitation of workers, or that its essence can be captured in the promulgation of management models. What all these highly variable approaches have in common is a focus on one best way of managing, organized in terms of an overarching principle: the pan-optical for Bentham; engineering for Taylor; authority for Fayol; human relations for Mayo; democracy for Follett; exploitation for Braverman; and abstract models for various standards and excellence-focused bodies. Max Weber, as we shall see, was somewhat more analytical than any of these other early theorists.

ORIGINS

Management ideas have spread globally for a long time. Simple ideas travel most easily: complex ideas usually become simplified in order to travel. Wherever economic activity has been spread across the globe then general management theories have developed, often suggesting that there is one best way to manage – what today is often called best practice. The earliest form of management best practice might be surprising to you.

Although long established, from the sixteenth century onwards one general form of work organization and management rapidly became global: slavery in the plantation economies of the Caribbean and the Americas. Slavery, an institution founded on human bondage, was one of the earliest and simplest ideas about how to manage large-scale organization. Many early ideas of modern management were developed in the context of slavery. The involuntary migration of millions of people from Africa to the Americas where they were sold into forced labour brought into sharp focus the necessity of managing to extract value from recalcitrant bodies. Slaves, bought and stolen from Africa, shipped to the Americas, laboured long and hard under the management of overseers who shared no language or culture, and often precious little sympathy, with their charges. A system of work and management had to be devised that was very simple, so that even people wrongly regarded as 'ignorant savages' could do it. From slavery, the beginnings of a formal discipline of work as a consciously designed set of tasks under the control of an overseer developed. Cooke (2003) suggests that the management of slaves in plantations anticipated many early modern management ideas.[1]

On the plantations, the central issue was how to produce disciplined labour in the service of those who owned the land and the people. Whereas the title to the land was enshrined in property deeds, ownership of a slave was denoted by the slave being branded with a hot iron with the insignia of the owner. The combination of black bodies, green fertile fields, and cash crops proved lucrative indeed for the owners of these properties. In his seminal *Black Jacobins*, published initially in 1938, James (2001: 9–10) described the horrific forms this efficient management took in French-run San Domingo:

> For the least fault the slaves received the harshest punishment. In 1685 the Negro Code authorized whipping … and slaves were not infrequently whipped to death. The slaves received the whip with more certainty and regularity than they received their food. It was the incentive to work and the guardian of discipline.

The good management of their assets was a major concern. Slave owners differed between those who sought to extract as much value from a slave before they died prematurely and those who wanted to avoid exhausting the usefulness of their slaves through overwork. The latter were acting as prudent investors seeking neither to underutilize nor to waste their investments, for allowing slaves to die prematurely represented a costly waste of these human resources. In everyday practice, discipline was settled through the employment of tight surveillance, the use of exemplary harsh punishment to keep the mass in line, together with routine management (Cooke, 2003).

In Europe slavery was an option that was only ever countenanced on people who were not recognized as being a part of the nation; the same was true in the United States. In the US, if you were a 'landed immigrant' you were a free person; if you were an immigrant through expropriation of your body by a slave trader or if your ancestors were, unless you had been 'emancipated' by the slave owners, you remained captive until slavery was abolished in the South after the US Civil War. Slavery was not much practiced in the domestic economy of Britain compared to the plantations of the West Indies and Americas, as industrial property owners preferred able and willing bodies in their service rather than slaves. Slavery ceased to be a legally available mode of production in Britain, having been outlawed by the British Parliament early in the development of modern industry, on 25 March 1807. Other systems for producing profits had to be found and exported globally. Initially, these focused on architectural design; later they focused on work and organizational design. What they all have in common is the assumption that there is one best way to manage. In this chapter we will meet a number of proposals for the one best way. Each of these has made a significant contribution to a theory of and for management.

DEVELOPING EARLY MODERN MANAGEMENT

Early modern management was based on the efficient extraction of value from the labour that was employed.

For **early modern management** those who were managing and being managed should create more value than would be paid out to them in wages and salaries, thus ensuring that there is a return to the capital – usually in the form of shareholdings – that is invested in the enterprise. For value to be extracted in this way reform of both asset holding and, as a consequence, of management, was necessary.

One of the most significant economic historians of management has suggested:

> The pioneers of the industrial revolution were forced to lay the foundations of the practices of labour management themselves, involving a subject as complex, novel and full of pitfalls as the other applied sciences they had to master …. We can hazard a guess as to how many of the survivors were successful … largely because they mastered … the tasks of management, [but] we shall probably remain forever ignorant of the number of those who failed because they did not. (Pollard, 1965: 160)

The numbers to be supervised were not great. As late as the early 1850s in the British cotton industry, a factory of 300 people could still be considered very large (Hobsbawm, 1975: 21), and, as late as 1871, the average British cotton factory employed only 180 people, whereas engineering works averaged only 85. One reason they were small was that finance was in scarce supply:

> By and large the characteristic enterprise of the first half of the century had been financed privately – e.g., from family assets – and expanded by reinvesting profits, though this might well mean that, with most of capital tied up in this way, the firm might rely a good deal on credit for its current operations. But the increasing size and cost of such undertakings as railways, metallurgical and other expensive activities requiring heavy initial outlays, made this more difficult, especially in countries newly entering upon industrialization and lacking large accumulations of private investment capital. (Hobsbawm, 1975: 214)

To grow large meant expending capital in the shape of money. Not that much capital was available. In the early days of the Industrial Revolution money was mostly tied up in aristocratic land-holdings. Mostly early entrepreneurs raised capital through credit. Merchants combined credit with rented buildings and machinery, together with cheap sources of labour. If the enterprise were to fail, the liability and exposure of the emergent entrepreneurs would be limited (Tribe, 1975). By keeping these commitments small, fortunes might be better insured.

Enterprises were enabled to grow beyond the financial capacities of their owners by the development of **limited liability legislation**. This enabled the incorporation of a company as a legal entity, limiting the liability of those who invest in it such that their personal fortunes are dealt with as legally separate from their investments in the asset. Such legislation was first pioneered in the UK in 1856 and then widely copied internationally almost immediately thereafter.

Limited liability legislation separated the private fortunes of entrepreneurs from investments in business, so that if the latter failed, the personal fortune was sequestered and the debtors' prison avoided.

Limited liability legislation was the key factor in fuelling the formation and growth of accountancy institutes in the UK, and thus the accounting profession. Before 1856, the situation was quite different. If the business failed, the owner's personal fortune could be seized against debtors. Not surprisingly, this limited the size of the enterprise, because a prudent investor would not want to be overexposed. Being able to risk the savings of investors freed up entrepreneurial energies and did much to prepare the ground for a widespread share market in which individuals might invest their savings in productive enterprises.

The scale effects of limited liability were dramatic. For example, the Krupp works at Essen in Germany had only 72 workers in 1848, but by 1873 it employed almost 12,000. Whole regions became dominated by huge commercial ventures. Limited liability legislation was an institutional form that rapidly spread globally.

Limited liability legislation

If limited liability legislation solved the problem of how to raise capital and increase scale, it did not resolve the problem of how to manage the vastly expanded enterprise. It was the '"master" rather than the impersonal authority of the "company"' that held sway in 'the enterprise, and even the company was identified with a man rather than a board of directors' (Hobsbawm, 1975: 214). But how could a single master exercise mastery over so many? How was the master to achieve effective governance over a vastly increased scale of operations?

One solution was based on the owners of previously independent business being re-employed as internal contractors to oversee the processes of labour in firms that were taken over by financiers. These were individuals skilled more in the art of raising capital than executing the mundane command of work. One consequence of internal contracting – where the contractor used materials, plant, and equipment supplied by the owners but managed the labour contracted to deliver a certain quantity of product – was that quite different methods of internal control could flourish in different plants in the same industry. Standards were highly variable. Here a benign and benevolent despot might be master, there the master might be acting on behalf of a labour-managed cooperative, while in another plant the master might be a ruthless and vicious tyrant, exploiting family members or those too weak in the market to resist downward pressure on their wages.

The system of internal contracting flourished from the late nineteenth through to the early twentieth century, with variable lags in different countries, being developed earliest and superseded fastest in the USA. Given that the internal contract was a fixed sum agreed between the internal contractor and the employers of capital, then the middleman, the internal contractor, stood to gain the most by paying the least for the quantity contracted, so there was plenty of opportunity for downward pressure on wages to occur. Not surprisingly, this fact was well understood by trade unionists as they sought to improve the lot of union members by standardizing conditions and wages (Clawson, 1980; Littler, 1982). Unionism exercised an upward pressure, standardizing the conditions of work, whereas, from the business owners and employers of finance, there was a downward pressure beginning to be exercised in the name of an efficient rate of return.

The downward pressure from finance and the upward pressure from the unions led, inexorably, to an increased standardization of workplace routines, so that they became increasingly the same across workplaces, modelled on the best practice from the employees' point of view. A military model provided the earliest template for this organizational design. By the early twentieth century, the most percipient observer of organizations, a German called Max Weber, noted that bureaucracy had become the fate of our times, modelled unambiguously on the military (Weber, 1976). As the economic historian Eric Hobsbawm put it, 'Paradoxically, private enterprise in its most unrestricted and anarchic period tended to fall back on the only available model of large-scale management, the military and bureaucratic' (1975: 216), noting the railway companies, with their 'pyramid of uniformed and disciplined workers, possessing job security, often promotion by security and even pensions', as an extreme example. Weber (1948: 261) put it even more sharply: 'No special proof is necessary to show that military discipline is the ideal model for the modern capitalist factory.'

The result of processes working towards standardization was that the blueprint for designing modern organizations was increasingly inherited from the design of professional armies, shaped within a framework of military discipline, even while being applied to market-based enterprises. Being disciplined and being visible were the key themes. Order, discipline, and authority were to become organizational watchwords, especially in the confined spaces of manufactories – or, as they became known, factories.

MANAGEMENT THEORY: FOUNDING FATHERS AND MOTHER

Management control was best assured through establishing routines disciplining those employed. Discipline was achieved when predictable and designated work was done unproblematically in a routine way. In small workshops, discipline was relatively easy to enact, especially where these workshops had a craft basis or were organized around mastery of a specific knowledge, such as how to make barrels, fabricate metal, or weave wool. In such a structure, the master was presumed to know the craft, which apprentices were presumed not to know and had every motive for learning, so that they too could become skilled workers.

The master exercised power by getting the apprentice to do things the way that he favoured. The basis of the master's authority was ownership of key resources, such as a workplace, materials, and distribution and manufactory networks, ownership that made them **capitalists**. On this basis, masters were easily able to enforce rules, to say when work was done correctly or incorrectly. They had knowledge of how to do the work in the workshop, which provided the basis for **direct management control**. While the master had these resources, the employees had little or none. The only thing they owned and controlled were their bodies and perhaps those of immediate family, which they could sell as labour power to owners of resources.

In small workshops the master's control was exercised face to face. In larger workshops, in contrast, it had to be enacted at a distance. Various methods of fusing discipline and surveillance over employees were tried. Early in the development of industrial capitalism one man had wondered if one could not design a building which had factory discipline built into it. He was familiar with a manufactory that his brother ran in Russia. Based on his knowledge of this factory, he designed an architectural innovation that was influential in early management control because it enabled that control to be built into the bricks and mortar: as a built form it was reproduced around the world, such that examples may be found in the West Indies, the Americas, as well as in Europe. The designer was a man called Jeremy Bentham.

The owners of capital were known as **capitalists** because they owned capital – the social relations and resources that made them masters over other men, women, and children.

Direct management control was possible because of the combination of ownership and control of resources as well as of knowledge of the means of production that enabled employers to exercise discipline over their employees.

Designing architecture for management: Jeremy Bentham

Jeremy Bentham was a prominent English philosopher who was the leading voice in founding a philosophical movement known as **utilitarianism** – a philosophy that sought to improve society through the application of rational calculation and efficient planning. He wrote in the late eighteenth and early nineteenth centuries in England and sought to reform many aspects of human life through the application of utilitarian philosophy. He proposed reform of many institutions, including the relations between religion and the state, proposed the abolition of slavery, sought to introduce equal rights for women, and sought to reform the institutions of marriage and divorce as well as employment and unemployment. His ideas travelled far. For instance, ideas that he initially developed for a model factory were quickly picked up and adapted for use in the design of prisons, as a systematic architecture for management, which sought to make oversight more efficient.

Bentham planned to reform work by using what he called the panoptical principle: establishing the possibility of inclusive surveillance, or

Utilitarianism is a moral philosophy that says we should always act for the greatest good of the greatest number.

Panopticism: The capacity to be all seeing. It was an attribute of the architectural structure known as a Panopticon, designed by Jeremy Bentham in the eighteenth century. What was most significant about the Panopticon, and what gave it its panopticism, was the fact that those under surveillance did not know when they were being watched, but were aware that they were potentially always under surveillance.

panopticism. Successful surveillance, according to Bentham, depended on architectural principles. Bentham designed something that he called a Panopticon. Its ingenuity resided in the economy of effort required to administer it, once it was designed and built.

Panopticism is not just an external attribute of the design; it is also a disposition of those under its sway. Those under panopticism are aware that they may be being observed but are never sure whether they are actually being watched at that moment.

As Image 12.1 shows, the Panopticon was a complex architectural design. It consisted of a central observation tower (which you can see clearly in the cutaway section) from which any supervisor, without being seen, could see the bodies arranged in the various cells of the building. In each cell, the occupants were backlit (neither electric nor gas lighting had yet been invented) and isolated from one another by walls, yet subject to scrutiny by the observer in the tower. Control was to be maintained by the constant sense that unseen eyes might be watching those under surveillance. You had nowhere to hide, nowhere to be private, and no way of knowing if you were being watched at any particular time. The situation was structured such that obedience in and through productive activity seemed the worker's only rational option, not knowing whether or not they were being watched but obliged to assume that they were (see also pp. 174). The Panopticon was a means not only for making work visible but also for making those being seen aware that they may be under scrutiny

IMAGE 12.1   Plan of the Panopticon (2nd edn, 11.6)

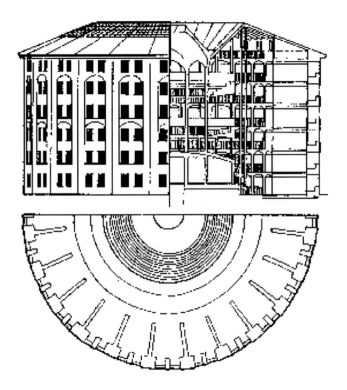

at any time. The Panopticon was not just a system of surveillance but also a system of records and rules. The authorities would have a complete file on the behaviour of each inmate. There would be rules governing time-tables, the nature of work, and the authority to exercise surveillance. The principle of inspection or surveillance instilled itself in the moral conscience of those who were being overseen. The aim was to produce a self-disciplining subject. The asymmetrical nature of seeing but not being seen, of knowing you were possibly being watched but not when or if you were, was designed to produce employees labouring under the threat of constant supervision.

Today, of course, the Panopticon has become electronic. The average person in the cities of the developed world is rarely out of range of a CCTV as they move around (see pp. 297–299). As people walk in the streets and through the halls of public spaces they are subject to cameras that follow their every move. However, they do so with little effect, except insofar as people are called into account retrospectively because of a perceived deviant event. It is not just in public space: almost all large organizations today will have multiple security cameras. Most of the time there is no one constantly monitoring the results of the watchful electronic eyes. It is usually only when it is established that some crime or misdemeanour has occurred that the tapes are checked. If it is not established fairly quickly, the evidence has often disappeared, as the tapes are routinely wiped and reused if nothing has come to notice. The mere fact of panoptical possibilities does not mean quite as much control as might initially be thought. Panoptical possibilities are not necessarily wholly inclusive.

QUESTION TIME

On your next trip into the city or the uni check how many CCTVs monitor your progress. Record them here.

_____

_____

_____

Are there other forms of surveillance that you have encountered on the journey? Record them here.

_____

_____

_____

Compare notes with your tutorial group.

Engineering design of jobs: F. W. Taylor

Engineers had long been fascinated by work. For instance, the nineteenth-century English engineer Charles Babbage made many contributions to early work study and, in fact, designed an early form of the computer as well as writing extensively *On the Economy of Machinery and Manufactures* (1971). Engineering had a natural affinity with work in a profit-based economy, because engineering's key concept was that of efficiency, defined as getting more output from less input. Practical managers and businesspeople find such a prospect especially appealing.

Engineering was a discipline with great reach and authority. It was being constructed by popular engineering journals and magazines of the day as *the* locus of professional managerial expertise (Shenhav, 1999). According to the new engineering approaches to management, corporations and organizations could be managed empirically, on the basis of facts and techniques, rather than experience, privilege, or an arbitrary position. Functions and responsibilities should be aligned in a scientifically proven manner by engineers trained in the management of things and the governance of people working.

Alfred Chandler, in *The Visible Hand* (1977), proposed that modern management began when the visible hand of management came to dominate the invisible hand of market forces. Management emerged as a systematic new solution to the issue of how to get others 'to get things done' (Hoskin, 2004: 745). The answer, suggests Hoskin (2004), emerged initially at the Springfield Armory, in the production of muskets through:

> establishing *prescribed* times required to make each musket part, and then reordering the space across which manufacture proceeded, so that the musket 'took shape' following a principle of linear flow. The trigger for this was a study that to all intents and purposes was a time-and-motion study, but 50 years before the work of F. W. Taylor. (Hoskin, 2004: 747)

Here, Daniel Tyler, Army Inspector of Contract Arms, established the precise time that *should* be required for producing each part of the army-issue musket (Hoskin and Macve, 1988):

> He did so simply by spending six months standing 'watch in hand', examining and recording the average time actually required to produce each musket part, and then extrapolating a norm or 'standard' time (naturally lower) that each part should take. On that basis Tyler then (a) constructed a table of daily piece-rate targets and rates for each part and (b) devised an overall production coordination system across the successive shops involved in the production process. Once he had covered the whole production process, he had the information necessary to work out, by cumulating his standard times, the standard time for the production of one musket (1772 minutes 36.2 seconds), and to calculate via the piece rates established for each item a daily production target of acceptable-quality pieces – a 'tough but attainable' target (equally naturally). (Hoskin, 2004: 747)

Tyler was a graduate at the US military academy of West Point. It was engineering as it was taught and developed at West Point that was decisive in the triumph of engineering in management theory. Students at West Point were the first people in the USA to learn a new way of engaging with and solving problems, which typically took the practices of writing, examining and numerically grading, and translating them to new situations demanding solutions. In the US context, the West Point graduates took these practices and applied them to solving the problems of coordination in workplace contexts. Within 50 years the lessons had become widely learnt in the USA, as Shenhav (1999) identifies, circulated through popular mechanics journals that enjoyed mass circulation. However, it was one particular engineer who, 50 years after their first emergence at West Point, was to have the distinction of turning the lessons into a practical lesson that changed management globally. The engineer in question systematized a concern for efficiency with a separate concern for surveillance and discipline. Armed with a checklist and a stopwatch, F. W. Taylor (1967 [1911]) developed **scientific management** around a set of ideas for making people's work more visible. He observed and timed work, and then redesigned it, so that tasks could be done more efficiently. Taylor, an engineer, proposed that scientific management could design the best way of performing any set of tasks on the shop floor, based on detailed observation, selection, and training.

Taylor's four principles of management are as follows:

1 *Developing a science of work*: This would be achieved by observing and measuring norms of output, using a stopwatch, and detailed observation of human movements. On this basis, improvements could be made to the design of workstations and tools, which could improve effectiveness. Given improvements in effectiveness, pay would be improved.

2 *Scientifically selecting and training the employee*: Not just anybody could earn the higher rates of pay – they had to be people scientifically selected and trained. Taylor believed that everyone had different aptitudes – it was really a question of fitting the worker to the job, and this was the task of management. When management did this job properly, all human resources would be developed to their utmost potential.

3 *Combining the sciences of work and selecting and training of employees*: The workers would easily perceive the good sense of systematic selection and training, thought Taylor. They would benefit from higher wages. Resistance was more likely to come from managers – who had to learn new systems of work and to give up privileges that they had, in Taylor's view, no right to.

4 *Management and workers must specialize and collaborate closely*: Management must focus on mental labour; on setting up systems, designing them, and supervising them. Workers must concentrate on manual labour and leave the higher order mental labour to the managers. If everyone keeps to one's assigned tasks, roles, and methods, then conflict in the workplace between management and workers will be eliminated, he thought. That is because science will show the one best way of doing things. Taylor had a very limited view of science. He regarded it as equivalent to making systematic measurement and observation, after which work would be redesigned on the basis of the data generated and inferences made about existing procedures and how they might be improved. A famous example, which is discussed critically by Braverman (1974), was the example of the Dutch worker Schmidt and the art of shovelling pig iron, heavy, demanding work. Taylor established that even a rather dumb worker, with a carefully designed tool, could increase productivity significantly if whatever scientific management said should be done was done.

Scientific management: The principle that there is one best way to organize work and organization, according to a science of management based upon principles of standardization of time and routinization of motion as decided by authoritative experts.

Check out the Companion Website www.sagepub.co.uk/ managingandorganizations3 for free access to an article by Keith Hoskin (2004) on the very earliest years of the discipline of management as a branch of engineering in the USA, from West Point to F. W. Taylor.

Management should be designed as a series of functions, said Taylor. These could actually be scientifically disaggregated and redefined so that different functional specialists would do different aspects of the task. Taylor was the founding father of work study – fitting the person to the job – and work design, and the pioneer of productivity-related pay systems.

Taylor's views were subject to severe criticism from several contemporary interests. They were not very popular with many people who fulfilled existing management roles. First, internal contractors – people who provided and supervised labour to work within factories owned by remote financiers, entrepreneurs, and industrialists – stood to lose their livelihoods if scientific management triumphed and replaced them with systematic managers, so they were opposed to it.

Second, the owners of capital were often opposed, particularly those with small workshops. These people were already fearful of the risk of being swallowed up or driven out of business by big businessmen gobbling up small enterprises into new centres of financial control, the men who became known as the robber barons (such as Andrew Carnegie and Theodore Vanderbilt). Moreover, they were fearful that the new knowledge would undermine the power of ownership. These fears were well founded. Prior to the enactment of US antitrust regulations, holding companies in the form of trusts, such as the Standard Oil Trust, dominated the rise of US industrial corporate capitalism.

Third, few managers were prepared to accept the productivity pay elements of Taylor's system (they preferred the efficiency outcomes without the costs of wages designed to achieve them). Employers tended to adopt his ideas piecemeal; they were keen on the efficiencies from the time measurement but not as keen on the rewards in the form of bonuses that Taylor proposed under his recommendations for the use of piece rates (Taylor, 1895).

Fourth, from the last quarter of the nineteenth century workers were increasingly organizing in unions that were opposed to the loss of craft skills that the engineering approach to management of standardization and systematization of work entailed (Shenhav, 1999).

Fifth, to workers, the fact that scientific management was often associated in the popular mind with layoffs, due to available work being completed sooner, appeared particularly threatening.

Taylor's ideas had the advantage of being quite easy to grasp (see Taylor, 1995; Wrege, 1995) and to adopt. However, they were controversial, as we have seen. Much of the opposition to Taylor's ideas came to a head when the US Congress, in 1912, held an inquiry into the use of his system of management, due to association of its adoption with strikes. However, the results of this enquiry did not do much to dampen the adoption of the schemes and the First World War did a great deal to encourage them. The reason was simple: craftworkers were being enlisted for the slaughter in Europe and untrained workers, especially young women, were flooding into mechanistic factory jobs that needed to be quickly learnt and simply done in the interests of meeting war production targets (Clegg and Dunkerley, 1980).

Check out the Companion Website www.sagepub.co.uk/ managingandorganizations3 for free access to an article by Mark Bahnisch (2000) on how F. W. Taylor sought to re-engineer subjectivity and bodies as the basis for management.

Mechanistic jobs have formalized structure with rigid job description and prescription. These jobs have a high degree of work **specialization** and the jobs tend to be organized in an equally rigid departmental structure of separate 'silos'. These jobs form vertical chains with a clear and strict hierarchy of authority, vertical communication, and a limited information network. Managers tend to have relatively small spans of control over a few specialized employees. Chains of command tend to be relatively long in consequence, and there is little participation in organizational design and decision-making by employees. The structure displays a high degree of centralization of knowledge, decision-making, and control at the top of the organization, resulting in an elongated organizational structure. It seeks to order the organization to run like clockwork, like a machine. It copes best with situations where the environment is subject to little change and discontinuity. In a machine bureaucracy, operating tasks are simple and repetitive, defined as such by technical analysts – scientific manager's successors – who do the standardizing.

Line managers have formal authority within mechanistic organizations but only within the terms of the organizational design configured by technical planners, budgeters, and work-study analysts, who do the designing. Managers in mechanistic bureaucracies are typically fixated on control; consequently conflict tends not to be resolved but repressed so that when it does occur it often flares up in a wildcat strike (Gouldner, 1954). Typically, the interior need for control is supported by operating in an environment that is simple, stable, and safely unchanging, such as a mass production firm in a placid rather than turbulent environment. Mechanistic models of management can cause unanticipated trouble even as they solve some problems. Their inhumane treatment of the people who work in them often leads employees to be resistant to the discipline imposed on them by the management system.

Specialization: The skill formation that occurs when labour is divided and defined into smaller specific tasks rather than being seen as a general task that anyone might do.

Engineering design of authority: Henri Fayol

It was another engineer, Henri Fayol, who is often regarded as the most significant European founder of modern management. He published *Administration Industrielle et Générale* in 1916 (see Fayol, 1949), in which he argued that better management not merely is concerned with improving output and disciplining subordinates, but also must address the training of the people at the top. Fayol was important for his stress on management training. Without training, it was too much to expect that either legitimacy or rationality would follow. The training should focus on preparing management to plan, organize, command, coordinate, and control for optimal performance. To outperform Taylor's idea of scientific management, presented in only four principles, the core of Fayol's training programme offered 14 principles to provide a manual for proper management, efficient organizations, and happy employees. Fayol's ideas received endorsement from leading industrialists and politicians of the time.

Fayol's promulgated 14 principles of management from his experiences managing in the mining industry as follows:

1   *Specialization of labour*: To encourage continuous improvement in skills and the development of improvements in methods.
2   *Authority*: Establishing the right to give orders and the power to exact obedience.
3   *Discipline*: There was to be obedience.
4   *Unity of command*: Each employee was to have one and only one boss.
5   *Unity of direction*: A single mind should generate a single plan.
6   *Subordination of individual interests*: To the interests of the organization.
7   *Remuneration policy*: Employees should receive fair payment for services.
8   *Centralization*: Consolidation of management functions so that decisions will be made from the top.
9   *Scalar chain*: A clear line of authority and formal chain of command running from top to bottom of the organization, as in the military.
10 *Order*: All materials and employees have a prescribed place, where they should be found.
11 *Equity*: There should be a principle of fairness involved in the way that the organization treats employees.
12 *Personnel tenure*: Limited turnover of personnel was a good thing, and lifetime employment should be offered to good employees.
13 *Initiative*: This requires designing a plan and doing what it takes to make it happen.
14 *Esprit de corps*: There should be harmony and cohesion among organization members.

Although Fayol developed his work about the same time as the era of scientific management, it is a different approach, one that focuses on positions rather than people. He doesn't strive to simplify people's work to fit simplified jobs but to capture the real nature of managerial work. His concern was less with workers and more with what and how managers did what they did. Fayol was not translated into English until the 1940s, so his impact on management outside the Francophone (and Latin) world was delayed.

Bureaucracy: Max Weber

Bureaucratic organization, seen at the turn of the nineteenth century as the hallmark of modern organization, depended above all else on the application of what Max Weber, a German scholar, termed 'rational' means for the achievement of specific ends. In a bureaucracy, techniques would be most rational when they were designed purely from the point of view of fitness for purpose: the better they fit their purpose, the more rational they were. Following Weber, theorists thought that the forms that organizations would take would be extremely limited around the world. Bureaucracies would triumph. Indeed, modernity would be advanced through the achievements of bureaucratic organization, in Weber's view. Bureaucracy has endured as the dominant organizational form for much of the time since.

Weber and subsequent theorists focused on bureaucracy because it has been seen as absolutely necessary to the running of large organizations. It was functionally necessary – unavoidable – that organizations should be bureaucracies if they had large and complex divisions of labour. Some theorists argue that this functional necessity may be seen as a culturally induced predisposition, in a specific case of a more general Weberian-influenced approach, which is known as institutional theory.

Below, we will illustrate this theory with a little story about French bread; thus, if nothing else, there is a lot of food in this chapter! The point of the story about French bread is to demonstrate that different organizational models for the design and delivery of a basic staple of life do not follow any necessary or universal pattern. This is important because, in the spirit of finding singular systems capable of managing everything in the same way, local variations and differences that are really important are neglected in the search for the universalizing, one best way – which for most of the last hundred years or so has meant, for many theorists and practitioners, bureaucracy.

A **bureaucracy** is a form of **organizational design**. In bureaucracy, action is supposed to be procedurally based on formal rules. When bureaucracies are classified as being of the rational–legal type, they are supposed to apply values and principles universally, without favour or prejudice.

If you move through one career track in a bureaucracy, in theory, you need not know anything about how things are done in other tracks. Whether the bureaucracy is a public or private sector organization would be largely immaterial. Day-to-day control involves the intermediation of experts whose expertise will always be specialized, partial, and fragmented. The notion of a career is essential to the practice of bureaucracy and the career is followed in a specialized area of expertise. There is differentiation of both expertise and careers.

The term bureaucracy began to be used in France in the eighteenth century by compounding the French word for an office – a bureau – with the Greek word for rule. By the nineteenth century, Germany provided the clearest examples of its success. The German state constructed by its first chancellor, Bismarck, was a model bureaucracy in both its armed forces and civil administration. The origins of the modern German state were innovations pioneered in Prussia, the heart of modern Germany. Weber realized that the creation of the modern state of Germany had only been possible because of the development of a disciplined state bureaucracy and standing army – inventions that became the envy of Europe. In the military, nothing exhibited bureaucratic discipline better than goose-stepping, which the Prussians invented in the seventeenth century. The body language of goose-stepping transmitted a clear set of messages. For the generals, it demonstrated the absolute obedience of their recruits to orders, no matter how painful or ludicrous these might be. For civilians, the message was that when men were drilled as a collective machine that could ruthlessly crush insubordination and eliminate individualism, a formidable apparatus was created (Davies, 1998). Not surprisingly, as modern industrial organizations emerged in Germany in the late years of the century,

Bureaucracy is an organizational form consisting of a hierarchy of differentiated knowledge and expertise in which rules and disciplines are arranged not only hierarchically in regard to each other but also in parallel.

An **organizational design** is the designated formal structure of the organization as a system of roles, responsibilities, and decision-making.

they incorporated some of the forms of bureaucracy whose success was everywhere around them.

At the core of Weber's (1978) conception of organization as bureaucracy was the notion that members of an organization adhere to the rules of that organization. He contrasted three types of authority, based upon the rule of *charisma*, the rule of *tradition*, and the rule of *rational*, *legal precepts*. Thus, there were three major bases of authority, thought Weber.

Rational-legal precepts: People obey orders as rational–legal precepts because they believe that the person giving the order is acting in accordance with a code of legal rules and regulations (Albrow, 1970: 43).

Rational organizations   Weber identified authority based on **rational–legal precepts** as the heart of bureaucratic organizations. Basically, this means that people follow rules because they respect the correctness of those rules, either because of their substantive legal content or because of their rationality – their appropriateness and correctness.

Members of a bureaucratic organization are expected to obey its rules as general principles that can be applied to particular cases and which apply to those exercising authority as much as those who must obey the rules. People do not obey the rules because of traditional deference or submission to charismatic authority; they do not obey the person but the office holder. Members of the organization 'bracket' the personal characteristics of the office holder and respond purely to the demands of office. Whether you like the office holder or not is supposed to be unimportant (see Image 12.2). Police officers may be disagreeable personally, but they hold an office that enables them to do what they do, within the letter of the law. The rule of law is the technical basis of their ability to take appropriate action, in terms of the definitions laid down in law.

IMAGE 12.2   Authority

Australia has government of the people by the departments for the cabinet. Its political philosophy is to keep the water on and the foreigners off, at the same time ensuring that the economic confusion is shared as democratically as possible. Although the woolsack in the House of Lords is symbolically stuffed with top grade merino, many believe it should be more appropriately stuffed in the Statue of Liberty.

COMMONWEALTH   BY AUTHORITY   OF AUSTRALIA
(USE BLOCK LETTERS)

SIGN HERE
(Usual signature of taxpayer)

WHAT DO YOU MEAN?

Weber's three types of authority

1 *Charismatic authority* means that deference and obedience will be given because of the extraordinary attractiveness and power of the person. The person is owed homage because of their capacity to project personal magnetism, grace, and bearing. For instance, management gurus such as Jack Welch, politicians such as Nelson Mandela, or popular characters such as Princess Diana have all been seen as charismatic authorities. People follow them because of what they believe to be the special nature of their personalities and the success they have achieved.

2 *Traditional authority* occurs where deference and obedience are owed because of the bloodline. The title held is owed homage because the person who holds it does so by birthright – they

are in that position by right of birth. Prince Charles, for instance, is not so much an authority because of his charisma but because of tradition: as oldest son of the queen, he is the future King of England because of the line of descent (see Image 12.3).

3 *Rational–legal authority* signifies that deference and obedience are owed not to the person or the title they hold but to the role they fill. It is not the officer but the office that is owed homage because it is a part of a rational and recognized disposition of relationships in a structure of offices. Examples are easy to find – just think of passport control or police. They are authorities although you do not know the people acting in the roles. The people who are actually acting are secondary; what is important is the office they represent.

IMAGE 12.3 Symbol of authority

Weber saw bureaucracy as an instrument or tool of unrivalled technical superiority. He wrote, '[p]recision, speed and unambiguity, knowledge of the files, continuity, discretion, unity, strict subordination, reduction of friction, and of material and personal cost. These are raised to the optimum point in the strictly bureaucratic administration' (Weber, 1948: 214). Bureaucracy is a rational machine that Weber defined as having 15 key dimensions:

1   Power belongs to an office and is not a function of the office holder.
2   Power relations within the organization structure have a distinct authority configuration, specified by the rules of the organization.
3   Because powers are exercised in terms of the rules of office rather than the person, organizational action is impersonal.
4   Disciplinary systems of knowledge, either professionally or organizationally formulated, rather than idiosyncratic beliefs, frame organizational action.
5   The rules tend to be formally codified.
6   These rules are contained in files of written documents that, based on precedent and abstract rule, serve as standards for organizational action.
7   These rules specify tasks that are specific, distinct, and done by different formal categories of personnel who specialize in these tasks and not in others. These official tasks would be organized on a continuous regulated basis in order to ensure the smooth flow of work between the discontinuous elements in its organization. Thus, there is a tendency towards specialization.
8   There is a sharp boundary between bureaucratic action and particularistic action by personnel, defining the limits of legitimacy.
9   The functional separation of tasks means that personnel must have authority and sanction available to them commensurate with their duties. Thus, organizations exhibit an authority structure.
10 Because tasks are functionally separated, and because the personnel charged with each function have precisely delegated powers, there is a tendency towards hierarchy.
11 The delegation of powers is expressed in terms of duties, rights, obligations, and responsibilities. Thus, organizational relationships tend to have a precise contract basis.
12 Qualities required for organization positions are increasingly measured in terms of formal credentials.
13 Because different positions in the hierarchy of offices require different credentials for admission, there is a career structure in which promotion is possible either by seniority or by merit of service by individuals with similar credentials.
14 Different positions in the hierarchy are differentially paid and otherwise stratified.
15 Communication, coordination, and control are centralized in the organization.

Weber saw that there were a number of rational foundations for modern bureaucratic organizations, such as a legal system based on rules rather than personal influence; an economy based on monetary exchanges; a formally free labour market in which people were not bought and sold but hired their labour time; the appropriation and concentration of the physical means of production as disposable private property; the representation of share rights in organizations and property ownership; and the 'rationalization' of various institutional areas, such as the market, technology, and education. The outcome of the process of rationalization, Weber suggests, is the production of a new type of person: the specialist or technical expert. Such experts master reality by means of increasingly precise and abstract concepts. Statistics, for example, began in the nineteenth century as a form of codified knowledge of everyday life and death, which could inform public policy. The statistician became a paradigm of the new kind of expert, dealing with everyday things but in a way that was far removed from everyday understandings. Weber sometimes referred to the results of this process as disenchantment, meaning the process whereby all forms of magical, mystical, traditional explanation is stripped away from the world (Clegg, 1995).

WHAT DO YOU MEAN?

What's good about bureaucracy?

1 Bureaucratic organizations provide satisfaction for those working within them because you know exactly what to do and what you will have to do to get to where you want to be in the organization.

2 They are fairly predictable, and they offer opportunities for careers for individual members to specialize and develop skills in what they most enjoy.

3 They limit arbitrary power and privilege. You must follow the rules but so must everyone else.

4 If you are a client or a customer of a bureaucracy, to the extent that the bureaucracy treats you as merely a case, you can expect to be treated according to precedents established by rules, rather than the whim of an officer.

5 You have a right of appeal in a bureaucracy. If the application of rules to cases is illegitimate, then you would have rational recourse to an appeal mechanism.

6 None are above the law, none can escape rules, and every office is accountable. In short, bureaucracy is a bulwark of civil liberty.

7 Bureaucracy frees people from arbitrary rule by powerful patrimonial leaders – those who personally own the instruments and offices of rule.

A cornerstone of bureaucracy, according to Weber, was that it operated 'without regard for persons'. Reading this phrase for the first time may resonate with what you already know about bureaucracy: that it is heartless, soulless, and cruel. It does not have a human face – it makes everybody a number. But Weber was arguing something far more fundamental. Essentially, Weber was saying that it does not matter if you are black or white, Muslim or Jew, gay or straight, rich or poor. It does not matter who or what you are. You are entitled to be judged not on the prejudices of the community or the person applying a rule, but strictly according to the

Check out the Companion Website www.sagepub.co.uk/ managingandorganizations3 for free access to an article by Stewart Clegg (2005) if you want to learn more about what happened to the Puritan ethic that lay behind the emergence of modern rational organizations and capitalism, according to Weber.

rules, without regard for the specificities of whatever might be your identity. Bureaucracy, when rational, legal, and fair is an efficient system for processing people.

Human relations: Elton Mayo

Not all of the early management thinkers saw the solutions to problems of managing and organizing in terms of engineering tighter control through making people more like machine parts. Rather, some theorists, such as the Australian, Elton Mayo, saw engineering as a part of the problem rather than the solution. Mayo developed what became known as the Human Relations School. The emphasis of this approach was on informal work group relations, the importance of these for sustaining the formal system, and the necessity of the formal system meshing with the informal system.

As a young man in Australia just after the Great War, Mayo had helped to develop therapeutic treatments for patients with shell shock and other 'nervous' conditions. From the treatment of maladjustment on the part of veterans, it was a small step to the treatment of industrial malaises: 'Industrial unrest is not caused by mere dissatisfaction with wages and working conditions but by the fact that a conscious dissatisfaction serves to "light up" as it were the hidden fires of mental uncontrol' (Mayo, 1922: 64, cited in Bourke, 1982: 226). Treating conflict at work meant treating industrial neuroses. Most people's actions were driven by the unconscious, he thought, following Freud, and this was as true of people at work as at war. Agitators and radicals were victims of neurotic fantasies that could be traced, invariably, to infantile history. If individuals could be guided by therapy in work, they would be healed of their neuroses. When he arrived in the USA, he brought these ideas with him as a highly successful public speaker on the lecture circuit. He eventually found a congenial home at Harvard, where he was invited in 1926.

At Harvard, Mayo became associated with what are known as the Hawthorne Studies. These studies have become a classic of modern management and were named thus because they were carried out in the Hawthorne Plant of the Western Electric organization in the suburbs of Chicago between 1924 and 1927. After the data had been collected and the experiments ended, he joined the project in April 1928 (Henderson, with Mayo, 2002 [1936]). In a range of experiments concerning the physical determinants of productivity, illumination and other physical variables were manipulated, with the surprising result that productivity kept rising even when unexpected – when the illumination was lowered rather than increased. Why was this so?

Mayo answered the question in terms of what became known as the Hawthorne Effect: when a group realizes that it is valued and forms social relations among its members, productivity rises as a result of the group formation. The Hawthorne Effect is what happens when informal organization formation occurs. It was this finding for which the study became famous. In this instance, it was presumed that the effect was an unanticipated consequence of the experimental interest taken in workers. Such formation will often be an unanticipated consequence of academic interest in people in organizational settings: research may have unanticipated effects. (His experiments have been widely criticized. See Carey (2002 [1967]) and O'Connor (2002) for the criticisms.)

Mayo's eight principles of management were as follows:

1 Work should be seen as a group rather than an individual activity.
2 Work is a central life interest for most people.
3 The lack of attention to human relationships was a major flaw in most other management theories.
4 In work, people find a sense of belonging to a social group and seek a need for recognition, satisfaction of which is vital for their productivity.
5 When workers complain, it may be a manifestation of some more fundamental and psychologically located issue.
6 Informal social groups at work have a profound influence on the worker's disposition and wellbeing.
7 Management can foster collaboration within informal groups to create greater cohesion and unity at work, with positive organizational benefits.
8 The workplace should be viewed as a social system made up of interdependent parts.

In the informal system, special attention was to be paid to the satisfaction of individual human needs, focusing on what motivates different people, in order to try to maximize their motivation and satisfaction. Mayo thought the manager had to be a social clinician, fostering the social skills of those with whom the manager worked. Therapeutic interviews were recommended as a management tool and training in counselling and personnel interviews was seen as an essential management skill. The advice was simple: pay full attention to the interviewee and make it clear that this is the case; listen carefully to what they have to say; do not interrupt; do not contradict them; listen carefully for what is being said as well as any ellipses in terms of what is left unspoken; try to summarize carefully what has been said by the speaker as feedback for the interviewee; and treat what has been said in confidence (Trahair, 2001).

Mayo had an agreeable message for many managers:

> What, after all, could be more appealing than to be told that subordinates are non-logical; that their uncooperativeness is a frustrated urge to collaborate; that their demands for cash mark a need for your approval [as a manager]; and that you have a historic destiny [as a manager] as a broker of social harmony? (Rose, 1975: 124)

Mayo undoubtedly believed that the technical competencies of managers had to be buttressed by social competencies. People had to be shown how to collaborate in the new complex organizations, and management's task, *par excellence*, was to aid this. Managers were to be the new conciliators and arbitrators of an accord with rational workers. While the workers would draw on local rationalities, variants of cultures of solidarity rooted in family, church, and community experience, the managers would draw on the rationality of science (Hogan, 1978; Weiss, 1981). In Mayo's view, it would be a one-sided contest where the reason of management should be self-evident.

Many of Mayo's ideas addressed the failure of modern management to consider collaboration as integral to modern enterprise. Mayo came to the conclusion that the real problems encountered in work were the lack of 'well-knit human groups'. Too little attention was being paid to social relations at work, especially those that enable people to get on well and cooperate with others. More training in social skills was required. Just as individual members should have a cooperative attitude, the organization should have an effective system of communications to foster social skills (see also Chapter 10). Organizations should organize teams and use personnel interviews to aid members, as Mayo (1985 [1951]) put it, to get 'rid of useless emotional complications', 'to associate more easily, more satisfactorily with other persons – fellow workers or supervisors – with whom he is in daily contact', and to develop in the worker a 'desire and capacity to work better with management'. Mayo's star faded fairly fast, although there was some renewed critical interest in the 1970s and 1980s (Clegg, 1979; Clegg and Dunkerley, 1980), and a sophisticated appreciation of his importance for contemporary human resource management in the work of writers such as O'Connor (1999; 2002).

Management, leadership, and the functions of the executive: Chester Barnard

The prosperous 1920s had seen modern corporate bureaucracies become legitimate. In the depression of the 1930s, however, their legitimacy came into question. The Depression of the 1930s saw many millions of people unemployed, reduced to welfare and soup kitchens. If managers were such great leaders, how come American firms were in such a mess? How could organizations be efficient and legitimate, when they also caused so much unemployment and turmoil?

For Chester Barnard, the key issue was leadership, of which he had considerable experience – he had been the president of New Jersey Bell Telephone and the Rockefeller Foundation. Barnard thought that those lucky enough still to have jobs should buckle down to the leadership of managers for it was only their good judgement that stood between them and the misery of unemployment.

Barnard wrote a book on leadership that had a major impact, *The Functions of the Executive* (1936). Leadership is required, said Barnard, to ensure both managerial authority and employee obedience. He knew that people were frequently capable of being, from an executive's point of view, mistaken about what they took their interests to be. Leaders should make followers' self-interest apparent, and this interest should be service to authority. Leaders created moral codes for subordinates to live by; subordinates needed tutelage in strong moral values, which it was management's duty to provide.

Barnard's five principles of management are as follows:

1 Individual behaviour is always variable and can never be easily predicted.
2 All individuals will have a 'zone of indifference' within which compliance with orders will be perceived in neutral terms without any questioning of authority. Managers should seek to extend the borders of this zone through material incentives but more especially through providing others with status, prestige, and personal power.
3 Communications, especially in informal organization, are absolutely central to decision-making. Everyone should know what the channels of communication are and should have access to formal channels of communications. Lines of communication should be as short and direct as possible.
4 Management's responsibility is to harness informal groupings and get them working for the organization, not against it.
5 Authority only exists insofar as the people are willing to accept it.

Barnard was the first significant modern executive to write on management and organization. In that sense, he was the genesis of the 'been there, done that, profited from the experience' type of text that executives are prone to write when they want to record how they did it 'my way' (karaoke management theory is what we call it). From the vantage point of his experience, he saw the manager's key task as ensuring that organizational systems motivated employees towards organization goals – because where individuals worked with common *values* rather than common *orders*, they would work much more effectively, he thought. The real role of the manager, he wrote, is to manage the values of the organization, which should be set by the chief executive (see also Chapter 8).

Management and social justice: Mary Parker Follett

Mary Parker Follett was born into a wealthy and privileged Boston family. After graduating from the Women's College at Harvard, she became involved in social work in a diverse Boston neighbourhood. What she learned in making community centres work for people lacking in the obvious resources of a wealthier society was that, with experience in 'modes of living and acting which shall teach us how to grow the social consciousness' (Follett, 1918: 363; 1924), many people were far more capable than they or others might have imagined.

Follett was the first woman to have had a book on management published, albeit after her death, called *Dynamic Administration* (1941). In this book, she argued that organizations, like communities, could be approached as local social systems involving networks of groups. Not for her the image of the all-knowing scientific engineer in control. Unlike scientific management, she believed in the full collaboration of employees and managers, and she sought their willingness to make these values compatible. Follett wanted to achieve not just productivity but also social justice.

She suggested that Taylor's ideas were incomplete. In particular, they had not been thought through for their democratic potential; Taylor's lone individuals, in a massive functional structure, under strict control, did not accord with American ideas of democracy. Something had to change in management thinking if this were to be the case. Mary Parker Follett signalled the changes. Her work continues to excite contemporary interest (Boje and Rosile, 2001; Calás and Smircich, 1996; Fox, 1968; O'Connor, 1999; 2002).

Central to Follett's worldview was the concept of power. She was concerned to democratize power, distinguishing between power-with and power-over (or coercive power rather than coactive power). She argues that it is the former that needs developing and the latter that needs diminishing. Organizations organize power and they create power. She saw power as legitimate and inevitable. But because power is so central, it does not mean that it need be authoritarian. Organizations must be developed democratically as places where people learn to be cooperative in power with others, especially managers and workers (see also pp. 287–288). Given democratic opportunities, she thought that people could make the most of their situation, even if they seemed relatively impoverished in their access to resources. Her view of democracy was that it should be participatory, because the experience of being participative was empowering and educative. In a democracy, Follett believed that people had to be able to exercise power themselves, at the grassroots level. Democratic diversity had great advantages, she said, over more authoritarian homogeneity. We should welcome difference because it feeds and enriches society, whereas differences that are ignored feed *on* society and eventually corrupt it (Follett, 1918). More modest than her male colleagues, she formulated her ideas in only three principles.

Follett's three principles of management are as follows:

1   Functions are specific task areas within organizations, which should be allocated the appropriate degree of authority and responsibility necessary for task accomplishment.
2   Responsibility is expressed in terms of an empirical duty: people should manage their responsibility on the basis of evidence and should integrate this effectively with the functions of others.
3   Authority flows from an entitlement to exercise power, which is based upon legitimate authority.

Mary Parker Follett was a unique management academic, a woman in a world of men, and a committed democrat in a world of macho managers. Notions of legitimate authority and civic responsibility were important to Follett's thinking. Thus, not surprisingly, when she turned her attention to organizations and management, she saw the concept of power as the essential basis for understanding business. She separated power from hierarchy, shunning the idea that some were born to rule and others to follow, which Taylor's ideas legitimated. She produced a rationale for authority distinct from Taylor's 'scientific' approach in which management is a responsible discharge of necessary functions. Authority and responsibility derive from function. Business requires an understanding of how to produce collaborative action between different people integrated in a common enterprise. Until her revival with the publication of Graham's (1995) edited volume, *Mary Parker Follett – Prophet of Management: A Celebration of Writings from the 1920s*, she was largely ignored. There are signs that her unique contribution and its relevance to current issues are now being recognized (Boje and Rosile, 2001).

EXPORTING MODERN MANAGEMENT IDEAS

With the exception of Fayol, these early influential ideas were developed in the USA and then exported. In the UK, engineers were regarded as lowly individuals with dirty hands and were remarkably unsuccessful in attaining occupational status and power. The term *engineer* was stretched to refer both to professional engineers with formal qualifications as well as to people who use tools to do manual labour.

British engineering owed far more to its craft origins than was the case either on the continent or in the USA, where professional engineering and scientific management were conflated in the 1920s. In France and Germany, engineering was an elite profession. Despite the early impact of approaches to industrial management (Littler, 1982), managerialism was slow to become really established in the UK. (In fact, Prime Minister Thatcher was still railing against the complacent inefficiency of British management in the 1980s when she was promoting 'efficiency in government', much as had Prime Minister Wilson in the 1960s when he was spreading what came to be known as the 'white heat of the technological revolution'.)

In France, the interwar state, under Clemenceau, introduced some elements of technocratic rationalization from above, befitting both the elite status of engineering and Fayol's eminence in its application to management. In Germany, although the USA became increasingly an inspiration for engineers from the early years of the century, it was not until the rise of the national socialist state that a management project premised on efficiency was widely adopted and diffused. In Italy, scientific management ideas were sponsored by notable industrialists, such as Gino Olivetti, in a counter-argument to ideas emerging from the workers' movement (Clegg and Dunkerley, 1980: 110–111), and were also espoused by Mussolini's fascist state – whose achievements, for many, were summed up in the idea that it 'got the trains running on time'. In Russia, in the new Soviet Union after 1917, Lenin, the head of state and major theorist of Bolshevism, the prevailing ideology, proclaimed that electrification plus Taylorism represented the basis for building scientific socialism.

Though the foundational ideas of modern management travelled far and wide, they were mostly cemented into place in the USA, from the 1930s onwards. As Grant and Mills (2006) argue, much of what became institutionalized in the USA as the normal account of management during the post-war period owed a great deal more to the context of the Cold War period in which it was produced than was acknowledged at the time. In the politically divided Europe after the Second World War, the importance of modern management was all too clear. The impact of US institutions on post-war Europe, through the Marshall Plan for post-war reconstruction, and Japan, through the immediate post-war occupation, ensured a process of widespread dissemination of US management and organization theory. In Europe business schools were created on explicitly American lines where they did not already exist. By the late 1960s in the UK, business and management schools were being developed by many universities, and even in a relatively under-industrialized country such as Australia, a national school of management was established by the late 1970s. In all of these schools, American management, by and large, became institutionalized as *the* template for modern management (see Locke, 1984). Curricula were developed, and writers examining organizations (Pugh and Hickson, 2007) studied, most of them American, although a few were not, such as the French Fayol, British Urwick, Anglo-Australians Clegg and Donaldson, and the Canadian Mintzberg.

Check out the Companion Website www.sagepub.co.uk/ managingandorganizations3 for free access to an article by James D. Grant and Albert J. Mills (2006) on the formative years of the discipline of management in the USA, from 1936 to 1960.

CONTEMPORARY MANAGEMENT MODELS

Many contemporary management approaches tend to ignore contemporary management theory. They tend instead to develop the management principles first expounded by Taylor and others. They use these principles to institute managerial control through establishing routines. The most notable of these are the many and various models of business excellence and quality management that are widely used in business, such as ISO 9000, the EFQM (European Foundation for Quality Management) model, the US Baldrige model, GE's Six-Sigma model, and so on.

In many respects the purposes of management principles and designs have not changed that much. Despite changing terms and fashions they are often oriented to making organizational behaviour predictable. They are normative and prescriptive models and, as Grant et al. (1994: 36) noted, rarely have any explicit theory. Being simple, lacking explicit theory, and being intellectually insubstantial, these models have been widely grasped by hard-pressed managers searching for common-sense solutions to complex problems. The models have travelled the world, seeking to translate local variations into common models.

However, they always have to do so in a context where individual sensemaking has the potential to make the best-laid plans and prescriptions imperfect. What is 'common sense' to managers is not always common sense for others, whether employees, supply chain managers, or customers. *From a sensemaking perspective, we would expect common sense* not *to be made easily*. Managing always involves making sense collectively and this is by no means an easy task. It certainly is not as easy as creating a list of management principles or developing a model and then expecting that the work of managing has been done and that all that is necessary is for people to accept one list of principles rather than another, or accept one model rather than another, and then use that one model systematically. The tools have to be used, and it is how they are used, with differential sense and interests attached to them, which is important. Hence, when confronted with management models we should attend not only to the content of the models themselves, but also to the meaning that they have for different stakeholders and the different uses to which they are put.

The search for alternative models of performance has produced a vast variety of organizational models to describe organizational performance. The processes through which these models are applied identify opportunities for improvement within organizations. Organizations that apply management models to areas such as quality, knowledge management, fair trade, corporate social responsibility, organizational excellence, and value chains will experience many challenges, not least of which will be the struggle to make the sense that senior management sees as inhering in these models coincide with the sense that other stakeholders also accept. Today, most of these models are internally developed, either by organizations or consultancies that sell models that they have devised.

Management models are a major source of organizational change: they prescribe both changes and change as a result of their use, as they run up against the different sense members, suppliers, customers, and other stakeholders make of them (see Guillen, 1994). Hence, there is a lot of churning in management models as consultancy companies need a constant stream of new products, and organizations discover new sensemaking gaps with the use of existing models.

In this chapter we have not surveyed the most contemporary models – they change too rapidly and are often generic to specific organizations – but have looked at the original formulations of management models by a number of influential theorists. Even contemporary models often retain elements derived from these early twentieth-century auspices. For instance, ISO 9000 and its subsequent variations, which are widely used in industry worldwide, are largely prescriptive models based on outmoded ideas about statistical process control, and an erroneous translation of the Japanese idea of *kaizen* as continuous improvement, quite disconnected from the main body of organization theory (Garvin, 1984).

Other influential models include the Balanced Scorecard (Kaplan and Norton, 1992), which focuses on performance measurement of financial, customer, internal, and knowledge and learning perspectives; the European Foundation for Quality Management Excellence model, which focuses on leadership, people, policies and strategy, alliances and resources, processes, results in people, results in customers, results in society, and key financial results. In this model we see elements of Taylor's and Fayol's concern with efficiency, Mayo's stress on people and human relations, together with Barnard's emphasis on leadership.

McDonaldization

McDonaldization refers to the application of goal-oriented rationality to all areas of human life.

The American sociologist George Ritzer coined the term **McDonaldization**. The model of McDonald's is a metaphor for a highly rationalized and 'cheap as chips' approach to business processes 'by which the principles of the fast food restaurants are coming to dominate more and more sectors of American society as well as the rest of the world' (Ritzer, 1993: 1). McDonaldization does not stop at the fast food store – it spreads to all areas of everyday life: to recreation, informal and interpersonal relationships, and even love and intimacy – think of 'speed dating'. As Ritzer says, even those places and activities that used to offer some release from a routinized world have now been rationalized through four major mechanisms:

1 *Efficiency* means utilizing the least output to gain the highest return. In mechanics, where the term comes from, efficiency is defined in terms of minimizing losses to extraneous physical activities, such as heat or friction in the transmission of energy. In business, given a goal, such as to maximize profits, what is the most efficient way of achieving this outcome? Or in simple terms, if the organization is a tool that is managed to achieve specific purposes, how can waste of resources be minimized around the tool's use? One way is to transfer the costs to the consumer. The McDonald's model dispenses with waitresses and offers only preformatted menus: it may not make for great choice or food but it creates a very efficient organization.

2 *Calculability* means cheapening the assembly costs of the standard product. It is calculably cheaper to make reality TV shows where there is no script development cost, no actors and agents' fees, just a bunch of people happy to try to grab their 15 minutes of 'fame' – or notoriety.

3 *Predictability* means that a McDonaldized service or product should be the same anywhere in the world every time. There should be no surprises. It means leaving nothing to the imagination; scripting everything – 'You want French fries with that?' – and using standardized procedures to produce always standardized outputs. Every day at Disneyland should be just the same experience, irrespective of the 'team members' inside the suits, on the rides, or serving in the cafeteria. And the team members are always young, cheap, and interchangeable.

4 *Control* means minimizing variation in every ingredient in the organizational assembly of people and things: customers and employees, raw materials, labour processes, and markets. It often means substituting machine processes that are utterly controllable for people who are not. Where people cannot be substituted, they can be drilled – just like the call centre operators and McDonald's staff – to perform always the same routines. And the organization can try to ensure that even physical appearance is controlled. Ritzer cites the example of the Euro Disney employees who had strict rules applied about their weight-to-height ratios, facial appearance, hair length, jewellery, makeup, and underwear. Control means learning to do and to be as one is told, even down to smiling on cue, as Mills (1996) demonstrates in his analysis of flight attendants.

MINI CASE

More do it yourself!

Go into your neighbourhood McDonald's. Ask for a standard burger minus one or other of the usual ingredients. How does the salesperson's standard response script vary from normal? Note how long you wait for the meal. Look around you, inside and outside the store. How much garbage is there in and out of the store? Think about Ritzer's four characteristics of McDonaldization. Count the number of things in which you find them embedded in the store. Take pictures. Report back to class.

• How efficient is McDonalds? What are the costs of this efficiency?

McDonald's may be instrumentally rational as a profit centre but it uses enormous quantities of grain to grow cereals to feed to cattle that will be killed in rationalized slaughterhouses (which were the original basis for Ford's idea of the moving production line). It packs the burgers in sweet bread that is unhealthy and serves it in containers that will be discarded and added to the planet's waste. Ritzer's McDonaldization kills spontaneity, creativity, and joy in discovery. When most things are reduced to the cheapest way of making them the same, there will be few surprises in store.

McDonaldization mostly employs young people, part-time, and students, who often put up with the work because they know that it is not a life sentence. Not everyone working in a McDonaldized organization is so fortunate. For some people, the segmentation of the labour market condemns them to a lifetime of junk jobs.

Check out the Companion Website www.sagepub.co.uk/managingandorganizations3 for free access to an article by Bryan Turner (2003) if you want to learn more about McDonaldization and how it is shaping consumer culture.

RESISTING MANAGEMENT: LABOUR PROCESS THEORY

As a result of the joint spread of modern capitalism and modern management around the globe, a common type of **labour process** became widely institutionalized – we have seen this in the case of McDonald's in the previous section. Some writers were convinced that this meant that as a common form of economic exploitation spread globally, universal forms of resistance to this economic exploitation would also develop. These were themes that had been developed in ideas about organizations that regarded Karl Marx's theory of economic **exploitation** as a point of departure.

Modern scientific management is regarded by labour process writers as the major means for the intensification of exploitation. Scientific management represented the accumulation, codification, and redesign of traditional craft knowledge in order to make enterprises more efficient. However, it was a codification of knowledge that was as much opposed to the laziness of early twentieth-century American management for allowing the efficiency benefits of innovative technology to be blunted by craft

Labour process may be defined as the social relations that people enter into when they are employed as well as the work that they actually do and the conditions under which it is done. Studying the labour process has given rise to a distinct labour process perspective that focuses on management as a struggle for control of the labour process between employees and managers.

Exploitation means simply that, assuming labour is the source of all value, then any value over and above that paid out in wages – from which profits must arise – derives from paying labour less than the value that it creates for the capital which hires it.

resistance, as much as it was a critique of these craft practices. For Taylor, management had been premised on relative ignorance rather than rational knowledge and was complicit with craft labour in maintaining inefficient working practices. While this insight is clearly inscribed in Taylor's work – as he sought to increase the value of the labour inputs by making them more efficient – it is not understood in Marx's terms.

Marx referred to profit as surplus value. According to Marx's ideas, employees must receive less value in wages than they created in profits, otherwise no profits would accrue. These terms focused on the notion of unequal exchange: when labourers exchanged their labour for a wage, then the capitalist must gain more from the exchange than the workers – a **surplus value** – otherwise no profit could be produced from the labour hired. Harry Braverman, in his book on the labour process (1974), saw the role of managers as central to the realization of surplus value.

In Braverman's view, managers anywhere in the world should be seen in terms of the structural role that they played as delegates of those who owned capital. Their job was to ensure the efficient extraction of surplus value. They did this by constantly seeking to increase productivity by simplifying jobs, by 'de-skilling' them (making them less craft-based and thus less likely to be controlled by a craftworker, using specialist craft knowledge, and more likely to be controlled by the manager who could insist that managerial rather than craft-approved methods be followed). The result was not only a 'degradation of labour' but also an increase in specialization (albeit at a lower level of skill) and thus the division of labour. It also contributed to longer organizational hierarchies, as organizations now needed supervisors to oversee routine de-skilled work in order to see that it was done correctly, according to management models (see also pp. 470–471). Scientific management was the epitome of the methods that managers instituted to de-skill and control labour. It can be said that scientific management, as Taylor and others conceived of it, was behind the development of **managerial capitalism**, in which personal and family ownership was increasingly fused with institutional and market-based investments, and the people on the shop floor were increasingly de-skilled as professional managers were increasingly employed, making artisanal craft knowledge less relevant.

In most large, complex, organizations today professional managers coordinate employees, technology, resources, and administrative structures. They do not necessarily own shares in what they govern and manage (although this is increasingly likely as stock-option incentive systems become widespread – at least for top management team members). As the visible hand of managers replaced Adam Smith's invisible hand of the market, managerial capitalism arose to manage large-scale organizations. Even companies such as Virgin, always associated with the buccaneering entrepreneur Richard Branson, are actually managed by rather bland organizational men and women of the corporation, as described by Whyte (1960) and Kanter (1976).

If capitalism was to be most efficient, argued Braverman, then management should seek to codify and 'own' all knowledge in an organization.

Surplus value is achieved by exploiting labour: working labourers for a greater return than they received and retaining the surplus value that they produced over and above that which they received.

Managerial capitalism sees capitalist entrepreneurs displaced by professional managers as the central, immediate, and direct agents of power within organizations.

Doing so strengthened the power of management and allowed experiments with more efficient ways of working. Codification would enable the radical separation of 'mental' (managerial) labour from 'manual' (worker) labour, allocating management to reconfigure production as it pleased. It rendered labour interchangeable as part of a large, efficiently managed machine. Management would achieve total control of the labour process and could set the pace of work.

De-skilling

Braverman argued that jobs were being de-skilled by the development of the capitalist labour process. Wherever jobs could be argued to be undergoing a process of fragmentation and where mental elements involved in the conception of work were being separated from their manual execution, a dynamic of de-skilling would be in process. The result would be increasingly routine and fragmented tasks, where individual employees lacked understanding of the principles underlying their relation with others. In a word, they would be alienated. The introduction of newer, simpler technologies would be used to transfer control over the labour process from workers to management (Braverman, 1974: 194). The result of de-skilling would be a downward pressure on wages and conditions of work, both within nation-states and globally. Junk jobs would emerge that had been de-skilled into easily learned low-paid tasks. Although these might initially open up a divide between those who held such jobs and those who were in more demanding work in particular countries, the long-term effect would be experienced in an international division of labour. Junk jobs could be set up anywhere in the world where there was compliant, cheap labour (see also pp. 604).

Braverman underestimated the range of strategies pursued by employers. In some cases, such as in the context of technical complexity, it might suit management to cede control of production to the workforce. In other cases, management might choose not to apply scientific management. For instance, even at its peak in 1920s' North America, there was only ever a partial take-up of scientific management. In Europe, employers generally tinkered with Taylorism, avoiding a full-blown implementation. Employers often avoided a full implementation of Taylorism as they wanted to retain operational flexibility. In the gentleman amateur boards of directors in the UK, there was a general contempt for ideas of management that came from North America.

The contemporary embrace of team working and culture initiatives raises different questions from those that Braverman was dealing with so that, in recent years, labour process theory has paid attention to the identity and subjectivities of workers and the surveillance regimes they work under. The research on surveillance draws on Foucault's use of the Panopticon metaphor borrowed from Bentham. This illustrates the way in which ideas from two centuries ago have a continued relevance to understanding organizations today. It also gives a sense of how ideas are constantly repackaged and reconfigured.

WHAT'S THE POINT?

What's wrong with labour process accounts of management?

1 *Resistance had been overlooked*: Michael Burawoy, for instance, highlighted the way in which workers successfully played games around production targets. Burawoy (1979) noted the prevalence of cooperation in most workplaces much of the time, which he saw as arising from participation in local 'games' on the shop floor – where the immediate elements of management control (such as a supervisor or payment system) became the object of worker ingenuity designed to beat the rules. He argued that the opportunity to gain small victories in local struggles over things close at hand to the immediate concerns of the employees softened the fundamentally skewed nature of the game in which any employee cooperates.

2 *Labour markets were complex rather than simply being subject to universal de-skilling*: Not all workers competed in a single labour market, because there were many labour markets, often exhibiting characteristics of 'dual labour market segmentation'. Rubery (1978) developed a theory of dual labour market segmentation. She argued that labour markets were structured not just by the actions of employers but also by the ability of workers 'to maintain, develop, extend and reshape their organisation and bargaining power' (Rubery, 1978: 34). Characteristically, dual labour markets divide between those segments that have some degree of career prospects, are full-time and better paid, and enjoy better conditions. The other segment is composed of less skilled jobs, often casual and part-time, with worse pay, prospects, and conditions. Often, labour market dualism was argued to have a gender dimension to it; that is, the pool of employees divided into those who had secure, better paid full-time work, largely men, whereas those who were in part-time, less secure, and lower paid work were disproportionately women (for

earlier labour process treatments of these themes, see Clegg and Dunkerley, 1980: 400–422; Knights and Willmott, 1986).

3 *Different controls targeted different types of employee*: Divisions made the task of control much easier because they concentrated employees' minds on the fact that they slotted into a huge hierarchy of labour, with the long-term unemployed at the bottom, and everyone competing for the minor qualitative differences available with shifting from one segment to the next – what Braverman called divide and rule prevailed. Hence, as Clegg (1981) argued, different types of control, using different principles, would be targeted at different categories of employees. Organizations were best seen as sedimented structures, revealing a complex layering of controls stratified in terms of their emergence, as temporal phenomena, as different innovations in control were layered on top of each other, subsuming but never entirely replacing what had gone before. Moreover, different strategies of control were oriented towards different levels in terms of the organizational hierarchy (also see the contributions in Knights et al., 1988).

4 *De-skilling was not for everyone*, the labour process theorists said. Friedman (1977: 78) argued that some employees, such as highly skilled and creative types, whose discretion management needed in work, meant that not all jobs could or would be de-skilled to the furthest point. Instead, some jobs would be designed to include elements of 'responsible autonomy'.

5 *Control was not just personal – the work of managers – but could be built into technology*: Edwards (1979) extended Braverman's analysis by highlighting that management also controlled employees through machinery and technological innovations, such as assembly lines, as well as through 'bureaucratic control'. The effects of technology, in particular, were much elaborated by labour process writers

(Continued)

(Continued)

(e.g. see the contributions of Knights and Willmott, 1988; also Friedman, 1990). These technologies were often associated with a decline in craft control by workers as their specialist craft knowledge became redundant with the introduction of more sophisticated technologies that replaced manual skill and dexterity with machine-coded reliability.

6 *The role of exploitation of surplus value is overstressed*: In many contemporary organizations, labour is a small element in the overall cost structure. The scene has changed greatly since Marx's day when factories were small and labour-intensive.

7 *The stress on the capitalist labour process does not allow for analysis of non-capitalist organizations*: A great deal of learning is translated from the private to the public sector and to the non-profit sector, and some may flow back the other way. Restricting analysis to business for profit organizations is unduly limiting.

Labour process theory began to develop many qualifications – but the qualifications eroded the core theory of exploitation, de-skilling, and resistance. Braverman and traditional labour process theorists were highly determinist. They argued from the existence of an analytical model of class structure that they superimposed on organizations and from which they saw necessary effects of exploitation and de-skilling as following. They minimized the capacity of ordinary people to exercise their human agency through resistance to control at work. They saw control as almost total, in a fatalistic way. Those human beings who were workers became ciphers in these views, shaped almost entirely by external structures – which, correlatively, were granted an almost total power as against the almost total subordination of those they controlled. Thus, it is not surprising that in terms of intellectual fashions, Marxist analyses fell out of favour in social science thinking. It was not only the bankruptcy of Marxism as a social system that caused its decline but also a shift in intellectual fashions. Structural and determinist thinking, in which immutable structures shaped the fates of ordinary people, fell out of fashion as entrepreneurial ideas became increasingly influential from the 1980s onwards. It has been post-structuralist thinking – the key idea of which is that there are no necessary structural divisions in society such as those between the classes of capital and labour but many more subtle and complex cleavages – that has influenced more recent debate.

Knights and Willmott (1989: 554) argued, from a post-structuralist position, that organizations were not places in which capitalists and managers had all the power and ordinary employees none. Instead, they argued that everyone in organizations has some power. People are defined not just by their job descriptions but also by the whole range of complex identities shaping them. It is not the case that some are ciphers and some are agents, that some can only do what only others can demand. It is not a case of power and autonomy on the one hand and subjection on the other.

Check out the Companion Website www.sagepub.co.uk/ managingandorganizations3 for free access to an article by David A. Spencer (2000) reviewing Braverman's legacy and the subsequent development of labour process analysis.

SUMMARY AND REVIEW

Taylor, notably, was an authoritarian, and believed that management's right to rule could be established scientifically, whereas for Fayol it seemed indubitable that the more rational and enlightened should lead – and lead wisely with care.

In management theory circles, the contributions of F. W. Taylor have been both overlauded and overdemonized. The Taylor system was simply one aspect of a widespread movement of systematization, articulated by engineers, that was afoot in late nineteenth- and early twentieth-century management, initially in the USA and then, in the era following the First World War, spreading throughout Europe and elsewhere.

Owners, managers, and employees alike frequently resisted Taylorism, and it was by no means a smooth path to a more rational future, as Taylor hoped. However, Taylor delivered the template for a systematic practice of management based on both universal principles and management science. Disguised, refined, and altered, his ideas are still at work in many contemporary approaches.

Mayo's Human Relations School contributed significantly to the development of management and organization theory. It manifests itself today in initiatives such as the 'learning organization' and 'empowerment' and it is in human relations that many of the personnel functions now associated with HRM were first developed, especially the idea of the counselling interview.

Although human relations focus on the soft, human side of business, it is often seen as the oil that is necessary to run smoothly the machine that Taylor designed. Follett and Mayo disagreed markedly with Taylor. Follett was much more of a democrat than Mayo, however. Mayo drew on his early experiences in Australia of a radicalized labour movement to point to the necessity of social integration and collaboration to overcome what he saw as the irrationality, the hatreds, and the futility of class struggle. Follett's experiences were more positive. She had seen at a community level what could be achieved by education, grassroots action, and social networks, and believed that these could deliver similar results in business.

In contemporary times, major critical currents – centred on labour process theory and the McDonaldization thesis – have re-engaged with the classic statements of management provided by early management theorists such as Taylor. In many respects these early management theories prepared the way for a great deal of modern management. Thus, the lineages of many contemporary or recent management fads go back to Taylor – such as business process re-engineering, total quality management, knowledge management, for instance – while others derive from Mayo's human relations – such as human resource management. But, as we have explained, formal principles always have to be seen in the context of their use, how they are interpreted, and understood in practice.

EXERCISES

1   Having read this chapter you should be able to say in your own words what each of the following key terms means. Test yourself or ask a colleague to test you.

- Surplus resources
  Scale
- Division of labour
- Supervision
- Direct management
  control
- Panopticon
- Scientific
  management
- Labour process
  theory

- Slavery
- De-skilling
- Human
  relations
- Bureaucracy
- Traditional
  authority
- Rational–legal
  authority
- Management
  models

2   What are the central features of bureaucracy?
3   Why did the expansion of scale in organization activities occur in the latter half of the nineteenth century and what were its implications for management?
4   What was Bentham's unique contribution to management?
5   What was innovative about Taylor's scientific management?
6   What did Fayol add to scientific management?
7   According to Follett, what were the unanticipated consequences of highly rational (scientific) management practices?
8   What aspects of management and organization did Mayo highlight?
9   How did Barnard conceptualize leadership?

10 Why do management plans sometimes meet resistance when managers try to implement them?

11 What strikes you as problematic with the proposition that labour is the only source of value?

ADDITIONAL RESOURCES

1 *Writers on Organizations*, written by Derek Pugh and David Hickson (2007), should be a staple resource for all introductory students. It provides thumbnail sketches of the life, times, and ideas of many of the key thinkers of management and covers almost all of those addressed here, plus plenty who were not. The current edition even includes an account of some of the work by one of the authors of this book, Stewart Clegg.

2 *Manufacturing Rationality: The Engineering Foundations of the Managerial Revolution* by Yehouda Shenhav (1999) is an excellent, very detailed, analysis of the engineering auspices of so many influential ideas and people in the early career of modern management.

3 As Boje and Rosile (2001) argue, Follett was the first advocate of situational models of leadership and cooperation – models that avoided general theories and approaches in favour of those that were contextually sensitive, that appreciated the detail of the situation that they were to be applied in. Other appreciations by distinguished management academics of Mary Parker Follett can be found in work such as *Prophet of Management: A Celebration of Writings from the 1920s*, which Pauline Graham (1995) edited, including commentary by Peter Drucker, Rosabeth Moss Kanter, and Henry Mintzberg, among others.

4 In his book *Recreating Strategy*, Stephen Cummings (2002: 79–131) 'deconstructs' management's history, and it is well worth reading for those who want to gain some idea of how the modern idea of management was socially constructed.

5 An earlier account by one of the present authors was published as *Organization, Class and Control* (Clegg and Dunkerley, 1980), and it contains detailed accounts of some other founding fathers of early management, of a more sociological bent, which have been omitted here.

6 We would recommend also the account by Peter Miller and Ted O'Leary (2002) of 'Hierarchies and American ideals, 1900–1940', from which we have drawn to frame this chapter.

7 There are many accounts that outline an interpretive approach. Many of them are referenced in Sandberg and Targama (2007), who provide an overall guide for the more sophisticated student. Perhaps the easiest account for the introductory student to follow is one that has been enormously influential and has been around for a long time. It is Chapter 6 of David Silverman's (1970) *The Theory of Organizations*, where he compares rational 'systems' perspectives with those that are 'interpretive', which he terms the 'action frame of reference'.

8 In films, there are plenty of examples of satire of various aspects of management, from Charles Chaplin's (1936) *Modern Times*, with its critique of the moving production line and associated efficiencies, through the 1948 John Farrow film *The Big Clock*, which is savage in its depiction of how one man's megalomania finds expression through a ruthless and amoral concern with efficiency centred on mastery of time.

9 In more contemporary films, science fiction classics such as the 1982 *Blade Runner* (Scott, 1982; there is a director's cut from 1992 as well) and *Gattaca* (Niccol, 1997) provide a bleak view of a future where modern management has become institutionalized as wholly corporate and in control, able to fit the person to the job almost perfectly, such that life outside its requirements can only be nasty, bleak, and poor. Both movies show the dark side of meritocracy wed to bureaucracy and science.

WEB SECTION

1 Our Companion Website is the best first stop for you to find a great deal of extra resources, free PDF versions of leading articles published in Sage journals, exercises,

video and pod casts, team case studies and general questions, and links to teamwork resources. Go to www.sagepub.co.uk/managing andorganizations3.

2 For state of the art briefings on how to manage organizations effectively, please visit the Henry Stewart Talks series of online audio-visual seminars on Managing Organizations, edited by Stewart Clegg: www.hstalks.com/r/ managing-orgs, in particular, Talk #13: *Organization design theory: its evolution within a changing context*, John Child.

3 A good introduction to Taylor can be found at http://onlinebooks.library.upenn.edu/webbin/ gutbook/lookup?num=6464.

4 One interesting early figure whom we do not discuss in the book but is well worth getting to know is Charles Babbage. He was an early engineer/manager and is credited with inventing the first computer or 'calculating machine'. For starters see www.en.wikipedia.org/wiki/ Charles_Babbage.

5 Henri Fayol is well served by the web: http:// en.wikipedia.org/wiki/Henri_Fayol.

6 The Hawthorne Studies, with many links, are discussed at http://psychology.about.com/od/ hindex/g/def_hawthorn.htm.

7 David Boje is an American academic who maintains a very lively website. One of his pages, http://tinyurl.com/3btjbd, contains a discussion of connections between Mary Parker Follett's work on power and empowerment and that of one of the authors of this book, Stewart Clegg.

LOOKING FOR A HIGHER MARK?

Reading and digesting these articles that are available free on the Companion Website www.sage-pub.co.uk/managingandorganizations3 can help you gain deeper understanding and, on the basis of that, a better grade:

1 On the Companion Website you will find Bahnisch, M. (2000) 'Embodied work, divided labour: subjectivity and the scientific management of the body in Frederick W. Taylor's 1907 "Lecture on Management"', *Body & Society*, 6 (1): 51–68, which looks at the way that modern management began by reforming the body of employees.

2 If you are interested in how management theory got to be the way it is, then it is useful to know a little history: the Companion Website contains a very useful source, Grant, J. D. and Mills, A. J. (2006) 'The quiet Americans: formative context, the Academy of Management leadership, and the management textbook, 1936–1960, *Management & Organizational History*, 1 (2): 201–224.

3 A good review article on the influential labour process account of management is to be found on the Companion Website, in the article by Spencer, D. A. (2000) 'Braverman and the contribution of labour process analysis to the critique of capitalist production – twenty-five years on', *Work, Employment & Society*, 14 (2): 223–243.

4 Try and read Turner, B. S. (2003) 'McDonaldization: linearity and liquidity in consumer cultures', *American Behavioral Scientist*, 47 (10): 137–153, before that next Macca's!

CASE STUDY

Innovation is as a key asset for any organization. Let us assume you agree with this statement and decide to bring innovation into your organization. If yours is a typical company it may fit the following profile: hundreds, maybe even thousands of employees; company work processes formalized over the years that seem to be doing their job pretty satisfactorily and shareholders who are more or less satisfied with the company's financials. Yet, there is a niggling sense that your company can be performing at a higher gear, and that *innovation* can make the difference. So what do you do? Do you change your workforce to include only the most creative people? Do you prioritize investment in new technologies? While these are steps in the right direction, their impact on the company may not be sustainable. Employees come and go and technologies are constantly changing. In this case study we describe a different approach that can make innovation a more sustainable asset for an organization. It involves changing the way people think, act, and work and an integrated effort at all levels of the organization: individual, team, and organizational.

Let us begin by looking at these three levels. On the individual level, *everyone* in the organization is required to acquire a skill-set that will allow them to think and act innovatively. This can make a crucial difference to many common (and uncommon) work tasks: from juggling projects within a time pressured and resource-scarce environment to dealing with the accidental deletion of an important file or a missing suitcase on an important week-long business trip. On the team level, providing the right tools and setting up the right work processes can enable real changes to be implemented. This can make a whole range of activities more effective: new product development, project management, inter-group communication and meetings (that great stealer of work time) that lead to better results. On the organizational level, the key move is to put in place a structure that encourages innovative thinking and supports implementation of innovative results. Many times organizations have lots of good will and motivate their employees to come up with new ideas (idea boxes and the like), but they are never followed up and gradually the hype falls. Proper structures and company guidelines, as uncreative as they sound, are essential in sustaining the motivation to keep on innovating.

The Bolivar Group is a Colombian-based conglomerate with an asset value in excess of $10bn. Its holding companies include banking, insurance, construction, mutual funds, and leisure resorts. For two years Bolivar had been searching for an innovation supplier to help them achieve the company's vision of long-term, sustainable leadership through innovation. They were looking to find a structured methodology that would allow everyone in their organization to be more innovative and so challenge the general consensus that innovation and creative thinking is an inherent trait among gifted individuals.

In 2007 Bolivar began working with SIT – Systematic Inventive Thinking® – a company with a structured innovation methodology that helps organizations create self-sustaining innovation. Bolivar was interested to teach its organization *how* to innovate. The methodology, known as the 'SIT Onion', consists of five layers and includes the tools, principles, skills, proficiencies, and activities required to deliver innovation.

Together, SIT and Bolivar launched Efecto-I! (The I-Effect): a comprehensive innovation programme that has created a culture and an attitude of innovation across the company's sub-businesses and 14,000 employees.

On the individual level, SIT provided Bolivar with innovation tools and principles that employees could apply on their own, at any time or in any situation – what is termed 'innovation on-demand'. From senior managers to salespeople to bank clerks, employees now have a method for coming up with fresh approaches to their daily tasks or solving problems.

On the team level, SIT established a cadre of specially trained innovation managers and coaches. The key responsibility of this group rests in actively disseminating the innovation methodology to the companies thousands of employees, and helping specific teams achieve innovation successes. Furthermore, SIT's work with Bolivar on project management proficiencies established processes that ensure that ideas generated in the innovation process are actually implemented, and more importantly, not discarded at the first sign of difficulty. These skills give the teams the means of working and thinking together, and ways to make sure that their decisions are carried out.

On the organizational level, SIT worked with Bolivar to design and implement an innovation structure to ensure all Bolivar's activities will be self-sustaining in the long run. This involved establishing dedicated innovation positions, new work processes, and success metrics. Existing company structures were utilized as far as possible, making it easier and more natural to implement the new innovation process within the organization.

Between 2008 and 2009, over 400 new products, services, business models, and work processes have been successfully implemented yielding new revenue on one hand, and cost saving and efficiency on the other. Two examples include: a) a new service in Bolivar's industrial machinery leasing company that created a new market, and b) new banking services that led to hundreds of thousands of dollars in cost saving.

Over 600 innovation coaches were trained throughout the entire Bolivar Group to lead systematic innovation inside the organization. These coaches use SIT methodology to manage daily business challenges in their teams. To date, close to 2000 employees have learned innovation tools from the coaches who run trainings on a regular basis.

Bolivar's innovation structure includes two vice presidents responsible for overseeing all innovation processes and two dozen innovation managers who support the cross-organization innovation coach activity. An innovation portal was established to support the innovation managers and innovation coaches by giving them access to innovation tools, workshop scripts, and examples that they can use in their work.

SIT worked with Bolivar to establish internal communication mechanisms that would update the entire organization on innovation activities and achievements. This continues to create a buzz in the company, getting everyone on board, and at the same time shows management support and commitment to the process. Bolivar regularly puts out quarterly booklets on new products and services in the company born out of the innovation process, corporate DVDs showcasing different divisions' accomplishments, and 'Innovation of the Day' emails giving both real Bolivar cases as well as information on innovation tools.

After less than three years of working together with SIT, Bolivar has much to show in terms of its ROI – return on innovation. The model they applied made innovation a concrete tool across all levels of the organization:

1 Individuals are more creative and give better performance.
2 Teams have enhanced work processes for rolling out their decisions.
3 The organization has the right structures to implement real changes across the entire company.

Question

1 What kind of changes to management relations and learning among employees would need to occur when implementing such a model in an organization that had a more traditional design, more oriented to command and control, rather than innovation and creativity?

Case prepared by Robyn Taragin-Stern and Grant Harris; see also SIT, www.sitsite.com.

NOTE

1   Although we tend to think of slavery as something that disappeared in the
nineteenth century, this is not the case. A recent study by the Joseph Rowntree
Foundation (Craig et al., 2007), in the UK, suggests that there are tens of thousands of people who work as virtual slaves in the modern British economy. The
bonds of modern slavery, experienced as a loss of free will and as being compelled to work irrespective of preferences, are sometimes shackles but are
much more likely to be debt bondage, theft of passport and ID, illegal status,
and fear because of the threat and use of violence. Thus, extreme economic
exploitation, absence of human rights, and actual or threatened violence characterize modern slavery in areas of the economy such as prostitution, hotel,
factory, and dock labour. Bales (2005) estimated the contemporary number of
slaves at 27 million people, globally.

CHAPTER THIRTEEN

MANAGING BEYOND BUREAUCRACY

Dysfunctions, Institutions, Isomorphism

LEARNING OBJECTIVES

By the end of this chapter, you will be able to:

- Understand how bureaucratic organizations' control over their members can be counterproductive

- Understand how and why so many organizations are similar in their design and practices

- Grasp how and why management action is always embedded in more or less implicit/ explicit theories about what is to be done

- Distinguish between (a) organizational exploitation and (b) organizational exploration of knowledge

- Know what is a 'failure trap' and what is a 'success trap'

BEFORE YOU GET STARTED . . .

Bureaucracy, the rule of no one, has become the modern form of despotism. (Mary McCarthy)

INTRODUCTION

During the twentieth century the ideas promulgated by writers such as Taylor, Fayol, Barnard, and Mayo seeped into practice. The major organizational event of the twentieth century was probably the Second World War, which saw a degree of management and organization hitherto not found before. Many of what we now take for granted as modern management ideas were first seen in action in the organization of events such as the Normandy Landing of 1944, which threw the weight of the United States into the war in Europe. The military approach was classically bureaucratic, involving detailed planning and organization. Ideas that had begun to be circulated in West Point, the US elite military academy, which had initially been imported from Germany in the nineteenth century and had been hooked up with the engineering approach of the scientific managers, were now seen in practice by Europeans as well as Americans. For a number of combatants who were subsequently enrolled as students in universities in the US, as well as other observers, it was evident that matters of organization were extremely important in the post-war world. Several of these students became organization researchers, often in sociology programmes in universities in cities such as New York at places like Columbia. As such they all learned from the plethora of translations of Max Weber that began to appear from the late 1940s, notably Weber's writings on bureaucracy.

Weber's approach was based on an analysis of how members of organizations use their sense of the organization and its rules as a resource in their everyday management (see Bittner, 2002 [1965]). Weber's account merely sought to systematize and accentuate elements of what had become ordinary bureaucratic practice by the beginning of the twentieth century. The model was neither prescriptive nor predictive: if these practices changed, then typologies would need to change. The new wave of organization researchers started to revise Weber's ideas to incorporate features of reality not captured in his model. As they conducted research into actual bureaucracies they found variants on the basic model.

RETHINKING BUREAUCRACIES

Who benefits?

Two researchers named Peter Blau and Richard Scott asked the question 'who benefits?' from the way an organization is designed. The notion of 'who benefits?' captures a dimension that Weber had not focused on. Blau and Scott (1963) focused on the relation of the organization to its members and beneficiaries. As they argued, there were at least four types of organization that could be distinguished on the basis of 'who benefits?'

1 Member-beneficent organizations, such as cooperatives.
2 Owner-beneficent organizations, such as businesses.
3 Client-beneficent organizations, such as schools or hospitals.
4 Public-beneficent organizations, such as a public postal service, which serves all members of a community.

It might be assumed that organizations served the person or persons who were their ostensive beneficiaries, such as shareholders or customers. Yet, just introducing these two categories can be problematic: many organizations serve both sets of interests, and while it is possible to argue that if, in the long run, customer interests are not served, then shareholder interests will suffer. But what about those organizations that exploit a near monopoly position to yield massive profits such as Microsoft, and who release software with many problems in it that they then expect their customers to alert them to and maybe even fix?

Further, many organizations seem to be run for the benefit of those who manage them rather than those who are, ostensibly, being served. Have you seen the John Cleese comedy *Fawlty Towers* in which he plays Basil Fawlty? Basil is authoritarian and incompetent, arrogant to those whom he despises, deferential to those whom he admires, and prone to making judgements and assumptions that are invariably managerially inappropriate and wrong. Nonetheless, the customers and the staff are always to blame, in his view. One reason why this show is so funny is that it is so easy to relate it to real-life situations. Most of us, to be sure, have encountered organizations similar to Fawlty Towers, where the managers seem to think that if they did not have to serve pesky customers (or students, patients, passengers, pupils, citizens, etc.), they could run a tightly managed organization.

The centrality of compliance

Other writers took different tacks. Etzioni (1961) focused on what he thought was the key issue in Weber's account – the relations of compliance. Why do people do what other people in organizations tell them to do when these people hold more powerful positions? What is the motivational basis for their compliance? Why do we obey directives? Two factors explain these questions, suggests Etzioni: subordinate involvement and management resources. Essentially, there are three types of power and three types of involvement, which tend to be internally consistent with each other.

Etzioni focused on compliance, asking what motives explain why people obey orders in organizations.

1 Coercive power elicits alienated involvement: 'I do this because I have no option other than to do so.'
2 Remunerative power elicits calculative involvement: 'I do this because I am being paid to do it and thus it is in my interests to do so.'
3 Normative power elicits moral involvement: 'I do this for the good of a greater cause, a higher glory.'

Trying to use the different types of power without the corresponding type of involvement will lead to unstable organizations and incongruent involvement, Etzioni suggests. You cannot run a business organization primarily on calculative involvement if you neglect to pay wages, as many formerly Soviet enterprises found after the fall of communism. Hence, these three types of relations will tend to be the coherent points about which actual organizations are organized. The more coherent the power/involvement relations, the more efficient the organizations will be, he suggests. There will be a tendency for coherence to emerge in the long run, so that misaligned organizations will tend to realign themselves. Things are rarely as simple and as clear-cut as the schema might lead us to believe. Organizations typically use all three patterns variably at different times. They try to increase moral involvement as well as paying wages; they try to coerce people while at the same time trying to maintain moral involvement. Nonetheless, empirical investigation has tended to support the consistency thesis that Etzioni puts forward (Hall et al., 1966).

Rule tropism

Bureaucracies might be technically superior in many respects, but it has been suggested that they make people sick. Merton (2002 [1940]), for instance, argued that, in bureaucracies, following the rules becomes an end in itself rather than a means to an end and that, as a result, people who work in bureaucracies become pathologically, psychologically maladjusted: he used a term from biology to explain this – tropism. The term 'tropism' is widely used in medicine, where it refers to an involuntary orienting response, a positive or negative reaction to a stimulus. In management, the stimuli are rules, and the response is one in which the existence of the rules in a bureaucracy immediately and involuntarily, through a learned response, structures actions within the organization.

WHAT DO YOU MEAN?

Job's Worth

Organization members in bureaucracies automatically shrink from innovation and creativity and retreat back to the rigidity of the rules. They become 'Job's Worths', summed up in phrases such as 'It's more than my job's worth, mate, to do what you want, even if it makes sense – see, it's against the rules.' With this proviso almost any kind of laziness, rigidity, and inability to be responsive can be defended.

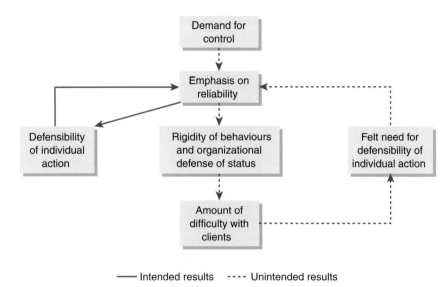

FIGURE 13.1
Merton's model of bureaucracy (after March and Simon, 1958: 41)

Highly bureaucratic rules, Merton argued, become a stimulus to which organization members show an involuntary response. Nobody wins through excessive rule following, says Merton. In such organizations, members show signs of what he calls rule tropism – following rules for their own sake. An unanticipated consequence of this is that the psychological maturity of organization members as adults capable of healthy learning and development is arrested. They learn only to follow the rules, for they can never be held to be irresponsible when doing this. Thus, organizational dysfunctions develop from organizations designed to create efficiency through rule-following behaviour.

Why does bureaucracy produce such responses? The answer resided in the normal processes of bureaucracy. Bureaucracies achieve an orderly transmission of instructions from top to bottom. Instructions are the major mechanism of control, and reliable obedience to instructions is the major mechanism of consent. Reliable subordinates perform accountably and predictably, according to the rules. Organization members realize that if they follow rules, they cannot be formally criticized. They can always 'cover their backs', even if following the rules produces a less good result. Rule following becomes the reason for people to adopt defensive behaviour, such as saying, 'I can't do that; it's more than my job is worth', meaning it is not part of my duty statement, job description, or responsibility. The more there is an emphasis on reliability, the greater becomes the reduction in personalized relationships and the more people are treated as a means to an end in terms of their role definitions; the rules of the organization become so internalized by members that they become almost an end in themselves, rather than a means to an end (Figure 13.1). Following the rule and applying the organizational categories strictly in order to make decisions becomes so much second nature that innovation is curtailed by conditioned responses – what people have become habituated to doing.

It is not just bloody-mindedness that is at work in rule tropism. Merton identified the phenomenon of 'trained incapacity', which he describes as:

> that state of affairs in which one's abilities function as inadequacies or blind spots. Actions based upon training and skills that have been successfully applied in the past may result in inappropriate responses under changed conditions. An inadequate flexibility in the application of skills will, in a changing milieu, result in more or less serious maladjustment. (2002: 358)

Strict adherence to rules often leads to a displacement of goals, because the aims of the organization become identified with following the rules that are only intended as a means to achieving the goals. Filling in forms correctly can quickly substitute for whatever action the forms were supposed to achieve. Formalism and ritualism develop as behavioural traits in consequence. The upshot of rigid adherence to bureaucratic rules is inefficiency.

Merton's recipe for bureaucratic inefficiency was quite simple and logical:

1 Effective bureaucracy demands reliability of response and strict devotion to regulations.
2 Rules become absolutes rather than means to an end.
3 Adaptation is minimized as rules are rigorously followed.
4 Elements designed in principle to enhance efficiency end up generating inefficiency as the letter of the law is observed rather than the spirit of the mission.

Changing interpretations of bureaucratic rules

Organization rules mean different things to different people in different contexts at different times. The meaning of rules is not fixed by what they say but how they are used. Gouldner (1954) tells a story illustrating this point. The story is set in a gypsum mine in which a new, younger manager, more focused on the bottom line, replaced a traditional CEO. Mining gypsum is hard, dirty, and dangerous work. Mining is the most dangerous of occupations according to ILO statistics.

From the perspective of the new mine manager, when he took over the plant, what he saw was considerable slackness. Employees 'borrowed' plant materials and used them at home. Safety regulations were violated. Authority relations were very familiar and flexible. The situation was one of 'mock bureaucracy', where the rules were seen as a result of external industry regulations that could be ignored for all practical purposes. Neither management nor workers' values were aligned with the rules, so they were widely regarded as lacking legitimacy. The rules simply got in the way of customary means of doing things. Informality reigned in the relations between management and the workers. Gouldner called this an 'indulgency pattern'. Everyone knew what the rules were but no one took them seriously. The new manager resolved to tighten control (Figure 13.2).

Tightening control did not solve the problems. Employees had become used to a slack regime. They saw the enhanced control as an imposition,

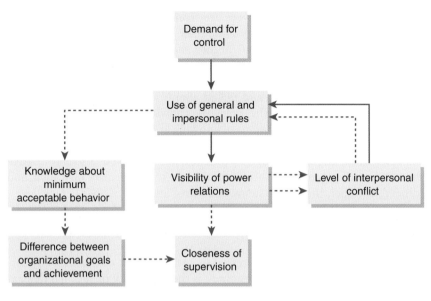

FIGURE 13.2
Gouldner's model of
bureaucracy (after March
and Simon, 1958: 41)

and failed to accept the legitimacy of the written rules over the customary ways of doing things. The consequence was an escalating resistance to increased managerial control by employees used to slackness as a norm. With the tighter policing of the rules, power relations became much more visible, raising the level of tension and resistance. Now management defined rule infringements as deliberate, given that the formal rules were being emphasized. The management response was to tighten supervision still further. Now, getting away with rule infringements became a serious game for the employees and a means of enhancing their prestige as successful 'larrikins' or rebels in the workplace, free and independent spirits whom management could not tame. The situation escalated out of control in a dynamic, unstable, and vicious cycle, as management saw such non-compliant behaviour as simply further warrant for rule enforcement. The final result was a sudden and illegal wildcat strike. The organization moved from a pattern of indulgency to one that was 'punishment centred'. After the strike, there was a concerted attempt to reinterpret and use the rules to create legitimate boundaries for action. During the whole cycle, the rules remained the same; it was their interpretation that changed. Managing the organization is less about knowing what the rules are per se and more about managing their meaning.

There are some optimists who think that managerial control, as we have analysed it here, is a thing of the past, at least under the apparent conditions of greater autonomy and discretion we have come to associate with knowledge work and knowledge workers and the advantage that this provides to tacit knowledge (Sewell, 2005). Can managers ensure that employees' cognitive efforts to apply what they know to what they do approach their full potential? Typically, the employees are 'empowered', that is, given discretion to use what they know to provide their organizations with solutions to workplace problems. As Sewell argues, however, this still requires the operation of disciplinary mechanisms that perpetuate managerial control. Such control will still be expressed in terms of *rules* about how knowledge is constituted, can be used, and talked about; in terms of subjects – what makes the *exemplary* (or the deviant) knowledge worker; in terms of *authority* – how some expressions of knowing are validated as organizational knowledge and others are not; and in terms of *practices* of elicitation and representation that supply not only practical knowledge but also a normative basis by which organization members are expected to regulate their own, and others', conduct, through systems of control and surveillance.

Check out the Companion Website www.sagepub.co.uk/ managingandorganizations3 for free access to an article by Graham Sewell (2005) if you want to learn how we should rethink and still use the notion of managerial control in the era of knowledge work.

Authority and delegation

Selznick (1943; 1949) was interested in authority, one of Weber's key categories. Where there is authority there is the possibility of rational delegation of duties that can be done by authorized others, according to rule. Delegation tends to increase the need for training in specialized competencies in order to ensure that the delegates are accountable for what has been assigned to them. It opens up opportunities for discretionary action on the part of delegates. Delegation occurs through defining different functional responsibilities, bifurcating organizational interests. Increased conflict can often occur between different responsibilities, in consequence; suboptimal goals will become paramount as departmental interests overrule overall organizational interests, especially where organizational goals are only weakly internalized by members (Figure 13.3). Consequently, a gap opens between the goals set by organizational elites and the performance delivered by departmental delegates. The normal workings of bureaucracies produce dysfunctional and counterproductive results, as delegation drives a wedge between goals and achievement.

Discretionary delegation rather than rule following

Blau (1955) studied two US government agencies: in one, rule-following was widely policed and observed, whereas in the other, the rules were creatively and interpretively followed. In the latter agency, rules were often bent or locally adjusted to ensure that a desired outcome was achieved. Performance assessment was premised on competition between officials. Blau found that those officials who collaborated rather than competed and who were more flexible in their reporting were more productive. Thus, the creative rule users performed better than the rule-followers. Where individuals were given more discretionary delegation in organizations, they performed better than when they worked according to rule. (Of course, working to rule is a classic industrial relations strategy for putting pressure on management.) In fact, in one of the two agencies, a federal office, Blau found that persistent and patterned infringement of the rules by officials made the organization more effective in achieving its

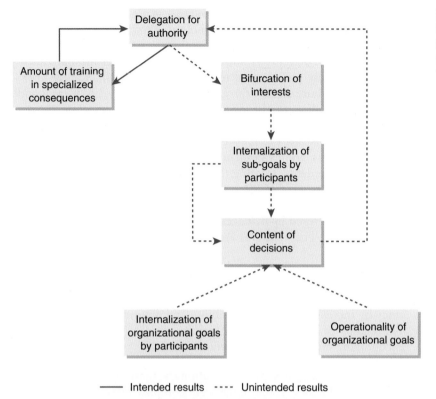

FIGURE 13.3
Selznick's model of
bureaucratic organization
(after March and Simon,
1958: 43)

formal goals. If the bureaucrats bent the rules they got better results!
Again, the logic is quite simple:

1   Local tacit knowledge and ways of doing things produce better outcomes
    than formally mandated ways.
2   More decentralized organization and less authoritarian management
    produce better practice outcomes.
3   Tightly stipulating rules and procedures does not produce best practice.
4   Best-practice outcomes occur where there is:

    a   Room for flexibility within a frame of employment security
    b   A professional orientation
    c   Collegiality in work groups
    d   An absence of entrenched conflicts within the hierarchy
    e   Evaluation by results rather than pressure to conform to processes.

Questioning bureaucracy

Weber identified bureaucracy with a growing pervasiveness of rational
calculation in all spheres of life. He made a moral case for bureaucracy as
rule without regard for persons as a positively democratic ideal, robust
against the blandishments of power and privilege. Against Weber, a number

of well-known critiques emerged: bureaucracy is not rational but produces action oriented to past precedents (Lindblom, 1959); it generates warped decisions (Cockett, 1995) and enables exploitation of uncertainty for sectional benefits (Crozier, 1964); bureaucratic personalities are individually and organizationally pathological (Merton, 2002 [1940]). Kanter (1984) wanted to reform bureaucracy through freeing creativity, broadening individuals' understanding of the overall organization, connecting them to others in it. The corollary of this process would be to improve management. Other writers saw even more reasons for distrusting bureaucracies. For instance, Peters and Waterman (1982) argue that bureaucratic rules privilege past precedents, freezing them for situations that could not have been anticipated, as we discussed in Chapter 6. Often these rules remain in existence because they served sectional interests, they diagnosed.

The diagnosis offered by management consultants Peters and Waterman was revolutionary. The logic was very clear:

1 Bureaucracy means that the employee is limited to being a cog in the organizational machine with a limited set of responsibilities.
2 Organization members can be liberated from the bondage of bureaucracy by increasing their responsibility and autonomy.
3 The chains of organizational hierarchy should be smashed through encouraging individual responsibility.

Peters and Waterman offered a revolutionary rhetoric, which sought to overthrow bureaucracy, seeing large-scale complex organizations as traps that ensnare creativity. Drawing on the research of March and Olsen (1976) and Weick (1969; 1979), Peters and Waterman argued that following bureaucratic rules would produce unimaginative outcomes. Instead, employees must share a managerial vision of their organization's culture and be prepared to go to extraordinary lengths to achieve it, not just follow rules. Often, the culture is expressed through a commitment to managing key performance indicators (KPIs) – rather than just following the rules; the newly liberated managers are expected to manage their own performance, in terms of striving, entrepreneurially, to exceed past performance.

MINI CASE

When KPIs rule, rationality does not always follow

Some unanticipated consequences can flow from this shift from the rules to the KPIs. For instance, privatized British railway services have, as one of their KPIs, being on time. In order to achieve on-time running as a KPI they adopted the practice of not stopping at scheduled stops when the train is running late. Thus, the train arrives on time but, unfortunately, the passengers do not, as their stop flashes by as the crew meets the KPIs. On paper, the performance is exemplary; in practice actually sticking to the rules in terms of required stops might lead to better service and customer

(Continued)

(Continued)

satisfaction (*Private Eye*, 1178, 1 March 2007: 12 'Cutting a good figure').

It is not only trains. The *Guardian* newspaper of Tuesday 20 February 2007 ('Irish Minister demands report on dangerous landings by Ryanair', p. 24) reported that the pilots union in the Republic of Ireland had reported that Ryanair's low-cost culture and fast turnaround times had led pilots to take unnecessary risks in their landing approaches:

> Last month the Irish Air Accident Investigation Unit issued a report on a 'serious incident' involving a Ryanair plane attempting to land at Cork airport in June last year. The captain failed to perform a standard procedure known as a 'go-around' after aborting a landing and instead banked in a tight circle to try again minutes later, bringing the plane within 425 feet [130 m] of the ground and alarming residents. It was the fourth incident within two years following a near-crash at Knock airport in March 2006, and troubled approaches at Rome airport in September 2005 and at Skavsta airport in Sweden in July 2004 … [Ryanair owner] Mr O'Leary said 25 minute turnarounds, which the Irish pilots union says puts pilots under severe pressure, are standard across the global budget airline industry. The three pilots who made the approaches at Knock, Stansted, and Skavsta have been demoted following the incidents. Mr O'Leary said he could not rule out similar incidents in the future despite the crackdown on pilots because of the sheer size of the airline, which will fly 42 million passengers on 454 routes this year … 'There will be more in the future, no doubt, no more than British Airways or easyJet. You cannot run an airline the size of ours without someone breaking a rule somewhere.'

- Why might the pilots union perceive low-cost air service providers' standard operating procedures as putting pilots under severe pressure?

New public management

Inspired in part by general management enthusiasms for entrepreneurialism, the doctrine of 'new public management' (NPM) substantially re-shaped the public sector bureaucracies of the neo-economically liberal English-speaking world from the 1980s onwards. At the core of the doctrine was a particular discourse of organizational change deployed as a rhetorical device for reshaping the identity of public service. As du Gay (2003) notes, much of this theorizing about contemporary economic and organizational change relied on a logic of overdramatic dichotomization constructing opposed and ethically juxtaposed categorical imperatives, where the dice was clearly loaded in favour of change. The discourse of organizational change mobilized support for attempts to re-invent and modernize public administration. In doing so, stark disjunctures and oppositions were deployed in simple narratives that politicians and their stakeholders could easily grasp, acting as catalysts for transformation. Simple answers positing universal and invariable managerial recipes predictably failed to deliver on their promise.

Neoliberal economic rationalist models inspired the changes over a period starting from the late 1970s. The consequence has been to create a public service, in Anglo-American polities at least, that has become less responsive in terms of public value and governance than it should be.

Moves towards efficiency and economy and concerns for transaction costs are important objectives of government but not always at the expense of public responsibility. The NPM, as a tendency, stressed a one-size-fits-all approach to public sector management. At its base was a simple idea: the public sector worked better the closer it approximated to private entrepreneurial practice. The introduction of quasi-markets and targets were the means whereby private sector managerial practices were applied to shape public sector management and governance (du Gay 2000a, 2001, 2002, 2006, 2008). It was assumed that the same management identities, practices, and roles could be applied across sectors, with incremental adjustments.

One of the most fundamental problems with the *New Public Management* movement has been its diminution of the statist and constitutional character of public bureaucratic office through the substitution of a language of political administration by a managerialist lexicon. This language, once learned, can be applied to managing hospitals as easily as managing transport. The language of the NPM spread like wildfire among ambitious and career-minded public servants in many jurisdictions. Not all welcomed it wholeheartedly, though, however much their political masters and mistresses in office might have embraced it. A micro-politics of resistance at the level of meanings and subjectivities, with multidirectional and generative effects for identity construction, characterized its reception in street-level bureaucracies. Focusing on the UK public services, Thomas and Davies (2005) used interviews with public service professionals in the police, social services, and secondary education to explore the meanings individuals ascribe to NPM discourse and how they see themselves within these meanings. These meanings did not posit NPM as the hegemonic discourse it is sometimes represented as being; instead it is seen as highly dynamic with individuals appropriating and 'conforming' to or 'resisting' disparate elements. The resistance that occurs is discursively produced within specific contexts, taking different form and emphasis with different groups.

Check out the Companion Website www.sagepub.co.uk/ managingandorganizations3 for free access to an article Robyn Thomas and Annette Davis (2005) on the impact of the NPM on managerial identities.

Institutional theory

There are three main explanations why so many organizations around the world adopted the bureaucratic form. One explanation stresses biological necessity: it might be genetic to create and order life according to hierarchies, and thus unavoidable: something imprinted in the species' way of doing things. Another explanation stresses efficiency: bureaucracy is functional, simply the one best way to organize large-scale activities under uncertain conditions. A third explanation is that bureaucracy has become so conventional that we find it normal to mimic the bureaucratic form because it has become so widely institutionalized. The reasons for its institutionalization (that it was associated with actions widely admired) have faded with time, such that it now seems natural, normal, and necessary.

Institutional theory: A theory that proposes that organizations have the structures that they do largely for cultural reasons. Some designs and practices become regarded, for whatever reasons, as highly esteemed, as displaying high 'cultural capital'. Through one or more of three specific mechanisms (coercive, mimetic, or normative isomorphism), the template becomes widely adopted.

This third argument is now widely accepted and is known as **institutional theory**. Institutional theory was developed in the 1950s and 1960s and early contributions emphasized the role of conflict and of the negotiated order between different interest groups. More recently, new institutional theory emerged and shifted emphasis towards understanding how organizations appear legitimate in the eyes of stakeholders.

Much modern institutional theory was developed from Berger and Luckmann's (1967) adaptation of some elements of Weber's social action approach into a generic 'social constructionist' perspective. Reality, they say, is socially constructed. This sounds more confusing than it actually is. Just think of being a student, enrolled in a first-year subject called Management. As a student, you are assigned a number, and then you have to enrol. The process of enrolling in a subject means choosing a code, standing in line on a particular day between 8 a.m. and 12 noon, then attending classes on a regular basis, passing assignments, until you either accumulate enough credits to graduate or pass final exams. You will not do these things just as you please but through skilful work in constructing answers to questions that are acceptably 'academic'. You must construct an academic persona and reality. All these things shape your reality as a student, but none of them are facts of nature – they do not have to be designed the way they actually are. At a certain point in history, universities simply decided to organize higher education in such a bureaucratic way, with registration, exams, graded assignments, and so on. Thus, much of what we take for granted as reality is, in fact, socially constructed.

Institutional theorists puzzle about questions such as, why, for instance, almost all public sector organizations in the Western world apply such similar models. To put it a bit more abstractly, what is at issue is the process by which actions are repeated and given similar meaning by oneself and others, which is defined as institutionalization. Institutional theory takes legitimacy as its master concept. It sees the quest for legitimacy as the driving force behind making organizations more alike. Meyer and Rowan (1977) argued that modern societies consist of many institutionalized rules, providing a framework for the creation and elaboration of formal organizations. Many of these rules are rationalized myths that are widely believed but rarely if ever tested. They originate and are sustained through public opinion, the educational system, laws, or other institutional forms. Thus, many of the factors shaping management and organization are not based on efficiency or effectiveness but on social and cultural pressures to conform to already legitimate practices. For instance, there is a lot of pressure on organizations to adapt to new tools invented by fashionable management gurus. Buzzwords such as TQM, *kaizen*, BPR, and so on are by no means proven to lead to success but are concepts that challenge organizations, since, if they do not apply them (and pay large fees to the not always so great consultants who are implementing them), they are seen as inert, reactive, and increasingly anachronistic. Institutional theory analyses the impact of this pressure on organizations and management decisions.

Few works are as widely cited as DiMaggio and Powell's (2002 [1983]) 'The iron cage revisited: institutional isomorphism and collective rationality in organizational fields'. Drawing on the new institutional theory pioneered by Meyer and Rowan in 1977, and influenced by Bourdieu's (1977) ideas about practice, the article considered how rationalized myths lodged in institutional settings shape organizational action to the extent that they can secure semblances of organizational legitimacy in order to capture resources and mobilize support. They sought to explain why organizations adopt similar forms and practices. They termed this process of copying **isomorphism**. The effect of institutional pressures is to constrain an organization's choice of structures to a set of arrangements that are acceptable within its field. The adoption of a particular initiative is a means of gaining legitimacy in the eyes of important stakeholders. In many cases an adopted initiative can be used to portray an *image* of rationality in the eyes of outside agencies. The ensuing symbolic display might well be decoupled from, or loosely coupled with, 'what actually happens'.

DiMaggio and Powell (2002 [1983]) stressed the importance of the concept of organizational fields and the focus on mechanisms of organizational change through institutional isomorphism. The organizational field was defined in relational terms as 'those organizations that, in the aggregate, constitute a recognized area of institutional life: key suppliers, resource and product customers, regulatory agencies, and other organizations that produce similar services or products' (DiMaggio and Powell, 2002 [1983]: 148).

Institutional isomorphism has become, perhaps, the key concept for much research during the past decade. Three ideal type mechanism of organizational change by institutional isomorphism have been sketched: coercive (when external agencies impose changes on organizations – most obviously through practices of state regulation), normative (when professionalization projects shape entire occupational fields), and mimetic mechanisms (essentially the copying of what is constituted as culturally valuable ways of doing or arranging things – cultural capital). Interest in the latter has far outweighed the former two in US empirical studies as Greenwood and Mayer (2008) note, while European researchers have been more oriented to the role of the state and other regulatory agencies, such as standards setting bodies (see Higgins and Hallström, 2007).

1   *Normative isomorphism*: Phenomena can become widespread because they are regarded as culturally positive norms, such as teamwork. Not meeting the expectations of what is regarded as a culturally positive norm would be regarded as either stupid or deviant. An organization's members become normatively predisposed through a long period of professional training and socialization, so that they favour certain sorts of practice. The widespread use of the partnership form by law and other professional firms is a case in point. The MBA qualification can be construed as a transmission mechanism for notions of best practice in management. In the traditional professions, **normative isomorphism** is often transmitted through continuing professional development such as a medical doctor attending a conference on the latest

Isomorphism: A term derived from biology, referring to a similarity in form of organisms of different ancestry. In organization and management theory, isomorphism is usually used in the context of institutional theory to refer to a situation in which organizational designs and practices in different organizations are nonetheless similar.

Normative isomorphism occurs when an organization's members are normatively predisposed, perhaps through a long period of professional training and socialization, to favour certain sorts of design and practices. The widespread use of the partnership form by low and other professional firms is a case in point.

developments in a particular aspect of medicine, or a lawyer keeping up with developments in case law. Thus, it is likely that there will be a received wisdom or a 'normative' view as to how best to treat a particular medical condition at a given time. This can change radically over time. For instance, today's medical professionals would look in horror at the ease with which their predecessors doled out Valium in the 1960s.

2 *Coercive isomorphism* is where an organization is compelled to institutionalize a particular policy, such as adopt an employment law or a tax standard. Coercive isomorphism is often found in global supply chains, where one powerful buyer coerces other parts of the supply chain to adopt a particular initiative or technology. Where the adoption of norms is forced by powerful agencies, such as the state, this is coercive isomorphism, which we associate with legal requirements. **Coercive isomorphism** occurs when some powerful institution obliges organizations in its domain, on threat of coercion, to comply with certain practices and designs. Think of the law; it obliges all organizations over a certain size to have equal employment opportunity practices. The managers may not want to provide equal opportunity, but they are obliged to do so under threat of legal penalty. As an example of coercive isomorphism, think why it is the case that all commercial airplanes have the same little speech and demonstration of safety features before you take off (including pointing out a whistle with which to attract attention in the unlikely event of an accident!). Because international aviation law says they must do so, because they are in breach of the law if they do not perform the ritual, they do it so as to be seen to observe the law. The state coercively shapes institutions by enforcing certain forms of legislation. For instance, in most advanced societies, there are usually legal rules outlawing discrimination on various grounds; thus mandated organizations collect data and present profiles of their activities. They do so to show the ways the organizations are in accord with these laws. Hence, organizations develop an equal employment opportunity officer and programmes – not necessarily because they want to or they think it is a good idea to do so, but because they are obliged, by law, to do so. Coercive isomorphism is generally associated with compliance to legal requirements but it is also evident when a powerful organization exerts its will on those in less privileged positions. For instance, the British food industry, as in most developed economies, is dominated by a number of powerful supermarkets – such as Tesco and Sainsbury's – which demand all sorts of standards from the farmers and others that supply them.

> **Coercive isomorphism** occurs when some powerful *institution* obliges organizations in its domain, on threat of coercion, to comply with certain practices and designs. Think of the law; it obliges all organizations over a certain size to have equal employment opportunity practices. The managers may not want to provide equal opportunity, but they are obliged to do so under threat of legal penalty.

3 *Mimetic isomorphism*: Sometimes organizations and their managers desire, consciously, to be similar to a particularly highly regarded exemplar, and when they copy it in this way, it is a case of **mimetic isomorphism**. In this type of action, something is regarded as so normatively attractive that the organization's managers desire to be similar because doing so easily defines what is proper, correct, and legitimate; hence, mimetic isomorphism is the process of copying organizational

> **Mimetic isomorphism**: In simple language, mimetic isomorphism means the process of copying. Organizational designs and practices that are seen to be successful are copied because they are associated with success.

devices or practices. Organizational designs and practices that are seen to be successful are copied because they are associated with success. Often organizations are held up as exemplars that other organizations attempt to emulate. This might be a successful competitor or it might be an organization from another industry. For instance, in the budget airlines industry many of the start-ups used the American Southwest Airlines as an exemplar to mimic. In university settings, business schools such as Harvard or London are often held up as being organizations that others want to copy. Some might argue that the case study – such an important feature of any business education – has its origins in Harvard, and has gone on to be mimicked across the world. The mimicry of so-called excellent organizations through best-practice benchmarking is an example of mimetic isomorphism. Similarly, adopting a management innovation such as knowledge management or, in the recent past, TQM or BPR, would also be an illustration of mimetic isomorphism. Mimetic isomorphism is demonstrated when a particular organizational practice, such as professors and teachers dressing up in academic gowns and making a procession as part of the ceremony of awarding a degree to new graduates, becomes widely diffused because people identify it as a central part of an institution. We know of no university that has dispensed with this ceremony for, as vice chancellors have frequently been known to remark, such a ceremony is symbolically representative of the university. So the ritual is widely adopted and diffused even in the newer universities. Stewart, co-author of this book, once worked somewhere in which many of the students who did the MBA were from overseas countries. Often, they had returned home prior to being awarded their degrees in order to return to careers and families and friends. Hence, they missed the ceremony and its photo opportunities, but nonetheless they clamoured for an opportunity to gain these mementos. The problem was that they did not want to have the expense of flying back to Australia from India or China, for instance, to get their pictures taken. Consequently, the university instituted a pre-degree ceremony, where a senior university dignitary would speak some formal words, during which the students would be told that this was not a degree ceremony, and then hand them something that was not a degree certificate but looked just like one. The students wore gowns that they were not yet entitled to wear – as they had not graduated – but the all-important pictures could be taken 'proving' that they had been at the university and had been 'awarded' their 'degree'. The pictures proved it! Thus, in this way their social reality was constructed. They had the pictures to prove they were graduates of, and belonged to, a specific university, with its appropriate ceremonies, rituals, and photo opportunities, even though none of it had really happened.

According to institutional theorists, the three forms of isomorphism combine to make organizations that are subject to isomorphic pressures appear increasingly alike, at least at a surface level – institutional isomorphism even structures the way that states define themselves. The idea of the state as the modern form of nationhood first emerged in the Treaty of Westphalia (1648) in which the idea of a modern Europe of nation-states was institutionalized, such that sovereign states pledged not to interfere in the activities, within their boundaries, of other sovereign states. Over the next few hundred years the artifacts, trappings, and rituals associated with a state spread globally.

Anderson (1982) analyses a specific case in terms of institutional theory by providing a fascinating account of the spread of the idea of the nation-state as an organizational form, with its appropriate modes of style, dress, and address, almost everywhere during the nineteenth century. The idea of the state continued to shape post-colonial policy after the Second World War when decolonizing territories were imagined into existence as if they were nation-states, whereas, often, there was precious little in the way of precedents to suggest that they ever had been. The legitimacy of the nation-state as the appropriate organizational form – even for tiny territories with a few thousand people or vast tracts of land containing tribal and linguistically distinct, defined groups – was so overwhelming that no other organizational form could be considered. Once produced, the state becomes subject to the normal pressures of economic growth and recession, demographic changes, civil war, policies of structural adjustment, and struggles to control it. Sometimes the state in question succeeds by surviving these struggles. For instance, if we think about the long period from the US Civil War to the civil rights struggles of the post-1960s, it is clear that although there have been major struggles to control and use the state for different and contradictory purposes, through it all something that is recognizable as the state of the USA has survived intact.

Sometimes states fail, as was the case in Rwanda and the neighbouring Great Lakes Region of Africa during its post-colonial history, most notably in the 1990s (Jefremovas, 2002). When states fail, rather than weakening the normative ideal, they strengthen it: that is how 'normative isomorphism' works – as an ideal metric. Failing the isomorphic test simply becomes further fuel for endorsing the normative model more strongly.

Institutions and entrepreneurs

Institutional theory was originally and mostly oriented to explaining why there were so few types of organizations and how things mostly seemed similar. The problem with this was what to do about change: how was change ever possible if everything seemed to be oriented to making things similar? In order to make change from isomorphized regimes possible, institutionalism introduced the category of the institutional entrepreneur. If so much energy goes into being similar to culturally valued organizations through mimesis how is it possible that organizations can change? This is the question the institutional entrepreneur is designed to answer.

Institutional entrepreneurs can be thought of as champions of change. Nelson Mandela was an institutional entrepreneur in South Africa, for instance, and has become one of the most widely admired men on the planet in consequence. Nonetheless, as is the case for the vast majority of institutional entrepreneurs, we cannot neglect the wider social fabric in which such institutions are embedded. Without the long struggle, armed resistance, and civil disobedience campaigns of the ANC Mandela could not have achieved much. Of course, he is a remarkable political actor but he is precisely that – a political actor tangled up in a complex web of power and political relations, including a deeply divided ANC.

Institutional entrepreneurs make strategic choices that have determinate consequences for an industry; however, these choices are limited by institutional rules that frame what are legitimate or viable strategies for action. Candace Jones' (2001) study of the early years of the American film industry from 1895 to 1920 takes from institutional theory the idea that firms' practices depend on the strategic choices that key agents make; these choices, in turn, depend on the social construction or enactment that they make of the environment in which they are operating, which frame their mental models of the institutional field. When a particular set of mental models becomes embedded in practice then a trajectory is launched for the development of an institutional field. Thus, initial conditions, especially an entrepreneurs' career history as defined by their choices, help shape the frame through which subsequent choices can be made by privileging certain frames. Organizations erect barriers to imitation based on their control of either property rights or knowledge; where they are successful in terms of consumer responses to their practices they entrench non-imitable competitive advantages that will depend on the unique mix of local resources and knowledge that they can continue to corral and control.

'From *Moby Dick* to *Free Willy*', by Tom Lawrence and Nelson Phillips (2004), is a study of the emergent industry of whale-watching in Pacific Canada, which charts the translation of whales from being the prey of Moby Dick to becoming an object of rare and organized appreciation by ecologically oriented tourists. The evolution was not naturalistic: key institutional entrepreneurs were involved in transforming an institutional field. The industry emerged in the context of macro-institutional changes discursively signalled by the emergence of an ecological consciousness in which the whale became a spectacle to be reverentially appreciated and commercially consumed – not in the flesh but in the spirit – the spirit of 'Free Willy'. The whale is essentially socially constructed in its meaning; for the Japanese and Norwegian authorities it is a source of food; for much of the rest of the world it is an object of wonder and delight rather than a dinner. The transition from being an object of prey to a source of delight is bounded by professionalized discourses of whaling and anti-whaling while, in turn, these are increasingly framed within a popular consciousness that is shaped by the changing representational practices of Hollywood.

A network of collaborative entrepreneurs began to colonize the previously unknown niche in which there was a demand for whale-watching by coordinating information on sightings. As the trade grew it became increasingly institutionalized at the regional level. New actors emerged representing the interests neither of tourists nor tour operators but the whales. All of these developments were local and emergent rather than central and planned. Thus was the fashion for whale-watching founded.

Institutions and professions

At the core of all modern organizations of some size and complexity are professionals. Professions, Scott maintains, define, interpret, and apply institutional elements such that they are the most influential contemporary creators of institutions. According to Scott (2008), professions as institutions rest on three different pillars: the regulative, normative, and cultural-cognitive pillars, familiar from DiMaggio and Powell (2002 [1983]).

Cultural-cognitive agents fix ontological frameworks, distinctions, typifications, and principles that range from the metaphysical realm of the theologian and philosopher to the material realm of engineers and applied scientists. Internal professional control is largely embedded in shared sensemaking. Normative agents do moral work of various kinds that stakes out areas of legitimated action premised on professional standards, codes, precepts, and rulings.

Within professions there are distinctions between different generic categories of social action, suggests Scott. Creative professionals are lodged in the universities, think tanks, and research centres. Carrier professionals are those who translate professional messages and spread them to new actors, arenas, and agencies: educators, trainers, consultants, and so on. The largest sub-category is comprised of the clinical professionals who deal with specific cases and clients. All professions are a component of Florida's (2002) creative class – a somewhat elastic and amorphous category. Typically, in terms of endogenous change, increasing professionalization leads to greater specialization within the primary profession, increased use of mechanization and routinization, and the consolidation and formalization of knowledge. Exogenously, these professionals are overwhelmingly organizational members rather than being the independent practitioners of the past. Not only that; their clients are increasingly corporate as well. One consequence is that the organizational form of the independent professions increasingly mirrors that of their clients in some important respects: they are becoming increasingly managerial. A shift is occurring from professional partnerships as the major organizing device to a managed professional business form (Hinings et al., 1999). Such managed professional businesses, as they grow in size, are likely to become more specialized and differentiated. These tendencies are altering the institutional logic of the professions away from the old ethos of altruism and service towards a more market-oriented provision of technical services. Both endogenous organizational changes such as increased organizational size as well as exogenous changes contingent on modernization lead to greater specialization and differentiation.

Check out the Companion Website www.sagepub.co.uk/ managingandorganizations3 for free access to an article by Tom Lawrence and Nelson Phillips (2004) on the emergence of whale-watching as an industry and the role that institutional entrepreneurs played in establishing it.

Check out the Companion Website www.sagepub.co.uk/ managingandorganizations3 for free access to an article by R. W. Scott (2008) on the professions.

Standards and institutionalization

One of the most symptomatic discourses of modern times has been the growth of formal written international standards, a major factor working to make organizations more alike globally. As Brunsson and Jacobsen (2000) have elaborated, standards are a major mechanism of institutional isomorphism rendering organization spaces, at least superficially, more alike, because they are defined by common rules. Since the late 1980s, starting from a concern with quality, international standards bodies have issued rules on an increasing number of arenas of organizational activity, such as ecological impact. A significant industry of global consultancy, auditing, certification, and accreditation accompanies these new managerial standards. Winton Higgins and Kristina Tamm Hallström (2007) have investigated 'Standardization, globalization and rationalities of government' with respect to organizations. They focus on the evolution of the national standards bodies, the participation in government of some of the pioneers of standardization, and how their relationship with public authorities developed in reference to rationally and consensually arrived-at 'technically-best' solutions, and the growing prestige of putatively independent expertise.

Standards, and the regulatory routines based on them, play a specific instrumental role in organizations. They create the manager as someone that is seeking to improve constantly. The role of the highly abstract ('generic') ISO 9000 quality assurance standards, and of ISO's subsequent management standards, elaborate 'practices of the self' for corporate managers to help them shape their identity as competent managers through following prescribed practices. Because these practices are subject to certification and recurring audit, the manager's and the organization's sense of legitimacy is enhanced. They must be doing the right things if they are following standards and are certified and audited as doing so! As audit never finds perfection – perfectability is impossible – then the manager must constantly live and manage with the need to constantly improve; any error or inadequacy uncovered by audit simply serves as further justification for improvements in the application of the standard.

Check out the Companion Website www.sagepub.co.uk/ managingandorganizations3 for free access to an article by Winton Higgins and Kristina Tamm Hallström (2007) on the role of standards in institutionalization.

Are managers dedicated followers of fashion?

Several pointers emerge from the previous discussions suggesting that management fashions are important. The combination of institutional entrepreneurship and the sheer centrality of professions to modern organizations both suggest transmission belts for organization fashions. The growth of the standards industry also aids the spread of fashion: the spread of the ILO 9000 standard for quality management in the 1990s saw a huge growth in total quality management in organizations globally. Institutional entrepreneurs help spread fashionable ideas, because they carve out new fields that others then copy; professions do so because they are one of the major sources of legitimation of new practices that can then be globally translated and disseminated, through devices such as professional publications and international conferences.

The global circulation of management ideas means that organizations that are self-evidently very different might talk about themselves in very similar ways. Over the last 25 years a huge array of new management techniques has been diffused across the organizational world. Many, like total quality management (TQM), business process re-engineering (BPR), downsizing, activity-based costing (ABC), cultural change programmes, and knowledge management, have had significant impacts on organizations. Very often they are referred to as new managerialist programmes of change.

In this context, writers such as Eric Abrahamson (1996; 1997), at Columbia University in New York, have suggested that managers are followers of fashion. The argument is that the management ideas industry – a loose but powerful network of management consultancies, management gurus, software firms, business schools, and the like – develop carefully packaged management initiatives, which are then commodified and sold across the organizational world. These ideas have a shelf life of two or three years before being replaced by the next initiative. These ideas are seen as the latest fashions in management, which are then consumed by managers who can be characterized as 'dedicated followers of fashion'.

The adoption of a fashion is an example of mimetic isomorphism – copying a best practice to appear legitimate and rational in the eyes of important external stakeholders. As with any fashion, there are early adopters who are at the very height of fashion – haute couture – and those that follow when the fashion becomes more commonplace.

Management academics often look down at managers for following fashion. Barbara Czarniawska, at Gothenburg University in Sweden, and Rene ten Bos, at Nijmegen University in The Netherlands, take issue with theorists who treat fashion pejoratively or look down on fashion as trivial (Czarniawska, 2005; ten Bos, 2000). Both point out that following fashion can be a positive and exciting experience for managers and organizations alike. Czarniawska alerts us to the paradoxical nature of fashion in that it is simultaneously about 'invention and imitation, variation and uniformity, preserving the status quo' (2005: 144).

Organizations are constructions, concocted out of whatever knowledge their members deem salient in specific locales. Child and Kieser (1979) found that a sample of German organizations was consistently more centralized than was a comparable sample of British firms, which they put down to local cultural difference that proved to be even more important than the impact of models of best practice retailed by international consulting agencies. These models did not produce convergence by eroding the value basis of a German cultural predisposition for more centralized control. Such findings, of a 'societal effect', are widely established (see Maurice and Sorge, 2002).

The structure of capital markets, interest rate regimes, and accounting conventions all provide specific institutional frameworks within which managerial judgement forms. While the trick of a successful management team is to achieve appropriate consensus, such consensus may well form around inadequate strategies, or subsequently come to be defined as such when a new rational metric is introduced. Think of what happens when the opposition wins an election. The new government will argue that all

Check out the Companion Website www.sagepub.co.uk/managingandorganizations3 for free access to an article by Jesper Strandgaard Pedersen and Frank Dobbin (2006) if you want to see how institutional analysis can help us understand how organization culture forms through processes of not only imitation but also what the authors call hybridization, transmutation, and immunization.

IMAGE 13.1   Inside the Boulangerie de l'Ille Barbe, Lyon, France

the policies of the recent past were errors and foolishness. New policies require new priorities and new measures of their achievement, which the new government will introduce. Something similar often happens when there is a contested takeover of a firm or a merger; sometimes it also happens when, as a result of the appointment of a new CEO, there is a change in the top management team. In with the new, out with the old – politics are a major mechanism of organizational change.

Rationality concerns not just technical efficiency, because it is always culturally framed. Managers seek to make their organizations similar to models that are already institutionalized as positive examples. They do not want to deviate too far from the forms that are already culturally valued. Thus, organizations end up being similar not because it is rationally efficient for them to be so, but because it is institutionally rational. Sticking to legitimate forms bestows legitimacy. Hence, organizations in similar fields of activity tend to be similar in their design, functioning, and structure. These are the basic insights of institutional approaches to organization analysis. If we take institutional theory seriously along with Weber's thoughts on bureaucracy, they give rise to the idea that we do not deal with rationality but rationalities. The example of French bread illustrates this more tangibly.

Why French bread is better – organizationally, in terms of taste, freshness, quality

In their research into 'Artisanal bakery in France: how it lives and why it survives', Bertaux and Bertaux-Wiame (1981) wrote, disparagingly, about industrial bread as 'industrial food wrapped in a shroud of cellophane which is sold in the supermarkets of the western world under the somewhat euphemistic label of "bread"'. Industrial bread accounts for most of the bread sold in the Anglo-Saxon countries of the USA, Canada, Australia, New Zealand, and the UK. The reasons for the supremacy of this industrial bread are evident from Chandler's account (1962). Bread is usually produced from within a division of a giant food conglomerate based around vertical integration from flour milling to bread and related food retailing. Chandler's thesis is that efficient, successful organizations in similar industries, cross-culturally, should adopt the same type of strategy and structure, irrespective of their location (see also Chapter 15).

In France, they do things differently. According to data from the French Ministry of Foreign Affairs (*Le Magazine*, 26 December 1996), the independent shops of artisan bakers comprise 75 per cent of the volume (probably more in value), while industrial bread has an 18 per cent market share, and retailers like Carrefour (bread produced most of the time in big artisanal units) have 7 per cent. There are still 35,000 *boulangeries artisanales*, and there are still 81 regional breads, with the baguette representing 80 per cent of the purchases. Each shop serves an average 1,570 inhabitants per shop.

Visitors to and residents of France know that the typical French bread is a crusty baguette or half-pound loaf. It looks good and it tastes good. However, to describe it does not tell us what French bread is. It is clearer, perhaps, if we determine what it is not. First, it is not a standardized, easily transportable, mass-produced product. It is not a heavily marketed, brand-identified, size-invariant, shrink-wrapped, and sliced product sold identically in virtually similar supermarket chains throughout the country. It provides the quality of 'freshness'. It is perishable, its value being that it is fresh, does perish, and cannot be bought other than on a daily basis. It incorporates everything that industrial bread could never be.

So how is French bread possible? How has the market dominance of conglomerate oligopoly bread been avoided? Why should it be that in France (and a number of Latin countries) most of the bread consumed is made by artisans rather than in factories, and only a small percentage of the market is for industrial bread, whereas in other countries, such as the UK and the USA, it is industrial bread that wins the market?

In France there is about one bakery for every thousand people, a decentralized scattering of small, independent bakeries that manufacture and sell bread, cakes, and croissants from the same premises. The shopkeeper is usually the baker's wife, and the couple is the real economic unit, the man as an artisan and the woman as a shopkeeper. On average, each bakery employs fewer than three workers, each usually less than 20 years old. Most of these young people leave the trade sometime between 20 and 25.

Many of these very small bakeries are in decline in depopulating urban areas and villages. Newer, larger (employing 10–15 people) bakeries making bread for large chains, such as Carrefour, have developed in suburban areas. However, these are still the same kinds of artisan bakeries, making the same kind of artisan bread, using the same methods of production. They are just larger.

In 1966, however, traditional methods of making French bread did seem to be under threat. The largest flour-milling group in France, which had a virtual monopoly on the supply of flour to the Paris market, was rumoured to be preparing a huge bread factory close to the Seine in order to supply industrial bread to the French market. One day, without warning, the flour-milling company changed the terms of trade. Henceforth, only full truckloads would be delivered, a crippling blow to bakers who had neither the market nor the storage capacity to warrant such an amount. However, after a week of panic, when it looked as if what the big millers desired – the eclipse of the small bakers – might occur, the small bakers discovered some independent mills still functioning in the regions outside Paris, which were on the verge of closing down, due to a lack of work, that were delighted to receive the orders of the small bakers.

Baking bread has always been, and remains, hard work, sometimes for relatively small returns. On a typical day, the shop opens from eight in the morning, or seven in working-class districts; it may shut from one till four, and then reopen, closing finally at eight. The wives are the street-level workers, the front-line marketers. Good bakers bake good bread, but it is good wives who sell it, who create a regular customer attracted to a particular bread and a particular shop. In addition, wives are also the accountants, cashiers, and trusted confidantes. Wives who become widows can hire bakery workers to continue the business, but husbands who have become widowers, or whose wives have left them, find it difficult to continue in the business without an unpaid and trustworthy partner. Good wives are good investments in more ways than one. It is to the wives' judgement that the reproduction of this whole enterprise falls.

Given the nature of the trade, only someone who had been apprenticed in it could possibly run the business, and, indeed, most present-day bakers were formerly workers who had become self-employed at an early age. The only people who can take over the trade are the young men who have been apprenticed in it. They are the only ones to know the trade intimately. Becoming a self-employed baker consummates the hard union of an apprenticeship with long hours and low pay. It is this possibility that makes being a lowly worker bearable.

How bakery workers become proprietors and old couples retire from the trade are inextricably linked. The retiring couple lends the necessary money to the bakery worker and his wife. For the incoming couple, its acceptance means eight years of relative hardship and privation as they save to repay the value of the goodwill (based on the value of an average month's sale of bread). For the retiring couple it means placing tremendous trust in the new couple, for the turnover may be a risky business.

To say economic action is **embedded** is to say that it must be understood in its cultural context.

The lesson we learn is simple: these bakers act rationally, as do their industrial counterparts equipped with methods of rational management seeking economies of scale, even though they each act radically differently. Thus, do not expect a singular scientific rationality to be played out in an industry; rather, there is more than one type of rationality. Each type is **embedded** and legitimized in its own logic. No rationality is *necessarily* 'more rational' than another.

IMAGE 13.2   A listing of some of the local breads provided from Le Boulangerie de L'Ille de Barbe, a celebrated boulangerie in Lyon, France

French bread is a testament to what Granovetter (2002 [1985]: 363), among others, has termed the **embeddedness** of economic action.

Granovetter focuses on the central role of networks of social relations in producing trust in economic life. Seen from this perspective, the reproduction of the *boulangerie* is not only a mode of organization but also a complex of cultural and economic practices. It is a classic case of embeddedness. One consequence of an embedded analysis is a perceptible transformation in the object studied. It enables one to appreciate that 'small firms in a market setting may persist … because a dense network of social relations is overlaid on the business relations connecting such firms' (Granovetter, 2002 [1985]: 385). The case of French bread demonstrates the importance of the institutionalization of value and the centrality of culturally framed economic mechanisms in ensuring the survival of a seemingly archaic form into contemporary times.

Embeddedness refers to the realization that economic relations can never be grasped purely in terms of their economic rationality but need to be seen as organically situated within specific features of social settings. For instance, in the garment industry, much of the manufacturing may take place through loosely coupled supply chains of organizations whose members share a neighbourhood and ethnicity. The economic action that ensues is embedded in these social relations.

ORGANIZATIONS EXPLOITING AND EXPLORING

Check out the Companion Website www.sagepub.co.uk/ managingandorganizations3 for free access to two articles on embeddedness. One is by Tina Dacin, Marc J. Ventresca, and Brent D. Beal (1999), while the other is by Simone Ghezzi and Enzo Mingione (2007).

French bread is consistent: it is produced through the exploitation of craft knowledge. This exploitation occurs through tacit knowledge of practice, which in this case is handed down by tradition. In less traditional industries the exploitation of knowledge focuses on repetition, precision, discipline, and control of existing capabilities, usually through explicit management controls. The hallmark is process improvement, deepening and refining existing knowledge about ways of doing things, which is risk averse and measurement oriented; it seeks measurable improvement in performance as a result of systematically identifiable causal factors. Exploitation is aided by strongly legitimated and uncontested organization cultures where people know and perform in highly institutionalized appropriate ways. March contrasts knowledge exploitation with knowledge exploration, which characterizes organizations that are premised on constant innovation, involving serendipity, accident, randomness, and chance.

WHAT'S THE POINT?

The failure trap and the success trap

Two traps confront organizations. One is the failure trap, the other is the success trap:

- In the *failure trap*, organizations explore too much, always trying new ideas; when they fail, they try something else new, which fails again, and so on. A culture of failure develops impatience with new ideas that do not work immediately, as well as an excess of exploration.
- The *success trap* arises from being too good at exploitation. It keeps on repeating actions that mimic what was successful previously, and consequently develops highly specific capabilities that new ideas do not match in action, thus encouraging aversion to exploration.

The moral of this story is that organizations should never be where they do not belong: being in too deep a groove is just as dangerous as

always searching for innovative futures. Organizations need both exploration and exploitation but not too much of either. But how are they to be designed to achieve this?

March suggests that those organizations that become specialists at short-run efficiency in exploitation will fail in the long run because of their inability to explore. Where a rigid organization fails to explore sufficiently, another will replace it by successfully mutating through exploiting what the previous one failed to explore.

March is less confident than the revolutionaries of management such as Peters (1994). From March's perspective, organizations that abandon what they know best in search of the new will be led only to error and failure. Only those few organizations that were able genuinely to exploit novelty – paradoxically by driving the unknown out of exploration rapidly – would survive, although not for too long.

Knowledge exploration requires more relaxed attitudes to controls and institutional norms. Evolving and adaptive organizations need to be able to exploit and explore simultaneously. If they are only good at exploitation, they will tend to become better and better in increasingly obsolescent ways of doing things; they will find themselves outflanked. And if they are only specialists in star trekking, in exploration, they are unlikely to realize the advantages of their discoveries, as they lack the exploitative capacities to be able to do so. Organizations have to learn to balance search and action, variation and selection, and change and stability (March, 2002: 271). Organizations will most often attempt risky exploratory behaviour when they are failing to meet targets rather than when they are achieving them; however, risks are best taken when sufficient slack or surplus resources mean that the organization can afford to risk different ways of doing things. In many respects, however, it is least likely that risks will be taken at this time because the grooves of success are already directing the organization.

MINI CASE

Imagining organizing business

Research the dot-com boom that collapsed in 2001, using the web. Find businesses that flourished briefly.

- To what extent did the development of these companies exemplify a system that sustained 'imaginative madness' at the individual level and to what extent did it allow the larger system to choose among 'alternative insanities'?

March offers a good diagnosis of why efficient forms of exploitation are likely to continue to be reproduced as the dominant organization form. Where innovation does occur, then it is likely to be rewarded only where its exploration rapidly becomes exploited. While particular organizations may come and go, the forms that they exhibit are much less likely to display the radical discontinuities that some of the gurus of management, such as Peters, would suggest. As March says, it is tenacity more than awareness that most revolutions require.

March (2002: 275) states that '[i]maginations of possible organizations are justified by their potential not for predicting the future (which is almost certainly small) but for nurturing the uncritical commitment and persevering madness required for sustained organizational and individual rigidity in a selective environment' (2002: 275). Many organizations must fail so that the few models of difference may survive 'in a system that sustains imaginative madness at the individual organizational level in order to allow a larger system to choose among alternative insanities' (March, 2002: 276). Empirical research thus far suggests that the majority of new organization practices remain incorporated within traditional organizational forms, that organizations may embrace new technologies and practices but do not necessarily change their forms in consequence (Palmer and Dunford, 2001).

WHAT'S THE POINT?

Exploration and exploitation

- If organizations fail to exploit what they know efficiently, they wither and atrophy.
- If organizations fail to explore so that they know how to do different things (double-loop learning) or the same things differently

(single-loop learning), they wither and atrophy.
- Organizing successfully involves managing both exploration and exploitation.
- They must be balanced.
- Too much of either pursued single-mindedly leads to atrophy.

March (2002) thinks that the framework of increasingly rapid organizational change will be more likely to create rapid incremental turnover in organizational forms than radical discontinuities. In an environment demanding greater flexibility and change of organizations, these changes will tend to play out not just in individual organizations but also in terms of the population of organizations. Some organizations will be selected as efficient, adaptive, and legitimate, whereas others will not survive because they do not match what the environment requires. He foresees a future of short-term organizations that are effectively disposable. These organizations will efficiently exploit what they know how to do until some other organizations emerge to do this better. Then they will die. Adaptability will occur at the population level rather than necessarily at the specific organizational level. Overall, efficiency will be served, although specific organizations may not survive. Not every organization can be a survivor.

For March's scenario to be realized, however, there has to be a pool of organizations that are discontinuously exploring learning through active imagining. Of course, without the pioneering of new forms and structures, there would be no new and more efficient mutations of organization forms to succeed those that already exist. Now, if March is right, what this probably means is a double-edged movement: McDonaldization of the efficient but relatively disposable exploiters of knowledge, with the exercise of imagination reserved for those organizations that seek to explore new forms of knowledge. What is foreseen is a type of *Blade Runner* scenario: highly innovative science-based knowledge organizations in gleaming towers for the highly paid, skilled, and educated, on the one hand, and, on the other hand, lots of street-level organizations that are exploitive and relatively impoverished, providing a poor working environment.

SUMMARY AND REVIEW

Max Weber made an important distinction between substantive and formal types of rationality and suggested that there was more than one way of being rational.

What was most important to Weber was the injunction to research how values became institutionalized in organization and management.

Subsequently, many theorists developed Weber's perspective into institutional theory to explain that organizations and the management action that occurs within them are culturally embedded, culturally framed, culturally reproduced, and culturally changed. In other words, whatever passes for rationality is culturally defined (rather than something that can be settled by reference to some external standard, of engineering or economic efficiency).

Bureaucracy was the dominant organizational form for much of the twentieth century. In the post-Second World War era, when systematic empirical study of bureaucracies occurred, it became clear that bureaucracies often functioned in ways that would not be expected from Weber's account. The stress shifted from rule-following as functional to a view of its dysfunctions, especially in terms of knowledge exploration.

EXERCISES

1 Having read this chapter you should be able to say in your own words what each of the following key terms means. Test yourself or ask a colleague to test you.

- Compliance
- Rule tropism
- Trained incapacity
- Mock bureaucracy

- Institutional isomorphism
- Normative isomorphism
- Coercive isomorphism
- Mimetic isomorphism
- Embeddedness
- Organizational exploitation
- Organizational exploration
- Indulgency pattern

2 How do different rules define different rationalities?
3 What are the main competing rationalities at work in the story of French bread?
4 What does embeddedness mean in practice?

ADDITIONAL RESOURCES

1 There is no substitute for reading great scholars in the original, and Weber is a case in point. Many of his books are very difficult to read today, as they are very formal and rather heavy going. However, *The Protestant Ethic and the Spirit of Capitalism* (1976) is probably the most accessible of his books, and has wonderfully prescient conclusions pointing to the world in which we live today.
2 If you find the ideas of institutional theory intriguing, there is a wealth of materials from which to choose. One thorough and useful contribution is that of Greenwood and Hinings (2002), which addresses 'old' and 'new' institutionalism, bringing them together. More recent and definitive is Lawrence and Suddaby's (2006) discussion of 'institutions and institutional work'.
3 A fascinating institutional account is provided by Allmendinger and Hackman (2002) of how the changes from there being an East and West Germany to a unified Germany had significant effects on the organization and survival of symphony orchestras from the two territories.
4 Scott (2002 [1987]) provides a synoptic overview of the wide variations in different types of institutional theory.
5 In terms of institutional theory, one film illustrates the general points particularly well. In Reed's *Down with Love*, the 2003 romantic comedy of sexual manners, starring Renée Zellweger and Ewan McGregor, when the female lead character starts up a magazine in opposition to the one that the male lead character is employed on, it is almost a clone of *KNOW* – the men's magazine – even to the name, which is *NOW* – the only difference being that *NOW* is pitched at a female demographic whereas *KNOW* is aimed at men. The crucial point is that in establishing the magazine, the successful form is copied. In fact, the whole film is a witty and extended scripting of institutional theory in its premises – all the main plot moves, on the part of the two lead actors, are generated by character mimesis.
6 In addition, there is also an excellent film of Kafka's *The Trial* (Jones, 1992), starring Kyle MacLachlan and Anthony Hopkins, which illustrates the dread and oppressiveness of bureaucracy at its worst.

WEB SECTION

1 Our Companion Website is the best first stop for you to find a great deal of extra resources, free PDF versions of leading articles published in Sage journals, exercises video and pod casts, team case studies and general questions, and links to teamwork resources. Go to www.sage pub.co.uk/managingandorganizations3.
2 For state of the art briefings on how to manage organizations effectively, please visit the Henry Stewart Talks series of online audiovisual seminars on Managing Organizations, edited by Stewart Clegg: www.hstalks.com/r/managing-orgs, in particular, Talk #13: *Organization design theory: its evolution within a changing context*, by John Child.
3 A good site that gives you a flavour of Weber on bureaucracy is http://www.maxweberstudies.org.

4 One writer diametrically opposed to Weber was the Austrian economist Ludwig Von Mises. At http://www.mises.org/etexts/mises/bureaucracy.asp, you can find his impassioned argument against bureaucracy. At the home page there are more links to his ideas, http://www.mises.org/, which have had a significant influence on many current economists' ideas.

LOOKING FOR A HIGHER MARK?

Reading and digesting these articles that are available free on the Companion Website www.sagepub.co.uk/managingandorganizations3 can help you gain deeper understanding and, on the basis of that, a better grade:

1 Capitalism emerged from religious ideas, according to Weber. What has happened to the legacy of Max Weber's Puritans in modern times? Look at Stewart's article to find out: Clegg, S. R. (2005) 'Puritans, visionaries and survivors', *Organization Studies*, 26 (4): 527–545.
2 Management control is a constantly evolving phenomenon: if you want to know where it has evolved to in high-intensity knowledge-based organizations, look at Graham Sewell's (2005) 'Nice work? Rethinking managerial control in an era of knowledge work', *Organization*, 12 (5): 685–704.
3 The paper by Jesper Strandgaard Pedersen and Frank Dobbin (2006) 'In search of identity and legitimation: bridging organizational culture and neoinstitutionalism', *American Behavioral Scientist*, 49 (7): 897–907, is available on the Companion Website, and is a very useful guide to some of the ways that fashion operates to shape management and organizations.
4 Embeddedness is an important concept – if only because the absence of it from most economics accounts tells you what is wrong with them! The Companion Website has two good articles that use the embeddedness concept: M. Tina Dacin, Marc J. Ventresca, and Brent D. Beal (1999) 'The embeddedness of organizations: dialogue & directions', *Journal of Management*, 25 (6): 317–356 and Simone Ghezzi and Enzo Mingione (2007) 'Embeddedness, path dependency and social institutions: an economic sociology approach', *Current Sociology*, 55 (1): 11–23.

CASE STUDY

CORRUPTION AT THE DOUALA PORT: A SPECIAL REPORT

What follows is a case study based on the Douala Seaport, the economic gateway into the central African region as a whole and Cameroon in particular. According to the National Port Authority, which controls the port, it is 'Open to the world, open to the future.' The much-heralded infrastructural developments of the last five years are often brandished as evidence that the port is a client-oriented one. These developments, it is argued are: 'Designed to make the port more efficient and operationally-focused ... while offering an exciting and expanding portfolio of investment opportunities to the private sector.'

Alas, the experience of the port's clients is much at odds with the glowing picture painted in glossy official brochures and on the Internet. Clients instead tell harrowing tales of institutionalized corruption, intimidation, and brazen theft, which have made the port a major obstacle to economic growth and private initiative in the country.

In this special report, *The Post* will chronicle the nightmarish stories of some individuals who have had the misfortune of dealing with officials at Cameroon's 'ideal port facility'. Those with similar stories are encouraged to send us their stories for publication.

In the meantime, those who want to contact the National Port Authority directly should write to:
PORT AUTHORITY OF DOUALA
Maritime Affairs Centre, SIMAR Bonanjo Building, PO Box 4020, Douala, Cameroon.

Tel: (237) 420133/427384, Fax: (237) 426797,
E-mail: portdedouala@camnet.cm
Thursday, 06 January 2005 at 12:40 PM in Special Report: Corruption at Douala Port | Permalink TrackBack
TrackBack URL for this entry:
http://tinyurl.com/ynlf5l
Listed below are links to weblogs that reference 'Corruption at the Douala Port: A Special Report'.

Comments

Contacting the National Port Authorities does not bring anything. I appreciate the effort being made here to address this long-term problem of corruption at the Douala port. I have been shipping cars from Germany to some people in Douala for the past 8 years and the complaints I receive about these port authorities are really frustrating. Corruption is not only at the port. It is a nation-wide bug that seems to be normality under Biyaism.

Imagine that one ships an old car from Germany that costs just 400 Euro to Cameroon. The cost of shipping this car is about 500 Euro. One understands because the size and weight of the car determines the cost of shipment. When this car arrives in Cameroon, the owner of the car has to spend about 1.3 million frs to claim this car from the port. This is about 5 times the cost of the car itself. Forgetting about the money 'chopped' by the so called clearing agent, the actual custom duty seems to be unreasonably high, the magnitude of which is never clearly known. How can a poor Cameroonian who buys a car for 250000 frs in Germany spend 1.3 million frs to get the car out of Douala port?

I shipped a Nissan Cherry in September 1999 to Douala with four computers, monitors and printers in the car. I was afraid that most of these things shall be stolen in the ship on its way to Douala. Fortunately, these things all arrived in Douala. My brother traveled to Douala and saw the things all intact, but one custom officer told the clearing agent that custom duties must be paid for each of those computers and printers etc. in the car, even the things I sent to some relatives as 'dash'. My brother then went back to Kumba to see how he could gather some money, so that he can bribe and collect all the items including the car because the custom duty he had to pay for one of the computers was far more than the cost of the four computers. Bribery is a thing that I have never encouraged, but Cameroonians are pushed into very frustrating situations that they regard bribery as the only way out because they can't even avoid it by complaining to the head of the institution. It all starts from the head and not the bottom! So giving the contact of the National Port Authorities means nothing here. Before my brother came to collect the things three days after, he noticed that some of the things had been stolen from the car. One clearing agent told him that the very custom officer came and removed some of the items and certainly kept them for himself. When he went to the custom officer, he directed him to settle his clearing business with another officer who finally took some of the items from the car for himself plus about 200000 frs before the business about clearance could start. Finally, my brother had to sell the car at the port for the buyer to arrange the clearance. He however got some of the computers and monitors out.

Some of us are just not interested in shipping cars to Cameroon even for our own use because of this very customs issue and the corruption at that Douala port. The custom duties are irrational and the path of clearance is extreme bribery and corruption. Just as the 'sans galon' police men collect from 100 frs to even 'winning cover beer' from taxi drivers and ensure that the commissioner in the office has his own share of the money, so too is the corruption at the port. If those custom officers and the other bandits running around the port do not heavily oil the mouth of their bosses, they shall either be transferred to an area where there is no

possibility to get 'chocco' or they are assigned unpleasant functions. So even the biggest boss knows all what is happening there. It is the system. Don't think that it shall be efficient to start fighting the corruption from the 'small-small' custom officers by reporting to the boss. The complaints will end in the dust bin of the boss because he does not want to read that kind of complaint against their 'business'. It is Cameroon! The twice most corrupt country in our planet.

If we have to efficiently combat corruption in any sector in our beloved country, then we must start from the chief executive. You know what I mean. These are the guys in a long time good-for-nothing government that has not only plundered the economy, but has done everything to ensure that foreign investors, even Cameroonians abroad, fear investing in Cameroon. However, we should explain our experiences. At least the public shall read if the head of the National Port Authority finds it frightening.

(Posted by: A. Che Mofor | Thursday, 06 January 2005 at 04:47 PM)

It is rather regretful to express to any Cameroonian abroad who wish to ship anything back home to rethink because Douala port is worse than a hell on earth. I have brought in goods to Germany, US and even Israel with no problem but was forced to abandon two of the three cars I brought in to Cameroon in 2000. I used 2.8 million to take out a car (now LT 0544N) which I was offered as a birthday gift by a friend. My experience there is not one I would like any other human being to go through. I will never for whatever reason bring in anything into Cameroon.

Even in the airport is the same scenario. Why must we have to pay a 10,000 frs fee in the small dirty Dla or Yde airports where no other airport on earth, even great airports such as JFK, Charles de Gaulle, Franfort Tel Aviv etc. ask for fees.

Sad that some of us who are opportuned to share the wealth of the West can not bring it back home due to the brokage in Dla. Dla port is the main reason of making Cameroon the most underdeveloped country on earth. Douala town itself is just an evident of depreciation.

(Posted by: Dr. Martin Salah | Friday, 07 January 2005 at 08:30 PM)

The previous comments make the case as to the nature and level of corruption at the air/sea ports in Douala so I will switch my attention to another direction of the bureaucratic malfunction in Cameroon. My view is that the collection of 10,000 frs at the airport in Douala may be a good idea if the funds are used to maintain the infrastructure but this has not been the case, so where do the funds go? The leaky roofs, dirty floors, and stinking restrooms (with no toilet tissue) at the airport in Douala, are prima facie evidence that the collection of 10,000 frs is just another form of extortion. [Are] the government delegate for Douala Urban Council and/or the senior divisional officer for Wouri aware of these problems? My guess is yes. Why are they administrators? What constitutes the wellbeing of a locality and who guarantees that wellbeing? When customs officers, on a daily basis, bring home extorted goods from merchants what do their spouses or family members say? (Darling, a good steal today; more grease to your elbows.) The families of these thieves have a moral obligation to let them know that what they are doing is wrong and should stop.

(Posted by: neba funiba | Saturday, 08 January 2005 at 05:47 PM)

Dear Brothers,

I realised some changes in the customs sector recently when I shipped 3 cars last year October and in January 2006 I removed them at the Douala port. Actually, I didn't spend that much to remove them, maybe due to the recent anti-corruption drive in the country. I hope with time there can be more drastic action against those perpetrators of any corruptive ideology at the port.

I didn't [have] to pay for any other charges than to pay just for the vehicles directly at the customs office. If the government can enforce strict laws governing this domain, I think things will change in Cameroon for the better. Since then I have been encouraging my friends to import and/or export and invest businesses back home. Only with this notion can there be a rapid economic boom and other socioeconomic benefits in Cameroon.

Fritzane Kiki
Hong Kong

(Posted by: Fritzane Kiki, Hong Kong | Wednesday, 07 June 2006 at 10:29 AM)

I personally thank the post newspaper in trying to air out the corrupt nature in which Douala port is operating, I don't really know which policy is Cameroon government operating, as regards the custom duty of imported goods. When you compare other countries in Africa, Cameroon has one of the highest customs duties. In fact it is a chain of corruption in that port that is hindering Cameroonians out of the country to invest in Cameroon, foreign nationals and companies have been sent away with our corrupt habit at the port in Douala. It takes about four to five working days to get out an old car of ten years old from Douala ports sometimes even longer, while it takes two days to get out your goods or car from a port in [Togo]. It is alarming what is happening at Douala ports, it is always a nightmare to clear your goods at the ports. As an importer of used spare parts in Cameroon, I find it easier doing business in countries like Togo and Ivory Coast that I have shipped many cars and containers there than Cameroon which is my home country. Douala ports scare a lot of Cameroonians out of the country to do business in Cameroon, high custom duty, lot of bureaucracy and constructive corruption of the ports is bringing our economy down. Please let the government do some thing about these malpractices at the Douala ports.

Joki Manga
Munich Germany

(Posted by: Joki Manga | Tuesday, 08 August 2006 at 05:16 PM)

I have been very sick about this corruption problem in Cameroon. I almost had a stroke last year. I talked to one community college in Maryland USA. When they were upgrading their computer. I was given 29 completed computers. I intended to send them to a new Government Technician School in Alanbukum Mankon Bamenda. After hauling the computers to my Home, I tried to contact friends who could help contribute for the shipment. I was informed that it will cost me millions to clear these computers at the custom. I became frustrated and finally gave some of the computers to a salvation unit.

I have an idea about fighting this corruption. If some of us who travel home could get pictures of this corrupted system or video tape their transactions. This information could be published and it could help.

(Posted by: anye | Friday, 09 February 2007 at 12:48 PM)

Question

1 You have been appointed to a UN Development Agency charged with remedying the corruption in the Port of Douala. How would you analyse the problem and what would you recommend as a solution?

Case sourced (and edited) from http://www.post-newsline.com/2005/01/strongcorruptio.html, accessed 26 February 2007.

CHAPTER FOURTEEN
MANAGING ORGANIZATIONAL DESIGN

Design, Environment, Fit

LEARNING OBJECTIVES

This chapter is designed to enable you to:

- Define organizations in terms of structural contingency theory
- Discuss size, technology, and environment as the key contingencies associated with organization structures
- Link organizational contingencies to organizational design
- Relate issues of organization structure to questions of organizational strategy

BEFORE YOU GET STARTED . . .

Organization design matters just as much as any other kind of design ... ugly organization design produces bad managing. (Stewart Clegg)

INTRODUCTION

An organizational design is the plan of an organization's rationally designed structure and mode of operation. The formal structure of an organization is its framework of roles and procedures. Since 'design' is a noun and a verb, organizational design can also be the process of creating such a plan. An organizational design creates a rational model of formal organization; what actually happens when the rational model is implemented is often called the informal organization, to the extent that what actually occurs differs from what the rational design intended. Thus, the study of organizational design is perhaps the most rationalistic part of organization theory as it is often the study of things that do not happen – but which should, according to the rational model. The dominant theory of organizational design is known as contingency theory.

Contingency theory

In management and organization theory a contingency is something that managers cannot avoid. Contingencies arise from routines rather than from emergencies, as facts of organizational life, and have to be acknowledged and dealt with. Different organizations face different contingencies. How they handle these contingencies is reflected in their organizational design. The contingencies of environment, technology, and size have been seen as the most important issues to be managed. It is argued that these are universal issues with which all organizations, with similar contingencies, anywhere in the world, will have to deal with.

- *Environment*: The more certain and predictable the environments in which organizations operate, the more probable it is that they will have bureaucratic structures.

- *Technology*: As organizations adopt more *routinized technologies* – technologies with repetition and routines associated with them – they tend to become more bureaucratic.

- *Size*: As organizations become bigger, they become more bureaucratic, in the sense of being characterized by higher scores on scales that measure the degree of formalization, standardization, and centralization.

Contingency theory in organization and management theory suggests that there are several key contingencies shaping organizations. The basic idea of contingency approaches is to stress that all organizations have to deal with a predictable number of contingencies and that these contingencies will shape the organization's design as it adapts to them.

Contingency theory argues that organizations, no matter where in the world they are, will have a similar design if they are similar in size and technology. It is the organizational design, they argue, rather than the culture in which it is embedded, that is important. Thus what gets globalized, as these organizations spread multinationally, are organizational designs. So, it will not matter if you start your career in India, China, or the USA: the organizations that you work for and the way that you do the job you do will be essentially the same; thus, on the basis of correlations between contingencies and organization structural variables, established through large-scale, survey-based studies, contemporary organization theorists argue that there is a tendency towards consistency in organizational designs (Etzioni, 1961). Those organizations whose structures are not well aligned with the contingencies that they currently deal with have to undertake structural adjustment to regain fit with those contingencies.

Recent discussion of the management of organizations has focused on the fit between an organization's structure and its contingencies – the inescapable things that it has to deal with – which can change over time. As these become misaligned, because contingencies change, a process of structural readjustment is required. The insight emerged out of studies that focus on the relation between mechanisms such as technology and size and organization structure. Prior to the development of contingency perspectives, most theorists had either written up case studies of particular organizations or focused on some specific substantive aspect of organizations, such as 'who benefits?'

The contingencies literature regards organizations as imperfect designs that can be improved when we know what contingencies they have to deal with. Modern organization and management theory poses a central question: how to design a structure specifically suited to the contingencies with which an organization has to deal? Earlier writers such as Taylor (see also pp. 483–487) presumed one best way to organize, irrespective of contingencies, rather than seeing that how to organize depends on the central factors that management faces. The organization is conceived as a system open to inputs from the environment and that sends outputs to the environment as a result of internal transformation processes.

The variations that occur in organization structure are seen to be a result of environmental contingencies by Burns and Stalker (1961): they identify mechanistic and organic structures. A **mechanistic organization** takes a machine as its basic model. It is designed to be formal and specialized, with precise role prescriptions for each task and responsibility, often expressed in detailed manuals of procedures or collections of job descriptions. There are many formal rules, procedures, and instructions. The division of labour is extensive and the specialized differentiation of functional tasks means that jobs are narrowly defined. Work coordination is based on the direct supervision of low-level employees by upper-level employees, front-line supervisors as they are usually termed – or, in older parlance, the 'foreman' or principal worker – literally the first man. The system of control is hierarchical, with restricted opportunities for mostly vertical communication expressed as imperative commands – telling people what to do – within narrow spans of expertise and control, all embedded in a rigidly departmentalized structure. A traditional factory in a traditional industry such as garment making would be a case in point.

A mechanistic organization is most frequently to be found in stable environments, especially those with a cost minimization strategy; also, mechanistic models are found more frequently in large organizations that employ a large number of people.

There, the designers design a garment that is produced by workers under supervision working on specialized parts of the overall garment: some on zips, others on sleeves, and so on. Mechanistic organizations deal with members who are treated as if they were simple by putting them to work in tightly prescribed jobs working on designs in whose composition they have no part.

Mechanistic organizations handle employee's aspirations for self-actualization badly; people have to slot into the structures rather than the structures being designed to handle individual variance. Consequently, employee commitment and satisfaction are often quite low even though the insistence on loyalty and obedience to superiors is quite high. Not surprisingly, under these conditions, there is a considerable potential for conflict. Repressing conflict with an insistence on strict adherence to the rules diminishes opportunities for alternative ideas and innovation to be expressed. As an organizational design, it minimizes participation and limits responsibility to obeying orders. It can work efficiently in a stable environment where change happens slowly.

An **organic organization** is more likely to be found in firms that are smaller, that operate in highly uncertain environments, and that are strongly oriented to discovery and learning – such as high-tech R&D firms or bio-pharmaceuticals.

While mechanistic organizations often have a hierarchy of command and control, **organic organizations** are simpler in structural terms, in which individuals are allowed space in which to develop their creativity. Think of a business such as Google where the stress is on constant innovation. Most contemporary organizations are far better designed on more organic lines because they have to deal with continuous and turbulent changes in markets, customer preferences, technologies, regulations, etc. These conditions require a great deal more imagination and creativity than the mechanistic design can deliver. Organizations appropriate to this kind of environment will be more like a living organism capable of adapting to its environment. When employee commitment is central to quality and productivity and market and technological conditions demand the decentralization of decision-making processes, organic, decentralized, flat organizational forms are far more appropriate.

TABLE 14.1 Burns and Stalker's structures

	Design	
Dimension	*Mechanistic*	*Organic*
Standardization	High	Low
Formalization	High	Low
Centralization	Concentrated	Diffuse
Discretion	Small	Extensive
Authority levels	Many	Few
Administrative component	Large	Small
Specialization	Depth	Breadth
Communication	Minimal	Extensive

Source: Pennings (2002: 6)

Table 14.1 contrasts the structural features of the two types of structure. Each is characterized by the same structural variables but they are formed in very different patterns. It is the patterning of the structure on these key variables that distinguishes the two types of structure; that they vary so sharply is an effect of the different environmental contingencies that each deals with. Stable environments allow for machine-like organizations while unstable ones do not; hence they are characterized by organic structures.

Structural contingency theory

One approach above all others reflected the emphasis on contingencies: the work of the Aston school (Pugh and Hickson, 1976). They read everything relevant that had been produced by writers on organizations, looking for convergence and divergence in the literature (Hickson, 2002 [1966]; Pugh et al., 1971). At the same time that they were involved in the literature review, they were also conducting interviews with practising managers. From these key informants they learned what seemed to be the most salient aspects of the manager's role. Between the literature review and the focal discussions with the managers, 'the concepts slowly crystallized' (Pugh and Hickson, 1976) to indicate the appropriate research procedures. These consisted of a great many questions about aspects of an organization's structure, design, and processes, which could be recorded in the form of a numerical score on a Likert scale. Thus, they were able to build a shorthand picture of how the organization did what it did through the responses to the scales they designed.

The Aston researchers used factor analysis to search statistically for patterns of variations in the data collected. These common factors could then be used to refine scales to align them more closely with those factors that were statistically robust. The scales were seen to represent real features of the empirical world as they are defined in terms of conceptual constructs. In the case of the Aston project, the scales coalesced around a contingency perspective.

The researchers' discussions and reflections finally focused on five variables drawn from Weber's initial list of 15 (which was discussed in Chapter 12):

1 *Specialization*: The extent to which the organization had highly specialized job descriptions and designs. It refers to the skill formation that occurs when labour is divided and defined into smaller specific tasks rather than being seen as a general task that anyone might do.
2 *Standardization*: The extent to which the organization has many standard manuals of procedures involving the prescription of constant and invariant ways of doing things.
3 *Formalization*: The extent to which the organization's total range of actions and procedures are covered by formal policies and agreements. Formalization refers to the phenomenon whereby roles, rights, and responsibilities attaching to positions in an organizational design are defined formally. A high degree of formalization implies that there are many formal rules and regulations surrounding these positions; in contrast, a low

degree of formalization describes a situation in which individuals in the positions have a high degree of relative autonomy in being able to define how they should do what they do, and, indeed, what they choose to do.

4 *Centralization*: The extent to which the organization ensures that decision-making is referred to the apex of the organization or distributed to lower levels. Centralization is the process whereby the roles and positions that exist in an organizational design are associated with each other through a series of relations traced to a common central position or set of positions of command and control. Some organizations are much more centralized than others; those with only a single centre of command and control that all matters of decision have to flow through are the most centralized. Typically, bureaucracies are thought of as being highly centralized.

5 *Configuration*: The shape of the authority structured as a system of role relationships, patterning structured formal relations between conceptually designated elements in an organizational design, such as centralization, formalization, and routinization. Centralization means that many decisions have to be referred to the centre; formalization means that most task elements are formally defined; while routinization means the extensive development of routines for action so that they become regular and predictable in their parameters and consequences.

Earlier researchers such as Gouldner emphasized what the phenomena of everyday organizational life meant, such as the changing meaning of the organization rulebook. The Aston researchers were less interested in meaning and more concerned with collecting considerable amounts of statistical data on a large number of organizations. They could correlate such data with the hypothetical dimensions and come up with some well-grounded empirical answers to the question they had set for themselves: what were the determinants of organization structure? The answer was that structure is determined by situational contingency.

 ## WHAT'S THE POINT?

The relation between size and bureaucracy is global

The Aston researchers regarded bureaucracy as unavoidable. In any country in the world where there are large organizations, irrespective of national culture or industry, environment or technology, these organizations would be more bureaucratic than smaller organizations in the same country.

For the Aston researchers, the crucial contingency is that 'size matters'. They had collected extensive data on the dimensions of organization structures for 44 organizations from the West Midlands of England. After analysis, they concluded that the variable that best explained why these organization dimensions had a certain shape or pattern of association between them was the size of the organization. Basically, the larger the organization, the more bureaucratic it seemed. And this is true all over the world they suggested, after further comparative research.

The findings of these 'structural contingency' theorists nicely unsettle some common misconceptions, the best known of which is Parkinson's Law (Parkinson, 1957). Parkinson was a civil servant who, on the basis of his experience and observations, argued that work expands proportionately with the time available for its completion. Following from this assertion, he argued that organizations therefore increase the number of administrators that they require disproportionately with their increases in size. Structural contingency theory demonstrates that this argument is not correct. For instance, Blau (2002 [1970]) measured differentiation in terms of the number of organization levels in the hierarchy, the number of departments, and the number of job titles. He found that increasing size is associated with increasing differentiation but that the rate of differentiation decreased with increasing size. Administrative overheads are lower in larger organizations, and the span of control for supervisors is greater. Administrative overheads are inversely related to size, whereas the span of control is positively related to size. Thus, larger organizations are able to achieve economies of scale *if* they can distribute delegation of authority efficiently and effectively in the organization. If they can do so, they can handle the costs of differentiation – an increased necessity for control and coordination of the differentiated activities – without piling a weighty administrative overhead on top of the hierarchy to control the complex differentiation. Thus, the larger the organization, *given that it is able effectively to delegate authority and line control of workflow*, the less necessity there is for centralized control and administrative overheads. This concept helps to explain the lack of association between size and concentration of authority/line control of workflow that the Aston researchers found. Size increases overhead costs but also increases the scope for economies of scale, which can be deepened further by effective delegation of authority and control.

Organizational design

Debate on organizational design crystallized when Henry Mintzberg, a prolific and very popular writer, published a seminal paper in 1981. He argued that five natural configurations fit the different tasks organizations have to accomplish. Like an ill-cut piece of clothing, some structures do not fit the purpose organizations want to achieve. This misfit leads to trouble and inefficiencies. Consistency and coherence between organizational structure and tasks, says Mintzberg, is the key to success. Rather like an organic structure that evolves in its environment, some organization structures should simply fit, naturally. They do not need to be chopped to size.

Decentralization is the opposite of centralization. Organizations often seek to decentralize when they feel that their systems and processes are becoming too slow because too much decision-making, even on small and inconsequential matters, is being referred to the centre. Often, organizations with low levels of trust are highly centralized because a decentralized decision structure requires that you trust those who are delegated to decide.

Structuring devices such as span of control, forms of decentralization and hierarchy, degrees of job enlargement, and so on, must be chosen in a

Decentralization is the opposite of centralization. Organizations often seek to decentralize when they feel that their systems and processes are becoming too slow because too much decision-making, even on small and inconsequential matters, is being referred to the centre. Often, organizations with low levels of trust are highly centralized because a decentralized decision structure requires that you trust those who are delegated to decide.

way that is consistent with an organization's specific situation (its size, strategy, competitors, production technology, and so on). Imagine a large manufacturing company that has experience and know-how in mass production buying a small supplier known for its innovation potential. Should management of the large company put its bureaucratic structure (suitable for mass production) into the smaller innovative daughter company? What effects would this have on its innovation potential?

Mintzberg (1983b) argues that, for every situation and task an organization is facing, there is one of five specific structures that fits best:

1 *Simple structure*: This configuration, the most basic structure, consists of top management, a few middle managers, and a task force. Power is centralized; management knows and supervises the whole company. According to Mintzberg, this structure is typical for entrepreneurial companies that are small and innovative but that work on relatively simple products. Most organizations start off as simple structures but struggle when they grow. Classic entrepreneurial owner-managed firms will start out as relatively small organizations in a simple yet dynamic environment, understanding of which is claimed by the founding figure. Of course, such organizations are highly vulnerable; to the extent that they are the creations of a single person who places themselves under high stress conditions of management, they are only a heartbeat away from potential disaster, if they have not evolved into professionally managed organizations.

2 *Machine bureaucracy*: This structure puts the emphasis on standardization and employs low skilled but highly specialized staff. It is a structure for mass production that focuses on simple products in a fairly stable environment. Taylor's scientific management ideas derived from such structures. In contrast to the simple structure, this design requires management of administration; the organization needs detailed planning and standardization, which leads to a bureaucratic system. The more bureaucratic the system is, the easier it can grow; the organization continues to do the same things, but instead of making 100,000 hamburgers a day, it produces 1,000,000 a day. McDonald's is Mintzberg's example for such a machine bureaucracy – very efficient in what it does but not very flexible and not very interesting to work for (see also pp. 472–473).

3 *Professional bureaucracies*: In contrast to machine bureaucracies, professional bureaucracies rely on standardized skills, not processes. Universities, large consulting firms, or hospitals are examples of this structure; they work like bureaucracies, but they need highly trained staff to deliver their services. Thus, employees in professional bureaucracies have more autonomy than workers in machine bureaucracies. Professional bureaucracies have relatively flat hierarchies, where professionals accredited through external institutions (having earned certificates from universities, and so on) do the central work. These people have considerable autonomy because of their specialized knowledge and the high demand for the services they can supply. Expertise is at a

premium and highly valued in such organizations. Professional employees enjoy a high degree of responsible autonomy. However, parallel to the professional staff, a large number of support staff back up the professionals. Their jobs are simpler, more routinized, and normally less well paid. (Think of a hospital with well-paid doctors, nurses who are not as well paid, and poorly paid auxiliaries, such as porters and cleaners, laundry staff, and ward orderlies.) These structures fit best into a complex but fairly stable environment. They are good at executing state-of-the-art tasks but not as adept when it comes down to changing them. Hospitals, for instance, develop great expertise in operating, but when they are challenged by alternative herbal medicines or natural therapies, they do not know how to integrate them, and their normal professional strategy is one of exclusion.

4 *Divisionalized form*: In contrast to the professional bureaucracy, this structure does not rely on highly trained professional individuals; instead, it uses expert units called *divisions*. Each division runs its own business by producing specialized products for a particular market. Hence, these divisions are relatively autonomous and enjoy a certain degree of freedom. But how does management make sure that the divisions are on track? Headquarters (HQ) normally measures their performance (the standardization of outputs, as Mintzberg puts it). Each division's performance is measured and compared with that of the other divisions. This arrangement keeps the division managers busy and HQ in charge. Put simply, top management imposes goals on divisions, which forces divisions to plan their activities properly, ultimately leading to the bureaucratization of the single divisions. As we saw previously in this chapter, machine bureaucracies are appropriate when standards are imposed and clear objectives need to be achieved. However, because the divisional form was chosen so that organizations can respond to a flexible environment, the dynamic that leads them to bureaucratization has a negative effect on the organization. Also, it has important consequences regarding ethical behaviour; because the goals the division must achieve are mostly formulated in terms of monetary targets for sales, rate of return, and so on, the social consequences (because they are hard to measure) tend to be ignored.

5 *Adhocracy*: None of the previous four structures really fits when put into a highly turbulent environment where constant innovation is the key to success. The *adhocracy*, a structure of interacting project teams, is the solution. An adhocracy may be defined as a type of organizational design that is not consciously structured but just develops spontaneously, in an ad hoc manner – hence, adhocracy. Creative think tanks, such as advertising agencies or design and architectural practices, need lots of experts who create products that cannot be standardized. With every job they do, they have to deliver the standards to be able to measure them. In those project teams that make up the adhocracy, power is distributed; everybody is a decision-maker, and strategies are not implemented top down but emerge while the teams explore new terrain (see also pp. 280–287). An operating adhocracy works directly for clients,

Check out the Companion Website www.sagepub.co.uk/ managingandorganizations3 for free access to an article by Eric J. Walton (2005) if you want to learn how and why we know that bureaucratic control is enduring.

as in the advertising agency example. An administrative adhocracy serves itself; think of an organization such as the Department of Homeland Security cobbled together by the Bush administration after 9/11 as a means of enhancing national security.

All these configurations have strengths and weaknesses. Each type represents a structure that best fits a certain environment. The consistency and coherence between structure and task is, above all, the most important thing.

Technology and organizational design

Once upon a time industrial technology nearly always involved smokestacks, but this is no longer the case. A scientific definition of technology does not just look at the motive force behind industry, whether coal, water, or wind, for example. A fuller definition of technology includes not just the machinery but also the organization relations associated with it in terms of people and processes, the knowledge and skills necessary to make the technologies work, as well as the infrastructure that they rely on. For instance, just-in-time technologies assume relatively cheap fuel and free-flowing roads. Broader still, technology may include a body of knowledge applied to practice where it is the usefulness of the technology that is important rather than other intrinsic properties. Woodward saw the relationship between technology and organizations to be a contingent relation mediated by organization structure.

Using a sophisticated conception of technology Joan Woodward, an English researcher, studied about 80 industrial firms in the southeast of England and focused on technology to make sense of the data that she collected (Woodward, 1965). She argued that the more routinized the technology, the more the firm had a structured set of organizational authority relations. Technologies were classified by Woodward into a number of types: *small batch and unit production* (where the products were largely tailored designs for different customers with small runs), *large batch and mass production* (where the production runs were much larger and the customers usually many fewer), and *process production* (where the system was a continuous flow on a 24/7 basis, with the major requirement being that the system stay to specifications and standards). These distinctions were made on the basis of the technical complexity of the operations, defined in terms of the degree of controllability of the production process and the extent to which results were predictable. Windmills, waterfrills, and smokestacks would differ organizationally.

Woodward found out, to her surprise, that firms with similar production systems were organized in a similar manner and that the degree of technical complexity was related to (a) the number of levels in the organization, (b) the span of control of front-line supervisors (how many people they supervised), and (c) the ratio of managers and administrative staff to the total workforce. Organizations using the least and the most complex technologies – unit and process production, respectively – showed a number

IMAGE 14.1 Alternative technology

of similarities. These organizations had a low level of specialization compared with the managers in the mass production firms.

The reason that specialists were less evident in unit and process firms differed in each case:

- Small-batch and unit production firms employed fewer specialists because these organizations required more generalist skills for more variable production runs; also, these firms tended to be smaller than mass production organizations, so staff had to be technically more competent.

IMAGE 14.2   Large-batch printing production

▓ In process production, staff specialists had a very high status and were sometimes difficult to distinguish from management, who also had to have a high level of technical expertise. Both process and unit and small-batch production had relatively low levels of bureaucracy compared with mass production.

Woodward related these differences in organization structure and technology to the central problems that each category of organization dealt with:

▓ For unit and small-batch production, it was product development – meeting specific customer requirements for single or small batches of a specialist product.

▓ For the process organizations, the central issue was marketing – they had to ensure that the continually flowing output from the production process met sufficient immediate demand. Thus, the type of innovation that was central depended on the type of organization.

▓ A formally bureaucratic structure, such as was common in a mass production technology-centred firm, seemed inimical to innovation; instead, the central issue was efficiency in administering standardized production.

Time span of discretion is a concept for thinking about the relation of power to do things, the magnitude of the effects these things will have, and the location of responsibility for the things done. It also functions as a rationale for different levels of remuneration.

Time span of discretion is a concept for thinking about the relation of power to do things, the magnitude of the effects these things will have, and the location of responsibility for the things done. It also functions as a rationale for different levels of remuneration.

Managers who do things that have long-term consequences, which affect major decision areas such as investment strategy, for which they are ultimately responsible, have an extensive **time span of discretion**.

Those with an extensive time span of discretion, said Elliot Jacques (1956), a contemporary of Woodward, should be remunerated more for the greater responsibility. Woodward's point was that the type of organization shaped the time span: in flow and mass production the time span of discretion would be much greater than in batch and unit production, for instance. It is not only the central organizational problem that is significant but also the time span of discretion exercised in making decisions:

- In batch and unit production, many decisions are made, but they typically have short-term consequences because they relate to an immediate design or production issue that will not necessarily have implications for the next, probably different, job. Decisions tend to be made on the line with little need for authorization from on high.

- In mass production, however, there are fewer decisions to be made because the process is so much more routinized and predictable, but those decisions have much longer implications because production runs are long-lasting and repeating. Because decisions about production have major resource and related implications, they tend to be referred up the management line to the level of the functional specialist responsible for the arena within which the decision issue falls.

- In process production, although fewer policy decisions are made, they have both longer term and more interdependent implications. In a continuous process, any change to any parameter may affect all others, so decision-making has to be pooled because of the sequential and reciprocal nature of the issues involved. Hence, a strongly bureaucratic structure would be inappropriate because it would place functional specialists in separate silos of knowledge rather than integrating and pooling them. In Woodward's research, technology is a crucial contingency because it enables her to construct a detailed narrative about the nature of organizational structuring and decision-making.

Check out the Companion Website www.sagepub.co.uk/ managingandorganizations3 for free access to an article by Lisl Klein (2006) if you want to learn more about the legacy of Joan Woodward.

Though Joan Woodward died in 1971, her ideas remain influential and are still discussed today, as you will see if you check out the next download.

Technology, rather than size, may be the crucial contingency variable (Aldrich, 2002 [1971]; Mindlin and Aldrich, 2002 [1975]). The American sociologist Howard Aldrich reached this conclusion after reanalysing the Aston data using a different logic of analysis. Whereas the Aston researchers relied primarily on factor analysis (a statistical technique that establishes high degrees of intercorrelational coherence and variance in a data set), Aldrich used causal path analysis to model the relations between variables. Causal path analysis makes theoretical assumptions that it seeks to justify, theoretically, about the likely explanation for structural relations. These assumptions can then be tested through various models. The Aston approach differed in that those researchers simply looked for the correlations that existed and then imagined how they might have come into being as a result of cross-sectional causal relations. For instance, if they had counted kitchen sinks, and the number of sinks had been shown to correlate highly with structure, they would have imagined a story that explained the relation. Aldrich would not do this unless he had some prior reason in theory for thinking that kitchen sinks were important.

External dependence occurs where top management depends on parent organizations for key resources.

Aldrich gives **external dependence** and technology high priority. Technology is what the organization's top management chooses to use as its method for doing what it does, similarly to Woodward's definition. More highly structured firms – those that seem more bureaucratic – need to employ more people, Aldrich suggests. Size is an effect rather than a cause, a dependent rather than an independent variable, and the major cause of the degree of structure, according to Aldrich's reanalysis, is the technology in use in the organization. From these flow the specifications, job descriptions, and so on, which compose the structural measures. The number of people employed does not precede the technologies used. The causal path that would assume so seems nonsensical. Technologies and people evolve together, and the structure adapts accordingly.

In brief, the development of an organization proceeds from its initial founding and capitalization in response to perceived market opportunities, through its design based on copying and modifying other organizations' structures, and finally to the employment of a workforce to staff the nearly completed organization. This obviously oversimplified view of the development of an organization leads to specific predictions about the causal ordering of observed organizational variables. Technology is causally prior to the size of the workforce, and organization structure is at least initially usually prior to size (Aldrich, 2002 [1971]: 355).

Essentially, Aldrich has a more plausible story to tell than the Aston researchers, who, as pioneers, made up the story as they went along, testing their *cross-sectional data* – data collected at the same time and place – in terms of the degree of its intercorrelation. Whereas the Aston narrative was driven by the correlations – the story was fitted to the variance observed in the data – Aldrich sought to refine the narrative structure and then model these assumptions in the causal path analysis. Also critical of the Aston and Woodward interpretations of the link between technology and structure were the US researchers, Blau and Schoenherr (1971), who also found that size determined technology, which in turn determined structure.

Later research suggested that technology does not determine organizational behaviour; in fact, it is the organizational relations of power and knowledge that are significant. This finding emerged from a study by Barley (1986) into the adoption of new scanning technology in hospitals. How the technology was used as 'an occasion for structuring' and the consequences of this depended on the local politics of knowledge in the hospital, as radiologists and technicians negotiated them. Orlikowski and Yates (1994) found that both the technologies in use and the organization structure change interactively as users engage in dialogue with designers and modify technologies in practice; again the changes in technology and structure are a result of local politics and negotiations over managerial adaptation that slowly lead to institutionalization.

QUESTION TIME

Interview five people at random from different jobs in any organization that you are familiar with – ask them a simple question: if you made a mistake concerning some significant decision in your work, how long would it be before it became evident?
  Enter the data below.

Job title	Nature of significant decision	Time span of discretion
Is the longest time span of discretion that of the most senior job?		

Strategic choice and organizational design

Control was a key element in early theoretical accounts of business organizations. Etzioni (1961) identified commitment and power as the interlocking basis of organization control (see also pp. 487–488). It was assumed that, as managers were hired to control the organization in the interest of its shareholders (a group that would often include themselves, of course, because their interests were aligned with those of shareholders through stock options), managerial control of the organization was a fundamental phenomenon. Managers were committed to control. Through controlling costs, overheads can be reduced, profits increased, and shareholder value enhanced. Managers make decisions – that is a key part of their job. The more senior the manager, the more their decisions will have implications for the time span of discretion.

Strategic choices, such as the size of the organization, its environment, and technology, may determine organization structures, and the top management team – or dominant coalition as they are sometimes called – exercise choice in the decisions fixing these things. The kinds of products of the organization will determine the markets entered, the technologies chosen, and the structural shape and size of the organization. Thus, for Child (2002 [1972]), the action of strategic choice should be thought of as preceding the structural factors that structural contingency theorists see as determining organizational structure.
The argument is very simple:

The most important decisions managers make are those that structure the future strategy of the organization. John Child (2002 [1972]) called these strategic choices.

1   Managers in positions of control make strategic choices about how they will configure the organizations they are responsible for. They will choose work plans, resources, and equipment. This is the nature of their work – it is what their plans and orders are meaningfully oriented towards.

2   The technologies and structures that ensue will be the result of these managers making decisions that link available resources with necessary tasks.

3   The top management team that constitutes the dominant coalition will constantly be evaluating the organization's competitive position.

4   This team will do so in terms of the values that it shares – the organization's dominant culture or ideology – from which it derives goal preferences for the organization.

5   For example, will the organization be innovative with respect to new technology, copy innovations developed elsewhere, or be a cost-cutting exercise to minimize the costs associated with innovation?

What the managers do on behalf of the organization is its strategic action, the imposition and subsequent negotiation of their sensemaking. It is this strategic choice that influences structural features. Hence, management decisions shape organizational design more powerfully than purely environmental influences because, to an extent, they choose the conditions under which they operate.

Structural adjustment to regain fit, or SARFIT

There is a lack of dynamism to the contingency models that the Aston researchers developed because of the historical specificity of the assumptions that framed them. One writer who appreciated that this was the case, while still remaining wedded to the basic contingency framework, was Lex Donaldson, who argued that, periodically, because any organizational design would slip out of kilter with the contingencies with which it had to deal, organizations had to undergo a structural change to regain fit with their contingencies – especially those in their environment (Donaldson, 2002 [1987]). He calls this approach the *SARFIT* model.

SARFIT means Structural Adjustment to Regain Fit.

All organizations make structural adjustments periodically, says Donaldson. The changes that *SARFIT* has to respond to are performance induced. There are eight key corporate factors that might signal the need for change.

There are four factors that might lead to adaptive – or functional – change. These are:

1   Changes induced by the business cycle of boom and bust.

2   Competition, increasing or diminishing market share.

3   Levels of indebtedness, either fuelling or dragging growth down.

4   Divisional risks, as some divisions fail to meet the performance targets set, and others exceed them.

Four other factors – diversification, divisionalization, divestment, and directors – are more likely to lead to dysfunction as a result of a lack of adaptive change:

5   Diversification can smooth out market, cyclical, and seasonal variations in business, making change less necessary.
6   Similarly, divisionalization can spread risks across a portfolio of products.
7   Divestment means that product lines can be eliminated, together with the structures that support them, if they consistently fail.
8   Finally, directors, especially non-executive ones, can be a break on what they, with their wider business horizons, are able to perceive as risk, and their counsel can diminish performance failures.

If good performance is to be maintained by a business organization, rather like a fine sports car it needs to be constantly fine tuned to adjust to the environmental factors it has to deal with. When the organization is out of alignment with its environment, then, rather like a sports car that is not perfectly well tuned, performance will suffer. Thus, an organization that has concentrated on a specific product range for its domestic market will typically have a structure organized around functions such as finance, sales, and production. As the firm diversifies into an increased number of products aimed at different markets, such a structure will no longer be well tuned to the changing circumstances. As Pugh and Hickson (2007: 18) suggest, 'Too much will be loaded on to the management apex, and responsibilities and priorities will become confused. There will be misfit between tasks and structure. Performance will suffer.' Under such circumstances firms will likely attempt a refit – or, as Donaldson calls it, a 'structural adjustment to regain fit (*SARFIT*)'.

As a theoretical approach Donaldson champions *SARFIT* to extend both the contingency determinism of the earlier Aston school as well as Child's strategic choice approach. *SARFIT* blends insights from the strategy literature with themes from the literature on organization structure and its determination, and develops the sociological theory of structural **functionalism**. For instance, when a firm develops a multi-product structure, in the interests of maintaining performance, it will shift to a divisional structure defined in terms of specific divisions for specific products. Each division would likely have its own internal functional structure. Should the firm expand multinationally then it might have to divide into several divisions organized on a geographical basis: for example, Europe, Asia, North America, and so on.

Donaldson argues that it is far more probable that the organizational design will shift as variables that moderate its performance change, such as its size or the tasks that it is designed to accomplish, than that the organization's top managers will choose to keep the same design and allow performance to suffer. These contingencies, such as size and task design, are related, although he sees size as the most fundamental. For instance, a firm may see its performance suffering because it has ceased to be innovative. In response to

Functionalism is an approach to analysis that assumes that phenomena exist to fulfil some function or other. Functionalism is often criticized for being conservative because, *ipso facto*, it assumes that what exists serves some purpose, therefore must be useful, and need not be replaced or revised.

this diagnosis the organization may hire more creative and design staff; consequently, the size of the organization increases and, to justify their existence, the staff come up with new products, processes, and related ideas.

Two sets of assumptions frame these views:

1 The first is that the organization will be operating in openly competitive markets; where this is not the case then the organization's top managers may expend a great deal of energy or resources in trying to fix the regulations, competitive structure, and illiberality of the business environment in which they operate. Under these circumstances, elements of strategic choice can affect organizational configuration as the result of actions taken by the dominant coalition. The elite group may choose to adapt to changing contingencies by protecting the present structure of the organization – for instance, by withdrawing from an arena in which there is a particular contingency challenge to deal with, such as a specific market or technology, or they may seek to gain political support in regulating that market with quotas, tariffs, or other protective measures that benefit their interests – at least as these are defined in the short term. The coalition will do this because of the role that their values, perceptions, and political influences play in creating a cultural comfort zone. Donaldson argues that changing contingencies to fit an extant structure, while feasible, is more difficult than changing structure so that it is better aligned with the changing contingencies; this will especially be the case in a competitive business environment where a firm's position is always going to be judged in relation to its competitors. Organizations and their dominant coalitions, he suggests, are more likely to readjust their structure than their contingencies to regain fit between it and the contingencies that they are obliged – by competitive pressures – to handle.

2 The second assumption is that the organization will actually hire more employees to increase its capabilities. It might, for instance, decide to outsource design to a creative agency, make the existing design team redundant in view of its lack of innovative performance, and thus shrink in employee size. The dynamics at play in such a situation would be quite different because of the solution to the perceived problem, with different consequences – shrinkage in size rather than increase and, following Donaldson's logic, a less bureaucratic structure. The first solution to the innovation problem increases size and makes the task design more uncertain. The second solution decreases size, makes the task design more uncertain, and will increase organizational interdependence as the firm comes to rely on the external agency.

Donaldson (2002 [1987]) draws on the well-known strategy/structure literature, sparked by the studies of Chandler (1962). The essential insight was that:

> as companies move from being undiversified to being diversified in their product range so they move from the functional to the product divisional form. Similarly, the shift from single to various geographic areas leads to a move from functional structure to geographic divisions, *ceteris paribus*

(Egelhoff, 1982) … There is a cycle of change in strategy leading to mismatch and low performance, then structural adjustment to a new match. There are relatively few cases where adjustment comes about by the alteration of the contingency to fit the structure. (Donaldson, 2002 [1987]: 383, 389)

How does *SARFIT* occur? Here are some likely steps:

1   As product diversity expands, the HQ of a functionally structured organization finds that its decision-making becomes increasingly complex because it has to manage greater product diversity with a corresponding requirement to know about more products, materials, technologies, markets, competition, and so on.
2   The HQ that does not delegate its decision-making to the divisions will soon become overwhelmed by more information than it is able to process.
3   In product divisional form organizations, the divisions are given relative autonomy by the corporate office. Control by corporate HQ is accomplished through comparisons of profitability across divisions. Low-performing divisions are axed or restructured.
4   Delegated decisions should be better decisions because they are made closer to market knowledge and organizationally specific know-how. They should be quicker and better quality because they are more specialized and expert based.
5   Decentralizing gives the top management team at corporate HQ more scope for strategic rather than for operational decision-making. It allows the division's top managers to have more autonomy in decision-making on matters such as design, manufacture, and marketing.
6   The HQ no longer has to assimilate so much information and has only to coordinate the decisions made at divisional level.
7   The costs of this increased efficiency are some measure of duplication of certain administrative functions in each division, which adds costs, thus: the functional form is best for more homogeneous product offerings because its unified control structure is cheaper; the functional form matches low product diversification; the product divisional form matches high product diversification.

Donaldson's reanalysis of a number of well-known longitudinal studies of structural changes tests whether the straightforward contingency determinism model, the strategic choice model, or the *SARFIT* model best explains the data. He finds that changes in contingency, such as moving to new markets or products, initially lower performance. Lower performance leads to a structural adjustment to regain fit and a new cycle of matched contingencies. The process is one of trial and error. Periodically, the organization will still require additional changes to stay in match as contingencies continue to change. Structures overwhelmingly adjust to contingencies rather than contingencies to structures. For instance, after a company diversifies, it needs to adjust its structure. Diversification disequilibrates the organization's fit with its contingencies, so it has to readjust structurally to regain fit. The top management dominant coalition will make choices to regain fit, but they are quite limited in the choices that they can make. Misfit from diversification leads to poor performance. Poor performance is tackled by making some structural adjustments, and in this way fit is regained. Thus, strategy leads to structure. The relation between the variables in the theory is dynamic because a change in either size or task design – conceptualized in terms of task uncertainty and interdependence – can change the resource equation. Greater or lesser size constraints have an impact on available capital, as do changes in task uncertainty and interdependence. As capital availability – the key resource of capitalist enterprises – shifts in supply for distribution in salaries, wages, and dividends, then the market will make judgements of fitness about the organization, affecting its valuation and through this mechanism the actions of its top management.

Of course, this assumes that the organization is a publicly listed corporation, although in other situations, such as a private equity fund, where the crucial variable is the length of time that debt has to be carried, there are other mechanisms working to encourage fit and fitness, as the markets define it. Thus, in terms of Child's strategic choice theory, Donaldson does not oppose managerial choice as such but points out that it is rather limited in nature. Managers have choice, but they choose to do what the contingencies would indicate.

McKinley (2008: 956) suggests, that managers are not like:

Check out the Companion Website www.sagepub.co.uk/ managingandorganizations3 for free access to an article by Lex Donaldson (2002 [1987]) if you want to learn more about how *SARFIT* works and how it fits into a long stream of scientific work.

> homing pigeons, equipped with an automatic guidance system that channels their restructuring efforts toward the condition of fit and prevents excessive change of structure. If managers did have such an automatic guidance system, the failure rates of organizations would probably be much lower than they actually are.

Managers may do *SARFIT* but to do so they have to make sense of a great deal of data and information, and sometimes they will get it wrong.

NEW ORGANIZATIONAL FORMS

The limits of the bureaucratic model

The heyday of contingency theory was the 1960s through the early 1980s. Since that time, other approaches have captured the imagination of many of the best research journals, but it is fair to say that contingency theory, although it may not be at the cutting edge of current research, underlies much normal understanding of contemporary management and organizations as machines within which we work.

In the early 1960s, when the Aston researchers first started to think about organizations, they had no reference point other than what existed at that time. And what existed were, by and large, variations on bureaucracy, so the measures that they devised to capture empirical data on the structure of organizations were largely normalized on these assumptions. Thus, their questions were all oriented towards capturing data that demonstrated whether there was more or less bureaucracy, as measured by the constructs of standardization, formalization, and so on in any specific organizations in a given sample.

But the world has changed. Some 50 years later, in the early twenty-first century, we have not only many new forms of organization but also technologies, environments, and strategies to sustain them that were unimaginable all those years ago. Of course, one can still go out and use the Aston measures to collect data on organizations, and, because of the questions one asks, one will still pick up a distribution of data around these bureaucratic constructs. However, is their saliency still the same? If the world has changed sufficiently, the assumptions on which these questions were constructed will no longer be the central issues but will have become more marginal. We may, therefore, require new questions.

Contingencies are conceptualized and measured through their regular, predictable effects. Thus, for instance, organization size is a matter of the number of people employed by an organization: as this number increases, the organization tends to become bureaucratic. If an organization shrinks in size, then, hypothetically, it should become less bureaucratic. But what happens if an organization lays off workers, develops outsourcing of previously internal functions, and focuses on its core competencies? It has certainly become smaller in terms of the number of employees, but is it a real change in form? If you were a maintenance employee on Friday, and on Monday you come in to work as an outsourced subcontractor employed by a firm other than the one that employed you on Friday and you are doing the same sort of job, has anything really changed that much? The organization still has an operations and maintenance (O&M) function, but instead of being remunerated through the payroll, it is now paid for through a contract with another firm, which pays the labour. Why should the change in contractual form through which a function is delivered change the overall nature of the organization? Certainly, the change means that there is one less area to manage in terms of day-to-day administration, but the effects of moving to an O&M outsourcing contract do not mean an end to responsibilities; instead, they are simply shifted to other areas of the organization and different mechanisms of control.

Size is a construct that made great sense in bureaucracies where virtually everything was internalized; however, as organizations become virtual in form or shift from employment to other forms of contracts, the simple assumption that their size equals the number of labour contracts they have written seems misguided. And if the fundamental mechanisms are not self-evident, the theories built on their basis will not be as secure as they seem.

One place where the basis of structural contingency theory becomes especially problematic is in considering new forms of organization. Given that these are designed around new and virtual contingencies, will they be consistent in their behaviour with those organizations designed around the bureau and written files of rules? Will the same categories apply? If we have ways of asking questions that already assume that organizations have certain properties, we will collect data based on these assumptions, irrespective of how relevant these are to the new organizational forms.

Defining a new organizational form

Various authors define an organizational form as the blueprint for a population of organizations, such as banks or automobile firms (Aldrich and Ruef, 2006; Hannan and Freeman, 1989). An organizational population is an aggregation of organizations that are all different instantiations of a typical form – thus they will exhibit some common features, whether it is a marketing strategy or an identity (see Aldrich and Ruef (2006) for an overview, and Hsu and Hannan (2005) for a developed analysis of organizational form as an identity). New populations of organizations, oriented towards different formal properties, develop in such a way that they are not merely contingency-led variations around the structural form of bureaucracy. What marks a new organizational form is either, as Hannan and Freeman (1989) define it, a goal, an authority structure, a core technology, and a marketing strategy, or, as Hsu and Hannan (2005) define it, its identity base, seen in terms of cultural frames. Thus, **new organizational forms** exhibit a structural–strategic difference, a cultural difference, or perhaps both.

Often the assumption is made that one form – bureaucracy – is being replaced with another, new organizational form, but, as Dunford and his colleagues (2007) suggest, it is more likely that we will, empirically, find hybrids, with some elements still retaining bureaucratic control features and others showing signs of new organizational forms.

M-form

One of the earliest of alternative or new organizational forms that emerged was the multi-divisional or **M-form** organization. The classical bureaucracy was a triangle with a broad base: it was superseded in the minds of many management writers by the multi-divisional form or M-form which emerged in the 1930s to become the dominant US form by the 1950s (Fligstein, 2002) and became dominant in Western Europe during the 1960s and 1970s. In an M-form organization there are many separate profit centres. Each profit centre has to meet centrally fixed performance criteria or else be axed. The M-form consisted of a multiplicity of smaller triangles connected by umbilical cords of financial control to the parental core company. The structure of 3M, with a division for every product, became the classic case of such an organization. Each division is a profit centre that can be assessed strategically; it can be encouraged to grow or it can be terminated if it is in decline, as markets change and evolve.

According to Alfred Chandler, the M-form facilitates growth through diversification across products, industries, and markets and includes the notion of delegation of power and authority to divisional managers. The growth of firms has seen an evolution from national to multinational corporations (MNCs). These MNCs adopt an internal structuring that includes operational and strategic integration of business functions that minimize costs and economize via internal coordination and control, and as such achieve governance economies. The M-form represents a combination

New organizational forms are organizational designs for structure seeking to be non-bureaucratic – indeed are often anti-bureaucratic – stressing flat structures rather than tall hierarchies, multiskilled capabilities rather than a rigid division of labour, informality rather than a high degree of formality.

Check out the Companion Website www.sagepub.co.uk/ managingandorganizations3 for free access to an article by Dan Kärreman and Mats Alvesson (2004) about a knowledge-intensive organization that seemed to have some characteristics of both a bureaucracy and a new organizational form, and find out how issues of power and individual identity are managed in such firms.

Check out the Companion Website www.sagepub.co.uk/ managingandorganizations3 for free access to an article by Dunford and his colleagues (2007) if you want to learn more about how bureaucratic control and new organizational forms may be mutually compatible.

The **M-form** organization is a hub-and-spokes model with a hub of central services serving spokes with profit centres at their end, which were based usually on either product or regional specialization.

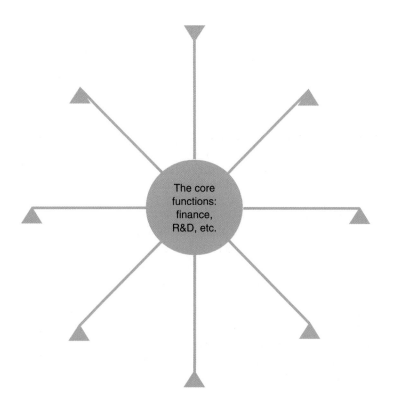

FIGURE 14.1
The multi-divisional form (MDF) structure. The many small triangles symbolize profit centres nurtured and controlled by the parental core company in the centre)

of a divisional structure with hierarchical control and functional flexibility (see Figure 14.1).

Chandler (1962) documented the transformation of the US corporate form from the holding company to the multi-divisional form (MDF) based on the 1932 assumption of separation of ownership and management control defined by Berle and Means in *The Modern Corporation and Private Property*. Chandler (1990) argued that the MDF is more efficient due to the cost advantages that 'scale and scope' provide. Chandler defined scale as plant size and scope as the use of many of the same raw materials to produce a variety of product. Among the top 100 firms, measured in terms of asset size, bureaucracy started to give way to the MDF in the USA from the 1920s, but especially after the Second World War, particularly in 1948–1949, according to research by Fligstein (2002).

The M-form of organizing was invented by General Motors to encompass central control and ownership; vertical integration of the production; formal internal coordination through vertical and horizontal linkages between decentralized divisions, and corporate head office function and specialized staff concentrated in departments and subunits.

After the lead of firms such as General Motors and DuPont it was largely firms that had strong and distinct product lines as their central strategy that made the switch early, setting up a divisional structure based on the product lines. Where the CEO of the firm had sales, marketing, or finance backgrounds the firm was also more likely to have switched to an MDF structure early. Over time, more and more CEOs came from a finance background and such CEOs were most likely to opt for an MDF organization.

Typically, it was established firms that were more likely to shift rather than newer firms. However, there is an interesting mimetic effect: as other firms in an industry change to the divisional form then any remaining firm is more likely to do so (Fligstein, 1985: 387). Overall, Fligstein concluded:

> those in control of large firms acted to change their organizational structures under three conditions: when they were pursuing a multiproduct strategy; when their competitors shifted structures and when they had a background in the organization such that their interests reflected those of the sales or finance departments. (Fligstein, 1985: 338)

The data seem to suggest that the ways of making sense of the business situation that were shared by sales and finance – perhaps being more focused on the numbers – oriented these people to be more favourably disposed to the M-form model. When others in the same industry saw that successful firms were making the switch, then they switched as well, in imitation.

Switching to an overall M-form structure did not mean the end of bureaucracy, merely its re-specification. Bureaucracy was located in the M-form in either the product- or region-centred divisions, which related as satellites to core centralized functions, such as finance. The devolved geographical or product-based divisions had to perform according to criteria fixed centrally – for instance, a certain return on investment (ROI). Thus, the rules were more oriented to *outcomes* rather than to processes, unlike the classic bureaucracy.

From the 1990s onward, the M-form came under increasing pressure (Pettigrew et al., 2002a) and, especially in the USA, has been changing towards a multi-subsidiary rather than multi-divisional form because of tax and antitrust regimes in the USA and their effects on the ownership and control of corporate capital (Zey, 2008b). The legal relationship between the parent corporation and its subsidiaries is one of capital interdependency, which is of far more importance than the notional legal independence.

The M-form enables internationalization and the emergence of MNCs as complex networks with centralized governance at the HQ coordinating activities through subsidiary units. The price mechanism is used to control subunit performance because they have to meet agreed performance targets or be sanctioned, with the ultimate sanction being their demise; interunit transactions are coordinated by transfer-pricing mechanisms, where value is determined by in-house accountancy rules and decisions. There are at least seven pressures simplifying MDF structures:

1 Heightened international competition through globalization, forcing firms to be both local and global.
2 Efficiency drives to reduce costs, concentrating manufacturing regionally and simplifying organization structures.
3 Improving learning and knowledge transfer in international firms, by using internal networks and alliances.
4 Technological changes producing shorter product life cycles, requiring more flexibly structured organizations.

5 Advances in IT, enabling less hierarchical controls and more lateral knowledge flows and networks.

6 Freed-up state-run bureaucracies, following deregulation of state control of the economy, offering new opportunities for flexibility, innovation, and radical change.

7 The emergence of a knowledge-based economy as the norm, requiring more autonomous and skilled employees.

Pettigrew et al. (2002b) suggest that what the organization is designed to be affects how well it can do what it does. Pettigrew (2003; Fenton and Pettigrew, 2000; Pettigrew et al., 2002b) investigated these changes during the 1990s in the top European and Japanese companies. Japanese organizations were less radical in adopting new forms but, nonetheless, even though they are often seen as the last redoubt of bureaucracies, they are changing in significant ways (Clegg and Kono, 2002; Kono and Clegg, 2001). A delayering of middle management hierarchies, accompanied by increased decentralization, both operational and strategic, is creating more incentive-based and leaner management, often organized in cross-functional and cross-boundary project teams. Organizations are becoming much more interactive, both vertically and horizontally, as a result of IT investments and the development of associated new knowledge and learning capabilities (see also pp. 355–359).

These new capabilities are not only intraorganizational but also interorganizational, involving suppliers and customers through supply chains and enhanced human resource management (HRM) functions. Such activities aim to foster horizontal relationships both internally and with external stakeholders, through conferences, seminars, interactions with business schools, and sometimes with rival firms, to create a 'boundaryless organization' (Nohria and Ghoshal, 1997). The hierarchy of large-scale vertical organization is being replaced with more horizontal relationships, focused more narrowly on core competencies. What is not core can be outsourced to some other organization that can provide the service cheaper, faster, and more innovatively – because it is its core business – or it can be delivered through an alliance (see also pp. 583–584).

Relatively simple mass production technologies gave rise to bureaucratic patterns of managing. Where technologies changed to become more flexible, more flexible styles of managing become possible. Fulk and DeSanctis (2002: 279–280) suggest that it is technologies that make these new styles more flexible: technologies that offer a dramatic increase in the speed of communication; decrease its cost; increase its bandwidth; have vastly expanded connectivity; enhance integration of communication with computing technologies; and open up communal, collaborative capabilities for communication help create alternatives to traditional bureaucratic organizations, making more decentralized and flexible approaches to organizational design imaginable (Daft and Lewin, 1993).

Indeed, as our world rapidly changes and is increasingly characterized and typified by uncertainty, ambiguity, and complexity, organizations have sought to become more adaptive or responsive. Today, organizations are finding it is nigh on impossible to predict and plan for the future in any way that is truly certain. As a result organizations must be much more inclined to improvisation, creativity in problem solving, and fluid in form and structure.

In an interesting article in the online version of *The Economist* (27 February 2007) Jeffrey Joerres, chief executive of Manpower Inc., argues that organizations should be thought of more as orchestras than as armies. Rather, organizations must be highly skilled and talented at the level of the individual, but also well coordinated and creative in order to make the beautiful and creative music that orchestras are capable of making. As with orchestras, organizing centres around a project and the team comes together for its performance and disbands until the next project comes along. What organizations do today is more like making music than making war (although we should point out that armies today act more like new organizational forms than as highly bureaucratized units – although the same forms of authority still remain in the army).

From *The Economist* article we get the impression that the military order, structure, command, and control that the term army elicits is an idea of the past. If we look at the extensive use of civilian contractors and supply chains on the side of the Coalition troops in the Second Iraq War, it is clear that warfare is just as much influenced by new organizational forms as is any other high-technology activity. Similarly, on the side of the 'insurgency' against the occupying armies, there is clear use of loosely coupled and networked organization, which appears to be almost virtual, and certainly creative in the use of improvised explosive devices. As such, critical organizational performances will require, in addition to individual talent and orchestrated coordination, **collaboration** and an emphasis on new organizational modes of operating (such as alliances, networks, and so on). So let us take a closer look at new forms of organizing, for all indications are that they will be a dominant feature of your future working life.

Collaboration is typically designed either to advance a shared vision or to resolve a conflict. It usually results in an exchange of information or a joint agreement or commitment to action between two or more parties, such as organizations.

Matrix organizations

Now you might think that matrix organizations were scary psychedelic organizations based on the famous movies – but you'd be wrong! **Matrix organizations** are a mixed organizational form in which traditional vertical hierarchy is overlaid by a horizontal structure consisting of projects, products, and business subsidiaries or geographical areas. The key characteristic of a matrix organization is a multiple command structure in which employees experience dual or multiple lines of authority, responsibility, and accountability. Jay R. Galbraith (1971) represented the matrix organization as a mixed form along the continuum of a range of organizational design alternatives. Matrix structures are best for temporary projects with designated cost, time, and performance standards. Classical matrix design is specified by the choice among the authority structure, integrating mechanisms such as teams, and by the formal information system (see Table 14.2). Wherever projects are a key component in the way that products or services are delivered then a matrix organizational design can be considered. It makes, in theory, for a more flexible organization.

Matrix organizations can be thought of as coordinative devices that blend the programme orientation of project staff with the speciality orientation of functional personnel in a synergistic relationship, and first emerged in the US aerospace programme in the 1960s.

TABLE 14.2   Advantages and disadvantages of matrix organizations

Advantages of a matrix organization structure	Disadvantages of a matrix organization structure
1 Increased frequency of communication in the organization	1 Creates ambiguity about resources and personnel assignments
2 An increase in the amount of information the organization can handle	2 Encourages organizational conflict between functional and project managers
3 Flexibility in the use of human and capital resources	3 Produces conflict among individuals who must work together but have very different backgrounds
4 Increased motivation, job satisfaction, commitment, and personal development as well as heightened ease in achieving technical excellence within the organization	4 Leads to insecurity for functional managers and erosion of their autonomy, making it more costly in terms of overhead and staff, more meetings, delayed decisions, and information processing

Matrix organization has been adopted by multinational firms with varying degrees of success, especially in large project-based organizations, such as civil engineering firms (see Chan (2008), from whom this account is derived).

Shamrock organizations

A shamrock organization is an organizational structure in which a core of essential executives and workers are supported by outside contractors and part-time help. We will often find this structure in design-oriented companies such as Nike. The employees in the shamrock do the designing, the manufacture of its products is contracted out.

The shamrock leaf shape is a symbolic representation of an organization with three distinct parts, as defined by Charles Hardy (1990). It is illustrated in Figure 14.2.

The first part, or leaf, represents the core staff of the organization. They are likely to be highly trained professionals who form the senior management. The second leaf consists of the contractual fringe and may include individuals who once worked for the organization but now supply services to it. These could be design professionals, for instance. These individuals operate within broad guidelines set down by the organization but have a high degree of flexibility and discretionary powers. The third leaf describes the consultancy services provided by IT specialist firms, for instance. These firms are sufficiently close to the organization to feel a degree of commitment to it, ensuring they maintain a high standard of work. The shamrock is one of many new organizational forms that have been developed in recent years.

Call centres

Not included explicitly in Handy's shamrock, call centres are an increasingly ubiquitous accoutrement of contemporary organizations. Call centres are

FIGURE 14.2
The shamrock organization

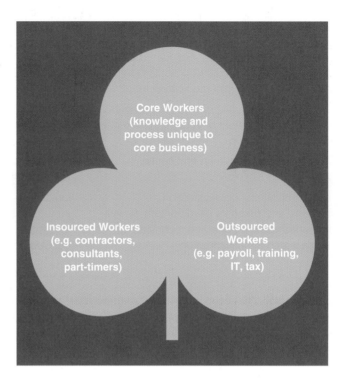

often the first point of contact that most customers have with virtual organizations. Call centres handle large volumes of telephone calls from and to internal and external customers. They emerged in the service sector in the late 1980s as an efficient way to conduct sales, marketing, and customer service functions. Usually they are unremarkable office buildings with many cubicles, within each of which is a computer monitor and telephony head-set. Usually the cubicles are about a metre deep, about 1.2 metres wide, and separated by a partition wall about 1.2 metres high. There might be many hundreds of these cubicles. With the development of VoIP (Voice over Internet Protocol), call centres can be located anywhere, in any country, and still dial at local rates. Many are located in countries such as India where labour costs are far cheaper than in the more developed economies and where the skill basis is well developed, especially language capabilities in English. Call centres are organized in shifts of teamworkers, with employees answering or making calls. Team leaders monitor targets and manage performance.

The technology behind call centres is twofold: first the menu of FAQs and scripted responses, and, second, automated call distribution (ACD), the technological backbone of call centres. For the former, some call centres will be dedicated – dealing with just one firm or an organization's incoming calls while others will handle multiple accounts. Most scripts are prewritten and appear on the screen in front of the agent handling the call. The only real problems that can arise are when the agent is 'off script' – when the question does not conform to the problems for which they have answers. The ADC routes calls to the different operators on the next available basis, thus minimizing 'hold times' and maximizing the number of calls that any agent can handle, as well as ordering the queue of calls. Once the calls have been queued then each operator can expect to handle relatively the same number of calls per shift. Thus, each operator can be subject to surveillance of his or her performance. Winiecki (2006: 25) notes that data on more than 20 statistical records are recorded by the ADC on the performance of each operative, such as how long each call takes, how long the operative pauses between calls, how much time is spent on other related work, such as preparing database records documenting the call, time logged on and off, break times and duration, and so on. It is, indeed, an Electronic Information Panopticon as Winiecki elaborates at length. Moreover, it is one that is capable of generating quite profound emotional dissonance, as Ball (2008) recognizes. The most common cause of emotional dissonance will be frustrated and abusive customers, the necessity of sticking to restrictive scripts, and the increased quantification of the performance management systems through the Panopticon. The call centre is another example of the electronic panopticon that was discussed in Chapter 12.

Inbound call centres handle customer queries; employees have to be good listeners, good at keeping customers to questions that they are scripted to deal with, and empathetic when dealing with customers. Length of time spent on each call is the major performance indicator. Efficiency is demonstrated by dealing with a greater volume of calls. Employees are also assessed according to the service quality levels they achieve. Outbound call centres try to sell goods and services to randomly chosen telephone customers and employees are assessed on the number of sales they make (Ball, 2008).

Call centres combine elements of three different technology-based organizational designs (Frenkel et al., 1998). First, they are white-collar bureaucracies, with extensive technical rules built into the design of the work process: the scripts, the electronic measures of performance, and close supervision. Second, they are mass production flow-based labour processes. What flows through them on a 24/7 basis are telephone calls rather than oil or petrochemicals. Third, each service encounter is a unique opportunity either to sell or service a customer satisfactorily. While each call will be different, the centres have high degrees of standardization in the available responses and sales pitches, although, because of the unpredictability of customer responses, operatives can display creativity and innovation in the way that they handle specific customers. Where more complex customer relationships exist, call centres can be innovative forms of work organization, suggest Wickham and Collins (2004).

Increasingly, call centres not only handle basic sales and customer services, but also are locales for work to be outsourced to third-party providers, such as specialist HRM firms. These may be entirely outsourced, or they could be co-sourced, where both internal staff and external resources process calls, or in-sourced where a business sets up its own call processes in an overseas location, such as India. Outsourced firms rely on the premise that they are specialists in services that are only peripheral to the core business of their contract partners, and thus they are able to achieve efficiencies of scale, scope, and quality in providing services, which are stipulated in the contract.

WHAT DO YOU MEAN?

What do knowledge workers do?

Three Accenture-affiliated consultants (Harris et al., 2001) have come up with the following list of successful capabilities for e-management, suggesting that there are seven key capabilities for e-managers to master in the new e-management systems. Some of these are quite generic and few seem to be technologically driven. Indeed the only aspect that seems really specific to the digital technology is the question of speed. Their research is less about call centres and more concerned with the types of people typically referred to as 'knowledge workers' – symbolic analysts who work with the new digital technologies in more creative and less scripted ways than the call centre operatives.

Harris et al. stress that e-managers will:

1 Be speedy in decision-making.
2 Be open to partnering, to identify and evaluate potential partnerships, build key relationships, and successfully negotiate deals.

3 Keep up with evolving technologies – reading, meeting with experts, and working with the technology first hand.
4 Develop a network of trusted technical experts, who can offer guidance and actively unlearn old technologies that may be barriers to accepting the new.
5 Be focused, while balancing the demands of multiple and diverse stakeholders – members of their own team, colleagues from other units in the company, external partners, customers, and shareholders.
6 Make sense of the future by constantly exploring the external environment and taking an experimental approach.
7 Be talent magnets – hiring and retaining good people through communicating a compelling vision and making sure that vision is understood by everyone in the company and, when it is not, being able to manage the emotions that will be expressed in conflicts and confrontations, and creating a learning environment.

Networks

Check out the Companion Website www.sagepub.co.uk/ managingandorganizations3 for free access to an article by Premilla D'Cruz and Ernesto Noronha (2006) that takes the reader inside Indian call centres.

Networks can be understood as a long-term relationship between organizations that share resources to achieve common goals through negotiated actions.

In *The Rise of the Network Society*, Castells (2000) claimed that forms of **networks** had begun to transform organizations.

Castells identified Cisco Systems as the world's leading and most typical network enterprise. Cisco Systems had provided about 80 per cent of the world's Internet hardware in 1999, by far the world's largest supplier of such equipment. Its market capitalization grew by over 2000 per cent in only five years, reaching a value of $220 billion in 1999. The following year it more than doubled to $550 billion, making Cisco the most valuable company in the world at that time. Cisco follows a 'networked business model' demonstrating that networks are a means of production at the same time as being the end product of the business. Cisco uses the Internet and web-based technology to maintain a global network of customers, employees, and suppliers. It is reasonable to assume that Accenture might have had Cisco as one of the companies in mind when producing its list of capabilities.

There is little from the Accenture list that suggests any great specificity about e-management in network-based firms whose business model sits astride the Internet. Indeed, further research suggests that for these new firms in the e-economy, many aspects of dissagregation of traditional organizational designs are more social than technological. Barbara Adkins and her colleagues have written that in the:

> knowledge economy … [t]he product is no longer tangible, the process is no longer straightforward, and the outcomes – 'success' or 'failure' – are no longer exclusively defined by the bottom line. The traditional firm that works independently no longer stands up in comparison with the organizational and professional networks that cross-cut and break down traditional organizational and disciplinary boundaries. (Adkins et al., 2007: 92)

Networking has become a core business competence for firms such as Cisco in a largely technical marketing and supply chain set of relations. However, there is one puzzling aspect of the knowledge economy: if digital disaggregation makes location anywhere possible, how come so many firms cluster close to each other in locations such as Silicon Valley – where Cisco Systems has stayed resolutely headquartered? The answer resides in that concept of 'embeddedness' that we encountered in Chapter 13. Certain places become magnets for particular fields of activity, like hi-tech in Silicon Valley, movie making in Hollywood or Mumbai, or creative design in Brisbane's Fortitude Valley. Let us look at the last one in a little more detail.

Fortitude Valley, or the Valley, as locals refer to it, has long been a slightly seedy area of the city, close to the old wharves on the Brisbane River, separated from the city of Brisbane by a ridge and the undeveloped site of a cathedral, in the past a place associated with prostitution and illegal gambling. But, like many other edgy areas of major cities, the Valley has become cool. Cheap leases, warehouses ripe for conversion, street-level access rather than anonymous high-rises, and a traditional café and restaurant scene have seen many new design businesses locate there. A specific ecology of business has developed in the Valley, where social and business networks overlay each other in a shared sense of identity and community, as well as dense networks of referrals and problem-solving. Much of the work that individual firms do is digitally based but often involves collaborative project-based work with other creative people in the same neighbourhood. So while much of the work is Internet mediated, it occurs between people involved in projects that are very much socially mediated. It is not so much the technology that creates new possibilities for organizational design that is disaggregated and project based, but a network of ties premised on social proximity, in both a spatial and cultural sense. Projects and project teams are the nodes that connect in a series of value-chain relationships that bind members and projects together. Connected by these nodes are team members, clients, suppliers, users, and other key stakeholders, who comprise a socioprofessional community. Digital capabilities maintain and make possible the network but they are not its essence: that resides in the deep embeddedness of the creative teams in a specific place and set of related spaces that constitute the Valley as these creative people experience and use it as a resource, or what the French sociologist Bourdieu (1998) called symbolic capital.

The ultimate contradiction of the Internet revolution is that although firms could be located anywhere in cyberspace, they still seem to cluster

Networking involves collaboration between different people or agencies such as organizations. Often, independent organizations join together with others to form a network in which the other organizations have complementary skills so that together they can do something that neither alone would be able to manage.

together in specific quarters of global cities such as New York, London, and Sydney (Castells, 2001). An obvious reason is that on the average in the Organization for Economic Cooperation and Development (OECD) economies, about 36–40 per cent of what is spent in the economy is spent by the national state, in terms of defence, health, education, and so on, and these sorts of expenditures tend to be well grounded in national capabilities and concentrated in national space.

QUESTION TIME

More do it yourself!

Are there any equivalents to the Valley near your university? Why do you think the cluster occurs? What concepts fit the case best?

The Internet enables space to supersede time because, in a world of trade in symbolic images such as software, currencies, and other forms of representation, time is no longer an issue. If you have trading facilities in the right time zones, for instance, you can trade 24 hours a day, moving money, or other 'signs' of commerce, symbolically, across the globe, from London to New York to Tokyo to Sydney to London. There is an increasing separation of the 'real' economy of production and its simulacra in the 'symbol economy' of financial flows and transactions. A new international division of labour compresses and fragments both space and distance in such a way that not only production but also various business service industries become distributed in unlikely places. Global currencies facilitate trade across the world: MBAs become global warriors in the new world order. New divisions restructure geographic space. In principle, anywhere is virtually immediately accessible by information and communication technologies. In practice, most national capitals can be reached within 24 hours of air travel.

The most radical expression of network organization is that of Michael Hardt and Antonio Negri (2000), who envisage a new form of global democratic potential in network organizations, which they term the 'multitude'. They conceive a network in terms inspired by Deleuze and Guattari (1984) who imagined a network as an open system with no underlying structure or hierarchy, which they termed 'the rhizome'. The term is used metaphorically and is drawn from botanical usage, where it means a thick underground horizontal stem that produces roots and has shoots that develop into new plants. The rhizome can be expressed in terms of several principles, suggests Munro (2008: 273):

1 Any point in a rhizome can be connected to any other (such as a distributed network), and objects of different kinds are connected within the rhizome. This is the principle of connection and heterogeneity.

2   The rhizome is defined by its lines of flight rather than by points internal to it. As the rhizome makes connections with the outside, it undergoes a metamorphosis; like a piece of music, it transforms itself with each new note. This is the principle of multiplicity.

3   The rhizome can be broken at any spot, and it will either sprout a new line of growth or continue along an old line. Deleuze and Guattari described this kind of network as 'the wisdom of plants', by means of which they move, expand, and develop their territory. The rhizome moves by following a flow, of wind, of rain, of water. This is the principle of a signifying rupture.

4   The rhizome does not have an underlying generative structure; intensive states and thresholds replace the idea of an underlying topology. This is referred to as the principle of cartography.

Virtual spaces in which information can spread in an unregulated, nomadic fashion would be examples of rhizomatic networks, such as online communities for file sharing such as Facebook, YouTube, or Linux, which function by making novel connections and expanding and maintaining internal communal relations. Rhizomatic networks, such as Limewire, are challenging the dominance of older bureaucratically organized music companies, for instance.

There has been a lot of excitement about the ability of virtual, digital technologies to lead to the erosion of bureaucracy. However, there are findings from empirical research that suggest that in large-scale organizations information and communication technologies tend to be framed by pre-existing organization structures. The imperatives of bureaucracy are not so much dissolved as translated into the new technologies, as Harris (2008) demonstrates in his analysis of the adoption of digital technology in the British Library. Where radically decentralized virtual forms of service delivery were adopted they were framed in such a way that that they were dependent on heavily managed forms of capacity building and information aggregation, thus ensuring the continuity of bureaucratic lines of power and authority.

Other researchers have also noted the ways in which the introduction of virtual technologies, such as e-business systems, has increased the hierarchy and the bureaucracy of organizations rather than reducing it. For instance, Eriksson-Zetterquist, Lindberg and Styhre (2009), argue that the introduction of an e-business system for purchasing not only increased hierarchy and bureaucracy but also threatened the purchasers' professional identities and established work procedures. Technological artifacts are not detached from the broader reformulating of managerial procedures and practices but reflect and embody them.

Check out the Companion Website www.sagepub.co.uk/ managingandorganizations3 for free access to an article by Martin Harris (2008), which critically evaluates the adoption of information and communication technologies by the British Library, and charts how virtuality does not necessarily trump bureaucracy; as well as an article by Ulla Eriksson-Zetterquist, Kajsa Lindberg and Alexander Styhre (2009) about the implementation of e-business systems in a large global corporation.

New organizational forms after bureaucracy

Many new forms of organization are emerging these days: the network and cellular form (Miles et al., 1997), the federal organization (Handy, 1993), the creative compartment (Fairtlough, 1994), the postmodern and flexible firm (Clegg, 1990; Volberda, 2002), the virtual organization (Goldman et al., 1995), and the individualized corporation (Ghoshal and Bartlett, 1997). Clarke and Clegg (1998) reviewed the mainstreams in the literature of these 'post' organizations – all of which have in common that they are conceived in terms that are opposed to and seen as superseding bureaucratic models of structure. Often, in a generic sense, these post organizations are referred to as **new organizational forms**. In Table 14.3 we indicate some of the terms and sources of new organizational forms.

New organizational forms are sometimes termed postbureaucratic organizations, as Fairtlough (2007) suggests. At their core he suggests are two main features: reduction of hierarchy and of coercive elements in bureaucracy and a move towards less rigid and perhaps apparently less rationalistic ways of organizing. Concepts of new organizational forms are characterized by being less sure about what they are than what they are not: they are opposed to bureaucracy because of its variously diagnosed pathologies. All point the way to some version or other of a postbureaucratic future (Heckscher, 1994), but no one term – other than, perhaps, 'new organizational forms' (Lewin et al., 2002) and 'virtual organization' (Ahuja and Carley, 1999; Black and Edwards, 2000; Davidow and Malone, 1992; DeSanctis and Monge, 1999) – has captured the imagination in the way that the term *bureaucracy* once did. Palmer and Dunford (2001) provide a succinct account of the relationships between design and form.

A further analysis of the literature identified 346 instances of the occurrence of the term 'new organizational forms' that were investigated across 135 articles (Palmer et al., 2007). The researchers concluded from their content analysis of these articles that there were five differences in language use and assumptions about new organizational forms. The five differences covered:

1 The *type* of change represented. While some analysts see the emergence of new organizational forms as evolutionary, others see it in terms of a radical revolutionary break with prior practices. There is little interchange between the perspectives.

2 The *outcome* of changing. Analysts are divided about the outcomes that occur as organizations shift to new organizational forms. On the one hand some see the shift as one of increasing simplification of forms while others see it as an increase in complexity. The former tendency stresses de-layering, flattening of hierarchy, and less division of labour, while the latter emphasizes the need for simultaneously different things to be accomplished, such as innovation and control, flexibility and efficiency, and differentiated decision-making authority and broad participation. Not surprisingly, the latter tendencies suggest that new organizational forms can be ambiguous and challenging because the rules of the new game are not at all clear to all the players in it. For Child and Rodrigues (2003), the reduction of organizational layers leads to an increasing complexity in organizational control because of the absence of traditional bureaucratic hierarchies. New governance

TABLE 14.3   Concepts of new organizational form structure

Adhocracy	This refers to organizations that have simply grown, without much explicit design. They are characterized by a lack of structure and formal rules. Often small, creative agencies are adhocracies, such as a design studio	Mintzberg (1983a)
Technocracy	Organization structure enabled by technological innovations. Organizations that comprise people who work on a common database from remote locations would be a good example. Research networks such as the Genome project would be a good example	Burris (1993)
Internal market	Flexible markets and internal contracts within an organization structure characterize these forms of organization, often adopted by public sector organizations in search of greater flexibility and efficiency	Malone et al. (1987)
Clans	An organization based on shared culture rather than formal rules, much as the members of an extended anthropological clan might be in a traditional society. The culture is overwhelmingly oral rather than recorded in formal rule-like statements. For instance, hi-tech start-ups in places such as Silicon Valley	Ouchi (1980)
Heterarchy	A form of organization resembling a network or fishnet. Rather than there being a single chain of authority – a hierarchy – there are plural connections between the individual members. Professional firms, such as law partnerships or accounting partnerships, often correspond to this model	Hedlund (1986)
Virtual organization	An organization linked through virtual networks rather than formal rules, often involving several ostensibly separate organizations, often project organized. *The crucial factor is that the network relations are virtually enabled.* Often data are moved with great rapidity around the virtual network and separate skill sets work on the data either in series or in parallel. This often is the preferred mode of design-oriented firms, such as architects' studios, working on large projects with many other specialist partners, such as engineers, project management firms, designers, etc.	Davidow and Malone (1992)
Network organization	An organization formed by intersecting and cross-cutting linkages between several separate organizations, usually connected on a project basis, such as large-scale civil engineering alliances between a public sector organization, such as a major utility, and other specialist construction, design, and project-management-related firms. *The crucial factor here is that the partners have a more formal and enduring relationship than in the virtual organization, and are not restricted to work on digital data, such as movies, designs, etc.*	Biggart and Hamilton (1992) Powell (1990) Rockart and Short (1991)
Postmodern organization	This is essentially a bureaucratic organization which has undergone a degree of de-differentiation of its structure; that is, it has become more integrated, less specialist, and more team based. Japanese automobile companies – learning bureaucracies that are seeking to become less bureaucratic – would be a case in point	Clegg (1990)

practices premised on trust and cooperation are required for a simpler, de-layered organizational form.

3   The *drivers* for changing. A strong emphasis in the literature suggests that management is the major driver, making strategic choices in response to a changing business environment of technologies and supply chains, as well as seeking to overcome existing bureaucratic inertias. While these arguments all emphasize managers' strategic choice there are other arguments that see the changes as far more environmentally driven. It is the emergence of new populations of organizations born in the digital age that are seen as the drivers, due to the centrality of new forms of knowledge and its management, new bases for legitimacy and institutionalization as firms such as Google become the icons of the new age.

4   The *level of analysis*. The different positions on levels of analysis stress that the changes are either occurring primarily internally to organizations or they are the result of new interorganizational relationships between and among organizations. The former position stresses *intra*-organizational change; the latter posits *inter*-organizational change as the primary mechanism. The former changes see managerial agency as central while the latter stress the importance of new industries emerging.

5   The *meaning of new*. Novelty is always problematic: is something innovative in an absolute or a relative way? If it is absolutely new this means that the innovation has never been seen before; if it is relatively new the innovation may have been known but not applied in the specific context in which it is now applied. The former is new in time; the latter new in context. The debates about the meaning of the 'new' in new organizational forms often relate to different paradigmatic assumptions and positions offered by the rich ecology of organization and management theories.

The upshot of their analysis is that there is a strong need for researchers to be more explicit about their assumptions and to develop increasing facility in enabling conversations across paradigms so that there can be greater clarity about these matters of interpretation and organizational design.

Rationalized myths and organizational change

All planned organizational change is an attempt to construct a specific design for an organization. Of late, especially since the global financial crisis, this design has been overwhelmingly driven by the mantra of improving corporate performance. In the wake of the subprime mortgage crisis in the US corporate failure has become the headline issue rather than corporate success. Lehman Brothers, Merrill Lynch, Ford, GM, Chrysler, BT, Rolls Royce, Sony, and many more: the litany of corporate cuts enacted in the name of improving performance rolled out remorselessly. In one month alone, in November 2008, 533,000 jobs were slashed in the US (*The Guardian* 6 December 2008). Organizational change invariably means downsizing and de-layering, designing the organization to cost less by shedding more labour. While this is true of the UK and the Euro zone as well as the United States it is in America that the trend is most evident.

Through aggressive policies of domestic wage cutting, downsizing, and delayering, combined with outsourcing overseas, corporate profits are increasing seven times faster than revenue. The *Washington Post* reports:

> How can America's corporations so defy gravity? Ever adaptive, they have evolved a business model that enables them to make money even while the strapped American consumer has cut back on purchasing. For one thing, they are increasingly selling and producing overseas. General Motors is going like gangbusters in China, where it now sells more cars than it does in the United States. In China, GM employs 32,000 assembly-line workers; that's just 20,000 fewer than the number of such workers it has in the States. And those American workers aren't making what they used to; new hires get $14 an hour, roughly half of what veterans pull down ... The GM model typifies that of post-crash American business: massive layoffs, productivity increases, wage reductions (due in part to the weakness of unions), and reduced sales at home; increased hiring and booming sales abroad. Another part of that model is cash retention. A Federal Reserve report last month estimated that American corporations are sitting on a record $1.8 trillion in cash reserves. As a share of corporate assets, that's the highest level since 1964. (Meyerson, 2010)

There is a particular rationale that drives these changes in most instances and it goes by the name of 'shareholder value'. It is a 'loose rhetoric' (Froud et al., 2000: 80–7; 2006: 36) that seems designed to play to financial and market analysts who have such a significant impact on stock valuations. Cutting costs by delayering and downsizing typically produces an instant result in terms of the market valuation of shares. The top management team typically receives a substantial slice of their income in the form of stock options so it is in their interests to drive the value ever higher.

As ever, there are winners and losers from these changes. The winners are evidently the top management team members having stock options; increasingly the losers are those survivors in middle management who have to try and manage the eviscerated corpus of the organizations that have been downsized. It is their responsibility to manage the consequences of formal changes to organization structures. Three authors – John Hassard, Leo McCann and Jonathan Morris – have conducted a major cross-national investigation of how these employees subjectively interpret the changes of working conditions contingent on these organizational structural changes. The research was published as *Managing in the Modern Corporation: The Intensification of Managerial Work in the USA, UK and Japan* (2009) and we will summarize the main findings here.

Being against bureaucracy, being in favour of leaner, meaner organizations became something of a rationalized myth in the 1980s. We can conveniently mark the emergence of this rationalized myth with the publication of a series of texts by 'management gurus' in the 1980s, especially Peters and Waterman's (1982) *In Search of Excellence* and Hammer and Champy's (1993) *Reengineering the Corporation*, which Best (1990) examines in *The New Competition*. These all contributed to creating a **rationalized myth** in modern business: in which institutional rules function as myths that depict various formal structures as rational means for the

Rationalized myths are rationalized and impersonal rules that bind different organizations through belief in their legitimacy. To be legitimate they will be pervasive features of the institutionalized environment in which the organizations operate. Their legitimacy is based on the belief that the practices sanctioned by the myths are efficient and effective. Organizations use these myths to increase the legitimacy of their structure and hence their survival prospects.

attainment of desirable ends (Meyer and Rowan, 1977). The institutional rule that has become increasingly accepted as a rationalized myth is that continuing competitiveness can only be achieved by a perpetual war on costs best served by 'slashing costs through mass downsizing exercises in an attempt to impress financial markets' (Hassard et al., 2009: 29). If businesses do this then they will, in the short term, satisfy financial and market analysts and drive up their stock values. The rationalized myth is not imposed on business: there is no central authority saying that this is what one must do, nor is it entirely the result of normative professionally organized pressures, although the major consulting companies have certainly contributed to the climate in which the rationalized myth flourished. Mostly it seems to have spread by mimesis, by imitation. As highly regarded firms seek to ensure the maintenance of their competitive edge through these strategies then their competitors, fearing that they will lose value in the eyes of the market if they are not seen to be doing the same things, seek to emulate their strategies.

While the 'gurus' heralded these organizational changes their results, when exposed to more sober analysis, have been decidedly mixed. Cuts to organizations have been unnecessarily damaging, suggest writers such as Burke and Nelson (1997), Sennett (1998) and Pfeffer (1998). Organizational knowledge that was embodied and embrained in under-valued workers has been allowed to leave the organization with insufficient regard for what was being lost; innovation has suffered as the remaining more hard-pressed managers seek to manage a greatly intensified workload. The costs of managing have increased enormously as the widespread adoption of new digital technologies make work a continuous irruption into life more generally: the BlackBerry messages that arrive from the boss at 9.00 p.m., demanding an instant response, or which arrive when you are at the kid's soccer on a Saturday morning; the mobile calls that announce an emergency that requires your urgent attention. These interruptions of everyday life are the surface manifestation of the larger structural pressures that are occurring in our economies and societies. These pressures are the result of the implementation of the rationalized myth – restructuring, financialization, downsizing, de-layering and the removal of employee entitlements, as Hassard et al. (2009: 37) observe. These pressures, despite the existence of the rationalized myth, are not natural but socially constructed – they result from the decisions made by executives as they respond to the changing political economy, especially as its signals are directed by leading politicians and market analysts.

Globalization, which we shall discuss in Chapter 15, has played an increasing role in these structural changes. Organizations that were once largely domiciled in their home countries now have supply chains and outsourcing arrangements that span the globe, bringing new opportunities for cost reduction into play as previously unincorporated regions and peoples of the planet are brought into the world economy in regions such as China, India, and the ex-Soviet Union. Accompanying this globalization of organizations and labour there has been an internationalization of financial markets, further easing the transmission of the rationale myth.

The results of this globalization have undoubtedly been impressive for consumers: we have more choice of more things of better quality for less money than was the case when economies were less integrated globally. Competition on the basis of price and quality has led to more demanding consumers who, in turn, maintain competitive pressure on firms. These competitive pressures are condensed and intensified within firms into expectations that middle managers can constantly manage a series of paradoxes; tighten cost control and be more innovative; deliver higher performance and greater commitment; live life through a series of projects with diminished job security and increased adherence to the corporate culture. The list of contradictions should be familiar to anybody working in major organizations today.

The major mechanism for translating the rationalized myth into action 'has been the substantial job cuts and reorganizations targeted specifically at managers (in addition to the long-standing threats to operatives)' as Hassard et al. (2009: 49) analyse. Some effects of this are easy to observe: the reduction of management layers; the outsourcing of non-core back-office functions to countries with much cheaper white-collar labour processes, such as India, and the development of international supply chains and overseas production. All of these tendencies have contributed to the growing complexity involved in managing organizations that are considerably smaller than was the case 30 or so years ago, with a greatly diminished managerial cadre whose roles and responsibilities are now stretched over many more areas of expertise. For instance, today's managers work in high-tech knowledge-intensive environments in which learning is a lifetime imperative and the mastery of new skills a mundane necessity. That managerial work and organizational design have changed so considerably is largely due to the massive increase in sophistication and prevalence of ICT systems – the digital revolution – that have made managing at a distance, across space and time, much more feasible. We have seen this widely discussed in the thesis of the 'network society' by Castells (1996). Leaner organizations lack buffer zones and loose coupling that can contain and limit crises if things go wrong. There is consequently far more probability of crisis and need for the firefighting that these entail. Contemporary managers also require considerable skills in managing alliances, networks, and supply chains that would have been a mystery to an earlier generation. The experience of time has changed as well. In consulting companies there is a saying current among managers that you earn your money from nine to five and the chances of promotions from five to nine. The intensification of work fills in not only all the spaces of the working day but also can creep into other areas of life.

One of the major changes in organizational designs that has paralleled the structural changes are changes in the identity of managers. Watch a TV show such as *Mad Men*, about Madison Avenue executives in the 1950s, and one thing is immediately evident: they are all white men and they all share a very common culture and identity. That is no longer the case; managers are no longer a caste. Female labour participation rates have increased significantly in most of the OECD countries, and organizations have to manage not only the career expectations of their managers but also their fertility expectations in a way that would not have been meaningful in older style bureaucracies that were largely the preserve of males. Work–life balance is a major issue not only because of the intensification of management work and its increasing commitments but also the increasing, if still limited, entry of women into management roles and the necessity for new domestic management strategies, particularly with respect to child-care. The extension of work into domestic life through home-working, home offices, and personal computers means that the home is no longer such a separate preserve from work and the organization but that the organization leaches into the family rather than being shut out as the front door closes. Modern managers are also not exclusively white anymore: the multi-cultural workforce is a reality in global cities such as Sydney, Paris, New York, and London. This introduces an additional complexity into organizational design – the management of and interaction between people of very different faiths, cultures, and background assumptions. Combined with the pressure of intensification and probability of recurring crises, the chances of causing inadvertent cultural offence in everyday work also increase.

The picture is not necessarily bleak and we should not be too one-dimensional about it: management has become more difficult, demanding, and more challenging – and for many managers this makes what might once have seemed a humdrum job one that is very exciting, intellectually, and emotionally rewarding. Yet, in their empirical investigation of the life world of middle managers in Japan, the UK, and the US, Hassard and his colleagues (2009) paint a picture of middle managers as the carriers of the costs of the evident restructuring that has been occurring these past 30 years or so. While they do not find convergence across the three countries, with Japan, especially, retaining more traditionally bureaucratic practices and the UK a more regulated environment, there are broad similarities occurring in the experiences of managers that have been subject to restructuring. Opposed to some of the more optimistic accounts in the literature – perhaps optimistic because they are derived from more extraordinary rather than ordinary organizations, which stress the participatory and empowering elements of new organizational forms – they did not find much evidence of positive decentralization.

> The kind of decentralisation we found involved devolvement of authority alongside cuts to employment numbers, which tended to mean a centralisation of core strategic goals and concepts and the re-establishment of top management prerogative. Senior management's core message in the 2000s is communicated down the hierarchy clearly and repetitively ... According to the managers spoken to in our study, so called 'devolvement' in this context usually meant loading extra work onto the shoulders of staff. If there were greater numbers of colleagues among whom to share the workload, then perhaps the downward devolvement of authority would be more welcome. Downwards devolution of authority and widening responsibilities are commendable concepts, but they rarely work out so well for employees in practice given the cost-cutting and job-reducing context in which such changes take place. Although one positive effect of restructuring reported by middle managers was that their work has become more interesting and rewarding, the downside was that it has certainly got tougher and more demanding. (Hassard et al., 2009: 23–24)

It is the middle managers that remain in downsized, de-layered structures who carry the burden of these organizational changes away from bureaucracy to flatter, leaner, newer organization forms. The findings of the study by Hassard et al. suggest that, almost universally across different industries in the UK, the US, and Japan, 'there is very strong evidence to suggest that the working lives of mid-level managerial employees are considerably more pressured and possibly more insecure than they once were' (2009: 228). There are financial pay-offs as well as more interesting work opportunities, 'but the overall feeling of being overwhelmed in work while the traditional promotional ladder has been largely removed was a major and wide spread finding'. These findings are backed up by various health and stress-related studies in each of the countries (see Hassard et al., 2009: 230–231), which document the costs of stress, pressure, and lack of physical fitness wreaked on middle level managers by the intensification of work and the encouragement of macho cultures that stress performance and results consistent with the rationalized myth of increasing shareholder value in the face of international competitive pressures over and above the costs incurred doing so. Of course, there are exceptions to the rule: some organizations do seek to ensure family-friendly, healthy working practices but these appear to be in the minority, with most firms regarding such 'soft stuff' as an unjustifiable cost incurred against the erosion of shareholder returns by the pressures of international competition.

The empirical material in the investigations by Hassard et al. (2009) is considerable and fascinating; unfortunately, there is far too much to report completely in the context of a textbook but we would urge readers to make themselves familiar with it at first hand. It is a rich and ethnographically detailed account of the lives that many readers of this book presently experience or are likely to experience in the future, unless there are strong counter pressures exerted to those that presently dominate. While there are advocates of such changes in business schools and in HRM it is difficult to see such advocacy being successful in the face of the repeated restructurings that are designed to deliver enhanced value to shareholders. Certainly, senior executives in the top management team, whose income is contingently linked to performance in these terms, are unlikely to be advocates for a more caring and less uncompromising work regime on their middle managers. Moreover, such a harsh regime is functional for elite recruitment: if middle managers can manage to thrive despite the pressures, they show themselves to be the kind of people whose elevation to upper level management may well be justified. And each time such a decision is made the vicious cycle is reinforced.

Design thinking

In the last few years, the notion of **design thinking** has gained popularity outside the design professions, especially in business school circles. In part, this is because of the accelerating changes in organizational designs and structures over the past 30 years, which has led to increasing calls for design thinking to be incorporated into the management curriculum. At its core,

Design thinking emerged as a term that was widely used in the 2000s. Its inspiration goes back to Simon (1969). Brown (2009) develops it as a conjoined process of inspiration, ideation, and implementation. Inspiration derives from making a problem material through mock-up, sketches, scenarios, and so on. Ideation is the process of generating, developing and testing ideas through building prototypes, piloting, and 'testing the waters' – idea work. Implementation is the clear development and specification of the idea, its effective communication, the enrolment of others in its support, and the translation of the idea into action or practice.

the call for design thinking seems to be recognition that the analytical frameworks usually dominant in business schools are somewhat limited. Typically, these have stressed deduction in research that seeks to define hypotheses a priori and then test them empirically, and induction, for those researchers that prefer more grounded and ethnographic approaches where they 'induct' findings from the specifics of the empirical situation. Against these currents, design thinking stresses what the American pragmatist, Peirce (1940), referred to as abduction.

Abduction is a term drawn from Aristotelian thought and used by Peirce to distinguish a distinct form of inference from the more common induction and deduction. Abduction is 'a process of interpretation in order to develop explanations based on observation [where] the explanation arrived at is not deduced or induced but "abduced" from the variety and complexity of experiences and observations' (Iedema et al., 2006: 1115). Abduction recognizes that social science theories do not function as grand narratives from which hypotheses can be deduced. Such theories are never sufficiently local and do not take account of the constructivist basis of the social reality that they seek to theorize: that social reality is constantly becoming rather than being constant (Kornberger et al., 2005). Given the assumption that whatever sense of order is constructed is co-produced by situated actors it follows that the analyst should turn to the discovery of the underlying rules that are implicitly embedded in the work of construction. These rules are neither the instantiation of some covering law nor are they explicitly constructed as such by those whose actions inscribe them. Furthermore, the analyst, as a situated actor, will also always be involved in this construction project. The best way of proceeding is to work collaboratively, through trial, error, and prototypes, to determine how best to put together an understanding of how to do what in order to create value.

Influenced by design thinking, the field of organization and management studies acknowledges the need to bring together practitioners and academics in order to develop knowledge that can be applied (Schön, 1992). One interesting recent development that attempts to overcome the gap between academics and practitioners is the connection of design studies to organization science (Romme, 2003; Zell, 1997). Romme (2003) claims that organization studies should include design as one of its primary modes of engaging in research. Organization science as design science has to go well beyond the familiar structural aspects of organizations and go beyond the prevailing conception of organizational entities as natural phenomena (Jelinek et al., 2008). A focus on design entails a set of tools, skills, and epistemologies for more grounded organizational enquiry (Romme, 2003). Bate and Robert (2007) claim that there are four lessons to be drawn from design sciences for organization and management theory. First, organizational design can include the user of the organization's products and services in the development of organizations. Second, applied design thinking can be used to address simultaneously all three issues of performance, engineering, and aesthetics/experience. Third, new diagnostic and intervention methods and approaches are useful. And fourth, design sciences show how and where energy can be applied to bring about and sustain change.

Drawing upon the work of Herbert Simon, Schön (1992) suggests that practitioners are, of necessity, designers; the production of artifacts is essential to their business. Therefore, practitioners in the field of design sciences, including, among others, professional designers, architects, and engineers, are focused on prototyping action and are solution centred (Michlewski, 2008). The idea of prototyping includes the objectives of creating a physical prototype to enable organizational thinking and learning to occur more rapidly by making prototypes small and thus, by testing them, being able to minimize the impact of failures. Prototypes also encourage employees to explore new behaviour (Coughlan et al., 2007: 127). Design approaches practise interventions that are improvement- and solution-centred (Trullen and Bartunek, 2007), based upon a set of fundamental values that include the view that collaboration between researchers and practitioners is important; that research focuses on solutions rather than on analysis; that experiment is necessary for the intervention process; that each situation is unique in its context, and that the intervention approach involves trying to reach stated goals (Trullen and Bartunek, 2007: 27) – even if these change in the process.

That there are strong organizational relationships between design and form is evident. Think of the image of a central business district and contrast a traditional townscape with a corporate cityscape, crowding out the small-scale domestic architecture in its surrounds. Could the corporate organization be easily headquartered in the townscape? Could the townspeople easily live in or adapt to the corporate scene? The literature on new organizational forms suggests that modern corporations can in fact become similar to high-tech cottage industries, as everyone is wired from anywhere. Working virtually, they may have no need to concentrate in a few blocks of central business district real estate. Not every organizational form is as tangible as those that are housed in city skyscrapers. In its most virtual new form, organization will be composed of networks of interdependent but independent knowledge-based teams working in different continents and time zones. Such work can be organized on a rolling 24-hour process and often involves multiple global collaborators (Clarke and Clegg, 1998: 293). The work activities are often associated with digital databased projects, such as film or copy-editing, computer programming, or graphic designing.

For Fairtlough (2007), a rare example of a successful CEO, research biologist, and organization theorist combined in one person, the alternatives to hierarchical bureaucracy are *heterarchy* and *responsible autonomy*. As he argues, heterarchy comprises dispersed leadership, dispersed power, and a balance of power, with mutual accountability. A good example of heterarchy would be the structure of professional service firms, such as law firms. Although these tend to become more hierarchical as they grow in size, the advantages of partnership continue to be recognized. The procedures in many successful law firms are quasi-democratic, with voting by all partners deciding key issues. A great deal of conversation between partners takes place before a vote. However, the nature of these conversations is strongly influenced by the prospect of the subsequent vote (Fairtlough, 2007: 1274).

Responsible autonomy depends on encapsulating relatively autonomous roles as responsible to rules, both explicit and tacit, which govern the interaction of autonomous actors or elements or divisions of an organization.

Organizations are essentially adaptive systems. To be adaptive can mean both preserving elements of what is and adopting elements of what is not already part of the organization's makeup. To that extent they are self-organizing systems. Making up managers and organizations as radically different may not be so easy, because both remembering and forgetting hamper organizations that seek to change radically. Organizations forget some of what they know when their managers presume they can ditch the past for a new future. In order to survive in any changing present, organizations have to remember a great deal of what they have been if they are to maintain cohesion and routine. But too much routine (i.e. too much remembering) can be lethal for organizations, just as can too much change. Simultaneously, organizations have to exploit what they know and explore what they do not if they are to be adaptive.

The Internet enables speedier, more efficient, and cost-effective access to resources and customers and a different set of ownership, location, and organizational capabilities than was possible just a decade before. Contrast Amazon with a traditional book retailer. Almost every organization today of any size is awash with e-technology and software. Most of the tools that are bought are not revolutionary in their managerial impact; they merely enable managers to do what they would have done anyway but do it better and faster. The new tools are based on technological innovations that drastically change the tools used to produce a good or service. For instance, e-mail replaces and speeds up the postal system, or search engines such as Google replace and speed up the reference library. As Beauvallet and Balle (2002) demonstrate, revolutionary new technologies do not necessarily produce managerial revolutions.

In the nineteenth century the typewriter was a profound mechanical invention. It speeded up clerical and recording systems that had been based on handwriting. In Weber's (1978) view the typewriter directly contributed to the creation of modern managerial bureaucracies. The computer vastly extends the capabilities of the keyboard, even while retaining many of its apparent features, but its digital capabilities also transform the possible nature of organizational design. Digital technologies can deliver business as usual much faster. Basic e-technologies, such as e-mail, websites, and search engines, can be used effectively to obtain office productivity improvements. They make it possible to generate new channels for communicating with customers, suppliers, and staff.

The digital revolution not only enhances service productivity but can transform what were once broadcast models of distribution – from a few centres to many customers – into narrow-cast communication where there are a great many points of distribution and reception – think of downloads, or the favourite blogs that you visit. Clearly, the music industry is undergoing rapid change. One of the major labels, EMI, is in major financial trouble at the time of writing, and the subject of takeover bids, despite having a huge back catalogue.

Additionally, and perhaps most importantly, digital technologies make extended supply chain operations feasible and reliable. Think about when you order a product – a CD or book – from Amazon. You can track the delivery of the product in virtual space, pay for it virtually, and view many of its features virtually – all from your office desk. You do not need to leave your chair. Of course, there is a downside to this from an employer's point of view: while you may appear to be working hard you might actually be doing anything! You could be doing the grocery shopping, fixing a date, flirting, looking at pornography, or selling secrets to a business rival. The web opens up new channels for business – making it possible to host new forms of marketing and advertising – but it also makes it harder for employers to control people's use of their time.

The major advantages of digital technologies for business and organizations are their virtual possibilities for disaggregating existing designs. Increasingly, organizations segment and specialize activities that are critical to their competitive advantage and those that are not. The non-core functions, such as back-office accounting, telemarketing, or programming, are outsourced to parts of the world where the wage is one-third to one-tenth the cost in the home market. This dramatically reduces operating costs and increases competitiveness. There are now very many new niche-based business opportunities that were not previously evident. Perhaps the one that we are all most familiar with is the call centre. When we have a problem with that new gadget or that bill we have just received, the number that we call is not that of the organization that supplied it to us. It will be a call centre that handles that organization's account. Digital technology means that organizations can hive off non-core elements of their business and contract other business, for which this is their core technology, to handle that aspect of the business.

SUMMARY AND REVIEW

Bureaucracy was the initial point of departure for empirical studies of organizations. Theorists studied organizations and analysed them in terms of their degree of difference from the ideal type of model that Weber had constructed. Clearly, they would differ, and they did. Although a number of classic and interesting studies were completed in this vein, there was a problem with the knowledge generated: how could it be made comparable and cumulative?

The Aston programme of research sought to make this scientific goal a centrepiece of inquiry and shifted analysis to a more sophisticated plane – that of contingency theory. However, the findings that the programme launched were contested almost from the start. Aldrich accused it of drawing obvious conclusions on the basis of inference that was guided purely by jumping to conclusions from the variance found in the data rather than considering deeply how plausible was the story that underlay the connections presumed. To build a more plausible narrative, he reanalysed the data using causal path analysis. Child also questioned the narrative; for him, it downplayed the role of the top management dominant coalition being able to exercise strategic choice.

Donaldson does not deny that such strategic choice occurs but thinks it most probable, on the basis of empirical enquiry, that the choice will tend to be exercised in favour of the organization structure being adjusted to regain fit with changing contingencies rather than the contingencies being changed to suit the existing structure.

Much recent debate has centred on the emergence of new organizational forms. From the perspective of contingency theory, whose classic conceptual dimensions were modelled on bureaucratic organizations, the emergence of new organizational forms may be challenging because their premises are less bureaucratic and written rules, and more IT and virtual designs. In the e-world, the old certainties may no longer hold.

EXERCISES

1 Having read this chapter you should be able to say in your own words what each of the following key terms means. Test yourself or ask a colleague to test you.

- Contingencies
- Multi-divisional form
- Structural contingency theory
- New organizational form
- Technology
- Call centres
- Structural adjustment to regain fit
- E-management
- Rhizome

2 What is the importance of developing a general theory for managing all organizations in terms of contingencies?

3 According to Burns and Stalker, why do organizations in stable environments have different structures than those in fast-changing and innovative environments?

4 According to the Aston school, why does an organization become more bureaucratic as its size increases?

5 According to Mintzberg, what are the five most feasible configurations of organization structure?

6 What were the major innovations of the multi-divisional form?

7 Does e-management destroy bureaucracy?

8 How creative are call centres?

9 What enables creative designers in the Valley to be creative?

ADDITIONAL RESOURCES

1 The debates that surround a somewhat arcane area of organization and management theory – namely, why organization structures are as they are – can sometimes be quite passionate. Topics that evoke lively discussion include the appropriate methodologies that researchers should use and the appropriate assumptions that they should make about the nature of organizational reality. Most analysts of organization structures regard these methodologies and assumptions as objectively real, as social facts, rather than as social constructions that analysts use to make sense of what they assume is reality. The strongest proponent of this approach, which insists that organization structures are real things that are representable in terms of a limited number of variables, is Lex Donaldson, who has been a prolific and robust debater. A clear statement of his views is to be found in Donaldson (2002 [1987]), an article titled 'Strategy and structural adjustment to regain fit and performance: in defence of contingency theory'.

2 Clegg has elsewhere criticized Donaldson for the tendency in his work to leave little or no room for any evolution in organizations' forms in other than a bureaucratic mode; see Clegg (1990), *Modern Organizations*, Chapter 2.

3 You might want to consult the overview of structural contingency theory offered by Pennings (2002). To be up to date with the latest changes in corporate form the excellent contribution by Zey (2008b) on the 'multisubsidiary form' should be read carefully. Finally, in the same encyclopedia there is an excellent analysis of neocontingency theory by McKinley (2008).

4 Films about organization structure do not easily spring to mind, although several demonstrate bureaucracy in use. One that is situated in the domestic bureaucracy of an Edwardian manor house is *Gosford Park* (Altman, 2001). Each servant is assigned a role and authority 'beneath stairs' that is contingent on that assumed by their masters above.

5 Films about the military often demonstrate bureaucracy in action. Think of all those films about prisoners of war seeking to escape but

first having to gain permission from the officers in captivity who run the escape committee. *The Great Escape* (Sturges, 1963) is one of the best of the genre.

6 Another military film worth looking at is *A Few Good Men* (Reiner, 1992). In this film, Dawson and Downey are two marines stationed in the US naval base at Guantánamo Bay in Cuba. They follow orders that cause harm to another marine, resulting in his death. They are put on trial for murder. The basis of their defence is that they were only following orders. Dawson and Downey were trained to exist strictly in terms of the hierarchy and structure of the corps. Even though they knew that what they were doing to the other marine was wrong and that they were endangering him, their life code was to follow orders from their senior officers without question. The contingency that the Marine Corps had established in its structure and authoritarian culture (see also pp. 271–274) resulted in their being able to commit and to rationalize certain acts that most people would ordinarily consider inhumane. By not using their own reason, they ultimately acted against the best interests of the Marine Corps. The colonel is imprisoned for giving the order, and the two marines are dismissed from duty. We see in this movie that the hierarchy and order in organizations such as the Marine Corps and the army, when followed unquestioningly, have the potential to result in a sequence of events that are not only immoral but against the best interests of the institution that they were designed to protect.

WEB SECTION

1 Our Companion Website is the best first stop for you to find a great deal of extra resources, free PDF versions of leading articles published in Sage journals, exercises, video and pod casts, team case studies and general questions, and links to teamwork resources. Go to www.sage pub.co.uk/managingandorganizations3.

2 For state of the art briefings on how to manage organizations effectively, please visit the Henry Stewart Talks series of online audio-visual seminars on Managing Organizations, edited by Stewart Clegg: www.hstalks.com/r/

managing-orgs, especially Talk #13 by John Child on *Organization design theory: its evolution within a changing context*.

3 One cool site for creative designers is http://www.cgart.com/. It has some great graphics and an insight into the ethos of the design ecology.

4 The website http://www.integrity-design.com/, from Duluth, Minnesota, provides a good insight into the range of business that a regional company in the e-commerce world might be involved in.

5 Wikipedia has an informative entry on call centres: http://en.wikipedia.org/wiki/Call_ centre.

6 For an interesting view of some of the unanticipated consequences of call centres, check out the following story: http://tinyurl.com/yzavt7.

7 http://tinyurl.com/27dfop is a good introduction by UNESCO to the idea of creative clusters.

8 The classic model of a multi-divisional firm is 3M: check its website at http://tinyurl.com/2dnc8s and explore a firm that is diversified and multi-divisional in both products and geographically defined markets.

9 You can explore the Cisco Systems website at http://www.cisco.com/.

LOOKING FOR A HIGHER MARK?

Reading and digesting these articles that are available free on the Companion Website www.sagepub.co.uk/managingandorganizations3 can help you gain deeper understanding and, on the basis of that, a better grade:

1 Joan Woodward's ideas remain influential, despite having been developed some time ago. On the Companion Website there is a paper that shows her contemporary relevance: Lisl Klein (2006) 'Joan Woodward Memorial Lecture: applied social science: is it just common sense?', *Human Relations* 59 (8): 1155–1172.

2 Lex Donaldson tells us about why he thinks **positivism** is the best approach to organization and management theory in a paper that you can download from the Companion Website: Lex Donaldson (2005) 'Vita contemplativa: following the scientific method: how I became a committed functionalist and positivist', *Organization Studies*, 26 (7): 1071–1088.

3 Eric J. Walton (2005) 'The persistence of bureaucracy: a meta-analysis of Weber's model of bureaucratic control', *Organization Studies*, 26 (4): 569–600, a researcher who has worked with Lex Donaldson, demonstrates the ways in which bureaucracy is a persistent phenomena in organization life.

4 The iron cage, Max Weber's metaphor, recurs constantly in studies of organizations: it is used in Dan Kärreman and Mats Alvesson (2004) 'Cages in tandem: management control, social identity, and identification in a knowledge-intensive firm', *Organization*, 11 (1): 149–175, which you can find on the Companion Website.

5 The extent to which bureaucracy persists or is being made redundant by new organizational forms is a matter that is addressed empirically in R. Dunford et al. (2007) 'Coexistence of "old" and "new" organizational practices: transitory phenomenon or enduring feature?', *Asia Pacific Journal of Human Resources*, 45 (1): 24–43, which is available on the Companion Website.

6 When you ring a call centre from an English-speaking country these days, often you will end up talking to someone in India. If you are interested in how these call centres shape the lives and identity of those who work there then the contribution by Premilla D'Cruz and Ernesto Noronha (2006) 'Being professional: organizational control in Indian call centres', *Social Science Computer Review*, 24 (3): 342–361, which is available on the Companion Website, makes very interesting reading.

7 It has been widely and somewhat erroneously asserted that digital technology meant the end of bureaucracy. Research by Martin Harris in the British Library suggests strongly that this is not necessarily the case: Harris, M. (2008) 'Digital technology and governance in transition: the case of the British Library', *Human Relations*, 61 (5): 741–758.

8 To add further skepticism to the view that new digital technologies facilitate there being less bureaucracy in organizations, you can take a look at Ulla Eriksson-Zetterquist, Kajsa Lindberg and Alexander Styhre (2009) 'When the good times are over: professionals encountering new technology', *Human Relations*, 62 (8): 1145–1170.

CASE STUDY

RECORD LABELS LOSE OUT AS BANDS BECOME BRANDS IN FIERCE MARKET

New roles are emerging for those closest to artists in a fragmented media world

Owen Gibson and Katie Allen

The upheaval wrought on the music industry in recent years, of which EMI's latest travails are just the latest manifestation, have inspired a change in bedtime reading among senior executives. Their book of choice is now less likely to be a classic tale of rock industry excess such as *Hammer of the Gods*, but *The Long Tail*, a book about how the Internet has brought about the death of shared culture.

The book, written by Chris Anderson of *Wired* magazine, sums up the challenges facing established media groups, including leading record labels: 'At this point, the artists don't need the labels any more. The consumers don't need the labels anymore and I think the labels, rather than trying to protect what business they have, need to ask themselves what is their relevance.'

Although sales of CDs are falling sharply, British artists are riding the crest of a creative wave – live music has never been more popular, festivals are selling out in record time and brands are paying millions to associate themselves with up and coming acts. It is a new music marketplace where the artist's brand is becoming as valuable as their recorded output.

But for all the rhetoric about artists being able to build their own fan bases online, a guiding hand – not to mention substantial investment and know-how – is still required to bring new artists to public attention in an increasingly fragmented media world. Many experts believe today's changes will result in individual artists emerging as 'cottage industries' in their own right, much less dependent on labels to produce and market their music.

As the ancillary revenues around each artist – from live appearances, merchandising, ringtones, advertising and licensing deals – become more important than dwindling recorded music royalties, new roles are emerging for those closest to artists. It is no coincidence that the likes of Island Records co-founder Tim Clark, who now manages Robbie Williams among others, and Creation Records founder Alan McGee now work in artist management.

Already, many majors rely on management companies to bring new artists to their attention. Now, some are starting to bypass them altogether. Mr Clark, who co-founded ie Music and was responsible for Robbie Williams' multi-faceted £80m contract with EMI, believes that deal could be the last of its kind. He likens the latest period of flux to the anything goes spirit of the 1960s before the major label consolidation of the late 1970s.

The company is pioneering a new form of investment in artists backed by Ingenious Media, the media-focused private equity fund launched last year by former Really Useful Group chief executive Patrick McKenna. Passenger, a new band who have been building local support in Brighton and release their first single today, are the guinea pigs for the new approach. Mr Clark is bypassing the big labels by going directly to Ingenious, which is putting up £1.3m to launch the band – investment matched by ie Music and external investors.

New model

Through the new financial model – dubbed Music Venture Capital Trusts – they claim that artists have more freedom and retain more of their own rights while their management are able to lavish care and attention on all aspects of an artist's career.

The artist retains ultimate control, they say, because managers tend to be employed on an annual contract.

'We work for our artists and we answer to our artists. At the end of the day, our artists can turn around and sack us,' says Mr Clark. He says he 'very nearly came to blows' with EMI over ie Music's determination to sign a global marketing deal with Sony Ericsson for Williams – a marriage that he says has been 'incredibly successful'. By being able to work with each part of an artist's 'basket of rights', he claims to stand a better chance of building a long-term brand than a record label more concerned with short-term returns.

'That's why management is having more success in doing this because they recognise that basket of rights and they recognise the value of those rights,' says Mr Clark.

Mr McKenna believes the majors should have cottoned on earlier: 'I think it's one of life's great mysteries why record companies haven't embraced this 360 degree business model.'

Bryan Calhoun, an Atlanta-based music consultant who works with Kanye West and Ludacris, is another who is thriving amid the music industry's shifting sands. He says artists are recognising how far they can leverage their brands and are going beyond what the major labels can offer them. Kanye West is signed to Universal Music as a recording artist but has been working with Mr Calhoun's StrategusPro company on creating a fan community.

Strategy

'It's about building an entire digital strategy and the fan club is a part of it,' says Mr Calhoun. 'Ringtones and mastertones, those things are controlled by the major because that is who Kanye is signed to. But then he has also retained rights for exploiting his other content, voicetones, images, those kind of things,' he says.

'A lot of people are looking to try to figure out exactly what they are going to do going forward and it doesn't necessarily have to do with the major labels.'

Terry McBride, who runs Canadian music management group Nettwerk, also claims that bypassing major labels can allow artists to hold on to more control. He helped Barenaked Ladies make $3m from 500,000 album sales, much more than they would have done if they had gone through a major label.

As major labels struggle to adapt to this new world, cutting costs and restructuring their business models, it is important to retain some perspective. Many employed by them retain enough faith to believe they will emerge from this transitory period stronger.

But the majority of those who stand to benefit from their potential demise, including Mr McKenna, believe the days of the major labels as we know them are numbered.

'I've always thought record companies believed they financed the music industry, manufactured and distributed pieces of plastic and did the marketing. The reality, in my view, is that I don't see them doing any marketing. And if manufacturing and distribution no longer count, then it's just the financing – and we can do that,' he says.

Off the record

With the music market in decline, artists and their managers are increasing their focus on building brands that can deliver revenue streams beyond traditional record sales. Notable examples are rapper 50 Cent buying a stake in Glaceau Vitamin Water as part of his new super-healthy image. More recently, style-conscious Lily Allen announced she was teaming up with fashion chain New Look. London-based music consultancy Entertainment Media Research has tapped into the trend with a new tool called PopScores that tracks the awareness and popularity of 200 artists. So who's up and who's down? The Beatles bagged the highest score this month while Peter Andre got the lowest. Amy Winehouse was the biggest winner, according to the latest survey of 4,500 music consumers aged 13–59.

The PopScores tool can also show up changes in popularity following specific events in a star's life. Madonna's score dropped after her controversial adoption of a Malawian boy. More recently, Robbie Williams – who has checked himself into rehab – has been losing PopScore points, despite some offsetting effect from growing support among 40 to 59-year-old women. The service can also pick up longer-term consumer trends and PopScore's most recent analysis explores the rarity of female artists among top favourites lists. For male consumers there is only one female artist, Kylie, in their top 20. There are six in the equivalent list for female music fans: Pink, Kylie, Christina Aguilera, Gwen Stefani, Anastacia and Sugarbabes.

Questions

1 To what extent are changes in technology making the bureaucratic model redundant?
2 What are the sources of value in the new model and where, if anywhere, do the old structures of the record companies fit in?

Source: *The Guardian*, 26 February 2007, available at http://business.guardian.co.uk/story/0..2021280. 00.html#article_continue (accessed 27 February 2007).

CHAPTER FIFTEEN
MANAGING GLOBALIZATION

Flows, Finance, People

LEARNING OBJECTIVES

By the end of this chapter, you will be able to:

- Debate the impact of globalization, especially on organizations
- Identify some key strategic issues involved in managing in a global economy
- Explain why resistance to globalization occurs
- Discuss the central role of knowledge workers in the global economy
- Understand that globalization has both positive and negative effects on individuals, organizations, societies, and nations

BEFORE YOU GET STARTED . . .

It has been said that arguing against globalization is like arguing against the laws of gravity. (Kofi Annan, ex-Head of the United Nations)

INTRODUCTION

Whereas the Cold War, the world wars, or the Age of Empires shaped previous generations of managers and organizations, the contemporary scene is shaped by globalization. Here we debate some key themes, focusing our discussion, eventually, on the winners and losers from globalization. You, as a management student, need to understand the global patterns within which your managing will be constituted. The fact is that we live in a globalizing world. What this implies is that anywhere/anything is potentially or actually linked to anywhere/anything else in the management of commerce, government, aid, or other globally exchanged goods and services, but especially in movements of international financial flows and foreign currency exchanges that now dwarf the value of international trade in goods. Financial services are fundamental to the operation of every aspect of the economic system. Thus, globalization is vitally important in terms of both the factors making this connectedness possible and the consequences flowing from it. Globalization, as the enveloping context, provides the big picture within which the rest of this book should be situated. However, it is also important because globalization is the phenomenon underpinning the contemporary contexts in which you will be managing and organizing.

MINI CASE

Wall St suffers biggest fall since 9/11

*Fears over Chinese and US economies trigger slump
Losses wipe out year's gains on main indices*

Larry Elliott, economics editor

The Guardian, Wednesday 28 February 2007
http://tinyurl.com/yurwk8

Wall Street suffered its biggest one-day fall yesterday since the immediate aftermath of the September 11 terrorist attacks, as a day of hefty stock market falls around the world culminated in a late panic sell-off in New York.

The Dow Jones industrial average closed more than 400 points down amid fears that the US and China – the twin locomotives for the global economy – were about to plunge into recession and that the White House might be preparing air strikes against Iran's nuclear capability.

At one stage, the savage mark down of equities on Wall Street left the Dow down 550 points, but a partial recovery meant that at the closing bell the average of blue chip stocks finished 415.86 points lower at 12,216.40.

The one-day loss more than wiped out this year's gains on the stock market for the Dow and New York's two other main share price indices – the S&P

(Continued)

(Continued)

500 and the Nasdaq – and was the biggest drop since September 17 2001, when trading recommenced six days after terrorists flew two planes into the World Trade Center. Wall Street went into retreat at the start of yesterday's trading, and was 200 points lower by lunchtime in New York. It dropped sharply during the afternoon, with the late flurry of selling coming too late in the day to trigger the automatic circuit breakers designed to calm the markets.

Oil prices, which earlier had climbed to more than $62 a barrel in early New York trading, later dropped back to close a dollar lower at just over $60 on concerns that the decline of almost 8% in US durable goods order announced in Washington yesterday was evidence that higher interest rates had finally taken their toll.

Despite news yesterday of a modest pick-up in sales of existing homes, yesterday's mini-crash was also blamed on the exposure of the US financial sector to subprime mortgages, a high-risk form of home loan that proved lucrative when the housing market was booming. The latest figures show that the price of existing homes in the US in January was 3.1% lower than a year earlier.

Bond prices rose as dealers sought a safe haven from the turmoil in the equity markets. Thomas Metzold, vice-president of Eaton Vance in Boston, said: 'Only time will tell if this is a correction or more. But I feel we had gotten the point of feeling that risk was nonexistent and maybe people have finally gotten a wake-up call.'

Earlier, a day of turmoil on the world's bourses from Hong Kong to Buenos Aires began with a fall of almost 9% in Shanghai, with the biggest drop in China's stock market in almost a decade blamed on hints from Beijing that action was being planned to combat the speculation that this week drove share prices to record highs.

Chris Low, economist at FTN Financial in New York said: 'What is striking to us is not the big move in Chinese stocks, but the contagion driving stocks down around the world. For the past couple of years, contagion was a thing of the past.'

The FTSE 100 closed almost 150 points down on the day at 6,286.1, with the fall of 2.31% the sharpest since last June. The FTSE 250 suffered its biggest one-day points fall, dropping by 431.5 to 11,180.9. The Nikkei dropped 0.52% to 18,119.92 after the yen's strength gave investors a reason to sell some exporters' shares. The FTSEurofirst 300, the pan-European index, dropped 2.8% to close unofficially at 1,507.06, its biggest one-day percentage loss since May 2003.

Foreign exchange markets were also thrown into turmoil by a jump in the yen. Investors have made big profits in recent years by borrowing money cheaply in yen and buying higher-yielding but riskier assets elsewhere. An unwinding yesterday of these so-called 'carry trades' led to a 2% decline in the value of the dollar against the yen – its biggest drop in a year. The dollar also lost ground against the sterling, with the pound ending the day in London little more than three cents away from the $2 level.

The ripple effect reminded some of the retreat in global markets of May 2006. 'There's near-term vulnerability a la May 2006 because of the sheer amount of risk that is on board across the world,' said Jim O'Neill, chief global economist at Goldman Sachs.

Explainer: carry trades

Currency carry trades involve an investor borrowing money in a currency where interest rates are low and buying assets in a currency where they are high.

The amount investors make on the deal depends on the riskiness of the asset they buy and the amount they are prepared to borrow to boost their initial investment. Evidence suggests that many investors have plumped for high-risk plays and dangerously magnified their exposure through borrowing.

In recent years, the prime target for the carry trade has been the Japanese yen, because a decade of deflation has forced the authorities to keep interest rates at zero. Even now, the official cost of borrowing is under 1%, compared to more than 5% in Britain and America (these rates are much lower now, in the wake of the global financial crisis).

The carry trade is not a one-way bet, however. The main risk comes from movements in exchange rates: if the yen goes up against the dollar, paying back the original borrowing becomes more expensive and can wipe out the profits of an investor who has borrowed heavily to fund the trade.

Copyright Guardian News & Media Ltd 2007.

- What do these 'Chinese whispers' tell you about the processes of contemporary globalization?
- What have been the further globalization effects of subprime loans?

CHINESE WHISPERS

Globalization can be thought of as worldwide integration in virtually every sphere achieved principally through markets, a process whereby the world becomes more interconnected and the fates of those people and organizations in it become more intertwined. In business terms, globalization means business without frontiers, crossing national boundaries, and dealing with the world, not just the home base.

Financialization means the pervasive influence of financial calculations and judgements. Applied to everyday organizational life, it means the way that financial calculations now constitute the primary criteria of value, even for mundane objects, practices, and processes. It can be summed up in the ubiquitous phrase 'what's the value proposition?'

On the evening of 27 February 2007 (GMT) the world's major stock markets appeared to be collapsing, losing as much in New York on a single day as they did on 9/11. The next day, the *Sydney Morning Herald*, *Independent*, *Guardian*, and the *New York Times* all carried the same lead business story. The Mini Case box shows how the *Guardian* ran it. It was a precursor of things to come.

These 'Chinese whispers' represent one side of the process of globalization – the international financialization of global investments. Linked by instantaneous technologies, the world's major markets are heavily interdependent. While this kind of spectacular domino effect demonstrates the global reach and interpenetration of financial markets and is emblematic of globalization, the process of globalization entails more than merely digitally connected markets. Forty years ago it was inconceivable that China, stalled in the depths of the Cultural Revolution, could have precipitated an economic meltdown anywhere. Then it was entombed in Maoist rhetoric and the struggles that this legitimated against those who were seen as taking the 'capitalist road'. Today, despite (or perhaps because of) being a one-party authoritarian state that is still nominally Marxist, it is building that capitalist road and using it to supply the world with an ever-increasing supply of cheaper goods. No one back then could have imagined that rumours in China could shake confidence in the global economy, but in a global world everything is connected, potentially, to everything else, as the *Guardian* commentary shows.

What makes globalization and financialization such a potent mix is the way that immediacy characterizes the consequences of decisions, as the 'Chinese Whispers' case demonstrates. Of course, moke recently the global financial crisis that began to unfold from late 2007 has made this even clearer. The implications of a market in finance that is technologically mediated make a global crisis possible. Karin Knorr-Cetina and Alex Preda (2007) noted that markets have moved from a network-based architecture, with human processing at its core, to one based on a mode of coordination that can technologically mediate and disperse information simultaneously to a large audience of observers. One consequence of this is the creation of a historically unprecedented, integrated system of new institutional components, electronic circuits, software, hardware, and systematic information processes, enabling a flow market to emerge that moves across time zones with the sun, 24/7, year in year out. These flow markets are stable only for long enough to enable transactions to occur and they change as a result of the transactions they enable – as financial crises make abundantly clear.

The most recent financial crisis began to unravel in late 2007 and, at the time of writing, is still in process, especially in the Eurozone. Within banking circles it was clear by late 2007 that the sector was in trouble. Ironically, this came after a record year of profits for most banks. Steeling themselves for larger losses, banks began to exercise much more caution in relation to each other. Most specifically, they were now reluctant to lend to each other in the short-term money markets. The freezing up of money on the short-term money markets in the UK led to the downfall of Northern Rock.

Subsequently, in the US, Bear Stearns was encountering difficulties in raising monies on the short-term money markets. In a sense, it was a replay of the problems that beset Northern Rock a few months previously. In addition, it had been rocked by the failure of its Bear hedge fund in 2007. Commercial investors started to withdraw their monies from Bear Stearns: in ten days during March 2008, over $10 billion in cash was taken out of the bank (Tett, 2009: 255). It was clear that Bear Stearns was no longer viable as a bank. The Federal Reserve exerted heavy pressure on JPMorgan Chase to intervene and help Bear Stearns. JPMorgan Chase had suffered some losses, but these were tiny when compared to their competitors. Their caution in the property market – for which they had been castigated a few years before – was now proving prescient. JPMorgan purchased Bear Stearns for £250 million ($2 a share, against the $100 it had been trading at in the year before), which was backed with a $30 billion Fed guarantee against losses. This was seen as a very low price for Bear Stearns. This was shortly after renegotiated with the government, when more liabilities were spotted: in return for government guarantees the price was lifted to $10 a share.

The markets briefly rallied hearing this news; many saw this as a decisive move to prevent what they feared could have been a financial meltdown. Monies started to flow once more into the short-term money markets. In many ways this was reminiscent of the 1929 Wall Street Crash, where at various junctures the markets rallied and commentators proclaimed the crisis to be over (Galbraith, 1954). By April 2008 the IMF speculated that total losses could be in the region of £1,000 billion.

In September 2008 Freddie Mac and Fannie Mae, two large American mortgage providers, were in trouble. They were highly leveraged, lending out large multiples of loans against their asset base and were seriously undermined by defaults in the mortgage market. The US government, in effect, nationalized the two mortgage providers. At this juncture the banking sector was descending into crisis, with something akin to a domino effect breaking out.

It is widely agreed that the tipping point in the recent banking crash came when the US government decided not to bail out Lehman Brothers. As an iconic Wall Street bank, Lehman Brothers had been at the forefront of much of the lending that had taken place, with particularly aggressive positions in the sub-prime mortgages market. Resonant with Bear Stearns and Northern Rock, Lehman Brothers obtained much of its financing from the short-term money markets. It was struggling to raise funds and investors were withdrawing assets. Critically, Dick Fuld, its chairman, failed to seek early help for the bank from potential suitors. Events started to spiral out of control and other bankers simply lost trust in Lehman's balance sheet: in their estimation Lehman was under-stating their huge exposure defaults on super senior collateralized debt obligations (CDOs). Banks were unwilling to trade with Lehman Brothers, which, among other things, led the Fed to call a meeting about the future of Lehman Brothers. The fascinating feature of this meeting – attended by the Fed and all the major American banks and some European ones – was that Lehman Brothers were not actually invited! At the meeting the bankers divided into groups and went into breakout rooms to discuss options to save Lehman Brothers. The bankers rejected the idea, mooted by the American government, of forming a consortium to bail out the bank.

Barclays was interested in purchasing the bank, but, following much deliberation, was stymied by the British government, which feared, correctly as it transpired, that Barclays' financial position was insufficiently strong to mount a takeover. Discussions went on between Barclays Capital, the UK Financial Services Authority, and Hank Paulson, the US Treasury Secretary. Barclays Capital wanted to make the deal, but the Financial Services Authority were less keen and were wary of being railroaded into agreement. When Alistair Darling, the British Chancellor, told Paulson that the deal was off, Paulson told his colleagues that 'the British don't want to import our cancer' (Ross-Sorkin, 2009). Paulson was keen for 'closure' by 7 p.m. on the Sunday evening, as that is when the Asian stock markets opened. Hank Paulson decided to let Lehman Brothers fail. Having pressured JPMorgan Chase to subsume Bear Stearns and having bailed out Freddie Mae and Fannie Mac, he decided that he was not willing to countenance any further rescues and that an example of the consequences of moral hazard needed to be evident. The decision not to rescue Lehman Brothers was a dramatic one and it sent shockwaves not just through the financial community but also through the broader economy and political sphere. On 14 September 2008, Lehman Brothers went into bankruptcy. The world was reeling from shock that an iconic Wall Street institution was being allowed to fail. By the Monday morning, following the bankruptcy announcement, stock exchanges around the world had lost a stunning $600 billion in a two-day period.

As the global financial crisis demonstrates, in contemporary financial markets, knowledge systems and sensemaking devices make available unprecedented data streams processed by divisions of analysts, model builders, and strategists located on the trading floors of major banks that are liable to catastrophic outcomes from seemingly rational individual decisions. The market rests on a system of observation and projection that assembles dispersed and diverse activities, interpretations, and representations, which in turn orient and constrain the response of an audience in a cycle that has no finitude. The reality attended to is one of flux and flow, a constant becoming, as action is enacted on the basis of observational cues that this action will necessarily, reflexively, change, in a self-regarding system without end, one in which finitude does not exist. Of course, as we learned in the most dramatic way, with the unfolding of the global financial crisis, these markets are not self-regulating.

The mass of individual enactments change the nature of that which is being enacted in a constant process whereby a new market reality is in the process of becoming, in an endless fluidity. The process of reality constantly changing on the screen is composed of an infinite succession of data that is the market, a series of devices for managing space, in which the world is comprised of time zones rather than physical features. Global markets have their own time reckoning systems: dates and hours set for important economic announcements and for the release of periodically calculated economic indicators and data, structuring participants' aware-ness and anticipation, and anchoring market developments in national or regional economies' fundamental characteristics.

DEFINING GLOBALIZATION

For some theorists globalization means the financialization of everyday organizational life (Martin, 2002). Others see it in terms of the integration of deregulating markets and technology facilitated by telecommunications and transport innovations. Additionally, globalization has been seen in terms of the Americanization of the world (Ritzer, 1993) because many of the phenomena described as global are American: American products, designs, and politics dominate the global world – even when they are being manufactured by Mexican or Brazilian companies. The USA dominates this world; it has the only military capable of global power projection and its form of English is fast becoming the global norm. American consumption, especially of energy, drains natural resources from this world.

Check out the Companion Website www.sagepub.co.uk/ managingandorganizations3 for free access to an article by Karin Knorr-Cetina and Alex Preda (2007) if you want to learn more about how global financial markets are organized.

The USA is not only hugely globalized, but also massively indebted – with much of that debt held in Chinese and Japanese banks. The global world floats on a sea of oil and other energy resources that, according to some analysts, are at a tipping point in terms of exploitable reserves and existing price mechanisms. Future reserves will only be had at historically much higher prices. Thus, what is increasingly being globalized are North American values, products, force, and debt, and unsustainable modes of production and consumption.

Most global corporations are domiciled in relatively few countries. Firms from Japan and the USA dominate the list of Global 500 firms. There are twice as many US firms (nearly 200) as Japanese (about 100). Germany, the UK, and France each have nearly half as many as Japan, with numbers distributed around 40. After these few countries, most other countries hardly rate, with the exception of Switzerland, Italy, South Korea, and Canada, which each have about ten such firms, and there are a handful of firms from the remaining OECD countries as well as one or two from China, Taiwan, Venezuela, and some other industrialized economies (Bergesen and Sonnett, 2001).

To the extent that the world is becoming *economically* global, it is a world dominated by US, East and South-East Asian, Western European, and allied interests. Technological, economic, and cultural integration is developing within and between these three regions and is evident in the patterns of international trade and investment flows. Interfirm strategic alliances are heavily concentrated among companies from these countries.

International activities enable firms to enter new markets, exploit tech-nological and organizational advantages, as well as reduce business costs and risks, and achieve more economic integration of their activities.

Transnational or **multinational organizations** – the terms are often used inter-changeably – have significant control over both production and consumption

Those organizations known as **transnational** or **multinational organizations**, because they extend beyond national space in their routine activities, are able to exert control either through ownership and/or through the coordination and control of operations, as a result of other mechanisms, such as a multisubsidiary form based on capital interdependency (as we discussed in Chapter 14). The acronyms TNC (TransNational Corporation) or MNC (MultiNational Corporation) are sometimes used.

IMAGE 15.1 Coca-Cola, the most global brand

in more than one country. They dominate world trade. In principle, they have sufficient geographical flexibility to shift resources and operations between global locations. In practice it may be a bit more difficult. There is a plurality of transnational corporations, which neither dominate national industrial sectors in all markets nor operate without regard for more or less sovereign states.

The power of transnationals can easily be overestimated. Only a small number of transnational corporations are truly global, and not all transnational corporations are necessarily large, in conventional definitions of that term. Global patterns differ markedly according to the national origin of the firms. New supplies and sources of transnational corporations evolve as the world economy evolves, so that we now have emergent market transnational corporations in newly industrializing countries. Nonetheless, the commanding heights of the world economy remain centred on Europe, the USA, and Japan, even as China, India, Brazil, Russia, and South Africa enter the ranks as major outposts jostling for possession of some of these heights.

Why globalization? Scale, scope, and access to key resources

In *Scale and Scope*, Chandler (1990) argues that the evolution of the global corporation is the final stage in the transformation of industries in search of *economies of scale* in production, *economies of scope* in marketing and distribution, and national differences in the availability and *cost of resources*:

1   In many industries, *economies of scale* are such that volumes exceed the sales levels individual companies can achieve in all but the largest countries, forcing them to become international or perish. The minimum efficient level for capital-intensive plants is 80 to 90 per cent of capacity in contrast to labour-intensive industries. The costs and profits of capital-intensive industries are determined by plant utilization and throughput, rather than by the simple amount produced. Less capital-intensive industries are not as affected by scale economies.

2   Opportunities exist for *economies of scope* through worldwide communication and transportation networks. Trading companies handling the products of many companies can achieve greater volume and lower unit cost.

3   Cutting the *costs of resources* by gaining access to cheap resources is often assumed to be a reason for globalizing. With changes in technology and markets came requirements for access to new resources as lower factor costs. Cheap labour may be important, but not as much as one might think. It is misleading to assume that the search for cheaper labour in itself is the central driving force of the increasing internationalization of many industries. In most industries there are more important factors than labour costs, including access to markets, technology, and other resources, among which one may be human resources. Increasingly, industry requires more highly skilled labour, and the possession of relevant skills is more immediately important than the price of labour. A focus on globalization that sees it in terms of economies of scale and scope, or the search for cheap labour, or in terms of the business strategies of transnational corporations, is not necessarily wrong. But it is limited, as we will see.

WHAT DO YOU MEAN?

Why do firms become global?

Firms become global in search of three advantages, according to Dunning (1998):

1   *Ownership advantages*: Reusing existing production techniques and management knowledge to produce existing goods and services elsewhere other than the home country can provide a significant return on the original investments that produced them. Thus, firms seek to replicate what they already know and do somewhere else, under different conditions. Managing these conditions is the major challenge – things

such as language, regulatory and political environment, markets, and so on.

2   *Locational advantages*: Firms sometimes go global in search of particular local advantages where there is some particular asset to exploit – things such as low wages or government subsidies or tax breaks – or there is a particular asset they wish to acquire – such as a new market, raw material supply, or new knowledge.

3   *Internationalization advantages*: These arise where there is a realization that working through local agents with a franchise or licence arrangement leaves the firm open to risks

(Continued)

(Continued)

such as brand mismanagement, or competition from firms already embedded locally.

How do firms become global?

Firms become global in a number of separate ways, according to Bartlett and Ghoshal (1989):

1 Where they have undifferentiated markets, such as Microsoft, organizations will tend to be strongly centralized using local subsidiaries mostly as pipelines to the market – what Bartlett and Ghoshal (1989) call *global firms*. Local subsidiaries are not great places to make a career from; what happens there is relatively overlooked from the centre.

2 Where the local markets are highly differentiated and market know-how and responsiveness are important, then the organizational form tends to be a series of independent national companies – what they call *multinational firms*. In such firms, people's careers can flourish in the global company if they are noticed for making a significant difference locally; automobile companies tend to operate like this to accommodate local preferences for vehicles, such as the prevalence of four-cylinder diesel cars in France or six-cylinder cars in the USA or Australia.

3 Where firms spread out from a home base that comprised their key assets, but marketed globally, they would be *international firms*. Achieving a balance between centralization and decentralization is the issue here; from the career perspective of managers, being a home-country manager has distinct locational advantages.

4 Where firms are most thoroughly global they consist of what Morgan (2008: 1566) refers to as 'a network of subsidiaries, divisions and central functions in which flows of information could be horizontal, not just vertical, allowing ideas to flow in all directions', which are true *transnational* firms. Hedlund (1986) characterizes these as having a heterarchic rather than hierarchic organizational form. From the point of view of a person making a career, these look like the ideal organizations to join because innovation and ability in one part of the heterarchy can be noticed more easily in other parts. Moreover, there are opportunities for advancement through the creation of internally competitive markets within the transnational firm.

Do different national firms become global in different ways and does this have implications for careers?

The characteristic imprinting of the national business system on the firm affects the way that it internationalizes, as Whitley (1999) has argued. For instance, Japanese firms tend to be highly centralized when they move overseas, using Japanese top management teams and Japanese supply chain partners, relying only on local labour. Their investment strategies are long term as they have strong bank financing of their operations; thus they build for the long term using the systems that work well in Japan. Careers by foreign nationals in such firms will face the barrier of their not being Japanese, which will limit their occupational mobility. Other countries, such as British transnationals, where stock market pressures for fast returns are far greater, expect subsidiaries to be profitable more quickly. Careers built in these subsidiaries by foreign nationals who achieve high leverage of their asset base as managers can be much more competitive because talent gets recognized and rewarded more easily.

Characteristics of globalization

Globalization has a technical core, which is organized in terms of flows of inputs, their distribution globally, transformation, and outputs, organized through global supply chains. These, in turn, are embedded in technological and logistical systems, which, in turn, are coupled with financial and governance systems. The key actors, without doubt, are transnational firms, whose ability to move facilities and resources globally sets in play the dynamics flows through global circuits, at the core of which is a production complex, incorporating material inputs, transformation processes, distribution networks, and channels to market for the consumption of goods.

Each of these is reciprocally interconnected, with feedback loops. Supporting the core are technological and logistical systems, which in turn are contained within a financial system and a governance system of regulation, coordination, and control (see Figure 15.1 on page 580). Financial systems, as the example with which we began this chapter indicates, are extremely important: they control the supply and value of the underlying key commodity, which of course is capital.

Circuits of global production have an impact in four ways:

1 *On the global relations between states*, as we see states flourish as a result of globalization, such as China and India in recent times. New opportunities for managers from, and within, these countries arise, with all the challenges of international placements for HRM (Brewster et al., 2007; Sparrow et al., 2004).

2 *On issues of sustainability*, as places such as China and India industrialize on the back of a fossil fuel industry that is ecologically most damaging. The levels of pollution in the Pearl River Delta, for instance, which is China's main export route, are absolutely dreadful. Managers may manage costs by outsourcing or setting up a supply chain – but they could end up having to manage damage that is far more than bargained for when they made their initial assessment of the value proposition of an outsourcing or supply chain partner.

3 *On people's conceptions of who they are*: This reaches into societies and enables people to migrate and move from one society to another – the millions of 'guest workers' in the Middle East oil-rich countries of the Gulf, for instance – or the people who become illegal migrants from Africa and Asia in search of a better life, so it has a considerable impact on changing conceptions of personal identity. People only develop a sense of self in relation to others. For most of human history, these others were framed by what was available at the local, often village, level. Today, even the most remote villager can see themselves in the mirror that the media project into their communities. Managers who employ such people may have to manage the contradictions that occur when the expectations of global business and local culture collide.

4 *On the multicultural diversity of organizations and communities*: In almost any of the world's great cities today there are people working with each other, competing with each other, and playing with each other, whose ancestors come from villages all over the globe. Multicultural society is normal. Managers today have to be able to manage complex differentiated workforces with sensitivity and skill.

FIGURE 15.1
Global flows, systems, and effects

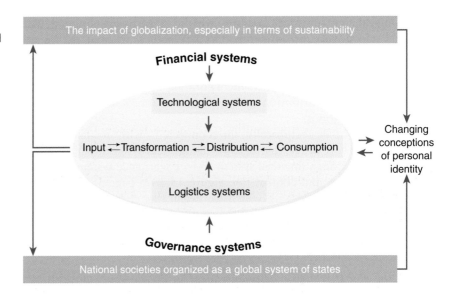

Transnational corporations often get a bad press for their subcontracting practices in the Third World. For instance, writers such as Naomi Klein are extremely critical of the role that transnationals play in the developing world. Her argument is that transnationals behave irresponsibly by employing subcontractors who pay low wages, have poor working conditions, and potentially abusive environments (Klein, 2001). She singles out the famous companies whose brands are known the world over.

In a campaign by Oxfam – the non-governmental organization – Nike has been taken to task over these issues. One thing that such campaigning activity has delivered is assurance from Nike that such concerns have been addressed, which for many is a contestable point. On balance, it is fair to say that transnational organizations may be positive agents of change. It is clear that they have the potential to create stable, long-term jobs with decent pay and conditions. Thus, potentially, they deliver better jobs and better wages in many economies. In addition, they set standards that local industry has to aspire to in both labour and industry practice.

Those transnationals that do not meet global standards can expect to be subject to campaigns throughout the Western world. Their good name represents their reputational capital. If there really were 'no logos', as Naomi Klein advocates, it would be much harder to police standards, because without brand names, no reputations would suffer. There would be no brand differentia offering opportunities for discrimination between the choice of one T-shirt or another. We would expect that in such a situation, price signals would be even more sovereign and would exercise still stronger downward pressure on local wages and conditions in the Third World. Fair logos rather than no logos might be better policy.

Subcontracted manufacturing jobs also create higher export earnings domestically, which potentially enhance the tax base of less developed national governments. We say 'potentially' because often these companies are quite sophisticated in moving tax losses around their global operations and using the pricing of internally traded goods to minimize liabilities where they will attract the highest regimes of tax – something referred to as transfer pricing.

Global flows of finance, knowledge, people, and politics

Globalization of production, distribution, and consumption flows through many circuits and networks linking the transit of material and non-material phenomena (such as services) in relationally patterned ways. There are many linkages and feedback loops (Hudson, 2004), as well as a few key nodes in the boardrooms of Tokyo, New York, London, and a few other centres.

The key agencies in these flows, as well as transnational firms, are states, global institutions such as the United Nations (UN), the International Labor Organization (ILO), the World Bank, the IMF, and the G8 – which frame the institutional rules of the global economy, which are largely neo-economically liberal – and international non-governmental organizations such as Greenpeace or Human Rights International, as well as civil society organizations (CSOs) such as the various anti-globalization movements.

These organizations create circuits and networks that are always in various stages of flux; shifting hither and thither in the search for alliances and pathways that suit their interests. They traverse varieties of capitalism in a global economy where to speak of capitalism per se is far too abstracted (Hall and Sostike, 2001). The boards of the transnational firms in the few really global cities seek to control the key assets of capital, technology, knowledge, labour skills, natural resources, and consumer markets.

Transnational organizations often have greater range and resources than some of the national states over whose territories their business interests run. There are exceptions, including those states that exercise a monopoly or oligopoly control over a key resource base, such as the OPEC states, or are strongly opposed to liberal economic governance, such as Russia or Venezuela, with their respective oil industries.

Transnational organizations are also flexible: at best, in terms of flexibility, they are private equity; if moderately flexible, they only have to account to shareholders in terms of a bottom line; if slightly less flexible, they may be accountable to a wider range of stakeholders on a wider range of measures, such as 'triple bottom-line' accounting for profits, people, and nature.

These stakeholders can sometimes include states and other interested parties such as financial institutions, unions, NGOs, and CSOs. Sometimes, in one arena the same firms, unions, states, NGOs, and CSOs may be collaborating, while they are competing ruthlessly in another arena.

Globalization is a multiplicity of processes, not a state of existence

We live in a globalizing rather than globalized world. Dicken (2007: 8), the foremost geographer of globalization, suggests that there is an interpenetration of four parallel processes creating globalization:

1   *Localizing processes*: These are where geographically concentrated activities with varying degrees of functional integration occur, playing a key role in the global economy. Key ports such as Rotterdam, Singapore, and Hong Kong or airports such as Heathrow and Frankfurt would be obvious examples.

2   *Internationalizing processes*: These are where there is a simple spread of economic activities across national borders but with low levels of functional integration. The *maquiladora* plants of Monterrey, in northern Mexico, which use cheap land and labour to service goods or produce components and goods for the US economy, would be a case in point. For instance, GE has a plant that services all of its North American radiological equipment there.

3   *Globalizing processes*: These are characterized by both an extensive geographical spread and a high degree of functional integration. The global auto industry would be a case in point, where new models may come from any of a number of countries, despite that we might think of them as 'national' cars. German cars, which many people prefer because of the perceived quality of German workmanship, might come from Brazil, the USA, South Africa, or the Czech Republic, for instance.

4   *Regionalizing processes*: These are characterized by globalizing processes that take place at a regionally supranational scale such as the EU or the European Free Trade Association, or other similar common markets.

Corporations sometimes have considerable potential to shape policy within nation-states. In countries that are competing with one another for foreign direct investment from these global entities, then, in a process more akin to a beauty contest than any economic planning model, less developed nations will sometimes compete against each other in terms of tax incentives, grants, and other inducements to attract firms to their country. Within countries, regional policies operate to try and bring investment to particular regions.

Corporations are not entirely footloose and fancy-free: often they are deeply embedded within specific locales, perhaps because of a specific infrastructure, suppliers, or university research centres. However, there are a lot more firms than the 193 countries in the world. UNCTAD (United Nations Centre on Transnational Corporations) estimates that there are 60,000 transnational corporations globally (UNCTAD, 2004). Because states are spatially fixed, they are immobile compared with firms, and so their governments have to struggle with the policy implications of globalization; they cannot decamp or disengage.

Global financial systems

A liberalization of the financial system took place in the 1980s, which accelerated through to 2008 when the global financial crisis stopped it in its tracks. This liberalization occurred together with the digital revolution in IT. The rapid spread of IT systems linked markets globally so that differentials in interest rates between states could lead to rapid, almost instant, transfers and movement of large volumes of capital, sometimes with speculative effect, as currency traders take a punt on short-term futures markets for the currency in question.

New financial instruments, such as junk bonds, leveraged buyouts, and currency speculation, became *de rigeur* as finance capital took on a hyper-real quality. One consequence of the widespread financialization that ensued, Harvey (1992: 194) suggests, was that the financial system achieved an unprecedented degree of autonomy from real production, becoming dominated by an economy of signs representing capital flows rather than an economy of things.

The global integration of financial markets collapses time differences, creating instantaneous financial transactions in loans, securities, and other innovative financial instruments while the deregulation and internationalization of financial markets creates a new competitive spatial environment (Harvey, 1992: 161). Globally integrated financial markets increase the speed and accuracy of information flows and the rapidity and directness of transactions.

The increasing coordination of the world's financial system emerged to some degree at the expense of the power of nation-states' public sector managers in reserve banks to control capital flows and hence fiscal and monetary policy. Instantaneous financial trading means that shocks felt in one market are communicated immediately around the world's markets, as we saw with the example of Chinese Whispers. The implementation of transfer taxes to discourage short-term capital flights has been suggested; however, the international economic polity has so far resisted these efforts (http://www.ceedweb.org/iirp/).

Global strategic alliances

Major mechanisms of global integration are collaborations and strategic **alliances**. The major strategic objectives of alliances are maximizing value, enhancing learning, protecting core competencies, and maintaining flexibility. 'The more a company becomes globalized, the more it is likely to lose its own identity within a tangle of companies, alliances and markets', suggests Petrella (1996: 76). Particularly in industries where there is a dominant worldwide market leader, strategic alliances and networks allow coalitions of smaller partners to compete against the leading companies rather than each other in several ways:

Alliances are essentially a strategic device connecting different organizations in a network or web that includes many transacting parties. Yoshino and Rangan (1995: 17) define alliances as 'cooperation between two or more independent firms involving shared control and continuing contributions by all partners'.

1   Strategic alliances help transfer technology across borders. Access to new markets is facilitated by using the complementary resources of local firms, including distribution channels, and product range extensions (recall the example of Cisco Systems from Chapter 14).

2 Alliances allow partners to leverage their specific capabilities and save costs of duplication (see also pp. 543–549). All other activities can be outsourced either through alliances or subcontracting.

3 Another way of looking at virtual companies, alliances, and joint ventures is as the outsourcing of risk, allowing organizations at arm's length from the parent companies to take risks more freely, something that the parent organizations wish to avoid.

Strategic alliances are a way of focusing investments, efforts, and attention only on those tasks that a company does well in its **value chain**. Only when the created value is higher than the cost of creating it will an organization be making a profit. Those activities and practices that are core to profit making can be differentiated from those that are secondary, such as corporate governance or human resource management.

The value chain core will differ from industry to industry. Managers can analyse the value chain in their organization and outsource or procure elsewhere those elements that are not contributing positively to profitability, a process referred to as deconstruction or disintermediation of the value chain. When they do this they establish what is often referred to as a supply chain, where rather than being created internally value is created through a network of interorganizational relations. Often, this process of deconstruction and disintermediation can unwittingly destroy subtly embedded social capital, competencies, and value that are not immediately apparent or amenable to simplistic analysis. Around half of all cross-border strategic alliances terminate within seven years. Often, where one or other of the partners purchases the alliance, then its termination does not necessarily mean failure – but it does suggest that management at a distance might tax managerial capabilities.

One strategy that firms that are deeply involved in alliance relations follow is to use formalization as a means to make sense of their partners, the interorganizational relationships in which they are engaged, and the contexts in which these are embedded. Formalizing relations helps to (a) focus participants' attention; (b) provoke articulation, deliberation, and reflection; (c) instigate and maintain interaction; and (d) reduce judgement errors and individual biases, and diminish the incompleteness and inconsistency of cognitive representations.

Mergers and acquisitions

Some firms globalize by merging with or acquiring others, often in other countries. The consulting company PricewaterhouseCoopers concludes that about 70 per cent of mergers and acquisitions are destined to fail and destroy value rather than make it (Feldman and Spratt, 1999). Being big and being global is no surefire success recipe, despite whatever the financial institutions – whose profits come from brokering these deals – might say. Going global seems to open firms to challenges and risks rather than global dominance and easy profits. Interfirm alliance through

---

The **value chain** is a concept for decomposing an organization into its component activities. Each activity can be analysed with regard to the value that it adds to the final product or service, which can be measured in terms of what the customer is prepared to pay for it, and the cost entailed in producing profit.

Check out the Companion Website www.sagepub.co.uk/ managingandorganizations3 for free access to an article by Paul W. L. Vlaar, Frans A. J. Van den Bosch, and Henk W. Volberda (2006) if you want to learn more about how managers involved in interorganizational relations often use formalization to try and make sense of their foreign partners' social and embedded contexts.

merger and acquisition is risky because it carries the cost of strategic and organizational complexity. As we have seen in Chapter 6, managing organization culture is not straightforward, and this is especially the case where the organization is the result of a merger between two or more quite distinct cultures.

Different institutional systems

Transnational activity is not easily managed precisely because it crosses the borders of so many institutional systems. Of particular importance are the sector-specific and national institutional features of the home and host countries. For manufacturing firms, what is crucial are the ways in which the firm is embedded in the home country and host country and how this shapes the (re)organization of tasks and work systems. As Geppert and Matten (2006) argue, the important question is how key actors – especially the top management team – shape the interaction of these institutional pressures and, hence, manufacturing approaches, location choices, and work system designs. Typically, they argue, these managers apply a 'cherry-picking' strategy where they selectively use elements of the way in which work is normally shaped by the host-country business system. It is not easy to import wholesale the manufacturing strategies of MNCs originating from highly coordinated business systems, because these are highly context specific and difficult (if not impossible) to transfer elsewhere. For instance, Japanese just-in-time manufacturing does not work very well in cities, such as Bangkok, where the traffic is gridlocked much of the time.

Check out the Companion Website www.sagepub.co.uk/ managingandorganizations3 for free access to two articles that Mike Geppert was involved in writing, one with Karen Williams (2003) and another with Dirk Matten (2006), if you want to learn more about how multinationals translate their operating systems from one country to another.

UK and US companies are stock price oriented, whereas, in contrast, Japanese, Dutch, and Swiss companies are less sensitive to stock prices. Indeed, there has been much debate on the role that the city and financial institutions play in Anglo-American organizations. Critics such as Hutton (1995) argue that the primacy of finance creates an atmosphere in which a short-term orientation prevails, as companies aim to satisfy shareholders, who can easily sell their stock. He contends that this stifles innovation and makes for capricious organizations. In contrast, he notes that ownership of German and Japanese companies, with stable and major bank investments, enables them to plan for the medium and long term.

National governments and transnational companies have different interests

The interests that transnational organization's managers have to advance often mean that they cannot owe loyalty to their national governments as they seek to advance company value. We can characterize the sometimes vexed relations between government and transnational managers by showing how what each wants clearly differs.

Transnationals' managers:

- Want unrestricted access to resources and markets throughout the world.

- Seek freedom to integrate manufacturing with other operations across national boundaries.

- Demand an unimpeded right to try to coordinate and control all aspects of the company on a worldwide basis.

- Endeavour to maximize shareholder value and minimize taxes.

- Minimize taxes by establishing corporate headquarters in low-tax regimes such as the Dutch Antilles or the Cayman Islands.

- Lobby for light regulatory frameworks and minimal government expenditures, so less tax is required.

- Have a bottom line to which they can reduce costs and benefits unambiguously.

- Think of how to achieve competitiveness globally without barriers.

- Want governments to offer grants and subsidies for local investment.

- Expect governments to cover the costs of basic infrastructure, such as funding of basic and high-risk research, universities, and vocational training systems; promotion and funding of the dissemination of scientific and technical information and technology transfer; as well as ensuring economic and physical security and a communications infrastructure, such as up-to-date and high-speed international rail links.

- Seek tax incentives for investment in industrial R&D and technological innovations, as well as guarantees that national enterprises from the given country have a stable home base.

- Expect privileged access to the domestic market via public contracts (defence, telecommunications, health, transport, education, and social services).

- Want appropriate industrial policies, particularly for those in the high-technology strategic sectors (defence, telecommunications, and data processing).

- Talk in terms of capital mobility and its logic. If the local state does not provide the required sweeteners, mobile capitalism will simply exit the scene and set up where the benefits sought can be ensured.

- Have to abide by the rules of the states in which they invest.

Governments:

- Have to manage changing definitions of what constitute 'citizenship rights', such as taxpayer-funded provisions of big-ticket items like health and education, or else they have to manage to persuade people who once saw themselves primarily as citizens to become consumers in markets that transnational corporations are only too keen to enter.

- Want external sources of investment, technology, and knowledge that transnationals can supply to create global competitiveness within the national economy.

- Apply investment regulations that define specific levels of local content, technology transfer, and a variety of other conditions in an effort to make transnational companies increase the extent of their local activities.

- Seek to reduce costs by downsizing, which often produces new commercial opportunities in fields such as defence contracting and telecommunications.

- Practice severe efficiency drives and privatization but still remain in charge of essential parts of their sovereignty, such as legislation and the formation of national economic policy.

The rationalities of government and commerce differ greatly. Neither home base nor host-country governments necessarily share interests with the transnational organizations that straddle them. It might be remarked that in business there are no allies, only interests.

COMPETITIVE ADVANTAGE

Innovation drives competitive advantage

Globalization is driven by the strategic responses of firms as they exploit market opportunities and adapt to changes in their technological and institutional environment, and attempt to steer these changes to their advantage. The most important competitive force in the global economy is the capacity for innovation, a thesis powerfully illustrated by Porter (1990) in *The Competitive Advantage of Nations*.

Porter correlates the advance of knowledge, achievement in innovation, and national competitive advantage. In his search for a new paradigm of national **competitive advantage**, Porter starts from the premise that competition is dynamic and evolving, whereas traditional thinking had a static view of cost efficiency due to factor or scale advantages. But static efficiency is always being overcome by the rate of progress in the change in products, marketing, new production processes, and new markets.

The crucial issue for firms, and nations, is how they 'improve the quality of the factors, raise the productivity with which they are utilized, and create new ones' (Porter, 1990: 21). The capacity to innovate successfully on a worldwide basis becomes the key competency of leading international companies. It frequently leads to substantive injustices as employees' knowledge in one part of the world is used to deliver cheaper and more efficient manufacturing in another part of the world, and then their jobs being scrapped (Clegg, 1999).

Check out the Companion Website www.sagepub.co.uk/managingandorganizations3 for free access to an article by Glenn Morgan and Peer Hull Kristensen (2006) if you want to learn more about how multinational – or transnational – companies behave.

Competitive advantage is gained by firms changing the constraints within which they and their competitors operate.

Intellectual property is information that derives its intrinsic value from creative ideas. It is also information with a commercial value that can be realized through its sale on the market.

Market imperfections and high transaction costs provide an incentive for firms to internalize firm-specific knowledge and expertise. In addition, another incentive is to protect **intellectual property** rights within the firm.

Intellectual property rights are bestowed on owners of ideas, inventions, and creative expression that have the status of property. Like tangible property, they give owners the right to exclude others from access to or use of their property. What protects intellectual property rights are national laws centred on specific legislative spaces and environments. Intellectual property rights are probably most easily understood through the example of music. As we saw in Chapter 14, with the case study, once music flows through the Internet in an immediate digital way, the central issue becomes how it is that corporations are able to retain their central nodal point in its distribution

IMAGE 15.2   Irn Bru – the drink that made it in Scotland but not elsewhere

and channel profit from the transactions. The answer appears to be, with difficulty. Although digitalization drives globalization, making intellectual property easily available anywhere in the world, national laws limit it – but are hard to enforce in any way other than as the occasional example.

It can sometimes be the case that competitive advantage is purely local, for local reasons. Take the field of soft drinks, for example. Coca-Cola is the undisputed world brand but in certain markets it has strong local competition that enjoys a competitive advantage that might not be found elsewhere. For instance, there are several brands of 'Muslim' Cola available in certain markets: the Mecca brand in France (and elsewhere in Europe) and Quibla-Cola, launched in the Muslim community in the UK. These drinks' intrinsic appeal is that they are not US brands. Of course, it is not just in the fields of religious identity and global politics that specific local brands may prosper without making it big globally: in Scotland one of the best-selling soft drinks is a brand that many of our non-Scottish readers may not have heard of, let alone know how to pronounce – Irn Bru. You can even buy it from dispensers specifically devoted to it (see Image 15.2 on page 588).

Local clusters in a globalizing world

A paradoxical consequence of increasing globalization is the concentration of clusters of world-class expertise in specialist industries in different local economies around the world. The significant local dimension of the globalization phenomenon consists of regional economies built upon inter-linked networks of relations among firms, universities, and other institutions in their local environment (see Storper and Scott, 1993). Early specialization is reinforced by the growth of similar firms and institutions to create highly competitive industrial and service clusters.

We can explain the rationale for the local concentration of specialist industry in terms of the advantages of being in the same location as similar firms, specialized suppliers, and contractors, as well as knowledgeable customers (see also pp. 549–550). In addition, these locations tend to provide a good technological infrastructure and specialist research institutions, as well as a highly skilled labour force, where specialization within firms enables extensive outsourcing (vertical disintegration) and encourages similar new firms to be set up in the location (horizontal disintegration). For instance, Lash and Urry (1994) discuss the importance of local concentration in the making of movies, and a number of UK authors have described the networks and clusters associated with 'Motorsport Valley', a small area north of London that accounts for most of the automotive innovation associated with Formula 1 motor racing (Tallman et al., 2004).

Local geographic concentrations of three broad groups of industrial and service activities have been noted:

1 Highly competitive traditional, labour-intensive industries, which are highly concentrated, including textiles and clothing in Italy.
2 High-technology industries that often cluster around new activities, such as biotechnology in San Francisco, semiconductors in Silicon

Valley, scientific instruments in Cambridge (UK), and musical instruments in Hamamatsu (Japan).

3   Services, notably financial and business services, such as advertising, films, fashion design, and R&D activities, concentrated in a few big global cities such as Los Angeles, Tokyo, London, Paris, Sydney, and Shanghai.

Globalization increases the competitiveness of these local economies by attracting international firms with their own specific advantages and enhancing established sourcing and supply relations. Local firms individually may respond to heightened competition through improving their innovative performance. Innovation may be extended through developing greater interactions between firms, suppliers, users, production support facilities, and educational and other institutions in local innovation systems.

Local firms, particularly if they are highly specialized, will cooperate with international firms seeking complementary resources in the specialized assets of small firms. Some writers, following Robertson (1992), such as Clarke and Clegg (1998), Helvacioglu (2000), and Ritzer (2004), have referred to the phenomenon of the interpenetration of the global in the local, and vice versa, as 'glocalization'. However, it is not only in areas of straightforward global business, such as manufacturing, that locality can become a source of competitive advantage; it can also be built from marginalized and stigmatized local cultures. Think of hip-hop, now the dominant popular music trend globally. It emerged from the ghetto culture of alienated black youth in the big cities of the USA.

WHO AND WHAT ARE THE GLOBALIZERS?

For global actions there have to be global ideas that travel and are translated widely. Over the last 25 years there has been an emergence of a powerful management ideas industry which has successfully packaged, communicated, and sold discontinuous innovation as a cultural ideal and a desirable good (Townley, 2000a; 2000b). A management ideas industry has been fuelled by the rise of business schools, especially through the provision of MBA degrees, the growth in management consultancies, and the emergence of self-styled management gurus. Taken together, this amounts to an actor network that has successfully packaged and commoditized managerial initiatives. These models of 'best practice' have been disseminated throughout the organizational world. These create blueprints of what organizations 'should' look like and what managers 'should' do. Collectively the key players of the management ideas industry have helped produce management fashions.

Large IT firms

The major actors in the management ideas industry have been the large IT companies, such as SAP and Cap Gemini. The changes in IT have been one of the major enabling factors behind globalization. IT firms have played an important role in the development of the management ideas industry. Recent initiatives such as enterprise resource planning and knowledge management rely very heavily on IT practices. Kipping (2002) has argued that consultancies go through waves of development. According to his analysis, large IT firms are riding the most recent wave and are becoming the dominant players in the consulting industry. We may think of them as the 'fifth column' of the management ideas industry: they penetrate businesses that need the technical capabilities that IT brings, but their entry becomes a beachhead for sustained attack by management ideas. The first of these are usually introduced by management consultants, often called in to try and make the IT systems that millions have been expended on work better, to live up to expectations.

Management gurus

The emergence of a global management project is in part a phenomenon spread through hugely influential 'guru' books. There is now a huge commercial market in popular management books and a circuit of celebrity for those who write them. They are the gurus of the modern age, the 'management gurus'. Earlier in this book we introduced Tom Peters. He is the most celebrated and, at the same time, infamous of the management gurus. Gurus are generally self-styled and known for their image and rhetoric intensity. Producing airport lounge bestsellers and conducting world lecture tours, gurus hawk their homespun nostrums throughout the corporate world.

Analysts of gurus have argued – in a McLuhan (1964) fashion – that the medium is the message: evangelical-style exhortations to change accompanied by convincing stories and snappy sound bites characterize the genre. The books follow a similar vein and, as we suggested earlier, are often taken to task for their theoretical and methodological failings, which is, perhaps, to miss the point. Even more managers are likely to listen to a guru presentation or perhaps read a guru book than are likely to attend business school (Clegg and Palmer, 1996).

Many of the gurus have enjoyed glittering corporate careers and their ideas on management are lent credibility by this corporate experience – such texts have elsewhere been characterized as 'karaoke texts', in a reference to their 'I did it my way' quality (Clegg and Palmer, 1996). Often, key texts will anchor key management consultancy products.

Management consultancy

Large-scale management consultancy has grown exponentially and consultants have become major actors in the creation and transmission of management ideas. Management consultants simultaneously instil a sense of security and anxiety in their clients: security, because they imbue managers with a sense of certainty and control over the future or whatever organizational problem it is that the consulting is concerned with; anxiety, because the managers are in a sense emasculated – unable to manage without the guidance of consultants (Sturdy, 2006).

While many US consultancies had been in existence for much of the last century – coming out of the systematic management movement of Taylor's day – it is over the last 20 years or so that demand for their services has boomed. Organizations such as McKinsey and the Boston Consulting Group have become high-status brands in their own right. Other consultancies emerged out of the large accountancy partnerships. Uniquely placed as the auditors to large firms, most major accountancy firms commercialized to the extent that their consultancy operations became at least as important as the core auditing business, which was notably the case with Arthur Andersen and its most infamous client, Enron.

The role of the large accounting firms is pivotal to understanding the story of the rise of consultancies. By the mid-1980s the market for financial audit was mature and had stagnated. In any case, outside of a few accounting firms in a few geographical locations, competition between these firms was frowned upon and for the most part regarded as being somewhat aggressive and ungentlemanly. What the large accounting firms possessed was a monopoly over the provision of audits to large firms. The 'full professional jurisdiction' (Abbott, 1988) was protected by law. The large accounting firms developed a number of capabilities, one of which was the ability to cultivate and sustain long-term relationships with clients. These connections were often cemented by their own accountants going to work in client firms after a number of years with the accounting partnership. Accounting partnerships also possessed highly sophisticated means of charging for audits and managing large-scale interventions in organizations.

The shifting context of accounting firms in the 1980s allowed them to diversify outside of audit activities, though their clients were generally those that they also sold audit services to. Audit became the wedge that opened the corporate door to the on-selling of additional services. Hanlon (1994) has demonstrated the way in which the large accounting firms commercialized themselves – pursuing capital accumulation strategies; also Greenwood et al. (1999) have written extensively on the unique characteristics of accounting firms that allowed them to globalize so successfully.

Power (1999) has argued that we increasingly live in an audit society, one in which the principles of verification and calculability underpin practices. During this time accountants and management consultants have risen to powerful positions within civil society. In the UK, for instance, large accounting firms played an important role in drafting privatization and private finance initiatives. They were simultaneously to profit from the implementation of such policies. Accountants and management consultants now often carry out government work that was once the sole preserve of mandarins.

What marks out a mandarin from a management consultant or an accountant is a different type of intellectual capital: the mandarin was most likely to be a classicist, schooled in a classical discipline, educated at a socially elite university, and drawn from a wealthy family background. The moral sentiments of the knowledge born by a management consultant are more technocratic and democratic, and are likely to be premised on less concern with social origins, and education in a business school, usually in an MBA.

Management education

Evolution of management education   Management education has long been a contested terrain: indeed, it could be argued that it has been such since the inception of its current form in the early twentieth century in the USA. Relatively recent signs of this contestation are evident in two influential reports on management education that were released in 1959: the Carnegie Report and the Ford Report. A significant response to these reports was the deployment of the American Assembly of Collegiate Schools of Business (AACSB) in 1961 as the standards body for masters-level graduate education. As was reported shortly thereafter (Oberg, 1963), among the chief criticisms made in these reports were that education standards were low, grading too easy, and the quality of research conducted in business schools substandard. It was also claimed that business curricula did not prepare students properly for work: there was too much narrow vocationalism in a curriculum with an insufficient number of subjects in the humanities, liberal arts, mathematics, statistics, languages, and the natural and social sciences (Oberg, 1963).

 WHAT'S THE POINT?

What's the point of management education?

At the same time that the American system was being challenged to make management education better quality and broader in content, it was being exported as an exemplar around the world. Indeed, the post-war phenomenon of the Americanization of management education on a global scale was instigated initially by the American involvement in the reconstruction of a devastated Europe. In the UK, this was later bolstered by the take-up of the 1963 Robbins Report, which not only created significant expansion of the higher education sector, but also resulted in the formation of the London Business School and the Manchester Business School, as 'national' business schools.

The longer term effects of this expansionism are manifest most particularly in the global adoption of the MBA as the model for the advanced education of managers. However, by the 1970s the Carnegie Commission reported that business schools were characterized by 'a lack of relevance in the topics under research, overly quantitative course content, and a lack of preparation for entrepreneurial careers' (Friga et al., 2003: 235). Instead of going back to the earlier idea of

broadening the curriculum to include non-vocationally specific subjects, the response was to 'include more organizational behaviour and teamwork topics' (Friga et al., 2003).

Despite this, another report in 1998 suggested that 'the major weaknesses of baccalaureate graduates from business schools center around communication skill' (Porter and McKibbin, 1998: 103). Further, it argued that the corporate sector gives business school graduates relatively low ratings in terms of their leadership and interpersonal skills (Porter and McKibbin, 1998). Management education, they argue, should:

- Be relevant to the needs of business.
- Develop leadership skills.
- Develop good communication skills.

To which we would add the importance of developing a substantive knowledge of the key topics covered in this book, especially the relation of *managing* to *management*, of actually knowing about the practice of management and not just its prescribed theory. The reason we recommend this is because what managers do rarely corresponds to what they are prescribed to do in (most of the other) textbooks.

Management education has penetrated the Anglo-American university system to a considerable degree. Sturdy (2006) reports that '25% of US university students currently major in business or management and in the UK, 30% of undergraduates study some management'. Equally, fast-emerging economies such as China and India have embraced the MBA with great enthusiasm. A small number of business school MBAs are rich in symbolic capital, while some such as Harvard enjoy iconic status. Thus, from being, once upon a time, the province of an elite cadre of American business aspirants, the MBA is now offered in ever-increasing volumes across the world, fast overshadowing the traditional undergraduate domains of academic endeavour.

In one sense, the growth of the MBA may be taken as a case in point of what some critical scholars have seen as the neo-colonial domination of an American educational model on a global scale (Miller and O'Leary, 2002). Hence, the cultural logic of the MBA, from its beginning in the neo-classical architecture and green pastures of Harvard University, has developed in the latter part of the twentieth century to become the model of management education. As such it is the principal vehicle for the normalization of disciplined expectations in the managers of tomorrow, while offering practical opportunities for the consultants of today to enrol others who will soon be influential to their ideas and to expound them in settings that proffer great legitimacy and legitimation. The interconnections become almost seamless; the managers in training are normalized into the idea that consultancy is a solution provider; the consultancies gain exposure to attract the brightest and the best from the top MBAs. The MBA-speak of PowerPoint slides and spreadsheets prepare the student of today for the consulting and management presentations of tomorrow. Thus, the MBA acts as a rationalizing device as well as a means of career advancement for individual students.

Management education, theory, and practice   One of the fascinating features of the MBA is its link with management practice. The promissory note of the MBA is to deliver more highly paid jobs to students. While there are a host of distance and part-time programmes available, the costs of participating in a full-time programme are considerable. Students have to be fairly sure that their investment will be worthwhile by providing them with a degree of fluency in the cultural capital of managerialism: of course, whether being able to be a smooth conversationalist in a particular rhetoric makes better managers or not is an open question. What it certainly does do is to allow them to communicate with other managers in a global management. As Victorian administrators were schooled in studies of long-dead languages and the histories of classical civilizations, the managerial classes of today study a syllabus that is remarkably uniform in its content. The MBA curriculum and skills are fast becoming the Latin of the modern world, with modern accounting the grammar, spreading to become a global institutional practice, through the ubiquity of MBA and professional management education, as Yong Suk Jang (2005) argues.

The MBA has been thought of as the solution to the problem of qualifying managers (du Gay and Salaman, 1992; Watson, 2004). Managers would not be people with skills merely learnt on the job but they would have been prepared, vocationally, beforehand. They would be well- prepared receptacles for the received forms of calculation with which, globally, management makes its ready reckoning.

From within business schools, however, there have been rumblings of disquiet about the MBA. Almost exactly a hundred years after its inception in the USA, the concept of the MBA has, as it were, swapped sides: it is now critically perceived as part of the problem rather than the solution. Some authors regard the MBA as an increasingly irrelevant model based on assumptions intrinsic to a less flexible age than today. Henry Mintzberg's 'hard look at the soft practice of managing and management development' (2004; see also Bennis and O'Toole, 2005) revealed in a popular tone what other scholars such as Parker and Jary (1995) and Sturdy and Yiannis (2000) theorized more critically earlier: the concept of the MBA is producing neither an educated workforce nor good managers.

That the MBA should have talismanic and iconic status might seem surprising when one contrasts the market reality with the conclusions drawn by significant figures in the field such as Jeffrey Pfeffer, who suggest that, in practice, 'there is scant evidence that the MBA credential, particularly from non-elite schools, or the grades earned in business courses – a measure of the mastery of the material – are related to either salary or the attainment of higher level positions in organizations' (Pfeffer and Fong, 2002: 92). It would seem that the cultural potency of the MBA is stronger than the realities of its effects or the vigour of its critique.

Problems with management education   Mintzberg makes a clear distinction between the practice of management and what the MBA produces (Mintzberg, 2004). His point is that (North American) MBA education is focused on an outmoded model of disciplinary business functions, analysis, and technique, rather than on the practice of administering.

There is a paradox here: his brief review of the series of crises that management education has faced over the years stands in stark contrast to the overwhelming international success of management education. In some English-speaking universities in the world today the MBA has become a commodity to be sold to overseas students in large numbers to help keep the university afloat in an era of declining funding. One corollary has been a deflation in the value of the credential. The value of the MBA was that it was a positional good; when few people possessed it, it had a high value. When it is increasingly sold to ever more people, some of whom have few claims to any mastery of business, its positional value will be sharply eroded. Today, the MBA is increasingly global *and* ubiquitous; its ubiquity is leading to increasing attempts to differentiate products in the market, generating more specialist versions of the overall generalist qualification, in order to enhance its value proposition.

The wave of accounting scandals and corporate collapses has led to further soul searching over the MBA. Enron was an enthusiastic recruiter of MBA graduates (Cruver, 2003). The company was originally involved in transmitting and distributing electricity and natural gas throughout the United States. Enron grew wealthy due largely to marketing, and was

Check out the Companion Website www.sagepub.co.uk/ managingandorganizations3 for free access to an article by Yong Suk Jang (2005) to see how modern accounting has become the grammar of business.

named 'America's Most Innovative Company' by *Fortune* magazine for six consecutive years, from 1996 to 2001. As discovered, in late 2001, when it collapsed, many of Enron's recorded assets and profits were inflated or fraudulently nonexistent. Sophisticated accounting presented a picture that was far from accurate. Cruver, a Texas A&M MBA graduate, chronicles his 18 months at Enron before the company collapsed. The enduring images are of highly motivated, bright MBA graduates not asking difficult questions, not raising concerns over dubious practices, and generally being socialized into the macho, competitive 'win at all costs' culture of Enron.

That these MBA graduates' professional education seeded ethical concerns so lightly is one thing, but some writers such as the late Sumantra Ghoshal have argued that the MBA actually made crashes such as Enron possible. And had he been around to see the global financial crisis of 2008 he might also have extended the argument against MBA graduates as managers. The lack of professional ethical formation of future managers makes them extremely plastic at the hands of those whose heroic leadership status in hotshot organizations defines that which the young managers aspire to be. It institutionalizes the possibility of management's ethical failure as the norm to which recruits will be socialized. By contrast with professions such as medicine and law there is little attention paid to professional ethics and civic morals, other than those that emphasize winning at all costs, being a corporate game player, and being the one who ends up with the most chips in the lottery of organizational life.

How has the MBA achieved the global significance that it has? In part this is an outcome that is dialectically related to globalization: globalizing processes encourage the employment and utilization of the technical knowledge associated with MBAs to maintain their momentum. In part, it is precisely because of these processes of standardization.

The future of management education   Recently, there have been two factors that have further influenced the development of the MBA: first, the introduction of *ranking systems for business schools*; and, second, the growing pressure towards, and internationalization of, *formal accreditation systems*. Together, these have placed management education in a 'regulatory field' (Hedmo et al., 2005) that is increasingly likely to shape its future.

1   It was in 1988 that the US media introduced ranking systems for business schools – allowing prospective students and potential employers to make easy cross-comparisons about the 'value' of different institutions. In the UK, the *Financial Times* produced its first rankings in 1999. The main result of this was largely limited to 'tinkering' with programmes and more attention being directed towards the marketing and packaging of programmes so as to attract students in an increasingly competitive market (Friga et al., 2003).

2   There is an increasing importance of standards for the MBA as a commodity circulating at a global level. The AACSB International – a body recognized as the 'largest and most prestigious accrediting institution for management education in the United States' (Hedmo et al., 2005:

202) and, increasingly, the rest of the world – plays a key role in standard setting. (There is also the much smaller European-based EQUIS programme, but it does not have the same global significance.)

MBAs are increasingly accredited from bodies such as the AACSB. It is an institute that bills itself, and is widely recognized, in its own words, as the premier accrediting agency for bachelors, masters, and doctoral degree programmes in business administration and accounting. Increasingly, when agencies such as the AACSB subject management programmes to assessment, scrutiny, and evaluation in order to accredit them (Hedmo et al., 2005: 3) it has been suggested that these 'accreditation and public-ranking systems appear to have become more recent bearers of Americanization' (Üsdiken, 2004: 89), standardizing the form of management knowledge.

Despite its eponymous emphasis on being 'international', the cultural specificity of the AACSB is also reflected in the history of its name. Until 1997 it was known as the American Assembly of Collegiate Schools of Business, which was founded in 1916. It then became AACSB International. In 2001, the current de-Americanized name was adopted but the acronym remained. The AACSB's emergence as the peak standards-making body has encouraged the move towards centralized standardization. To win membership of the AACSB grants global legitimacy; one consequence of the AACSB and its framing of the field is that, across the world, students will be tutored in similar lessons in management, finance, marketing, human resources, and so forth.

While such developments can be seen as a form of decentralized cultural imitation and emulation, what is striking in recent times is the concerted attempt to impose a centralized set of standards on the geographically and culturally dispersed practice of MBA education. Most particularly, such centralization has been achieved by the way in which the AACSB has become normatively mimetic and, as such, an obligatory passage point for global legitimacy. The AACSB, an international standards-setting body based in the USA, now offers accreditation to business/management school programmes in universities across the world. Promising a guarantee of quality and credentials, the AACSB is today an important and influential force in MBA education, and is likely to be so increasingly.

QUESTION TIME

Globalizing education

What are the indications that your university or college is involved in globalization? What would count as evidence and why? Jot down what you take to be evidence, and compare notes with others in your class.

Systematic management standards

Perhaps one of the most important and most underrated mechanisms assisting in globalization is the central role played in organizations today by systematic management standards. These are structured, acontextual, standardized, and more or less similar self-assessment frameworks (Cole, 1999) such as the Malcolm Baldrige Quality Award (MBNQA), the European Foundation for Quality Management (EFQM) Excellence Model, and the Swedish Institute for Quality (SIQ) Model for Performance Excellence. Such standards act as both a coordination mechanism and a regulatory instrument, and what they do is to make globally coordinated control much easier to achieve.

The most important of these standards, without a doubt, is ISO 9001, dating from 1987. This standard, produced by a technical committee of the International Standards Organization (ISO), while only seven pages in length, when originally produced, has been adopted globally in all sizes and forms of organizations. It is the rational management plan *par excellence*, being a standard for *all* management *anywhere*. In excess of 800,000 organizations have been *certified* to ISO 9001, but as insiders to the ISO world point out, it is likely that several times that number have applied the standard without seeking certification. Judged on sales of the standard alone, hundreds of millions of employees throughout the world have had contact with, or have been influenced by, ISO 9001 or one of its industry-specific derivatives, such as ISO/TS 16949:2000 and ISO 22000:2005.

Standards are produced by a complicated and lengthy process that occurs in committees composed of representatives of various national standards organizations. The members of these committees are not management academics but technical standards writers, perhaps with some public and private sector representation as well, producing the standard as a result of a consensus between the various national representatives and stakeholders. These standards are very influential because they become rational ideals that function as rhetorical devices that are used to shape what global organizations actually do. As such ideals they do not need to be justified outside of the committee system of the ISO. Nor are they held accountable to processes of peer-reviewed research.

Academic research has had a negligible influence on the emergence of the ISO 9001 standard. Brunsson and Jacobson (2000), who have done the most to advance our understanding of *A World of Standards*, suggest that, in fact, research has been ignored at times when that best suited the interests of the standard writers. It is probably more accurate to say that explicit management research is something that occurs in a parallel institutional universe with very little seepage or porosity across its borders into the standards world of practice. Yet, the latter, the world of standards, has done far more to shape practice, demonstrating that in management the relation between theory and practice that is often presumed, by which ideas flow from theory to shape practice, lacks truth value. Management practice is far more likely to be shaped by standards in which theory has had little or no role to play than by the knowledge disseminated in academic journals, texts, and conferences.

Such standards, much as most highly rationalized accounts of what manage-ment should do, probably have more effect on what managers represent themselves as doing rather than what they necessarily do. Standards largely shape representations rather more than practices, and thus increase hypocrisy. Nonetheless, to the extent that global firms adopt global standards, such as ISO 9001, it introduces a powerful rhetorical device into management any-where to make it more accountable in terms of the standard. In part this is the way in which the institutionalization of ISO 9001 has been achieved, largely through a new job classification (the quality manager), who can use the tool to shape the work environment of all employees under their supervision. Especially, in the spread of global outsourcing and manufacturing, the ISO 9001 standard has been very important in translating rationalized manage-ment knowledge into local contexts far from the core of the global economy.

Audit according to the standard is the key mechanism by which rhetoric is translated into practice. Power (1999) points out that from being a rela-tively marginal instrument of control, audit has become a central mecha-nism in what, after Foucault (1979), he refers to as new regimes of governmentality. Audit, Power (1999) suggests, is the control of control, a capacity to act at a distance upon systems of control. In enterprises, this is said to mean that the introduction of audit processes can spread power at the micro level through the capillaries of the organization without the necessity of any centralized control at all: this is the institutional beauty of standards. And, as Rose (1999: 154) suggests, '[r]endering something auditable shapes the process that is to be audited: setting objectives, pro-liferating standardized forms, generating new systems of record-keeping and accounting, governing paper trails'.

Accountability is created in conformance with a set of norms of transpar-ency, observability, and standardization that make accountability and inspec-tion in its name a new norm. While such arguments are elegant, they may be overstated. There is no guarantee that the rules will be followed, and it is the very rule-followers who have the discretion in following and interpret-ing the rules (Brunsson and Jacobsen, 2000). The challenge for particular programmes entering into the accreditation process rests on the creativity of the interpretation as much as the accuracy of the rule following.

Of course, the other realm in which standards assist globalization is by ensuring that specific products work globally, because they all meet a com-mon standard. Think of mobile phones and the emergence of 3G for instance, or think of Microsoft Word – these standards make globalization that much easier because everyone is using the same standard.

GLOBAL MANAGERS AND GLOBAL JOBS

Knowledge work

The management ideas industry of gurus, consultants, educators, and IT firms has reshaped the corporate world. They have changed the linguistic and ideational context in which organizations operate by ushering in a new grammar for organizations. Most large organizations' managers today can talk about their 'strategy', articulate their 'mission', their 'values', and their 'corporate culture'. There is no doubt that globalization spreads certain universal values and attachments through its world of global consumer products and brands. Rolex, Chivas Regal, and Porsche spell success in just about every language. All young global symbolic analysts, whether working on the semiotics of money, films, or words, would recognize such symmetry.

From Reich's (1991) perspective, symbolic analysts include:

- Research scientists
- Professional engineers
- Public relations executives
- Investment bankers
- Lawyers
- Real estate developers
- Creative accountants
- Management, financial, tax, energy, armaments, agricultural, and architectural consultants
- Management information and organization development specialists
- Strategic planners
- Corporate headhunters

- Systems analysts
- Advertising executives
- Marketing strategists
- Art directors
- Architects
- Cinematographers
- Film editors
- Production designers
- Publishers
- Writers and editors
- Journalists
- Musicians
- Television and film producers
- University professors

These knowledge workers are all symbolic analysts manipulating symbols to solve, identify, and broker problems. They simplify reality into abstract images by rearranging, juggling, experimenting, communicating, and transforming these images, using analytic tools, such as mathematical algorithms, legal arguments, financial analysis, scientific principles, or psychological insights that persuade, amuse, induce, deduce, or somehow or other address conceptual puzzles (Reich, 1991). They comprise the creative class who populate creative cities (Florida, 2000). They are probably who you want to be.

To what degree are these symbolic analysts or knowledge workers, comprising the creative class, different from those who have gone before? What marks out their professional identity? Management analysts such as Mats Alvesson (1993; Alvesson and Kärreman, 2001) have argued that what marks such work as different are its linguistic and symbolic accomplishments in circumstances of high ambiguity and uncertainty. In such circumstances, there is not one correct answer; instead, there are a number of competing, plausible alternatives. It places the persuasive abilities of the knowledge worker to the fore, comprising both their image intensity (the suit they wear, the briefcase they carry, the sleekness of their PowerPoint presentation) and the persuasiveness of their rhetoric (the robustness of their argument, their vocabulary, their accent).

Knowledge workers are global, working for Big 4 firms or their small boutique equivalents. They regularly move between the great commercial capitals of the world, creating genuinely international corporate elites. Such transience, perhaps, fosters networking skills and alters sensibilities around risk, two other important characteristics of the symbolic analysts. In summary, they are the stressed-out but well-remunerated shifters and shapers of money, meanings, and markets, doing deals, making business, moving from project to project (Garrick and Clegg, 2001).

Global business elites are easy to spot: on the one hand, those who are highly skilled and educated and employed in global organizations; on the other hand, those in the service economy of legal and financial advice – both sometimes closely related through the dependence of the former on the expertise of the latter. These expatriate and international managers comprise the globalizing elites who not only partake in similar forms of communication power flows, such as common media, technologies, and messages, but also they have shared work experiences in international companies and organizations, working and living in global financial and economic centres. Expatriates are the most liquid human element in these global elites if only because they flow with and are shaped by globalizing capital. While globalizing is not exclusively organized by elites from North American dominated institutions it is significant that multinational financial institutions, governments, and markets all recruit individuals socialized in elite business schools.

The prominence and wealth of financial centres in the high period of late modernity, from the 1980s onwards, deepened links between national elites and institutions of higher education, ensuring the reproduction of the 'financial man'; individuals, mostly male, embedded in a moral community and organizational system that motivated them to enrich themselves, their corporation and, from the perspective of state elites, able to advance core national interests. Business schools, especially the *Financial Times* elite, were at the core of this activity.

Better than sex: how a whole generation got hooked on work

> The dream of a leisure society was the great twentieth-century delusion. Work is the new leisure. Talented and ambitious people work harder than they have ever done, and for longer hours. They find their only fulfilment through work. The men and women running successful companies need to focus their energies on the task in front of them, and for every minute of the day. The last thing they want is recreation … Creative work is its recreation. If you're drafting the patent on a new gene or designing a cathedral in São Paulo, why waste time hitting a rubber ball over a net? (Ballard, 2001: 254)

A few years after J. G. Ballard published *Super-Cannes*, in 2001, two Australian authors, Helen Trinca and Catherine Fox, published a book with the title of *Better Than Sex: How a Whole Generation Got Hooked on Work* (2004), which researched a similar view to that which the character Wilder Penrose articulates in Ballard's novel. The authors asked a number of respondents some simple questions:

 What does work mean to you?

 Why do you like it?

 Why is work so important?

 Why do we give it such a place in our lives?

 What is it about work that makes us feel good?

They show how work now pervades the whole of our lives, both inside and outside the workplace. They examine the reasons why this is so, and they show how corporations operate to capture the hearts and minds of their employees. As the authors say, 'the central thesis of this book is that many people are consumed by work because it is the element of their lives which is most affirming' (Trinca and Fox, 2004: 69). The book provides a subtle, insightful, and amusing commentary about an essential part of commercial life and the participants in that life. The authors do not postulate that work is invariably better than sex but they say in their conclusion that 'work is intensely complex and potentially life changing, and sometimes, just sometimes, it is indeed better than sex' (Trinca and Fox, 2004: 218).

After the publication of their book the following boxed column appeared in the *Sam and the City* page of the *Sydney Morning Herald* website.

MINI CASE

Hooked on work

Forget oysters and strawberries – it seems that work has become the new aphrodisiac of the 21st Century. Yet with tough deadlines, rough deals and hefty sales targets, what makes us so addicted to the hard grind?

'Our lust for the job erodes our lust for each other,' wrote authors Helen Trinca and Catherine Fox in *Better Than Sex: How a Whole Generation Got Hooked on Work*.

'Work better than sex? Pah! Give us sex any day over prickly bosses, irksome colleagues and demanding budgets,' we angrily retorted when the book was released in 2004.

Yet fast forward today and there seems to have been a rapid and seismic shift in our perceptions and actions.

Instead of designer accessories, it's whiz-bang gadgets that we're stocking up on. We're spending big on high-fangled devices like USB Pen

(Continued)

(Continued)

drives (portable computer hard drives), laptop computers with built-in wireless connections, buzzing BlackBerrys (portable emailing devices) and snazzy O2 Atoms which are small enough to sit in our pockets and allow us to surf the net any place, any time.

Our work has expanded well beyond the drab four walls of our office buildings. We do it while we're shopping for groceries, walking on the treadmill, commuting on the train, waiting in the line at the bank and even sitting at the dinner table.

So are we obsessed? 'Addicted to work? Totally!' confesses Roxy Jacenko, owner of swanky PR agency Sweaty Betty. 'I love the buzz of running my own business and watching everything unfold that I have created. I am a slave to my job, but only because I love it and because I care.'

Ah, the 'slave to the job' syndrome. Suddenly, out of sheer necessity, we're decreasing the hours spent with our partners, narrowing our personal time to a measly spin class on the weekends (if we're lucky) and cutting out social activities to spend more time chained to our desks.

And if we compare ourselves to the rest of the world, Australians are working way too many hours for comfort. The *Australian Bureau of Statistics* reports that the number of us working more than 60 hours per week has shot up a whopping 81 per cent, making us the hardest working OECD country in the world. Either that's a whole lot of googling, ebaying and hotmailing, or we've become serious workaholics.

'There is this great belief you are going to get more out of the work environment than other areas of your life,' says Trinca. 'Work is taking the place of other relationships. Yes, work can be a bit messy and difficult but personal relationships can sometimes be even worse.'

Janelle Miller, a 33-year-old real estate agent, concurs. 'After spending a full day at work, and quite often throwing in a few hours of overtime, I spend what seems like an eternity in peak hour before getting home. I'm exhausted, cranky and just want to get to bed before doing the whole thing over again in the morning. I certainly don't have time for a partner at this point in my career.'

Yet according to Trinca, work might not be favoured over sex for much longer. 'In the last three or four years, we've seen Generation Y really arguing a little bit more strongly for balance. They're ambitious and keen, but are also ambitious for private time. After slogging away for a few years, they'll take a break, and it will be a long one.'

Written by author and blogger Samantha Brett, first published on her *Sydney Morning Herald* blog 'Ask SAM' (www.smh.com.au/asksam), ranked #1 Australian news blog.

- Why might knowledge workers think work better than sex? Interview a small sample and see what their views are. Do their responses support or refute the 'better than sex' hypothesis?

Global work

The international flow of expert migrant professional and knowledge workers helps create a global labour market in a growing number of occupations. The evidence of these jobs suggests that, despite attention to the issues of wages and associated cost of taxes raised by journalists and politicians, transnational companies do not, by and large, invest their main facilities where wages and taxes are the lowest. If they did, the theory of comparative costs would work far better than it does. The reasons are self-evident: wages are often a minor cost factor; greater transaction costs are associated with the presence or absence of densely embedded networks for business in particular locales, such as the world cities of New York, London, Paris, and Tokyo, which are likely to remain so. Creative cities act as magnets for talent, offering lifestyle and recreational attractions that draw the creative class to live there and often provide the melting pot of experiences necessary for their inspiration. In addition, many businesses reap great advantage from their cultural and geographic relationships with institutions of education, finance, government, and so on. Government–business relations typically have an exclusive rather than open character, and can be an important component in building national competitive advantage (Porter, 1990), which then attracts globally skilled knowledge workers.

Knowledge work and dirty work

Globally skilled knowledge workers generate job opportunities for less skilled workers. Supporting the cars, shopping, apartments, and travel of these wealthy symbolic analysts is all the dirty work done by those who cook, wash, and clean up, who pack and sell convenience foods, who park and service cars, who tend and care for appearance: the face workers, nail workers, and hair workers – the necessary body maintenance to keep all the wealthy and beautiful people sweet. In global cities such as Hong Kong and Singapore, you can see street-level globalization in the form of the mainly Filipina and Sri Lankan female domestic workers who congregate in the public spaces of the central business district on Sunday, their day of rest. The rest of the week it is more likely to be thronged with global business people while the maids, chauffeurs, and other domestic servants make global households run smoothly.

In addition, there is a shadow labour force of workers in the symbolic sphere – but workers who are tightly scripted, operating in unambiguous and simple environments, unlike their symbolic analyst counterpoints. Outside the confines of the corporate glitterati and the symbolic analyst elite there is a category of disaggregated work quintessentially associated with globalization: that of call centres. Enabled by developments in technology, call centres were ushered into existence in the 1990s, the idea being particularly attractive to corporations, as it allowed them to downsize parts of the organization and establish call centres in relatively deprived areas where wage, rent, and utility rates were lower and the workforce more pliable. The growth of IT allowed for the increasing codification of knowledge, reducing the need for physical contact between producers and consumers, of which call centres are the perfect example – they can be located anywhere. Work is cheapened by routinization of existing tasks; re-engineered tasks can then be moved to places where wages are cheaper. The transaction costs associated with relocation are not great: satellites and computers can ensure virtual linkage. The blueprint is clear: rationalize parts of the organization; introduce jobs at just over minimum wage in deprived, postindustrial parts of the country or another country; and institute a system of surveillance aimed at maximizing efficiency (see pp. 545–547).

In terms of globalization, there are also 'grunge jobs' (Jones, 2003: 256). Jones sees grunge jobs as essentially bifurcated. First there are the semi-skilled workers who work in the lower reaches of the supply chains established by the global giants. It is a contingent, easily dismissible, and re-employable mass of people who can be used and laid off to absorb transaction costs and cushion demand for the core transnational companies globally. In a word, these lower reaches of the supply chain are 'sweatshops' (Teal, 2008) that routinely and intensively exploit employees under labour conditions that would not be tolerated elsewhere. When these transnational companies react to signs of economic distress, then it is these subcontract workers in the supply chain who bear the pain first, buffering the core company employees. These workers are low skill, add little value, and are easily disposable, but at least they may have social insurance and may work in the formal economy, although they have few organized rights and little representation. Many sweatshops are 'informal', meaning that they are illegal and thus evade legal requirements.

The second element in the composition of the grunge economy comprises an underclass of workers who are often illegal immigrants working sporadically in extreme conditions outside the formally regulated labour market: think of sweatshops in the garment industry or the Western world's many illegal sex-workers, for instance. As you sit reading this book, you are probably wearing clothes (possibly designer clothes) that have been manufactured in the developing world. What are the conditions like for those producing the clothes that you are now wearing? As Jones (2003) reports, there is research from Deloitte & Touche (1998) that suggests that informal sector activity ranges from 40 per cent in the Greek economy to 8–10 per cent of the British economy. States often encourage the informal sector as an arena from which street-level and taxable entrepreneurs might develop in enterprises other than the marketing of drugs, prostitutes, and the proceeds of crime (Deloitte & Touche, 1998; Sassen, 1998).

GLOBAL RIGHTS

Globalization in the cultural sphere has meant the global proliferation of norms of individualized values, originally of Western origin, in terms of a discourse of 'rights' (Markoff, 1996). Such discourse is not unproblematic. It meets considerable opposition from religious, political, ethnic, sexual, and other rationalities tied to the specificities of local practices, but it does provide a framework and set of terms through which resistance to these might be organized. Managers seeking to standardize HRM practices globally will probably follow a 'rights-based' template that will often conflict sharply with local realities.

One theorist who has realized this is Barber (1996), who has popularized the idea that the world is set on a collision between McWorld and Jihad, where convergence in the form of primarily US business interests meets stubborn and deep-seated sources of local resistance, embedded in religious worldviews. From this perspective, the trajectory of convergence produces a globalization of culture, technologies, and markets against which local forms of retribalization, through Jihad, will react.

In many ways, suggests Moghadam (1999: 376), working-class and poor urban women have been the 'shock absorbers' of neo-liberal economic policies having suffered in both domestic and industrial/productive capacities. Structural adjustment policies that increase prices, eliminate subsidies, diminish social services, and increase fees for essentials hitherto provided by the state place women at greater risk of ill-health and poverty. However, to the extent that transnationals enter into employment in these regions, then they represent unparalleled opportunities for employment outside of either the informal sector of dubious work and conditions or outside domestic service – opportunities that are often accompanied by education programmes, as governments seek to equip their human capital with the upgradeable skills that will attract further investment.

The ecosystem as a whole is now often ascribed rights and interests, in the name of sustainability. Other entities incapable of interest representation, such as fetuses, those who are on life-support systems, and so on, are also ascribed rights. Animals are ascribed rights (Singer, 1976). Whales have rights that are violated by global organizational actors from Japan; domesticated farm animals such as factory-farmed pigs, hens, and turkeys are routinely treated in ways that deny their right to a 'natural' life. It matters not whether a cow is British or French in an economy where meat, sperm, livestock, and meat-derived products, such as gelatin and cosmetic additives, as well as avian influenza, mad cow, and foot-and-mouth disease, can trade globally. Greenpeace, as an organization for expressing a standardized moral consciousness that can mobilize activists anywhere, can represent Canadian seals as easily as those that are Russian and, through global media, can act its way into the global consciousness. Local species can become global icons. Mismanage these and you will be in deep trouble!

GLOBAL SUSTAINABILITY

Economic growth and population growth place simultaneous demands on the natural environment by depleting resources, eliminating species, and spreading disease. Globalization is resource hungry: the boom in the Chinese economy is swallowing finite raw materials such as wood, rubber, minerals, ores, or oil from every part of the world. Global interdependence between human and ecological health is both causing and spreading global diseases such as HIV/AIDS (French, 2003; Garrett, 1994) and avian influenza.

Increasingly, we live in 'risk societies' where national and geographic boundaries cannot insulate us from human-made or natural disasters generated elsewhere (Beck, 2002). Recall the 2004 tsunami – with good management and prediction in place ahead of the likely impact of such events we can better cope with them. Whereas the Pacific had in place such management systems – in Hawaii – the Indian Ocean did not due to the relative poverty of the region compared with the Pacific, and many thousands of people died, partially in consequence.

Another example, which Beck discusses, is Chernobyl, but the examples are legion: the illegal logging of Sumatran rainforest and the burning off of waste that casts dense smoke palls all over the South-East Asian region, causing health problems in far-away Singapore. The pollution from industrial China blankets Hong Kong and occasionally drifts across the Pacific to the US West Coast. The use of cyanide in mining in Romania, at Aural Gold Plant, allowed 3.5 million cubic feet (100,000 m^3) of cyanide-contaminated waste to enter the Tisza River on 30 January 2000, poisoning the Danube and infecting over 250 miles (400 km) of rivers in Hungary and Yugoslavia. Cyanide leaching is widely used in the global mining industry. That engagement ring may be not only potentially tainted with 'Blood Diamonds' but also cyanide-leached gold. Local actions can have global consequences.

GLOBAL WINNERS AND LOSERS

News Corp and some other global media companies such as CNN are undoubtedly winners from globalization – but there are also losers. Some of these losers are the organizational behemoths created in response to the opportunities for global action that the digital world presents, companies that simply overreached their corporate governance and integrative capabilities. A case in point, staying in the media space, would be the Time Warner/AOL merger, which created an overvalued corporate entity with a difficult blend of organization cultures (see also pp. 236–237). Indeed, ungovernable entities that are too complex culturally, organizationally, and financially could be seen as one aspect of the collateral damage that globalization has sustained on the ranks of business. But these are neither the primary nor the most desperate casualties.

The main beneficiaries of globalization are undoubtedly the skilled employees of the transnational companies and those symbolic analyst professionals who service these companies: lawyers, researchers, consultants, IT experts, and so on. Meyer (2000: 240–241) is unequivocal that those who organize scientific and professional activity on a global scale are the real winners. Professional associations represent such people; international knowledge businesses, universities, and research laboratories employ such people, as do international governmental associations and agencies. These are the people at home in airport lounges, with frequent flyer programmes and portable computers as global talismans of their universality.

The winners also include not just those whom Meyer identifies as being able to make universalistic claims about rights, science, or any other form of expert knowledge, as well as the digital content providers, but also those who are experts in various global sports, representing sponsors such as Nike, Adidas, and other transnational sports companies whose brands are ubiquitous, as well as the global entertainers, the J.Lo's and Kylies. Global brands and those whom they sustain are unequivocal winners from globalization.

With the emergence of global brands, international outsourcing, and supply chains, there is a natural tendency for the market leader to get further ahead, causing a monopolistic concentration of business (Arthur, 1996). Real dangers attach to winning when the losers are excluded and abandoned to their situation. The winners can come together and increasingly integrate with one another. Where such processes occur within societies, serious consequences may result in terms of increased poverty, unemployment, alienation, and crime. But the consequences are of a higher order of magnitude when the processes of exclusion and alienation involve countries and whole regions of the world. The share of world trade in manufactured goods of the 102 poorest countries of the world is falling as the share of the developed world increases. There is a delinking of the less from the more developed world, particularly in Africa. The core of an increasingly globally integrated world economy excludes those countries from the margins.

Poverty in South Asia increased from 20 per cent in 1981 to 43 per cent in 2005, while in sub-Saharan Africa it has more than doubled from 11 per cent to 28 per cent between 1981 and 2005. In 2005 the World Bank redefined the poor as those living on less than UD$ 1.25 a day. The World Bank saw global poverty decline from 1.9 billion in 1981 to 1.4 billion in 2005. The United Nations *Rethinking Poverty: Report on the World Social Situation 2010* (available from http://www.un.org/esa/socdev/rwss/2010. html) contests these figures, which it argues underestimate global poverty.

The primary casualties of globalization appear to be low-skilled grunge workers in traditional manufacturing countries who either lose their jobs as they slip overseas or experience a painful slide in their wage rates as employers strive to reduce costs. Particularly vulnerable are the relatively unskilled and undereducated, especially in labour market systems that do not develop very active and interventionist labour market policies. Wood (1994) reckons that trade with developing countries is the prime suspect for the increase in inequality *within* industrial countries. He estimates that it has reduced the demand for low-skilled workers in rich economies by more than a fifth. Against this, however, one must balance the fact that most jobs are still in spatially discrete and non-tradeable sectors. A wharfie in Australia cannot easily relocate to become a longshoreman in the USA. And even for the 16 per cent of US workers who make their living in manufacturing, the overlap of production with low-wage countries is relatively small. Their main competitors in most sectors are workers in other high-wage countries, as is true of most OECD states.

In the world at large, the effects of globalization can be seen through studying the GNPs of the world of nations in the post-war eras. Those that have been phenomenally successful in lifting themselves up those tables have, by and large, engaged, and been engaged with, the world globally. The states that have not been engaged or have remained disengaged have remained poor and are the real losers from globalization.

RESISTING GLOBALIZATION

Resistance to globalization began to be seen from the late 1990s onwards in the 'anti-globalization movement'. Since then, terms such as the 'social justice movement' have gained currency. The first major protests occurred in

1999, often taking the name of the date on which they occurred (e.g. J16 for 'June 16th') or the city where the protests were held (e.g. the 'Battle for Seattle'). Protests regularly occur in connection with economic policy-making institutions such as the WTO, the World Bank, the IMF, as well as conferences such as the Davos World Economic Forum and the G8 summits. The political and business elites who gather at these are seen as the chief architects of globalization by the protestors. The protests often have a libertarian and carnival quality to them. The resistance often conceives of itself as 'globalization from below' opposed to 'globalization from above', expressing a global solidarity. Since 2001, the World Social Forum has been held as a sort of annual counter-summit to the World Economic Forum. The World Social Forum has done a great deal to place issues such as environmental destruction, the need for sustainability, and Third World poverty on the agenda.

New Right politicians are against globalization; it brings people they do not want to their nation, it threatens them with ideas they do not like, and while it sells them lots of cheap goods that they can afford, it does so at the cost of vulnerable jobs in previously protected parts of the domestic economy – the heartland of their political support. They see globalization as fragmenting national identities. Those under threat demand to be protected from its adverse effects. Ethnically distinct identities (those who do not share what extremists constitute as national identity, usually because of skin colour or religion, or both) are denounced and marginalized as denying the majority of 'ordinary people' their rights to economic surplus, relief, jobs, housing, or whatever.

Resistance to globalization is adept at using some of its tools – such as digitalization – against it: international organizations such as the Global Justice Movement are able to influence global policy-making through their websites. Sometimes the tactics of culture jamming are used: hackers attacked Nike's site in June 2000 and substituted a 'global justice' message for Nike's corporate message. Many anti-Nike websites and listserves have emerged, circulating information about and organizing movements against Nike, which have forced it to modify its labour practices. The management academic, David Boje, is particularly active in this respect.

Greenpeace created an anti-McDonald's website. This site was developed by supporters of two British activists, Helen Steel and Dave Morris, who were sued by McDonald's for distributing leaflets denouncing the corporation's low wages, advertising practices, involvement in deforestation, cruel treatment of animals, and patronage of an unhealthy diet. With help from supporters these two fought back, organizing a McLibel campaign, creating a McSpotlight website criticizing the corporation. The three-year libel trial, the UK's longest ever, ended with the judge defending some of McDonald's claims against the activists while substantiating some criticisms. The activists sought public support to help pay their costs and the fine. The case created unprecedented adverse publicity for McDonald's and, in retrospect, the libel action could hardly be seen to have done the corporation any good.

The New Right sometimes meets the Old Left in the shadows cast by politics. We also find S11 anarchists agreeing, in Sklair's (1999: 158) words, that 'globalization is often seen in terms of impersonal forces wreaking havoc on the lives of ordinary and defenceless people and communities'. As he goes on to say, it 'is not coincidental that interest in globalization over the last two decades has been accompanied by an upsurge in what has come to be known as New Social Movements (NSM) research' (Sklair, 1998; Spybey, 1996). NSM theorists argue for the importance of identity politics (of gender, sexuality, ethnicity, age, community, and belief systems) in the global era. S11 are a perfect example of this – and their strategies are based on global tactics. They do not seek to build effective conventional political alliances and positions, but use the tools of globalization, such as the Internet, to create activist happenings as spectacular media events whenever the leading global players meet internationally. But if you are against a concept such as globalization, which seeks to capture a broad array of social detail, which bits of it are you most against? And what is the alternative to globalization? Is it protectionism? Of course, there is an argument that sometimes protectionism, especially where it preserves unique intellectual/cultural property, such as national cinema or television, is necessary if the juggernaut of cheap US mass-produced and McDonaldized products is not to eliminate cultural differences. Such arguments are common in France, for example.

THE DARK SIDE OF GLOBALIZATION

Banerjee (2008) developed the concept of necrocapitalism, which he defines as those contemporary forms of organizational accumulation that involve dispossession and the subjugation of life to the power of death. Such a process is integral to, and an essential element of, globalization, he suggests. It is a form of natural power involving violence and coercion as a substitute for the creation of social power. Organizationally, this coercive power works institutionally, materially, and discursively in the political economy, resulting in violence and dispossession. Examples include the impact of the resources industry in developing countries and the privatization of war and the military. Globalization is blurring the boundary relations between states and corporations, especially in matters of warfare, where the state is increasingly outsourcing elements of war to the private sector.

Banerjee draws on contributions from classic social science discussions of colonialism and imperialism. Three characteristics of colonialism are the domination of physical space, usually to extract resources, creating not only long-standing dependency relations in economic terms but also cultural domination through the reformation of the indigenous and subjugated people's minds (particularly in terms of knowledge systems and culture), and the incorporation of local economic histories into a Western perspective.

Historically, as a result of imperialism, the globe was carved up into a series of Western centres and 'other' peripheries. Organizations such as the major trading companies and mining companies played a key role in the map-making that transpired. We live with the consequences of that map-making today. For instance, the British carved Iraq out of the Ottoman Empire after the collapse of that Empire as a result of the First World War. On 11 November 1920 it became a mandated protectorate of the British

Empire under the imprimatur of the League of Nations with the name *State of Iraq*. The British government laid out the political and constitutional framework for Iraq's government, one consequence of which was that the new political system lacked legitimacy, because it was seen as an alien imposition. Britain imposed a monarchy on Iraq and defined its territorial limits with little regard for natural frontiers and traditional tribal and ethnic settlements. It was, to all intents and purposes, an artificial and puppet state in which British Petroleum interests were paramount.

In Africa prior to colonization, indigenous people controlled 80 per cent of the territory. At the Berlin Conference of 1884–1885, called by Bismarck, the European powers created geometric boundaries that divided Africa into 50 irregular countries. The new map of the continent was superimposed over the one thousand indigenous cultures and regions. The new countries divided coherent groups of people and merged together disparate groups who really did not get along. Nearly all of Africa's contemporary problems can be seen to have their roots in this initial map-making (see http://geography.about.com/cs/politicalgeog/a/berlinconferenc.htm).

Today, Banerjee suggests, imperialism also operates in economic, political, and cultural guises and is operationalized through different kinds of power: institutional power (agencies such as the IMF, WTO, and the World Bank), economic power (of corporations and nation-states), and discursive power that constructs and describes uncontested notions of 'development', 'backwardness', 'subsistence economies' while disallowing other narratives from emerging. Banerjee not only traces these manifestations of power but also provides a number of examples, easily drawn from recent histories, of organizational violence committed on employees and citizens by both imperial states and imperialist corporations. Colonialism and imperialism created export-oriented, often single resource-based economies, centred on plantation agriculture of cash crops, or resource extraction, and today it is particularly the latter arena, dominated by a few global companies, that routinely commit violence and rain down devastation, in the process of developing regions and consorting with local elites, on communities that have the misfortune to be the recipients of their investments.

The institutional auspices of organizations studies are something overwhelmingly situated in European and US universities. The hegemonic intellectualism of Western ways of knowing have been critiqued widely in the humanities and social sciences more generally in recent years, following critiques that flow from the post-colonial literature that Banerjee draws on, as they have been developed in management and organization theory by Frenkel and Shenhav (2006). They draw on theories of orientalism, associated with the work of Edward Said (1978), and hybridity as a third space, associated with the work of Homi Bhabha (1994). Orientalism is founded on a binary epistemology that necessitates a sharp distinction between colonizers and the colonized, whereas Bhabha's work represents a hybrid epistemology, taking into consideration the fusion and the mutual effects of colonizers and the colonized. Orientalism and hybridity are often described as mutually exclusive: either as two consecutive phases in post-colonial theory or as two competing epistemologies. Their contribution

Check out the Companion Website www.sagepub.co.uk/ managingandorganizations3 for free access to an article by Subhabrata Bobby Banerjee (2008) on necrocapitalism.

examines the effect of the colonial encounter on the canonization of organization studies and management more generally as well as on the boundaries of it as a canon. Banerjee argues, theoretically, that orientalism and hybridity are neither competing nor mutually exclusive concepts, but rather, two complementary aspects of the same process. The argument is that the identity that has been canonized as the mainstream of management and organization studies followed two contradictory principles simultaneously at work: hybridization and purification. Hybridization refers to the mixing of practices between colonizers and the colonized, to the translation of texts and practices from the colonies to the metropolis, and vice versa. Purification refers to the mechanisms that construct colonizers and colonized as two distinct and incommensurable, ontological zones. Examined from this point of view, such encounters were always hybrids albeit that they were represented in purified binary terms of West versus the rest. Historically, the construction of Western management discourse was clearly based on a system of omissions and exclusions, largely of the experiences of slavery and plantation modes of production, which fed directly into early industrial practices but were excluded from formal academic accounts of the origins of management thought and practice. Similar processes are seen to be at work in the evolution of international management as a field where the good is exclusively (rational) Western and the bad (irrational) non-Western practice. At its worst, this genre lapses into pure condescension and stereotyping of non-Western practice that would not have been out of place in a 'Black Sambo' book or *Uncle Tom's Cabin*. Management has adopted an essentially colonial viewpoint casting the non-Western as the inferior 'other' while seeing Western culture as a universal model. Much of international human resource management fits this pattern, for example. Management became the spearhead of neo-colonialism in the age of decolonization. Furthermore, it assists in the reproduction of the West's control of the global economy and culture, while at the same time increasing management's ostensibly scientific legitimacy.

Check out the Companion Website www.sagepub.co.uk/ managingandorganizations3 for free access to an article by Michal Frenkel and Yehouda Shenhav (2006) on a postcolonial reading of management and organization studies.

SUMMARY AND REVIEW

Our everyday life is global. Wherever we live, we cannot escape globalization. Next time you go to the shopping mall, take a look at the people around you – in fact, take a look at yourself and what you are wearing. As we noted at the outset, there are no frontiers to fashion. We are all the result of globalization benefiting from the movement of

people as they seek new opportunities, markets, lives, resources, land, and so on. Organizations sometimes globalize to access new markets and other times to access cheaper resources, while sometimes they do so for both reasons.

Globalization involves many processes interacting with each other, which are dynamic and unstable. The major elements of globalization are global flows of finance, knowledge, people, and politics.

The key circuits through which globalization processes flow are: global financial systems, global strategic alliances, and mergers and acquisitions. Managing in a globalized world exposes the manager to different institutional systems. Globalization occurs because of economies of scale, scope, and resources acquisition. The major agencies advancing globalization are: large IT firms, management gurus, management consultancies, MBAs, and systematic management standards.

The knowledge industries are a major component of globalization, including the education context in which you are probably reading this book. As well as knowledge workers, globalization also encourages the spread of dirty jobs. The good news for you is that because you are reading this book, you probably will not end up doing one of these dirty jobs!

Management cannot avoid responsibility to other humans and the environment in which they live, as well as shareholders. There is no simple, disembedded global rationality, focused only on accounting fictions, which a manager can apply as if it were a powerful talisman, ritual, or incantation. There is no special method to inure you against, and insure your organization from, the perils that occur when an irresistible force, such as globalization, meets an old immovable object, like a deeply embedded local reality with its own ways of being, thinking, and feeling.

Being a global manager today entails moral as well as personal responsibilities, ethical as well as financial obligations, power as well as pleasure, a commitment to the production of better lives, not just the consumption and spewing out of goods and services.

Globalization, at its best, would mean that all of us cannot prosper from being rapacious to any of us; to harm, damage, and blight any of us in the name of some of us is a crime against all. We are in this life together, on one fragile planet, one globe, one people, the human race, and we should try to manage on that basis. Sustainability matters because, simply, once used up, non-renewable resources are gone.

Globalization means that singular strategic visions that managers produce for organizations will collide with a world composed of many local realities. Globalization presents many management problems *and* opportunities. In this chapter we have identified the major areas of concern with which such managers will have to grapple. These include managing the intersection of national societies and all their tacit assumptions, with an increasingly systemic, patterned, and interconnected world. You will also have to manage the impact of these systemic processes on yourself and those with whom you work and whom you employ, globally. You will have to manage the impact of your global activities, and those of the organization that employs you, on the fate of humankind in general.

EXERCISES

1 Having read this chapter you should be able to say in your own words what each of the following key terms means. Test yourself or ask a colleague to test you.

- Globalization
- Globalization processes
- Global circuits
- Global strategic alliances
- Resistance to globalization
- Global strategies
- Transnationals
- Global jobs
- Grunge economy
- Creative class
- Dirty work
- Global rights
- Clusters
- Knowledge workers
- Necrocapitalism

2 What are the key processes defining globalization? How do they shape the phenomenon?
3 Who are the major global actors?
4 What are the different kinds of global jobs?
5 How does globalization shape human consciousnesses?
6 Who are the winners and who are the losers from globalization?
7 Why is it not a paradox to say that the global is always local?

ADDITIONAL RESOURCES

1 The BBC Radio Reith Lectures of 1999 by Anthony Giddens, published as *Runaway World: How Globalization is Reshaping our Lives* (2000), are a clear and useful sociological introduction to globalization as a broad phenomenon.

2 Thomas Friedman's (1999) *The Lexus and the Olive Tree* is one of the very best sources on globalization – and beautifully written, as befits a *New York Times* correspondent.

3 The definitive text on globalization, written by an economic geographer, is Peter Dicken's (2007) *Global Shift: Mapping the Changing Contours of the World Economy*. It contains extensive discussion of a number of specific industries: clothing and textiles; automobiles; semiconductors; agro-food industry; financial services and logistics.

4 An interesting guide to globalization is written by sociologist Dennis Smith (2006) *Globalization: The Hidden Agenda*, which raises some quite worrying scenarios.

5 Glenn Morgan's (2008) entry on 'Transnationals' in the *International Encyclopedia of Organization Studies* is a very useful introduction to these key actors in globalization.

6 The debate between Barbara Parker (2003) and Marc Jones (2003) in *Debating Organizations* (Westwood and Clegg, 2003) is worthwhile for those deeply interested in the topic. For others it might be a bit heavy. Barbara Parker, together with Stewart Clegg (2006), contributed a chapter on globalization to the *Sage Handbook of Organization Studies* (edited by Clegg et al., 2006b), which is also well worth study.

7 In terms of films, there are a number of good documentaries, such as *Gap and Nike: No Sweat?* It is a BBC *Panorama* production, focusing on Nike and Gap, both of which claim that they have strict codes of conduct for manufacturing. They claim that they do not use sweatshops or child labour. They say they routinely 'monitor' their factories, to make sure their codes are followed. But when the BBC's *Panorama* team visited Cambodia, it found severe breaches of these codes within days. By talking with workers and using hidden cameras, the team shows how one factory, used by both Gap and Nike, has sweatshop conditions and employs children. All the workers interviewed were working seven days a week, often up to 16 hours a day, and some of the employees were children as young as 12. After these findings, *Panorama* went back to speak with Gap and Nike, to hear what they had to say. The team

also shows how US companies can use foreign sweatshops and still claim that the goods are made in the USA. See the Global Exchange Fair Trade Store at http://globalexchange.org/tapes.html (*Global Exchange Fair Trade Store*, 2004). You might also want to look at www.caa.org.au/campaigns/nike (Oxfam, 2004).

8 More commercially, there is the 2003 Stephen Frears film, *Dirty Pretty Things*, which dramatizes life in the grunge jobs that illegal immigrants fill in any global city, in this case London.

9 The film *Blood Diamond* (Zwick, 2006) looks at the role of transnational corporations in the troubled diamond mining industry of Africa in Sierra Leone.

WEB SECTION

1 Our Companion Website is the best first stop for you to find a great deal of extra resources, free PDF versions of leading articles published in Sage journals, exercises, video and pod casts, team case studies and general questions, and links to teamwork resources. Go to www.sagepub.co.uk/managingandorganizations3.

2 For state of the art briefings on how to manage organizations effectively, please visit the Henry Stewart Talks series of online audiovisual seminars on Managing Organizations, edited by Stewart Clegg: www.hstalks.com/r/managing-orgs, in particular, Talk #18: *Transnational corporations and climate change: towards a global governance framework*, Bobby Banerjee.

3 You can find David Boje's web page at http://business.nmsu.edu/~dboje/. There are many links to explore.

4 The World Bank maintains a useful resource page on globalization: http://www1.worldbank.org/economicpolicy/globalization/.

5 The consulting company, A. T. Kearney has a globalization index that you can find on http://tinyurl.com/ypvjmk. The most globalized countries, according to this index, are Singapore, Ireland, Switzerland, the USA, The Netherlands, and Canada while Egypt, Indonesia, India, and Iran are the least.

6   Kearney is not the only provider of an index of globalization. The Swiss Think Tank KOF maintains a very useful page, which provides an index of how globalized countries are: http://globalization.kof.ethz.ch/. The index measures the three main dimensions of globalization: economic, social, and political. In addition to the three indices measuring these dimensions, an overall index of globalization and sub-indices referring to actual economic flows, economic restrictions, data on personal contact, data on information flows, and data on cultural proximity are calculated. Data are available on a yearly basis for 122 countries. According to the index, the world's most globalized country is Belgium, followed by Austria, Sweden, the UK, and The Netherlands. The least globalized countries according to the KOF index are Haiti, Myanmar, the Central African Republic, and Burundi.

7   Wikipedia has a good page on one of the main agents of anti-globalization, the Global Justice Movement, at http://en.wikipedia.org/wiki/Global_Justice_Movement.

8   The IMF has a web page with a 2000 briefing paper in it at http://tinyurl.com/ytnbbr.

9   The United Nations maintains a Global Policy Forum page at http://www.globalpolicy.org/globaliz/index.htm, with some quite useful links on it.

10 There is an academic site maintained by Emory University in the USA that has many links on it: http://www.sociology.emory.edu/globalization/.

11 Mining is one of the great global offenders against nature: check out http://www.earthworksaction.org/pubs/Cyanide_Leach_Packet.pdf.

12 The anti-McDonald's page can be found at www.mcspotlight.org.

13 The online journal *Globalization* can be accessed at http://globalization.icaap.org/editorialboard.php. The publisher, Polity Press, maintains a website supporting several of its books in the Global Transformations series. Again, there are many links that can be easily accessed through this page.

14 Dennis Smith maintains a website related to his 2006 book, *Globalization: The Hidden Agenda*, http://www.globalhelix.org/.

LOOKING FOR A HIGHER MARK?

Reading and digesting these articles that are available free on the Companion Website www.sagepub.co.uk/managingandorganizations3 can help you gain deeper understanding and, on the basis of that, a better grade:

1   Paul W. L. Vlaar, Frans A. J. Van den Bosch, and Henk W. Volberda (2006) have written a paper that we have made available on the Companion Website that is a very good guide to 'Coping with problems of understanding in interorganizational relationships: using formalization as a means to make sense', *Organization Studies*, 27 (11): 1617–1638.

2   A crucial issue in managing multinational organizations is how much you should manage centrally in terms of home-country characteristics, or go with the local flow. On the Companion Website we have three papers that address this issue:

    a   Mike Geppert and Karen Williams (2003) 'Change management in MNCs: how global convergence intertwines with national diversities', *Organization Studies*, 27 (4): 491–515.

    b   Mike Geppert and Dirk Matten (2006) 'Institutional influences on manufacturing organization in multinational corporations: the "cherrypicking" approach', *Organization Studies*, 27 (4): 491–515.

    c   Glenn Morgan and Peer Hull Kristensen (2006) 'The contested space of multinationals: varieties of institutionalism, varieties of capitalism', *Human Relations,* 59 (11): 1467–1490.

3   Many users of this book will also be studying accounting: in one paper that we have put on the Companion Website you can read how important and influential being a part of the accounting community really is: Yong Suk Jang (2005) 'The expansion of modern accounting as a global and institutional practice', International *Journal of Comparative Sociology*, 46 (8): 297–326. No more jokes about accountants after reading this!

4   Globalization can be a violent and bloody process, as Subhabrata Bobby Banerjee (2008) argues in 'Necrocapitalism', *Organization Studies*, 29 (12): 1541–1563.

5   Michal Frenkel and Yehouda Shenhav's (2006) 'From binarism back to hybridity: a postcolonial reading of management and organization studies', *Organization Studies*, 27 (6): 855–876, introduces debates from the humanities and social sciences into management and organization theory.

6   Financial markets and their dictates and rhythms are at the heart of modern globalization, as Karin Knorr-Cetina and Alex Preda (2007) examine in 'The temporalization of financial markets: from network to flow', *Theory, Culture & Society,* 24: 116–138.

CASE STUDY

TASTE AND THE GLOBALIZATION OF FISH

Hi, this is Tyrone Pitsis writing. I used to be an executive chef before I wrote books such as this. When I was a chef, one of the most popular choices at my restaurant was a fish dish made with wild Orange Roughy Perch fillet, pan fried in a sea salt, pepper, and chilli crust served on a bed of wilted greens (rocket, baby spinach, and radicchio) topped with char-seared Tasmanian scallops and citrus butter sauce with Cointreau. Sounds good? It was, but it was also very expensive! Why was it expensive? Partly because people in Sydney, as in any other global city, will pay almost anything for very good food, but also because of the hidden story behind the Orange Roughy. This story is all about the globalization, access, and ownership of the world's scarce resources, and how global partnerships attempt to manage such resources in a sustainable way but are prone to failure for all the reasons we have covered in this entire textbook. Therefore, this story is highly relevant to this closing chapter.

The story begins with the oddly named Orange Roughy. The fish is an excellent eating fish with sweet, light white flesh suited to several types of cooking methods (pan frying, poaching, grilling, and so on). As such it is a highly sought-after fish, and while the fish is farmed, diners at the top restaurants demand and expect the wild variety. For this reason the fish is very high on many fishing industries' agendas, so much so that it is in danger of being fished to extinction. Indeed, there are several new technologies designed specifically for locating and catching the fish, such as sonar and mega-fishing boats. So, herein lies a real problem because, farmed or wild, compared with you and I the Orange Roughy takes a very long time to reach maturity (approximately 100 years). The long juvenile period, combined with the fact that the fish stocks are not being replenished sufficiently to sustain them, has meant that these and many other fish stocks are fast depleting.

To respond, international governments and fishing industries have had to establish a global compact to manage the fish stocks in an enduring and sustainable way, or risk an entire industry becoming extinct along with an entire species of fish. However, the complexity of managing such fish stocks is just too much for one country to deal with for one very simple reason. The 'Roughy', like many other fish, are what we call 'straddling' fish stocks. That means they really do like to swim, and they do it far and wide to the extent that they can swim through the waters of several countries. For example, the Roughy will typically swim through Australian waters, New Zealand waters, Russian, Norwegian, and North Korean waters, then into international waters, and so on. Now, in the ocean there are no checkpoints or immigration officers so the fish cannot know or care which country's water they currently are swimming in. The fishermen and fisherwomen of that country do, however, because while in Australian waters, for example, they are Australian fish – in international waters they are technically anybody's. Traditionally, for pure economic reasons, when the fish are in your waters the practice has been to catch as many of them as you can.

As fishermen and fisherwomen were noticing less fish, and that the fish they caught were younger and smaller, they started to become quite concerned. The global demand for the fish meant local fisheries would most certainly become things of the past. Now, while many of the local fishermen and fisherwomen were thinking locally, and in terms of their own interest, the reality is that the issue of what can be fished is truly a global one. To complicate the issue further, several international environmental and scientific groups are lobbying hard to place a complete moratorium (suspension) on fishing. Clearly, any attempt to address the problem goes beyond any local fishing authority or concern, and implies knowledge, skills, and abilities in a range of international management capabilities, including international diplomacy, human relations, conflict management and negotiation, communications, networks and relationship building, culture and values, corporate social responsibility, business ethics and sustainability, and global leadership.

The ability to manage what at face value seems benign – that is, some fish – can and will have serious global implications.

To illustrate the complexity of this issue, at one stage several of the Orange Roughy fishing nations agreed to have controlled catches, to conduct research, and to collaborate to ensure the long-term sustainability of not only their fish, but also the entire global industry, environmental and scientific groups, industry and consumers. The problem was that a major South African multinational corporation, I&J, relied heavily on the fish for some of its very popular products, and would chase the fish in massive fishing vessels. At one point the corporation offered 'kickbacks' (or payment) to some of the less ethical fishermen and fisher-women in New Zealand to inform them when the fish 'straddled' out of Australian waters and into international waters – upon which a ship would be ready to haul the fish in at over two times the legal quota allowed for the participating nations (see, http://www.journeyman.tv/?id=9212).

Clearly, this global issue is not a simple one to manage and requires immense international relations and international management knowledge and experience. Who would have thought a nice meal in a restaurant could have such a story to tell? So, let us assume that you and your team are responsible for drafting a policy document for dealing with the problem and call it a draft paper on *Global fish management and sustainability*.

IN YOUR PAPER:

1 Define what you think is the problem, as you see it, and explain to what extent you think the problem is local or global.
2 Thinking about the issues covered in this chapter, how might what you have learned be applied to the research and write-up of your report? Provide clear links between your report and this chapter.
3 What would you recommend should be done to deal with the global resource problem? To what extent will it satisfy all the interested parties involved, including local fisheries, governments, industry, scientists, and conservationists alike? Can this outcome actually be achieved?

Case prepared by Tyrone S. Pitsis, School of Management, UTS, University of Newcastle-upon-Tyne.

BIBLIOGRAPHY

Abbott, A. (1988) *The System of Professions: An Essay on the Division of Expert Labor*. Chicago: Chicago University Press.

Abbott, J. D. and Moran, R. T. (2002) *Uniting North American Business: NAFTA Best Practice*. Burlington, MA: Butterworth-Heinemann.

Abrahamson, E. (1996) 'Management fashion', *Academy of Management Review*, 21: 254–285.

Abrahamson, E. (1997) 'The emergence and prevalence of employee management rhetorics: the effects of long waves, labour unions, and turnover, 1875 to 1992', *Academy of Management Journal*, 40 (3): 491–533.

Achbar, M. (Director) (2003) *The Corporation* [Motion picture]. Los Angeles: Films Transit International.

Adams, J. S. (1963) 'Towards an understanding of inequity', *Journal of Abnormal and Social Psychology*, 67: 422–436.

Adkins, B., Foth, M., Summerville, J. and Higgs, P. L. (2007) 'Ecologies of innovation: symbolic aspects of cross-organizational linkages in the design sector in an Australian inner-city area', *American Behavioral Scientist*, 50: 922–934.

Adler, S. (2011) 'The Human Experience of Working: Richer Science, Richer Practice', *Industrial and Organizational Psychology*, 4 (1): 98–101.

Ahuja, M. K. and Carley, K. M. (1999) 'Network structure in virtual organization', *Organization Science*, 10 (6): 741–757.

Albrow, M. (1970) *Bureaucracy*. London: Pall Mall.

Aldrich, H. (2002) 'Technology and organizational structure: a reexamination of the findings of the Aston Group', in S. R. Clegg (ed.), *Central Currents in Organization Studies I: Frameworks and Applications*, Volume 2. London: Sage, pp. 344–366; originally published in *Administrative Science Quarterly* (1971) 17: 26–42.

Aldrich, H. E. and Ruef, M. (2006) *Organization Evolving*, 2nd edn. London: Sage.

Allison, G. T. (1971) *Essence of Decision: Explaining the Cuban Missile Crisis*. Boston: Little Brown.

Allmendinger, J. and Hackman, J. R. (2002) 'Organizations in changing environments: the case of East German Symphony Orchestras', in S. R. Clegg (ed.), *Central Currents in Organization Studies I: Frameworks and Applications*, Volume 3. London: Sage, pp. 217–252; originally published in *Administrative Science Quarterly* (1996) 41: 337–369.

Allport, G. W. and Odbert, H. S. (1936) 'Trait names: a psycholexical study', *Psychological Monographs*, 47 (1, Whole No. 211).

Altman, R. (Director) (2001) *Gosford Park* [Motion picture]. United States: USA Films.

Alvesson, M. (1993) 'Organizations as rhetoric: knowledge intensive firms and the struggle with ambiguity', *Journal of Management Studies*, 30 (6): 997–1015.

Alvesson, M. (1995) *Management of Knowledge-Intensive Companies*. Berlin: de Gruyter.

Alvesson, M. (2004) *Knowledge Work and Knowledge-Intensive Firms*. Oxford: Oxford University Press.

Alvesson, M. and Berg, P. O. (1992) *Corporate Culture and Organizational Symbolism*. Berlin: de Gruyter.

Alvesson, M. and Kärreman, D. (2001) 'Odd couple: making sense of the curious concept of knowledge management', *Journal of Management Studies*, 38 (7): 995–1018.

Amabile, T. (1998) 'How to kill creativity', *Harvard Business Review*, September–October: 77–87.

Ambrose, S. (2007) 'The decline (& fall?) of the IMF or, chronicle of an institutional death foretold'. Available at http://www.focusweb.org/focus-on-trade-number-128-march-2007.html?Itemid=94 (last accessed 1 April 2007).

Ambrose, S. E. (2001) *The Band of Brothers*. New York: Simon & Schuster.

Anandakumar, A., Pitsis, T. S. and Clegg, S. R. (2007) 'Everybody hurts, sometimes: the language of emotionality and the dysfunctional organization', in J. Langan-Fox, C. L. Cooper and R. J. Klimoski (eds), *Research*

Companion to the Dysfunctional Workplace: Management Challenges and Symptoms. Cheltenham: Edward Elgar, ch. 12, pp. 187–215.

Anderson, B. (1982) *Imagined Communities: Reflections on the Origins and Spread of Nationalism.* London: Verso.

Anderson, R. (1999) *Mid Course Correction: Toward a Sustainable Enterprise: The Interface Model.* Atlanta: Peregrinzilla Press.

Anspaugh, D. (Director) (1986) *Hosiers* [Motion picture]. Los Angeles: Metro-Goldwyn-Mayer Pictures.

Antonacopoulou, E. (2008) 'Practice', in S. R. Clegg and J. R. Bailey (eds), *The Sage International Encyclopedia of Organization Studies.* Thousand Oaks, CA: Sage, pp. 1291–1298.

Antonakis, J. and House, R. J. (2002) 'An analysis of the full-range leadership theory: the way forward', in B. J. Avolio and F. J. Yammarino (eds), *Transformational and Charismatic Leadership: The Road Ahead.* Amsterdam: JAI Press, pp. 3–34.

Antonakis, J. and House, R. J. (2004) 'On instrumental leadership: beyond transactions and transformations', Paper presented at the Gallup Leadership Institute Conference, University of Nebraska.

Antorini, Y. M. (2007) '*Brand community innovation: an intrinsic case study of the adult fans of LEGO community*', PhD thesis, Copenhagen Business School.

Appelbaum, E. and Hunter, L. (2005) 'Union participation in strategic decisions of corporations', in R. Freeman and L. Mishel (eds), *Emerging Labor Market Institutions for the 21st Century.* Cambridge, MA: National Bureau of Economic Research, pp. 265–291.

Arendt, H. (1994) *Eichmann in Jerusalem: A Report on the Banality of Evil.* New York: Penguin.

Argenti, P. and Forman, J. (2000) 'The communication advantage: a constituency-focused approach to formulating and implementing strategy', in M. Schultz, M. Hatch and M. Larsen (eds), *The Expressive Organization: Linking Identity, Reputation, and the Corporate Brand.* Oxford: Oxford University Press, pp. 233–245.

Argyris, C. (1960) *Understanding Organizational Behaviour.* London: Tavistock.

Argyris, C. and Schön, D. (1978) *Organizational Learning: A Theory of Action Perspective.* Reading, MA: Addison-Wesley.

Aronson, E. (1960) *The Social Animal.* San Francisco: W. H. Freeman.

Arthur, B. (1996) 'Increasing returns and the two worlds of business', *Harvard Business Review*, Reprint 96401.

Arvey, R. D. and Murphy, K. R. (1998) 'Performance evaluation in work settings', *Annual Review of Psychology*, 49: 141–168.

Asch, S. (1955) 'Opinions and social pressure', *Scientific American*, 193: 31–35.

Ashkenasy, N. (2003) 'The case for culture', in R. Westwood and S. R. Clegg (eds), *Debating Organizations: Point-Counterpoint in Organization Studies.* London: Blackwell, pp. 300–310.

Ashkenasy, N., Hartal, C. E. J. and Dauss, C. S. (2002) 'Diversity and emotion: the new frontiers in organizational behaviour research', *Journal of Management*, 28: 307–338.

Ashkanasy, N. M., Wilderom, C. P. M. and Peterson, M. F. (2000) *Handbook of Organizational Culture and Climate.* London: Sage.

Ashkanasy, N. M., Wilderom, C. P. M. and Peterson, M. F. (2011) *Handbook of Organizational Culture and Climate (Second Edition).* London: Sage.

Atkin, R. S. and Conlon, E. J. (1978) 'Behaviorally anchored rating scales: some theoretical issues', *Academy of Management Review*, 3 (1): 119–128.

Babbage, C. (1971) *On the Economy of Machinery and Manufactures.* New York: Kelley; original work published 1832.

Bacharach, S. A. (2005) *Get Them on Your Side: Win Support, Convert Skeptics, Get Results.* Avon, MA: Platinum Press.

Bachrach, P. and Baratz, M. S. (1962) 'Two faces of power', *American Political Science Review*, 56: 947–952.

Bachrach, P. and Baratz, M. S. (1970) *Power and Poverty: Theory and Practice.* New York: Oxford University Press.

Badaracco, J. L. (1991) *The Knowledge Link: How Firms Compete Through Strategic Alliances.* Boston, MA: Harvard Business School Press.

Bagozzi, R. (2003) 'Positive and negative emotions in organizations', in K. Cameron, J. Dutton and R. Quinn (eds), *Positive Organizational Scholarship: Foundations of a New Discipline.* San Francisco: Berrett Koehler.

Bahnisch, M. (2000) 'Embodied work, divided labour: subjectivity and the scientific management of the body in Frederick W. Taylor's 1907 "Lecture on Management"', *Body & Society*, 6 (1): 51–68.

Baird, M. (2004) 'Orientations to paid maternity leave: understanding the Australian debate', *Journal of Industrial Relations*, 46 (3): 259–275.

Baldwin, M. W. (1992) 'Relational schemas and the processing of social information', *Psychological Bulletin*, 112: 461–484.

Bales, K. (2005) *Understanding Global Slavery: A Reader*. Berkeley, CA: University of California Press.

Ball, K. (2008) 'Call centers', in S. R. Clegg and J. R. Bailey (eds), *The Sage International Encyclopedia of Organization Studies*. Thousand Oaks, CA: Sage, pp. 139–142.

Ballard, J. D. (2001) *Super-Cannes*. New York: Picador.

Bandura, A. (1986) *Social Foundations of Thought and Action: A Social-Cognitive Theory*. Englewood Cliffs, NJ: Prentice Hall.

Banerjee, S. B. (2008) 'Necrocapitalism', *Organization Studies*, 29 (12): 1541–1563.

Bangle, C. (2001) 'The ultimate creative machine: how BMW turns art into profit', *Harvard Business Review*, January: 47–55.

Bansal, P. and Hunter, T. (2003) 'Strategic explanations for the early adoption of ISO 14001', *Journal of Business Ethics*, 46: 289–299.

Barber, B. (1996) *Jihad vs. McWorld*. New York: Ballantine.

Barbuto, J. E., Fritz, S. M., Matkin, G. S. and Marx, D. B. (2007) 'Effects of gender, education, and age upon leaders' use of influence tactics and full range leadership behaviors', *Sex Roles*, 56 (1–2): 71–83.

Barclay, L. A. and Markel, K. S. (2007) 'Discrimination and stigmatization in work organizations: a multiple level framework for research on genetic testing', *Human Relations*, 60 (6): 953–980.

Barker, J. (2002) 'Tightening the iron cage: concertive control in self-managing teams', in S. R. Clegg (ed.), *Central Currents in Organization Studies II: Contemporary Trends*, Volume 5. London: Sage, pp. 180–210; originally published in *Administrative Science Quarterly* (1993) 38: 408–437.

Barker, P. (1998) *Michel Foucault: An Introduction*. Edinburgh: Edinburgh University Press.

Barker, R. A. (2001) 'The nature of leadership', *Human Relations*, 54: 469–494.

Barley, S. R. (1986) 'Technology as an occasion for structuring: evidence from observations of CT scanners and the social order of radiology departments', *Administrative Science Quarterly*, 31 (1): 78–108.

Barley, S. R. and Kunda, G. (1992) 'Design and devotion: surges of rational and normative ideologies of control in managerial discourse', *Administrative Science Quarterly*, 37: 363–399.

Barley, S., Meyer, G. and Gash, D. (1988) 'Cultures of cultures: academics, practitioners and the pragmatics of normative control', *Administrative Science Quarterly*, 33: 24–60.

Barnard, C. (1936) *The Functions of the Executive*. Cambridge, MA: Harvard University Press.

Barrett, F. J. (2002) 'Creativity and improvisation in jazz and organizations: implications for organization learning', in K. Kamoche, M. P. Cunha and D. V. J. Cunha (eds), *Organizational Improvisation*. London: Routledge, pp. 138–165.

Barry, D., Carroll, B. and Hansen, H. (2006) 'To text or context? Endotextual, exotextual, and multi-textual approaches to narrative and discursive organizational studies', *Organization Studies*, 27 (8): 1091–1110

Bartholomew, S. (1998) 'National systems of biotechnology innovation: complex interdependence in the global system', *Journal of International Business*, 2: 241–266.

Bartlett, C. and Ghoshal, S. (1989) *Managing Across Borders: The Transnational Solution*. London: Century Press.

Bass, B. M. and Avolio, B. J. (2000) *Multifactor Leadership Questionnaire*. Redwood City, CA: Mind Garden.

Bass, B. M. and Avolio, B. (2003) *Multifactor Leadership Questionnaire: Feedback Report*. Redwood City, CA: Mind Garden Inc.

Bate, S. P. and Robert, G. (2007) 'Towards more user-centric OD: lessons from the field of experience-based design and a case study', *Journal of Applied Behavioral Science*, 43: 41–66.

Bauman, Z. (1989) *Modernity and the Holocaust*. Cambridge: Polity.

Bauman, Z. (1992) *Intimations of Postmodernity*. London: Routledge.

Bauman, Z. (1993) *Postmodern Ethics*. Oxford: Blackwell.

Bauman, Z. (1995) *Life in Fragments*. Cambridge: Polity Press.

Baumeister, R. F. and Leary, M. R. (1995) 'The need to belong: Desire and interpersonal attachments as a fundamental human motivation', *Psychological Bulletin*, 117: 497–529.

Beauvallet, G. and Balle, M. (2002) *E-Management Work: The Internet and the Office Productivity Revolution*. London: Writers Club Press.

Beck, U. (2002) *Risk Society: Towards a New Modernity*. London: Sage.

Becker, B. and Gerhart, B. (1996) 'The impact of human resource management on organizational performance: progress and prospects', *Academy of Management Journal*, 39 (4): 779–801.

Becker, B. E. and Huselid, M. (2006) 'Strategic human resources management: where do we go from here?' *Journal of Management*, 32 (6): 898–925.

Belbin, R. M. (1993) *Team Roles at Work*. Oxford: Butterworth–Heinemann.

Belbin, R. M. (2000) *Beyond the Team*. Oxford: Butterworth–Heinemann.

Benard, S. and Correll, S. J. (2010) 'Normative discrimination and the motherhood penalty'. *Gender & Society*, 24 (5): 616–646.

Benfari, R. C., Wilkinson, H. E. and Orth, C. D. (1986) 'The effective use of power', *Business Horizons*, 29 (3): 12–16.

Bennis, W. G. and O'Toole, J. (2005) 'How business schools lost their way', *Harvard Business Review*, May: 96–104.

Bennis, W. G., Berkowitz, N., Affinito, M. and Malone, M. (1958) 'Authority, power and the ability to influence', *Human Relations*, 11: 143–156.

Benson, J. and Brown, M. (2011) 'Generations at work: are there differences and do they matter?' *The International Journal of Human Resource Management*, 22 (9): 1843–1865.

Berger, P. and Luckmann, T. (1967) *The Social Construction of Reality: A Treatise in the Sociology of Knowledge*. Harmondsworth: Penguin.

Bergesen, A. J. and Sonnett, J. (2001) 'The Global 500: mapping the world economy at century's end', *American Behavioral Scientist*, 44 (10): 1602–1615.

Berle, A. A. and Means, G. C. (1932) *The Modern Corporation and Private Property*. New York: Harcourt, Brace & World.

Bertaux, D. and Bertaux-Wiame, I. (1981) 'Artisanal bakery in France: how it lives and why it survives', in F. Bechofer and B. Elliot (eds), *The Petite Bourgeoisie: Comparative Studies of the Uneasy Stratum*. London: Macmillan, pp. 121–154.

Best, M. H. (1990) *The New Competition: Institutions of Industrial Restructuring*. Cambridge: Polity.

Beukman, T. L. (2005) '*The effect of selected variables on leadership: behavior within the framework of a transformational paradigm*', Doctoral dissertation. University of Pretoria.

Beyer, J. M. and Nino, D. (1999) 'Ethics and cultures in international business', *Journal of Management Inquiry*, 8 (3): 287–297.

Bhabha, H. (1994) *The Location of Culture*. London: Routledge.

Biggart, N. W. and Hamilton, G. G. (1992) 'On the limits of a firm-based theory to explain business networks: the Western bias of neoclassical economics', in N. Nohria and R. Eccles (eds), *Networks and Organizations: Structure, Form and Action*. Boston, MA: Harvard Business School Press, pp. 471–490.

Bittner, E. (2002) 'The concept of organization', in S. R. Clegg (ed.), *Central Currents in Organization Studies I: Frameworks and Applications*, Volume 2. London: Sage, pp. 76–87; originally published in *Social Research* (1965) 32: 239–255.

Bjørkeng, K., Clegg, S. R. and Pitsis, T. S. (2009) 'Becoming a practice', *Management Learning*, 40 (2): 145–159.

Black, J. A. and Edwards, S. (2000) 'Emergence of virtual or network organizations: fad or feature', *Journal of Organization Change Management*, 13 (6): 567–576.

Blake, R. R. and McCanse, A. A. (1991) *Leadership Dilemmas–Grid Solution*. Houston: Gulf.

Blake, R. R. and Mouton, J. S. (1985) *The Managerial Grid III*. Houston: Gulf.

Blanchflower, D. G., and Oswald, A. J. (2011) *International Happiness*. National Bureau of Economic Research working paper series (w16668), Cambridge, MA. Available at http://www.nber.org/papers/w16668 (last accessed 14 July 2011).

Blau, P. M. (1955) *The Dynamics of Bureaucracy*. Chicago: University of Chicago Press.

Blau, P. M. (1964) *Exchange and Power in Social Life*. New York: Wiley.

Blau, P. M. (2002) 'A formal theory of differentiation in organizations', in S. R. Clegg (ed.), *Central Currents in Organization Studies I: Frameworks and Applications*, Volume 2. London: Sage, pp. 276–298; originally published in *American Sociological Review* (1970) 35: 201–218.

Blau, P. M. and Schoenherr, R. (1971) *The Structure of Organizations*. New York: Basic Books.

Blau, P. M. and Scott, W. (1963) *Formal Organizations: A Comparative Approach*. London: Routledge & Kegan Paul.

Bloom, D. E. and Canning, D. (2000) 'Public health: the health and wealth of nations', *Science 287* (5456): 1207–1209.

Bogard, W. (1996) *The Simulation of Surveillance: Hypercontrol in Telematic Societies*. Cambridge: Cambridge University Press.

Boje, D. M. (2002) 'Stories of the storytelling organization: a postmodern analysis of Disney as "Tamara-Land"', in S. R. Clegg (ed.), *Central Currents in Organization Studies II: Contemporary Trends*, Volume 7. London: Sage, pp. 29–66; originally published in *Academy of Management Journal* (1995) 38: 997–1035.

Boje, D. M. and Dennehey, R. (1999) *Managing in the Postmodern World*. Dubuque, IA: Kendall-Hunt. Available at http://cbae.nmsu.edu/~dboje/pages/CHAP5LEA.html (last accessed 22 July 2011).

Boje, D. M. and Rhodes, C. (2006) 'The leadership role of Ronald McDonald: double narration and stylistic lines of transformation', *Leadership Quarterly*, 17 (1): 94–103.

Boje, D. M. and Rosile, G. A. (2001) 'Where's the power in empowerment? Answers from Follett and Clegg', *Journal of Applied Behavioral Science*, 37 (1): 90–117.

Bolden, R. and Gosling, R. (2006) 'Leadership competencies: time to change the tune?' *Leadership*, 2 (2): 147–163.

Bone, J. (2007) 'Black's lawyer protests at perks and privileges strategy', *The Times*, 23 May: 45.

Bordow, A. and Moore, E. (1991) *Managing Organizational Communication*. Melbourne: Longman.

Borman, W. C., Hanson, M. A. and Hedge, J. W. (1997) 'Personnel selection', *Annual Review of Psychology*, 48 (2): 299–337.

Bourdieu, P. (1977) *Outline of a Theory of Practice*. Cambridge and New York: Cambridge University Press.

Bourdieu, P. (1998) *Practical Reason: On the Theory of Action*. Cambridge: Polity.

Bourke, H. (1982) 'Industrial unrest as social pathology: the Australian writings of Elton Mayo', *Historical Studies*, 20 (79): 217–233.

Boyd, M. and Pikkov, D. (2005) 'Gendering migration, livelihood and entitlements: migrant women in Canada and the United States', United Nations Research Institute for Social Development (UNRISD) Occasional Paper written for the preparation of the report *Gender Equality: Striving for Justice in an Unequal World*, Occasional Paper 6: United Nations Research Institute for Social Development. Geneva, Sweden: UNRISD. Available at www.unrisd.org/publications/opgp6 (last accessed 14 July 2011).

Brass, D. J., Butterfield, K. D. and Skaggs, B. C. (1998) 'Relationships and unethical behavior: a social network perspective', *Academy of Management Review*, 23 (1): 14–31.

Braun, R. and Krieger, D. (2005) *Einstein – Peace Now! Visions and Ideas*. Chichester: Wiley.

Braverman, H. (1974) *Labor and Monopoly Capital*. New York: Monthly Review Press.

Braybrooke, D. and Lindblom, C. E. (1963) *A Strategy of Decision*. New York: Free Press.

Brewster, C. (1995) 'Towards a "European" model of human resource management', *Journal of International Business Studies*, 26 (1): 1–21.

Brewster, C., Sparrow, P. and Vernon, G. (2007) *International Human Resource Management: Contemporary Issues in Europe*. London: Routledge.

Bronfenbrenner, K. (1998) *Organizing to Win: New Research on Union Strategies*. Ithaca, NY: Sage.

Brown, A. D. (2005) 'Making sense of the collapse of Barings Bank', *Human Relations,* 58 (12): 1579–1604.

Brown, A. D. and Coupland, C. (2004) 'Constructing organizational identities on the Web: a case study of Royal Dutch/Shell', *Journal of Management Studies*, 41 (8): 1325–1347.

Brown, J. and Duguid, P. (2001) 'Creativity versus structure: a useful tension', *Sloan Management Review*, 42 (4): 93–94.

Brown, S. L. and Eisenhardt, K. (1997) 'The art of continuous change: linking complexity theory and time-paced evolution in relentlessly shifting organizations', *Administrative Science Quarterly*, 42 (1): 1–34.

Brown, T. (2009) *Change by Design: How Design Thinking Transforms Organizations and Inspires Innovation*. New York: HarperCollins.

Browning, B. W. (2007) 'Leadership in desperate times: an analysis of endurance: Shackleton's incredible voyage through the lens of leadership theory', *Advances in Developing Human Resources*, 9 (2): 183–198.

Brunsson, N. (1985) *The Irrational Organization*. Chichester: Wiley.

Brunsson, N. (1989) *The Organization of Hypocrisy*. Chichester: Wiley.

Brunsson, N. (1998) 'Non-learning organizations', *Scandinavian Journal of Management*, 14 (4): 421–432.

Brunsson, N. (2006) *Mechanisms of Hope*. Oslo/Copenhagen: Liber/Copenhagen Business School Press.

Brunsson, N. and Jacobsson, B. (2000) *A World of Standards*. Oxford: Oxford University Press.

Buchanan, D. and Badham, R. (1999) *Power, Politics and Organizational Change: Winning the Turf Game*. London: Sage.

Buchanan, D. and Huczynski, A. (2004) 'Images of influence: *12 Angry Men* and *Thirteen Days*', *Journal of Management Inquiry*, 13 (4): 312–323.

Buckholz, R. A. (1998) *Principles of Environmental Management: The Greening of Business*. Upper Saddle River, NJ: Prentice Hall.

Burawoy, M. (1979) *Manufacturing Consent: Changes in the Labor Process Under Monopoly Capitalism*. Chicago: University of Chicago Press.

Burchielli, R. (2006) 'The purpose of trade union values: an analysis of the ACTU1 Statement of Values', *Journal of Business Ethics*, 68 (2): 133–142.

Burgelman, R. (1983) 'A process model of internal corporate venturing in the diversified major firm', *Organizational Science Quarterly*, 28: 223–244.

Burke, R. J. (1994) 'Generation X: measures, sex and age differences', *Psychological Reports*, 74 (2): 555–562.

Burke, R. J. and Nelson, D. L. (1997) 'Downsizing and restructuring: lessons from the firing line for revitalizing organizations', *Leadership & Organization Development Journal*, 18 (7): 325–334.

Burns, T. and Stalker, G. M. (1961) *The Management of Innovation*. London: Tavistock.

Burris, B. H. (1993) *Technocracy at Work*. Albany, NY: State University of New York Press.

Calás, M. B. and McGuire, J. B. (1990) 'Organizations as networks of power and symbolism', in B. Barry (ed.), *Organizational Symbolism*. Berlin: de Gruyter, pp. 95–113.

Calás, M. B. and Smircich, L. (1996) 'Not ahead of her time: reflections on Mary Parker Follett as a prophet of management', *Organization*, 3 (1): 147–152.

Calás, M. B. and Smircich, L. (2006) 'From the "woman's point of view" ten years later: towards a feminist organization studies', in S. R. Clegg, C. Hardy, T. B. Lawrence and W. Nord (2006) *The Sage Handbook of Organization Studies*. London: Sage, pp. 284–346.

Camelo-Ordaz, C., Garca-Cruz, J., Sousa-Ginel, E. and Valle-Cabrera, R. (2011) 'The influence of human resource management on knowledge sharing and innovation in Spain: the mediating role of affective commitment', *International Journal of Human Resource Management*, 22 (7): 1442–1463.

Cameron, J. (Director) (1997) *Titanic* [Motion picture]. United States: Paramount.

Cameron, K. S. and Spreitzer, G. (2011) *Oxford Handbook of Positive Organizational Scholarship*. Oxford: Oxford University Press.

Cameron, K. S., Dutton, J. E. and Quinn, R. E. (2003a) 'Foundations of positive organizational scholarship', in K. S. Cameron, J. E. Dutton and R. E. Quinn (eds), *Positive Organizational Scholarship: Foundations of a New Discipline*. San Francisco, CA: Berrett-Koehler Publishers, pp. 3–12.

Cameron, K. S., Dutton, J. E. and Quinn, R. E. (2003b) *Positive Organizational Scholarship: Foundations of a New Discipline*. San Francisco, CA: Berrett-Koehler Publishers.

Campbell, F. (Producer) (2000) *Gap and Nike: No Sweat?* [Television broadcast]. United Kingdom: BBC.

Campos, G. P., Ramos, C. S. and Bernal, J. J. Y. (1999) 'Emotion discourse "speaks" of involvement: commentary on Edwards', *Culture & Psychology*, 5 (3): 293–304.

Cappozzoli, T. K. (1995) 'Resolving conflict within teams', *Journal for Quality and Participation*, 18 (7): 28–30.

Carey, A. (2002) 'The Hawthorne Studies: a radical criticism', in S. R. Clegg (ed.), *Central Currents in Organization Studies I: Frameworks and Applications*, Volume 1. London: Sage, pp. 314–322; originally published in *American Sociological Review* (1967) 32: 403–416.

Carnegie, D. (1944) *How to Win Friends and Influence People: How to Stop Worrying and Start Living*. London: Chancellor.

Carr, A. (1968) 'Is business bluffing ethical?' *Harvard Business Review*, January/February: 143–153.

Carson, T. (1993) 'Second thoughts about bluffing', *Business Ethics Quarterly*, 3 (4): 317–343.

Carter, C., Clegg, S. R. and Kornberger, M. (2008) *A Very Short, Fairly Interesting and Reasonably Cheap Book about Studying Strategy*, London: Sage.

Carter, C., Clegg, S. R., Kornberger, M., Messner, M. and Laske, S. (eds) (2007) *Business Ethics as Practice: Representation, Discourse and Performance*. Edward: Cheltenham Elgar.

Casey, C. (1995) *Work, Self and Society: After Industrialism*. London: Routledge.

Castells, M. (1996) *The Rise of the Network Society, The Information Age: Economy, Society and Culture Vol. I*. Oxford: Blackwell.

Castells, M. (2000) *The Rise of Network Society: The Information Age: Economy, Society and Culture. Volume 1*, 2nd edn. London: Blackwell.

Castells, M. (2001) *The Internet Galaxy: Reflections on the Internet, Business, and Society*. New York: Oxford University Press.

Castles, S. and Miller, M. J. (2003) *The Age of Migration: International Population Movements in the Modern World*. London: Guilford.

Cathay Pacific Airways (1997) *Recruitment and Corporate Socialization Program Statement*, Hong Kong.

Chan, A. (2003) 'Instantiative versus entitative culture: the case for culture as process', in R. Westwood and S. R. Clegg (eds), *Debating Organizations: Point-Counterpoint in Organization Studies*. Oxford: Blackwell, pp. 311–320.

Chan, A. (2008) 'Matrix organizations', in S. R. Clegg and J. R. Bailey (eds), *The Sage International Encyclopedia of Organization Studies*. Thousand Oaks, CA: Sage, pp. 884–886.

Chandler, A. D. (1962) *Strategy and Structure: Chapters in the History of the American Industrial Enterprise*. Cambridge, MA: MIT Press.

Chandler, A. D. (1977) *The Visible Hand*. Cambridge, MA: Harvard Belknap Press.

Chandler, A. D. (1990) *Scale and Scope*. Cambridge, MA: Harvard University Press.

Chaplin, C. (Director) (1936) *Modern Times* [Motion picture]. United States: Kino International.

Chen, J. and Wang, L. (2007) 'Locus of control and the three components of commitment to change', *Personality and Individual Differences*, 42 (3): 503–512.

Cheney, G. and Christensen, L. T. (2001) 'Organizational identity: linkages between internal and external communication', in F. M. Jablin and L. L. Putnam (eds), *New Handbook of Organizational Communication*. Thousand Oaks, CA: Sage, pp. 231–270.

Child, J. (2002) 'Organizational structure, environment and performance: the role of strategic choice', in S. R. Clegg (ed.), *Central Currents in Organization Studies I: Frameworks and Applications*, Volume 2. London: Sage, pp. 323–343; originally published in *Sociology* (1972) 6: 1–21.

Child, J. and Kieser, A. (1979) 'Organization and managerial roles in British and West German companies: an examination of the culture-free thesis', in C. J. Lammers and D. J. Hickson (eds), *Organizations Alike and Unalike: International and Inter-Institutional Studies in the Sociology of Organizations*. London: Routledge & Kegan Paul, pp. 251–271.

Child, J. and Rodrigues, S. (2003) 'Corporate governance and new organizational forms: issues of double and multiple agency', *Journal of Management and Governance*, 7: 337–360.

Christensen, C. (1997) *The Innovator's Dilemma: When New Technologies Cause Great Firms to Fail*. Boston, MA: Harvard Business School Press.

Christensen, L. and Cheney, G. (2000) 'Self-absorption and self-seduction in the corporate identity game', in M. Schultz, M. Hatch and M. Larsen (eds), *The Expressive Organization: Linking Identity, Reputation, and the Corporate Brand*. Oxford and New York: Oxford University Press, pp. 246–270.

Cicirelli, V. G. (1987) 'Locus of control and patient role adjustment of the elderly in acute-care hospitals', *Psychology and Aging*, 2 (2): 138–143.

Clark, P. (2003) *Organizational Innovations*. London: Sage.

Clarke, J., Hall, S., Jefferson, T. and Roberts, B. (eds) (1976) *Resistance Through Rituals*. London: Hutchinson.

Clarke, T. (ed.) (2004) *Corporate Governance: Critical Perspectives on Business and Management*. London: Routledge.

Clarke, T. and Clegg, S. R. (1998) *Changing Paradigms: The Transformation of Management for the 21st Century*. London: Collins.

Clawson, D. (1980) *Bureaucracy and the Labor Process: The Transformation of U.S. Industry 1860–1920*. New York: Monthly Review Press.

Clegg, S. R. (1979) *The Theory of Power and Organization*. London: Routledge & Kegan Paul.

Clegg, S. R. (1981) 'Organization and control', *Administrative Science Quarterly*, 26 (4): 545–562.

Clegg, S. R. (1989) *Frameworks of Power*. London: Sage.

Clegg, S. R. (1990) *Modern Organizations: Organization Studies in the Postmodern World*. London: Sage.

Clegg, S. R. (1994) 'Power and the resistant subject', in J. Jermier, D. Knights and W. R. Nord (eds), *Resistance and Power in Organizations: Agency, Subjectivity and the Labor Process*. London: Routledge.

Clegg, S. R. (1995) 'Weber and Foucault: social theory for the study of organizations', *Organization*, 1 (1): 149–178.

Clegg, S. R. (1999) 'Globalizing the intelligent organization: learning organizations, smart workers, (not so) clever countries and the sociological imagination', *Management Learning*, 30 (3): 259–280.

Clegg, S. R. (2005) 'Puritans, visionaries and survivors', *Organization Studies*, 26 (4): 527–545.

Clegg, S. R. (2010) *SAGE Directions in Organization Studies (Volume II)*, London: Sage.

Clegg, S. R. and Bailey, J. R. (eds) (2008) *The Sage International Encyclopedia of Organization Studies*. Thousand Oaks, CA: Sage.

Clegg, S. R. and Dunkerley, D. (1980) *Organization, Class and Control*. London: Routledge & Kegan Paul.

Clegg, S. R. and Hardy, C. (1996) 'Representations', in S. R. Clegg, C. Hardy and W. R. Nord (eds), *Handbook of Organization Studies*. London: Sage, pp. 676–708.

Clegg, S. R. and Kono, T. (2002) 'Trends in Japanese management: an overview of embedded continuities and disembedded discontinuities', *Asia Pacific Journal of Management*, 19 (2 & 3): 269–285.

Clegg, S. R. and Kornberger, M. (2003) 'Modernism, postmodernism, management and organization theory', in E. Locke (ed.), *Postmodernism in Organizational Thought: Pros, Cons and the Alternative*. Amsterdam: Elsevier, pp. 57–89.

Clegg, S. R. and Palmer, G. (1996) *The Politics of Management Knowledge*. London: Sage.

Clegg, S. R. and Rhodes, C. (2006) *Management Ethics: Contemporary Contexts*. London: Routledge.

Clegg, S. R., Carter, C. and Kornberger, M. (2004) 'Get up, I feel like being a strategy machine', *European Management Review*, 1 (1): 21–28.

Clegg, S. R., Courpasson, D. and Phillips, N. (2006a) *Power and Organizations*. Thousand Oaks, CA: Sage.

Clegg, S. R., Carter, C., Kornberger, M. and Schweitzer, J. (2011) *Strategy: Theory & Practice*. London: Sage

Clegg, S. R., Hardy, C., Lawrence, T. B. and Nord, W. R. (eds) (2006b) *The Sage Handbook of Organization Studies*. London: Sage.

Clegg, S. R., Pitsis, T. S., Rura-Polley, T. and Marosszeky, M. (2002) 'Governmentality matters: building an alliance culture for interorganizational collaboration', *Organization Studies*, 23 (3): 317–337.

Coch, L. and French, J. R. P. (1948) 'Overcoming resistance to change', *Human Relations*, 1: 512–532.

Cockett, R. (1995) *Thinking the Unthinkable: Think Tanks and the Economic Counter-Revolution, 1931–1983*. London: HarperCollins.

Cohen, M. D., March, J. G. and Olsen, J. P. (1972) 'The garbage can model of organizational choice', *Administrative Science Quarterly*, 17 (1): 1–25.

Cole, R. E. (1999) *Managing Quality Fads*. Oxford: Oxford University Press.

Collins, D. (1998) *Gainsharing and Power: Lessons from Six Scanlon Plans*. Ithaca, NY: Cornell University Press.

Collins, L. R. and Schneid, T. D. (2001) *Physical Hazards of the Workplace*. Boca Raton, FL: CRC Press.

Collinson, D. L. (1994) 'Strategies of resistance: power, knowledge and subjectivity in the workplace', in J. Jermier, D. Knights and W. R. Nord (eds), *Resistance and Power in Organizations: Agency, Subjectivity and the Labor Process*. London: Routledge, pp. 25–68.

Colson, C. and Pearcey, N. (1999) *Shattering the Grid: How Now Shall We Live?* Wheaton, IL; Tyndall House Publishers.

Colville, I., Waterman, R. and Weick, K. (1999) 'Organizing and the search for excellence: making sense of the times in theory and practice', *Organization*, 6 (1): 129–148.

Conger, J. A. (2000) 'How generational shifts will transform organizational life', in F. Hesselbein, M. Goldsmith and R. Beckhard. (eds), *The Organization of the Future*. San Francisco: Jossey-Bass, pp. 17–24.

Cooke, B. (2003) 'The denial of slavery in management studies', *Journal of Management Studies*, 40 (8): 1895–1918.

Cooney, N. (2011) *Change of Heart: What Psychology Can Teach Us About Spreading Social Change*. Brooklyn: Lantern Books.

Coppola, F. F. (Director) (1972, 1974, 1990) *The Godfather: Parts I, II, and III* [Motion pictures]. United States: Paramount.

Coppola, F. F. (Director) (1974) *The Conversation* [Motion picture]. United States: Paramount.

Corman, S. R. and Poole, M. S. (2000) *Perspectives on Organizational Communication: Finding Common Ground*. New York: Guilford Press.

Cornelissen, J. P., Kafouros, M. and Lock, A. R. (2005) 'Metaphorical images of organization: how organizational researchers develop and select organizational metaphors', *Human Relations*, 58 (12): 1545–1578.

Costa, P. T., Jr and McCrae, R. R. (1999) *NEO Personality Inventory: Revised (NEO PI-R)*. Available from Psychological Assessment Resources, Inc. at www.parinc.com/products_search.cfm?Search=General (last accessed 12 July 2011).

Coughlan, P., Fulton Surwe, J. and Canales, K. (2007) 'Prototypes as (design) tools for behavioral and organizational change: a design-based approach to help organizations change work behaviors', *Journal of Applied Behavioral Science*, 43: 122–134.

Courpasson, D. (2002) 'Managerial strategies of domination: power in soft bureaucracies', in S. R. Clegg (ed.), *Central Currents in Organization Studies II: Contemporary Trends, Volume 5*. London: Sage, pp. 324–345; originally published in *Organization Studies* (2000) 21: 141–161.

Coutu, D. (2000) 'Creating the most frightening company on Earth: an interview with Andy Law of St. Luke's', *Harvard Business Review*, September–October: 143–150.

Cozijnsen, A. J., Vrakkin, W. J. and Van Izerloo, M. (2000) 'Success and failure of 50 innovation projects in Dutch companies', *European Journal of Innovation Management*, 3 (3): 150–159.

Craig, G., Gaus, A., Wilkinson, M., Skrivankova, K. and McQuade, A. (2007) 'Modern slavery in the United Kingdom', 26 February. Available at http://www.jrf.org.uk/publications/modern-slavery-united-kingdom (last accessed 22 July 2011).

Crane, A. and Matten, D. (2004) *Business Ethics: A European Perspective: Managing Corporate Citizenship and Sustainability in the Age of Globalization*. Oxford: Oxford University Press.

Crick, B. (1962) *In Defence of Politics*. Chicago: University of Chicago Press.

Crosby, F. J., Iyer, A., Clayton, S. and Downing, R. A. (2003) 'Affirmative action: psychological data and the policy debates', *American Psychologist*, 58 (2): 93–115.

Crozier, M. (1964) *The Bureaucratic Phenomenon*. London: Tavistock.

Crozier, M. and Friedberg, E. (1980) *Actors and Systems: The Politics of Collective Action*, trans. A. Goldhammer. Chicago: University of Chicago Press.

Cruver, B. (2003) *Enron: The Anatomy of Greed: The Unshredded Truth from an Enron Insider*. London: Arrow.

Cullen, J. B., Parboteeah, K. P. and Victor, B. (2003) 'The effects of ethical climates on organizational commitment: A two-study analysis', *Journal of Business Ethics*, 46: 127–41.

Cummings, S. (2002) *Recreating Strategy*. London: Sage.

Cusumano, M. A. and Gawer, A. (2002) 'The elements of platform leadership', *MIT Sloan Management Review*, 43: 51–58.

Cyert, R. M. and March, J. G. (1963) *A Behavioral Theory of the Firm*. Englewood Cliffs, NJ: Prentice Hall.

Czarniawska, B. (2005) 'Fashion in organizing', in B. Czarniawska and G. Sevón, *Global Ideas: How Ideas, Objects and Practices Travel in the Global Economy*. Oslo/Copenhagen: Liber/Copenhagen Business School Press, pp. 129–46.

Dacin, M. T., Ventresca, M. J. and Beal, B. D. (1999) 'The embeddedness of organizations: dialogue & directions', *Journal of Management*, 25 (6): 317–356.

Daft, R. and Lewin, A. Y. (1993) 'Where are the theories for the "new" organizational forms? An editorial essay', *Organization Science*, 4: i–iv.

Darwin, C. (1859) *On the Origin of Species by Means of Natural Selection, or the Preservation of Favoured Races in the Struggle for Life*. London: John Murray.

Das, T. K. and Teng, B. (2000) 'A resource-based theory of strategic alliances', *Journal of Management*, 26: 31–61.

Davidow, W. H. and Malone, M. A. (1992) *The Virtual Corporation: Structuring and Revitalizing the Corporation for the 21st Century*. New York: HarperCollins.

Davies, N. (1998) *Europe: A History*. New York: Harper Perennial.

Davis, M. (1959) *Kind of Blue* [Record album]. New York: Columbia.

Dawson, P. (2003) *Reshaping Change: A Processual Perspective*. London: Routledge.

D'Cruz, P. and Noronha, E. (2006) 'Being professional: organizational control in Indian call centers', *Social Science Computer Review*, 24 (3): 342–361.

Deal, T. E. and Kennedy, A. A. (1982) *Corporate Cultures: The Rites and Rituals of Corporate Life*. Reading, MA: Addison-Wesley.

Deardon, J. (Director) (1999) *Rogue Trader* [Motion picture]. United Kingdom: Newmarket Capitol, Granada Film Productions.

De Certeau, M. (1988) *The Practice of Everyday Life*. London: University of California Press.

DeCharms, R. (1968) *Personal Causation*. New York: Academic Press.

Deci, E. L. (1975) *Intrinsic Motivation*. New York: Plenum.

Deci, E. L. and Ryan, R. M. (1985) *Intrinsic Motivation and Self-Determination in Human Behavior*. New York: Journal Plenum.

Deci, E. L. and Ryan, R. M. (1987) 'The support of autonomy and the control of behavior', *Journal of Personality and Social Psychology*, 53: 1024–1037.

Deci, E. L. and Ryan, R. M. (2000) 'The "what" and "why" of goal pursuits: human needs and the self-determination of behavior', *Psychological Inquiry*, 11 (4): 227–268.

De Dreu, C. K. W. and Van Vianen, A. E. M. (2001) 'Managing relationship conflict and the effectiveness of organizational teams', *Journal of Organizational Behavior*, 22: 309–328.

de Geus, A. (1988) 'Planning as learning', *Harvard Business Review*, March–April: 70–74.

Deleuze, G. and Guattari, F. (1984) *A Thousand Plateaus: Capitalism and Schizophrenia*, Volume 2. London: Athlone.

Deloitte & Touche (1998) *Informal Economic Activities in the EU*. Brussels: European Commission.

Deming, E. (2000) *Out of the Crisis*. Boston: MIT Press.

Den Hartog, D. N. and Koopman, P. L. (2001) 'Leadership in organizations', in N. Anderson, D. S. Ones, H. Kepir-Sinangil and C. Viswesvaran (eds), *Handbook of Industrial, Work and Organizational Psychology*. London: Sage, pp. 166–187.

Denison, D. (1990) *Corporate Culture and Organizational Effectiveness*. New York: Wiley.

Derrida, J. (1988) 'Afterword: toward an ethic of discussion', in *Limited Inc.*, ed. G. Graf. Evanston IL: Northwestern University Press, pp. 111–154.

Derrida, J. (1994) 'Nietzsche and the machine: interview with Jacques Derrida', *Journal of Nietzsche Studies*, 7: Spring.

Derrida, J. (1995) *Points-Interviews 1974–1994*. Stanford, CA: Stanford University Press.

Derrida, J. (1996) 'Remarks on deconstruction and pragmatism', in C. Mouffe (ed.), *Deconstruction and Pragmatism*. London: Routledge, pp. 77–88.

DeSanctis, G. and Monge, P. (1999) 'Communication processes for virtual organizations', *Organization Science*, 10 (6): 693–703.

Devos, T., Spini, D. and Schwartz, S. (2002). 'Conflicts among human values and trust in institutions', *British Journal of Social Psychology*, 41 (1): 481–494.

Dicken, P. (2007) *Global Shift: Mapping the Changing Contours of the World Economy*, 5th edn. London: Sage Publications.

Diefendorff, J., Morehart, J. and Gabriel, A. (2011) 'The influence of power and solidarity on emotional display rules at work', *Motivation & Emotion*, 34 (2): 120–132.

DiMaggio, P. and Powell, W. W. (2002) 'The iron cage revisited: institutional isomorphism and collective rationality in organizational fields', in S. R. Clegg (ed.), *Central Currents in Organization Studies I: Frameworks and Applications*, Volume 3. London: Sage, pp. 324–362; originally published in *American Journal of Sociology* (1983) 48: 147–160.

d'Iribarne, P. (2008) 'National cultures', in S. R. Clegg and J. Bailey (eds), *The Sage International Encyclopedia of Organization Studies*. Thousand Oaks, CA: Sage, pp. 945–949.

Dobbin, F. (1994) 'Cultural models of organization: the social construction of rational organizing principles', in D. Crane (ed.), *The Sociology of Culture: Emerging Theoretical Perspectives*. Oxford: Basil Blackwell, pp. 117–141.

Dodgson, M. (2000) *The Management of Technological Innovation: An International and Strategic Approach*. Oxford: Oxford University Press.

Does, S., Derks, B. and Ellemers, N. (2011) 'Thou shalt not discriminate: how emphasizing moral ideals rather than obligations increases Whites' support for social equality', *Journal of Experimental Social Psychology*, 47 (3): 562–571.

Donaldson, L. (1992) 'The Weick stuff: managing beyond games', *Organization Science*, 3 (3): 461–466.

Donaldson, L. (1999) *Performance-Driven Organizational Change: The Organizational Portfolio*. London: Sage.

Donaldson, L. (2002) 'Strategy and structural adjustment to regain fit and performance: in defence of contingency theory', in S. R. Clegg (ed.), *Central Currents in Organization Studies I: Frameworks and Applications*, Volume 2. London: Sage, pp. 379–389; originally published in *Journal of Management Studies* (1987) 24: 1–24.

Donaldson, L. (2005) 'Vita contemplativa: following the scientific method: how I became a committed functionalist and positivist', *Organization Studies*, 26 (7): 1071–1088.

Donaldson, R. (2000) *Thirteen Days* [Motion picture]. Los Angeles: Buena Vista.

Dooley, R. S., Fryxell, G. E. and Judge, W. Q. (2000) 'Belaboring the not-so-obvious: consensus, commitment, and strategy implementation speed and success', *Journal of Management Studies*, 23 (5): 501–517.

Douglas, C. and Ammeter, A. P. (2004) 'An examination of the leader political skill construct and its effect on ratings of leader effectiveness', *Leadership Quarterly*, 15: 537–550.

Drucker, P. (1998) *Management Challenges for the 21st Century*. Oxford: Butterworth–Heinemann.

Drummond, H. (2002) 'Living in a fool's paradise: the collapse of Barings' Bank', *Management Decision*, 40 (3): 232–238.

Dubrin, A. J. (2005) *Coaching and Mentoring Skills*. Englewood Cliffs, NJ: Pearson Prentice Hall.

du Gay, P. (1996) *Consumption and Identity at Work*. London: Sage.

du Gay, P. (2000a) *In Praise of Bureaucracy*. London: Sage.

du Gay, P. (2000b) 'Enterprise and its futures: a response to Fournier and Grey', *Organization*, 7 (1): 165–183.

du Gay, P. (2001) 'A common power to keep them all in awe: a comment on "governance"', *Journal of Social Research*, 6 (1): 11–27.

du Gay, P. (2002) 'How responsible is "responsive" government?' *Economy & Society*, 31 (3): 461–482.

du Gay, P. (2003) 'The tyranny of the epochal: change, epochalism and organizational reform', *Organization*, 10: 663–684.

du Gay, P. (2004) 'Against "Enterprise" (but not against "enterprise", for that would make no sense)', *Organization*, 11 (1): 37–57.

du Gay, P. (2006) 'Machinery of government and standards in public service: teaching new dogs old tricks', *Economy & Society*, 35 (1): 148–167.

du Gay, P. (2007) *Organizing Identity: Persons and Organizations after Theory*. London: Sage.

du Gay, P. (2008) 'Max Weber and the moral economy of office', *Journal of Cultural Economy*, 1 (2): 129–144.

du Gay, P. and Salaman, G. (1992) 'The cult[ure] of the customer', *Journal of Management Studies* 29 (5): 615–633.

du Gay, P., Hall, S., Janes, L., Mackay, H. and Negus, K. (1997) *Doing Cultural Studies: Story of the Sony Walkman*. London: Sage.

Dunford, R., Palmer, I., Benveniste, J. and Crawford, J. (2007) 'Coexistence of "old" and "new" organizational practices: transitory phenomenon or enduring feature?' *Asia Pacific Journal of Human Resources*, 45 (1): 24–43.

Dunlop, J. T. (1958) *Industrial Relations Systems*. New York: Holt, Reinhart and Winston.

Dunning, J. (1998) 'Reappraising the eclectic paradigm in an age of alliance capitalism', in M. Colombo (ed.), *The Changing Boundaries of the Firm*. London: Routledge.

Dunphy, D. and Pitsis, T. S. (2003) 'Leadership wisdom', in C. Barker and R. Coye (eds), *The Seven Heavenly Virtues of Leadership*. Melbourne: McGraw-Hill.

Durkheim, E. (1982 [1895]) *Durkheim: The Rules of Sociological Method and Selected Texts on Sociology and its Method*. Edited and introduction by Steven Lukes, select translations by W. D. Hallis. New York: The Free Press.

Dutton, J. E., Glynn, M. A. and Spreitzer, G. M. (2006) 'Positive organizational scholarship', in J. Greenhaus and G. Callanan (eds), *Encyclopedia of Career Development*. Thousand Oaks, CA: Sage, pp. 641–644.

Dutton, J. E., Lilius, J. M. and Kanov, J. M. (2007) 'The transformative potential of compassion at work', in S. K. Piderit, R. E. Fry and D. L. Cooperrider (eds), *Handbook of Transformative Cooperation: New Designs and Dynamics*. Stanford, CA: Stanford University Press, pp. 107–124.

Dutton, J. E., Morgan Roberts, L. and Bednar, J. (2010) 'Pathways for positive identity construction at work: four types of positive identity and the building of social resources', *The Academy of Management Review*, 35 (2): 2265–2293.

Dutton, J. E., Frost, P., Worline, M. C., Lilius, J. M. and Kanov, J. M. (2002) 'Leading in times of trauma', *Harvard Business Review*, 80 (1): 54–61.

Dylan, B. (1978) 'Changing of the guards', on *Street Legal* [Record album, Copyright 1978 Special Rider Music]. United States: CBS.

Easterby-Smith, M. (1997) 'Disciplines of organizational learning: contributions and critiques', *Human Relations*, 50 (9): 1085–1113.

Edelman, J. and Crain, M. B. (1993) *The Tao of Negotiation: How to Resolve Conflict in All Areas of Your Life*. London: Piatkus.

Edelman, M. (1964) *The Symbolic Uses of Politics*. Champaign, IL: University of Illinois Press.

Edelman, M. (1971) *Political Language*. London: Academic Press.

Edquist, C. (2000) 'Systems of innovation approaches: their emergence and characteristics', in C. Edquist and M. McKelvey (eds), *Systems of Innovation: Growth, Competitiveness and Employment*, Volume 1. Cheltenham: Edward Elgar, pp. 3–37.

Edwards, R. (1979) *Contested Terrain: The Transformation of the Workplace in the Twentieth Century*. New York: Basic Books.

Effron, M., Gandossy, R. and Goldsmith, M. (eds) (2003) *Human Resources in the 21st Century*. Hoboken, NJ: Wiley.

Egelhoff, W. G. (1982) 'Strategy and structure in multinational corporations: an information-processing approach', *Administrative Science Quarterly*, 27 (3): 435–458.

Ehigie, B. O. and Ehigie, R. I. (2005) 'Applying qualitative methods in organizations: a note for industrial/ organizational psychologists', *Qualitative Report*, 10 (3): 621–638.

Eichengreen, B. (2007) *The European Economy since 1945: Coordinated Capitalism and Beyond*. Princeton, NJ: Princeton University Press.

Ekman, P. and Friesen, W. V. (1986) 'A new pan-cultural facial expression of emotion', *Motivation and Emotion*, 10: 159–168.

Ellis, R. J. (1988) 'Self-monitoring and leadership emergence in groups', *Personality and Social Psychology Bulletin*, 14: 681–693.

Emerson, R. M. (1962) 'Power-dependence relations', *American Sociological Review*, 27 (1): 31–41.

Endler, N. S. and Speer, R. L. (1998) 'Personality psychology: research trends for 1993–1995', *Journal of Personality*, 66: 621–629.

Enz, C. A. (1988) 'The role of value congruity in interorganizational power', *Administrative Science Quarterly*, 33: 284–304.

Epstein, N. B. and Baucom, D. H. (2002) *Enhanced Cognitive-behavior Therapy for Couples: A Contextual Approach*. Washington, DC: American Psychological Association Press.

Erickson, G. (2007) 'The day I almost sold the company'. Available at http://www.clifbar.com/ourstory/ document. cfm?location=journey&id=137 (last accessed 2 February 2007).

Eriksson-Zetterquist, U., Lindberg, K. and Styhre, A. (2009) 'When the good times are over: professionals encountering new technology', *Human Relations*, 62 (8): 1145–1170.

Esser, J. K. and Lindoerfer, J. S. (1989) 'Groupthink and the Space Shuttle Challenger accident: toward a quantitative case analysis', *Journal of Behavioral Decision Making*, 2 (1): 167–177.

Etzioni, A. (1961) *A Comparative Analysis of Complex Organizations: On Power, Involvement, and Their Correlates*. New York: Free Press.

European Industrial Relations Observatory On-line (2004) 'Trade Union Membership 1993–2003'. Available at http://www.eurofound.europa.eu/eiro/2004/03/update/tn0403105u.html (last accessed 23 February 2007).

Ewenstein, B. and Whyte, J. (2007) 'Beyond words: Aesthetic knowledge and knowing in organizations', *Organization Studies*, 28 (5): 689–708.

Fairtlough, G. (1994) *Creative Compartments: A Design for Future Organizations*. London: Adamantine Press.

Fairtlough, G. (2007) *Three Ways of Getting Things Done: Hierarchy, Heterarchy and Responsible Autonomy in Organizations* (International Edition). Axminster: Tricarchy Press.

Falkner, R. (1973) 'Career concerns and mobility motivations of orchestra Musicians', *Sociological Quarterly*, 14 (Summer): 334–349.

Farrow, J. (1948) (Director) *The Big Clock* [Motion picture]. Hollywood: Paramount Pictures.

Fayol, H. (1949) *General and Industrial Management*. London: Pitman.

Feldman, M. L. and Spratt, M. F. (1999) *Five Frogs on a Log: A CEO's Field Guide to Accelerating the Transition in Mergers, Acquisitions, and Gut Wrenching Change*. New York: HarperCollins.

Fenton, E. M. and Pettigrew, A. (2000) 'Theoretical perspectives on new forms of organizing', in A. M. Pettigrew and E. M. Fenton (eds), *The Innovating Organization*. London: Sage, pp. 1–46.

Festinger, L. (1957) *A Theory of Cognitive Dissonance*. Stanford, CA: Stanford University Press.

Festinger, L. and Carlsmith, J. M. (1959) 'Cognitive consequences of forced compliance', *Journal of Abnormal and Social Psychology*, 58: 203–210.

Fiedler, F. E. (1964) *A Theory of Leadership Effectiveness*. New York: McGraw-Hill.

Fisher, S. G. (1996) 'Further evidence concerning the Belbin Team Role Self-perception Inventory', *Personnel Review*, 25 (2): 61–67.

Fleming, P. (2008) 'Resistance to change', in S. R. Clegg and J. R. Bailey (eds), *The Sage International Encyclopedia of Organization Studies*. Thousand Oaks, CA: Sage, pp. 1376–1379.

Fleming, P. and Spicer, A. (2003) 'Working at a cynical distance: implications for power, subjectivity and resistance', *Organization,* 10 (1): 157–179.

Fleming, P. and Spicer, A. (2007) *Contesting the Corporation: Struggle, Power and Resistance in Organizations*. Cambridge: Cambridge University Press.

Fletcher, G. J. O. and Sydnor Clark, M. (2003) *Blackwell Handbook of Social Psychology: Interpersonal Processes*. Malden, MA: Blackwell Press.

Fligstein, N. (1985) 'The spread of the multidivisional form', *American Sociological Review*, 5 (3): 377–391.

Fligstein, N. (2002) 'The spread of the multidivisional form among large firms, 1919–1979', in S. R. Clegg (ed.), *Central Currents in Organization Studies I: Frameworks and Applications*, Volume 4. London: Sage, pp. 343–364; originally published in *American Sociological Review* (1985) 5 (3): 377–391.

Florida, R. (2002) *The Rise of the Creative Classes*, New York: Basic Books.

Flyvbjerg, B. (1998) *Rationality and Power: Democracy in Practice*. Chicago: University of Chicago Press.

Foley, J. (Director) (1992) *Glengarry Glen Ross* [Motion picture]. United States: New Line.

Follett, M. P. (1918) *The New State: Group Organization, the Solution for Popular Government*. New York: Longman, Green.

Follett, M. P. (1924) *Creative Experience*. New York: Longman, Green.

Follett, M. P. (1941) *Dynamic Administration: The Collected Papers of Mary Parker Follett*, ed. H. C. Metcalf and L. Urwick. New York: Harper & Bros.

Fong, G. T. and Markus, H. (1982) 'Self-schemas and judgments about others: seeking information about others', *Social Cognition*, 1: 191–204.

Ford, J. (Director) (1941) *How Green Was My Valley* [Motion picture]. Los Angeles: Twentieth Century Fox.

Forman, M. (Director) (1975) *One Flew Over the Cuckoo's Nest* [Motion picture]. United States: United Artists.

Foucault, M. (1965) *Madness and Civilization: A History of Insanity in the Age of Reason*. New York: Vintage.

Foucault, M. (1979) *Discipline and Punish*. Harmondsworth: Penguin.

Foucault, M. (1983) 'The subject and power: afterword', in H. Dreyfus and P. Rabinow (eds), *Michel Foucault: Beyond Structuralism and Hermeneutics*. Brighton: Harvester, pp. 208–226.

Foucault, M. (2003) *Society Must Be Defended*, trans. D. Macey. Harmondsworth: Penguin.

Fox, E. M. (1968) 'Mary Parker Follett: the enduring contribution', *Public Administration Review*, 28 (6): 520–529.

Francis, R. and Armstrong, A. (2003) 'Ethics as a risk management strategy: the Australian experience', *Journal of Business Ethics*, 45: 375–385.

Frank, A. and Brownell, J. (1989) *Organizational Communication and Behaviour: Communicating to Improve Performance*. New York: Dryden.

Frears, S. (Director) (2000) *High Fidelity* [Motion picture]. United States: Buena Vista.

Frears, S. (Director) (2003) *Dirty Pretty Things* [Motion picture]. United States: Miramax.

Freedom, R. B. and Medoff, J. L. (1984) *What Do Unions Do?* New York: Basic Books.

Freeman, K. E. (1984) *The Feminist Case Against Bureaucracy*. Philadelphia: Temple University Press.

French, H. (2003) *Vanishing Borders: Protecting the Environment in the Age of Globalization*. New York: Norton Paperbacks.

French, J. P. R. and Raven, B. (1968) 'The bases of social power', in D. Cartwright and A. Zander (eds), *Group Dynamics*. New York: Harper & Row, pp. 150–167.

Frenkel, M. and Shenhav, Y. (2006) 'From binarism back to hybridity: a postcolonial reading of management and organization studies', *Organization Studies*, 27 (6): 855–876.

Frenkel, S., Tam, M., Korczynski, M. and Shire, K. (1998) 'Beyond bureaucracy? Work organization in call centres', *International Journal of Human Resource Management*, 9 (6): 957–979.

Freud, S. (1935) *A General Introduction to Psychoanalysis*. New York: Carlton House.

Frey, K. and Lüthje, C. (2011) 'Antecedents and consequences of interaction quality in virtual end-user communities', *Creativity and Innovation Management*, 20, (1): 22–35.

Frey, L. R. (2004) 'The symbolic-interpretive perspective on group dynamics', *Small Group Research*, 35 (3): 277–306.

Friedman, A. (1977) 'Responsible autonomy versus direct control over the labour process', *Capital and Class*, 1: 43–57.

Friedman, A. (1990) 'Managerial strategies, activities, techniques and technology: towards a complex theory of the labour process', in D. Knights and H. Willmott (eds), *Labour Process Theory*. London: Macmillan.

Friedman, M. (1982) *Capitalism and Freedom*. Chicago: University of Chicago Press.

Friedman, T. (1999) *The Lexus and the Olive Tree*. London: HarperCollins.

Friedman, T. (2005) *The World Is Flat: A Brief History of the Twenty-First Century*. New York: Farrar, Straus and Giroux.

Friga, P. N., Bettis, R. A. and Sullivan, R. S. (2003) 'Changes in graduate management education and new business school strategies for the 21st century', *Academy of Management Learning and Education*, 2 (3): 233–249.

Frost, P. J. (1999) 'Why compassion counts', *Journal of Management Inquiry*, 8 (2): 127–133.

Frost, P. J. (2003) *Toxic Emotions at Work: How Compassionate Managers Handle Pain and Conflict*. Cambridge, MA: Harvard Business School Press.

Frost, P. J. and Egri, C. P. (2002) 'The political process of innovation', in S. R. Clegg (ed.), *Central Currents in Organization Studies II: Contemporary Trends, Volume 5*. London: Sage, pp. 103–161; originally published in *Research in Organizational Behaviour* (1991) 13: 229–295.

Frost, P. J. and Robinson, S. L. (1999) 'The toxic handler: organizational hero and casualty', *Harvard Business Review*, July–August: 96–106.

Froud, J., Sukhdev, J., Williams, K. and Leaver, A. (2006) *Financialization and Strategy: Narrative and Number*. London: Routledge.

Frost, P. J., Dutton, J. E., Maitlis, S., Lilius, J. M., Kanov, J. M. and Worline, M. C. (2006) 'Seeing organizations differently: three lenses on compassion', in S. R. Clegg, C. Hardy, T. B. Lawrence and W. R. Nord (eds), *The Sage handbook of Organization Studies*. London: Sage, pp. 843–866.

Froud, J., Haslam, S., Johal, S. and Williams, K. (2000) 'Shareholder value and financialization: consultancy promises, management moves', *Economy and Society*, 29: 80–110.

Fulk, J. and DeSanctis, G. (2002) 'Electronic communication and changing organization forms', in S. R. Clegg (ed.), *Central Currents in Organization Studies II: Contemporary Trends*, Volume 2. London: Sage, pp. 278–289; originally published in *Organization Science* (1995) 6: 337–349.

Fulop, L. and Rifkin, W. (1999) 'Management knowledge and learning', in L. Fulop and S. Linstead (eds), *Management: A Critical Text*. South Yarra, Victoria: Macmillan, pp. 14–47.

Gabriel, Y., Fineman, S. and Sims, D. (2000) *Organizing and Organizations*. London: Sage.

Gagliardi, P. (1990) 'Artifacts as pathways and remains of organizational life', in P. Gagliardi (ed.), *Symbols and Artifacts: Views of the Corporate Landscape*. Berlin: de Gruyter, pp. 3–38.

Galbraith, J. K. (1954) *The Great Crash of 1929*. New York: Houghton Mifflin.

Galbraith, J. K. (1969) *The Affluent Society*. Boston: Houghton Mifflin.

Galbraith, J. K. (2011) 'Inequality and economic and political change: a comparative perspective', *Cambridge Journal of Regions, Economy and Society*, 4 (1): 13–27.

Galbraith, J. R. (1971) 'Matrix organization designs', *Business Horizons*, 14: 29–40.

Gambetta, D. (2009) *Codes of the Underworld: How Criminals Communicate*. Princeton, NJ: Princeton University Press.

Gambrell, K. M., Matkin, G. S. and Burbach, M. E. (2011) 'Cultivating leadership: the need for renovating models to higher epistemic cognition', *Journal of Leadership & Organizational Studies* (In print).

Gandz, J. and Murray, V. V. (1980) 'The experience of workplace politics', *Academy of Management Journal*, 23 (2): 237–251.

Gardiner, L. R. and Armstrong-Wright, D. (2000) 'Employee selection under anti-discrimination law: implications for multi-criteria group decision support', *Journal of Multi-Criteria Decision Analysis*, 9 (1–3): 99–109.

Gardner, W. L., Avolio, B. J., Luthans, F., May, D. R. and Walumbwa, F. O. (2005) 'Can you see the real me? A self-based model of authentic leader and follower development', *Leadership Quarterly*, 16 (3): 343–372.

Garrett, L. (1994) *The Coming Plague: Newly Emerging Diseases in a World Out of Balance*. New York: Farrar Straus and Giroux.

Garrick, J. and Clegg, S. R. (2001) 'Stressed-out knowledge workers in performative times: a postmodern take on project-based learning', *Management Learning*, 32 (1): 119–134.

Garvin, David A. (1984) 'What does quality really mean?' *Sloan Management Review*, 26 (1): 25–43.

Gatewood, R. D. and Carroll, A. B. (1991) 'Assessment of ethical performance of organization members: A conceptual framework', *Academy of Management Review*, 16 (4): 667–690.

Gazi, I. and Zyphur, M. (2007) 'Ways of interacting: the standardization of communication in medical training', *Human Relations*, 60 (5): 769–792.

George, J. M. (1992) 'The role of personality in organizational life: issues and evidence', *Journal of Management*, 18 (2): 185–213.

Georgopoulos, B. S., Mahoney, G. M. and Jones, N. W. (1957) 'A path goal approach to productivity', *Journal of Applied Psychology*, 41: 345–353.

Geppert, M. and Matten, D. (2006) 'Institutional influences on manufacturing organization in multinational corporations: the "cherrypicking" approach', *Organization Studies*, 27 (4): 491–515.

Geppert, M. and Williams, K. (2003) 'Change management in MNCs: how global convergence intertwines with national diversities', *Organization Studies*, 27 (4): 491–515.

Gersick, C. J. G. (1988) 'Time and transition in work teams: toward a new model of group development', *Academy of Management Journal*, 31 (1): 9–41.

Gersick, C. J. G. (1989) 'Marking time: predictable transitions in task groups', *Academy of Management Journal*, 32 (2): 274–309.

Gersick, C. J. G. (1994) 'Pacing strategic change: the case of a new venture', *Academy of Management Journal*, 37 (1): 9–45.

Ghezzi, S. and Mingione, E. (2007) 'Embeddedness, path dependency and social institutions: an economic sociology approach', *Current Sociology*, 55 (1): 11–23.

Ghoshal, S. (2005) 'Bad management theories are destroying good management practices', *Academy of Management Learning and Education*, 4 (5): 75–91.

Ghoshal, S. and Bartlett, C. A. (1997) *The Individualized Corporation: A Fundamentally New Approach to Management: Great Companies Are Defined by Purpose, Process, and People*. New York: HarperBusiness.

Gibney, A. (Director) (2005) *Enron: The Smartest Guys in the Room* [Motion picture]. Los Angeles: Magnolia Pictures.

Giddens, A. (2000) *Runaway World: How Globalization Is Reshaping Our Lives*. London: Routledge.

Giesen-Bloo, J., van Dyck, R., Spinhoven, P., van Tilburg, W., Dirksen, C., van Asselt, T., Kremers, I., Nadort, M. and Arnoud Arntz, A. (2006) 'Outpatient psychotherapy for borderline personality disorder randomized trial of schema-focused therapy vs transference-focused psychotherapy', *Archives of General Psychiatry*, 63 (6): 649–658.

Gilliland, S. W. (1993) 'The perceived fairness of selection systems: an organizational justice perspective', *Academy of Management Review*, 18 (4): 694–734.

Gioia, D. (2006) 'On Weick: an appreciation', *Organization Studies*, 27 (11): 1709–1721.

Goffman, E. (1961) *Asylums*. Harmondsworth: Penguin.

Goldman, B. M., Gutek, B. A., Stein J. H. and Lewis, K. (2006) 'Employment discrimination in organizations: Antecedents and consequences', *Journal of Management*, 32 (6): 786–830.

Goldman, S. L., Nagel, R. N. and Preiss, K. (1995) *Agile Competitors and Virtual Organizations: Strategies for Enriching the Customer*. New York: Van Nostrand Reinhold.

Goleman, D. (1997) *Emotional Intelligence: Why it Can Matter More than IQ*. New York: Bantam Books.

Goleman, D., Boyatzis, R. and McKee, A. (2002) *The New Leaders: Transforming the Art of Leadership into the Science of Results*. London: Time-Warner.

Golsorkhi, D., Rouleau, L., and Seidl, D. (2010) *Cambridge Handbook of Strategy as Practice*. Cambridge: Cambridge University Press.

Gordon, G. and DiTomaso, N. (1992) 'Predicting corporate performance from organizational culture', *Journal of Management Studies*, 29 (6): 783–798.

Gordon, P. J. (2001) *Lean and Green: Profit for your Workplace and the Environment*. San Francisco: Berrett-Koehler.

Gordon, R. D. (2002) 'Conceptualizing leadership with respect to its historical-contextual antecedents to power', *Leadership Quarterly*, 13: 151–167.

Gordon, R. E. (2007) *Power, Knowledge and Domination*. Copenhagen and Oslo: CBS Press & Liber.

Gouldner, A. W. (1954) *Patterns of Industrial Bureaucracy*. New York: Free Press.

Graham, G. (2002) 'If you want honesty, break some rules', *Harvard Business Review*, April: 42–47.

Graham, P. (ed.) (1995) *Mary Parker Follett – Prophet of Management: A Celebration of Writings from the 1920s.* Boston, MA: Harvard Business School Press Classic.

Gramsci, A. (1971) *Selections from the Prison Notebooks.* New York: International Publishers.

Granovetter, M. (2002) 'Economic action and social structure: the problem of embeddedness', in S. R. Clegg (ed.), *Central Currents in Organization Studies I: Frameworks and Applications*, Volume 3. London: Sage, pp. 363–389; originally published in *American Journal of Sociology* (1985) 93: 481–510.

Granstrom, K. and Stiwne, D. (1998) 'A bipolar model of groupthink: an expansion of Janis's concept', *Small Group Research*, 29 (1): 32–56.

Grant, D. (2008) 'Metaphor and organization', in S. R. Clegg and J. R. Bailey (eds), *The Sage International Encyclopedia of Organization Studies*. Thousand Oaks, CA: Sage, pp. 896–900.

Grant, J. D. and Mills, A. J. (2006) 'The quiet Americans: formative context, the Academy of Management leadership, and the management textbook, 1936–1960', *Management & Organizational History,* 1 (2): 201–224.

Grant, R. M., Shani, R. and Khrishnan, R. (1994) 'TQM's challenge to management theory and practice', *Sloan Management Review*, 35 (2): 25–35.

Green, F. (1997) 'Union recognition and paid holiday entitlement', *British Journal of Industrial Relations*, 35 (2): 243–255.

Greenberg, J. and Baron, R. A. (2003) *Behavior in Organizations*, 8th edn. Englewood Cliffs, NJ: Prentice Hall.

Greener, I. (2006) 'Nick Leeson and the collapse of Barings Bank: socio-technical networks and the "Rogue Trader"', *Organization*, 13 (3): 421–441.

Greenwood, R. (2008) 'Resource dependence', in S. R. Clegg and J. R. Bailey (eds), *The Sage International Encyclopedia of Organization Studies*. Thousand Oaks, CA: Sage, pp. 1383–1385.

Greenwood, R. and Hinings, C. R. (2002) 'Understanding radical organizational change: bringing together the old and the new institutionalism', in S. R. Clegg (ed.), *Central Currents in Organization Studies I: Frameworks and Applications*, Volume 4. London: Sage, pp. 120–150; previously published in *Academy of Management Review* (1996) 21: 1022–1054.

Greenwood, R. and R. Meyer (2008) 'Influencing ideas: a celebration of DiMaggio & Powell (1983)', *Journal of Management Inquiry*, 17 (4): 258–264.

Greenwood, R., Rose, T., Brown, J., Cooper, D. and Hinings, B. (1999) 'The global management of professional services: the example of accounting', in S. Clegg, E. Ibarra-Colado and L. Bueno-Rodriquez (eds), *Global Management: Universal Theories and Local Realities*. London: Sage, pp. 265–296.

Gregory, K. L. (1983) 'Native-view paradigms: multiple cultures and culture conflicts in organizations', *Administrative Science Quarterly*, 28: 359–376.

Greifeneder, R., Bless, H. and Pham, M. T. (2011) 'When do people rely on affective and cognitive feelings in judgment? A review', *Personality and Social Psychology Review*, 15 (2): 107–141.

Gudergan, S., Josserand, E. and Pitsis, T. (2005) 'Close encounters of the virtual kind: the structuration of online communities', Paper presented at the 21st EGOS Colloquium, Berlin.

Guest, D. E. (2004) 'The psychology of the employment relationship: an analysis based on the psychological contract', *Journal of Applied Psychology*, 53 (4): 541–555.

Guest, D. E. (2011) 'Human resource management and performance: still searching for some answers', *Human Resource Management Journal*, 21 (1): 3–13.

Guggenheim, D. (Director) (2006) *An Inconvenient Truth* [Motion picture]. Los Angeles: Paramount Classics.

Guillen, M. F. (1994) *Models of Management: Work, Authority, and Organization in a Comparative Perspective.* Chicago: University of Chicago Press.

Haggis, P. (2006) *Crash* [Motion picture]. Vancouver: Lionsgate Films.

Hall, C. S. and Lindzey, G. (1957) *Theories of Personality.* London: Wiley.

Hall, P. and Sostike, D. (2001) *Varieties of Capitalism: The Institutional Foundations of Comparative Advantage.* Oxford: Oxford University Press.

Hall, R. (1993) 'A framewok linking intangible resources and capabilities to sustainable competitive advantage', *Strategic Management Journal*, 14: 607–618.

Hall, R. H., Haas, J. E. and Johnson, N. J. (1966) 'An examination of the Blau-Scott and Etzioni typologies', *Administrative Science Quarterly*, 12: 118–139.

Hamann, R., Acutt, N. and Kapelus, P. (2003) 'Responsibility versus accountability? Interpreting the world summit on sustainable development for a synthesis model of corporate citizenship', *Journal of Corporate Citizenship* (Spring) 9: 32–48.

Hamel, G. (1996) 'Strategy as revolution', *Harvard Business Review*, July–August: 69–82.

Hamel, G. (2002) *Leading the Revolution*. New York: Plume.

Hamel, G. and Prahalad, C. K. (1996) *Competing for the Future*. Boston, MA: Harvard Business School Press.

Hamilton, T. and Sharma, S. (1997) 'The violence and oppression of power relations', *Peace Review*, 9 (4): 555–561.

Hammer, M. and Champy, J. (1993) *Reengineering the Corporation: A Manifesto for Business Revolution*. New York: HarperBusiness.

Hancock, P. and Tyler, M. (2001) *Work, Postmodernism and Organisation: A Critical Introduction*. London: Sage.

Handy, C. (1993) *Understanding Organizations*. London: Penguin.

Handy, C. (2002) *The Elephant and the Flea*. Boston, MA: Harvard Business School Press.

Haney, C., Banks, C. and Zimbardo, P. (1973) 'Interpersonal dynamics in a simulated prison', *International Journal of Criminology and Psychology*, 1: 69–97.

Hanks, P. (ed.) (1986) *Collins Dictionary of the English Language: An Extensive Coverage of Contemporary International and Australian English*. Sydney: Collins.

Hanlon, G. (1994) *Commercialisation of the Service Class*. London: Macmillan.

Hannan, M. T. and Freeman, J. (1989) *Organizational Ecology*. Cambridge, MA: Harvard University Press.

Hardt, M. and Negri, A. (2000) *Empire*. Cambridge, MA: Harvard University Press.

Hardy, C. (1995) *Managing Strategic Action: Mobilizing Change: Concepts, Readings, and Cases*. London: Sage.

Hardy, C. and Clegg, S. R. (1999) 'Some dare call it power', in S. R. Clegg and C. Hardy (eds), *Studying Organizations: Theory and Method*. London: Sage, pp. 368–387.

Hardy, C. and Clegg, S. R. (2006) 'Some dare call it power', in S. R. Clegg, C. Hardy, T. B. Lawrence and W. R. Nord (eds), *The Sage Handbook of Organization Studies*. London: Sage, pp. 754–775.

Harkins, S. G. and Szymanski, K. (1989) 'Social loafing and group evaluation', Journal of Personality and Social Psychology, 56 (3): 934–941.

Harris, M. (2008) 'Digital technology and governance in transition: the case of the British Library', *Human Relations*, 61 (5): 741–758.

Harris, J. G., De Long, D. W. and Donnellon, A. (2001) 'Do you have what it takes to be an e-manager?' *Strategy & Leadership*, 29 (4): 10–14.

Harter, S. (1978) 'Effective motivation re-considered: toward a developmental model', *Human Development*, 21: 36–64.

Harvey, D. (1992) *The Condition of Postmodernity*. Oxford: Blackwell.

Hassard, J., McCann, L. and Moriss, J. (2009) *Managing in the Modern Corporation: The Intensification of Managerial Work in the USA, UK and Japan*. Cambridge: Cambridge University Press.

Hatch, M. and Schultz, M. (2001) 'Are the strategic stars aligned for your corporate brand?' *Harvard Business Review*, February: 129–134.

Hatcher, L. and Ross, T. L. (1991) 'From individual incentives to an organization-wide gainsharing plan: effects on teamwork and product quality', *Journal of Organizational Behavior*, 12 (3): 169–183.

Havemann, H. A. (1993) 'Ghost of managers past: managerial succession and organizational mortality', *Academy of Management Journal*, 36 (4): 864–881.

Hawken, P. (1993) *The Ecology of Commerce: A Declaration of Sustainability*. New York: HarperCollins.

Heckscher, C. (1994) 'Defining the post-bureaucratic type', in C. Heckscher and A. Donellon (eds), *The Post-Bureaucratic Organization: New Perspectives on Organizational Change*. Thousand Oaks, CA: Sage, pp. 14–62.

Hedlund, G. (1986) 'The hypermodern MNC: a heterarchy?', *Human Resource Management Journal*, 25 (1): 9–35.

Hedmo, T., Sahlin-Andersson, K. and Wedlin, L. (2005) 'Fields of imitation: the global expansion of management education', in B. Czarniawska and G. Sevón (eds), *Global Ideas: How Ideas, Objects and Practices Travel in the Global Economy*. Oslo: Liber, pp. 190–212.

Heider, F. (1958) *The Psychology of Interpersonal Relations*. New York: Wiley.

Held, B. S. (2004) 'The negative side of positive psychology', *Journal of Humanistic Psychology*, 44 (1): 9–46.

Helvacioglu, B. (2000) 'Globalization in the neighbourhood: from the nation-state to Bilkent Centre', *International Sociology*, 15 (2): 326–342.

Henderson, L. J. (2002) 'The effects of social environment' (with Elton Mayo), in S. R. Clegg (ed.), *Central Currents in Organization Studies I: Frameworks and Applications*, Volume 2. London: Sage, pp. 299–313; originally published in *Journal of Industrial Hygiene and Technology* (1936) 18: 401–416.

Hendrickson-Eagley, A. (1987) *Sex Differences in Social Behavior: A Social-role Interpretation*. Hillsdale, NJ: Lawrence Erlbaum Associates.

Herman, S. (2007) 'Leadership training in a "not-leadership" society', *Journal of Management Education*, 31 (2): 151–155.

Herman-Wurmfeld, C. (Director) (2003) *Legally Blonde 2* [Motion picture]. United States: MGM.

Herscovitch, L. and Meyer, J. P. (2002) 'Commitment to organizational change: extension of a three-component model', *Journal of Applied Psychology*, 87: 474–487.

Hersey, P., Blanchard, K. H. and Johnson, D. (1996) *Management of Organizational Behavior: Utilizing Human Resources*, 7th edn. Upper Saddle River, NJ: Prentice Hall.

Hetrick, W. P. and Boje, H. R. (1992) 'Postmodernity, organisation and hyperchange', *Journal of Organizational Change Management*, 5 (1): 5–8.

Hickson, D. J. (2002) 'A convergence in organization theory', in S. R. Clegg (ed.), *Central Currents in Organization Studies II: Contemporary Trends*, Volume 1. London: Sage, pp. 380–389; originally published in *Administrative Science Quarterly* (1966) 11: 224–237.

Hickson, D. J., Miller, S. J. and Wilson, D. C. (2003) 'Planned or prioritized? Two options in managing the implementation of strategic decisions', *Journal of Management Studies*, 40 (7): 1803–1836.

Hickson, D. J., Butler, R. J., Cray, D., Mallory, G. R. and Wilson, D. C. (1986) *Top Decisions: Strategic Decision-Making in Organizations*. San Francisco: Jossey-Bass.

Hickson, D. J., Hinings, C. R., Lee, C. A., Schneck, R. E. and Pennings, J. M. (2002) 'A strategic contingencies theory of intra-organizational power', in S. R. Clegg (ed.), *Central Currents in Organization Studies II: Contemporary Trends*, Volume 5. London: Sage, pp. 3–19; originally published in *Administrative Science Quarterly* (1971) 16: 216–229.

Higgins, C. (1980) *Nine to Five* [Motion picture]. United States: Fox.

Higgins, W. and Hallström, K. T. (2007) 'Standardization, globalization and rationalities of government', *Organization*, 14 (5), 685–704.

Hill, R. P. (2002) 'Managing across generations in the 21st century: important lessons from the ivory trenches', *Journal of Management Inquiry*, 11 (1): 60–66.

Hinings, C. R., Greenwood, R. and Cooper, D. (1999) 'The dynamics of change in large accounting firms', in D. M. Brock, M. J. Powell and C. R. Hinings (eds), *Restructuring the Professional Organization: Accounting, Health Care and Law*. London: Routledge, pp. 131–153.

Hinings, C., Hickson, D., Pennings, J. and Schneck, R. (1974) 'Structural conditions of intraorganizational power', *Administrative Science Quarterly*, 19 (1): 22–44.

Hirschbiegel, O. (Director) (2001) *Das Experiment* [Motion picture]. Germany: Samuel Goldwyn.

Hirschhorn, L. (2002) 'Campaigning for change', *Harvard Business Review*, July: 98–104.

Hobsbawm, E. (1975) *The Age of Capital 1848–1875*. London: Weidenfeld & Nicolson.

Hofstede, G. (1980) *Culture's Consequences: International Differences in Work-Related Values*. London: Sage.

Hofstede, G. (1991) *Cultures and Organizations: Software of the Mind*. McGraw-Hill.

Hofstede, G. and Peterson, M. F. (2000) 'National values and organizational practices', in N. M. Ashkanasy, C. P. M. Wilderom and M. F. Peterson (eds), *Handbook of Organizational Culture and Climate*. London: Sage, pp. 401–405.

Hogan, D. (1978) 'Education and the making of the Chicago working class, 1880–1930', *Historical Education Quarterly*, 18: 227–270.

Hogg, M. A. (1996) 'Intragroup processes, group structure and social identity', in W. Robinson (ed.), *Social Groups and Identities: Developing the Legacy of Henri Tajfel*. Oxford: Butterworth, pp. 65–93.

Höllerer, Markus A. (2010) *Between creed, rhetoric façade, and disregard. Dissemination and theorization of corporate social responsibility (CSR) in Austrian publicly traded corporations*. Doctoral dissertation, WU Vienna University of Economics and Business.

Holly, T. M. (2003) 'A hire standard: improving employee selection can keep you fully staffed – and out of court – legal trends', *Human Resources Magazine*, 48 (7): 109–112.

Holt, D. B. (2003) 'What becomes an icon most?' *Harvard Business Review*, March: 43–49.

Hopkins, W. E. (1997) *Ethical Dimensions of Diversity*. London: Sage.

Hornby, N. (1995) *High Fidelity*. London: Riverhead.

Horowitz, M. J. (1991) *Person Schemas and Maladaptive Interpersonal Patterns*. Chicago: University of Chicago Press.

Hoskin, K. (2004) 'Spacing, timing and the invention of management', *Organization*, 11 (6): 743–757.

Hoskin, K. and Macve, R. (1988) 'The genesis of accountability: the West Point connections', *Accounting, Organizations and Society*, 13 (1): 37–73.

House, R. J. (1971) 'A path-goal theory of leadership effectiveness', *Administrative Science Quarterly*, 16: 321–338.

House, R. J. (1996) 'Path-goal theory of leadership: lessons, legacy, and a reformulated theory', *Leadership Quarterly*, 7: 323–352.

House, R. J. and Mitchell, T. R. (1974) 'Path-goal theory of leadership', *Journal of Contemporary Business*, 4: 81–97.

House, R. J., Shane, S. A. and Herold, D. M. (1996) 'Rumors of the death of dispositional research are vastly exaggerated', *Academy of Management Review*, 21: 203–224.

House, R. J., Hanges, P. J., Javidan, M., Dorfman, P. and Gupta, V. (2004) *Culture, Leadership, and Organizations: The GLOBE Study of 62 Societies*. Thousand Oaks, CA: Sage.

Howard, G. S. (1988) 'On putting the person back into psychological research', in D. M. Deluca (ed.), *Essays on Perceiving Nature: How the Humanities, Arts, and Sciences View Our World*. Honolulu: University of Hawaii Press, pp. 207–214.

Howard, P. J. and Howard, J. M. (2006) *The Owners Manual for Personality at Work: How the Big Five Personality Traits Affect Performance, Communication, Teamwork, Leadership and Sales*. Austin, TX: Bard Press.

Howard, R. (Director) (1995) *Apollo 13* [Motion picture]. United States: Universal.

Howcroft, D. and Wilson, M. (2003) 'Participation: "Bounded freedom" or hidden constraints on user involvement?', *New Technology, Work, and Employment*, 18 (1): 2–19.

Howitt, P. (Director) (1998) *Sliding Doors* [Motion picture]. United States: Miramax.

Hsu, G. and Hannan, M. T. (2005) 'Identities, genres, and organizational forms', *Organization Science*, 16 (5): 474–490.

Hudson, R. (2004) 'Conceptualizing economies and their geographies: spaces, flows, and circuits', *Progress in Human Geography*, 28: 447–471.

Hurley-Hanson, A. E. and Giannantonio, C. M. (2006) 'Recruiters' perceptions of appearance: the stigma of image norms', *Equal Opportunities International*, 25 (6): 450–463.

Hutton, W. (1995) *The State We're In*. London: Vintage.

Iedema, R., Rhodes, C. and Scheeres, H. (2006) 'Surveillance, resistance, observance: exploring the teleo-affective volatility of workplace interaction', *Organization Studies*, 27 (8): 1111–1130.

Irwin, H. and More, E. (1994) *Managing Corporate Communication*. St Leonards: Allen & Unwin.

Iyer, A. and Ryan, M. K. (2006) *Challenging Gender Inequality in the Workplace: Men's and Women's Pathways to Collective Action*, SPSSI-EAESP Small Group Meeting on Multiple Perspectives on Real World Helping and Social Action, Long Beach, USA.

Jackson, A. (2011) *Appearance, Rationality and Justified Belief. Philosophy and Phenomenological Research*, forthcoming.

Jackson, P. (Director) (2001–2003) *The Lord of the Rings* trilogy [Motion pictures]. United States, New Zealand: New Line.

Jacques, R. (1996) *Manufacturing the Employee: Management Knowledge from the 19th to 21st Century*. London: Sage.

James, C. L. R. (2001) *Black Jacobins*. Harmondsworth: Penguin; original work published 1938.

Jang, Y. S. (2005) 'The expansion of modern accounting as a global and institutional practice', *International Journal of Comparative Sociology*, 46 (8): 297–326.

Janis, I. L. (1982) *Groupthink*. Boston: Houghton Mifflin.

Jaques, E. (1956) *Measurement of Responsibility*. London: Tavistock Publications.

Jeffcutt, P. (1994) 'From interpretation to representation in organizational analysis: postmodernism, ethnography and organisational symbolism', *Organization Studies*, 15 (2): 241–274.

Jefremovas, V. (2002) *Brickyards to Graveyards: From Production to Genocide in Rwanda*. Albany, NY: State University of New York Press.

Jelinek, M., Romme, A. G. and Boland, R. J. (2008) 'Special issue on design studies', *Organisation Studies*, 29 (3).

Jermier, J. M. (1996) 'The path-goal theory of leadership: a subtextual analysis', *Leadership Quarterly*, 7: 311–316.

Jermier, J., Knights, D. and Nord, W. R. (eds) (1994) *Resistance and Power in Organizations: Agency, Subjectivity and the Labor Process*. London: Routledge.

Jermier, J., Forbes, L. C., Benn, S. and Orsato, R. J. (2006) 'The new corporate environmentalism and green politics', in S. R. Clegg, C. Hardy, T. B. Lawrence and W. R. Nord (eds), *The Sage Handbook of Organization Studies*. London: Sage, pp. 618–650.

Joachimsthaler, E. and Aaker, D. (1997) 'Building brands without mass media', *Harvard Business Review*, January–February: 39–50.

Johnson, G., Langley, A., Melin, L. and Whittington, R. (2007) *Strategy as Practice: Research Directions and Resources*. Cambridge: Cambridge University Press.

Jolijn Hendriks, A. A., Kuypera, H., Lubbers, M. J. and Van der Werfa, M. (2011) 'Personality as a moderator of context effects on academic achievement', *Journal of School Psychology*, 49 (2): 217–248.

Jones, C. (2001) 'Co-evolution of entrepreneurial careers, institutional rules and competitive dynamics in American Film, 1895–1920', *Organization Studies*, 22 (6): 911–944.

Jones, C. (2004) 'Jacques Derrida', in S. Linstead (ed.), *Organization Theory and Postmodern Thought*. London: Sage, pp. 34–63.

Jones, C., Parker, M. and ten Bos, R. (2005) *For Business Ethics: A Critical Approach*. London: Routledge.

Jones, D. (Director) (1993) *The Trial* [Motion picture]. United Kingdom: Angelika.

Jones, M. (2003) 'Globalization and the organization(s) of exclusion in advanced capitalism', in R. Westwood and S. R. Clegg (eds), *Debating Organizations: Point-Counterpoint in Organization Studies*. Oxford: Blackwell, pp. 252–270.

Joo-Kee, H. (2006) 'Glass ceiling or sticky floor? Exploring the Australian gender pay gap', *Economic Record*, 82 (259): 408–427.

Judge, M. (Director) (1999) *Office Space* [Motion picture]. United States: Fox.

Jupp, J. (2002) *From White Australia to Woomera: The Story of Australian Immigration*. Cambridge: Cambridge University Press.

Kaarsemaker, E. and Poutsma, E. (2006) 'The fit of employee ownership with other human resource management practices: theoretical and empirical suggestions regarding the existence of an ownership high-performance work system', *Economic and Industrial Democracy*, 27 (4): 669–685.

Kahneman, D., Krueger, A. B., Schkade, D., Schwarz, N. and Stone, A. (2006) 'Would you be happier if you were richer? A focusing illusion', *Science*, 312 (5782): 1908–1910.

Kameda, T., Tsukasaki, T., Hastie, R. and Berg, N. (2011) 'Democracy under uncertainty: the wisdom of crowds and the free-rider problem in group decision making', *Psychological Review*, 118 (1): 76–96.

Kamoche, K., Cunha, M. P. E. and Cunha, D. V. J. (eds) (2002) *Organizational Improvisation*. London: Routledge.

Kanov, J. M., Maitlis, S., Worline, M. C., Dutton, J. E., Frost, P. J. and Lilius, J. M. (2004) 'Compassion in organizational life', *American Behavioral Scientist*, 47 (6): 808–827.

Kanter, R. M. (1976) *Men and Women of the Corporation*. New York: Basic Books.

Kanter, R. M. (1984) *The Change Masters: Corporate Entrepreneurs at Work*. Sydney: Allen & Unwin.

Kanter, R. M. (1990) *When Giants Learn to Dance*. London: Unwin Hyman.

Kaplan, R. S. and Norton, D. P. (1992) 'The balanced scorecard – measures that drive performance', *Harvard Business Review*, 70 (1): 71–79.

Kärreman, D. and Alvesson, M. (2004) 'Cages in tandem: management control, social identity, and identification in a knowledge-intensive firm', *Organization*, 11 (1): 149–175.

Kärreman, D. and Rylander, A. (2008) 'Managing meaning through branding – the case of a consulting firm', *Organization Studies*, 29 (1): 103–125.

Katz, D. and Kahn, R. L. (1978) *The Social Psychology of Organizations*, 2nd edn. New York: Wiley.

Kaufman, P. (Director) (1983) *The Right Stuff* [Motion picture]. United States: Warner Bros.

Kawakami, K., Dion, K. L. and Dovidio, J. F. (1998) 'Racial prejudice and stereotype activation', *Personality and Social Psychology Bulletin*, 24 (4): 407–416.

Keele, L. and Wolak, J. (2006) 'Value conflict and volatility in party identification', *British Journal of Political Science*, 36 (3): 671–690.

Kelman, H. C. (1973) 'Violence without moral restraint', *Journal of Social Issues*, 29 (4): 25–61.

Keneally, T. (1982) *Schindler's Ark*. London: Hodder & Stoughton.

Kerr, S. and Jermier, J. M. (1978) 'Substitutes for leadership: their meaning and measurement', *Organizational Behavior and Human Performance*, 22: 375–403.

Kim, L. (1998) 'Crisis construction and organisational learning: capability building in catching-up at Hyundai Motor', *Organization Science*, 9 (4): 506–521.

Kipping, M. (2002) 'Trapped in their wave: the evolution of management consultancies', in T. Clark and R. Fincham (eds), *Critical Consulting: New Perspectives on the Management Advice Industry*. Oxford: Blackwell, pp. 28–49.

Kirkbride, P. (2006) 'Developing transformational leaders: the full range leadership model in action', *Industrial and Commercial Training*, 38 (1): 23–32.

Kirkman, B. L., Rosen, B., Tesluk, P. E. and Gibson, C. B. (2004) 'The impact of team empowerment on virtual team performance: the moderating role of face-to-face interaction', *Academy of Management Journal*, 47 (2): 175–192.

Kirkpatrick, S. A. and Locke, E. A. (1991) 'Leadership: do traits matter?', *Academy of Management Executive*, 5: 48–60.

Kjonstad, B. and Willmott, H. (1995) 'Business ethics: restrictive or empowering?' *Journal of Business Ethics*, 14: 445–464.

Klein, L. (2006) 'Joan Woodward Memorial Lecture: applied social science: is it just common sense?' *Human Relations*, 59 (8): 1155–1172.

Klein, N. (2001) *No Space, No Choice, No Jobs, No Logo: Taking Aim at the Brand Bullies*. New York: Picador.

Knafo, A., Roccas, S. and Sajiv, L. (2011) 'The value of values in cross-cultural research: a special issue in honor of Shalom Schwartz', *Journal of Cross-Cultural Psychology*, 42 (2): 178–185.

Knights, D. (1990) 'Subjectivity, power and the labor process', in D. Knights and H. Willmott (eds), *Labour Process Theory*. London: Macmillan, pp. 297–335.

Knights, D. and Vurdubakis, T. (1994) 'Foucault, power and all that', in J. Jermier, D. Knights, and W. Nord (eds), *Resistance and Power in Organizations*. London: Routledge, pp. 167–198.

Knights, D. and Willmott, H. (eds) (1986) *Gender and the Labour Process*. Aldershot: Gower.

Knights, D. and Willmott, H. (eds) (1988) *New Technology and the Labour Process*. London: Macmillan.

Knights, D. and Willmott, H. (1989) 'Power and subjectivity at work: from degradation to subjugation in the labour process', *Sociology*, 23 (4): 535–558.

Knights, D., Willmott, H. and Collinson, D. (eds) (1988) *Job Redesign*. Aldershot: Gower.

Knorr-Cetina, K. and Preda, A. (2007) 'The temporalization of financial markets: from network to flow', *Theory, Culture & Society*, 24: 116–138.

Knowles, M. and Knowles, H. (1972) *Introduction to Group Dynamics*. Chicago: Follett.

Kochan, T. A., Eaton, A. E., McKersie, R. B. and Adler, P. (2009) *Healing Together: The Kaiser Permanente Labor Management Partnership*. Ithaca, NY: Cornell University Press.

Kolk, A. (2000) *Economics of Environmental Management*. Harlow: Prentice Hall.

Kondo, D. K. (1990) *Crafting Selves: Power, Gender, and Discourses of Identity in a Japanese Workplace*. Chicago: University of Chicago Press.

Kono, T. and Clegg, S. R. (1998) *Transformations of Corporate Culture: Experiences of Japanese Enterprises*. Berlin and New York: de Gruyter.

Kono, T. and Clegg, S. R. (2001) *Trends in Japanese Management*. London: Palgrave.

Kornberger, M. (2009) *The Brand Society*. Cambridge: Cambridge University Press.

Kornberger, M. and Brown, A. D. (2007) '"Ethics" as a discursive resource for identity work', *Human Relations*, 60 (3): 497–518.

Kornberger, M., Carter, C. and Clegg, S. R. (2006) 'Rethinking the polyphonic organization: managing as discursive practice', *Scandinavian Journal of Management*, 22: 3–30.

Kornberger, M., Clegg, S. R. and Rhodes, C. (2005) 'Learning/Becoming/Organizing', *Organization*, 12 (2): 147–167.

Kotler, P. (2000) *Marketing Management*. Upper Saddle River, NJ: Prentice Hall.

Kotter, J. and Heskett, J. (1992) *Corporate Culture and Performance*. New York: Free Press.

Kouzes, J. M. and Posner, B. Z. (1995) *The Leadership Challenge: How to Keep Getting Extraordinary Things Done in Organizations*. San Francisco: Jossey-Bass.

Kreiner, K. and Schultz, M. (1993) 'Informal collaboration in R&D: the formation of networks across organizations', *Organization Studies*, 14: 189–209.

Kubrick, S. (Director) (1987) *Full Metal Jacket* [Motion picture]. United States: Warner Bros.

Kung, I. C. and Wang, H. Z. (2006) 'Socially constructed ethnic division of labour', *International Sociology*, 21 (4): 580–601.

Kupiszewski, M. and Kupiszewska, D. (2011) '*MULTIPOLES*: a revised multiregional model for improved capture of international migration', in J. Stillwell and M. Clarke, *Population Dynamics and Projection Methods*, Volume 4. Springer: London, pp. 41–60.

Lam, K. C. H., Buehler, R., McFarland, C., Ross, M. and Cheung, I. (2005) 'Cultural differences in affective forecasting: the role of focalism', *Personality and Social Psychology Bulletin*, 31 (9): 1296–1309.

Lampel, J. and Bhalla, A. (2007) 'The role of status seeking in online communities: giving the gift of experience', *Journal of Computer-Mediated Communication*, 12 (2): 434–455.

Landsorganisationen I Sveirge (2006) 'The collective agreement'. Available at http://www.lo.se/home/lo/home.nsf/ unidView/ F53218717022F344C1256E4C004F02EF (last accessed 23 February 2007).

Landy, F. J. (2005) *Employment Discrimination Litigation: Behavioral, Quantitative, and Legal Perspectives*. San Francisco: Jossey-Bass.

Lash, S. and Urry, J. (1994) *Economies of Signs and Space*. London: Sage.

Latané, B. (1981) 'The psychology of social impact', *American Psychologist*, 36: 343–356.

Latané, B. and Wolf, S. (1981) 'The social impact of majorities and minorities', *Psychological Review*, 88: 438–453.

Laughlin, P., Hatch, E., Silver, J. and Boh, L. (2006) 'Groups perform better than the best individuals on letters-to-numbers problems: effects of group size', *Journal of Personality and Social Psychology*, 90 (4): 644–651.

Lawler, III, E. E. (2005) 'Creating high performance organizations', *Asia Pacific Journal of Human Resources*, 43 (1): 10–17.

Lawler, III, E. E., Worley, C. G., Creelman, D. and Crooke, M. (2011) *Management Reset: Organizing for Sustainable Effectiveness*. California, CA: John Wiley.

Lawrence, T. B. and Phillips, N. (2004) 'From *Moby Dick* to *Free Willy*: macro-cultural discourse and institutional entrepreneurship in emerging institutional fields', *Organization*, 11 (5): 689–711.

Lawrence, T. B. and Suddaby, R. (2006) 'Institutions and institutional work', in S. R. Clegg, C. Hardy, T. B. Lawrence and W. R. Nord (eds), *The Sage Handbook of Organization Studies*. London: Sage, pp. 215–255.

Leahy, R. L. (2011) 'Personal schemas in the negotiation process: a cognitive therapy approach', in F. Aquilar and M. Galluccio (eds), *Psychological and Political Strategies for Peace Negotiation: A Cognitive Approach*. Springer: New York.

Lean, D. (Director) (1962) *Lawrence of Arabia* [Motion picture]. United States: Columbia.

Lench, H. C., Safer, M. A. and Levine, L. J. (2011) 'Focalism and the underestimation of future emotion: when it's worse than imagined', *Emotion*, 11 (2): 278–285.

Leonard, D. and Sensiper, S. (1998) 'The role of tacit knowledge in group innovation', *California Management Review*, 40: 3.

Levitt, B. and March, J. (1988) 'Organizational learning', *Annual Review of Sociology*, 319–340.

Lewin, A. Y., Long, C. P. and Carroll, T. N. (2002) 'The coevolution of new organizational forms', in S. R. Clegg (ed.), *Central Currents in Organization Studies II: Contemporary Trends: Volume 8*. London: Sage, pp. 323–347; originally published in *Organization Science* (1999) 10: 535–550.

Lewin, K. (1951) *Field Theory in Social Science: Selected Theoretical Papers*. London: Tavistock.

Likert, R. (1979) 'From production- and employee-centeredness to systems 1–4', *Journal of Management*, 5 (2): 147–156.

Lilius, J. M., Worline, M. C., Maitlis, S., Kanov, J. M., Dutton, J. E. and Frost, P. J. (2008) 'The contours and consequences of compassion at work', *Journal of Organizational Behavior*, 29: 193–218.

Lilja, S. and Luddeckens, E. (2006) 'Women in middle management in Germany, Sweden and the United Kingdom', Masters thesis in Business, Hogskolan I Jonkoping, Internationella Handelshogskolan, Sweden. Available at http://hj.diva-portal.org/smash/get/diva2:4150/FULLTEXT01 (last accessed 22 July 2011).

Lindblom, E. (1959) 'The science of "muddling through"', *Public Administration Review*, 19 (2): 79–88.

Lindeman, M. and Verkasalo, M. (2005) 'Measuring values with the short Schwartz's value Survey', *Journal of Personality Assessment*, 85 (3): 170–178.

Linstead, S. and Grafton-Small, R. (2002) 'On reading organizational culture', in S. R. Clegg (ed.), *Central Currents in Organization Studies II: Contemporary Trends, Volume 7*. London: Sage, pp. 227–250; originally published in *Organization Studies* (1992) 13: 331–355.

Littlejohn, S. (1983) *Theories of Human Communication*, 2nd edn. Belmont, CA: Wadsworth.

Littlejohn, S. (1989) *Theories of Human Communication*, 6th edn. Belmont, CA: Wadsworth.

Littler, C. (1982) *The Development of the Labour Process in Capitalist Societies*. London: Heinemann.

Locke, R. R. (1984) *The End of the Practical Man: Entrepreneurship and Practical Education in Germany, France and Great Britain*. London: JAI.

Lönnqvist, J.-E., Leikas, S., Paunonen, S. V., Nissinen, V. and Verkasalo, M. (2006) 'Conformism moderates the relations between values, anticipated regret, and behavior', *Personality and Social Psychology Bulletin*, 32 (11): 1469–1481.

Lounsbury, M. and Crumley, E. T. (2007) 'New practice creation: an institutional perspective on innovation', *Organization Studies*, 28 (7): 993–1012.

Lucas, G. (Director) (1977–2002) *Star Wars* trilogy [Motion pictures]. United States: 20th Century Fox.

Lukes, S. (1974) *Power: A Radical View*. London: Macmillan.

Luketic, R. (Director) (2001) *Legally Blonde* [Motion picture]. United States: MGM/United Artists.

Lumet, S. (1957) *12 Angry Men* [Motion picture]. Los Angeles: United Artists.

Luthans, F. (2002) 'Positive organisational behaviour: developing and managing psychological strengths', *Academy of Management Executive*, 16 (1): 1–11.

Luthans, F. and Avolio, B. (2003) 'Authentic leadership development', in K. S. Cameron, J. E. Dutton and R. E. Quinn (eds), *Positive Organizational Scholarship: Foundations of a New Discipline*. San Francisco: Berrett-Koehler, pp. 241–258.

Luthans, F. and Youssef, C. M. (2004) 'Human, social and now positive psychological capital management: investing in people for competitive advantage', *Organizational Dynamics*, 33 (2): 143–160.

Luthans, F., Avolio, B. J., Avey, J. B. and Norman, S. M. (2007) 'Positive psychological capital: measurement and relationship with performance and satisfaction', *Personnel Psychology*, 60: 541–572.

Luthans, F., Luthans, K. W., Hodgetts, R. M. and Luthans, B. C. (2002) 'Positive approach to leadership (PAL): implications for today's organizations', *Journal of Leadership Studies*, 8: 3–20.

Lynham, S. A. and Chermack, T. J. (2006) 'Responsible leadership for performance: a theoretical model and hypotheses', *Journal of Leadership & Organizational Studies*, 12 (4): 73–88.

Lyon, D. (1994) *The Electronic Eye: The Rise of Surveillance Society*. Cambridge: Polity.

Lyons, S., Duxbury, L. and Higgens, C. (2005) 'Are gender differences in basic human values a generational phenomenon?' *Sex Roles*, 53 (9/10): 763–778.

Macaulay, S. (1966) *Law and the Balance of Power: The Automobile Manufacturers and Their Dealers*. New York: Russell Sage Foundation.

Madsen, S. R. and Gygi, J. (2005) 'An interview with John H. Zenger on extraordinary leadership', *Journal of Leadership and Organization Studies*, 11 (3): 119–125.

Maguire, S. and Hardy, C. (2006) 'The emergence of new global institutions: a discursive perspective', *Organization Studies*, 27 (1): 7–29.

Maignan, I. and Ferrell, O. C. (2004) 'Corporate social responsibility and marketing: an integrative framework', *Journal of the Academy of Marketing Science*, 32 (1): 3–19.

Makridakis, S., Hogarth, R. M. and Gaba, A. (2010) 'Why forecasts fail: what to do instead', *MIT Sloan Management Review*, 51 (2): 83–90.

Malone, T. W., Yates, J. and Benjamin, R. I. (1987) 'Electronic markets and electronic hierarchies', *Communications of the ACM*, 30: 6.

Mann, M. (Director) (1999) *The Insider* [Motion picture]. United States: Touchstone.

March, J. G. (1988) 'The technology of foolishness', in J. G. March (ed.), *Decisions and Organizations*. Oxford: Blackwell, pp. 253–265.

March, J. G. (2002) 'The future, disposable organizations and the rigidities of imagination', in S. R. Clegg (ed.), *Central Currents in Organization Studies II: Contemporary Trends, Volume 8*. London: Sage, pp. 266–277; originally published in *Organization* (1995) 2: 427–434.

March, J. G. (2007) 'The study of organizations and organizing since 1945', *Organization Studies*, 28 (1): 9–19.

March, J. G. and Olsen, J. (1976) *Ambiguity and Choice in Organizations*. Bergen: Universitetsforlaget.

March, J. G. and Simon, H. A. (1958) *Organizations*. New York: Wiley.

March, R. M. (1996) *Reading the Japanese Mind: The Realities Behind Their Thoughts and Actions*. Tokyo: Kodansha International.

Margolis, J. D. and Walsh, J. P. (2003) 'Misery loves company: rethinking social initiatives by business', *Administrative Science Quarterly*, 48: 268–305.

Markoff, J. (1996) *Waves of Democracy: Social Movements and Political Change*. Thousand Oaks, CA: Pine Forge.

Markus, H. R. (1977) 'Self-schemata and processing information about the self', *Journal of Personality and Social Psychology*, 35: 63–78.

Martin, J. (1992) *Culture in Organizations: Three Perspectives*. New York: Oxford University Press.

Martin, J. (2000) 'Hidden gendered assumptions in mainstream organizational theory and research', *Journal of Management Inquiry*, 9 (2): 207–216.

Martin, J. and Frost, P. (1996) 'The organizational culture war games: a struggle for intellectual dominance', in S. R. Clegg, C. Hardy and W. Nord (eds), *Handbook of Organization Studies*. London: Sage, pp. 599–621.

Martin, J., Knopoff, K. and Beckman, C. (1988) 'An alternative to bureaucratic impersonality and emotional labor: bounded emotionality at The Body Shop', *Administrative Science Quarterly*, 43: 429–469.

Martin, R. (2002) *Financialization of Daily Life*. Philadelphia: Temple University Press.

Martínez-Córcoles, M., Gracia, F., Tomás, I. and Peiró, J. M. (2011) 'Leadership and employees' perceived safety behaviours in a nuclear power plant: a structural equation mode', *Safety Science*, 49, (8–9): 1118–1129.

Marx, K. and Engels, F. (1969) *Marx/Engels Selected Works, Volume One*. Moscow: Progress Publishers.

Maslow, A. (1965) *Eupsychian Management: A Journal*. Homewood, IL: Irwin.

Maslow, A. (1968) *Toward a Psychology of Being*. Princeton, NJ: Van Nostrand.

Maslow, A. (1970) *Motivation and Personality*. New York: Harper & Row.

Maurice, M. and Sorge, A. (2002) *Embedding Organizations*. Amsterdam: Benjamins.

Mayer, J. D. (1999) 'Emotional intelligence: popular or scientific psychology?' *APA Monitor Online*, 30 (8). Available at http://www.apa.org/monitor/sep99/sp.html (last accessed 22 June 2007).

Mayer, J. D., Salovey, P., Caruso, D. R. and Sitarenios, G. (2001) 'Emotional intelligence as a standard intelligence', *Emotion*, 1: 232–242.

Mayer, J. D., Salovey, P., Caruso, D. R. and Sitarenios, G. (2003) 'Measuring emotional intelligence with the MSCEIT V2.0', *Emotion*, 3 (1): 97–105.

Mayes, B. T. and Allen, R. W. (1977) 'Towards a definition of organizational politics', *Academy of Management Review*, 2: 674–678.

Mayo, E. (1922) 'Industrial unrest and "nervous breakdowns"', *Industrial Australian and Mining Standard*, 63–64.

Mayo, E. (1946) *The Human Problems of an Industrial Civilization*. Cambridge, MA: Harvard University Press.

Mayo, E. (1985) *The Psychology of Pierre Janet*. Westport, CT: Greenwood; original work published 1951.

McCrae, R. R. and Costa, P. T., Jr (1996) 'Toward a new generation of personality theories: theoretical contexts for the five-factor model', in J. S. Wiggins (ed.), *The Five-Factor Model of Personality: Theoretical Perspectives*. New York: Guilford, pp. 51–87.

McEwan, I. (2002) *Atonement*. Toronto: Vintage Canada.

McGregor, D. (1960) *The Human Side of Enterprise*. New York: McGraw-Hill.

McKinley, W. (2008) 'Neocontingency model', in S. R. Clegg and J. Bailey (eds), *The Sage International Encyclopedia of Organization Studies*, Thousand Oaks, CA: Sage, pp. 955–957.

McLuhan, M. (1964) *Understanding Media: The Extensions of Man*. New York: McGraw-Hill.

McNay, L. (1994) *Foucault: A Critical Introduction*. Cambridge: Polity.

McSweeney, B. (2002) 'Hofstede's model of national cultural differences and their consequences: a triumph of faith – a failure of analysis', *Human Relations*, 55 (1): 89–118.

Mendoza, J. L., Bard, D. E., Mumford, M. D. and Ang, S. C. (2004) 'Criterion-related validity in multiple-hurdle designs: estimation and bias', *Organizational Research Methods*, 7 (4): 418–441.

Menefee, M. L., Parnell, J. A., Powers, E. and Ziemnowicz, C. (2006) 'The role of human resources in the success of new businesses', *Southern Business Review*, 32 (1): 23–33.

Merton, R. K. (1957) *Social Theory and Social Structure* (revised and expanded edn). Glencoe, NY: Free Press.

Merton, R. K. (2002) 'Bureaucratic structure and personality', in S. R. Clegg (ed.), *Central Currents in Organization Studies I: Frameworks and Applications, Volume 1*. London: Sage, pp. 357–366; originally published in *Social Forces* (1940) 18: 560–568.

Mesch, D. J., Rooney, P. M., Steinberg, K. S. and Denton, B. (2006) 'The effects of race, gender, and marital status on giving and volunteering in Indiana', *Non-profit and Voluntary Sector Quarterly*, 35 (4): 565–587.

Meyer, J. W. (2000) 'Globalization: sources and effects on national states and societies', *International Sociology*, 15 (2): 233–248.

Meyer, J. W. and Rowan, B. (1977) 'Institutionalized organizations: formal structure as myth and ceremony', *American Journal of Sociology*, 83: 340–363.

Meyerson, D. (1991) '"Normal" ambiguity? A glimpse of an occupational culture', in P. Frost, L. Moore, C. Louis, C. Lundberg and J. Martin (eds), *Reframing Organizational Culture*. Newbury Park, CA: Sage, pp. 131–144.

Meyerson, D. E. and Kolb, D. M. (2000) 'Moving out of the "armchair": developing a framework to bridge the gap between feminist theory and practice', *Organization*, 7: 553–571.

Meyerson, H. (2010) 'The job machine grinds to a halt', *Washington Post*, 28 July. Available at http://www.washingtonpost.com/wp-dyn/content/article/2010/07/27/AR2010072704791.html?wpisrc=nl_opinions (last accessed 12 August 2010).

Michlewski, K. (2008) 'Uncovering design attitude: inside the culture of designers', *Organization Studies*, 29 (3): 373–392.

Miles, R. E., Snow, C. C., Matthews, J. A. and Coleman, H. J. (1997) 'Organizing in the knowledge area: anticipating the cellular form', *Academy of Management Executive*, 11 (4): 7–20.

Milgram, S. (1971) *The Individual in a Social World*. Reading, MA: Addison-Wesley.

Milgram, S. (1974) *Obedience to Authority*. New York: HarperCollins.

Mill, J. S. (1962) *Utilitarianism: On Liberty – Essay on Bentham, Together with Writings of Jeremy Bentham and John Austin*, ed. with an introduction by M. Warnock. London: Collins.

Miller, P. and O'Leary, T. (2002) 'Hierarchies and American ideals, 1900–1940', in S. R. Clegg (ed.), *Central Currents in Organization Studies I: Frameworks and Applications, Volume 1*. London: Sage, pp. 192–221; originally published in *Academy of Management Review* (1989) 14: 250–265.

Miller, S. J. and Wilson, D. C. (2006) 'Perspectives on organizational decision-making', in S. R. Clegg, C. Hardy, T. B. Lawrence and W. R. Nord (eds), *The Sage Handbook of Organization Studies*, 2nd edn. London: Sage, pp. 469–484.

Mills, A. J. (1996) 'Corporate image, gendered subjects and the company newsletter: the changing face of British Airways', in G. Palmer and S. Clegg (eds), *Constituting Management: Markets, Meanings and Identities*. Berlin: de Gruyter, pp. 191–211.

Mindlin, S. E. and Aldrich, H. (2002) 'Interorganizational dependence: a review of the concept and reexamination of the findings of the Aston Group', in S. R. Clegg (ed.), *Central Currents in Organization Studies I: Frameworks and Applications, Volume 2*. London: Sage, pp. 367–378; originally published in *Administrative Science Quarterly* (1975) 20: 382–392.

Mintzberg, H. (1973) *The Nature of Managerial Work*. New York: Harper & Row.

Mintzberg, H. (1981) 'Organizational design, fashion or fit?' *Harvard Business Review*, 59 (1): 103–116.

Mintzberg, H. (1983a) *Power In and Around Organizations*. Englewood Cliffs, NJ: Prentice Hall.

Mintzberg, H. (1983b) *Structure in Fives: Designing Effective Organizations*. Englewood Cliffs, NJ: Prentice Hall.

Mintzberg, H. (1984) 'Power and organizational life cycles', *Academy of Management Review*, 9 (2): 207–224.

Mintzberg, H. (1985) 'The organization as political arena', *Journal of Management Studies*, 22: 133–154.

Mintzberg, H. (2002) 'The organization as a political arena', in S. R. Clegg (ed.), Central Currents in Organization Studies II: Contemporary Trends, Volume 5. London: Sage, pp. 50–69; originally published in *International Studies of Management and Organizations* (1985) 1: 78–87; 20: 382–392.

Mintzberg, H. (2004) *Managers not MBAs: A Hard Look at the Soft Practice of Managing and Management Development*. San Francisco: Berrett-Koehler.

Mintzberg, H., Raisinhani, D. and Theoret, A. (1976) 'The structure of "unstructured" decision processes', *Administrative Science Quarterly*, 21: 246–275.

Mir, R. and Mir, A. (2009) 'From the colony to the corporation', *Group and Organization Management*, 34 (1): 90–113.

Mitchell, C. (2002) 'Selling the brand inside', *Harvard Business Review*, January: 99–105.

Moberg, D. J. (2006) 'Ethics blind spots in organizations: how systematic errors in persons' perception undermine moral agency', *Organization Studies*, 27 (3): 413–428.

Moghadam, V. M. (1999) 'Gender and globalization: female labour and women's mobilization', *Journal of World-Systems Research*, 5 (2): 367–388.

Monte, C. F. (1991) *Beneath the Mask: An Introduction to Theories of Personality*. Fort Worth, TX: Holt, Rinehart & Winston.

Moore, G. and Beadle, R. (2006) 'In search of organizational virtue in business: agents, goods, practices, institutions and environments', *Organization Studies*, 27 (3): 369–389.

Moore, M. (Director) (2002) *Bowling for Columbine* [Motion picture]. United States: United Artists.

Morgan, G. (1986) *Images of Organizations*. London: Sage.

Morgan, G. (1989) *Creative Organization Theory: A Resource Book*. London: Sage.

Morgan, G. (2008) 'Transnationals', in S. R. Clegg and J. R. Bailey (eds), *The Sage International Encyclopedia of Organization Studies*. Thousand Oaks, CA: Sage, pp. 1565–1567.

Morgan, G. and Kristensen P. H. (2006) 'The contested space of multinationals: varieties of institutionalism, varieties of capitalism', *Human Relations*, 59 (11): 1467–1490.

Morin, E. (1984) 'El error de subestimar el error', in E. Morin, *Ciencia con Conciencia*. Barcelona: Anthropos, pp. 273–289.

Morris, E. (Director) (2003) *The Fog of War: Eleven Lessons from the Life of Robert S. McNamara*. Los Angeles: Sony Classics.

Mostow, J. (Director) (2003) *Terminator 3: Rise of the Machines* [Motion picture]. United States: Warner Bros.

Mouzelis, N. (1967) *Organization and Bureaucracy*. London: Routledge & Kegan Paul.

Mowday, R. T. (1991) 'Equity theory predictions of behavior in organizations', in R. M. Steers and L. W. Porter (eds), *Motivation and Work Behavior*. New York: McGraw-Hill.

Mumby, D. (1987) 'The political function of the narrative in organizations', *Communication Monograph*, 54: 113–127.

Mumby, D. K. and Stohl, C. (1991) 'Power and discourse in organizational studies: absence and the dialectic of control', *Discourse and Society*, 2: 313–332.

Munro, I. (1992) 'Codes of ethics. Some uses and abuses', in P. Davies (ed.), *Current Issues in Business Ethics*. London: Routledge, pp. 97–106.

Munro, I. (2008) 'Network society and organizations', in S. R. Clegg and J. Bailey (eds), *The Sage International Encyclopedia of Organization Studies*. Thousand Oaks, CA: Sage, pp. 971–975.

Murray, R., Caulier-Grice, J. and Mulgan, G. (2010) *The Open Book of Social Innovation*. London: Young Foundation. (Available at http://www.youngfoundation.org/publications/reports/the-open-book-social-innovation-march-2010), accessed 21 September 2011.

Myers, D. G. (2001) *Psychology*, 6th edn. New York: Worth.

NAFE Magazine (2004) and the National Association for Female Executives (Fourth Quarter). 2004 Salary Survey. *NAFE Magazine*, 27 (4): 20–21.

Nathan, B. R. and Alexander, R. A. (1985) 'The role of inferential accuracy in performance rating', *The Academy of Management Review*, 10 (1): 109–115.

Nelson, R. R. and Rosenberg, N. (1993) 'Technical innovation and national systems', in R. R. Nelson (ed.), *National Systems of Innovation: A Comparative Analysis*. Oxford: Oxford University Press.

Newell, M. (1997) (Director) *Donnie Brasco* [Motion picture], United States: Mandalay Films.

Ng, T. W. H. and Feldman, D. C. (2011) Locus of control and organizational embeddedness. *Journal of Occupational and Organizational Psychology*, 84 (1): 173–190.

Nguyen, H. N. and Mohamed, S. (2011) 'Leadership behaviors, organizational culture and knowledge management practices: an empirical investigation', *Journal of Management Development*, 30 (2): 206–221.

Niccol, A. (Director) (1997) *Gattaca* [Motion picture]. United States: Columbia.

Nicholson, N. (2000) *Executive Instinct: Managing the Human Animal in the Information Age*. New York: Crown Business Books.

Nicol, B. (2009) *The Cambridge Introduction to Postmodern Fiction*. Cambridge: Cambridge University Press.

Nietzsche, F. (1974) *The Joyful Wisdom*. New York: Gordon Press.

Nijhof, A., Cludts, S., Fisscher, O. and Laan, A. (2003) 'Measuring the implementation of codes of conduct. An assessment method based on a process approach of the responsible organisation', *Journal of Business Ethics*, 45: 65–78.

Nohria, N. and Ghoshal, S. (1997) *The Differentiated Network: Organizing Multinational Corporations for Value Creation*. San Francisco: Jossey-Bass.

Nolan, C. (2001) *Memento* [Motion picture]. Los Angeles: New Market Films.

Nolan, C. (2010) *Inception* [Motion picture]. United States: Dreamworks.

Nonaka, I. (1991) 'The knowledge-creating company', *Harvard Business Review*, 71 (4): 65–77.

Nonaka, I. and Takeuchi, H. (1995) *The Knowledge-Creating Company: How Japanese Companies Create the Dynamics of Innovation*. Oxford: Oxford University Press.

Norrish, J. M. and Vella-Brodrick, D. A. (2007) 'Is the study of happiness a worthy scientific pursuit?' *Journal of Social Indicators Research*. Available at http://www.springerlink.com/content/45w28664j25545r5 (last accessed 14 July 2011).

Nowecki, M. and Summers, J. (2007) 'Changing leadership styles', *Healthcare Financial Management*, 61 (2): 118–120.

Nutt, P. C. (1984) 'Types of organizational decision processes', *Administrative Science Quarterly*, 29 (3): 414–450.

Nystrom, P. C. (1978) 'Managers and the high-high leader behavior myth', *Academy of Management Journal*, 19: 325–331.

Oberg, W. (1963) Education for business: a balanced appraisal', *American Management Association Bulletin*, No. 34.

O'Connor, E. S. (1999) 'The politics of management thought: a case study of Harvard Business School and the Human Relations School', *Academy of Management Review*, 24 (1): 117–131.

O'Connor, E. S. (2002) 'Minding the workers: the meaning of "Human" and "Human Relations" in Elton Mayo', in S. R. Clegg (ed.), *Central Currents in Organization Studies I: Frameworks and Applications, Volume 1*. London: Sage, pp. 333–356; originally published in *Organization* (1999) 6: 223–246.

O'Doherty, J., Winston, J., Critchley, H., Perrett, D., Burt, D. M., Dolan, R. J. and Adolphs, R. (2003) 'Beauty in a smile: the role of medial orbitofrontal cortex in facial attractiveness', *Neuropsychologia*, 41 (2): 147–155.

Olins, W. (2000) 'How brands are taking over the corporation', in M. Schultz, M. Hatch and M. Larsen (eds), *The Expressive Organization: Linking Identity, Reputation, and the Corporate Brand*. Oxford and New York: Oxford University Press, pp. 51–65.

Oliver, C. (1990) 'Determinants of interorganizational relationships', *Academy of Management Review*, 15 (2): 241–265.

Olson, J. B. and Hulin, C. (1992) 'Information processing antecedents of rating errors in performance appraisal', *Journal of Vocational Behavior*, 40 (1): 49–61.

Ordiorne, G. (1981) *The Change Resisters*. Englewood Cliffs, NJ: Prentice Hall.

O'Reilly, Charles A. III and Michael L. Tushman (2004) 'The ambidextrous organization', *Harvard Business Review*, 82 (4): 74–81.

O'Reilly, Charles, and Michael Tushman (2008) 'Ambidexterity as a dynamic capability: resolving the innovator's dilemma', *Research in Organizational Behavior*, 28: 185–206.

Orlikowski, W. (1993) 'Learning from notes: organizational issues in groupware implementation', *Information Society Journal*, 9: 237–250.

Orlikowski, W. J. and Yates, J. (1994) 'Genre repertoire: examining the structuring of communicative practices in organizations', *Administrative Science Quarterly*, 39: 541–574.

Orsburn, J. D., Moran, L., Musselwhite, E. and Zenger, J. H. (1990) *Self-Directed Work Teams: The New American Challenge*. Homewood, IL: Irwin.

Orwell, G. (1949) *Nineteen Eighty-Four: A Novel*. Harmondsworth: Penguin.

Osborne, D. and Gaebler, T. (1992) *Re-inventing Government*. Reading, MA: Addison-Wesley.

Osborne, P. (2011) 'Phone hacking: David Cameron is not out of the sewer yet', *The Telegraph*, 9 July. Available at http://www.telegraph.co.uk/news/uknews/phone-hacking/8626421/Phone-hacking-David-Cameron-is-not-out-of-the-sewer-yet.html (last accessed 9 July 2011).

O'Toole, J. (1996) *Leading Change: The Argument for Values-Based Leadership*. New York: Ballantine Books.

Ouchi, W. G. (1980) 'Markets, bureaucracies and clans', *Administrative Science Quarterly*, 25: 129–141.

Oxfam (2004) 'Oxfam Community Aid Abroad. The NikeWatch Campaign'. Available at www.caa.org.au/campaigns/nike (last accessed 14 July 2011).

Oz, F. (Director) (2004) *Stepford Wives* [Motion picture]. Los Angeles: Paramount.

Palmer, I. and Dunford, R. (2001) 'Design and form: organizational', in N. J. Smelser and P. B. Bates (eds), *International Encyclopedia of the Social and Behavioral Sciences*. Oxford: Elsevier, pp. 3535–3538.

Palmer, I., Benveniste, J. and Dunford, R. (2007) 'New organizational forms: towards a generative dialogue', *Organization Studies*, 28 (12): 1829–1846.

Parashar, S., Dhar, S. and Dhar, U. (2004) 'Perception of values: a study of future professionals', *Journal of Human Values*, 10 (2): 143–152.

Parker, B. (2003) 'The disorganization of inclusion: globalization as process', in R. Westwood and S. R. Clegg (eds), *Debating Organizations: Point-Counterpoint in Organization Studies*. Oxford: Blackwell, pp. 234–251.

Parker, B. and Clegg, S. R. (2006) 'Globalization', in S. R. Clegg, C. Hardy, T. B. Lawrence and W. R. Nord (eds), *The Sage Handbook of Organization Studies*. London: Sage, pp. 651–674.

Parker, M. (1992) 'Post-modern organizations or postmodern organization theory?' *Organization Studies*, 13 (1): 1–17.

Parker, M. (2000) *Organizational Culture and Identity*, London: Sage.

Parker, M. and Jary, D. (1995) 'The McUniversity: organization, management and academic subjectivity', *Organization*, 2 (2): 319–338.

Parkinson, B., Totterdell, P., Briner, R. B. and Reynolds, S. (1996) *Changing Moods: The Psychology of Mood and Mood Regulation*. London and New York: Longman.

Parkinson, C. N. (1957) *Parkinson's Law*. Boston: Houghton Mifflin.

Parry, E. and Urwin, P. (2011) 'Generational differences in work values: a review of theory and evidence', *International Journal of Management Reviews*, 13 (1): 79–96.

Pascale, R. (1999) 'Surfing the edge of chaos', *Sloan Management Review*, 40 (3): 83–94.

Pascale, R. and Athos, A. (1981) *The Art of Japanese Management*. New York: Warner.

Pedersen, J. S. and Dobbin, F. (2006) 'In search of identity and legitimation: bridging organizational culture and neoinstitutionalism', *American Behavioral Scientist*, 49 (7): 897–907.

Peirce, C. S. (1940) *The Philosophy of Peirce: Selected Writings*. New York: Dover.

Pennings, J. M. (2002) 'Structural contingency theory: a reappraisal', in S. R. Clegg (ed.), *Central Currents in Organization Studies I: Frameworks and Applications, Volume 3*. London: Sage, pp. 3–41; originally published in *Research in Organizational Behaviour* (1992) 14: 267–309.

Peters, T. (1988) *Thriving on Chaos: Handbook for a Management Revolution*. New York: Knopf.

Peters, T. (1994) *The Pursuit of Wow! Every Person's Guide to Topsy Turvey Times*. New York: Random House.

Peters, T. and Waterman, R. (1982) *In Search of Excellence: Lessons From America's Best-Run Companies*. Sydney: Harper & Row.

Peterson, S. J., Luthans, F., Avolio, B. J., Walumbwa, F. O. and Zhang, Z (2011) 'Psychological capital and employee performance: a latent growth modeling approach', *Personnel Psychology*, 64 (2): 427–450.

Petrella, R. (1996) 'Globalization and internationalization: the dynamics of the emerging world order', in R. Boyer and D. Drache (eds), *States Against Markets: The Limits of Globalization*. London: Routledge.

Pettigrew, A. (1973) *The Politics of Organizational Decision-making*. London: Tavistock.

Pettigrew, A. (1985) *Awakening Giant: Continuity and Change in ICI*. Oxford: Blackwell.

Pettigrew, A. (1990) 'Longitudinal field research on change: theory and practice', *Organization Science*, 1 (3): 267–292.

Pettigrew, A. (1997) 'What is processual analysis?' *Scandinavian Journal of Management*, 13 (4): 337–348.

Pettigrew, A. (2002) 'Strategy formulation as a political process', in S. R. Clegg (ed.), *Central Currents in Organization Studies II: Contemporary Trends, Volume 5*. London: Sage, pp. 43–49; originally published in *International Studies of Management and Organization* (1977) 1: 78–87.

Pettigrew, A. (2003) *Innovative Forms of Organizing*. London: Sage.

Pettigrew, A., Ferlie, E. and McKee, L. (1992) *Shaping Strategic Change: Making Change in Large Organizations: The Case of the National Health Service*. London: Sage.

Pettigrew, A., Massini, S. and Numagami, T. (2002a) 'Innovative forms of organizing in Europe and Japan', in S. R. Clegg (ed.), *Central Currents in Organization Studies II: Contemporary Trends, Volume 8*. London: Sage, pp. 323–347; originally published in *European Management Journal* (2000) 18: 259–273.

Pettigrew, A., Thomas, H. and Whittington, R. (eds) (2002b) *Handbook of Strategy and Management*. London: Sage.

Pfeffer, J. (1981) *Power in Organizations*. Marshfield, MA: Pitman.

Pfeffer, J. (1992) *Managing With Power: Politics and Influence in Organizations*. Cambridge, MA: Harvard Business School Press.

Pfeffer, J. (1998) 'Six dangerous myths about pay', *Harvard Business Review*, May–June, 108–119.

Pfeffer, J. (2005) 'Why do bad management theories persist? A comment on Ghoshal', *Academy of Management Learning and Education*, 4 (1): 96–100.

Pfeffer, J. and Fong, C. T. (2002) 'The end of the business school', *Academy of Management Learning and Education*, 1 (1): 78–95.

Pfeffer, J. and Salancik, G. (1978) *The External Control of Organizations: A Resource Dependence Perspective*. New York: Harper & Row.

Pfeffer, J. and Salancik, G. (2002) 'The bases and uses of power in organizational decision making: the case of a university', in S. R. Clegg (ed.), *Central Currents in Organization Studies II: Contemporary Trends, Volume 5*. London: Sage, pp. 21–42; originally published in *Administrative Science Quarterly* (1974) 19: 453–473.

Phillips, J. M. (1998) 'Effects of realistic job previews on multiple organizational outcomes: a meta-analysis', *Academy of Management Journal*, 41 (6): 673–690.

Phillips, N. and Hardy, C. (1997) 'Managing multiple identities: discourse, legitimacy and resources in the UK refugee system', *Organization*, 4 (2): 159–186.

Phillips, N., Lawrence, T. and Hardy, C. (2004) 'Discourse and institutions', *Academy of Management Review*, 29 (4): 635–652.

Piliavin, J. A. and Unger, R. K. (1985) 'The helpful, but not helpless female: myth or reality?' in V. O'Leary, R. K. Unger and B. S. Wallston (eds), *Women, Gender, and Social Psychology*. Hillsdale, NJ: Lawrence Erlbaum Associates, pp. 149–186.

Pitsis, T. S. (2008a) 'Theory X', in S. R. Clegg and J. Bailey (eds), *The Sage International Encyclopedia of Organization Studies*. Thousand Oaks, CA: Sage, pp. 1545–1547.

Pitsis, T. S. (2008b) 'Theory Y', in S. R. Clegg and J. Bailey (eds), *The Sage International Encyclopedia of Organization Studies*. Thousand Oaks; CA: Sage, pp. 1547–1549.

Pitsis, T. S. (2008c) 'Positive psychology', in S. R. Clegg and J. Bailey (eds), *The Sage International Encyclopedia of Organization Studies*. Thousand Oaks, CA: Sage, pp. 1266–1270.

Pitsis, T. S. and Clegg, S. R. (2007) 'We live in a political world: the paradox of managerial wisdom', in E. Kessler and J. Bailey (eds), *The Handbook of Managerial and Organizational Wisdom*. Thousand Oaks, CA: Sage.

Pitsis, T., Clegg, S. R., Marosszeky, M. and Rura-Polley, T. (2003) 'Constructing the Olympic dream: managing innovation through the future perfect', *Organization Science*, 14 (5): 574–590.

Plato (1968) *The Republic*, trans. with notes and an interpretive essay, by A. Bloom. New York: Basic Books.

Podsakoff, P. M., Niehoff, B. P., MacKenzie, S. B. and Williams, M. L. (1993) 'Do substitutes for leadership really substitute for leadership? An empirical examination of Kerr and Jermier's Situational Leadership Model', *Organizational Behavior and Human Decision Processes*, 54: 1–44.

Polanyi, M. (1962) *Personal Knowledge: Towards a Post-Critical Philosophy*. Chicago: University of Chicago Press.

Polanyi, M. (1983) *The Tacit Dimension*. Gloucester, MA: Peter Smith.

Pollard, S. (1965) *The Genesis of Modern Management: A Study of the Industrial Revolution in Great Britain*. London: Edward Arnold.

Porter, L. W. and McKibbin, L. E. (1998) *Management Education and Development: Drift or Thrust into the 21st Century?* New York: McGraw-Hill.

Porter, M. (1987) 'From competitive advantage to corporate strategy', *Harvard Business Review*, May–June: 43–59.

Porter, M. (1990) *The Competitive Advantage of Nations*. Basingstoke: Macmillan.

Porter, M. (1996) 'What is strategy?' *Harvard Business Review*, November–December: 61–78.

Porter, M. and van der Linde, C. (1995) 'Green and competitive', *Harvard Business Review*, 18: 599–620.

Porter, M. E. and Kramer, M. R. (2002) 'The competitive advantage of corporate philanthropy', in the *Harvard Business Review on Corporate Social Responsibility*. Boston: Harvard Business School Press, pp. 27–64.

Poster, M. (1990) *The Mode of Information: Poststructuralism and Social Context*. Cambridge: Polity.

Powell, W. W. (1990) 'Neither market nor hierarchy: network forms of organization', *Research in Organizational Behavior*, 12: 295–336.

Power, M. (1999) *The Audit Society: Rituals of Verification*, 2nd edn. Oxford: Oxford University Press.

Price, A. (2004) *Human Resource Management in a Business Context*. New York: Thompson Press.

Proffet-Reese, M., Rowings, L. and Sharpely, T. (2007) 'Employee benefits of the future', *Employee Benefit Plan Review*, 61 (7): 21–25.

Pugh, D. S. and Hickson, D. J. (1976) *Organizational Structure in Its Context: The Aston Programme 1*. London: Saxon House.

Pugh, D. S. and Hickson, D. J. (2007) *Writers on Organizations*. London: Sage.

Pugh, D. S., Hickson, D. J. and Hinings, C. R. (1971) *Writers on Organizations*. Harmondsworth: Penguin.

Quindlen, A. (2000) *A Short Guide to Happiness*. New York: Random House.

Quinn, D. and Jones, T. M. (1995) 'An agent morality view of business policy', *Academy of Management Review*, 20: 22–42.

Quinn, J. B. (1978) 'Strategic change: logical incrementalism', *Sloan Management Review*, 20 (Fall): 7–21.

Quinn, J. B. (1980) *Strategies for Change: Logical Incrementalism*. Homewood, IL: Irwin.

Rahim, M. A. (1997) 'Relationships of stress, locus of control, and social support to psychiatric symptoms and propensity to leave a job: a field study with managers', *Journal of Business and Psychology*, 12 (2): 159–174.

Räisänen, C. and Linde, A. (2004) 'Technologizing discourse to standardize projects in multi-project organizations: hegemony by consensus?' *Organization*, 11 (1): 101–121.

Rao, H. (2009) *Market Rebels: How Activists Make or Break Radical Innovations*. Princeton, NJ: Princeton University Press.

Ray, T. and Clegg, S. R. (2007) 'Can we make sense of knowledge management's tangible rainbow? A radical constructivist alternative', *Prometheus*, 25 (2): 161–185.

Reardon, J. (2006) 'Are labor unions consistent with the assumptions of perfect competition?' *Journal of Economic Issues*, 40 (1): 171–182.

Reed, P. (Director) (2003) *Down With Love* [Motion picture]. United States: 20th Century Fox.

Reed, S. K. (2009) *Cognition: Theory and Application*, 8th edn. Belmont, CA: Wadsworth.

Reeder, G. D., Pryor, J. B., Wohl, M. J. A. and Griswell, M. L. (2005) 'On attributing negative motives to others who disagree with our opinions', *Personality and Social Psychology Bulletin*, 31 (11): 1498–1510.

Rees, H. T. and Sprecher, S. K. (2009) *Encyclopedia of Human Relationships*. Thousand Oaks, CA: Sage.

Reich, R. B. (1991) *The Work of Nations*. New York: Vintage Books.

Reiner, R. (Director) (1992) *A Few Good Men* [Motion picture]. United States: Columbia.

Reis, H. T. (1994) 'Domains of experience: investigating relationship processes from three perspectives', in R. Erber and R. Gilmour (eds), *Theoretical Frameworks for Personal Relationships*. Hillsdale, NJ: Lawrence Erlbaum, pp. 87–110.

Riesman, D., Glazer, N. and Denney, R. (2001) *The Lonely Crowd: A Study of the Changing American Character*. New Haven, CN: Yale University Press; original work published 1950.

Reitman, J. (Director) (2005) *Thank You for Smoking* [Motion picture]. Los Angeles: 20th Century Fox.

Rhodes, C. (2001) 'D'Oh: *The Simpsons*, popular culture, and the organizational carnival', *Journal of Management Inquiry*, 10 (4): 374–383.

Riley, P. (1983) 'A structurationist account of political cultures', *Administrative Science Quarterly*, 28: 414–437.

Ritzer, G. (1993) *The McDonaldization of Society*. Newbury Park, CA: Pine Forge.

Ritzer, G. (2004) *The Globalization of Nothing*. Thousand Oaks, CA: Pine Forge.

Roberts, S. J., Scherer, L. L. and Bowyer, C. J. (2011) 'Job stress and incivility: what role does psychological capital play?' *Journal of Leadership & Organizational Studies*, May 9 (in press).

Robertson, R. (1992) *Globalization: Social Theory and Social Culture*. London: Sage.

Robey, D. (1981) 'Computer information systems and organization structure', *Communications of the ACM*, 24: 679–687.

Robins, K. and Webster, F. (1985) '"Revolutions of the Fixed Wheel": information technology and social Taylorism', in P. Drummond and R. Paterson (eds), *Television in Transition: Papers From the First International Television Studies Conference*. London: British Film Institute, pp. 36–63.

Robinson, S. L., Kraatz, M. S. and Rousseau, D. M. (1994) 'Changing obligations and the psychological contract: a longitudinal study', *Academy of Management Journal*, 37 (1): 137–152.

Roche, E. (2001) 'Words for the wise', *Harvard Business Review*, January: 26–27.

Rockart, J. F. and Short, J. E. (1991) 'The networked organization and the management of interdependence', in M. S. Scott Morton (ed.), *The Corporation of the 1990s: Information Technology and Organizational Transformation*. Oxford: Oxford University Press.

Rode, J. C., Arthaud-Day, M., Mooney, C. H., Near, J. P. and Baldwin, T. T. (2006) 'Ability and personality predictors of salary, perceived job success, and perceived career success in the initial career stage', *International Journal of Selection and Assessment*, 16 (3): 292–299.

Roethlisberger, F. J. and Dickson, W. J. (1939) *Management and the Worker*. Cambridge, MA: Harvard University Press.

Rogers, C. (1967) *On Becoming a Person: A Therapist's View of Psychotherapy*. London: Constable.

Rogers, C. (1991) 'Barriers and gateways to communication', *Harvard Business Review*, November–December: 105–111.

Rohan, M. J. (2000) 'A rose by any name? The values construct', *Personality and Social Psychology Review*, 4: 255–277.

Rokeach, M. R. (1968) *Beliefs, Attitudes and Values*. San Francisco: Jossey-Bass.

Rokeach, M. R. (1973) *The Nature of Human Values*. New York: Free Press.

Romme, A. G. L. (2002) 'Domination, self-determination and circular organizing', in S. R. Clegg (ed.), *Central Currents in Organization Studies II: Contemporary Trends, Volume 5*. London: Sage, pp. 273–303; originally published in *Organization Studies* (1999) 20: 801–831.

Romme, A. G. L. (2003) 'Making a difference: organization as design', *Organization Science*, 14 (5): 558–573.

Rose, M. (1975) *Industrial Behaviour: Theoretical Developments Since Taylor*. London: Allen Lane.

Rose, N. (1999) *Powers of Freedom: Reframing Political Thought*. Cambridge: Cambridge University Press.

Rosen, M. (2002) 'Breakfast at Spiro's: dramaturgy and dominance', in S. R. Clegg (ed.), *Central Currents in Organization Studies II: Contemporary Trends, Volume 7*. London: Sage, pp. 334–352; originally published in *Journal of Management* (1985) 11: 31–48.

Rosenthal, R. and Jacobson, L. (1992) *Pygmalion in the Classroom: Teacher Expectation and Pupils' Intellectual Development*. New York: Irvington.

Rosenzweig, P. (2007) *The Halo Effect: ... and the Eight Other Business Delusions That Deceive Managers*. New York: Free Press.

Ross, N. (2005) 'Health, happiness, and higher levels of social organisation', *Journal of Epidemiology & Community Health*, 59 (8): 614.

Rossouw, G. J. and van Vuuren, L. J. M. (2003) 'Modes of managing morality: a descriptive model of strategies for managing ethics', *Journal of Business Ethics*, 46 (4): 389–402.

Ross-Sirkin, A. R. (2009) *Too Big to Fail: The Inside Story of How Wall Street and Washington Fought to Save the Financial System from Crisis – and Themselves*. Harmondsworth: Allen Lane.

Roth, L. M. (2006) 'Because I'm worth it? Understanding inequality in a performance-based pay system', *Sociological Inquiry*, 76 (1): 116–139.

Rotter, J. B. (1966) 'Generalised expectancies for internal vs. external control of reinforcement', *Psychological Monographs*, 80: 1–28.

Rousseau, D. M. (1996) 'Changing the deal while keeping people', *Academy of Management Executive*, 10: 50–56.

Rousseau, J.-J. (2006 [1762]) *The Social Contract*. Harmondsworth: Penguin.

Rubery, J. (1978) 'Structured labour markets, worker organisation and low pay', *Cambridge Journal of Economics*, 2: 17–36.

Russell, N. and Gregory, R. (2005) 'Making the undoable doable: Milgram, the Holocaust, and modern government', *American Review of Public Administration*, 35 (4): 327–349.

Ryan, A. M. and Ployhart, R. E. (2000) 'Applicants' perceptions of selection procedures and decisions: a critical review and agenda for the future', *Journal of Management*, 26 (3): 565–606.

Ryan, P. J. (2002) *Peter Ryan: The Inside Story*. Sydney: Viking.

Ryan, R. M. and Deci, E. L. (2000) 'Self-determination theory and the facilitation of intrinsic motivation, social development, and well-being', *American Psychologist*, 55 (1): 68–78.

Sagiv, L. and Schwartz, S. H. (2000) 'A new look at national culture: illustrative applications to role stress and managerial behavior', in N. M. Ashkenasy, C. P. M. Wilderom and M. F. Peterson (eds), *The Handbook of Organizational Culture and Climate*. London: Sage.

Said, E. (1979) *Orientalism*. New York: Vintage.

Sandberg, J. and Targama, A. (2007) *Managing Understanding in Organizations*. London: Sage.

Sassen, S. (1998) *Globalization and Its Discontents*. New York: New Press.

Schank, R. C. and Abelson, R. P. (1977) *Scripts, Plans, Goals, and Understanding: An Inquiry into Human Knowledge Structures*. Hillsdale, NJ: Lawrence Erlbaum Associates.

Schattschneider, E. E. (1960) *The Semi-sovereign People: A Realists' View of Democracy in America*. New York: Holt, Rinehart and Winston.

Schatzki, T. R. (2006) 'On organizations as they happen', *Organization Studies*, 27 (12): 1863–1873.

Schein, E. (1997) *Organizational Culture and Leadership*. San Francisco: Jossey-Bass.

Schein, E. (2002) 'Organizational culture', in S. R. Clegg (ed.), *Central Currents in Organization Studies II: Contemporary Trends, Volume 7*. London: Sage, pp. 196–205; originally published in *American Psychologist* (1990) 45: 109–119.

Schein, E. (2006) 'From brainwashing to organizational therapy: a conceptual and empirical journey in search of "systemic" health and a general model of change dynamics: a drama in five acts', *Organization Studies*, 27 (2): 287–301.

Schmitt, D. P., Allik, J., McCrae, R. R. and Benet-Martinez, V. (2007) 'The geographic distribution of Big Five personality traits: patterns and profiles of human self-description across 56 nations', *Journal of Cross-Cultural Psychology*, 38 (2): 173–212.

Schön, D. A. (1992), 'The theory of inquiry: Dewey's legacy to education', *Curriculum Inquiry*, 22: 119–139.

Schuler, R. S. and Jackson, S. E. (2000) 'HRM and its link with strategic management', in J. Storey (ed.), *Human Resource Management: A Critical Text*. New York: Thomson International.

Schuler, R. S. and MacMillan, I. C. (1984) 'Gaining competitive advantage through human resource management practices', *Human Resource Management*, 23 (3): 241–255.

Schultz, M., Hatch, M. J. and Larsen, M. H. (eds) (2000) *The Expressive Organization: Linking Identity, Reputation and the Corporate Brand*. Oxford: Oxford University Press.

Schumpeter, J. A. (2006 [1942]) *Capitalism, Socialism and Democracy*, London: Routledge.

Schuster, M. (1983) 'The impact of union-management cooperation on productivity and employment', *Industrial and Labor Relations Review*, 36 (3): 415–430.

Schuster, M. (1984) 'The Scanlon Plan: a longitudinal analysis', *Journal of Applied Behavioral Science*, 20 (1): 23–38.

Schwartz, S. (1992) 'Universals in the content and structure of values: theoretical advances and empirical tests in 20 countries', in M. P. Zanna (ed.), *Advances in Experimental Social Psychology, Volume 24*. San Diego, CA: Academic Press, pp. 1–65.

Schwartz, S. (1994) 'Are there universal aspects in the structure and contents of human values?' *Journal of Social Issues*, 50: 1–18.

Schwartz, S. (1996) 'Value priorities and behavior: applying a theory of integrated value systems', in C. Seligman, J. M. Olson, and M. P. Zanna (eds), *The Ontario Symposium: The Psychology of Values, Volume 8*. Mahwah, NJ: Lawerence Erlbaum Associates, pp. 1–24.

Schwartz, S. (2011) 'Studying values: personal adventure, future directions', *Journal of Cross-Cultural Psychology*, 42 (2): 307–319.

Scott, J. C. (1990) *Domination and the Arts of Resistance: Hidden Transcripts*. New Haven, CT: Yale University Press.

Scott, R. (Director) (1982) *Blade Runner* [Motion picture]. United States: Warner Bros.

Scott, R. (Director) (2000) *Gladiator* [Motion picture]. United States: Dreamworks SKG.

Scott, W. R. (2001) *Institutions and Organizations*. Thousand Oaks, CA: Sage.

Scott, W. R. (2002) 'The adolescence of institutional theory', in S. R. Clegg (ed.), *Central Currents in Organization Studies I: Frameworks and Applications, Volume 4*. London: Sage, pp. 390–410; previously published in *Administrative Science Quarterly* (1987) 32: 493–511.

Scott, W. R. (2008) 'Lords of the dance: professionals as institutional agents', *Organization Studies*, 29 (2): 219–238.

Searle, T. P. and Barbuto Jr, J. E. (2011) 'Servant leadership, hope, and organizational virtuousness: a framework exploring positive micro and macro behaviors and performance impact', *Journal of Leadership & Organizational Studies*, 18 (1): 107–117.

Seifert, B., Morris, S. A. and Bartkus, B. R. (2003) 'Comparing big givers and small givers: financial correlates of corporate philanthropy', *Journal of Business Ethics*, 45 (3): 195–211.

Seligman, M. E. P. and Csikszentmihalyi, M. (2000) 'Positive psychology: an introduction', *American Psychologist*, 55: 5–14.

Seligman, M. E. P., Steen, T. A., Park, N. and Peterson, C. (2005) 'Positive psychology progress: empirical validation of interventions', *American Psychologist*, 60 (5): 410–421.

Selznick, P. (1943) 'An approach to a theory of bureaucracy', *American Sociological Review*, 8: 47–54.

Selznick, P. (1949) *TVA and the Grass Roots: A Study in the Sociology of Formal Organization*. Berkeley, CA: University of California Press.

Semler, R. (1993) *Maverick: The Success Story Behind the World's Most Unusual Workplace*. New York: Warner Books.

Senge, P. (1990) *The Fifth Discipline: The Art and Practice of the Learning Organization*. New York: Doubleday.

Senior, B. (1997) 'Team roles and team performance: is there "really" a link?' *Journal of Occupational and Organizational Psychology*, 70 (3): 241–258.

Sennett, R. (1998) *The Corrosion of Character: The Personal Consequences of Work in the New Capitalism*. New York: Norton.

Sewell, G. (2001) 'What goes around, comes around inventing a mythology of teamwork and empowerment', *Journal of Applied Behavioral Science*, 37 (1): 70–89.

Sewell, G. (2002) 'The discipline of teams: the control of team-based industrial work through electronic and peer surveillance', in S. R. Clegg (ed.), *Central Currents in Organization Studies II: Contemporary Trends, Volume 5*. London: Sage, pp. 211–245; originally published in *Administrative Science Quarterly* (1998) 43: 397–428.

Sewell, G. (2005) 'Nice work? Rethinking managerial control in an era of knowledge work', *Organization*, 12 (5): 685–704.

Seybold, P. (2001) 'Get inside the lives of your customers', *Harvard Business Review*, May: 81–89.

Shah, P. and Kleiner, B. (2005) 'New developments concerning age discrimination in the workplace', *Equal Opportunities International*, 24 (5/6): 15–23.

Shaw, G. (2000) 'Planning and communicating using stories', in M. Schultz, M. Hatch, and M. Larsen (eds), *The Expressive Organization: Linking Identity, Reputation, and the Corporate Brand*. Oxford and New York: Oxford University Press, pp. 182–195.

Sheehan, N. T. (2005) 'Why old tools won't work in the "new" knowledge economy', *Journal of Business Strategy*, 26 (4): 53–61.

Sheldon, K. M. (1995) 'Creativity and self-determination in personality', *Creativity Research Journal*, 8: 25–36.

Sheldon, K. M., Ryan, R. M. and Reis, H. (1996) 'What makes for a good day? Competence and autonomy in the day and in the person', *Personality and Social Psychology Bulletin*, 22: 1270–1279.

Shen, J. and Edwards, V. (2004) 'Recruitment and selection in Chinese MNEs', *International Journal of Human Resource Management*, 15 (4): 814–835.

Shenhav, Y. (1999) *Manufacturing Rationality: The Engineering Foundations of the Managerial Revolution*. Oxford: Oxford University Press.

Sheridan, A. (1998) 'Patterns in the policies: affirmative action in Australia', *Women in Management Review*, 13 (7): 243–252.

Silverman, D. (1970) *The Theory of Organizations*. London: Heinemann.

Simon, H. A. (1957) *Administrative Behavior*. New York: Macmillan.

Simon, H. A. (1960) *The New Science of Management Decisions*. New York: Harper & Row.

Simon, H. A. (1969) *The Sciences of the Artificial*. Cambridge: MIT Press.

Singer, P. (1976) *Animal Liberation: A New Ethics for Our Treatment of Animals*. London: Cape.

Sklair, L. (1998) 'Social movements and global capitalism', in F. Jameson and M. Miyoshi (eds), *Cultures of Globalization*. Durham, NC: Duke University Press.

Sklair, L. (1999) 'Competing conceptions of globalization', *Journal of World-Systems Research*, 5 (2): 143–162.

Slaughter, J. E. and Zicker, M. J. (2006) 'A new look at the role of insiders in the newcomer socialization process', *Group & Organization Management*, 31 (2): 264–290.

Smircich, L. (2002) 'Concepts of culture and organizational analysis', in S. R. Clegg (ed.), *Central Currents in Organization Studies II: Contemporary Trends, Volume 7*. London: Sage, pp. 152–174; originally published in *Administrative Science Quarterly* (1983) 28: 393–413.

Smith, A. (1961) *An Enquiry into the Nature and Causes of the Wealth of Nations*. Indianapolis, IN: Bobbs-Merrill; original work published 1776.

Smith, D. (2006) *Globalization: The Hidden Agenda*. Oxford: Polity Press.

Smith, K. (Director) (1994) *Clerks* [Motion picture]. United States: Miramax.

Smither, J. W., London, M. and Reilly, R. R. (2005) 'Does performance improve following multisource feedback? A theoretical model, meta-analysis, and review of empirical findings', *Personnel Psychology*, 58 (1): 33–66.

Smola, K. W. and Sutton, C. D. (2002) 'Generational differences: revisiting generational work values for the new millennium', *Journal of Organizational Behavior*, 23 (4): 363–382.

Soares, C. (2003) 'Corporate versus individual moral responsibility', *Journal of Business Ethics*, 46: 143–150.

Spar, D. L. and La Mure, L. T. (2003) 'The power of activism: assessing the impact of NGOs on global business', *California Management Review*, 45 (3): 78–101.

Sparrow, P., Brewster, C. and Harris, H. (2004) *Globalization of Business: Tracking the Business Role of International HR Specialists*. London: Routledge.

Spector, P. (1982) 'Behaviour in organizations as a function of employee's locus of control', *Psychological Bulletin*, 91: 482–497.

Spector, P. E. (1994) 'Using self-report questionnaires in OB research: a comment on the use of a controversial method', *Journal of Organizational Behavior*, 15 (5): 385–392.

Spencer, D. A. (2000) 'Braverman and the contribution of labour process analysis to the critique of capitalist production – twenty-five years on', *Work, Employment & Society*, 14 (2): 223–243.

Spielberg, S. (Director) (1993) *Schindler's List* [Motion picture]. Los Angeles: Universal.

Spybey, T. (1996) *Globalization and World Society*. Cambridge: Polity.

Sroufe, L. A. (1996) *Emotional Development*. New York: Cambridge University Press.

Stacey, R. (1999) 'Creative organizations: the relevance of chaos and psychodynamic systems', in R. Purser and A. Montuori (eds), *Social Creativity*. Cresskill, NJ: Hampton, pp. 61–88.

Starbuck, W. (1983) 'Organizations as action generators', *American Sociological Review*, 48: 91–102.

Starbuck, W. (1992) 'Learning by knowledge-intensive firms', *Journal of -Management Studies*, 29: 713–740.

Stark, D. (2009) *The Sense of Dissonance: Accounts of Worth in Economic Life*. Princeton, NJ and Woodstock, Princeton University Press.

Starke, F. A., Sharma, G., Mauws, M. K., Dyck, B. and Dass, P. (2011) 'Exploring archetypal change: the importance of leadership and its substitutes', *Journal of Organizational Change Management*, 24 (1): 29–50.

Stein, M. (2000) 'The risk taker as shadow: a psychoanalytic view of the collapse of Barings Bank', *Journal of Management Studies*, 37 (8): 1215–1230.

Stensaker, I. and Falkenberg, J. (2007) 'Making sense of different responses to corporate change', *Human Relations*, 60 (1): 137–177.

Stiglitz, J. (2002) *Globalization and Its Discontents*. Victoria, British Columbia: Allen Lane, Penguin.

Stone, O. (Director) (1986) *Platoon* [Motion picture]. United States: Orion.

Stone, O. (Director) (1987) *Wall Street* [Motion picture]. United States: Fox.

Storper, M. and Scott, A. J. (1993) 'The wealth of regions: market forces and policy imperatives in local and global context', *Lewis Center for Regional Policy Studies, Working Paper No. 7*, Los Angeles: University of California Press.

Strauss, A., Schatzman, L., Ehrlich, D., Bucher, R. and Sabshin, M. (1963) 'The hospital and its negotiated order', in E. Friedmann (ed.), *The Hospital in Modern Society*. New York: Macmillan.

Sturdy, A. (2004) 'The adoption of management ideas and practices: theoretical perspectives and possibilities', *Management Learning*, 35 (2): 155–179.

Sturdy, A. (2006) 'Management education', in C. Carter and S. Clegg (eds), *The Encyclopedia of the Sociology of Management*. Oxford: Blackwell.

Sturdy, A. and Yiannis, G. (2000) 'Missionaries, mercenaries or used car salesmen? Teaching MBA in Malaysia', *Journal of Management Studies*, 37 (4): 979–1002.

Sturges, J. (Director) (1963) *The Great Escape* [Motion picture]. United States: United Artists.

Styhre, A. (2001) 'Kaizen, ethics, and care of the operations: management after empowerment', *Journal of Management Studies*, 38: 795–810.

Subramanian, S. V., Kim, D. and Kawachi, I. (2005) 'Covariation in the socioeconomic determinants of self rated health and happiness: a multivariate multilevel analysis of individuals and communities in the USA', *Journal of Epidemiology & Community Health*, 59 (8): 664–669.

Sudnow, D. (1967) *Passing On: The Sociology of Dying*. Englewood Cliffs, NJ: Prentice Hall.

Suh, A. and Shin, K. (2010) 'Exploring the effects of online social ties on knowledge sharing: a comparative analysis of collocated vs dispersed teams', *Journal of Information Science*, 36 (4): 443–463.

Sutton, R. I. and Rafaeli, A. (1988) 'Untangling the relationship between displayed emotions and organizational sales: the case of convenience stores', *Academy of Management Journal*, 31 (3): 461–487.

Swann, J., Newell, S., Scarbrough, H. and Hislop, D. (1999) 'Knowledge management and innovation: networks and networking', *Journal of Knowledge Management*, 3 (4): 262–275.

Szabo, I. (Director) (1985) *Colonel Redl* [Motion picture]. United States: Orion Classics.

Tallman, S., Jenkins, M., Henry, N. and Pinch, S. (2004) 'Knowledge clusters and competitive advantage', *Academy of Management Review*, 29 (2): 258–271.

Tannenbaum, A. S. (1968) *Control in Organizations*. New York: McGraw-Hill.

Tarique, I. and Schuler, R. S. (2010) 'Global talent management: literature review, integrative framework, and suggestions for further research', *Journal of World Business*, 45 (2): 122–133.

Taylor, A. (2006) 'Call for law to help close gender pay gap', *Financial Times*, 5 January.

Taylor, F. W. (1895) *A Piece Rate System*. New York: McGraw-Hill.

Taylor, F. W. (1967) *Principles of Scientific Management*. New York: Harper; original work published 1911.

Taylor, F. W. (1995) 'Report of a lecture by and questions put to Mr. F. W. Taylor: a transcript', *Journal of Management History*, 1 (1): 8–32.

Teal, G. (2008) 'Sweatshops', in S. R. Clegg and J. R. Bailey (eds), *The Sage International Encyclopedia of Organization Studies*. Thousand Oaks, CA: Sage, pp. 1495–1498.

Tehrani, N. and Haworth, J. T. (2004) *Workplace Trauma: Concepts, Assessment and Interventions*. New York: Brunner–Routledge.

ten Bos, R. (2000) *Fashion and Utopia in Management Thinking*. Amsterdam: Benjamins.

ten Bos, R. and Rhodes, C. (2003) 'The game of exemplarity: subjectivity, work and the impossible politics of purity', *Scandinavian Journal of Management*, 19 (4): 403–423.

Teo, S. and Crawford, J. (2005) 'Indicators of strategic HRM effectiveness: a case study of an Australian public sector agency during commercialization', *Public Personnel Management*, Spring: pp. 1–16.

Tett, G. (2009) *Fool's Gold: The Inside Story of J. P. Morgan and How Wall St. Greed Corrupted Its Bold Dream and Created a Financial Catastrophe*, New York: Free Press.

Tharenou, P. (1997) 'Organisational, job, and personal predictors of employee participation in training and development', *Applied Psychology*, 46 (2): 111–134.

The Economist (2007) 'Making music: companies need to be more like orchestras than armies', *The Economist*, 27 February. Available at http://www.economist.com/sponsor/ukpeopleready/index.cfm?pageid=article 102top (last accessed 27 February 2007).

The Shell Report (2003) 'Meeting the energy challenge – our progress in contributing to sustainable development'. Available at http://sustainabilityreport.shell.com (last accessed 22 July 2011).

Thomas, R. and Davies, A. (2005) 'Theorizing the micro-politics of resistance: new public management and managerial identities in the UK public services', *Organization Studies*, 26 (5): 683–706.

Thompson, J. D. (1956) 'Authority and power in identical organisations', *American Journal of Sociology*, 62: 290–301.

Thorndike, E. L. (1920) 'A constant error in psychological ratings', *Journal of Applied Psychology*, 4: 469–477.

Thrash, T. M. and Elliot, A. J. (2002) 'Implicit and self-attributed achievement motives: concordance and predictive validity', *Journal of Personality*, 70 (5): 729–755.

Tidd, J., Bessant, J. and Pavitt, K. (2001) *Managing Innovation: Integrating Technological, Market and Organizational Change*. Chichester: Wiley.

Tönnies, F. (2001) *Community and Civil Society*. Cambridge: Cambridge University Press.

Toor S. and Ofori, G. (2009) 'Ethical leadership: examining the relationships with full range leadership model, employee outcomes, and organizational culture', *Journal of Business Ethics*, 90 (4): 533–547.

Townley, B. (1993) 'Foucault, power/knowledge and its relevance for human resource management', *Academy of Management Review*, 18 (3): 518–545.

Townley, B. (1994) *Reframing Human Resource Management: Power, Ethics and the Subject at Work*. London: Sage.

Townley, B. (2002a) 'Managing with modernity', *Organization*, 9 (44): 549–573.

Townley, B. (2002b) 'The role of competing rationalities in institutional change', *Academy of Management Journal*, 45 (1): 163–179.

Trahair, R. (2001) 'George Elton Mayo', *Biographical Dictionary of Management*. Thoemmes Press. Available at http://www.thoemmes.com/encyclopedia/mayo.htm (last accessed 2 January 2006).

Trejo, S. J. (1993) 'Overtime pay, overtime hours, and labor unions', *Journal of Labor Economics*, 11 (2): 253–278.

Tribe, K. (1975) 'Capitalism and industrialization', *Intervention*, 5: 23–27.

Trinca, H. and Fox, C. (2004) *Better Than Sex: How a Whole Generation Got Hooked on Work*. Sydney: Random House Australia.

Trullen, J. and Bartunek, J. M. (2007) 'What a design approach offers to organization development', *Journal of Applied Behavioral Science*, 43: 23–43.

Tsui, A. S., Nifadkar, S. S. and Yi Ou, A. (2007) 'Cross-national, cross-cultural organizational behavior research: advances, gaps, and recommendations', *Journal of Management*, 33 (3): 426–478.

Tuckman, B. (1965) 'Developmental sequence in small groups', *Psychological Bulletin*, 63 (6): 384–399.

Tuckman, B. and Jensen, M. A. (1977) 'Stages of small group development revisited', *Group and Organisation Studies*, 2 (4): 419–427.

Turner, B. S. (2003) 'McDonaldization: linearity and liquidity in consumer cultures', *American Behavioral Scientist*, 47 (10): 137–153.

Turner, J. C. (1987) *Rediscovering the Social Group: A Self-Categorization Theory*. New York: Basil Blackwell.

Tziner, A., Joanis, C. and Murphy, K. R. (2000) 'A comparison of three methods of performance appraisal with regard to goal properties', *Group Organization Management*, 25 (2): 175–190.

UNCTAD (2004) *Development and Globalization: Facts and Figures*. Geneva: UNCTAD.

Urry, J. (2007) *Mobilities*. London: John Wiley and Sons.

Üsdiken, B. (2004) 'Americanization of European management education in historical and comparative perspective: a symposium', *Journal of Management Inquiry*, 13 (2): 87–89.

Utting, P. (2003) 'Promoting development through corporate social responsibility – prospects and limitations', *Global Future*, 3: 11–13.

Vaast, E. (2007) 'What goes online comes offline: knowledge management system use in a soft bureaucracy', *Organization Studies*, 28 (3): 282–306.

van der Schalk, J., Fischer, A., Doosje, B., Wigboldus, D., Hawk, S., Rotteveel, M. and Hess, U. (2011) 'Convergent and divergent responses to emotional displays of ingroup and outgroup', *Emotion*, 11 (2): 286–298.

Vanderveen, G. (2006) *Interpreting Fear, Risk and Unsafety*. The Hague: BJU Legal Publishers.

Van de Ven, A. and Poole, M. (1995) 'Explaining development and change in organizations', *Academy of Management Review*, 20 (3): 510–540.

Van de Ven, A., Polley, D., Garud, R. and Venkataraman, S. (1999) *The Innovation Journey*. Oxford: Oxford University Press.

Van Dorsten, S. (2004) NAFE Magazine and the National Association for Female Executives (Fourth Quarter). 2004 Salary Survey. *NAFE Magazine*, 27 (4): 20–21.

Van Maanen, J. (1988) *Tales of the Field: On Writing Ethnography*. Chicago: Chicago Guides to Writing, Editing, and Publishing.

Van Maanen, J. (1991) 'The smile factory: work at Disneyland', in P. Frost, L. Moore, M. Louis, C. Lundberg and J. Martin (eds), *Reframing Organizational Culture*. Newbury Park, CA: Sage, pp. 58–76.

Vansteenkiste, M., Simons, J., Lens, W., Sheldon, K. M. and Deci, E. L. (2004) 'Motivating learning, performance, and persistence: the synergistic effects of intrinsic goal contents and autonomy-supportive contexts', *Journal of Personality and Social Psychology*, 87 (2): 246–260.

Veenhoven, R. (2004) 'Happiness as an aim in public policy: the greatest happiness principle', in A. Linley and S. Joseph (eds), *Positive Psychology in Practice*. Hoboken, NJ: Wiley, ch. 39.

Veenhoven, R. (2010) 'Capability and happiness: conceptual difference and reality links', *Journal of Socio-Economics*, 39: 344–350.

Veenhoven, R. (2011) 'Greater happiness for a greater number: is that possible? If so, how?', in K. M. Sheldon, T. B. Kashdan and M. F. Steger (eds), *Designing Positive Psychology: Taking Stock and Moving Forward*. Oxford University Press, New York, ch. 26, pp. 396–409.

Vinkenburg, C. J., van Engen, M. L., Eagly, A. H. and Johannesen-Schmid, M. C. (2011) 'An exploration of stereotypical beliefs about leadership styles: is transformational leadership a route to women's promotion?', *The Leadership Quarterly*, 22 (1): 10–21.

Vlaar, P. W. L., Van den Bosch, F. A. J. and Volberda, H. W. (2006) 'Coping with problems of understanding in interorganizational relationships: using formalization as a means to make sense', *Organization Studies*, 27 (11): 1617–1638.

Vogel, D. (2005) *The Market for Virtue: The Potential and Limits of Corporate Social Responsibility*. Washington, DC: Brookings Institution Press.

Volberda, H. W. (2002) 'Toward the flexible form: how to remain vital in hypercompetitive environments', in S. R. Clegg (ed.), *Central Currents in Organization Studies II: Contemporary Studies, Volume 8*. London: Sage, pp. 298–322; originally published in *Organization Science* (1998) 7: 359–374.

Von Hippel, E. (1986) 'Lead users: a source of novel product concepts', *Management Science*, 32: 791–805.

von Stamm, B. (2003) *Managing Innovation, Creativity and Design*. Chichester: Wiley.

Voronov, M. and Coleman, P. T. (2003) 'Organizational power practices and a "practical" critical postmodernism', *Journal of Applied Behavioral Science*, 39 (2): 169–185.

Walton, E. J. (2005) 'The persistence of bureaucracy: a meta-analysis of Weber's model of bureaucratic control', *Organization Studies*, 26 (4): 569–600.

Ward, P. R. and Coates, A. (2006) 'Health and happiness in a materially deprived, ethnically mixed locality', *Journal of Epidemiology & Community Health*, 60 (1): 87.

Warren, D. E. (2003) 'Constructive and destructive deviance in organizations', *Academy of Management Review*, 28: 622–632.

Wasik, J. F. (1996) *Green Marketing and Management*. Cambridge, MA: Blackwell.

Watkins, L. M. and Johnston, L. (2000) 'Screening job applicants: the impact of physical attractiveness and application quality', *International Journal of Selection and Assessment*, 8 (2): 76–84.

Watson, T. J. (2003) 'Ethical choice in managerial work: the scope for managerial choices in an ethically irrational world', *Human Relations*, 56 (2): 167–185.

Watson, T. J. (2004) 'Managers, managerialism and the tower of babble: making sense of managerial pseudo-jargon', *International Journal for Sociology of Language*, 166: 67–82.

Watzlawick, P., Beavin, J. and Jackson, D. (1967) *Pragmatics of Human Communication: A Study of Interactional Patterns, Pathologies, and Paradoxes*. New York: W. W. Norton.

Weber, M. (1948) *From Max Weber: Essays in Sociology*, trans., ed. and with an introduction by H. H. Gerth and C. W. Mills. London: Routledge & Kegan Paul.

Weber, M. (1976) *The Protestant Ethic and the Spirit of Capitalism*. London: Allen & Unwin.

Weber, M. (1978) *Economy and Society: An Outline of Interpretative Sociology*. Berkeley, CA: University of California Press.

Weick, K. E. (1969) *The Social Psychology of Organizing*. Reading, MA: Addison-Wesley.

Weick, K. E. (1979) *The Social Psychology of Organizing*, 2nd edn. Reading, MA: Addison-Wesley.

Weick, K. E. (1991) 'The vulnerable system: an analysis of the Tenerife air disaster', in P. Frost, L. Moore, C. Louis, C. Lundberg and J. Martin (eds), *Reframing Organizational Culture*. Newbury Park, CA: Sage, pp. 117–130.

Weick, K. E. (1995) *Sensemaking in Organizations*. Thousand Oaks, CA: Sage.

Weick, K. E. (2004) 'Mundane poetics: searching for wisdom in organization studies', *Organization Studies*, 25 (4): 653–668.

Weick, K. E. (2006) 'Faith, evidence, and action: better guesses in an unknowable world', *Organization Studies*, 27 (11): 1723–1736.

Weick, K. E. (2008) 'Sensemaking', in S. R. Clegg and J. R. Bailey (eds), *The Sage International Encyclopedia of Organization Studies*. Thousand Oaks, CA: Sage, pp. 1403–1406.

Weick, K. E. and Sutcliffe, K. M. (2003) 'Hospitals as cultures of entrapment: a re-analysis of the Bristol Royal Infirmary', *California Management Review*, 45 (2): 73–84.

Weick, K. E. and Westley, F. (1999) 'Organizational learning: affirming an oxymoron', in S. R. Clegg, C. Hardy and W. R. Nord (eds), *Managing Organizations*. London: Sage, pp. 190–208.

Weiner, B. (1980) *Human Motivation*. Hillsdale, NJ: Lawrence Erlbaum Associates.

Weiner, B. (1992) 'A cognitive (attribution)-emotion-action model of motivated behavior: an analysis of judgments of help-giving', *Journal of Personality and Social Psychology*, 39 (2): 186–200.

Weir, P. (Director) (2003) *Master and Commander: The Far Side of the World* [Motion picture]. United States: 20th Century Fox.

Weiss, B. (1981) *American Education and the European Immigrant*. Urbana, IL: University of Illinois Press.

Weiss, H. M. and Rupp, D. E. (2011) 'Experiencing work: an essay on a person-centric work psychology', *Industrial and Organizational Psychology: Perspectives on Science and Practice*, 4: 83–97.

Wellins, R. S., Byham, W. C. and Wilson, J. M. (1991) *Empowered Teams: Creating Self-Directed Works Groups That Improve Quality, Productivity and Participation*. San Francisco: Jossey-Bass.

Wenger, E. (1998) *Communities of Practice: Learning, Meaning and Identity*. New York: Cambridge University Press.

Wenger, E. (2002) 'Communities of practice and social learning systems', in S. R. Clegg (ed.), *Central Currents in Organization Studies II: Contemporary Trends, Volume 8*. London: Sage, pp. 29–48; originally published in *Organization* (2000) 7: 225–246.

Wennes, G. (2002) 'Skjønnheten og udyret: Kunsten å lede kunstorganisasjonen', Norwegian School of Economics and Business Administration, Bergen.

West, M. (2003) *Effective Teamwork: Practical Lessons from Organizational Research: Psychology of Work and Organizations*. London: Blackwell.

West, M. A. (2008) 'Team performance', in S. R. Clegg and J. Bailey (eds), *The Sage International Encyclopedia of Organization Studies*. London: Sage.

West, M., Tjosvold, D. and Smith, K. (2003) *International Handbook of Organizational Teamwork and Cooperative Working*. Chichester: Wiley.

Westbrook, D. and Kirk, J. (2005) 'The clinical effectiveness of cognitive behaviour therapy: outcome for a large sample of adults treated in routine practice', *Behaviour Research and Therapy*, 43 (10): 1243–1261.

Westwood, R. and Clegg, S. R. (eds) (2003) *Debating Organisation: Point-Counterpoint in Organization Studies*. Oxford: Blackwell.

White, R. W. (1963) *Ego and Reality in Psychoanalytical Theory: Psychological Issues*, Vol. III, No. 3, Monograph II. New York: International Universities Press.

Whitely, B. E. (1999) 'Right wing authoritarianism, social dominance orientation, and prejudice', *Journal of Personality and Social Psychology*, 77: 126–134.

Whitley, R. (1999) *Divergent Capitalisms*. Oxford: Oxford University Press.

Whyte, W. (1960) *The Organization Man*. Harmondsworth: Penguin.

Wickham, J. and Collins, G. (2004) 'Call centres as innovation nurseries', *Service Industries Journal*, 24 (1): 1–18.

Wiedow, A. and Konradt, U. (2011) 'Two-dimensional structure of team process improvement: team reflection and team adaptation', *Small Group Research*, February, 42 (1): 32–54.

Willmott, H. (1998) 'Towards a new ethics? The contributions of poststructuralism and posthumanism', in M. Parker (ed.), *Ethics and Organizations*. London: Sage, pp. 76–121.

Willmott, H. (2002) 'Strength is ignorance; slavery is freedom: managing culture in modern organizations', in S. R. Clegg (ed.), *Central Currents in Organization Studies II: Contemporary Trends, Volume 7*. London: Sage; originally published in *Journal of Management Studies* (1993) 30: 515–582.

Wilson, T. D. and Gilbert, D. T. (2005) 'Affective forecasting knowing what to want', *Current Directions in Psychological Science*, 14 (3): 131–134.

Winiecki, D. J. (2006) *Discipline & Governmentality at Work: Making the Subject and Subjectivity in Modern Tertiary Labor*. London: Free Association Press.

Wolfe, T. (1979) *The Right Stuff*. New York: Farrar, Straus and Giroux.

Wolinsky, F. D., Vander Weg, M. W., Martin, R., Unverzagt, F. W., Willis, S. L., Marsiske, M., Rebok, G. W., Morris, J. N., Ball, K. K. and Tennstedt, S. L. (2010) 'Does cognitive training improve internal locus of control among older adults?' *J Gerontol B Psychol Sci Soc Sci* 65 (5): 591–598.

Womack, J. P., Jones, D. T. and Roos, D. (1990) *The Machine That Changed the World*. New York: Rawson/Macmillan.

Wood, A. (1994) *North-South Trade, Employment and Inequality*. Oxford: Clarendon.

Wood, J. R. T. (1997) *Royal Commission into Corruption in the New South Wales Police Service*. Sydney: The Government of the State of New South Wales.

Woodward, J. (1965) *Industrial Organizations: Theory and Practice*. London: Oxford University Press.

Workman, J. (1993) 'Marketing's limited role in new product development in one computer systems firm', *Journal of Marketing Research*, 30: 405–421.

World Bank (2001) *Poverty Report*. Available at www.worldbank.org/poverty/wdrpoverty/index.htm (last accessed 14 July 2011).

Wrege, D. (1995) 'F. W. Taylor's lecture on management, 4th June 1907: an introduction', *Journal of Management History*, 1 (1): 4–7.

Wren, D. and Greenwood, R. (1998) *Management Innovators: The People and Ideas That Shaped Modern Business*. New York: Oxford University Press.

Wu, Y. (2010) 'An exploration of substitutes for leadership: problems and prospect', *Social Behavior and Personality: An International Journal*, 38 (5): 583–595.

Wyer, N. A. (2007) 'Motivational influences on compliance with and consequences of instructions to suppress stereotypes', *Journal of Experimental Social Psychology*, 43 (3): 417–424.

Yoshino, M. Y. and Rangan, U. S. (1995) *Strategic Alliances: An Entrepreneurial Approach to Globalization*. Boston, MA: Harvard Business School Press.

Young, E. (1989) 'On the naming of the rose: interests and multiple meanings as elements of organizational culture', *Organization Studies*, 10: 187–206.

Young, J. E., Klosko, J. S. and Weishaar, M. (2003) *Schema Therapy: A Practitioner's Guide*. New York: Guilford.

Zell, D. (1997) *Changing by Design: Organizational Innovation at Hewlett-Packard*. Ithaca, NY: Industrial and Labour Relations Press.

Zey, M. (2008a) 'Rational choice theory', in S. R. Clegg and J. R. Bailey (eds), *The Sage International Encyclopedia of Organization Studies*. Thousand Oaks, CA: Sage, pp. 1355–1356.

Zey, M. (2008b) 'Multisubsidiary form', in S. R. Clegg and J. R. Bailey (eds), *The Sage International Encyclopedia of Organization Studies*. Thousand Oaks, CA: Sage, pp. 934–938.

Zuboff, S. (1988) *In the Age of the Smart Machine*. New York: Basic Books.

Zwick, E. (Director) (2006) *Blood Diamond* [Motion picture]. Los Angeles: Warner Bros.

Affective forecasting refers to the process of making basic decisions in the present based on predictions about your emotions in some future act or event.

Affirmative action is controversial because it attempts to address long-standing and institutionalized discrimination against people of diverse backgrounds – such as gender, race, etc. – by discriminating in favour of people perceived as belonging to categories that are disadvantaged.

Agency is anything that can cause effects, usually delimited to people, but should not necessarily be so. Machines, viruses, animals, and many other non-human actors can cause important effects.

Alliances are essentially a strategic device connecting different organizations in a network or web that includes many transacting parties. Yoshino and Rangan (1995: 17) define alliances as 'cooperation between two or more independent firms involving shared control and continuing contributions by all partners'.

Artifacts are those things with which we mark out territory: the decorations and art in a building; the furnishings and fittings; the styles of clothes that people wear; the types of desks, offices, and computers that they use – these are all artifacts that tell us, subtly, about the environments we occupy or are in.

Attribution theory in its simplest definition refers to how people 'attribute' cause to their own and other people's behaviour (Heider, 1958).

Authentic leaders have the qualities of transformational leaders but also work on moral and ethical grounds; possess great self-awareness, integrity, confidence, and self-control; are positive and optimistic; are resilient (bouncing back from adversity); and are future oriented.

Authority attaches to forms of domination over others that are viewed as legitimate.

Basic assumptions are defined by Schein as the core, or essence, of culture, represented in difficult to discern, largely unconscious, and tacit frames that subconsciously shape values and artifacts, formed around deep dimensions of human existence such as the nature of humans, human relationships and activity, reality and truth.

To talk of **bounded rationality** means accepting that there are limitations and constraints on human behaviour. People are cognitively limited, producing 'satisficing' rather than optimally rational decisions (March and Simon, 1958; Simon, 1957). Individuals act inconsistently (and therefore irrationally) under conditions of uncertainty, which are characteristic of any decision-making situation. Satisficing means accepting decisions that are both sufficient and satisfying.

Brand A simple definition is the image of an organization that is created through design (e.g. its name, ads, logo, etc.), its behaviour (e.g. employees), and its products and services.

Bureaucracy is an organizational form consisting of a hierarchy of differentiated knowledge and expertise in which rules and disciplines are arranged not only hierarchically in regard to each other but also in parallel.

Capital is an abstract concept that might take many material forms. Traditionally, it was thought of purely in economic terms, as wealth invested in an asset with the intention of its delivering a return to the owner of that asset. As such, capital implies complex sets of relations of ownership and control of the asset and employment in its service.

The owners of capital were known as **capitalists** because they owned capital – the social relations and resources that made them masters over other men, women, and children

Capitalism is an economic system founded on the sanctity and dominance of private property rights organized through markets, in which the majority of people sell their labour power in a market for labour to owners of capital which is consolidated in an enterprise.

Change refers to a transition that occurs from one state to another.

Chaos is a Greek word that is in opposition to cosmos (an orderly and harmonious system). Normally chaos is related to the unpredictability of a system.

Charismatic leadership is a leadership type that emphasizes the articulation of a vision and mission that promises a better life. Sometimes such leaders develop a cult following.

Closed groups have several limitations or barriers to joining, maintaining, and ceasing membership.

Coaching is the process of developing and enhancing employees' job competencies and capabilities through constructive suggestions and encouragement.

Coercive isomorphism occurs when some powerful *institution* obliges organizations in its domain, on threat of coercion, to comply with certain practices and designs. Think of the law; it obliges all organizations over a certain size to have equal employment opportunity practices. The managers may not want to provide equal opportunity, but they are obliged to do so under threat of legal penalty.

Cognitive dissonance refers to the anxiety and discomfort we experience when we hold inconsistent and conflicting sets of cognitions (or schemas).

Collaboration is typically designed either to advance a shared vision or to resolve a conflict. It usually results in an exchange of information or a joint agreement or commitment to action between two or more parties, such as organizations.

Collaborative relations involve the process of sharing resources including ideas, know-how, technologies, and staff between two or more different organizations in order to create a solution to a given problem.

Collective agreement is a written agreement, made between the employer and the employees, which sets out terms and conditions of employment. Usually it is made between a union, as a body representing employees, and an employer. Collective agreements are typical of social democratic approaches to industrial relations.

Communication can be defined as exchange of ideas, emotions, messages, stories, and information through different means including writing, speech, signals, objects, or actions. It may be intentional, such as a carefully phrased letter, or unintentional, such as the inferences another person may make about one's body language.

Communication with stakeholders describes communication between an organization and other relevant parties (stakeholders) such as media, community groups, labour unions, politicians, etc.

Community of practice, according to Etienne Wenger, can be defined as the process of social learning that occurs when people who have a common interest in a problem, collaborate to share ideas, and find solutions.

Competitive advantage is gained by firms changing the constraints within which they and their competitors operate.

Concertive control is exercised in teamwork situations where the sense of responsibility that you have to the immediate members of the team impels you to work intensively and to not let them down.

Conflict In organizational contexts we can define conflict as one or more people perceiving that their interests are or will be negatively affected by the interests of others. Such conflict occurs when people want the same thing (power, job, resources, land, space, etc.), and access to those things is limited. Conversely, conflict may occur because parties may actually want different things (such as different outcomes).

Content theories of motivation refer to those 'contents' within us that drive or push us.

Contingency theory in organization and management theory suggests that there are several key contingencies shaping organizations. The basic idea of contingency approaches is to stress that all organizations have to deal with a predictable number of contingencies and that these contingencies will shape the organization's design as it adapts to them.

Corporate greening is a process that involves trying to adopt green principles and practices in as many facets of the business as it is possible to do so.

Corporate social responsibility (CSR) occurs when organizations seek to meet or exceed legal and normatively mandated standards, by considering the greater good of the widest possible community within which they exist, both in local and global terms, with regard to the environmental, social, economic, legal, ethical, and philanthropic impact of the organizations' way of conducting business and the activities they undertake.

Cultural anthropology is the study of specific societies and cultures, using the methods, concepts, and data of field-based research in its descriptions and analyses of the diverse peoples of the world. Sometimes called social anthropology it developed as an adjunct of imperialism in the nineteenth century, mapping largely small-scale (or 'primitive'), non-Western societies, but in the twentieth century has developed its fieldwork methods of inquiry into areas as diverse as youth cultures and corporate cultures.

Culture represents the totality of everyday knowledge that people use habitually to make sense of the world around them through patterns of shared meanings and understandings passed down through language, symbols, and artifacts.

Cybernetics can be defined as studying feedback and other communication mechanisms in machines, living organisms, and organizations.

Decentralization is the opposite of centralization. Organizations often seek to decentralize when they feel that their systems and processes are becoming too slow because too much decision-making, even on small and inconsequential matters, is being referred to the centre. Often, organizations with low levels of trust are highly centralized because a decentralized decision structure requires that you trust those who are delegated to decide.

Descriptive approach to business ethics would not seek for normative guidelines that ought to be applied in practice, but rather monitor and describe what actually happens.

Design thinking emerged as a term that was widely used in the 2000s. Its inspiration goes back to Simon (1969). Brown (2009) develops it as a conjoined process of inspiration, ideation, and implementation. Inspiration derives from making a problem material through mock-up, sketches, scenarios, and so on. Ideation is the process of generating, developing and testing ideas through building prototypes, piloting, and 'testing the waters' – idea work. Implementation is the clear development and specification of the idea, its effective communication, the enrolment of others in its support, and the translation of the idea into action or practice.

Dialectics refers to the contradiction between two conflicting forces, where each shapes the other, often against the pressure that is being exerted.

Differentiation perspective stresses that the normal divisions to be found in organizations – of departments and disciplines, of spatial locations, of gender, religiosity, ethnicity, age, and other attributes of human beings – will all tend to be potential bases for specific local cultural formation. The assumption is that experience of more than one culture is likely to be the organizational norm.

Direct management control was possible because of the combination of ownership and control of resources as well as of knowledge of the means of production that enabled employers to exercise discipline over their employees.

Diversity, in an organizational context, can most simply be defined as variety in geography, culture, gender, spirituality, language, disability, sexuality and age.

Division of labour produces a more specialized labour force. Instead of everybody trying to be a jack of all trades and a master of none, capable of doing everything in an organization, labour becomes more specialized by breaking down large jobs into many tiny components.

Double-loop learning means changing the frame of reference that normally guides behaviour.

Dyadic communication means two-party communications. Dyadic communication can be impersonal when two people interact without direct personal contact as well as face to face and unmediated.

Early modern management was based on the efficient extraction of value from the labour that was employed.

Efficiency means the most economical use of resources to achieve ends.

Embedded, to say economic action is embedded is to say that it must be understood in its cultural context.

Embeddedness refers to the realization that economic relations can never be grasped purely in terms of their economic rationality but need to be seen as organically situated within specific features of social settings. For instance, in the garment industry, much of the manufacturing may take place through loosely coupled supply chains of organizations whose members share a neighbourhood and ethnicity. The economic action that ensues is embedded in these social relations.

Emotional intelligence has been popularized by Daniel Goleman who conceives of it as the capacity to recognize our own emotions and the emotions of others, and the ability to manage our emotions in our relationships with others (Goleman, 1997).

Empowerment means giving someone more power than they had previously. Transferring power to the individual by promoting self-regulating and self-motivating behaviour through innovative human resource policies and practices, such as self-managing work teams, enhanced individual autonomy, and so on.

Entrepreneur The term, entrepreneur (adjective entrepreneurial), is associated with risk-taking activity, where someone seeks to innovate in a way that is discontinuous with existing ways of doing things.

Environment Organization and management theory conceives of organizations as existing in an environment composed of other organizations – what is sometimes referred to as an organization field.

Espoused values are a person's or social group's consistent beliefs about something in which they have an emotional investment as they express them; they are articulated in speeches, writings, or other media.

Ethics is usually understood as reflecting on and recommending concepts of right and wrong behaviour.

Ethnography is an approach to research that attempts to understand social phenomena, such as organizational life, as it happens and in its own terms. It involves in-depth interviews, participant observation, and detailed case study, and generally approaches research from the point of view of understanding what the subjects themselves think. It starts from the premise that meanings and understandings are socially constructed.

Explicit knowledge is the knowledge you can consciously talk about and reflect on, usually elaborated and recorded in such a way that others can easily learn it.

Exploitation means simply that, assuming labour is the source of all value, then any value over and above that paid out in wages – from which profits must arise – derives from paying labour less than the value that it creates for the capital which hires it.

Exploitation of knowledge occurs through routinization, standardization, and formalization of what is already known and done: doing it more cheaply, quickly, efficiently.

Expressive organization captures different levels of organizational expressions and their impact on processes such as strategy making, human resources, marketing, and others.

External attribution refers to attributing the cause of an individual's behaviour to an external or situational factor such as being 'Catholic' or 'Jewish'.

External dependence occurs where top management depends on parent organizations for key resources.

Financialization means the pervasive influence of financial calculations and judgements. Applied to everyday organizational life, it means the way that financial calculations now constitute the primary criteria of value, even for mundane objects, practices, and processes. It can be summed up in the ubiquitous phrase 'what's the value proposition?'

Formal groups refer to those groups where people have been specifically selected and are recognized as a team in order to complete a task, innovate, solve a problem, or provide a service or a product. **Fragmentation perspective** is suspicious of the desire to make culture clear. According to the fragmentation view, culture is neither clearly consistent nor *clearly* contested, but likely to be muddled and fragmentary. A fragmented organizational culture is one that forms around specific issues and then dissolves as these fade or are resolved. The nature of fragmentation is that specific and opportunistic cultural coherencies form at different times around different issues.

Frame is a term that comes from the cinema: a director frames a shot by including some detail and omitting other detail. A frame defines what is relevant.

Frames enable us to do **framing**. They focus us in on specific relevancies: by framing we decide on what is relevant from the infinite number of stimuli, behavioural cues, sense data, and information that surround us.

Functionalism An approach to analysis that assumes that phenomena exist to fulfil some function or other. Functionalism is often criticized for being conservative because, *ipso facto*, it assumes that what exists serves some purpose, therefore must be useful, and need not be replaced or revised.

Fundamental attribution error is the tendency to make internal attributions when explaining the causes of the behaviour of others.

Garbage can refers to situations characterized by 'problematic preferences', 'unclear technology', and 'fluid participation'.

Generations The idea that the different generations of specific societies can be captured in their essential features in a typology suggests that the values, beliefs, attitudes and cultural norms of a society are fragmented and centred on temporal-spatial features which mark specific generations in specific ways.

Globalization can be thought of as worldwide integration in virtually every sphere achieved principally through markets, a process whereby the world becomes more interconnected and the fates of those people and organizations in it become more intertwined. In business terms, globalization means business without frontiers, crossing national boundaries, and dealing with the world, not just the home base.

Group can be defined as two or more people working towards a common goal, but there is no psychological contract between them; the outcomes are less dependent on all the members working together, and there is usually no shared responsibility and accountability for outcomes.

Group dynamics is concerned with how groups form, their structure, processes, and how they function as a unit. Group dynamics is relevant in both formal and informal groups of all types. In essence, group dynamics is concerned with the study and analysis of any form of interaction that occurs within group contexts.

Groupthink refers to the tendency of members of a group to seek and maintain harmony in a group, at the cost of ignoring or avoiding important decisions that may disrupt harmony.

Halo effect The concept of the halo effect was first developed by psychologist Edward Thorndike (1920) and refers to the process by which if we ascribe certain characteristics to a person in one situation based on one trait, we tend to apply those characteristics to that person in other situations and to other traits.

Happiness can generally be defined as positive thoughts and feeling about one's life and can range from elation (being present when your team wins a grand final on the weekend), to a general feeling of satisfaction and contentment with one's life; it includes feeling calm, contented, satisfied, fulfilled, inspired, positive, and free.

Hard model of HRM: managers tend to have a Theory X orientation and believe most people would rather not be at work; for this reason management monitoring and control is integral, and typically extrinsic rewards such as pay rises and bonuses are used.

Hegemony signifies a system of rule or domination where those who are being dominated, or ruled, consent to that rule. It is a state of ideological conformance said to have been imposed on a subordinated group of people because of the concepts through which they think – concepts that do not enable them to assert a point of view that reflects a better understanding of their interests and the situation they are in.

Hierarchy implies status differentia based on relations of super- and subordination and associated privileges and distinctions.

HRM is the process and practice of managing and advising management on the recruitment, selection, retention, and development of staff in an increasingly complex legal and social environment with the aim of achieving the organization's objectives as they are made sense of by its managers or consultants.

Ideology is a coherent set of beliefs, attitudes, and opinions. The meaning is often pejorative, with a contrast drawn between ideology and science.

Impact bias may be considered to be the overestimation of the intensity and duration of the feelings actually experienced when we achieve that future event or goal (Wilson and Gilbert, 2005).

Individual agreements, as the term suggests, refers to the process of individuals negotiating the terms and conditions of their work, including pay, rewards and remuneration and so on.

Industrial relations (IR) refer to the relationship between employers and employees.

Informal groups are groups that are not necessarily sanctioned or even accepted by the organization and its management, but which still play a significant role in organizational outcomes.

Information Panopticon Increasingly, people in organizations and everyday life generally are subject to electronic surveillance, through instruments such as closed-circuit TV (CCTV), speed cameras, security cameras, and so on. These forms of surveillance have been referred to as the Information Panopticon.

In-group bias refers to the process in which members of a group favour or treat members of their own group with preference over others.

Innovation can be defined as the creation of either a new process (process innovation) or a new product or service (product/service innovation) that has an impact on the way the organization operates.

Institutional entrepreneurs are those people who occupy key positions with wide legitimacy attached to them, who are capable of bridging between the interests of diverse stakeholders, and have the capacity to introduce new practices and persuade stakeholders of the good fit of these practices with the routines and values that they embrace (Phillips et al., 2004).

Institutional tendencies are social structures that persist and endure and in doing so strongly shape the way that people, especially professionals, in organizations do the things they do.

Institutional theory A theory that proposes that organizations have the structures that they do largely for cultural reasons. Some designs and practices become regarded, for whatever reasons, as highly esteemed, as displaying high 'cultural capital'. Through one or more of three specific mechanisms (coercive, mimetic, or normative isomorphism), the template becomes widely adopted.

Institutions are recognizable in as much as specific practices are widely followed, accepted largely without debate, and exhibit properties of endurance.

Integration perspective According to Martin and Frost (1996), adherents of the integration perspective define culture as a phenomenon that is consistent and clear. Because they define organization culture in terms of unitary and shared assumptions, they include in their evidence only manifestations of it that accord with this definition, thus excising all the plural and non-integrative aspects of the culture.

Intellectual property is information that derives its intrinsic value from creative ideas. It is also information with a commercial value that can be realized through its sale on the market.

Internal attribution refers to explaining or attributing the cause of behaviour of an individual due to internal or dispositional factors such as being mean or being generous.

Interorganizational communication takes place between members of different organizations.

Interpersonal communication refers to direct interaction between two or more people.

Intraorganizational communication occurs inside an organization and typically engages organizational members.

Irrationality literally means the non-interpretability of a rule or rules underlying action; in practice, it more often means action whose rationality runs counter to that which is dominant and authorized.

Isomorphism A term derived from biology, referring to a similarity in the form of organisms of different ancestry. In organization and management theory, isomorphism is usually used in the context of institutional theory to refer to a situation in which organizational designs and practices in different organizations are nonetheless similar.

Knowledge That which is a part of the stock of ideas, meanings, and more or less explicit understandings and explanations of how phenomena of interest actually work or are structured or designed and relate to other phenomena: facts, information, and skills acquired by a person through experience or education.

Knowledge exploration involves serendipity, accident, randomness, chance, and risk-taking, not knowing what one will find.

Knowledge-intensive firms create value by solving their clients' problems through the direct application of knowledge. Whereas knowledge plays a role in all firms, its role is distinctive in knowledge-intensive firms. Rather than being embodied in the process or product, knowledge resides in experts and its application is customized in real time based on clients' needs (Sheehan, 2008: 54).

Knowledge management is the process of managing knowledge to meet existing and future needs. Put simply, knowledge management is all about know-how and know-why.

Labour process may be defined as the social relations that people enter into when they are employed as well as the work that they actually do and the conditions under which it is done. Studying the labour process has given rise to a distinct labour process perspective that focuses on management as a struggle for control of the labour process between employees and managers.

Leader (a) Leads people as a ruler; (b) inspires people as a motivator; and (c) facilitates or guides them as a coach and mentor.

Leadership is the process of directing, controlling, motivating, and inspiring staff towards the realization of stated organizational goals.

Learning is the process of acquiring knowledge and capabilities in addition to those already known. Usually thought of as something that individuals do, it is often associated with specific institutions, such as a school or a university. However, recently there has been a shift of emphasis to informal and work-based learning that occurs outside these specific institutional areas and in employing organizations.

Legitimacy attaches to something, whether a particular action or social structure, when there is a widespread belief that it is just and valid.

Limited liability legislation separated the private fortunes of entrepreneurs from investments in business, so that if the latter failed, the personal fortune was sequestered and the debtors' prison avoided.

Management is the process of communicating, coordinating, and accomplishing action in the pursuit of organizational objectives while managing relationships with stakeholders, technologies, and other artifacts, both within as well as between organizations.

Managerial capitalism sees capitalist entrepreneurs displaced by professional managers as the central, immediate, and direct agents of power within organizations.

Managerialism is the view that organizations should be normatively integrated by shared values expressed within a single source of authority, legitimacy, and decision-making embedded in the managerial hierarchy and serving the interests of the owners of that organization.

Managers are middletons: they intercede between executive authority, howsoever lodged, and those whose task it is to execute it. Historically, they were the supervisors, who had superordinate vision over subordinates, who were the hired 'hands'.

Managing is an active, relational practice which involves doing things. The things that managers do are supposed to contribute to the achievement of the organization's formal goals.

Marketing The shortest definition of marketing is meeting customer needs profitably.

Market–technology linking involves integrating the firm's unique competencies with customer needs, market structure, and technologies, together with its manufacturing, sales, and distribution capabilities.

Mass communication goes from one point to many receivers.

Matrix organizations can be thought of as coordinative devices that blend the programme orientation of project staff with the speciality orientation of functional personnel in a synergistic relationship, and first emerged in the US aerospace programme in the 1960s.

McDonaldization refers to the application of goal- oriented rationality to all areas of human life.

Mechanistic organization is most frequently to be found in stable environments, especially those with a cost minimization strategy; also, mechanistic models are found more frequently in large organizations that employ a large number of people.

Mentoring is the process of passing on the job expertise, skills, and knowledge in order to develop a protégé.

Metaphors use terms other than those of the subject under discussion to describe it. 'Dream-machine' is a recognizable metaphor.

M-form organization is a hub-and-spokes model with a hub of central services serving spokes with profit centres at their end, which were based usually on either product or regional specialization.

Mimetic isomorphism In simple language, mimetic isomorphism means the process of copying. Organizational designs and practices that are seen to be successful are copied because they are associated with success.

Motivation is defined as the psychological processes that drive behaviour towards the attainment or avoidance of some object (be that object a person or relationship, an abstract concept such as love, or a material good such as money, an iPod, or a BMW).

Networking is a collaboration between different people or agencies such as organizations. Often, independent organizations join together with others to form a network in which the other organizations have complementary skills so that together they can do something that neither alone would be able to manage.

Networks can be understood as a long-term relationship between organizations that share resources to achieve common goals through negotiated actions.

New organizational forms are organizational designs for structure seeking to be non-bureaucratic – indeed are often anti-bureaucratic – stressing flat structures rather than tall hierarchies, multiskilled capabilities rather than a rigid division of labour, informality rather than a high degree of formality.

Normative ethics seeks to establish means of judging whether business practices are right or wrong.

Normative isomorphism occurs when an organization's members are normatively predisposed, perhaps through a long period of professional training and socialization, to favour certain sorts of design and practices. The widespread use of the partnership form by law and other professional firms is a case in point.

Norms represent the tacit and unspoken assumptions and informal rules, the meaning of which people negotiate in their everyday interactions.

Occupational health and safety (OHS) refers to legislation, policies, acts, practices, and processes that are aimed at protecting all workers from injury and death in the workplace.

Open groups usually have free membership and no barriers to exit, and attract people due to shared interest.

Open systems In an open systems approach, organizations were viewed as systems that were open to inputs from their environments and that sent outputs to their environments as a result of their internal transformation processes.

Operationalize To operationalize a variable simply means deciding that the meaning of a concept can be best determined by proxy measures. Operationalization turns abstract concepts into measurable, clearly defined constructs by specifying certain operations for the collection of data that are presumed to represent accurately the characteristics of the concepts.

Organ Another key metaphor for modern management and organizations is the assumption that organizations are a collective body in which all the component parts should function much as do healthy organs in a human or animal body.

Organic organization is more likely to be found in firms that are smaller, that operate in highly uncertain environments, and that are strongly oriented to discovery and learning – such as high-tech R&D firms or bio-pharmaceuticals.

Organizational behaviour (OB) refers to the study of human behaviour in organizational contexts. OB is an applied discipline that concerns itself with individual-level, group-level, and organizational-level processes and practices that inhibit or enable organizational performance.

Organizational design is the designated formal structure of the organization as a system of roles, responsibilities, and decision-making.

Organizational identity usually means that organizations are assumed to have clear boundaries, a large degree of autonomy, and distinctive characteristics that differentiate them from other organizations.

Organizational learning Argyris (1960) defines organizational learning as the process of detection and correction of errors. In many respects, organizational learning is similar to individual learning. The idea is that organizations learn when the *knowledge* that their members have is explicitly known and codified by the organization. Organizations should seek to make as much of what their members do as explicit as possible. If members leave, the *explicit knowledge* that they developed in their jobs should stay.

Organizational politics, broadly speaking, refer to the network of social relations between people in and around organizations, between employees and their managers, customers, suppliers, competitors, etc., all of whom can be involved in organizational politics, insofar as they are involved, whether wittingly or not, in practices of power.

Organization culture comprises the deep, basic assumptions and beliefs, as well as the shared values, that define organizational membership, as well as the members' habitual ways of making decisions, and presenting themselves and their organization to those who come into contact with it.

Organizations are systematically arranged frameworks relating people, things, knowledge, and technologies, in a design intended to achieve specific goals.

To be **organized** thus means being characterized by the systematic arrangement of parts into a unified, organic whole.

Out-group refers to those people within one's own group, or in another group, that are treated inequitably or more negatively because they are not seen as belonging to one's own in-group.

Outsourcing occurs when an organization decides to contract a service provider who specializes in a particular area of service provision to do more economically and efficiently something that it previously did itself, such as catering, cleaning, maintenance, or IT.

Oxymoron is a figure of speech that combines two normally contradicting terms (such as deafening silence or military intelligence).

Panopticism The capacity to be all seeing. It was an attribute of the architectural structure known as a Panopticon, designed by Jeremy Bentham in the eighteenth century. What was most significant about the Panopticon, and what gave it its panopticism, was the fact that those under surveillance did not know when they were being watched, but were aware that they were potentially always under surveillance.

Paradigm A coherent set of assumptions, concepts, values, and practices that constitute a way of viewing reality for the community that shares them, especially in an intellectual discipline, in which the views are widely shared as a result of training and induction into the methods of the discipline. In more mature disciplines, there is usually a single dominant or normal paradigm, whereas less developed disciplines are characterized by a plurality of paradigms because there is a lack of shared agreement on what the discipline entails.

Perception is the process of receiving, attending to, processing, storing, and using stimuli to understand and make sense of our world. The stimuli can be experiences through any and all of the senses such as sight, sound, smell, taste, and touch.

Personality refers to the stable patterns of behaviour and internal states of mind that help explain a person's behavioural tendencies (Monte, 1991).

Person schemas are structures of meaning that affect thinking, planning, and behaviour concerning others; there are idealized person schemas which serve as prototypes that we compare all other persons by (see Horowitz, 1991).

Platform An evolving eco-system that is created from many inter-connected pieces.

Polyphony means literally the presence of many voices and hence different ideas and perspectives.

Positive psychology is the study, research, and theorizing of the psychological bases for leading the best life possible through positive thinking, feelings, and behaviour. In a management sense, positive psychology seeks to understand and to foster civic virtues, social responsibility, altruism, tolerance, happiness, and psychological wellbeing.

Positive psychological capital (PsyCap) refers to positive states such as hope, resilience, optimism, and self-efficacy through leadership and organizational behaviour that is oriented towards the positive psychological wellbeing and health of its members (Anandakumar et al., 2008).

Positivism models itself on natural science; it seeks theoretical generalizations of a broad scope through explanations that address objective mechanisms in terms of their causal regularities, a view of knowledge that privileges a conception of science focused on explanation more than understanding, where explanation is best served by specifying formal causal relations between abstract concepts conceived as variables.

Power The most common definition of power is that it is the chance of an actor to realize their own will in a social action, even against the resistance of others. The actor may be an individual or a collective entity. At its most mechanical, power means forcing others to do things against their will; however, power can be far more positive and less mechanical when it shapes and frames what others want to do – seemingly of their own volition.

Process theories of motivation concern themselves with the processes that are involved in motivation. Some argue that the process is one of expecting that behaving in a certain way will realize certain outcomes.

The term **psychology** is derived from the Greek word *psyche*, meaning one's own thoughts and feelings, and the English suffix 'ology' derived from the Greek *logos*, meaning reason, which in English is rendered as 'ology', denoting a field of study.

A **psychological contract** can be defined as the assumptions, beliefs, and expectations held between one person and another or within a group, organization, or some other collective entity, about the nature and function of the relationship between them. Typically a psychological contract refers to a contract made in the context of work.

Rational being rational means systematic application of various techniques to achieve some given end or goal.

Rational choice is a theory that adopts the view that all social interaction is a basically economic transaction undertaken by self-interested, goal-oriented individuals who exercise choice among alternative known outcomes that are based on their knowledge of, and the incentives that exist in, their immediate environment.

Rationality Action that is produced according to some rule; action that is not random or unpatterned.

Rationalized myths are rationalized and impersonal rules that bind different organizations through belief in their legitimacy. To be legitimate they will be pervasive features of the institutionalized environment in which the organizations operate. Their legitimacy is based on the belief that the practices sanctioned by the myths are efficient and effective. Organizations use these myths to increase the legitimacy of their structure and hence their survival prospects.

Rational–legal precepts People obey orders as rational–legal precepts because they believe that the person giving the order is acting in accordance with a code of legal rules and regulations (Albrow, 1970: 43).

Reciprocal determinism Bandura meant that our personality is a product of our behaviour, our thoughts, and our feelings in interaction with our environment.

Recruitment refers to the processes and practices used to attract suitable employees to the organization.

Reflexivity is the process of thinking about the effect of one's role, assumptions, and behaviour on a given action or object and considering the effect that the action has upon how we continue to think and behave.

Resistance to change consists of those organizational activities and attitudes that aim to thwart, undermine, and impede change initiatives. It is a widely observed phenomenon in organizations. The resistance can be overt, in the form of wildcat strikes, campaigns, or other forms of collective action, or it can be covert, through attempts at undermining change programmes through widespread adoption of cynicism, irony, and ambivalence.

Retained retention refers to the practices and process used to retain staff, and often includes staff development which refers to the processes, procedures, and policies designed and implemented to enhance and update the skills, knowledge, and capabilities of staff in relation to their career and their job.

Risk society is one in which the life-threatening disasters that it might be subject to cannot be controlled within a specific territory: Chernobyl or global warming are good examples.

Role schemas refer to schemas about appropriate and inappropriate behaviour in specific contexts (e.g. a woman's role as a mother, daughter, professional, wife, friend, etc.).

SARFIT means Structural Adjustment to Regain Fit.

Schemas are sets of cognitive constructs developed through social interactions that organize our thoughts, feelings, and attention (Baldwin, 1992; Epstein and Baucom, 2002).

Scientific management The principle that there is one best way to organize work and organization, according to a science of management based upon principles of standardization of time and routinization of motion as decided by authoritative experts.

Script schemas refer to schemas about how we operate upon our world and understand and remember information.

Selection refers to the tools, methods, and criteria upon which people will be, and are, selected for a given position, and includes job applications, interviews, tests, and measurement. Selection is related to the recruitment stage of the HRM function.

Self-determination theory (SDT) is a theory of motivation that emphasizes our intrinsic needs for being seen as competent, liked, and free from control of others.

Self-fulfilling prophecy The concept of the self-fulfilling prophecy was originally conceptualized by the sociologist Robert Merton (1957), to refer to the process by which a person who holds a belief or expectation, irrespective of the validity of that belief or expectation, causes that prediction to come true because people behave and act is if it is true.

Self-schemas are specific self-conceptions we hold about ourselves and we believe are self-descriptive and highly important to possess (Fong and Markus, 1982; Markus, 1977).

When a **self-serving bias** comes into play, people attribute their own successes to internal causes and their failure to external causes.

Sensemaking Managers have to be highly skilled and competent in managing to make sense of what they do. In management, the key competency has become known as sensemaking, which has been defined by Weick (2008) as the ongoing retrospective development of plausible images that rationalize what people are doing.

Single-loop learning means, basically, optimizing skills, refining abilities, and acquiring knowledge necessary to achieve resolution of a problem that requires solving.

Social impact refers to the strength of ties between individuals interacting in a group, the spatio-temporal closeness of the individuals, and the size of the group.

Social loafing – colloquially known as shirking, bludging, free riding, or laziness – is a phenomenon that we have all experienced. It refers to a situation in which members of a group exert less work effort than their peers.

Social schemas, as the name suggests, refer to our social knowledge (such as knowledge about public affairs, laws, politics, media and the arts, and anything else socially important).

Soft domination is characterized by the administration of rules that give managerial discretion to managers while reinforcing the strength of centralized authorities, because those who are delegates know that their obligation is to act creatively but to do so within the systems of authority (Courpasson, 2002).

Soft model of HRM takes a humanistic approach to HRM; typically soft HR managers have a Theory Y orientation which emphasizes that people are intrinsically motivated.

Specialization The skill formation that occurs when labour is divided and defined into smaller specific tasks rather than being seen as a general task that anyone might do.

Stakeholders are key individuals or groups of individuals with vested interests or 'stakes' in a given decision or project. The stakeholder can be a direct or an indirect stakeholder. A direct stakeholder is a customer, supplier, a government body, or anyone else formally linked to the organization(s). An indirect stakeholder is a member of the community who is not directly involved in the organization(s) but who is affected by its behaviour, such as a resident in its immediate community.

Stereotyping refers to the process of grouping objects into simplistic categories based on one's generalized perceptions of those objects.

Strategic choices The most important decisions managers make are those that structure the future strategy of the organization. John Child (2002 [1972]) called these strategic choices.

Strategic HRM In the formulation stage strategic HRM can contribute to the organization's objectives by ensuring that all key HRM functions such as the recruitment, retention, and development of staff are consistent with the business strategy. In the implementation stage HRM can contribute by ensuring that people understand the key strategic intentions and objectives, and ensure that people are abiding by those strategic intentions through measurement of performance consistent with those objectives.

Structural functionalism argues that the existence of an organization structure is explained by its function; thus those practices that persist are argued to do so because they are efficient.

Surplus value is achieved by exploiting labour: working labourers for a greater return than they received and retaining the surplus value that they produced over and above that which they received.

Sustainability means, literally, ensuring that resources are renewed. A sustainable use of resources would leave the world short of nothing that was depleted in any process – that resources would be renewed – and would ensure that nothing deleterious to the world's natural systems resulted from whatever processes were being undertaken.

Tacit knowledge is the knowledge you actually use when you do things but you cannot necessarily articulate it. An example is the knowledge required to ride a bike.

Team can be defined as two or more people psychologically contracted together to achieve a common organizational goal in which all individuals involved share at least some level of responsibility and accountability for the outcome.

A **theory** is an account of how things work, which is, at its best, coherent in its terms and applicable to phenomena that it seeks to interpret, understand and explain.

Theory X orientation assumes that people are lazy, require structure, direction and control, and want to be rewarded with money for a job well done.

Theory Y orientation assumes that people crave responsibility and autonomy, want to be treated with respect, and are driven towards self-actualization (Pitsis, 2008a; 2008b).

Time span of discretion is a concept for thinking about the relation of power to do things, the magnitude of the effects these things will have, and the location of responsibility for the things done. It also functions as a rationale for different levels of remuneration.

Top management team comprises the senior executives in any organization, the people who set strategy, direction, and purpose.

Total institutions are those organizations that share the essential feature of controlling almost the totality of the individual member's day-to-day life. Boarding schools, barracks, prisons, and asylums can be categorized as total institutions.

Traits refer to a mixture of biological, psychological, and societal influences that characterize a person's thoughts and actions throughout their lives.

Transactional leadership epitomizes the initiating structure, concern for production, and task-oriented themes of the behavioural leadership literature.

Transformational leadership, as you probably could guess, epitomizes consideration and concern for people and similar relations-oriented themes.

Transnational or multinational organizations, because they extend beyond national space in their routine activities, are able to exert control either through ownership and/or through the coordination and control of operations, as a result of other mechanisms, such as a multisubsidiary form based on capital interdependency (as we discussed in Chapter 13). The acronyms TNC (TransNational Corporation) or MNC (MultiNational Corporation) are sometimes used.

Trans-situational values are those that, irrespective of the situation in which you find yourself, your values do not change; you take them with you wherever you go.

Tropism means the involuntary response of an organism or one of its parts towards or away from a stimulus such as heat or light. In management the term is usually used to refer to rule tropism, where the stimuli are rules, and the response is one in which the existence of the rules in a bureaucracy immediately and involuntarily, as a learned response, structures actions within the organization.

Uncertainty can be defined as the inability to know how to continue some action, a lack of a rule, or undecidability about which rule to apply.

Unions can be defined as an association of wage-earning employees mobilized and organized in order to represent their constituents' interests. These interests can often be counter to the interests of employers, but not always necessarily so.

Utilitarianism is a moral philosophy that says we should always act for the greatest good of the greatest number.

Value chain is a concept for decomposing an organization into its component activities. Each activity can be analysed with regard to the value that it adds to the final product or service, which can be measured in terms of what the customer is prepared to pay for it, and the cost entailed in producing profit.

Value priorities refer to the order of values in terms of their importance to us as individuals.

Values are a person's or social group's consistent beliefs about something in which they have an emotional investment. Schwartz defines values as desirable goals, varying in importance, which serve as guiding principles in people's lives (Schwartz, 1992; 1994).

Variables are characteristics distributed across an entire population or sample of that population that will vary in the extent to which they are displayed. For instance, a student class varies in terms of the variables of height, weight, and so on. Such variables are defined by certain measures, such as inches, kilos, and so on.

Virtual teams are teams that operate across space, time, and organizational boundaries in order to complete a project. Typically, they use computer-mediated communication technologies and collaborative software in order to communicate and share information.

INDEX

CREDITS

"The Changing of the Guards" written by Bob Dylan. Copyright © 1978 Special Rider Music. All rights reserved. International copyright secured. Reprinted by permission.

Image I.2 Jean-Jacques Rousseau (1712–1778) by Allan Ramsey © National Gallery of Scotland.

What Do You Mean section, Chapter 2, p. 77. Reprinted with permission from Dr Timothy Sharp.

Figure 3.2 adapted from De Dreu, C.K.W and Van Vianen, A.E.M (2001) 'Managing relationship conflict and the effectiveness of organizational teams', *Journal of Organizational Behaviou*r 22: 309–328. Reprinted with permission.

Image 3.3 artwork courtesy of Catherine Reinke (recycled artist) http://recycledartist.net/

Figure 4.1 adapted from Blake and Mouton's (1985) registered model. Reprinted with permission from www.mindtools.com.

Figure 4.2 © 2002 Centre for Leadership Studies Inc. All Rights Reserved. Situational Leadership © is a registered trade mark of the Centre for Leadership Studies. Reprinted with permission.

Image 9.1 Nike Air Force 1 Low White/Red: from the Kix and the City online magazine dedicated to sneaker culture. www.KixandtheCity.com (http://www.kixandthecity.com/wp/wp-content/uploads/2007/01/RWProf.jpg)

Table 9.1 adapted from Clark, P. (2003) *Organizational Innovations*. Reprinted with permission from SAGE.

Image 12.2 reprinted with thanks to Bruce Petty.